11 - 50.

# THE ECONOMICS OF MONEY AND BANKING

# STEPHEN M. GOLDFELD · LESTER V. CHANDLER
Princeton University                    Emeritus, Princeton University

**EIGHTH EDITION**

# THE ECONOMICS OF MONEY AND BANKING

*1817*

**HARPER INTERNATIONAL EDITION**

**HARPER & ROW, PUBLISHERS, New York**

Cambridge, Hagerstown, Philadelphia, San Francisco,
London, Mexico City, São Paulo, Sydney

1332395

Sponsoring editor: John Greenman
Project editors: Claudia Kohner/Jon Dash
Designer: Gayle Jaeger
Production manager: William Lane
Compositor: Ruttle, Shaw & Wetherill, Inc.
Printer and binder: The Murray Printing Company
Art studio: Eric G. Hieber Associates, Inc.

**THE ECONOMICS OF MONEY AND BANKING, Eighth Edition**

Copyright © 1948, 1953 by Harper & Row, Publishers, Incorporated. Copyright © 1959,
1964, 1969, 1973 by Lester V. Chandler. Copyright © 1977 by Lester V. Chandler and
Stephen M. Goldfeld. Copyright © 1981 by Stephen M. Goldfeld and Lester V. Chandler.

All rights reserved. Printed in the United States of America. No part of this book may be
used or reproduced in any manner whatsoever without written permission except in the
case of brief quotations embodied in critical articles and reviews. For information
address Harper & Row, Publishers, Inc., 10 East 53rd Street, New York, N.Y. 10022.

Library of Congress Cataloging in Publication Data
Goldfeld, Stephen M.
    The economics of money and banking.

    Seventh ed. entered under L. V. Chandler.
    Includes index.
    1. Money.  2. Banks and banking.  I. Chandler,
Lester Vernon, Date-        Economics of money and
banking.  II. Title.
HG221.C448   1981        332.4              80-27895
ISBN 0-06-041236-4

Harper International Edition
35-02382
Cover design by Lorna Laccone

# CONTENTS

**v**

Though extensively revised and rewritten, this edition is quite similar in purpose, approach, and treatment to the seven editions that preceded it. It is addressed primarily to college and university undergraduates who are just beginning their formal study of money and banking. In the selection and presentation of materials we have kept the needs of the students in mind constantly and have not tried to write to our professional colleagues.

This is not an exhaustive treatment of money and banking. Not even a book many times the size of this one could claim to deal exhaustively with the vast amounts of theoretical, legal, institutional, empirical, and historical materials that have been accumulated in the field of money and banking. Furthermore, we do not believe it appropriate that the newcomer should be forced to wade through an encyclopedic treatment of this broad and complex subject. We have therefore selected what we believe to be the most important principles, processes, and problems and have attempted to deal with them fully enough to clarify their significance and interrelationships.

The ultimate interest of this book is in policy. However, policy cannot be understood without a theory of the interrelationships of money and banking and the functioning of the economy as a whole, a clear understanding of the institutions and processes involved, and an appreciation of the social and historical context within which policy makers operate and by which their policies are shaped. This book therefore employs theoretical, institutional, and historical approaches. It emphasizes an evolutionary view, attempting not only to explain how present-day structures, attitudes, and policies evolved but also to suggest some possible directions of future change. This view seems particularly appropriate in the light of recent developments.

**MAJOR CHANGES IN THE EIGHTH EDITION**

The field of money and banking has undergone substantial changes in the relatively short period of time since the publication of the previous edition. Indeed, notions of what constitute both "money" and a "bank" have altered perceptibly in the last several years. Furthermore the forces that have brought about these changes, financial innovation and regulatory reform, will inevitably provide further stimulus for change. Consequently, one major goal of this edition is to provide the reader with a firm understanding of the dynamic nature of the field of money and banking.

To accomplish this, the present edition introduces a number of major changes in both the exposition and coverage. The most extensive revisions appear in the new Part V devoted to monetary policy. This includes new chapters on the evolution of financial intermediaries and the actual conduct of monetary policy. These chapters document the growing similarities among financial institutions, examine in detail the role of interest rate ceilings, and contain an extended discussion of the important new legislative reforms embodied in the Depository Institutions Deregulation and Monetary Control Act of 1980.

Recent changes in the definition of money introduced by the Federal Reserve are also analyzed, and the question of the appropriateness of monetary rules is examined in the light of these new definitions. Elsewhere in the book, some of the more important changes include the following: an expanded discussion of the rationale of bank competition, supervision, and regulation; a fuller treatment of inflation; a more extensive analysis of the money supply process and money multipliers; and a considerably revised and updated discussion of international monetary relations.

Many individuals have made helpful contributions in the preparation of this edition. We would particularly like to thank our Princeton colleagues Dwight Jaffee and Robin Bauer, and Paul Howell of Baruch College. We also wish to thank Professors Harold R. Williams and Henry W. Woudenberg for preparing the *Instructor's Manual* that accompanies the text. Last, but not, as any author knows, least, we would like to thank Constance Dixon for her cheerful and efficient assistance in putting it all together.

Stephen M. Goldfeld
Lester V. Chandler

# THE NATURE AND FUNCTIONS OF MONEY AND FINANCE

# 1

One need not be an economist to be acutely aware that money plays an important role in modern life; one need think only of one's own experience and recall the headlines of recent years. From personal experience one knows that the process of getting a living is a process of getting and spending money, and that how well one can live depends on how many dollars one can get and how many goods and services each dollar will buy. One also knows that dollars are harder to get at some times than at others, and that the buying power of each dollar has varied widely, sometimes to one's benefit and sometimes not.

It is equally evident, even to the most casual observer, that the behavior of money is also vitally important to the operation of the national and international economies. When we recall the events of history, we are reminded that the periods of major economic contraction in the United States were frequently characterized by banking or monetary crises and invariably accompanied by substantial reductions in the stock of money. In particular, significant reductions of the money supply accompanied the major economic contractions of 1873–1879, 1893–1894, 1907–1908, 1920–1921, 1929–1933, and 1937–1938. Banking crises occurred in 1873 and again in 1907, the latter providing a stimulus for the subsequent creation of the Federal Reserve System.

During our most severe economic contraction, the Great Depression of 1929–1933, we witnessed a collapse of the banking system with the consequent disappearance via failure or merger of nearly 40 percent of the nation's banks. Newspapers of the 1930s headlined stories of "deflation and depression"; the drastic decline of output, job opportunities, and prices accompanying the shrinkage of effective demand; of widespread want and suffering while millions of unemployed workers and other productive facilities that were both willing and able to work were standing idle because of insufficient "demand"; and of wholesale failures of debtors to meet their obligations because of the decline of their money incomes and of the prices of their assets.

Headlines in other periods told different sorts of stories—not stories of deflation and shrunken employment, but stories of "inflation," of rising living costs, and of discontent and distress among those whose income and wealth were relatively fixed in terms of money. For example, in the periods surrounding the two World Wars—1914–1920 and 1939–1948—prices more than doubled. During each period the stock of money outstanding likewise more than doubled.

History also provides ample evidence that the movement of money between nations can have an important influence on economic developments throughout the world. In the United States, for instance, we have had to worry about the international position of the dollar, about the continuing deficit in our balance of international payments, the deterioration of our net international reserve position, speculation against the dollar, and conflicts among the domestic and international objectives of our monetary policies. These developments, it should be emphasized, are of more than historical interest. Aggravated by increasing oil prices, international monetary problems continued unabated in the 1970s. On the domestic front, we seemed to have the worst of both worlds, with the nation struggling to cope simultaneously with inflation and excessive unemployment. Indeed, for the first time in nearly 30 years, "double-digit" inflation surfaced in the United States in 1974. The subsequent contraction of the economy produced the worst U.S. recession of the post-World War II era, with the unemployment rate rising to 9 percent by mid-1975. A similar pattern seemed to be repeating itself in 1980, and as in earlier episodes, the newspapers were filled with a wide range of views as to the proper course for monetary policy.

In short, personal experience as well as some knowledge of history and economics makes it clear to everyone that money plays an important role in the economic system and that the behavior of money is somehow causally related to the behavior of employment, the rate of real output, the level of prices, the distribution of wealth and income, and so forth. What are not so clear, however, are the answers to questions such as these: Just what are the functions of money in the economy, and just how does money perform these functions? To what extent do economic disturbances "arise on the side of money and monetary policy"? To what extent do money and monetary policy amplify and spread through the economy disturbances originating in nonmonetary factors? What are the effects of the various types of money and monetary policies? Which ones promote economic objectives generally considered desirable, and which ones militate against the attainment of those objectives? With how much success can we use monetary policy to prevent unemployment, promote a steadily advancing level of output, and maintain a stable purchasing power of the dollar while preserving a basically free enterprise economy?

Such questions are the central concern of this book. The primary interest throughout is in the functioning of the monetary, credit, and banking systems and in their relationships to the functioning of the economy as a whole. Though much space will be devoted to historical, structural, and legal aspects of the various institutions that create, transfer, and destroy money, these aspects will not be studied primarily for their own sakes, but rather for their contribution to our understanding of the functioning of the economic system.

**THE BASIC FUNCTION OF MONEY**

Money has one fundamental purpose in an economic system: to facilitate the exchange of goods and services—to lessen the time and effort required to carry on trade. A person living and working in complete isolation from others has no use for money. It cannot be eaten or worn or used to promote productive processes; having no occasion to exchange either goods or services with others, such a person has no need for money. Even if a dozen persons lived together in isolation from all others, the use of money would be of only limited benefit to them; they could barter their goods and services among themselves with but little loss of time and effort. As groups become larger, however, and wish to increase their degree of specialization and the size of their trade area, they find the direct barter of goods and services increasingly inconvenient and increasingly wasteful of time and effort. They therefore search for something that will enable them to escape the wasteful processes of barter; they invent money.

We may say, then, that the sole purpose of money in the economic system is to enable trade to be carried on as cheaply as possible in order to make feasible the optimum degree of specialization, with its attendant increase of productivity. We are all familiar with the high degree of specialization that characterizes modern economies—specialization of persons, of business firms, of regions, and of types of capital. We know that without this high degree of specialization, which enables us to utilize the various regions to maximum advantage, to make the most advantageous use of native abilities, to develop skills, to amass huge amounts of specialized and useful knowledge, to employ large aggregations of specialized capital, and to achieve economies of scale, our productive powers and living standards would be far below their present levels. But this specialization would be impossible without an equally highly developed system of exchange or trade. Money is productive, therefore, in the sense that it is an essential part of the modern exchange mechanism and thereby facilitates specialization and production.

<table>
<tr><td>

**BARTER EXCHANGE**

</td><td>

We have carefully avoided saying that exchange is impossible without money. People can, of course, carry on trade by a direct bartering of goods and services. Primitive trade was often carried on in this way, and bartering is not unknown even now. Yet pure barter is so wasteful of time and effort that little trade would be feasible if this were the only available method of exchange.

</td></tr>
</table>

The first serious shortcoming of pure barter is the lack of any common unit in terms of which to measure and state the values of goods and services. (By the *value* of a good or service is meant its *worth*, the quantity of other goods and services that it can command in the market.) In this situation, the value of each article in the market could not be stated simply as one quantity, but would have to be stated in as many quantities as there were kinds and qualities of other goods and services in the market. For example, if there were 500,000 kinds and qualities of goods and services in the market, the value of each would have to be stated in terms of 499,999 others. Moreover, no meaningful accounting system would be possible. A balance sheet would consist of a long physical inventory of the kinds and qualities of the various goods owned and another inventory of those owed; consequently, the net worth of the person or firm could be ascertained, if at all, only by a prolonged and tedious study of the numerous barter rates of exchange prevailing in the market. Profit and loss statements would be equally difficult to draw up and interpret. A firm could only list the various kinds and qualities of goods and services acquired during the period as income and those paid out as expenses, so that again the net results could be discovered, if at all, only by a laborious study of barter rates of exchange. It is almost inconceivable that even a small department store, not to mention General Motors Corporation, could keep meaningful accounts in the absence of a monetary unit.

The second serious disadvantage of barter is often described as "the lack of a double coincidence of wants." Stated more simply, it would happen only rarely that the owner of a good or service could easily find someone who both wanted that commodity more than anything else and possessed the commodity that our trader wanted more than anything else. For example, suppose that a farmer owned a three-year-old draft horse and wished to trade it for a certain kind of two-wheeled cart. To find someone who already owned or could build with maximum economy exactly the kind of cart the farmer wanted and who would be willing to trade it, and who also wanted more than anything else the kind of horse that was being offered, would likely be a laborious and time-consuming process, if such a person existed at all. The farmer would probably have to accept something less desirable than the cart, or else carry through a number of intermediate barter transactions, for example, trading the horse for a cow, the cow for a boat, the boat for some sheep, and the sheep for the desired cart. Barter presents even more serious difficulties when the articles to be exchanged are not of the same value and cannot be divided without loss of value. Imagine, for example, the plight of the farmer who wanted to trade the horse for a pair of overalls, a hat, three dishes, an aluminum skillet, 50 cartridges, schoolbooks, and numerous other inexpensive articles.

A third disadvantage of pure barter is the lack of any satisfactory unit in terms of which to write contracts requiring future payments. Contracts involving future payments are an essential part of an exchange economy; individuals must enter into agreements as to wages, salaries, interests, rents, and other prices extending over a period of time. But in a pure barter economy these future payments would have to be stated in terms of specific goods or services. Though this would be possible, it would lead to three grave difficulties: (1) It would often invite controversy as to the quality of the goods or services to be repaid; (2) the parties would often be unable to agree on the specific commodity to be used for repayment; (3) both parties would run the risk that the commodity to be repaid would increase or decrease seriously in value over the duration of the contract (e.g., wheat might rise markedly in value in terms of other commodities, to the debtor's regret, or decrease markedly in value, to the creditor's regret).

A fourth disadvantage of pure barter, which results from its first two shortcomings, is the lack of any method of storing generalized purchasing power. People could store purchasing power for future use only by holding specific commodities or claims against specific commodities. This method of storing purchasing power has often been used, and as we shall see later, is used extensively even today. Yet it has serious disadvantages when it is the only method available. The stored commodity may deteriorate (or appreciate) in value, its storage may be costly, and it may be difficult to dispose of quickly without loss if its holder wishes to buy something else.

Because of the four disadvantages outlined above, pure barter is a highly inefficient means of trade. It was to overcome these difficulties that virtually every society invented some kind of money early in its development.

**THE SPECIFIC FUNCTIONS OF MONEY**

Money serves its basic purpose as "the great wheel of circulation, the great instrument of commerce" by performing four specific functions, each of which obviates one of the difficulties of pure barter described above. These functions are to serve as: (1) a unit of value, (2) a medium of exchange, (3) a standard of deferred payments, and (4) a store of value. The first two are usually called the *primary* functions of money. The last two are called *derivative* functions because they are derived from the primary functions.

**Money as a Unit of Value**   The first function of money has been given many names, of which the most common are *unit of value, standard of value, unit of account, common measure of value,* and *common denominator of value.* Through all these names runs one common idea: The monetary unit serves as the unit in terms of which the value of all goods and services is measured and expressed. As soon as a group develops a monetary unit such as a dollar, a peso, a franc, a pound sterling, or a pengo, the value of each good or service can be expressed as a *price,* by which we mean the number of monetary units for which it will exchange. For example, we say that the value of a certain hat is $10, that beef of a certain grade has a value of $2 a pound, and so on. Ours is certainly a pecuniary society in the sense that values typically are measured and expressed in monetary units.

The practice of measuring the values of goods and services in monetary units greatly simplifies the problem of measuring the exchange values of commodities in the market. One has merely to compare their relative prices in terms of monetary units. For example, if pig iron is $10 per hundredweight and corn is $2.50 per bushel, a hundredweight of pig iron is worth 4 bushels of corn. This practice also simplifies accounting. Assets of all kinds, liabilities of all kinds, income of all kinds, and expenses of all kinds can be stated in terms of common monetary units to be added or subtracted.

Money is not the only common unit of measurement employed in the economic system. Units such as feet, inches, and meters are used to measure linear distance; ounces, grams, pounds, and short tons, to measure weight; gallons, liters, and barrels, to measure liquid volume; and so on. These units of physical measurement are, themselves, constant quantities. Confusion would surely result if these units of physical measurement were to shrink 25 percent one year and expand 10 percent the next. Yet the unit of value (money), perhaps the most important unit of measurement in the economic system, has too often undergone wide fluctuations in its value or *purchasing power.* The latter is the inverse of the average or general level of prices of a large number of goods and services, as measured by the consumer price index, the wholesale price index, or by an index of the prices of all goods and services included in the gross national product. For example, if the general or average level of prices doubles—if twice as many dollars are required to buy a given assortment of goods and services—the value or purchasing power of a dollar decreases by 50 percent. But if the general or average level of prices falls by 50 percent—if only half as many dollars are required to purchase a given assortment of goods and services—then the value or purchasing power of a dollar is doubled. Some of the consequences of fluctuating price levels will be discussed later.

**Money as a Medium of Exchange**

Various names have been given to the second function of money: *medium of exchange, medium of payments, circulating medium,* and *means of payment.* This function of money is served by anything that is generally (not necessarily universally, but very commonly) accepted by people in exchange for goods and services. The "thing" may be porpoise teeth, bits of gold, copper coins, pieces of paper, or credits on the books of a bank; the only essential requirement of an object to be used as money is that people in general be willing to accept it in exchange for goods and services. When a group has developed such a mechanism, its members need no longer waste their time and energy in barter trade. Our farmer can simply sell the horse to the person who offers the most money for it and then buy the supplies from those who offer the best bargain. The Ford worker need not barter his bolt-tightening services directly for the various things that he needs; he can sell his services for money in the most favorable market and spend the money as he sees fit. In the final analysis, all trade is, of course, barter; one good or service is traded indirectly for others, with money acting as the intermediary. But by serving this purpose, money greatly increases the ease of trade.

The fact that money is often referred to as *generalized purchasing power* or as *a bearer of options* emphasizes the freedom of choice that the use of money affords. The owners of goods or services need not secure their supplies from the people to whom they trade those goods or services; they can use their money to buy the things they want most, from the people who offer the best bargain, and at the time they consider most advantageous.

Here, again, money can function properly only if it maintains a relatively stable purchasing power. If a dollar is a bearer of fluctuating amounts of generalized purchasing power, it is likely to cause confusion and injustice in trade.

**Money as a Standard of Deferred Payments**

As soon as money comes into general use as a unit of value and a medium of payments, it almost inevitably becomes the unit in terms of which deferred or future payments are stated. Modern economic systems require the existence of a large volume of contracts of this type. Most of these are contracts for the payment of principal and interest on debts in which future payments are stated in monetary units. Some of these contracts run for only a few days or a few months, many run for more than 10 years, and some run for 100 years or more. By the end of 1978, the volume of outstanding debts of American governmental units, nonfinancial business firms, and households was $3.7 trillion, and debts of financial institutions were $3.2 trillion. There are also many contracts other than debts that are fixed or semifixed in terms of monetary units; among these are dividends on preferred stock, long-term leases on real estate and other property, and pensions.

The disadvantages of writing contracts for future payments in terms of specific commodities have already been noted. But money is a satisfactory standard of deferred payments only to the extent that it maintains a constant purchasing power through time, or if it changes in value, does so in a predictable way. If money increases in value through time, especially in an unpredictable way, it injures the groups who have promised to pay fixed amounts of money and gives windfall gains to those who receive these fixed amounts. If, on the other hand, money loses value through time, it injures those who have agreed to receive the fixed amounts and lightens the burden of payers.

**Money as a Store of Value**

We have already noted the disadvantages of holding specific commodities as a store of value. As soon as money comes to be used as a unit of value and as a generally acceptable means of payment, it is almost certain to be widely used as a store of value. The holders of money are, in effect, holders of generalized purchasing power that can be spent through time as they see fit for the things they want most to buy. They know that it will be accepted at any time for any good or service and that it will remain constant in terms of itself. Money is thus a good store of value with which to meet unpredictable emergencies and especially to pay debts that are fixed in terms of money. This does not mean that money has been a stable and wholly satisfactory store of value; it can meet this test only if its purchasing power does not decline. In actual practice, it has performed this function most capriciously.

Money is not, of course, the only store of value. This function can be served by any valuable asset. One can store value for the future by holding short-term promissory notes, bonds, mortgages, preferred stocks, household furniture, houses, land, or any other kind of valuable goods. The principal advantages of these other assets as a store of value are that they, unlike money, ordinarily yield an income in the form of interest, profits, rent, or usefulness (as in the case of an auto or a suit of clothes); and they sometimes rise in value in terms of money. On the other hand, these assets have certain disadvantages as a store of value, among which are the following: (1) They sometimes involve storage costs; (2) they may depreciate in terms of money; and (3) they are "illiquid" in varying degrees, because they are not generally acceptable as money and because sometimes the only way to convert them into money quickly is to exchange them at a loss of value.

All persons and business firms are free to choose for themselves the form in which they will store their value, to determine the proportions they will hold in the form of money and in various nonmonetary forms, and to alter these from time to time to achieve what seem to them the most advantageous proportions on the basis of income, safety, and liquidity. The decisions are much influenced by people's expectations as to the future behavior of prices. If they come to believe that the prices of other things are less likely to decline and more likely to rise, they will be inclined to hold less of their wealth in the form of money and more in the form of other things. But if they come to believe that prices of other things are less likely to rise and more likely to fall, they will be inclined to hold an increased part of their wealth in the form of money and a smaller part in other forms.

We shall see later that this freedom of people and business firms to determine for themselves the distribution of their holdings as between money and other assets and to shift from one form of assets to another may initiate or aggravate fluctuations in the flow of money expenditures and in prices and business activity. Sometimes people as a group show a tendency that is variously described as a desire to hold more of their wealth in the form of money and less in other forms, to use more money as a store value and less as a means of payment, to transfer money from active use to idle balances, to hoard money, to hold money longer before spending it, or to decrease the velocity or rapidity of circulation of money. But regardless of the name applied to it, such a development tends to decrease the flow of money expenditures for securities, goods, and services, thereby exerting a downward pressure on the national money income, employment, and price levels. On the other hand, a widespread tendency that has been variously described as a general movement to hold less wealth in the form of money and more in other forms, to use less money as a store of value and more as a means of payment, to transfer money from idle balances to active use, to dishoard money, to hold money only a short time before spending it, or to speed up the velocity or rapidity of circulation of money serves to raise the rate of money expenditures and to raise money incomes, price levels, and under some conditions, employment and real output. Such fluctuations in the velocity of money, or the demand for money to hold, will occupy a very important position in our later discussions of the relationships between money and the behavior of the economy.

**DEFINITION OF MONEY**   Having considered the various functions performed by money, we must now ask: What "things" are included in money and what "things" excluded? Money should be defined precisely, for we shall deal at length with the supply (stock) of money and its behavior. Unfortunately, it is impossible to find a completely clear-cut answer to this basic question.

**Examples of Money**

Anyone who begins the study of money with a belief that there is some one thing that is "by nature" money and has been used as money at all times and in all places will find monetary history very disconcerting, for a most heterogeneous array of things have served as circulating media. An incomplete list is given in Table 1–1.

Some of these things are animal, some vegetable, some mineral; some, such as debts, defy classification. Some are as valuable for nonmonetary purposes as they are in their use as money; some at the other extreme have almost no value in nonmonetary uses. Some are quite durable; other could be classified as perishable. About the only characteristic that all these things had in common was their ability, at some time and place, to achieve general acceptability in payment. And the reasons for their general acceptability certainly varied from place to place and from time to time.[1]

**Legal Definitions of Money**

Some people have tried to define money in purely legal terms, contending that "money is what the law says it is." Legal provisions are certainly relevant. A "thing" is likely to have difficulty in achieving general acceptability in payments if the law prohibits its use for this purpose, although violations of such laws are far from unknown. Laws can also help a thing to achieve general acceptability by proclaiming it to be money. They may go further and endow it with *legal-tender* powers, decreeing that it has the legal power to discharge debts and that a creditor who refuses it may not demand anything else in payment of an existing debt.

---

[1] The variety of things that have served as money is reflected in our language. For example, the word *pecuniary*, meaning "monetary," comes from the Latin word *pecus*, which means "cattle," while *salary* derives from the Latin word for salt, *salarium*. Similarly, the expression "to shell out," meaning "to pay," reflects the early use of shells as money.

---

**TABLE 1–1**

*An incomplete list of things that have served as money*

| | | | | |
|---|---|---|---|---|
| clay | pigs | wool | porcelain | iron |
| cowry shells | horses | salt | stone | bronze |
| wampum | sheep | corn | iron | nickel |
| tortoise shells | goats | wine | copper | paper |
| porpoise teeth | slaves | beer | brass | leather |
| whale teeth | rice | knives | silver | pasteboard |
| boar tusks | tea | hoes | gold | playing cards |
| woodpecker scalps | tobacco | pots | electrum | debts of individuals |
| cattle | pitch | boats | lead | debts of banks |
| | | | | debts of governments |

However, legal definitions of money are not satisfactory for purposes of economic analysis. For one thing, people may refuse to accept things that are legally defined as money and may even refuse to sell goods and services to those who offer legal tender in payment. Moreover, things that are not legally defined as money may come to be generally acceptable in payment and even to become a major part of the circulating medium. Commercial bank notes and deposits are an outstanding example. We must conclude, therefore, that legal provisions are an important, but certainly not the only, determinant of the things that do and the things that do not serve as money.

**Functional Definitions of Money**

To be useful for purposes of economic analysis, the definition of money must be in functional terms. Money includes all those things that perform the functions of money and excludes all others. But this definition raises still other questions, notably, "performs *what* functions?" Two of the functions—those of serving as a unit of value and as a standard of deferred payment—do not help determine which "things" to include in the money supply and which to exclude, for they are abstract units that can relate to many different things. For example, we could measure values in dollars whether or not our money, denominated in dollars, was composed of gold, paper money, or porpoise teeth. And we could state contracts extending over time in dollars without reference to the nature of the things to be used in payment.

Virtually all economists agree that the money supply should include all those things that are in fact generally acceptable in payment of debt and as payment for goods and services. If a thing is in fact generally acceptable in payment and generally used as a medium of payments, it is money, whatever its legal status may be.

Applying this criterion to U.S. money, our supply includes at least coins, paper money, and demand deposits (or checking deposits) at banks. All our coins and paper money are not only generally acceptable in fact, they are also endowed with full legal-tender powers to discharge debts. Checking-deposit claims against banks do not have legal-tender powers, but they are in fact generally acceptable as payment, so much so that the vast majority of all payments in this country are made by transferring deposit claims against banks from payers to payees.

If, in measuring the money supply, we confine our attention to the public's holding of coin and paper money (collectively known as *currency*) and demand deposits at commercial banks, we have what is called the money supply, "narrowly defined." For many years this definition was the most commonly used one and was denoted both in official government statistics and in the press by the symbol M-1. Recently, for reasons to be described shortly, this definition was officially designated M-1A.

As Table 1–2 indicates, at the end of 1979 the U.S. money supply as measured by M-1A totaled $371.5 billion, with $28\frac{1}{2}$ percent in the form of currency and the remaining $71\frac{1}{2}$ percent in the form of demand deposits at commercial banks. Table 1–2 also demonstrates the rather general finding that a growing economy will typically be accompanied by an increasing money supply. For example, from 1960 to 1969 the annual growth of M-1A was 3.7 percent while the corresponding growth rate for the period of 1970–1979 was 6 percent. Subsequent chapters elaborate on both the sources of this monetary growth and its economic consequences.

**A New Definition of Money**

As was hinted at by the introduction of the ungainly symbol M-1A, there have been some changes in the official definitions of money. These changes were occasioned by the evolution of the financial system. Specifically, during the 1970s there emerged a number of financial instruments that were capable of serving as substitutes for demand deposits in making transactions. Two of the more important of these instruments can be readily identified.

1   NOW ACCOUNTS. A NOW account is an interest-bearing savings deposit that permits the holder to withdraw funds by writing what is, for all practical purposes, a check. NOWs are currently available at commercial banks, savings and loan associations, and mutual savings banks, although only in selected states. Recently passed legislation, however, will extend NOWs nationwide as of the start of 1981.

2   AUTOMATIC TRANSFER SERVICES (ATS). An ATS account, available at commercial banks, enables a depositor to keep his or her transactions balances in an interest-bearing savings account. As checks are written on what is essentially a zero-balance checking account, funds are automatically transferred from the ATS account to cover the check when it clears. Mechanics aside, ATS and NOW accounts clearly accomplish the same thing.

---

**TABLE 1–2**

*The public's money supply on selected dates*

| Type of money | AMOUNT OUTSTANDING (IN BILLIONS OF DOLLARS)* | | |
| --- | --- | --- | --- |
| | December 1960 | December 1969 | December 1979 |
| Currency | 29.0 | 46.1 | 106.1 |
| Demand deposits | 112.7 | 158.5 | 265.4 |
| Subtotal (= M-1A) | 141.7 | 204.6 | 371.5 |
| Other checkable deposits | 0.0 | 0.1 | 16.2 |
| Total (= M-1B) | 141.7 | 204.7 | 387.7 |

*Note:* The data shown are monthly averages of daily figures and are adjusted for seasonal variation. The latest data appear in the monthly *Federal Reserve Bulletin.*
*Source:* Board of Governors of the Federal Reserve System.

As should be evident, both ATS and NOW accounts can serve as substitutes for demand deposits in making payments. Thus, if we wish to count as money anything that is used as a medium of payments, we should clearly include ATS and NOW accounts for our definition. Indeed, it was precisely this line of reasoning that prompted the Federal Reserve—the official keeper of money data—to introduce a revised definition of money in February 1980. This revised definition (denoted, as one might have guessed, by the symbol M-1B) simply added to M-1A what were termed "other checkable deposits" (i.e., ATS, NOW accounts, and the like). As Table 1–2 shows, at the end of 1979 such deposits amounted to about $16 billion, but the potential for future growth in this category is enormous.[2] If anything, what this recent change shows is that what constitutes a medium of payment cannot be settled once and for all. Rather, those assets that function as media of payment may well change with the evolution of institutional practices and advances in technology.

**Near-Money vs. Money**

While the narrow definition of money based on the function of money as a medium of payment is the most widely accepted money supply concept, a number of economists consider this definition, even as revised, too restrictive. They admit that only currency and checkable deposits are generally accepted in payments, but they prefer to expand the money category to include some other things that have a high degree of moneyness and are widely used as a store of value. None would include everything used as a store of value; the concept of money would become meaningless if expanded to include land, structures, livestock, business inventories, and other such risky and illiquid assets. But some economists would include time and savings deposits at commercial and mutual savings banks, claims against credit unions, and shares of savings and loan associations in their definition of money. Some would go further and include U.S. Treasury bills and other short-term debts of the federal government and even short-term debts of safe private debtors.

These things are not generally acceptable in payment, and in most cases there is at least a short delay or other cost in exchanging them for money in the sense in which we have defined it. Yet they do indeed have a high degree of moneyness or *liquidity*. Those who favor a broader definition of the money supply believe these assets should be included because a dollar held in these forms may have almost the same effect on the willingness and ability of the public to spend as would a dollar of money in our restricted sense.

---

[2] In addition to ATS and NOW accounts, "other checkable deposits" includes credit union share drafts and checking accounts at mutual savings banks and savings and loans. For a detailed treatment of all these financial instruments as well as a full discussion of the latest official definitions of money, see Chapter 17.

We do not deny that the availability of these *near-moneys* can affect economic behavior. Nevertheless, for several reasons we think it desirable to adhere to the more commonly accepted narrow definitions. For one, since all assets possess the quality of moneyness in various degrees, any broad definition would have troublesome borderline cases. Second, money and near-moneys are only imperfect substitutes, and consequently we doubt that a dollar's worth of near-money affects the public's willingness to spend to the same extent as a dollar's worth of money proper. Finally, the public's spending behavior depends not only on the supply of money and other liquid assets but also on many other things, such as people's total wealth. Including these other liquid assets in the money supply simply because they affect the rate of spending would raise questions as to why all other determinants of spending were not also included. We believe these reasons are sufficient to warrant the use of a relatively narrow definition of money, and we shall do so throughout this book.[3]

Although we exclude these near-moneys from our definition of the money supply, we shall not ignore their effects on the behavior of the rate of spending. We include these in our analysis by taking into account the public's demand for money balances. We shall argue that the behavior of spending depends not only on the supply (stock) of money, but also on the demand function of the community for money balances. The characteristics of near-moneys will thus enter the equation as one, but only one, of the determinants of the community's demand function for money balances. In addition, the supply of money itself will be seen to be sensitive to the quantities of near-moneys held by the public.

| | |
|---|---|
| **MONEY AND THE ECONOMY** | The study of money and banking is a means for understanding the influence of money and monetary policy on the functioning of our economic system. The existence of this book is premised on the view that the behavior of money is an important element in explaining observed economic outcomes and that intelligent monetary policies can contribute to the attainment of socially desirable economic goals. |

While this upbeat view of money and monetary policy is shared by many economists of the present day, this was not always the case. Indeed, many of the writings of the so-called classical economists, who dominated British and American economic thinking in the nineteenth and early twentieth centuries, tended to accord money only an unimpor-

---

[3] We do, however, consider some broader definitions in Chapter 17.

tant causative role. Such a view of the significance, or rather the insignificance, of money was clearly stated by John Stuart Mill:

> It must be evident, however, that the mere introduction of a particular mode of exchanging things for one another by first exchanging a thing for money, and then exchanging the money for something else, makes no difference in the essential character of transactions. . . .
>
> There cannot, in short, be intrinsically a more insignificant thing, in the economy of society, than money; except in the character of a contrivance of sparing time and labor. It is a machine for doing quickly and commodiously, what would be done, though less quickly and commodiously, without it; and like many other types of machinery, it only exerts a distinct and independent influence of its own when it gets out of order.
>
> The introduction of money does not interfere with the operation of any of the Laws of Value . . . The reasons which make the temporary or market value of things depend on the demand and supply, and their average and permanent values upon their cost of production, are as applicable to a money system as to a system of barter. Things which by barter would exchange for one another, will, if sold for money, sell for an equal amount of it, and so will exchange for one another still, though the process of exchanging them will consist of two operations instead of only one. The relations of commodities to one another remain unaltered by money; the only new relation introduced is their relation to money itself; how much or how little money they will exchange for; in other words how the Exchange Value of money itself is determined.[4]

Two aspects of Mill's statement should be noted before jumping to the conclusion that money deserves no more attention than each of the other labor-saving devices in the economy. First, Mill conceded that money "exerts a distinct and independent influence of its own when it gets out of order." This suggests the importance of keeping money "in order" to avoid disturbances. Second, he was speaking primarily of *equilibrium conditions*—those conditions that would rule after sufficient time had elapsed for all factors of production, output, costs, and prices to become so adjusted that there would be no incentive for further changes. Associated with this long-run equilibrium was a presumption that there would be full employment of both labor and capital.

As already indicated, modern economists tend to accord money and monetary policy a more prominent role in their analysis. In the first

---

[4] John Stuart Mill, *Principles of Political Economy*, Book III, chap. 7, p. 3.

place, they believe money is frequently "out of order" in the sense in which Mill used the term. The coincidence of severe economic contractions and the disruptive behavior of money cited earlier is one reason for this altered view. In the second place, economists now devote much more attention to conditions and periods of disequilibrium: to business cycles, periods of unemployment or inflation, and periods of transition from one equilibrium position to another. The late Lord Keynes once quipped, "In the long-run we are all dead." This does not suggest that long-run consequences are unimportant, but it does emphasize that we cannot afford to neglect short runs or disequilibrium conditions which may persist for long periods and have serious social consequences. Indeed, as we shall see later, once economists focused on conditions of less than full employment, it became apparent that expansionary monetary policy was an effective tool for producing increases in both output and employment. It thus became clear that proper monetary management had an important role to play in achieving national economic objectives.

While we believe this view is the correct one, one should be wary of overemphasizing the influence of money. Some reformers, noting that the ability of individuals to obtain goods and services depends on the amount of money they can command, have erroneously assumed that the same must always hold true for an entire nation. They would therefore abolish poverty and usher in the economic millenium by greatly expanding the money supply. How wonderful it would be if we could all become rich in any real sense simply by creating great batches of money! Unfortunately, it is not that easy. We have already noted that an expansion of money spending may serve to expand real production if it occurs in a period of unemployment, when the labor force and other productive factors are not working at full capacity. Economic policy must not ignore this fact. But neither can it safely ignore the fact that the most that monetary policy can do to promote production—and it may not accomplish this without the aid of other wise economic policies—is to achieve and maintain full employment. It cannot compensate for a paucity of natural resources or a scarcity of capital goods or a backward state of technology or sluggish and unintelligent labor or unimaginative and unenterprising economic management or inefficiency in government economic activities. In other words, a wise monetary policy may help to raise and maintain the actually realized rate of production closer to potential productive capacity (although we should not assume that it can always achieve even this objective). However, monetary policy usually is not one of the major determinants of this potential capacity. Nor is a wise monetary policy by any means the only factor determining the distribution of income and wealth among the members of the community. We shall have wiser monetary policy, and certainly wiser economic policies as a whole, if we recognize the limitations of monetary policy as well as its power.

**SELECTED READINGS**

Board of Governors of the Federal Reserve System, "A Proposal for Redefining the Monetary Aggregates." *Federal Reserve Bulletin*, January 1979, pp. 13–42.

———, "The Redefined Monetary Aggregates." *Federal Reserve Bulletin*, February 1980, pp. 97–114.

Galbraith, J. K., *Money, Whence It Came, Where It Went.* Boston, Houghton Mifflin, 1975.

Having surveyed the various roles played by money in economic systems, we now consider the principal types of money that have been used. This is a highly important subject, for the types of money employed can influence greatly the behavior of a nation's money supply, the value or purchasing power of its monetary unit, and the ability of monetary authorities to control the money supply. The main development traced in the chapter is the movement from commodity money, such as gold coin, to credit money, such as checking deposits. Specifically, after examining the various types of money we consider the forces that led to the demise of the so-called gold standard and the rise of the modern banking system. This will have two side benefits. First, it will provide a glimpse at the workings of money in an international setting, a topic we shall return to in later chapters. Second, it will illustrate that, from the first, national economic policy often faced conflicting and potentially irreconcilable objectives — a frustration that policy makers live with to this day.

**CLASSIFICA-TIONS OF MONEY**

Money can be classified on several different bases, such as the following: (1) the physical characteristics of the materials of which money is made; (2) the nature of the issuer, such as a government, central bank, commercial bank, or other; and (3) the relationship between the value of money as money and the value of money as a commodity. We shall use all these classifications, but it will be convenient to start with the third. Table 2–1 shows the various types of money on this basis.

Since 1933, the United States has had only credit or debt money; both full-bodied and representative full-bodied money were discontinued and withdrawn at that time. The latter two should be analyzed, however, for they have played important roles in monetary history and are still remembered nostalgically by many people.

**Full-bodied Money**

Full-bodied money is money whose value as a commodity for nonmonetary purposes is as great as its value as money. Most of the early commodity moneys, such as cattle, rice, wool, and boats, were as valuable for nonmonetary purposes as they were in their monetary uses. The principal full-bodied moneys in modern monetary systems have been coins of the standard metal when a country is on a metallic standard: a gold standard, a silver standard, or a bimetallic standard using gold and silver. We shall use gold in our examples, but the same principles apply to full-bodied money made of any other commodity.

Full-bodied coins were typically issued by governments. Three steps were involved:

1   Define the gold value of the monetary unit. This may be done in either of two ways, but both amount to the same thing: Stipulate the gold content of the monetary unit or stipulate the money price of each unit of gold.

2   At the stipulated price, purchase all the metal that is offered and coin it without limit and virtually without charge. This prevents the market price of gold from falling below the mint buying price.

3   Permit the melting of coins to get gold for nonmonetary uses and/or stand ready to sell, at the fixed price, all of the commodity that is demanded. It is usually unnecessary to give permission to melt coins; people do it anyway if they find that it is the cheapest way to get gold. The effect of this is to prevent the market price of gold from rising above the mint price as long as gold can be acquired for nonmonetary uses. However, when the monetary

**TABLE 2-1**

*Classifications of money*

I. Full-bodied money
II. Representative full-bodied money
III. Credit money
   A. Issued by government
      1. Token coins
      2. Representative token money
      3. Circulating promissory notes
   B. Issued by banks
      1. Circulating promissory notes issued by central banks
      2. Circulating promissory notes issued by other banks
      3. Demand deposits subject to check

system is unable or unwilling to supply the commodity, the market price of gold can rise above the mint price; that is, the monetary unit can depreciate in terms of gold.

Figure 2–1 indicates that all this may be viewed as an arrangement whereby the price of gold is stabilized in terms of money. The curve $S_T S_T$ represents the total supply of gold in the sense of the total stock at various possible prices. The curve $D_C D_C$ represents the demand function for gold for nonmonetary purposes. The figure indicates that the price of gold cannot fall below the level $OE$ as long as the government stands ready to buy (represented by curve $D_M D_M$) at that price all that is offered for monetary purposes. And the price cannot rise above that level as long as gold can be supplied for nonmonetary uses by melting full-bodied gold coins. The supply of gold from melting coins is represented by the curve $S_M S_M$.

Another important point is this: When the government has fixed the price of gold and stands ready to buy in unlimited amounts and to permit melting of gold coins, it loses control of the quantity of full-bodied coins. The amount of gold in monetary use will be a residual equal to the total gold stock minus the amounts demanded for nonmonetary uses. In the figure, the amount of gold in monetary use is equal to the total stock ($OB$) minus the amount absorbed in nonmonetary uses ($OA$). The monetary value of the full-bodied coins is equal to the number of ounces in this form multiplied by the price per ounce. This is represented by the area $ADCB$.

Some consider it a merit of this type of money that its supply is limited by the cost of enlarging the gold stock and by competing demands for nonmonetary uses. They see this as a safeguard against overissue.

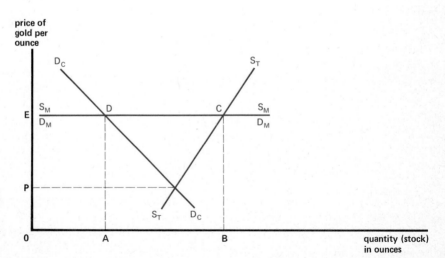

*Stabilization of the price of gold*

**FIGURE 2–1**

Others see little merit in leaving the quantity of money in this form to be determined by the vagaries of gold mining and of competing demands.

Two points on which there has been much misunderstanding need to be clarified:

1   To say that full-bodied coins have the same value as money as they have in nonmonetary uses of the metal is not to say that they have a constant value or purchasing power in terms of other things. If the price of a unit of gold is fixed in terms of money, its purchasing power varies reciprocally with the prices of other things. Thus, the purchasing power of gold will fall by half if the price level of other things doubles, and the purchasing power of gold will double if the price level falls by half. There is no reason to expect that the price level of other things will remain constant simply because the price of gold has been stabilized. (Think through, for example, the effects of a huge new discovery of gold deposits.)

2   It is not true, as some have inferred, that the value of a full-bodied coin (in the sense of its purchasing power over other things) is simply the reflected value of the metal as determined by its total supply (stock) and its demand for nonmonetary uses. Its value is determined by the total supply (stock) of the material and by its total demand for monetary and nonmonetary uses. And the monetary demand may come to be the major part of the total demand. The price and value of the material could fall greatly if the monetary demand were withdrawn and the total supply made available for nonmonetary uses.

**Representative Full-bodied Money**

Representative full-bodied money, which is usually made of paper, is in effect a circulating warehouse receipt for full-bodied coins or their equivalent in bullion. The representative full-bodied money itself has no significant value as a commodity, but it "represents" in circulation an amount of metal with a commodity value equal to the value of the money. Thus, the gold certificates that circulated in the United States before their recall in 1933 represented fully equivalent amounts of gold coin or gold bullion held by the Treasury as backing for them. The main advantage of representative money over full-bodied money is that the latter, involving as it did a physical commodity, typically became quite inconvenient when large sums were transacted. In all other important respects the two types of full-bodied money are equivalent.

**Credit Money**

By credit money, or debt money, we mean any money, except representative full-bodied money, that circulates at a value greater than the commodity value of the material from which it is made. In some cases, the market value of the money material is insignificant, as in the case of most paper money. In other cases, such as copper coins, the market value of the material may be substantial, but may still be below the value of the money.

How can a money achieve and maintain a value or purchasing power as money greater than the value of the commodity of which it is made? Essentially, the method is to limit the quantity of the money by preventing the free and unlimited transformation of the commodity into money. The most common way is for the issuing authority to fix the quantity of the particular type of money to be issued and to buy only as much of the money material as is needed for the purpose. The remainder of the supply of that commodity is left for nonmonetary uses, and this residual supply may be so large relative to demands for nonmonetary uses that the market value of the commodity will fall far below the value of the money. Note that in this case the issuing authority itself determines the quantity of debt or credit money to be issued and the amount of the money material to be purchased for the purpose.

Credit or debt money can also result as the issuing authority buys all the money material offered to it, but at a price significantly below the monetary or face value of the money into which it is transformed. Suppose, for example, that the monetary authority issues pesos, each containing $\frac{1}{2}$ ounce of silver, but stands ready to buy all silver offered to it at a price of only 1 peso an ounce. The issuing authority is clearly in a position to make large gross profits by purchasing silver at 1 peso an ounce and converting each ounce into 2 pesos of money. This gross profit to the issuer is called *seigniorage*. But the main point here is that this is a way of maintaining the value of credit money above the market value of the commodity of which it is made. Each ounce of silver in the form of money is obviously 2 pesos, but the price of silver in the market could fall as low as 1 peso an ounce, the price at which the monetary authority will buy it.

Credit money can take various forms:

1   TOKEN COINS. Our coins (half-dollars, quarters, dimes, nickels, and pennies) are indeed the "small change" of our monetary system; they make up only a very small fraction, about 3 percent, of our total money supply. These coins are all token money, with a value as money considerably above the market values of the metals contained in them. In general, the government creates and issues those amounts of the various denominations of coins that the public demands as "small change."

The history of silver coins provides a vivid example of one potential problem with token money. Until the mid-1960s dollars, half-dollars, and dimes were 90 percent silver and 10 percent alloy. During this period the price of silver remained low enough to keep the market values of the silver in these coins significantly below their face values. The situation changed in the 1960s as nonmonetary demands for silver—demands for silver to be used in silverware, electronics, and photographic film—rose sharply relative to silver supplies. The market price reached $1.293 an ounce, at which price it became profitable to melt down silver dollars and to exchange silver certificates for the silver bullion backing them. Silver dollars disappeared from circulation; some were converted to bullion for nonmonetary uses and some were added to rare-coin collections. As the market price of silver continued to rise, it became profitable to melt down half-dollars, quarters, and dimes. Congress modified this situation by changing the commodity content of these coins from silver to copper and nickel; once again the money value of small change is far above its market value as a commodity. This episode is a good illustration of Gresham's law, which, simply put, states that "bad money drives good money out of circulation." This happens because "bad" money (with less valuable metallic content) is passed on in transactions while individuals try to hold onto "good"money (with more intrinsic value). In the extreme, if a coin is worth more as a commodity than as money it will cease to circulate as money.

2   REPRESENTATIVE TOKEN MONEY. This is usually paper which is, in effect, a circulating warehouse receipt for token coins or for an equal weight of bullion that has been deposited with the government. This type of money is like representative full-bodied money, except that the coin or bullion held as "backing" is worth less as a commodity than it is as money. Silver certificates, which circulated in varying amounts from 1878 to 1967, are the only example of this type of money in the United States.

3   CIRCULATING PROMISSORY NOTES ISSUED BY GOVERNMENTS. Governments also issue credit money in a form that is usually, but sometimes inaccurately, called *circulating promissory notes.* These are usually made of paper and are sometimes called *fiat* money. The only circulating promissory notes issued by the U.S. government and still in circulation are the U.S. notes, or greenbacks, which were issued to assist in financing the Civil War. Over $400 million of them were originally issued, but they were reduced to $347 million by 1878 and have since remained at approximately that level.

Many people oppose the use of government paper money, fearing that it will be issued in excessive amounts. Monetary history provides a real basis for this fear, since these issues provide an attractive source of revenue to governments. By spending a small amount for paper, engraving, and printing, a government can pay its debts or cover its expenses by producing millions of dollars' worth of paper money. The temptation to sacrifice proper monetary management to budgetary needs is often strong. It should be pointed out, however, that most of the excessive issues of paper money have occurred during war periods when nations felt that their very existence was at stake and when they were in dire need of money to meet military requirements. There is no reason why a properly managed government paper money should not function well.

4    CIRCULATING PROMISSORY NOTES ISSUED BY PRIVATE BANKS. Circulating promissory notes issued by privately owned banks have played an important role in monetary systems. Promissory notes issued by state-chartered banks and by the First and Second Banks of the United States provided a large part of the circulating medium in this country before the Civil War, and the national banks chartered by the federal government issued such notes from the time of the Civil War until 1935.

5    CIRCULATING PROMISSORY NOTES ISSUED BY CENTRAL BANKS. The largest part of the hand-to-hand currency that is used in most advanced countries is in the form of circulating promissory notes issued by central banks, such as our Federal Reserve banks, the Bank of England, and the Bank of France.

6    CHECKING DEPOSITS AT BANKS. The major part of the money supply in this country, as well as in most other advanced countries, is in the form of demand deposits at banks. These so-called deposits are merely bank debts payable on demand and are claims of creditors against a bank which can be transferred from one person or firm to another by means of checks or other orders to pay. These claims against banks are generally acceptable in payment of debts and for goods and services. The popularity of checking deposits can be traced to their advantages:

a. They are not so liable to loss or theft as other types of money.

b. They can be transported very cheaply, regardless of the amount of the payment or the distance between payer and payee.

c. Because checks can be written for the exact amount of the payment, there is no need to make change and count bills and coins.

d. When endorsed by the payee, checks serve as a convenient receipt for payment.

The principal disadvantage of checking deposits is that checks drawn on them may not be accepted from an unknown person, but this is largely remedied by such devices as certified checks, cashier's checks, and traveler's checks, which in effect guarantee payment to the payee or to anyone to whom he or she transfers the claim.

**Overview**    Full-bodied money, representative full-bodied money, and the various types of credit money just described have all played a role in monetary systems. Modern economies, however, rely almost exclusively on credit money and, in particular, on the last two categories — currency and checkable bank deposits. Despite these developments, through the years the feeling has persisted, at least in some quarters, that money cannot be "good" unless it is based on some commodity — preferably gold.[1] At the risk of repetition, we must reiterate that this view is erroneous. That credit money can be overissued, and on too many occasions has been, is undeniable. But if it is properly limited, credit money can be given a scarcity value and can circulate at least as satisfactorily as any full-bodied money. In fact, with proper management the quantity of credit money can be adjusted to the needs of the economy better than the quantities of a gold or silver full-bodied money. As we shall now see, it was precisely this lack of flexibility that led to the disappearance of commodity money and commodity standards.

**MONETARY STANDARDS**    As noted above, it has been common for a country to try to maintain its monetary unit and its various types of money in that unit at a constant value in terms of some commodity. Any commodity could be chosen, but *gold standards* and *silver standards* have been the most commonly used. The first full-bodied money in the United States was, in fact, on a joint gold–silver standard, the most common type of *bimetallic* standard.

**Bimetallism**    In its first major monetary legislation, the Coinage Act of 1791, the United States established a bimetallic standard. It adopted the dollar as its monetary unit and gave it a fixed value in terms of silver and also in terms of gold. The mint price of silver was fixed at $1.293 an ounce and that of gold at $19.395 an ounce. Thus, the "mint ratio" was 15 to 1. Or, in other words, the mint price of gold was 15 times that of silver. The government stood ready to mint, at these values, all the gold and silver offered to it. And people were free to melt down or export coins. The clear intent of the legislation was to provide the new nation with full-bodied

---

[1] That the supposed critical role of gold has been stressed by writers of a "conservative" persuasion is well known. Perhaps less well known is Karl Marx' comment that "only in so far as paper money represents gold . . . is it a symbol of value." This may simply serve to show that Freud was on to something when he observed that the human attachment to gold was deep in the subconscious.

gold and silver coins, gold coins for the larger denominations and silver for the smaller ones.

However, the scheme failed; silver "drove gold out of circulation" because the mint ratio in the United States valued silver more highly relative to gold than did the mint ratios of several other important countries that were also on bimetallic standards. In those countries the mint ratio was $15\frac{1}{2}$ to 1. This discrepancy created an opportunity for a profitable chain of exchanges of gold and silver. For example, a person could get an ounce of gold in the United States, export it to another country in exchange for $15\frac{1}{2}$ ounces of silver, use 15 ounces of the silver to buy an ounce of gold here, and have $\frac{1}{2}$ ounce of silver left to cover expenses and yield a profit. However, gold would have disappeared from circulation in the United States even in the absence of such round-robin exchanges. This is because Americans making payments abroad found it cheaper to pay in gold, while foreigners making payments to Americans found it cheaper to pay in silver.

Responding to complaints against the de facto silver standard, Congress attempted to reestablish a bimetallic standard by altering the mint ratio in 1834. Leaving the silver content of the dollar and the mint price of silver unchanged, it lowered the gold content of the dollar so as to raise the mint price of gold from $19.395 to $20.67 an ounce. The new mint ratio was 16 to 1, while that abroad remained at $15\frac{1}{2}$ to 1. The situation was now reversed; the United States' mint parity valued gold more highly relative to silver than did other countries. The results, although apparently unintended, should have been predictable. Gold now drove silver out of circulation. Not only silver dollars but also half-dollars, quarters, and dimes disappeared, creating inconvenience in trade. The nation came to be on a de facto gold standard.

This experience provides another example of the workings of Gresham's law and also suggests the desirability of having a prerequisite in arithmetic for membership in Congress. We turn now to the more basic issue, the operation of a pure gold standard.

**The Gold Standard**    While a precise description of the gold standard would vary from place to place and time to time, in its pure form the gold standard simply involved the steps already described, namely, the definition of the monetary unit in terms of gold (e.g., by valuing gold at $20.67 an ounce) and the permission of full convertibility between gold and money and between money and gold. This mechanical connection between gold and the monetary unit undoubtedly encouraged confidence in the value of the monetary unit, but it was not without its problems. The most serious of these was that changes in the stock of monetary gold would tend to produce corresponding changes in the stock of money. For example, in the United States, which operated on a relatively pure gold standard from 1879 to 1933, the stock of dollars would increase as new dollars were issued to acquire new gold. This, in turn, would exert an expansionary and potentially inflationary influence on the economy. Alternatively, the stock of money would decrease whenever someone returned dollars to the government in exchange for gold (or melted down gold coins), and this would produce contractionary and deflationary forces. These inflationary and deflationary results often occurred whether they were wanted or not.

How would such changes in the stock of gold occur? One way was via an increase in the domestic production of gold. Indeed, on a number of occasions in U.S. history new gold discoveries led to substantial increases in the stock of money and were ultimately translated into significant increases in the price level. But this was neither the only nor the most important source of variation in our gold stock. Rather, as in the case of the demise of bimetallism, international factors proved to be of major significance.

Specifically, if a country had an adverse balance of payments – if it was importing more goods and services from other countries than it was exporting to them – this trade deficit had to be covered by shipping gold abroad. While countries kept *gold reserves* to accommodate temporary outflows, a persistently adverse balance of payments would eventually wipe out any stock of reserves. Under such conditions the international "rules of the game" called for the deficit country to deflate its domestic economy and lower its prices. This would tend to make its own products relatively more attractive to foreigners, since they were now cheaper and would make foreign goods relatively less attractive to its own citizens. Thus, exports would be promoted and imports inhibited. With the appropriate degree of deflation, the balance of payments would again "balance" and the gold outflow would cease.[2]

The difficulty with this scenario was that the cure was often more painful than the disease in that deflation of the domestic economy did more than reduce prices. It also tended to reduce output and employment and produce business failures. Increasingly, the social costs associated with such things as higher unemployment, labor unrest, and falling stock prices came to be regarded as too high a price to pay for maintenance of the gold standard. Countries wanted more freedom to issue money to promote output and employment, finance government deficits, or use for other purposes. The final straw in the United States was the Great Depression; in 1933, after several years of deflation and widespread unemployment, we abandoned the pure gold standard. While a

---

[2] For a fuller description of this process, including the role of foreign exchange rates, see Part VI.

limited gold standard lingered on until 1971, the age of pure gold standards essentially ended in the mid-1930s.

Such marked changes in the monetary role of gold remind us that monetary systems, far from remaining static, are subject to continuous, and sometimes abrupt, changes in both form and function.

## THE EVOLUTION OF THE MODERN PAYMENTS MECHANISM

As indicated earlier, modern payment systems now rely on credit money in the form of checkable bank deposits as the major component of the money supply. This section briefly sketches some of the critical forces that have brought about this development. Understanding these forces will provide both insight into the nature of banks and a basis for forecasting the nature of future developments in the payment mechanism.

### Coinage

As we have seen, primitive economies overcame the inconvenience of barter by the use of uncoined metals, such as copper, gold, and silver, as circulating media. These metals probably came to be generally acceptable in payment because they were widely desired for religious and ornamental purposes, they did not deteriorate, their large value relative to their weight and bulk made them relatively easy to transport, and so on. At this stage money was not differentiated from the material of which it was made; the metals flowed freely into and out of monetary uses. The use of bullion as money had serious disadvantages, however, especially if payers were not averse to short-weighing and adulteration. Precision weighing apparatus was not widely available and assaying was both laborious and inaccurate. Coinage solved both these problems. At first, coinage amounted merely to an official certification as to the weight and purity of a lump of metal. The imprint of a king's stamp meant in effect, "I hereby certify that this contains a certain weight of metal of a certain purity." The names of many monetary units (such as pounds, lire, livres, and shekels) that were originally units of weight attest to this fact.

### The Evolution of Banking

While coinage was an important monetary innovation, both coins and uncoined metal shared some disadvantages of those who held them or used them to make payments. These included (1) danger of theft or robbery, either in storage or in transporting the commodity or coin; (2) costs of transporting to make payments over distances; and (3) absence of interest or any other return on the money.

Largely because of the danger of theft and robbery, the practice arose of leaving gold and silver in the custody of some reputable person (a wealthy merchant, a money changer, or a goldsmith) who owned a strong box or other means of safekeeping. At this stage the "depositor" undoubtedly expected that the custodian would indeed hold all the specie intact. The custodian performed this service as a favor for friends or made a charge for it. It is also probable that at this initial stage a depositor who wished to make payments would go to the goldsmith or other custodian, get the required amount of coins, and use the coins themselves to make payment. But this was inconvenient; how much easier it would be to transfer claims against the metal. And such claims were at hand, for the goldsmith or other custodian usually gave some sort of evidence to the depositor. One type was a receipt, which said in effect, "IOU so many florins." The next step was for payers to make payment by giving these IOUs to a payee. The latter could then claim the specie from the goldsmith, or use the IOU to make payments to others. As these IOUs came to be used in payments, the bank note was born. A bank note is simply a bank debt or promise to pay, evidenced by a piece of paper. The earliest bank notes may have been acceptable only because they were believed to be fully backed by specie. Nevertheless, this was an important step in the evolution of money, for the community was becoming accustomed to using in payment not the precious metals themselves but paper claims against those metals.

Another method of payment soon developed. The person leaving gold or silver with the "banker" would not receive a piece of paper representing the debt of the banker, but simply a "deposit credit" evidenced by an entry on the bank's books. The practice soon arose of making payments by writing an order on the banker to pay someone else. For example, Jones would write an order on the bank saying, "Pay Smith X florins and charge to my account." Smith might then claim the gold or silver. But as such orders became more widely acceptable in payment, it became increasingly common for payees to leave the specie with the goldsmith or other banker and to pay others by transferring claims to deposits. Thus, deposit claims, not specie itself, came to be used as a means of payment.

The high cost and risk of transporting precious metals over distances created an opportunity for profit that did not go unnoticed by shrewd goldsmiths and merchants. One can imagine a canny goldsmith-banker in Lübeck writing to a counterpart in Genoa,[3]

> *As we both know, trade between our areas has grown rapidly in recent years. Large amounts of specie flow every month from my area to yours, at great cost to the merchants and great risk to property and life. At the same time, almost equally large amounts*

---

[3] The illustrative use of Genoa and florins (a gold coin first issued in thirteenth-century Florence) is meant to convey the important role of the Italians in the development of commercial banking. Indeed, the word *bank* itself derives from the Italian word *banco*, meaning "bench," reflecting the fact that early Italian bankers conducted their business from a bench in the street.

*of specie flow from the Genoa area to the Lübeck area, at comparable cost and risk. We can easily abolish these unnecessary costs, spur the development of trade, and add to our own pitifully low incomes by cooperating with each other. When someone in your area wishes to make a payment in the Lübeck region, you get from him the required amount of specie and give him an order on me to give specie to the payee, and I will do so. Then, when someone in my area wishes to make payments in the Genoa region, I will collect from her the required amount of specie and give her an order on you, which I hope you will honor. We will have to ship specie between Lübeck and Genoa only to the extent that the payments I make for your account and the payments you make for my account do not balance out, and I forecast that the net shipments required will be very small indeed relative to the total payments effected by us. In fairness to our customers and in the interest of promoting our business we should not charge for these services as much as it would cost our customers to ship specie equal to the total value of all payments, but in fairness to ourselves and our families our charges should exceed our actual costs.*

Such were the motivations that led to the establishment of business relationships among emerging bankers in the leading commercial centers. Bills of exchange or orders to pay became an increasingly popular way of effecting payments, and the things transferred were claims against goldsmith-bankers or merchant-bankers.

Up to this point we have dealt with only two forces that contributed to the evolution of banking: the disadvantages of full-bodied coins because of their liability to theft and robbery, and the high cost and risk of transporting them. But these two forces alone were sufficient to concentrate large amounts of the precious metals in the hands of an emerging class of bankers. At first, these were primarily goldsmiths, money changers, or merchants who took on safekeeping of specie and related functions as a sideline. Gradually, however, these functions increased in relative importance and profitability, and specialized bankers began to emerge. Note that in this earliest stage all deposits and bank notes were fully backed by specie, and the income of the emerging bankers came from charges for safekeeping and for transmitting payments.

Then came a discovery that was to be momentous for the evolution of banking. The emerging bankers discovered that, to meet their promises to pay in specie on demand, they did not need to hold gold and silver equal to 100 percent of their outstanding debts in the form of deposits and bank notes. A banker who was in fact holding specie fully equal to the value of his deposit and bank note liabilities might have put it this way:

> *I do not need to hold all that specie because those people are not all going to demand payment at any one time or even over a short period. Of course, there will be withdrawals. Some will want gold or silver for circulation. Also, I must be prepared to pay gold or silver to other banks who acquire claims against me in the form of deposit and bank note claims that I have issued. But such outpayments will be largely balanced by new inflows of gold and silver. I could meet any net drain that is likely to occur if I held gold and silver equal to only a small fraction — perhaps only a tenth — of my outstanding note and deposit liabilities. To hold more is terribly wasteful. Look at all the gold and silver lying there, idle and earning nothing! I think I'll lend out some of it and earn some interest.*

And if his conscience was troubled by his contemplated breach of trust, he may have soothed it by replying, "I didn't promise my customers in so many words that I would hold all the gold and silver; I merely promised that I would pay them gold and silver when they asked for it. If I keep the promise why should it be any concern of theirs if I increase my income a little?"

So were banks transformed from mere custodians holding specie reserves equal to 100 percent of the deposit and bank note liabilities into lenders who held specie equal to only a fraction of their liabilities. *Fractional reserve banking* was born. Such banking may indeed have originated as a surreptitious breach of trust. But the secret was soon out, and fractional reserve banking gained widespread support. A banker could now say to the public in effect,

> *It will be to our mutual advantage if you leave most of your gold and silver with me and hold and use as money the bank notes and deposits. The advantage to me as a banker is obvious; I can make loans and earn an income. But I will share this with you by providing valuable services at little or no cost to you. If you want currency that is convenient to hold or transport, I will provide you with bank notes. If you want the convenience of checking facilities I will provide those too. I will hold your funds in safekeeping, provide you with checkbooks, make payments for you over long distances, and do much of your bookkeeping for you.*

Many banks also paid interest on deposit balances, an advantage not offered by coins. Moreover, those who were depositors often received preferred treatment when they applied for loans.

In these various ways the public was persuaded to hold more and more of its money in the form of bank notes and deposit claims against banks. Increasing proportions of the gold and silver money came to lodge in the banks, there to serve as a fractional reserve against the banks' note and deposit liabilities.

The fractional reserve principle gave banks a great power that will be emphasized in later chapters — the power to increase and decrease the total money supply. Banks did not have this power when they issued bank notes and deposits only in exchange for an equal value of gold and silver; they merely substituted in the hands of the public one type of money for another. Suppose, for example, that the public has entrusted $100 of gold and silver to the banks in exchange for bank notes and deposits. This will appear as follows on the balance sheets of the public and the banks:

| BALANCE SHEET OF THE PUBLIC | | | BALANCE SHEET OF THE BANK | | |
|---|---|---|---|---|---|
| **ASSETS** | | **LIABILITIES** | **ASSETS** | | **LIABILITIES** |
| Gold and silver | −$100 | | Gold and silver | +$100 | Note and deposit liabilities  +$100 |
| Bank notes and deposits | +$100 | | | | |

The public's total holdings of money remain unchanged, its larger holdings of bank notes and deposits being offset by its smaller holdings of gold and silver. And the banks have issued note and deposit liabilities equal to only the $100 of gold and silver surrendered by the public.

Suppose now that, starting from this situation in which both their gold and silver holdings and their note and deposit liabilities are $100, the banks decide they can meet any likely demands for payments if they hold gold and silver reserves equal to only 10 percent of their liabilities. They come to believe that any gold and silver holdings in excess of 10 percent of their liabilities can be used as a basis for lending. Consider two extreme cases:

1. As the banks lend, the borrowers withdraw from the banks gold and silver equal to the full amount of the loans. If the banks lend $90, their holdings of gold and silver will fall by that amount, and they will increase their assets in the form of outstanding loans (debt claims against borrowers) by the same amount. The banks' balance sheets will now appear as follows:

| **ASSETS** | | **LIABILITIES** | |
|---|---|---|---|
| Gold and silver | $10 | Note and deposit liabilities | $100 |
| Loans | 90 | | |

The effect of this transaction is to increase the public's money supply by $90, the amount of the increase in loans. Thus, in addition to the $100 of notes and deposits still held by the public, the borrowers now have the $90 of gold and silver paid out by the banks. So we find that by making loans or buying other assets, the banks can increase the public's money supply even if borrowers take all their loan proceeds in gold and silver.

However, once the public has become accustomed to using bank notes and deposits as money, borrowers are unlikely to withdraw gold and silver equal to the full amount of their borrowings. They are likely to accept bank notes or deposits instead. Let us therefore consider the other extreme case.

2. As the banks lend, the borrowers take all the loan proceeds in the form of bank notes and deposits, and there is no net drain of gold and silver from the banks. Suppose the banks lend $900, giving note or deposit claims to the borrowers. The balance sheet of the banks will appear as follows:

| ASSETS | | LIABILITIES | |
|---|---|---|---|
| Gold and silver | $100 | Note and deposit liabilities | $1,000 |
| Loans | 900 | | |

In this process the banks have increased the public's money supply by $900, and have done so by issuing new note and deposit liabilities in exchange for debt claims against borrowers. The banks feel secure because their gold and silver reserves are still equal to 10 percent of their liabilities. In a sense, each $1 of gold and silver is supporting, or serving as a basis for, $10 of note and deposit liabilities. But most of these notes and deposits were created as banks purchased assets other than money itself. We shall later analyze these processes in more detail and also review the process through which banks decrease the total money supply by decreasing their holdings of loans and other debt claims. But have a try at explaining this yourself. What would happen to the money supply if, starting from the last situation described, the banks decreased by $500 their outstanding loans?

In broad outline, such are the processes through which the public came to hold much of its money in the form of claims against banks. Even when full-bodied gold and silver coins were available and the public could have refused to accept or hold anything else, it chose to hold much of its money in the form of bank notes and deposits, and the banks found it profitable to manufacture these claims. Thus, in large part, the development of credit or debt moneys reflected private choices

—the public's choices among the various types of money and the choices of bankers as lenders and creators of money.

**Government and Credit Money**

Although the composition of the money supply and the trend toward greater use of credit moneys have been greatly influenced by the choices of the public and the bankers, governments have exerted important influences in many ways. We shall mention here only a few of the most important.

1   Governments themselves have been issuers of credit money. In some cases, the purpose has been to provide more convenient types of money, such as token coins or paper money; in others, it has been to remedy an alleged shortage of money; and in still others, it has been to finance government expenditures. In the United States, government credit money is now issued by the Treasury (coin) and the Federal Reserve (paper money).

2   Governments regulate the availability of full-bodied and representative full-bodied moneys and the redeemability of moneys in precious metals. As noted earlier, the trend has been toward more and more restricted redeemability in gold, thus encouraging the expansion and use of credit moneys.

3   Governments influence the establishment and operation of banks in various ways. For example, they have both encouraged the establishment of banks and regulated their operations. At an early stage, they encouraged the issue of bank notes; later they moved toward the abolition of bank notes. And in various ways they regulate the volume of bank deposits. Indeed, one of the major functions of the Federal Reserve is to regulate money creation and money destruction by the banks.

Most of these points will be developed further in later chapters.

**Possible Future Developments in the Payments Mechanism**

Our discussion of the evolution of banking has traced the emergence of bank deposits as the primary medium of payments. However, recent advances in computer technology and the rapid growth in credit card usage have suggested to some that, just as coin and currency gradually gave way to the convenience and efficiency of checking deposits, such deposits may give way to yet another type of payments mechanism. Indeed, these days one hears the phrases "checkless society," "cashless society," and "electronic money" bandied about. Furthermore, there is ample evidence that neither the banks nor the Federal Reserve is fully content with the payments mechanism as it now stands. A brief review of the reasons for this discontent will both provide us with some further insights as to the nature of money and allow us to indulge in a bit of speculation as to the form of future payments media.

As detailed earlier, a payments mechanism is merely a set of institutional arrangements by which exchanges of resources are accomplished.

Barter, the use of coin or paper currency, and the use of checking deposits are all forms of payment mechanisms. As with any economic institution, the question naturally arises as to whether the existing payments mechanism is accomplishing its function as cheaply and as efficiently as possible. This is an important issue, since resources devoted to making payments tend to reduce the output of other goods and services that increase economic welfare.

The most obvious costs of the payments mechanism in the United States are the following: the costs of producing the supply of coin and paper currency, the costs of distributing and storing currency, and the costs of clearing checks. The first two categories include the expenses of operating the U.S. mint and the need for a stock of capital goods to safeguard the stock of currency. For example, it has been estimated that the total value of cash registers in the United States is approximately $4 billion.

Although the costs of producing, distributing, and storing currency are hardly inconsequential, by far the most important costs are those involved in clearing checks. In 1977 over 27 billion checks were written in the United States. It has been estimated that each check is handled an average of 10 times and passes through $2\frac{1}{3}$ banks before being returned to its source. The cost of this in 1977 has been put at about 30¢ per check, for a total of $8 billion. Projections for 1985 suggest that the number of checks written could exceed 50 billion, with an associated clearing cost of $16 billion.

Faced with these prospects for continued growth in the volume of checks, both the banks and the Federal Reserve have become increasingly concerned about the substantial resources devoted to shuffling pieces of paper among various parts of the country. To stem this tide the Federal Reserve has urged the use of wire transfers to replace processing of vast quantities of paper and has issued a set of guidelines for the implementation of "regional (check) clearing centers . . . provided with automated clearing and telecommunications capabilities to serve as a basis for transition to widespread checkless–electronic–fund transfers."

Many economists see the natural evolution of these developments as leading to the ultimate emergence of an *electronic money transfer system* (EMTS). Although the details of such a system are still quite speculative, some leading authorities forsee the following scenario:

> *Each economic unit in the society will have an account through which it can instantaneously effect funds transfers to any other member of the system. The EMTS will consist of a nationwide computer network which keeps track of individuals' credits and debits as trading occurs in the economy. Business firms and government offices will tie into the EMTS network using their own computers, while private individuals' means of*

*access to the system will be a plastic identification card, quite
similar to today's credit cards. Every retail establishment will have
one or more on-line terminals which have the capacity to read
identification cards and transmit sales and payment information
to the local EMTS computer center.*[4]

While the implementation of an EMTS clearly requires that many technical and legal problems be surmounted, for purposes of discussion let us assume that at some point in the future we have made the transition to an electronic payments mechanism. What differences are we likely to observe in the operation of the system as compared with our present structure? At the most mundane level we would, of course, see a marked reduction in the use of the conventional checking instrument. But what of the volume of deposits and the appropriate definition of the supply of money? It seems plausible that many transactions would involve transferring funds out of interest-bearing savings accounts. This would further blur the distinction between demand and savings deposits (or money and near-money), a trend that is already taking place. Clearly, in such a world a broader definition of the money supply would be needed, although the most appropriate definition would depend on the precise details of the payments mechanism.

An electronic payments mechanism would undoubtedly have other far-reaching implications for the operation of the financial system. For instance, if transactions are to be made from savings deposits, then savings banks and savings and loan associations, as well as commercial banks, would have to be an integral part of the payments network. This would undoubtedly change the nature of competition among these various financial institutions and require a change in the structure of government regulation of these institutions. We shall return to these issues in a later chapter. For the present, the mere possibility of an electronic transfer system should serve to reemphasize that appropriate definitions, such as that for money, are continually evolving and require constant review in the light of institutional changes in our economy.

**SELECTED
READINGS**

Angell, N., *The Story of Money*, New York, Harper & Row, 1929.

Del Mar, A., *The Science of Money*, London, Bell, 1885.

Flannery, M. J., and D. M. Jaffee, *The Economic Implications of an Electronic Monetary Transfer System*, Lexington, Mass., Heath, 1973.

Galbraith, J. K., *Money: Whence It Came, Where It Went*, Boston, Houghton Mifflin, 1975.

---

[4] Mark J. Flannery and Dwight M. Jaffee, *The Economic Implications of an Electronic Monetary Transfer System*, Lexington, Mass., Heath, 1973, p. 5.

# DEBT, CREDIT, AND FINANCIAL MARKETS AND INSTITUTIONS

This chapter has two major objectives. First, we examine the nature of debt or credit. Although in some quarters the notion of being in debt has an evil ring, we shall see that debt performs a vital role in channeling savings into productive investment. Put another way, just as money (which is in fact a form of debt) enables an economy to overcome the inefficiencies of barter, the existence of a broad range of debt instruments can help in achieving an efficient allocation of resources and a higher rate of economic growth.

After analyzing the economic functions of debt, we turn to the second objective of this chapter: exploring the actual process of debt creation. Specifically, we examine the vital role of financial markets and financial institutions in transmitting funds from lenders to borrowers or from savers to investors. A firm understanding of the general principles involved will prove critical in later chapters, where we examine the role of money and monetary policy in more detail.

## THE NATURE OF CREDIT OR DEBT

Debt and credit are merely the same thing looked at from two different points of view. They are an obligation to pay in the future; and since money is so widely used as a standard of deferred payments, they are usually obligations to pay fixed sums of money. From the point of view of the person to whom the future payment is to be made, the obligation is a credit; it is a claim against another person for payment. But from the point of view of the one who is obliged to pay in the future, the obligation is a debt. Since debt and credit are the same thing looked at from different points of view, it is obvious that the amount of debt outstanding at any time is equal to the amount of credit outstanding.

Credit or debt usually originates in economic and financial transactions in which creditors surrender something of value at one point of time in exchange for debtors' promises to pay in the future. The "something of value" surrendered may be money, services, goods, or some sort of financial claim such as stocks or bonds. However, the resulting debt is usually payable in money. We are all familiar with the creation of debt by the sale of goods or services "on credit." For example, Ms. Jones buys groceries, promising to pay at the end of the month. A corporation gets raw materials from its suppliers with the understanding that it will pay at the end of the quarter. Much of the outstanding debt at any time has arisen from such extensions of credit by sellers of goods and services. Most of the remainder has arisen out of money-lending transactions in which creditors surrendered money at one point of time in exchange for promises of debtors to pay later, usually with interest.

## ECONOMIC FUNCTIONS OF DEBT

The basic economic functions of debt and financial instruments can be understood most easily and clearly by considering a relatively simple society made up of spending units or households. Each household or unit receives during any income period, such as a month, some flow of money income resulting from the household's or unit's contribution to the value of current output of goods and services. During each income period each unit also spends some amount for the current output of goods and services to be used for consumption purposes. A unit's income and consumption need not be exactly equal during any income period. The difference between them will be called *saving*. During any period, therefore, households can be separated into three categories based on their pattern of saving. (1) *Zero savers* are those whose current consumption is exactly equal to their current income. (2) *Positive savers*, or simply *savers*, are those who consume less than their current income. Their saving represents the amount of their current income that they do not use to demand goods and services for their own current consumption. (3) *Negative savers* or *dissavers* are people whose current consumption exceeds their current income. Their consumption demands for output exceed their current incomes.

Let us now explore why a household may elect to be a saver or dissaver during a period, and why it may be a saver in some periods and a dissaver in others.

### Debt and Consumption

One problem faced by each household or unit is that of allocating its consumption through time, recognizing that with given current and expected future incomes, "the more we consume in one period the less can we consume in others." To achieve maximum total utility or satisfaction through time, each unit would have to take into consideration its current income, expected future income streams, present needs, and expected future needs. At any given time, different units are likely to attach differing relative values to consumption in the present as against consumption in the future. One unit may value present consumption very highly and be willing to sacrifice large amounts of future consumption in order to consume now in excess of its current income. Another may place a much lower premium on present consumption and demand little or no reward for consuming less than its current income.

Differing time patterns of income and needs contribute strongly to differences in valuations of present versus future consumption. For example, some units may have large needs in the present — such as needs for expensive medical care or educational services for their children — but expect their future needs to be lower. And their current income may be well below that expected in the future. Such units are likely to place a high premium on present consumption and to want to consume in excess of their current incomes. Other units may be in the reverse position. Their present needs may be small relative to those expected in the future, when their children reach college age or their parents face retirement. And their present incomes may be high relative to those expected in the future. Such units are likely to place little or no premium on present consumption and to want to consume less than their current incomes.

When households place different relative valuations on present and future consumption, all can be made to feel better off — to increase their total utility — through exchange or trade of present consumption against future consumption. Those units that place lower premiums on present consumption can transfer their current saving, representing claims on current output, to those units that place a higher premium on present consumption. Later, the borrowing units will return consuming power to the lenders, who can then decide whether to use it immediately for consumption or to save it for later. Thus, all units may be enabled to increase their total utilities through an optimal spreading or allocation of their consumption through time.

In the absence of debt or credit, exchanges of present consumption against future consumption are likely to be inefficient and so limited in extent that large potential increases in utility will fail to be realized. Suppose, for example, that a community has not yet invented consumer credit and has available only two types of assets — physical assets and some form of money, such as coins or paper money, which yields no interest. Households that wished to consume in excess of their current incomes could do so only by drawing down their money balances or by selling their physical assets. However, they may not have any excess money balances or any physical assets that they could sell without serious deprivation or loss. Those who wish to save are faced with only very limited alternative uses of their saving; they can only increase their money balances or buy physical assets. Increased money balances would provide additional liquidity and safety for the saver, but would yield no income. Physical assets might yield an income but be unattractive because of the transactions costs, illiquidity, and risk involved. As a consequence, savers might save less, and in any case, transfers of their money saving to dissavers would be limited. The situation can be improved by the invention and use of consumer debt or credit. This enables savers to transfer their money saving, representing claims against current output, to dissavers in exchange for their promises to repay in the future.

In summary, then, consumer credit (or debt) enables households to better space their consumption through time. It also involves the creation of financial instruments that enrich the menu of assets available to savers. Finally, consumer credit serves to bolster aggregate demand for output and to maintain the circular flow of income. As already noted, a household's saving during a period is simply that part of its income for the period that is not spent during the period for consumption. Thus, saving, considered by itself, is deflationary in the sense that it tends to lower total money demands for output and to shrink the circular flow of income. However, these deflationary effects are offset to the extent that money representing saving is transferred to dissavers, who spend it for consumption. We shall discuss this in more detail later.

**Debt and Investment**

Although consumer credit is widely used and the outstanding stock of consumer debt is very large, a much larger part of the total debt outstanding was created in the process of investment or capital formation — the process of adding to the nation's stock of capital goods. The stock of capital goods at any point of time is the accumulated stock of goods that were produced in the past and not yet consumed or used up. An outstanding characteristic of modern industrial societies is the huge stock of capital. Some types of capital render services directly to consumers. Outstanding examples are houses and apartments, which provide shelter and comfort. However, a larger part of the capital stock renders services as instruments in processes of production. Examples are structures and many types of durable equipment used in manufacturing, transportation, communications, and wholesale and retail trade; office buildings; farm machinery and other equipment; business inventories; and so on. In an industrial economy this huge stock of capital is a major reason for the high output per capita. Technological advances and increases in the stock of capital relative to labor are the two principal sources of growth of output per capita and of output per unit of labor. It is partly because of this that we are so interested in processes of capital formation or investment.

Saving is a necessary condition for capital formation. A society could not add to its stock of capital goods if its members insisted on using for current consumption all of the income or output that its labor and other productive resources could produce. Saving, or abstinence from current consumption, frees some part of available productive resources to produce output to be used to increase the stock of capital. However, although the ability and willingness to save is a necessary condition for capital formation, it is not by itself sufficient to assure that capital formation will occur. The productive resources that are not used to produce output for current consumption may remain unemployed or go to waste if no one employs them to produce goods to be added to the stock of capital. Thus, investment is another necessary condition for capital formation. *Investment* means the amount spent during a stated period for current output to be used to increase the stock of capital goods of the various types noted previously. It is through investment that the amounts of income or output, and more basically the productive resources that are saved, are translated into capital accumulation.

One can imagine an economic system in which each household spent for investment in each period an amount exactly equal to its own saving, no more and no less. Such a system would be highly inefficient, for at least two reasons:

1   DIFFERENCES IN THE MARGINAL PRODUCTIVITY OF CAPITAL. For some units, including some with high rates of saving, the marginal productivity of capital—the addition to output resulting from additions to capital stock—may be very low. There may be many reasons for this—lack of interest or ability in entrepreneurship and management, inadequate education or experience, possession of an already large stock of capital assets, and so on. For other units, including some with low rates of saving, the marginal productivity of capital may be much higher because of, for example, high interest and ability in entrepreneurship and management, excellent education and experience, an inadequate stock of capital relative to needs, and so on.

2   DISECONOMIES OF SMALL SCALE. If each household or unit could command only an amount of capital equal to its own accumulated savings, many enterprises would be too small to achieve the greater output made possible by the economies of scale. They would not be able to mass enough capital of specialized types, to command the necessary array of special talents, or to reap the other economies of large-scale production.

It is therefore clear that if capital is to make its maximum contribution to productivity, ways must be found to transfer savings, and thus the power of investment, to those who can achieve the highest marginal productivity of capital, and that savings must be pooled and used for investment in entities large enough to achieve economies of scale. In some industries the latter requires the pooling of hundreds of millions or even billions of dollars' worth of assets. In this process, if not earlier, a new type of institution differentiated from households—the specialized business firm—appears.

These business firms in turn create financial instruments or claims against themselves. In effect, savers surrender funds to those who wish to invest, receiving in return newly created financial instruments that represent claims against both the income of firms and their assets. Thus, the process of creating real capital usually has its counterpart in the creation of financial claims that are issued to raise the funds used to buy the capital.

Actual financial claims are of two broad types: equity claims and debt claims. *Equity claims*, such as common stock, are shares of ownership in the firm, necessarily involving both the possibilities of profits and the risk of loss. Alternatively, the saver may prefer to hold a *debt claim*, such as a corporate bond. In this case the firm promises to pay a stated amount of interest and to repay a stated amount of principal at a later date. While the factors that influence a saver's choice between equity and debt claims will be touched upon later, for our present purposes we simply wish to emphasize that large amounts of business investment are financed through the issue of debt and equity claims.

**Debt and Other Institutions**

For almost all other types of institutions in our society, debt and credit serve functions quite comparable to those served for households and business firms. Other such institutions include federal, state, and municipal governments; educational institutions; churches; charitable institutions; country clubs; fraternities; and many others. In any stated period these institutions receive flows of income and spend for current output. However, many do not wish to spend for output in a period an amount exactly equal to their current income. Some wish to spend for consumption and investment in capital formation an amount less than their current income. They are in a position to extend credit—to transfer to others claims against current output, receiving in return debt or equity claims. Others wish to be deficit units, to buy output to be used for consumption and investment in amounts exceeding their current incomes. Creation of debt claims against themselves enables them to command more output now in exchange for their obligations to repay later.

**Debt and the Level of Income**

Up to this point we have stressed the contribution of debt to the efficient allocation of resources in the economy. Of course, an efficient allocation of resources is necessary if the economy is to achieve its development and growth potential. Thus, the existence of debt and the attainment of increases in national income go hand in hand. Indeed, a casual inspection of the historical record provides evidence for the view that growth and prosperity have flourished when overall indebtedness has been rising rapidly. However, this observation should not be interpreted as prescribing unlimited debt creation. The issue is rather like the one that faced Goldilocks—avoiding debt creation that is "too small" or "too big" and hoping to get it "just right." We can gain some perspective on what this might involve by considering a specific illustration.

Suppose we start from a situation in which national income, or expenditures, is flowing at some annual rate and this income level is consistent with "full employment." This entire amount will accrue as income to the units in the society—households, business firms, governmental units, and so on. If every one of these units spent for consumption and investment purposes an amount exactly equal to its current income, the flow of national income would proceed at a stable rate. All income receipts flowing from the value of output would return to the market as expenditures for output, thus maintaining the level of output and income. Note that in such a case the maintenance of a stable flow of income could be achieved without any net creation of debt. Every unit would spend all its own income, and only that.

However, this balance of income and spending is unlikely to occur in the American economy. Some units spend less than their current income for consumption and investment purposes, and thus are called *surplus units*. If these surpluses of current income over expenditures for output are not somehow offset, they will cause a decline in the flow of expenditures for output and thus will decrease the level of national money income.

How, in an economy with surplus units, can such a fall of money income be averted? It can be averted only if there are other units—such as households, business firms, or governmental units—that spend more for consumption and investment than they receive in current incomes. These are called *deficit units*. To counterbalance the effect of the surplus units, the deficit units must somehow be enabled and persuaded to purchase the extra output that the surplus units did not purchase. A principal way of achieving this is by the creation of new debts. By this method, the surpluses of surplus units can be channeled to deficit units to be spent for consumption or investment.

In later sections we shall analyze at length the determinants of the behavior of national money income. Here we shall emphasize only one major point. In an economy like that of the United States, that includes many surplus units during any period, very large total surpluses will be generated when national money income is at a level consistent with "full employment." This level can be maintained only if there are deficit units able and willing to incur deficits as large as the total surpluses of surplus units. To achieve this requires a high rate of creation of new debt.

THE STOCK OF
OUTSTANDING
DEBT

The preceding sections stressed the role of debt and debt creation in transferring funds from surplus to deficit units, whether these are households, business firms, governments, or others. As a result of this process, at any point in time there is a stock of debt or credit outstanding. This stock is equal to the total of all debt issues in preceding periods minus amounts retired through repayment or default.

There are a variety of ways to summarize the stock of outstanding debt. One perspective is provided in Table 3–1, which contains data for the stock of credit market instruments on selected dates. A number of features of this table deserve emphasis. One is the huge volume of outstanding credit market debt — approximately $4,250 billion at the end of 1979. Another is the rate of growth of outstanding debt. For the last thirty years its annual growth has averaged $128 billion, and its annual average growth in the past decade was $276 billion.

To some pessimists, both the size of outstanding debt and its rate of growth are frightening. They lament that we shall never be able to pay off the debt and that as a nation we are borrowing ourselves into bankruptcy. To refute such primitive theses one does not have to argue that the growth rate of debt has been "just right" or that all debt has been wisely incurred. Several facts are relevant:

1  "We owe it to ourselves." Although many consider debt as the antithesis of thrift, savers need debt in order to find an outlet for savings. Thus, the debts of some American units are the assets of others.[1]

2  There is no reason why the outstanding debt should be retired or even reduced in total volume. Some debts will be repaid or reduced, and new debt will be created. But artificial attempts to

---

[1] This statement, which is specifically illustrated in Table 3–2, needs to be qualified in that a small part of this debt is owed to foreigners.

**TABLE 3–1**

*Outstanding credit market debt in the United States (end-of-year figures in billions of dollars)*

| Type of debt | 1949 | 1959 | 1969 | 1979 |
|---|---|---|---|---|
| U.S. government securities | 219.1 | 244.8 | 321.2 | 916.7 |
| State and local obligations | 21.0 | 65.5 | 133.1 | 312.7 |
| Corporate and foreign bonds | 38.4 | 84.8 | 178.0 | 455.7 |
| Mortgages | 62.9 | 191.9 | 443.2 | 1,333.7 |
| Consumer credit | 20.9 | 60.7 | 137.7 | 382.3 |
| Bank loans | 20.2 | 53.2 | 144.0 | 406.8 |
| Other debt | 20.7 | 39.5 | 133.4 | 438.0 |
| Total | 403.3 | 740.4 | 1,490.7 | 4,246.0 |

*Source:* Board of Governors of the Federal Reserve System, *Flow of Funds Accounts, 1949–1978,* Washington, D.C., December 1979.

reduce total outstanding debt or even to prevent its increase would inevitably damage investment and deflate national income.

3   The increase of total debt and of service charges on that debt has been accompanied by increases in ability to pay, whether this is measured in terms of income or in terms of the value of national assets. For example, between 1946 and 1979 the gross national product at annual rates and at current prices rose from $210 billion to $2,369 billion. The rise in corporate debt has been a financial counterpart of a high rate of investment in plant, equipment, and inventories. State and local government debt has been incurred mainly to finance public investment in new schools, streets, sanitation systems, and so on.

Some additional perspective on the role of debt in the economy can be gleaned from Table 3–2, which gives a more comprehensive snapshot of the stock of outstanding financial instruments for the year 1978. The data, which are taken from the extremely useful *Flow of Funds Accounts* compiled and published by the Federal Reserve System, illustrate the importance of debt for all the major sectors of the economy. Several facts stand out:

1   *Households* are the economy's largest lender group, with total financial assets of $3,422 billion and total liabilities of $1,210

**TABLE 3–2**

*Financial assets and liabilities
(in billions of dollars,
year-end 1978)*

| TYPE OF INSTRUMENT | HOUSEHOLDS ASSETS | HOUSEHOLDS LIABILITIES | BUSINESS ASSETS | BUSINESS LIABILITIES | GOVERNMENT ASSETS | GOVERNMENT LIABILITIES | FINANCIAL ASSETS | FINANCIAL LIABILITIES |
|---|---|---|---|---|---|---|---|---|
| Demand deposits and currency | 222.1 | | 81.3 | | 32.6 | | 22.1 | 405.3 |
| Time and savings accounts | 1,096.3 | | 31.2 | | 66.2 | | 26.5 | 1,242.3 |
| Life insurance and pension reserves | 729.3 | | | | | 68.5 | | 660.5 |
| Corporate stock | 808.5 | | | | | | 235.6 | 42.6 |
| Government securities | 278.8 | | 7.8 | 15.8 | 90.8 | 901.0 | 601.6 | 199.9 |
| Corporate and foreign bonds | 64.8 | | | 318.3 | | | 346.6 | 60.8 |
| Mortgages | 106.2 | 766.1 | | 392.4 | 25.5 | 0.8 | 1,040.8 | 13.3 |
| Consumer credit | | 340.0 | 43.6 | | | | 296.4 | |
| Bank loans | | 19.2 | | 260.2 | | | 358.2 | 28.8 |
| Miscellaneous | 116.0 | 84.7 | 661.7 | 479.4 | 154.6 | 45.5 | 421.3 | 520.3 |
| Total | 3,422.0 | 1,210.0 | 825.6 | 1,466.1 | 369.9 | 1,015.8 | 3,349.1 | 3,173.8 |

*Note:* Blanks indicate zero or insignificant entries. For a given row in the table, assets and liabilities do not necessarily balance because we have omitted the "Rest of the World" category and because of minor discrepancies in the data.

*Source:* Board of Governors of the Federal Reserve System, *Flow of Funds Accounts 1949–1978,* Washington, D.C., December 1979, p. 88.

billion. Much of the household-owned debt is highly liquid, being in the form of money or near-money. The major household liabilities are residential mortgages and consumer credit. The excess of financial assets over financial liabilities of $2,212 billion, which might be termed *financial net worth*, is only part of the overall net worth of the household sector. To arrive at total *net worth* one must include net nonfinancial assets, including real estate and other tangible property such as consumer durables. For 1978, total household net worth amounted to a hefty $6,577 billion.

2   *Businesses* as a group are net financial debtors. Most business debts are owed to financial institutions, with the household sector holding the bulk of the equity shares outstanding. Missing from Table 3–2 are the important nonfinancial assets held by businesses in the form of plant, equipment, and inventory.

3   *Governments*, like businesses, have liabilities that exceed their debt claims on other sectors. Federal debt vastly exceeds state and local debt, but includes large amounts of federal obligations held by federal agencies and trust funds (e.g., Social Security) and by the Federal Reserve.

4   *Financial institutions* such as commercial banks, savings and loan associations, and insurance companies have amassed huge amounts of funds. The bulk of their liabilities are owed to the household sector. Their assets are widely distributed in claims against the household, business, and government sectors. They clearly serve as an important middleman between surplus and deficit units, a role that we shall examine in more detail shortly.

As should be evident from this brief survey of the stock of outstanding financial assets and liabilities, debt instruments are a permanent and important feature of any modern economy. We turn now from the critical role served by debt instruments in channeling funds from surplus to deficit units to the actual *process* of channeling funds from lenders to borrowers.

Figure 3–1 schematically illustrates the twin nature of this process. The first way in which funds are transmitted is *direct* finance, in which ultimate borrowers and lenders are directly matched. Typically, such transactions are arranged by brokers or dealers serving as middlemen who maintain markets for trading both new and outstanding issues of debt instruments. The columns in Table 3–2 for households, business, and government give some indication of the extent of direct finance.

The second method of channeling funds from surplus to deficit units is indirect, through financial intermediaries. The importance of this channel is indicated by the vast sums in the "financial" column of Table 3–2. A *financial intermediary* is simply a financial institution—such as a commercial bank, a savings bank, a pension fund, or an insurance company—that issues claims against itself (acquired by ultimate lenders) and uses the proceeds to acquire financial claims against others (the ultimate borrowers). The claims issued by financial intermediaries are called *indirect securities*. Since both brokers and financial intermediaries are serving as middlemen, it is not the absence of a middleman that distinguishes between direct and indirect finance. Rather, it is the issuance of indirect securities such as savings deposits that provides the key distinguishing feature between the two methods of finance. The importance of this distinction will become clearer as we proceed.

**FINANCIAL MARKETS AND DIRECT FINANCE**

We shall first take up the role of financial markets in direct finance. As just indicated, the operation of financial markets is facilitated by a number of specialized financial institutions. These institutions perform services such as gathering and disseminating information about sources and uses of funds and creditworthiness of potential borrowers, serve as middlemen between issuers and ultimate buyers of debt and equity claims, and act as brokers and dealers to facilitate trading in outstanding claims. However, debt, credit, and instruments representing debt and ownership claims could be used even in the absence of these specialized institutions. Deficit units could sell newly created debt or equity claims directly to surplus units, with no go-between. The buyer might then hold the claim until it was redeemed by the issuer. If the buyer wished

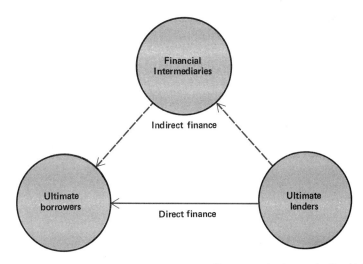

*Flows of funds via direct and indirect finance*

**FIGURE 3–1**

Economic units that raise funds by selling their liabilities to ultimate lenders (direct finance) or to financial intermediaries (indirect finance)

Economic units that acquire financial assets from ultimate borrowers (direct finance) or from financial intermediaries (indirect finance)

to sell it, he or she could search for someone who would be willing to buy it.

Such a simple set of arrangements could function, but only so inefficiently as to increase the cost and inhibit the development of financial processes. For one thing, it could not produce and disseminate the information and analysis required for rational and efficient valuation of claims. Such instruments are only claims against future asset values and future flows of income, and they can be valued rationally only to the extent that buyers and sellers can forecast what these future values are likely to be and the probabilities that they will be realized. This requires information and analysis concerning many relevant things: the past performance of the issuer in meeting its obligations, forecasts of the future performance of the issuer; comparison with other available claims, and so on. If buyers and sellers had to gather and analyze information for themselves, the cost would be so high that only very limited amounts of information would be gathered and analyzed; ignorance would remain widespread. This ignorance would limit the scope of markets, inhibit regional mobility of funds, and increase risk. Inefficiency in the allocation of funds and of capital investment would be inevitable.

In such a system the creation and sale of new claims would be inefficient and expensive. The issuer would have to seek out buyers, perhaps by ringing doorbells. Markets would be localized, and it would be difficult to move funds from areas of credit plenty to areas of greater scarcity. In the absence of facilities for trading in the stock of outstanding claims, each buyer might hold a security until it matured. If this were necessary, many buyers would be unwilling to acquire claims with longer maturities, or would buy them only at very high yields, because buyers might not want these funds unavailable to them for long periods of time. As an alternative to holding long-term credits, a buyer might seek out other buyers, but this would in many cases be time-consuming, and the scarcity of prospective buyers might cause the claim to be sold at low prices. The claims would be illiquid and the risk of loss of capital value would be high.

To remedy such shortcomings many types of financial institutions have been developed. As already emphasized, these institutions play an important role in the collection, analysis, and dissemination of financial information. We shall now examine two of their other functions: primary distribution of securities and the provision of secondary markets for securities.

**Primary Distribution of Securities**

Primary distribution of securities means the initial sale of newly created debt or equity claims. This function is best illustrated by investment banks, which do not buy securities with the intention of holding them but, like any other merchant, buy for the purpose of resale. Suppose some entity—a corporation or a governmental unit—decides to issue new securities and to sell them through an investment bank or group of investment banks. It may select the investment bank by competitive bidding or through negotiation. The investment bank performs four functions:

1   INVESTIGATION. This involves analysis of the present status and probable future performance of the issuer, the quality of the proposed issue, prices and yields on other comparable securities, and prospective market conditions. This culminates in determining a price and yield for the new issue.

2   UNDERWRITING. The investment bank guarantees the issuer a fixed price and assumes the risk of resale. If the issue is small, a single investment bank may underwrite it. If it is larger, two or more investment banks may form an underwriting syndicate, each assuming a share of the risk. Some underwriting syndicates include fifty or more investment banks.

3   WHOLESALE DISTRIBUTION. In some cases the underwriters sell at least a part of the issue to other dealers.

4   RETAIL DISTRIBUTION. This is the function of selling the new securities to their ultimate buyers. In some cases, the underwriters do this themselves. In others, they sell part of the issue to hundreds of dealers located throughout the nation and even in foreign countries. Their contribution to the regional mobility of funds is evident.

Investment banks are commonly used to distribute issues by many corporations, foreign governments, state governments, municipalities and many types of local authorities, and some agencies of the federal government. In a few cases the federal government has distributed its own direct issues through investment banking syndicates. Usually, however, this function is performed for federal securities by the Federal Reserve and commercial banks.

Commercial paper houses are another example of an institution that assists in primary distribution of newly issued short-term claims. *Commercial paper*, in this technical sense, refers to short-term promissory notes issued by finance companies and other corporations of high standing. Much of this is sold by the issuer directly to the ultimate buyer, the latter being primarily financial institutions and nonfinancial corporations with funds to invest for short periods. Some commercial paper is issued to dealers, who pay the issuer and distribute the paper to buyers all over the country. Only well-known firms find it feasible to sell their paper in this market.

We find, then, that institutions engaged in primary distribution of new debt and equity instruments serve, to the extent that they are effective, to reduce the cost of new issues, to increase the mobility of funds over wide areas, and to improve the allocation of investible funds and of investment in real capital.

**Secondary Markets for Securities**

By *secondary markets* we do not mean facilities for the initial sale of new issues but facilities for trading in outstanding debt and equity claims. If the term were not derogatory we would call it "the market for secondhand securities." The term *securities* is used here in its broadest sense to include ownership shares and debt obligations of all maturities. Sometimes a distinction is made between *securities markets* or *capital markets*, in which ownership shares and long-term debt obligations are bought and sold, and *money markets*, in which short-term debt obligations are traded.

The secondary securities market in the United States is highly complex, including central securities exchanges and thousands of persons and firms serving as brokers and dealers. Securities dealers buy and sell for their own accounts; they are like any secondhand merchant whose income is derived from the difference between buying price and selling price. However, in serving the brokerage function, brokers do not buy or sell for their own accounts; they act as go-betweens for buyers and sellers. In some cases, they learn who wants to sell and who wants to buy, and then put the prospective buyer and seller in contact with each other so they can enter into a transaction. In others, they act as agent for a buyer or seller.

Some securities command more efficient secondary markets than others. The *marketability* of a security, its ability to be sold quickly without a large decrease of its price, depends heavily on at least two factors:

1 HOW WIDELY ITS ISSUER AND ITS OWN QUALITIES ARE KNOWN. If both are widely known, there are likely to be many actual and potential buyers who will stand ready to bid for the security. However, if only a few know about the security, it may be salable only after a considerable delay or decline of price.

2 THE AMOUNT OF THE SECURITY OUTSTANDING AND THE NUMBER OF ITS HOLDERS. If a large amount of it is outstanding and it is widely held, transactions are likely to be frequent and buyers easy to find. But if the amount outstanding is small or most of it is held by only a few, the market for it is likely to be erratic. Many securities meet both these tests and enjoy a continuous market in which individual sellers or buyers can sell or buy considerable amounts quickly with little effect on price. Other, less fortunate securities lack marketability and can be sold only after a delay or a significant decline of price.

The existence of a highly efficient secondary market for a security markedly increases its liquidity and safety of principal value. Its marketability serves one of the requirements of liquidity—ability to be converted to money quickly. Of course, the other requirement—stability of value—is not assured by the existence of an efficient market. The value of a security may indeed fall because of less optimistic assessments of its issuer, the appearance of more attractive securities, or general changes in financial markets. But the holder is at least assured that there are many potential buyers who will complete for the security at a price commensurate with the prices of comparable issues.

To the extent that secondary markets enhance the expected liquidity and safety of value of securities, buyers are encouraged to hold more of them and at lower yields. Issuers of securities can acquire funds at lower costs, which promotes capital formation. Enhanced marketability of securities also makes it less advantageous for buyers to purchase only those securities that mature at or before the time when they will want to use the funds for some other purpose; they can buy issues with longer maturities and recover the money at any time by selling in the secondary market—but only by assuming some risk of loss of value, which may or may not be offset by possibilities of capital gains.

Liquidity through marketability thus helps solve a problem that would exist in a system in which buyers of claims would have to hold them to maturity or could sell them only with difficulty—deficit units would want to issue large amounts of long-term claims, considering heavy reliance on short-term financing too risky, while buyers would demand short-term claims because they thought they soon would, or might, want to use their money for other purposes.

Let us now survey briefly a few branches of the secondary market for securities, emphasizing functions rather than institutional detail. We start with the national securities exchanges, which include the New York Stock Exchange and the American Stock Exchange in New York City and lesser exchanges in several other cities. The exchanges themselves do not engage in trading. Their functions are to provide physical facilities, including the trading floor; to provide reporting and communications facilities; to determine what issues will be admitted to trading on the exchange; to regulate the conduct of their members; and so on. Actual trading is done by brokers and dealers who are members of the exchanges. These brokers and dealers are interlinked with all parts of the nation and with other countries in various ways. Offers to buy and sell flow through this network to the floor of the exchange from all parts of the country and from other countries. These offers meet on the floor of the exchange, where brokers and dealers conduct what is in effect an auction market, with the securities being sold to those who offer the highest prices. Both equities and bonds of major corporations are traded on these exchanges.

Another type of secondary market for securities is popularly called the *over-the-counter* market. This is not a market in the sense of some central place at which supply and demand meet and at which purchases and sales are consummated. Rather, it is a set of arrangements involving brokers and dealers who are located all over the country and are linked to each other and to buyers and sellers by telephone, teletype, computers, and written communications (including lists of offers to buy or sell). When an offer to buy or sell is received by a dealer or broker, the broker may sell or buy for his or her own account or for a customer, or communicate the offer to other brokers and dealers in the network. Some brokers and dealers specialize in a few types of securities; others interest themselves in a wide variety.

Many types of securities are traded in the over-the-counter market: shares of corporations, corporate bonds and some types of shorter-term corporate debt, debts of foreign governments, debts of the federal government, debts of states and municipalities, and so on. However, there are many corporate stocks and many types of debt issues that are not widely enough known or large enough in value to have access to this market.

We shall later deal further with some branches of the over-the-counter market that play important roles in the functioning of the banking and financial system. Among these are the following:

1   The market for U.S. government securities, including dealers who maintain continuous markets for marketable issues of the federal government.
2   The market for negotiable certificates of deposit (CDs), which are transferable instruments representing time-deposit claims against banks.
3   The federal funds market, in which are bought and sold claims against deposits at the Federal Reserve banks.

We shall find that such markets play important roles in enhancing the liquidity of some of these assets, in providing liquidity for various financial institutions and others, and in increasing the mobility of funds.

**DEVELOPMENT OF FINANCIAL INTERMEDIARIES**

As noted above, the second major channel for transmitting funds from lenders to borrowers is via institutions known as financial intermediaries. There are many types of financial intermediaries, such as savings banks, commercial banks, credit unions, and insurance companies, and the details of their operations vary considerably. What they share in common, however, is that they all issue liabilities to the public (e.g., savings deposits and savings and loan shares) and then turn around and use these funds to buy direct securities (e.g., stocks and bonds). To contrast them with the direct securities traded in financial markets, the liabilities of financial intermediaries are termed *indirect securities*.

We have already seen that households and other ultimate owners of savings can and do acquire and hold very large amounts of direct securities. The fact that ultimate owners of savings have the alternative of making up their own portfolios of money and many varieties of direct securities raises key questions: How can a financial intermediary make a living? What can it do for ultimate owners of savings that will induce them to pay an amount large enough for its services to cover its operating costs and leave a profit? In general terms, the answer is that, for at least some savers, a financial intermediary can do what the savers cannot do for themselves, or can do only at higher cost.

Especially for those individuals whose total accumulated savings are not large and for those whose current flow of saving is small, the acquisition and holding of direct securities involves high costs and other disadvantages:

1   HIGH COST OF INFORMATION AND ANALYSIS OF DIRECT SECURITIES. Many of those who do not acquire expert knowledge about securities in their regular course of business find it costly in terms of time, money, or both to gather and analyze information about any large number of direct securities. This is especially true when people have only small sums to invest.

2   HIGH COST OF BUYING, HOLDING, AND SELLING DIRECT SECURITIES. Most brokerage fees and other charges for buying and selling vary inversely in percentage terms with the sums involved. Brokers and dealers commonly impose a minimum flat charge in dollars, plus a diminishing percentage charge on sums in excess of that covered by the flat charge. Thus, transactions costs, in percentage terms, are often prohibitive when the sums involved are small or when the securities are to be held only a short time.

3   HIGH COST OF DIVERSIFICATION. The safety of principal value can be enhanced by holding a variety of direct securities whose prices do not move in a parallel way. Thus, total default risk can be reduced by holding debt claims against a variety of debtors, and greater stability of value may be achieved by holding a wide variety of ownership shares rather than concentrating on one or a few issues. Wealthy holders, with millions at their disposal, may achieve a high degree of diversification at relatively low cost, but this is not true of those with a smaller volume of assets. These holders must be content with only a few issues or incur the high transactions costs involved in buying small amounts of large numbers of issues.

4   HIGH COSTS OF LIQUIDITY. Most units wish to hold some liquid assets with which to meet foreseen or unforeseen excesses of expenditures over receipts. This can be expensive in terms of

foregone income or explicit costs if the only assets available for this purpose are money and direct securities.

Such are the principal disadvantages and diseconomies of a financial system containing only money itself and direct securities. These account for the establishment and growth of financial intermediaries. Enterprisers have found a source of profit: Members of the community were willing to accept, on the indirect securities issued by financial intermediaries, a rate of return sufficiently below the rates earned on the direct securities acquired by the intermediaries to cover operating costs and yield a net return. Individual financial intermediaries have succeeded in drawing funds from thousands and even hundreds of thousands of ultimate owners of savings, and many have amassed great pools of assets. Intermediaries with total assets in the hundreds of millions are commonplace, those with assets in the billions are numerous, and there are even some intermediaries with assets over $100 billion.

For the economy as a whole, Table 3–3 presents a list of the major financial intermediaries, ranked by asset size. Commercial banks are by far the largest, followed by savings and loan associations and life insurance companies. The growth in nonbank financial intermediaries has been particularly dramatic since 1945. For example, savings and loan shares have increased from less than $10 billion in 1945 to $579 billion in 1979. In recent years credit unions have grown particularly rapidly, with credit union shares rising from less than $6 billion in 1959 to over $60 billion in 1979. We shall have considerably more to say about the marked growth of financial intermediaries as we proceed.

## ECONOMIES OFFERED BY INTERMEDIARIES

We have just outlined the disadvantages of a financial system containing only money and direct securities, and suggested that these disadvantages provide profitable opportunities for financial intermediaries. While the actual growth and development of financial intermediaries bears ample witness to these opportunities, it will be instructive to explore more fully just why these opportunities arise.

The ability of financial intermediaries to survive and prosper is derived from several types of economies of specialization and scale. An intermediary operating with a large pool of funds can command experts in its various functions; reap the increased productivity and lower costs resulting from a high degree of specialization; employ efficient machinery and equipment, such as computers; and often succeed in purchasing services at prices lower than those charged to individual investors. For example, it can gather and analyze information at low cost per unit by spreading the total cost over a large volume of assets. Also, intermediaries can achieve lower transactions costs in buying, holding, and selling direct securities. The preceding sources of economies are highly relevant, but we shall stress the importance of "the law of large numbers." This law is basic to both diversification of assets and the principle of off-setting receipts and withdrawal of funds.

**Diversification of Assets**

If relevant future events were always predictable, there would be little or no reason for diversifying one's security holdings. If investors knew in advance what future returns—including both price changes and current incomes—on all securities would be, they would simply put all their funds into the security yielding the highest return. However, perfect certainty is not a characteristic of security markets. No matter how much time one may spend in gathering information, analyzing it, and making forecasts, the best that one can do is to identify possible outcomes and to estimate a subjective probability distribution for the various possible outcomes. For example, one may estimate the average expected return on a security to be 6 percent, but recognize that there is some probability that the return will be higher and some probability that it will be lower or even negative. Even if one feels confident about the probability distrubition, one cannot know which outcome will be realized. Even the improbable can happen. One will, of course, be happy if the actual return is higher than one expected. However, one will hardly welcome the risk that the actual outcome will be lower or even negative. If one holds only a single security, one faces a risk that a lower return or even a negative return will depress by a large percentage one's asset value or current income, or both.

*Diversification*—the holding of more than one security—can decrease the total risk of a portfolio, because lower-than-expected returns on some issues can be offset by higher-than-expected returns on others. However, the extent to which diversification can lower total risk does

**TABLE 3–3**

*Financial intermediaries ranked by asset size (year-end 1979, in billions of dollars)*

| Type of institution | Asset size |
| --- | --- |
| Commercial banks | 1,253 |
| Savings and loan associations | 579 |
| Life insurance companies | 421 |
| Private pension funds | 237 |
| State and local government retirement funds | 179 |
| Sales and consumer finance companies | 169 |
| Mutual savings banks | 165 |
| Property and casualty insurance companies | 157 |
| Credit unions | 62 |
| Open-end investment companies | 46 |
| Money market funds | 45 |
| Security brokers and dealers | 31 |

*Source:* Board of Governors of the Federal Reserve System, *Flow of Funds Accounts: Assets and Liabilities Outstanding,* Washington, D.C., February 1980.

not depend only on the number of issues held; it is highly dependent on the diversity of behavior of returns on the various securities. Diversification could eliminate risk entirely if returns on different securities were perfectly negatively correlated—if, for example, a fall in the price of one security was always offset exactly by a rise in the price of another. Combining the two risks would completely eliminate the overall risk. Unfortunately, because all securities are subject to some common forces, it is rarely, if ever, possible to find securities whose returns are perfectly negatively correlated.

At the other extreme, diversification could not reduce total risk at all if returns on all securities were perfectly positively correlated—if, for example, the prices of all securities always rose or fell simultaneously and in the same proportions. Fortunately, returns on all securities are not perfectly correlated; there is some degree of independence and diverse behavior. This is partly because some issues are subject to forces that do not affect others and partly because forces impinging on all issuers affect them in different ways and degrees. For example, managements of some companies inprove while others deteriorate; demands for products of some companies rise while demands for the products of others remain static or decline; companies in different industries are not affected in the same way and degree by such external events as cyclical fluctuations of business, inflation, and deflation; and so on. It is because of some degree of diversity of behavior of different securities that diversification can reduce total risk.

Thus, financial intermediaries are reducers of risk and manufacturers of safety. Through diversification of assets, they reduce risk to a degree that could not be achieved, or could be achieved only at higher cost, by the ultimate owners of savings. Operating with a large pool of funds, an intermediary can acquire and hold a large number of different securities; it can buy each in lots large enough to achieve low transactions costs; and through expert management, it may select a combination or portfolio of securities in which the risks best offset each other.

In short, one basic economic function of financial intermediaries is to reduce risk and enhance safety.

**Offsetting Receipts and Withdrawals of Funds**

Another fundamental basis for the origin and success of financial intermediaries is the phenomenon of offsetting receipts and withdrawals, which is also related to the law of large numbers. This principle was mentioned briefly in connection with our earlier discussion of commercial banking, but it is also broadly applicable to other types of financial intermediaries. To illustrate the principle, let us assume that some financial intermediary has received funds from a thousand households and has issued to them financial claims against itself, that it stands ready to accept new funds, and that it allows claimants to withdraw funds on demand or after only short notice. The management of the intermediary will expect that during any period some claimants will withdraw funds and that others will bring in additional funds. That all claimants will withdraw funds at the same time is not impossible but is highly improbable. In other words, it is quite improbable that withdrawals by all claimants will be perfectly positively correlated. On the basis of its own experience and the experience of other intermediaries and based on its knowledge of the income and expenditure flows of its customers, the management will expect that withdrawals will be at least partially, and perhaps fully or more than fully, offset by inflows of funds. It may even estimate a subjective probability distribution of the possible outcomes. For example, it may estimate that during some stated future period there is an 80 percent probability that net inflows will increase its net assets by at least 5 percent, a 95 percent probability that inflows will be at least equal to withdrawals, only a 5 percent probability that net withdrawals will amount to as much as 5 percent of its assets, and only a 1 percent probability that net withdrawals will amount to as much as 10 percent of its assets.

Operating on the basis of such expectations, an intermediary can create and issue to ultimate owners of savings financial claims against itself that are more liquid than the assets that it acquires and holds. For example, the claims that it issues may be fixed in terms of dollars, payable on demand or on short notice, and thus almost as liquid as money itself. Yet the great bulk of its assets can be in the form of longer-term illiquid securities, such as mortgages or bonds. Expecting that there is only 1 chance in 20 that net withdrawals will amount to as much as 5 percent of its assets and only 1 chance in 100 that such net withdrawals will be as high as 10 percent, it will feel secure in holding no more than 10 percent of its assets in liquid form. Even this small fraction need not all be in the form of money; most of it may be in the form of liquid short-term earning assets, such as obligations of the U.S. Treasury or loans to security dealers. Its holdings of liquid assets can be even smaller to the extent that it can confidently rely on borrowing to meet net withdrawals.

The transactions costs incurred by an intermediary can be far below those that would be necessary if ultimate owners of savings managed their liquidity individually. To only a minor extent is this due to the fact that an intermediary, buying and selling in large lots, can buy transactions services at lower prices. It is largely the result of the fact that an intermediary need not engage in as many transactions as the individual owner. If the ultimate owners of savings provided their own liquidity, they would either have to hold money, which yields no income, or pay transactions costs every time they bought a security and every time they sold a security to get money. However, because of the principle of offsetting receipts and withdrawals, an intermediary needs to sell securities only to the extent of net withdrawals. For example, if its receipts are exactly equal to withdrawals, thus leaving total assets unchanged, the intermediary need not sell any securities regardless of how large gross withdrawals may be.

**Overview**     Financial intermediaries are manufacturers of liquidity and safety. Through the processes described previously, the intermediary can create against itself financial claims that have characteristics that differ markedly from those of the assets that they acquire and hold. In these ways, intermediaries create financial claims with combinations of safety, liquidity, and yield that conform more closely to the tastes and preferences of many ultimate owners of savings. For these reasons, intermediaries have been able to attract huge amounts of funds. However, intermediaries also provide important benefits to issuers of direct securities, enabling them to issue at lower costs types of securities conforming more closely to the issuers' needs and preferences. For example, a business firm may wish to issue a long-term security that is itself relatively risky and illiquid, while individual investors place a high premium on safety and liquidity and would purchase and hold the security only if rewarded by a very high yield. An intermediary can help to solve such a problem by purchasing the risky and illiquid security conforming to the issuer's preferences and, on the basis of this security, pooled with others, create financial claims conforming to the preferences of investors. It is for this reason that intermediaries are said to intermediate between the preferences of issuers of direct securities and the preferences of asset-holders.

It should be quite evident by now that the existence of financial intermediaries leads to a more efficient flow of funds from lenders to borrowers. As a consequence, financial intermediaries, along with financial markets, play an important role in fostering productive investment and, consequently, economic growth.

**AN OVERVIEW OF THE FINANCIAL SYSTEM**     Having looked at its various parts, we are now in a position to survey the American financial system as a whole. It includes three broad sets of elements:

1   Huge amounts of direct securities of widely varying characteristics issued not only by households, business firms, and governmental units but also by almost every other type of nonfinancial entity. Great stocks of these are outstanding at any point of time and large new issues are generated when the economy is operating near its capacity levels.

2   Market facilities for trading in securities—facilities for primary distribution of newly issued securities and secondary market

facilities for trading in securities issued earlier. Many securities, whose issuers are well and favorably known, enjoy national and international markets in which they can be bought or sold quickly at competitive prices. When they function efficiently, securities markets add significantly to the liquidity and safety of direct securities.

3   A wide variety of financial intermediaries, which hold huge amounts of direct securities and issue huge amounts of indirect securities with characteristics differing significantly from those of the direct securities held. Depository types of intermediaries are outstandingly manufacturers of liquidity.

This complex financial system should be kept in mind as we continue our study of processes and institutions. To do so will facilitate understanding of the vital processes of saving, capital accumulation, and determination of the behavior of national income. To be sure, considerable amounts of investment are undertaken by ultimate savers, who finance their investment out of their own current flows of saving without recourse to any branch of the financial markets. However, much investment requires the creation of new securities or trading of old ones. Thus, the saving–investment process involves transactions in financial markets and via financial intermediaries.

A pictorial overview of the entire process is provided in Figure 3–2. The flow of funds from nonfinancial lenders to borrowers is channeled either directly through capital markets or indirectly through commercial banks and other nonbank financial intermediaries. As the figure illustrates, the major lender groups are identical to the major borrowing groups. This reflects the fact that financial markets and intermediaries are simply serving as the "middlemen" between lenders and borrowers.

*Direct and indirect flows of funds.*

Source: William N. ox, III, "Impairment n Credit Flow: Fact r Fiction?," *Monthly Review,* Federal Reserve Bank of Atlanta, February 1970, p. 25.

**FIGURE 3–2**

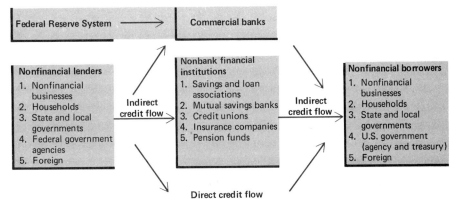

**Direct vs. Indirect**
**Finance: Some**
**Data**

Figure 3–3 documents the actual flow of funds from nonfinancial lenders to nonfinancial borrowers for 1979. It should be emphasized that these data are different in kind from those given earlier in the chapter (in Tables 3–1, 3–2, and 3–3). The earlier data are *financial stocks;* that is, they are dollar amounts outstanding *at a point of time*. The data in Figure 3–3 are *financial flows,* which measure the volume of funds borrowed or lent *during some time period*—in this case, the year 1979. Stocks and flows are, of course, related in that a stock of some asset is simply the sum of all previous flows of that asset.[2] Despite this close relationship, it is often useful to look at financial data from both perspectives. For example, this is commonly done when analyzing a business firm. The balance sheet of all the firm's assets and liabilities is a stock concept, while the income (or profit and loss) statement measures financial flows. This distinction between stocks and flows will also play an important role in later chapters, where we consider the relationship between the stock of money outstanding and the flow of national income.

Returning to Figure 3–3, several facts stand out. For one, in 1979 nearly $400 billion was raised in credit markets by the nonfinancial sector. Households and businesses were the major borrowers, but governments at various levels and foreigners also borrowed sizable sums. A second noteworthy fact is that $297 billion, or approximately three-quarters

---

[2] The distinction between stocks and flows applies to real (i.e., physical) assets as well as financial assets. Thus, for example, the stock of all automobiles outstanding is the cumulated flow of all past net flows of purchases. In this context *net* flow refers to total purchases less depreciation of the existing stock.

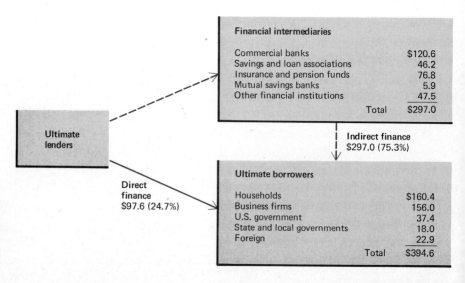

*Total funds raised by*
*nonfinancial sectors*
*in 1979 by direct and*
*indirect finance (in*
*billions of dollars)*
**FIGURE 3–3**

of the total funds raised, were channeled indirectly through financial intermediaries. Not surprisingly, commercial banks were quantitatively most significant in this regard.

While Figure 3-3 provides evidence that indirect finance through financial intermediaries accounted for the bulk of funds channeled through the financial system in 1979, the data in Figure 3–4 indicate that there was nothing special about this particular year. Indeed, from 1960 to 1979, on average indirect finance accounted for 74 percent of all funds —almost precisely the fraction in 1979. There were, of course, years in which financial intermediaries played a somewhat lesser role, such as 1966, 1969, and 1974–1975. As we shall later discuss in detail, these years correspond to "credit crunches" or periods of "disintermediation," when financial intermediaries came under severe pressure. But even in these years indirect finance remained the dominant pattern.

**Federal Reserve and Commercial Banks**

In subsequent chapters we shall be especially interested in the role played by the Federal Reserve and the commercial banks in the operation of the financial system. Indeed, Parts 2 and 3 of this book will be devoted to exploring what lies inside the Federal Reserve and commercial bank "boxes" of Figure 3–2.

Therefore, in concluding we should note that various facts discussed in this chapter are also relevant in many ways to the operations of the Federal Reserve and commercial banks.

1   The Federal Reserve wields its most powerful instrument for monetary management—open-market operations—by purchasing and selling in two branches of the over-the-counter market, the markets for government securities and acceptances. In so doing, it can influence the stock of money outstanding.

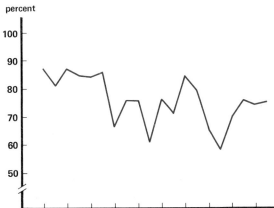

*Percentage of total funds raised by nonfinancial sectors accounted for by indirect finance*

**FIGURE 3–4**

2   Individual commercial banks do extend significant amounts of credit directly to their local customers. But they also have access to securities markets of national and even international scope, where they can buy and sell both newly issued and already-outstanding securities. This enables them to acquire securities of types not generated in their local markets and to diversify their portfolios. A large part of their liquidity needs are met by holding *secondary reserves*, which are liquid types of earning assets that gain much of their liquidity through the marketability provided by financial markets. These markets are also a major channel for the geographic mobility of bank funds.

3   As banks seek to acquire earning assets, they meet competition not only from ultimate owners of savings but also from a wide array of other financial intermediaries with huge assets.

4   The volume of demand deposits that the public is willing to hold depends in part on the volume and liquidity of other available claims and on the level of yields on these claims. Thus, when banks are prohibited from paying interest on demand deposits, they can expect that the quantity of demand deposits demanded by the public will decline if interest rates on other assets rise.

5   In attempting to issue and keep outstanding savings and time-deposit claims against themselves, commercial banks compete not only with direct securities of varying liquidity and yield, but also with claims issued by other financial intermediaries.

| SELECTED READINGS |

Board of Governors of the Federal Reserve System, *Introduction to Flow of Funds*, Washington, D.C., 1975.

Chandler, L. V., *The Monetary–Financial System*, New York, Harper & Row, 1979.

Goldsmith, R., *Financial Intermediaries in the American Economy Since 1900*, Princeton, N.J., Princeton University Press, 1958.

Gurley, J. G., and E. S. Shaw, *Money in a Theory of Finance*, Washington, D.C., Brookings Institution, 1960.

Smith, P. F., *Economics of Financial Institutions and Markets*, Homewood, Ill., Irwin, 1971.

*Report of the President's Commission on Financial Structure and Regulation*, Washington, D.C., Government Printing Office, 1971.

In the preceding chapter we considered the operation of financial markets, in which supplies and demands for funds are brought into balance. These magic words — *market*, *supply*, and *demand* — should immediately bring to mind another key concept, namely, that of a market-clearing price. While the notion of a price that equilibrates supply and demand is simple enough in principle, the details of price setting in financial markets can sometimes be confusing. Part of the reason for this is terminology, since people often refer to both the *price of a financial instrument* and the *price of borrowing money*. These two concepts of price are closely related, but they are not the same. Indeed, this should be apparent from the more common name of the price of borrowed money — the *interest rate*.

The purpose, then, of this chapter is to explore the nature of interest rates and the relationship of the interest rate to the price of a financial instrument. This topic is of considerable importance if we are to understand the portfolio choices of various groups in the economy and the workings of monetary policy.

**ATTRIBUTES OF DEBT INSTRUMENTS**

Financial instruments are the evidences of debt that originate in borrowing and lending, that is, in financial transactions in which purchasing power is transferred from surplus spending units to deficit spending units. In valuing any financial claim and in choosing among alternative financial claims, actual and potential buyers and holders consider the full range of rights and obligations carried by each claim. This suggests that, prior to discussing the interest rate or yield on a financial instrument, it will be helpful to explore some of the important characteristics of financial instruments that can influence the interest rate. Specifically, we shall concentrate on three attributes: maturity, liquidity, and safety of principal value.[1]

**Maturity**

By *maturity* we mean the time that must elapse before the borrower must repay the debt in full. Maturity is most meaningfully measured relative to the current point in time. For example, a bond issued in 1970 and due to be repaid in the year 2000 would have a 30-year maturity at issue but a 20-year maturity in 1980. When issued, most debts have a well-defined maturity that may range from a single day to many years. Two exceptions to this occur at either end of the maturity spectrum. At one extreme are bonds, called *consols* or *perpetuities*, under which the borrower agrees to make interest payments indefinitely into the future without ever repaying the principal. Consols, which thus have an infinite maturity, are in common use in England. At the other end of the spectrum are debts, such as demand deposits in a bank (which are liabilities or debts of the bank to the depositor), which are due on demand. Such debts are due whenever the holder wishes to cash them in, and consequently have no specific maturity.

**Liquidity**

By the *liquidity* of an asset we mean its capability of being converted into money quickly and without loss of value in terms of money. Money is perfectly liquid; it can be used immediately to pay debts or to spend, and it always remains at a constant value in terms of money. An asset is illiquid to the extent that its conversion into money requires time or entails loss of value either through a decline in its market value or through conversion costs in terms of inconvenience, brokers' fees, dealers' margins, and so on. As we have seen, the actual liquidity of an asset depends in part on the market facilities for it. However, certain assets, even though they are not marketable, can still be quite liquid. For example, the ownership of U.S. savings bonds cannot be transferred, but such bonds can be redeemed with relatively minor inconvenience. In general, a debt instrument is more likely to achieve a high degree of liquidity to the extent that it possesses two characteristics. First, it is a claim on an issuer with an excellent reputation for meeting its obligations promptly and in full. Second, it is of short maturity — payable on demand or within a few months. With maturity so short, any rise of market rates of interest will reduce its value only slightly.

Most holders consider liquidity to be a desirable characteristic in an asset and are willing to forgo some income to buy some liquidity. However, holders differ widely in the amounts of liquidity demanded in the form of earning assets and in the amounts of yield they are willing to sac-

---

[1] Some aspects of these attributes were touched on in the previous chapter.

rifice in order to obtain liquidity. Some, expecting or fearing large excesses of spending over receipts in the near future, may be willing to forgo considerable amounts of yield in order to demand large amounts of liquidity in this form. Others, expecting excesses of receipts over payments in the near future, may be willing to sacrifice very little yield to buy liquidity.

To the extent that liquidity requires short maturities, desires of holders may conflict with those of issuers. To the issuer, the short maturity can be a source of illiquidity; it subjects him or her to the possibility of having to repay inconveniently soon or to refinance in an unfavorable market at higher rates of interest.

**Safety of Principal**

By *safety of principal* we mean freedom from risk that the market value of the debt instrument will decline. "Safety" is used here in its relative sense. Instruments that are highly liquid are also highly safe; they are convertible into money not only quickly but also at a stable price. But some instruments that lack liquidity may be relatively safe; they can be collected or sold without loss over a longer period of time.

Risks of loss of principal value are of two types:

1   RISK OF DEFAULT. This is the risk that promised payments of interest and repayment of principal will not be met fully and on schedule. Default risks on debt instruments obviously differ from one issuer to another; the risk of default on debt instruments of the federal government is far below the risk of default on issues of a business concern whose future is doubtful. However, different issues of any given debtor may carry quite different risks of default because of differences in priority of claim against assets or income, or both. Some classes of debt are given prior claim to a debtor's income or assets, while other classes claim only such income and assets as may remain after satisfaction of all other debts. Other things equal, holders prefer instruments with lower default risk to those with greater default risk, but at least some can be induced to hold those with higher default risk if the promised income is higher.

2   MARKET RISK. This is the risk that the market price of a debt instrument will decline even if there is no risk of default. As we shall see shortly, this tends to come about when interest rates rise. We shall return to the issue of market risk after we examine the source of the inverse relationship between interest rates and prices of debt instruments.

**YIELD ON DEBT INSTRUMENTS**

By the *yield* of a debt instrument we mean its annual rate of return over cost, taking into consideration not only annual interest payments but also any difference there may be between its cost and its sale value. Since it reflects both interest payments and possible capital appreciation or depreciation, such a yield is sometimes called the *effective interest rate*. For many purposes it is most natural to calculate the yield under the assumption that the debt instrument is held to maturity. That is, it is sold or redeemed at maturity for its face value. In such cases the effective interest rate is termed the *average yield to maturity*. In order to indicate how the average yield to maturity is calculated, it is helpful to proceed in stages.

We shall assume that we are dealing with a conventional *bond*, which is an obligation by the seller (or, looked at another way, the borrower of the money) to pay the buyer a fixed sum of dollars per year over the life or maturity of the bond. This fixed sum is called the *coupon*.[2] In addition, when the bond matures, the borrower is obligated to pay the lender the *par value* or *principal* of the bond.

The coupon expressed as a percent of the par value is termed the *coupon yield* or *nominal yield* of the bond. Consider, for example, a bond promising to pay a par value of $1,000 at the end of ten years and $60 (the coupon) at the end of each year. Since $60/$1,000 = .06, or 6 percent, the coupon yield of the bond is 6 percent. It should be emphasized that since the par value and the coupon remain constant throughout the life of the bond, the coupon yield is likewise constant.

Armed with this introduction, we can now spell out how to compute the effective rate of interest as measured by the average yield to maturity. As indicated, the average yield to maturity takes into consideration the current market value, annual interest receipts (the coupon), and the relationship between the current market value and the value at which the debt will be paid off at maturity (the par value). How these ingredients are combined can best be illustrated by some examples.

Let us again consider a 10-year bond issued with a par value of $1,000 and a coupon of $60 or, equivalently, a coupon yield of 6 percent. Further assume that nine years have elapsed since the issue of the bond and that the market value of the bond (i.e., price of the bond) is now $965. (For the moment the reader is asked simply to accept the fact that the market value of the bond can change; reasons for the change are given in the next section.) An individual who buys this bond for $965 will receive a coupon payment of $60. However, since the bond will mature in one year at the par value of $1,000, the purchaser will also receive a capital gain or capital appreciation of $35 ($1,000 − $965). Thus, the total return for the year will be $95. Since the initial investment was $965, the average yield to maturity will be $95/$965, or 9.84 percent.

---

[2] The reader may be fortunate enough to be related to one of those happy souls whose primary form of work and/or exercise is the "clipping" of coupons. This phrase stems from the fact that on many bonds the coupon is removed by clipping with scissors (or, perhaps, a gold-plated coupon clipper) and sent to an agent for collection.

As a second example, let us consider the same 10-year bond with one year left until it matures. It is now selling for $1,020. The total return for the year will be $40, consisting of $60 in interest payments *minus* the $20 capital loss. In this instance, the average yield to maturity is $40/$1,020, or 3.92 percent.

Thus, in general, the coupon yield and the effective rate of interest will not be the same. This should hardly be surprising, since the coupon yield remains fixed over the life of the bond while the effective interest rate varies with market forces. The only case in which the two yields will be the same is one in which the market value of the bond is equal to its par value. But as we have suggested, this will not be true in general. Indeed, the bond may not even have been sold initially at its par value. For example, when the debtor originally issued a promise to pay $1,000 at the end of ten years and $60 of interest at the end of each year, interest rates in the market on comparable obligations may have been below 6 percent, so that the bond could be sold above par, say, for $1,050. Or, interest rates on comparable obligations may have been well above 6 percent, so that the debtor had to sell the bond below par, say, for $950. In any case, the market value after issue can deviate from par value. We shall see how this comes about when we discuss the relationship between the yield and the price or market value of a bond.

**YIELDS AND MARKET VALUES**

In the previous section we had occasion to refer to two important concepts—the average yield to maturity and the capital (market) value or price of a bond. These two concepts are obviously closely intertwined, and we shall now explore their relationship.

The present capital value of an income-producing asset is arrived at by a process termed *capitalization*, by which we mean discounting the expected flow of money receipts. *Discounting* means taking out interest in advance. Buyers who paid the full amount of future dollar returns for an obligation would receive no net interest at all. They usually will not buy an obligation unless the purchase price is such that the yield on the purchase price will be as great as that available on other comparable obligations. Of course, they would like to buy at a lower price, but this is likely to be prevented by competition from other purchasers.

The discounting process is easier to understand when only simple interest or discount is involved. To make things concrete, let us consider an individual who plans to invest in a 1-year bond at a time when the currently prevailing market yield or effective rate of interest on such bonds is $i$ percent per year. Suppose our potential investor is now offered a debt instrument that carries a promise to pay $1,060 one year later. What will he be willing to pay for this instrument? Our potential buyer will reason as follows: "This piece of paper is of value today only because it represents a claim against money receivable in the future. I will buy it only at such a price that I will receive the going rate of return on my money, and this 'price' is that amount which, if put out at the prevailing yield rate, would be worth $1,060 a year hence." In other words, the individual wants to determine the amount of money ($P$) that, if put out at the current rate of yield ($i$) on this type of obligation, will be worth $1,060 a year from now. That is, we must have

$$P(1 + i) = \$1,060$$

or

$$P = \frac{\$1,060}{1 + i}$$

If the prevailing interest rate is 6 percent, that is, $i = 0.06$, we then have

$$P = \frac{\$1,060}{1.06} = \$1,000$$

Thus, when the market yield is 6 percent, the individual would be willing to pay $1,000 for the asset under consideration. What happens if the interest rate differs from 6 percent? It is evident from our formula that the present value of $1,060 receivable one year hence will be lower if interest rates are higher and higher if interest rates are lower. For example, if the market yield is 8 percent, the formula becomes

$$P = \frac{\$1,060}{1.08} = \$981.48$$

If, however, the market yield is 4 percent,

$$P = \frac{\$1,060}{1.04} = \$1,019.23$$

The general formula for simple discount is

$$P = \frac{A}{(1 + i)}$$

where $P$ is the present value, $A$ is the dollar amount receivable at the end of the interest period, and $i$ is the rate of interest for that period stated in hundredths such as 0.08 or 0.04.[3]

The process of arriving at a present capital value for a longer-term obligation such as the 10-year bond described previously, is based on the same principle, but it is a bit more complicated, for two reasons.

---

[3] Here and later we shall assume that the interest period is one year and that the interest rate is the rate per year. We shall also assume that interest is compounded annually. In some cases the interest period is less than a year. For example, it may be six months. In such cases the $i$ in our formula will be the interest rate for half a year and the number of interest periods will be twice as large as it would be if the interest period were one year.

First, the obligation is to make a number of payments through time rather than a single payment; second, it involves compound interest or discount. Each prospective buyer will reason as follows: "This obligation is of value only because it represents a claim against $60 at the end of each of the next ten years and $1,000 at the end of the 10-year period. I will buy it only at such a price that I will receive the going rate of return on my money." The price $(P)$ is the sum of the discounted values of all the individual payments expected in the future. For example, there is some amount of money $(P_1)$ that, if put out at the prevailing yield rate, would be worth $60 a year hence. That is,

$$P_1(1 + i) = \$60$$

or

$$P_1 = \frac{\$60}{1 + i}$$

There is another smaller amount of money $(P_2)$ which, if put out at compound interest at the prevailing rate, would be worth $60 at the end of two years. Compound interest is used because during the second year, interest would be received on the first year's interest. That is,

$$P_2(1 + i)^2 = \$60$$

or

$$P_2 = \frac{\$60}{(1 + i)^2}$$

Similarly, there is a yet smaller amount of money $(P_3)$ that, if put out at compound interest, would be worth $60 at the end of three years.

$$P_3(1 + i)^3 = \$60$$

or

$$P_3 = \frac{\$60}{(1 + i)^3}$$

The present values of the other interest payments can be arrived at in the same way. There remains the $1,000 of principal payable at the end of ten years. Its present value is $\$1,000/[(1 + i)^{10}]$. The present value of the bond is the sum of the present values of the various payments to be received on it.

The general formula for arriving at present capital value by discounting is

$$P = \frac{A_1}{1 + i} + \frac{A_2}{(1 + i)^2} + \frac{A_3}{(1 + i)^3} + \ldots + \frac{A_n}{(1 + i)^n} + \frac{F}{(1 + i)^n}$$

where $P$ is the present value, the $A$'s are the dollar amounts receivable at the ends of the various interest periods, $F$ is the amount of the principal repayment, $i$ is the rate of discount, and $n$ is the number of interest periods. Fortunately, potential buyers need not solve such equations themselves; bond tables are easily available to do this for them.

Columns 5, 6, and 7 of Table 4–1 show the present value of the bond at discount rates of 4, 6, and 8 percent. It will be worth $1,000 if the rate is 6 percent, only $865.80 if the rate is 8 percent, and $1,162.22 if the rate is 4 percent.

One special case is worth noting because of its simplicity: the case of an obligation to pay fixed annual amounts in perpetuity. In this case the preceding formula becomes simply

$$P = \frac{A}{i}$$

Thus, the present value of the right to receive $60 a year in perpetuity becomes

$$P = \frac{\$60}{0.06} = \$1,000 \quad \text{if the discount rate is 6 percent}$$

$$P = \frac{\$60}{0.04} = \$1,500 \quad \text{if the discount rate is 4 percent}$$

**TABLE 4–1**

*Discounting and present values*

| End of year | Formula | (1) VALUES OF COL. (1) AT INTEREST RATES OF | | | (5) PERCENT VALUES* OF $60 AT END OF INDICATED YEARS AT DISCOUNT RATE OF | | |
|---|---|---|---|---|---|---|---|
| | | 4% | 6% | 8% | 4% | 6% | 8% |
| 1 | $(1+i)$ | 1.0400 | 1.0600 | 1.0800 | $57.692 | $56.604 | $55.556 |
| 2 | $(1+i)^2$ | 1.0816 | 1.1236 | 1.1664 | 55.473 | 53.400 | 51.440 |
| 3 | $(1+i)^3$ | 1.1249 | 1.1910 | 1.2597 | 53.340 | 50.377 | 47.630 |
| 4 | $(1+i)^4$ | 1.1699 | 1.2625 | 1.3605 | 51.288 | 47.526 | 44.102 |
| 5 | $(1+i)^5$ | 1.2167 | 1.3382 | 1.4693 | 49.316 | 44.836 | 40.835 |
| 6 | $(1+i)^6$ | 1.2653 | 1.4185 | 1.5869 | 47.419 | 42.298 | 37.810 |
| 7 | $(1+i)^7$ | 1.3159 | 1.5036 | 1.7138 | 45.595 | 39.903 | 35.009 |
| 8 | $(1+i)^8$ | 1.3686 | 1.5938 | 1.8509 | 43.841 | 37.645 | 32.416 |
| 9 | $(1+i)^9$ | 1.4233 | 1.6895 | 1.9990 | 42.155 | 35.139 | 30.015 |
| 10 | $(1+i)^{10}$ | 1.4802 | 1.7908 | 2.1589 | 40.534 | 33.504 | 27.792 |
| Subtotal | | | | | $486.65 | $441.61 | $402.61 |
| Present value of $1,000 receivable at the end of 10 years | | | | | 675.57 | 558.39 | 463.19 |
| Total | | | | | $1,162.22 | $1,000.000 | $865.80 |

* The values in columns 5, 6, and 7 are arrived at by dividing $60 by the numbers shown in columns 2, 3, and 4, respectively.

$$P = \frac{\$60}{0.08} = \$750 \qquad \text{if the discount rate is 8 percent}$$

**Implications of the Results**

Both the formulas just presented and the illustrative examples clearly point up the negative or inverse relationship between the level of market rates and the market value of a debt obligation. The numbers presented previously can also be arranged in a slightly different way to bring out another important point, namely, that the longer the maturity of an obligation, the greater is the effect of any given change of market rates of interest on its present value. From our previous examples we can construct Table 4–2. At a market rate of 6 percent each of three assets is valued at $1,000. If the market rate were 8 percent, while all the bonds have a lower value (the inverse relationship just noted), the decline in value is least for the 1-year bond and the greatest for the perpetuity.

We can also use these results to reconsider the notion of market risk mentioned earlier. From Table 4–2 it might be inferred that, other things equal, holders will prefer short maturities over long ones because of their lower market risk, and that they will purchase and hold longer maturities only if rewarded by a higher interest yield. This is sometimes true, but not always. For one thing, longer maturities carry the possibility not only of a larger loss of value if interest rates rise but also the possibility of a larger capital gain if interest rates fall. When interest rates are expected to fall in the future, the interest yield on longer maturities may be below that on shorter maturities, and holders will expect to make up the difference, or more than the difference, in capital gains. Moreover, even with given expectations as to the future course of interest rates, different holders are likely to have differing preferences for shorter and longer maturities. Some, expecting to need their funds soon, will prefer short maturities in order to lessen their market risk. Others, looking forward to a very long holding period and wanting an assured rate of return, prefer longer maturities. This also enables them to avoid the expense of buying a succession of shorter maturities. Here again we en-

| **TABLE 4–2** | | PRESENT VALUE IF DISCOUNTED AT | | |
|---|---|---|---|---|
| *Effects of maturity* | **Description of debt** | **6%** | **4%** | **8%** |
| | An obligation to pay $1,060 at the end of the year | $1,000.00 | $1,019.23 | $941.48 |
| | An obligation to pay $60 annually for ten years and $1,000 at the end of ten years | 1,000.00 | 1,162.22 | 865.80 |
| | An obligation to pay $60 a year in perpetuity | 1,000.00 | 1,500.00 | 750.00 |

counter the important fact of differences among buyers' tastes and preference functions.

The discussion to this point has been couched in terms of how a potential buyer would value bonds with different payment streams at alternative discount rates or market rates of interest. It is important to emphasize that the relationships we have developed are also relevant for the holder of an *outstanding* debt obligation. Consider, for example, an investor who purchased a perpetuity paying $60 a year when the market interest rate was 6 percent. The purchase price of such a bond clearly must have been $1000. Now assume that after one year the market rate on *new* perpetuities rises to 8 percent and that our bondholder needs to cash in his existing bond. Since potential purchasers can earn 8 percent by buying new perpetuities, they will be unwilling to settle for a lower rate of return. As the outstanding perpetuity promises to pay only $60 per year, as we have seen it must be priced at $750 to yield 8 percent to the holder. Thus, sale of the perpetuity will produce a capital loss of $250 for the bond owner. While he has earned $60 in interest payments, he will suffer a net loss of $190 on the purchase and subsequent sale of the bond. Given his need for funds and the change in interest rates, our investor obviously would have been better off had he kept his funds in a demand-deposit account paying no interest, although this is not to suggest that this would have been the best option. Purchase of a 1-year bond would have earned the investor $60 and returned his capital intact at the end of the year.

Such is the arithmetic of the negative relationship between the level of market rates of interest and the market values of *outstanding* debt obligations that have maturity values and interest returns that are contractually fixed in terms of dollars. The economic reason for this relationship is that in competitive markets, average yields to maturity on issues already outstanding must be in line with yields on new issues. Thus, when yields on new issues are rising, the prices on old issues must fall enough to make their yields equally attractive to investors. And when yields on new issues are falling, investors will bid up the prices of outstanding issues until their yields are no longer higher than those on new issues.

**A Realistic Example**     While we have explored the relationship between market yields and bond values with artificially chosen bonds, the same points can be illustrated with reference to some realistic debt instruments. In Table 4–3 we have listed actual historical data on market price and the yield to maturity for two different U.S. government bonds. Both bonds were issued with coupon interest rates of 4 percent but with different terms to maturity. One bond, issued in 1959, had an initial maturity of 21 years, whereas the second, issued a few years later in 1962, was for a 10-year maturity. As is evident from the table, prices and yields of the outstanding bonds fluctuated substantially and in the expected inverse fashion. In addition, as expected, during the period in which both bonds coexisted the bond with the longer maturity fluctuated in price over a much wider range (72.14 to 102.16) than the shorter-maturity bond (91.16 to 101.01). This indicates that shorter-maturity bonds, by virtue of being more stable in price, possess greater liquidity.

We noted earlier that many investors consider liquidity to be a desirable characteristic for which they would be willing to sacrifice interest income. To the extent that this is an important consideration, market yields on short-term bonds should be less than those on long-term bonds. However, the data in Table 4–3 indicate that the reverse was true for six of the year-end dates presented.[4] Obviously, liquidity considerations do not fully explain the relationship between these two interest rates. This clearly needs further examination.

---

[4] These differences need to be interpreted cautiously, since a significant part of the return from the longer-maturity bond is in the form of capital gains, which are taxed at a lower rate.

**TABLE 4–3**

*Year-end price and yield for two 4 per-cent United States government bonds*

| Date | BOND ISSUED 1/23/59 BOND MATURED 2/15/80 | | BOND ISSUED 11/15/62 BOND MATURED 2/15/72 | |
| | Market price† | Yield to maturity | Market price† | Yield to maturity |
| --- | --- | --- | --- | --- |
| 1979 | 98.24 | 14.42 | * | * |
| 1978 | 93.27 | 9.93 | * | * |
| 1977 | 93.28 | 7.17 | * | * |
| 1976 | 95.02 | 5.75 | * | * |
| 1975 | 88.12 | 7.32 | * | * |
| 1974 | 86.04 | 7.30 | * | * |
| 1973 | 85.20 | 6.92 | * | * |
| 1972 | 87.08 | 6.25 | * | * |
| 1971 | 87.14 | 5.98 | 100.04 | 2.86 |
| 1970 | 83.08 | 6.46 | 97.25 | 5.46 |
| 1969 | 72.14 | 8.03 | 91.16 | 8.48 |
| 1968 | 83.08 | 6.01 | 94.06 | 6.07 |
| 1967 | 85.02 | 5.67 | 93.16 | 5.80 |
| 1966 | 94.00 | 4.61 | 96.16 | 4.78 |
| 1965 | 94.08 | 4.56 | 95.30 | 4.77 |
| 1964 | 97.28 | 4.19 | 98.24 | 4.21 |
| 1963 | 98.08 | 4.15 | 99.06 | 4.12 |
| 1962 | 101.00 | 3.92 | 101.01 | 3.86 |
| 1961 | 99.18 | 4.03 | * | * |
| 1960 | 102.16 | 3.81 | * | * |
| 1959 | 93.22 | 4.48 | * | * |

\* Prior to issue of bond or subsequent to maturity.
† Price decimals are 32nds; e.g., the 1974 price of 86.04 is read 86 4⁄32 per $100.

At various times we shall refer to "the" interest rate, which suggests that there is but one interest rate in a given market at a given time. This is a useful device in making the exposition both simple and brief, but we have just seen that this is an oversimplification. The fact is that, at any point in time, there is a complex of rates in the market, and these can differ widely and steadily. How can differences in rates persist? Why do lenders not shift their funds from debts with low yields to those with higher yields until all yield differentials have been wiped out?

**The Term
Structure of
Interest Rates**
In attempting to answer these questions, it is helpful to begin our analysis with a relatively homogeneous group of financial instruments, namely, the bonds issued by the U.S. government. As they call for payment in legal tender, such bonds are free of the risk of default, since the government can always "print" money to meet its obligations. Consequently, the only major differences between various government bonds are with respect to coupon rate and maturity. A group of bonds with a particular combination of coupon rate and maturity is termed an *issue.* We saw two examples of such issues in Table 4–3, but there are, in fact, numerous government issues. For example, on September 28, 1979, there were 173 different issues outstanding. Of these, 74 were short term, due to mature in one year or less. The bulk of the short-term issues were *Treasury bills,* which are typically issued with maturities of three or six months. However, 22 of the short-term issues had an original maturity exceeding one year. The remaining 99 had maturities running from 1 year to 30 years.

As one might suspect from Table 4–3, these various issues exhibited substantial differences in yields to maturity, with actual yields ranging from about $9\frac{1}{2}$ to 12 percent. These yields are plotted in Figure 4–1, with yields on the vertical axes and the date of maturity (or, equivalently, the number of years to maturity) on the horizontal axes. Clearly, the yields plotted in Figure 4–1 do form a regular pattern, and this has been emphasized by drawing a smooth curve through the data.[5] This curve is known as the *yield curve,* and it portrays the *term structure of interest rates* at a point in time. That is, it shows how the yields to maturity vary with the maturity of the debt instrument on a given date.

As was already hinted at by Table 4–3, the yield curve can take a variety of shapes. The four most common shapes are portrayed in Figure 4–2 and are known as the flat yield curve, the ascending yield curve, the descending yield curve, and the humped yield curve. The ascending

---

[5] The pattern of yields in Figure 4–1 is regular, but not precisely so, since there appear to be some outliers off the curve. For the most part these outliers reflect some special features (such as taxes), and these issues are customarily ignored in drawing a yield curve.

yield curve is the "normal" one we had in mind when we suggested that liquidity considerations would tend to make yields on short-term securities less than those on long-term securities. Clearly, however, other shapes are quite common as well. What explains these various patterns?

The most commonly given explanation is termed the *expectations theory*, under which the shape of the yield curve is based on investors' expectations of *future* interest rates, in particular, future short-term rates.[6] The nature of this theory can be seen most easily with the aid of an example.

Suppose an individual wishes to invest funds for two years, and for

---

[6] As characterized by a 10-year-old named Keith Goldfeld, the issue is one of *futurizing*.

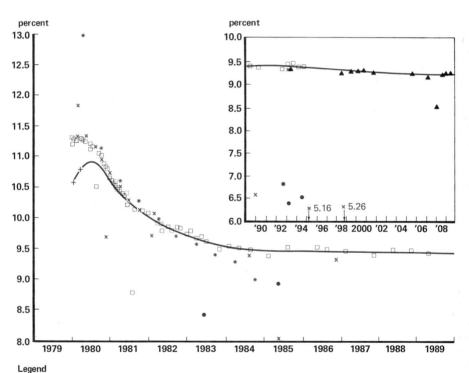

Yields of Treasury securities, September 28, 1979 (based on closing bid quotations)

Source: *Treasury Bulletin*, October 1979, p. 88.

**FIGURE 4–1**

Legend

× Fixed coupon issues
• Callable issues
* 1½ % exchange notes
+ Bills — coupon equivalent of 3mo., 6mo., and 1yr. bills

□ High coupon issues — 7% and higher fixed maturity issues

▲ High coupon callable issues — plotted to earliest call date when prices are above par par and to maturity date when prices are at par or below

Note: The curve is fitted by eye and based only on the most actively traded issues. Market yields on coupon issues due in less than 3 months are excluded.

simplicity assume that she considers the following two alternatives: She may purchase a 1-year Treasury security and, when it matures, acquire another 1-year bond; or she may initially purchase a 2-year bond and hold it until maturity. If our investor is a profit maximizer, she will choose that security (or combination of securities) that gives her the greatest return over the two-year period. For concreteness, suppose that 1-year bonds are currently yielding 7 percent and that our investor expects that 1-year bonds *issued a year from now* will yield 9 percent (this is the expected short-term rate). From one of her options she thus anticipates an average return over the two-year period of roughly 8 percent. Given these expectations, she would buy a 2-year bond only if it yielded more than 8 percent per year but would purchase a sequence of two 1-year bonds if the two-year rate was less than 8 percent. If all investors expected a future short-term rate of 9 percent, this line of reasoning implies that the yield on 2-year bonds would have to be approximately 8 percent for the bond market to be in equilibrium. If it was higher, investors would regard 2-year bonds as a good thing and bid *up* their price (driving *down* their yield) until an 8 percent rate was established and investors

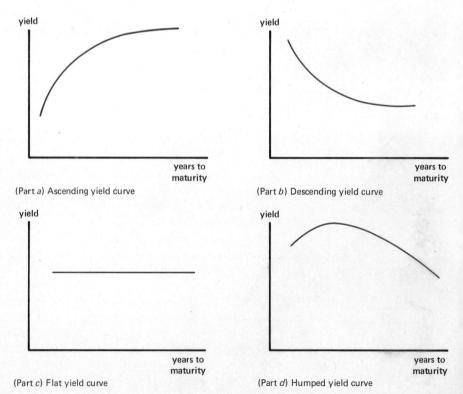

(Part a) Ascending yield curve

(Part b) Descending yield curve

*Common shapes of
yield curves*

**FIGURE 4–2**

(Part c) Flat yield curve

(Part d) Humped yield curve

were indifferent between the various options. Conversely, if the 2-year bond yield was lower than 8 percent, holders of 2-year bonds would attempt to sell such bonds and buy 1-year bonds (driving bond prices down and bond yields up) until an 8 percent rate was established. Thus, *arbitrage* would establish equilibrium in the bond market.

What this example suggests is that, in general, we should find that yields on long-term bonds will be averages of current and expected future short yields. This simple observation is, in fact, sufficient to account for all the possible yield curve patterns portrayed in Figure 4–2. For example, if short-term rates are expected to rise, long-term rates, being an average of current and future short rates, would be above current short rates, producing an ascending yield curve. If lower short-term rates are expected in the future, long rates will lie below current short rates, giving us a descending yield curve. Finally, if investors expect short-term rates first to rise and then to fall to much lower levels, a humped yield curve will result.

In many respects the expectations theory is a natural extension of the principles on market yields and bond prices developed previously. We saw earlier that the actual return from a bond sold before maturity could differ substantially from the yield to maturity that prevailed when the bond was purchased. The expectations theory explicitly recognizes the possibility that individuals may need funds after two, three, or ten years whatever the maturity of the security they happen to own. Thus, what the individual investor is assumed to maximize is the return over some particular *horizon* or *holding period*. Since different investors will have different holding periods, this serves to bring long-term rates into line so as to equalize *expected holding-period yields* for different horizons.

This then is the essence of the expectations theory of the term structure of interest rates. While it provides a reasonably satisfactory explanation of observed yield curves, there are several reasons why it may not hold exactly.

1  DIVERSE EXPECTATIONS. Not all investors have the same expectations, so that the arbitrage among various maturities, in some loose sense, only responds to "average" expectations.

2  TRANSACTIONS COSTS. Because there are costs, such as brokers' fees, for shifting funds among maturities, complete arbitrage may not take place.

3. LIQUIDITY CONSIDERATIONS AND UNCERTAINTY. Investors may not hold expectations with complete confidence and consequently may still prefer short-term maturities because of their liquidity. This would suggest that, for example, if current and all future short-term rates are 6 percent, even though the expectations theory predicts a long rate of 6 percent (a flat yield curve), the

actual long-term rate may have to exceed 6 percent to compensate investors for the greater price volatility of long-term bonds.

4   LONG MATURITY PREFERENCES. In contrast to those investors who are willing to pay a premium for liquidity, certain groups of investors may prefer longer maturities so as to balance better the maturity structure of their assets and liabilities. For example, life insurance companies that issue long-term liabilities typically invest in long-term bonds so as to be assured of a profit regardless of the course of interest rates over the life of the insurance contract. As with the case of liquidity needs, this could lead to a certain amount of bond market *segmentation*, which interferes with the arbitrage process.

**The General Structure of Interest Rates**

Our discussion of the market for U.S. government securities has documented the existence of numerous interest rates for such bonds. If interest differentials exist within this class of relatively homogeneous securities, it is hardly surprising that an even greater range of possible interest rates emerges once we look at other market instruments. In Figure 4–3 we have plotted a sample of such interest rates for several different types of market instruments. It is to be stressed that even this figure conceals many additional interest rate differentials. For example, the single long-term corporate bond rate that we have plotted is necessarily an average of many different rates that are paid by corporations with widely different borrowing capabilities. The diversity underlying an

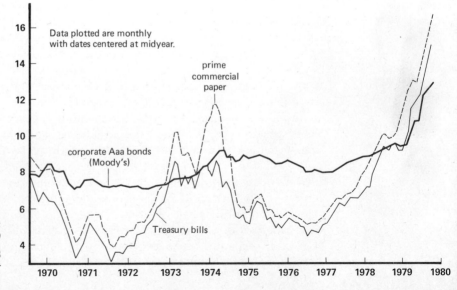

*Selected interest rates, 1970–1980*

**FIGURE 4–3**

average rate is relevant for the other series plotted in the figure as well. This complication aside, what accounts for the general structure of rates portrayed in Figure 4–3?

Our previous discussion of the term structure has noted some of the possible factors, such as liquidity and market risk, and we here consider a number of additional ones. A factor of primary importance, once we move away from U.S. government securities, is the risk of default. For example, there is a relatively constant differential between the rate on high-grade corporate bonds and the rate on long-term U.S. government securities and this reflects such a *risk premium*. Perhaps an even more vivid illustration of the risk element, is the enormous 4 percentage point difference between interest rates on prime commercial paper and U.S. Treasury bills that prevailed in mid-1974. Like Treasury bills, commercial paper is a short-term instrument. As it is only issued by large and well-known corporations (e.g., General Motors), the historical differential has been a percentage point or less. This might be taken as a measure of the normal risk premium. In mid-1974, however, we were in the midst of the oil crisis, when, at least according to the popular press, safety became of prime concern (especially with Arab oil sheiks). Consequently, the risk premium rose to unprecedented levels. Not coincidentally, mid-1974 was also a period in which short-term rates exceeded long-term ones. The other noteworthy feature of Figure 4–3 is the record-breaking level of interest rates that prevailed at the beginning of 1980. In March 1980, for example, the Treasury bill rate averaged a whopping $15\frac{1}{2}$ percent. We shall have more to say on the causes and consequences of this in a later chapter.

In addition to default risk, there are a number of other explanations of interest rate differentials that can be listed more briefly. Among these we have the following:

1   DIFFERENCES IN COSTS OF ADMINISTRATION PER DOLLAR OF LOAN PER YEAR. Interest charges usually include an amount to cover costs of investigating the creditworthiness of the borrower, of holding the loan, and of collecting principal and interest. On some loans, these costs are very low per dollar per year. For example, the annual administrative cost per dollar on a very large loan to a corporation whose credit standing need not be investigated may be almost negligible. On the other hand, such costs per dollar of loan per year may be very high on a small installment loan to a consumer when his or her credit standing must be investigated and interest and principal collected in weekly or monthly installments.

2   DIFFERENCES IN TAXABILITY. An example of such differences is the fact that income on securities issued by states and municipalities is exempt from federal income taxes, which

enables these securities to be sold at lower yield rates. During the period 1965–1979 interest rates on municipal securities averaged 1.3 percent less than the rates on 10-year Treasury bonds.

3   MARKET IMPERFECTIONS. Another part of the explanation of interest rate differentials is to be found in imperfections in the credit market, which inhibit the mobility of loan funds from one branch of the market to another. Some of the most important of these are lack of knowledge by lenders or borrowers, legal limitations on the types of loans that can be made by some financial institutions, and differing degrees of monopoly power in the various branches of the market. There are also a variety of restrictions that directly limit the rate of interest on certain types of debt obligations. Here we include state usury laws and legal restrictions that have limited the interest rate the federal government could pay on new long-term issues.

4   TECHNICAL FEATURES. A number of technical features of market instruments can also affect their yield. For example, bonds may be *callable* in that the borrower may have the right (usually after a certain date) to prepay the debt. Since borrowers are likely to do this only if interest rates have fallen, investors will generally require some compensation for accepting this feature. On the other hand, certain types of bonds may be *convertible* (e.g., into equities), and some investors may find this a desirable feature.

CONCLUSION   From our discussion of yields and other attributes of financial instruments, there are several points worth emphasizing:

1   The price or market value of a financial instrument results from equilibrating the forces of supply and demand. The interest rate or yield on a financial instrument is inversely related to its price. Thus, for example, an increase in the supply of a bond (say, by new issuers who wish to raise additional funds) will tend to reduce the price of the bond and raise the interest rate on the bond. In subsequent chapters we shall discuss how underlying economic developments shift the balance between supply and demand and thus change interest rates. Not surprisingly, the Federal Reserve, through its conduct of monetary policy, is of particular importance in this regard.

2   While the exposition of certain economic principles is often facilitated by the use of a single interest rate, this is a rather marked simplification. As we have seen, there are numerous market rates of interest, and these can differ widely. Moreover, these various rates may not move in a parallel manner through time, although they usually move in the same direction.

3   It is possible to elaborate a substantial number of characteristics of market instruments that explain differences in market yields. As investors differ with respect to preferences, expectations, and opportunities, it would be surprising if they chose to hold their assets in exactly the same form. In fact, there is substantial diversity of asset portfolios across different groups of investors. Or, put another way, because of differences in preferences among buyers and among issuers, securities come to be highly differentiated with differing claims on assets and income. These come to be reflected in differences in liquidity, safety of principal value, and yield. Holders are presented with a varied menu from which to choose. Subsequent chapters examine these portfolio decisions for the public, the banks, and other financial intermediaries and spell out the implications of alternative portfolio choice for the behavior of the economy and the operation of monetary policy.

**SELECTED READINGS**

First Boston Corporation, *Handbook of the United States Government and Federal Agencies and Related Money Market Instruments*, Boston, 1970.

Malkiel, B. G., *The Term Structure of Interest Rates: Theory, Empirical Evidence, and Applications*, Morristown, N.J., General Learning Press, 1970.

Stigum, M., *The Money Market: Myth, Reality, and Practice*, Homewood, Ill., Dow Jones-Irwin, 1978.

# COMMERCIAL BANKING

# 5

With this chapter we begin a detailed investigation of commercial banking in the United States. As already indicated, commercial banks are our most important financial institutions. Their importance stems both from their size and from the fact that their liabilities in the form of demand deposits account for the bulk of the money supply. Thus, commercial banks play a key role in the functioning of the economy. It is therefore natural that we should be concerned with whether the banking industry is structured so as to provide banking services in an efficient manner.

More specifically, in this chapter we shall examine issues like the following: How are banks born and how do they die? How did we get so many banks, and is this a good thing? What legal forms can banks take, and does this matter? Is the banking system safe, efficient, and competitive? Who regulates banks, how are they regulated, and why are they regulated? As we attempt to answer these questions, the reader should gain an appreciation of the complexities of the commercial banking industry and the problems faced by those policy makers who are charged with ensuring that the banking system functions smoothly.

**WHAT'S
IN A NAME?**  While we have used the term *commercial banks* in several instances, we have yet to describe what a commercial bank is. Since there are a variety of kinds of "banks"—investment banks, mutual savings banks, and even blood banks—the key is clearly meant to be the word *commercial*. In this context, the word is a legacy of the so-called *commercial-loan theory* of banking. This theory, which originated in the early days of banking, held that, aside from cash, bank assets should consist of short-term loans to

businesses to finance the transportation of goods and the holding of inventories. As industry developed, this theory was modified to admit the propriety of short-term loans to cover production costs, but it continued to exclude long-term loans such as those used for financing machinery, factories, and other real estate.

For a number of reasons, the phrase "commercial banking" is no longer particularly satisfactory. For one, even from the start commercial banks did not confine themselves to short-term loans. And with the passage of time they have increasingly acquired longer-term assets. Secondly, there are now many institutions for financing short-term business needs, so that the exclusivity implied by the phrase "commercial banking" is somewhat misleading.

What, in fact, differentiates commercial banks from other financial intermediaries is not the assets they hold but, rather, their liabilities. In particular, with minor exceptions only commercial banks can issue demand deposits, the primary component of the money supply. They thus have the power to create and destroy money, a feature that accounts for our close focus on commercial banking. Another feature distinguishing commercial banks from other financial institutions is the scope of their activities. Most of them are department stores of finance, not specialty shops. They not only offer checking services but also offer savings services, operate trust departments, underwrite securities, and deal in foreign exchange. As is stressed in their advertisements, they aspire to provide "one-stop" banking.

With the passage of time, some of the distinguishing features of commercial banks may blur. We have already noted the growing "moneyness" of the liabilities of nonbank financial intermediaries. Many of these institutions are also expanding the scope of their activities. While we shall later study the consequences of the growing similarity of financial intermediaries, for our present purposes we may regard commercial banks as relatively unique financial institutions.

**DUAL BANKING AND BANK SUPERVISION**

For those who like legal definitions, there is another way to define a commercial bank, namely, as any institution that is chartered to be a commercial bank. As this bit of sophistry suggests, one needs permission to start a bank, and this takes the form of securing a charter to engage in the business of commercial banking. If one makes a convincing case on grounds of worthiness and need, a commercial bank charter may be obtained from the federal government (through the Comptroller of the Currency) or from the various state banking authorities. Banks that have been granted charters by the federal government are known as *national banks;* the remainder are called *state banks*. National and state banks exist side by side in every state; hence the characterization of the United

States as having a *dual banking system.*[1] As of 1978 roughly two-thirds of the banks had state charters, but they accounted for only 45 percent of total assets (Table 5–1). National banks are evidently less numerous but larger than state banks.

As indicated in Table 5–1, there are two additional supervisory layers that serve to distinguish among banks. The first of these is Federal Reserve membership. All national banks are rquired to be members of the Federal Reserve System, but membership is optional for state banks. As of 1978 only 10 percent of the state banks were members. Overall, therefore, 38 percent of all banks were members, although they had 73 percent of all bank assets.

Another way in which banks can be distinguished from one another is with respect to insurance status. All Federal Reserve member banks are required to have their deposits insured by the Federal Deposit Insurance Corporation (FDIC). While this is optional for state nonmember banks, as shown in Table 5–1 virtually all of these have elected to be insured. (We shall have more to say about the FDIC shortly.)

**The Choice of a Charter**

Why do banks choose a national or a state charter? As already noted, national banks must join the Federal Reserve, so the choice of a charter is intertwined with the desirability of membership in the Federal Reserve. A key element is the fact that reserve requirements are much stiffer for banks that are members of the Federal Reserve in terms of both percentage requirements and the form in which reserves must be held. The high level of interest rates that has prevailed in recent years has meant that idle reserves (which pay no interest) carry a substantial opportunity cost. Consequently, banks seeking more advantageous reserve

[1] The historical reasons for the evolution of a dual banking system are traced in Chapter 8.

**TABLE 5–1**

*Three ways of classifying commercial banks°*

| | Number of banks | Percent of total number | Assets (in billions of dollars) | Percent of total assets |
|---|---|---|---|---|
| National banks | 4,564 | 31 | 671 | 55 |
| State banks | 10,148 | 69 | 544 | 45 |
| Federal Reserve member banks | 5,564 | 38 | 888 | 73 |
| Nonmember banks | 9,148 | 62 | 327 | 27 |
| FDIC-insured banks | 14,379 | 98 | 1,173 | 97 |
| Uninsured banks | 333 | 2 | 42 | 3 |
| All commercial banks | 14,712 | 100 | 1,215 | 100 |

° Number of banks at year-end 1978, assets as of midyear 1978.

requirements often elect or convert to a state charter.[2] As a result of this process, membership in the Federal Reserve has been declining in recent years.[3]

Some writers have expressed concern over the fact that individual banks get to choose either a national or a state regulator. The fear, perhaps, is that competition among regulators would lead to banking abuses. Or, put another way, Gresham's law might apply to bank regulation, with bad regulators driving out good ones. Whatever its merits as a historical description, in recent years this has not been much of an issue. At least one reason for this is that the FDIC examines the balance sheets of virtually all banks, be they national or state chartered.

**Regulatory Problems**

As expected, the existence of dual banking and the multiplicity of regulatory authorities is a source of complexity (and confusion) in the U.S. banking industry. Even within the federal bureaucracy, harmony does not always reign supreme. At various times considerable controversy has erupted among the Comptroller of the Currency, the FDIC, and the Federal Reserve. Proposals to consolidate these three groups have been advanced on a number of occasions, although with differing visions of which agency would survive the consolidation.

Once one introduces both federal and state jurisdictions, even more complexity results. Specifically, national and state banks are governed by different laws (even in the same state), and banking practices that are prohibited in one state may be permitted in another. Despite these quirks, dual banking has many staunch defenders, who argue that it stimulates innovation by letting each state function as an experimental laboratory. We shall see some examples of this below in Chapter 17. Nevertheless, whatever the merits of this argument, the dual banking system works reasonably well, and there seems to be little pressure for drastic surgery.

**THE NUMBER OF COMMERCIAL BANKS**

As noted in Table 5–1, as of year end 1978 there were 14,712 commercial banks in the United States. This number, however, has fluctuated considerably over time. In 1840 the country had roughly 900 banks. By 1900 the number of banks had expanded to nearly 9,000. This remarkable

---

[2] Capital requirements also tend to be lower for state-chartered banks than for national banks. National banks do generally enjoy more flexibility in the nature of the activities they are permitted to engage in, and Federal Reserve membership also provides a number of benefits.

[3] We shall examine this issue in Chapters 9 and 18. We should note that legislation signed into law on March, 31, 1980, provides for the gradual imposition of certain kinds of reserve requirements on nonmember banks. Over the longer run, this should minimize the importance of Federal Reserve membership as a policy issue.

growth continued up to 1920, at which time there were nearly 30,000 banks in the United States. However, between 1920 and 1940 the trend reversed and the number of banks declined by about 50 percent, falling to roughly 14,000. Since that time it has fluctuated more narrowly, declining a little during the earlier part of the period and showing an increase more recently.

In order to explain changes in the number of commercial banks it is necessary to examine new-bank chartering, bank failures, and bank mergers. The net change in the number of banks during any period is equal to the number of new banks created in the period minus the number that disappear through suspension or voluntary liquidation and also those that disappear by being consolidated or merged into other banks. For convenience we shall refer to these respectively as new banks, bank failures, and bank absorptions.

Table 5–2 shows that between the end of 1920 and year end 1978 the number of banks declined by about 14,500. More than 13,000 new banks were chartered in this period, but these additions were more than offset by over 13,500 failures and nearly 15,000 absorptions of banks through mergers.[4]

**New Banks**    Table 5–2 indicates that more than 13,000 new banks were chartered between 1921 and 1978. The rate of creation of new banks was high in the 1920s, much lower from 1929 through World War II, and

---

[4] The careful reader will note some statistical inconsistencies in Table 5–2. These arise partly from discrepancies in the original data and partly from shifts of institutions between the categories of commercial banks and noncommercial banks.

---

**TABLE 5–2**

*Changes in the number of United States commercial banks during selected periods, 1920–1978*

| Period | Number at end of period | New Banks | Bank failures | Bank absorptions | Net change during period |
|---|---|---|---|---|---|
| 1920 | 29,206 | | | | |
| 1921–1929 (inclusive) | 23,695 | 3,253 | 5,067 | 3,963 | −5,511 |
| 1930–1933 (inclusive) | 14,352 | 674 | 7,763 | 2,322 | −9,343 |
| 1934–1941 (inclusive) | 14,225 | 890 | * | 1,127 | −  127 |
| 1942–1945 (inclusive) | 14,011 | 258 | 201 | 327 | −  214 |
| 1946–1970 (inclusive) | 13,688 | 3,277 | 252 | 3,399 | −  323 |
| 1971–1978 (inclusive) | 14,712 | 2,060 | 42 | 994 | +1,024 |
| Total, 1921–1978 | | 13,081 | 13,549 | 14,972 | −14,494 |

*Source:* Board of Governors of the Federal Reserve System, *Banking and Monetary Statistics,* Washington, D.C., 1943; Federal Reserve Board, various annual reports, and *Federal Reserve Bulletin,* various issues.
* Data not reliable because of some reopenings of banks suspended earlier.

higher again in the postwar period, although still considerably below the rates of the 1920s. The rate of creation of new banks depends directly on the supply and willingness of private investors to establish and finance new banks, which presumably is based on prospective profitability, and on the availability of charters from the banking authorities. Both have undergone wide changes since World War I.

Free banking prevailed in the United States during the latter half of the nineteenth century and through World War I; the Comptroller of the Currency and most state banking authorities were empowered to grant charters to all who met the requirements of the general banking laws. It was under this policy of free banking that the number of banks grew to more than 29,000 in 1920. Following the banking debacle of the early 1930s, important modifications of the free-banking principle resulted from the Banking Act of 1935. Under this law a new bank still must meet the requirements of the relevant general banking laws, but the Comptroller of the Currency may issue a charter for a new national bank and the FDIC may insure the deposits of a new state-chartered bank only if they find it in the public interest to do so after investigating such things as the qualifications and experience of the proposed bank directors and officers, the prospects of success of the new bank, and the need of the community for additional banking facilities. Most state banking authorities have adopted somewhat similar policies, if only because a new state bank would have but limited chances of success if it were denied deposit insurance.

The prospective profitability of establishing new banks has also fluctuated widely. It is easy to understand why so few new banks were created during the Great Depression and also during and immediately following World War II, when interest rates were abnormally low. However, one might have expected that the rate of new-bank creation would have increased even more than it has since about 1950 in view of the generally higher level of interest rates, high and rising levels of economic activity, growth of population, and spread of metropolitan areas. A major part of the explanation is to be found in the growth of branch banking as branch offices have been established in areas that would otherwise have attracted new banks. We shall have more to say about this shortly.

**Bank Absorptions**    As shown in Table 5–2, between 1920 and 1978 some 14,972 banks disappeared through absorption in mergers. The absorption rate was high during the 1920s and somewhat lower from 1930 to 1933. After falling sharply from the end of 1933 to the end of World War II, the bank absorption rate again rose to high levels in the postwar period. It would be even higher if it were not restricted by the banking authorities and the Department of Justice.

What are the reasons for this high rate of bank mergers and for pressures toward even higher rates? Such mergers can occur only if owners of the bank to be absorbed are willing to sell at a price attractive to the owners and management of the acquiring bank. There are many reasons why the owners of an absorbed bank may be willing to sell at such a price. One is the imminence of failure. An unknown number of the absorbed banks would have suspended operations if they had not been bought. Banking authorities have often assisted such mergers. Other reasons for merging include various diseconomies of small scale that come to be reflected in low net earnings, difficulties in providing for management succession at salaries that the bank can afford to pay, and the low liquidity and marketability of shares in a small bank.

There are also many reasons why an acquiring bank is willing to pay an attractive price. Since a merger produces a larger bank, the acquiring bank may be able to reap cost savings due to economies of scale. Merger may also offer the possibility of obtaining new lines of business, new customers, or geographic diversification.

**Bank Failures**

Even in the nineteenth and early twentieth centuries, the United States had the dubious distinction of possessing one of the highest, if not the highest, bank failure rates of any important nation with a commercial banking system. Nearly 3,000 banks failed between 1864 and 1920. But the worst was yet to come. Another 5,067 had suspended operations by the end of 1929, and still another 7,763 were defunct by the end of 1933. The mortality rate was especially high among smaller banks, but many large ones also failed.

To generalize about the reasons for failure of any type of business enterprise is difficult, for the reasons vary from case to case, and even in a particular case failure usually results not from a single cause but from a combination of conditions. Nevertheless, it is possible to isolate some of the most important factors responsible for high bank-failure rates prior to 1934.

As just noted, the era of free banking, which prevailed until the mid-1930s, meant that it was relatively easy—some would say too easy—to start a bank. The net result was "overbanking." For example, it was not unusual for a village with 2,000 inhabitants to have three or more banks. These banks were inevitably small and, therefore, unable to capitalize on economies of scale. Furthermore, a large percentage of the assets of these small banks were typically in the form of loans to local borrowers. Thus, the banks were likely to be weak in the face of unfavorable economic developments, not only in the economy at large but also in their own localities. And some banks in overbanked areas would have failed even under favorable economic conditions; the adverse economic developments that materialized ensured disaster.

Adverse economic conditions for many banks began in the 1920s with gradual shifts in the location of business brought about in part by the revolution in highway transportation. Prior to the days of hard-surfaced roads, automobiles, and farm trucks, farmers took much of their

---

### HOW TO AVOID A BANK FAILURE

A firsthand account of a run on a bank in 1931 brought on by the closing of a neighboring bank.

I told . . . [the staff] what they would have to face in a few hours. "If you want to keep this bank open," I said, "you must do your part. Go about your business as though nothing unusual was happening. . . . We can't break this run today. The best we can do is slow it down. People are going to come here to close out their savings accounts. You are going to pay them. But you are going to pay them very slowly. . . . You know a lot of depositors by sight, and in the past you did not have to look up their signatures, but today when they come here with their deposit books to close out their accounts, you are going to look up every signature card. And take your time about it. And one other thing: When you pay out, don't use any big bills. Pay out in fives and tens, and count slowly." . . .

In the meantime a call had been put through to the Federal Reserve Bank in Salt Lake City to send currency to our [bank] . . . The armored car that brought funds to us in Ogden arrived on the scene as in the movies when the Union cavalry charged in to save all from the Indians. . . .

Mounting the counter, I raised my hand and called for attention: . . .

"I want to make an announcement. It appears that we are having some difficulty handling our depositors with the speed to which you are accustomed. Many of you have been in line for a considerable time. I just wanted to tell you that instead of closing at the usual hour of three o'clock, we have decided to stay open just as long as there is anyone who desires to withdraw his deposit or make one. Therefore, you people who have just come in can return later this afternoon or evening if you wish. There is no justification for the excitement or the apparent panicky attitude on the part of some depositors. As all of you have seen, we have just had brought up from Salt Lake City, a large amount of currency that will take care of all your requirements. There is plenty more where that came from." (This was true enough—but I didn't say we could get it.)*

* Mariner S. Eccles, *Beckoning Frontiers,* New York, Knopf, 1951, pp. 58–60. The bank and Eccles both survived, with Eccles going on to become chairman of the Board of Governors of the Federal Reserve System.

business to nearby agricultural villages or small towns. Here they sold many of their products, bought supplies, and did their banking. But as new roads and motor vehicles increased the speed and reduced the cost of transportation, farmers took their business (including deposits and borrowing) to the county seat or some other larger city. The smaller village or town was left to wither on the vine; its banks were fortunate if they escaped a less lingering death. Other shifts of business also contributed to the failures of individual banks: shifts of plants from one area to another, the replacement of small firms by larger ones that did their banking business elsewhere, and so on.

While shifts in the location of business contributed to a substantial number of bank failures, a more important factor was the periods of deflation and depression that the economy endured. Bank failures and business depressions are mutually aggravating; a depression tends to break banks, and bank failures deepen a depression. Falling prices, incomes, sales, and employment lessen the abilities of debtors to meet their obligations and thereby threaten both the solvency and the liquidity of banks. Many banks were destroyed or seriously weakened during the sharp deflation starting in May 1920. The failure of agriculture to recover fully during the 1920s injured banks that were heavily dependent on farming. Then came the Great Depression. Thousands of banks failed to survive under its strains, and bank failures and threats of failure played an important role in deepening and prolonging the depression.

Since 1934 bank-failure rates have been much lower than in preceding years. There appear to be many reasons for this, including the protection afforded by better supervision of banks, improved bank management, and more frequent absorptions of weak banks in mergers. However, a basic factor has been the maintenance of high and generally rising levels of income and economic activity. The FDIC, through its role in insuring deposits, also merits attention in this regard.

**THE FEDERAL DEPOSIT INSURANCE CORPORATION (FDIC)**

The FDIC was established in direct response to the dramatic number of bank failures experienced in the early 1930s.[5] It began operation in 1934, the year following the worst debacle in banking history, when some 4,000 commercial banks suspended operations. Initially the FDIC insured the first $5,000 of each deposit account in an insured bank, but the limit was later raised in several steps. In 1974 the limit was set at $40,000 and in 1980 it was raised to $100,000, where it now stands.

---

[5] Despite the evident need for deposit insurance, when it was proposed it had many vociferous opponents. Indeed, the prestigious American Bankers Association, fighting the plan to the bitter end, declared it to be "unsound, unscientific, unjust, and dangerous" (cited in J. K. Galbraith, *Money*, Boston, Houghton Mifflin, 1975, p. 197).

Even under the current system there remains a sizable volume of uninsured deposits. A part of this (roughly 2 percent of total deposits) is in the roughly 300 state banks that have elected to remain uninsured. Another part results from the insurance limit. For example, the $40,000 limit was sufficient to provide full insurance for 98 percent of the *number* of depositors, but only for about two-thirds of the *dollar amount* of total deposits. Naturally, raising the insurance limit to $100,000 reduced the volume of uninsured deposits, but it is estimated that 30 percent of deposits remain uncovered. While some readers may be disturbed by the existence of uninsured deposits, the operating procedures of the FDIC do in fact reduce its significance.

One reason for this is that the FDIC engages in an extensive program of bank examination and supervision that fosters sound management in the banking system. In so doing, it protects depositors by preventing bank failures. If, despite these procedures, a bank does experience financial difficulties, the FDIC may bring about a merger of the distressed bank with a healthy insured bank. To facilitate a merger it can purchase assets of the distressed bank or lend funds to it. When a successful merger results, depositors suffer no losses, so that the system functions as if full insurance were in effect.[6]

By any reasonable standard the operation of the FDIC has been a significant success. Since its inception in 1934 bank failures have been relatively few in number. Furthermore, those that have occurred have not spread in an infectious way through the banking system. Despite this success, there is one aspect of the FDIC that has come under criticism. This concerns the method of financing. The FDIC is financed by annual insurance premiums of 1/12 of 1 percent of the total (not just insured) deposits of its member banks. Out of this premium the FDIC adds to its insurance reserves (currently about $9 billion), pays operating expenses, and returns the residual to its member banks. Many large banks regard the setting of insurance premiums in relation to total deposits as unfair, arguing that this forces them to provide a subsidy to small banks. One reason for this is that small banks have historically had a higher failure rate than large banks—although this has not been true in recent years. From this perspective they argue that the premium should be higher for small banks. A second reason stems from the fact that large banks have a disproportionately high share of uninsured deposits, that is, a disproportionately large fraction of accounts that exceed the insurance limit. Since

---

[6] Even if a distressed bank fails and is permitted to go into receivership, depositors typically recover funds beyond the technical insurance limit. The proceeds for this result from the sale of the failed bank's assets. FDIC records indicate that roughly 90 percent of uninsured deposits are eventually recovered, although often a wait of several years is involved.

premiums are based on total deposits, large banks argue that they are paying for insurance that they are not getting. There are merits in both these arguments, and indeed some economists have called for a restructuring of insurance premiums to address these problems. In partial defense of the current system, it should be noted that many of the activities of the FDIC tend to protect (if not insure) all deposits of its member banks. Consequently, the arguments of the larger banks probably overstate the inequities inherent in the present setup.

## ORGANIZATIONAL FORMS IN BANKING

While we have touched on several aspects of the structure of the banking system, our treatment would not be complete without an examination of the various organizational forms of banking found in the United States. By the formidable-sounding phrase "organizational form" we simply mean whether a bank is set up as an independent bank with one office, has branch offices, or is grouped with other banks (or even nonbanks) in some legal or informal way. As we shall see, there is a considerable diversity of organizational forms—a diversity that reflects the legalistic hodgepodge stemming from our dual banking system.

### Unit Banks

The most common form of banking in the United States is what is termed *unit banking*. A unit bank is a banking corporation that operates only a single office. Largely as a result of state laws that limited or prohibited branching, unit banks have always dominated American banking. In 1900, for example, 99 percent of the roughly 8,700 banks were unit banks. Today, unit banks account for about 60 percent of all banks. Most unit banks are independent in that they are not controlled by a corporation that controls other banks. Furthermore, the average independent unit bank tends to be relatively small. We shall explore the consequences of this fact later.

### Branch Banking

A *branch bank*, as the name suggests, is a banking corporation that directly owns and operates two or more banking offices. Branching can occur through the creation of a new office from scratch, called *de novo branching*, or through the absorption of a bank through merger and the conversion of its facilities into branch offices. Banks often find it more feasible and economical to branch through absorption. For one thing, they may establish branches only with the permission of the banking authorities, and the latter often permit branching by absorption where they would deny *de novo* branches. Also, branching by absorption often gives access to a highly desirable banking site, brings with it bank assets and an established banking business, and eliminates one competitor from the local banking market.

Over time there has been a strong trend toward branch banking, with a marked increase in both the number of banks operating branches and the total number of branches. As the data in Table 5–3 show, in 1900 the U.S. banking system was overwhelmingly a unit-banking system; of the 8,738 banks existing at that time, only 87 had even one branch office, and the total number of branches was only 119. In 1920, only 530 of the 29,087 banks operated one or more branches, and the total number of branches was 1,281. Since then, branch banking has continued to grow, interrupted only during the Great Depression. Its growth has been especially rapid since World War II. For example, between 1950 and 1978 the number of banks operating branches increased from 1,291 to 6,381 and the number of branch offices climbed from 4,721 to 34,408. Despite this increase, unit banks still predominate in numbers, although not in total assets.

As a consequence of the expansion of branch banking, it is evident from Table 5–3 that the total number of bank facilities has increased markedly since 1950. The expansion of bank facilities via branching is common in other countries as well. For example, both Canada and Great Britain have on the order of only ten banks; each, however, has many branches. In fact, despite the small number of commercial banks, both of these countries have more banking facilities per capita than the United States.

While branch banking has grown significantly in the United States, it would expand even faster in the absence of official restrictions. These restrictions stem from the various state laws that govern branch banking —laws that cover a complete spectrum of possibilities. As of the late 1970s, some 22 states allowed statewide branching, 17 permitted limited branching, and the remaining dozen or so could be characterized as unit banking states. Branching across state lines is prohibited by all states. A vivid illustration of the differences among states can be seen by compar-

**TABLE 5–3**

*Number of United States commercial banks and branch offices on selected dates (end-of-year figures)*

| Year | Total number of banks | Number of banks with branches | Total number of branches |
|------|----------------------|-------------------------------|--------------------------|
| 1900 | 8,738 | 87 | 119 |
| 1920 | 29,087 | 530 | 1,281 |
| 1930 | 22,172 | 751 | 3,522 |
| 1940 | 14,344 | 954 | 3,525 |
| 1950 | 14,121 | 1,291 | 4,721 |
| 1960 | 13,472 | 2,329 | 10,216 |
| 1970 | 13,688 | 3,994 | 21,424 |
| 1974 | 14,457 | 5,123 | 28,434 |
| 1978 | 14,712 | 6,381 | 34,408 |

*Source:* Board of Governors of the Federal Reserve System, *banking and Monetary Statistics,* 1940–1970, Washington, D.C., 1976; *annual Statistical Digest,* various issues.

ing California, which has statewide branching, with Texas, a unit banking state. At the beginning of 1978 California had 235 banks, of which 158 maintained 3,750 branches or additional offices. Texas, by contrast, had 1,382 banks, of which 156 maintained 157 additional offices. California had about 16 branches per bank while Texas had 1/10 of a branch per bank.

Another point that deserves emphasis is that state branching laws also apply to banks with federal charters. That is, national banks must obey the branching laws of the state in which they are located. This practice, which helps preserve dual banking, stems from congressional acquiescence rather than from any constitutional principle. Indeed, there have been some recent attempts to circumvent this policy by administrative rather than legislative means. One illustration of this is a 1974 ruling by the Comptroller of the Currency concerning the use of electronic funds transfer terminals by commercial banks. More specifically, the ruling permitted national banks to operate customer–bank communication terminals (CBCTs). These facilities would be physically removed from existing bank premises and could be either manned or fully automated. Through CBCTs bank customers could make deposits or withdrawals from their accounts, transfer funds between checking and savings accounts, and transfer funds from their own accounts to those maintained by other bank customers. A substantial number of CBCTs may be in the offing, located in places such as shopping centers, train stations, factories, mobile home parks, and university campuses.

From the perspective of our present discussion, the most interesting aspect of this development is that the Comptroller ruled that such "minibank" facilities are *not* branch banks. Consequently, they do not come under the myriad of restrictions pertaining to branch banking. This ruling has not gone unchallenged, however, as a number of state banking authorities have either ruled to the contrary or instituted legal proceedings against banks that have opened CBCTs. On the other hand, some states, even a number that prohibit branch banking, have authorized the use of CBCTs. Evidently, then, whether or not CBCTs will ultimately be regarded as branch banks is as yet an unsettled issue. What is clear from this episode, however, is that bank regulation continues to be marked by disputes between the various regulatory authorities. Perhaps more fundamentally, this episode suggests that new technological developments may produce considerable strains in interpreting branching laws. A relevant analogy is the problems we are currently experiencing with our copyright laws in the face of readily available facilities for copying publications and transmitting them via computer terminals.

In summary, although the general trend of public policy is toward the liberalization of branching powers, many restrictions remain. Those who favor increased branching stress the desirability of geographic diversification and the benefits of economies of scale as one moves away from small unit banks. Opponents of branching argue that unit banks provide a more personal kind of service and that branching carries with it the danger of monopoly. We shall assess these various arguments after we have considered two remaining organizational forms.

**Group Banking**

Aside from branching, the other principal mechanism for establishing multiple-office banking is "group" or holding company banking. This refers to arrangements under which a corporation has ownership control of two or more separately incorporated banks, which are called its subsidiaries. The latter may be either unit banks or branch banks. Also important is the fact the group banks may cross state lines. That is, a holding company may control banks situated in several states.

As in all matters pertaining to bank regulation, state control of group banking is quite varied. About a dozen states prohibit group banking entirely, while more than two dozen have no specific legislation in this area. At the federal level, as a result of the Bank Holding Company Act, there is considerable regulation of bank holding companies. Among the act's most important provisions is that it requires holding companies to register with the Federal Reserve and gives the Federal Reserve power to prescribe the kinds of business activities that are open to bank holding companies.

Like branch banking, group banking has expanded greatly since World War II. By the end of 1978, there were 314 group systems that controlled some 2,300 banks that operated a total of nearly 11,000 branches. These banks held $338 billion of deposits, or about 33 percent of total commercial bank deposits. (See Table 5–4.) In contrast, in 1965 group banks held only 8 percent of total deposits.

The rapid growth of group banking is attributable both to the forces that have stimulated the growth of branch banking and to legal limita-

**TABLE 5–4**

*Selected data for one-bank and multi-bank holding company groups (year-end 1978, dollar amounts in billions)*

| | Number of groups | Number of banks controlled | Number of branches controlled | Assets | Deposits |
|---|---|---|---|---|---|
| One-bank holding companies | 1,799 | 1,791 | 10,740 | $468 | $353 |
| Multi-bank holding companies | 314 | 2,310 | 10,773 | 437 | 338 |
| Total | 2,113 | 4,101 | 21,513 | $905 | $691 |

*Source:* Board of Governors of the Federal Reserve System, *Annual Statistical Digest,* 1974–1978, Washington, D.C., p. 266.

tions on branching. Thus, to a substantial degree group banking has served as a way of getting around intrastate branching laws. This is evidenced by the fact that the vast majority of bank groups are located in states with predominantly unit banking or limited branching. Furthermore, given that group banks may cross state lines, group banking has been a popular device for circumventing prohibitions on interstate branch banking as well.[7]

**Holding Companies: One Bank vs. Multi-bank**

As we have seen, group banking involves the creation of a holding company that controls two or more banks. Such *multi-bank* holding companies need to be distinguished from what are known as *one-bank* holding companies. The purpose of a one-bank holding company is not to bring two or more banks under common control; instead, it is to enable a bank to engage in nonbank types of business. The number of one-bank holding companies has expanded very rapidly since the mid-1960s. Currently, about one-eighth of the banks are one-bank holding companies, but these banks hold more than one-third of total deposits (Table 5–4). As these data might suggest, many of the larger banks have reorganized as one-bank holding companies. This generally works as follows.

In a typical case the shares of a bank—often a large bank—are transferred to a newly created holding company, and the former shareholders of the bank receive in exchange shares of stock in the holding company. The latter then forms subsidiary corporations to provide services to the bank and to others. Among such activities are provision of computer services, selling or writing insurance, provision of investment and management advisory services, extension of real estate credit, equipment leasing, and so on.

The rapid expansion of one-bank holding companies in the 1960s, in terms of both number of banks and the scope of the activities of their subsidiaries, aroused considerable controversy. At the heart of this controversy was the fact that one-bank holding companies were not initially subject to the Bank Holding Company Act of 1956. They were thus free to engage in activities that were prohibited both to banks per se and to multi-bank holding companies. Critics of the situation pointed to possible adverse effects on the soundness of banks, conflicts of interest, unfair competition, and undue concentration of financial power. Some went so far as to raise the specter of a Japanese *zaibatsu syndrome*, with multi-industry combinations of banking and commerce coming to dominate the

---

[7] While to a substantial extent group banking serves as a substitute for branch banking, some groups may involve only a rather loose-knit arrangement with more local autonomy than would be found in a branch bank. In this regard, mention should be made of *chain banking*, which is like group banking except that no holding company is involved.

American economy. These concerns led, in 1970, to a revision of the 1956 act that restricted both one-bank and multi-bank holding companies to the same range of activities. This revision served to blur the distinction between the two types of holding companies. The 1970 amendments also liberalized the criteria that the Federal Reserve was to follow in defining allowable bank-related activities. Table 5–5 contains a recent list of approved, denied, and pending activities. As evidenced by this list, commercial banks are seriously striving to live up to their reputation as department stores of finance.

**TABLE 5–5**

*Status of bank holding company nonbanking activities*

**Activities approved by the Board**

1. Dealer in bankers' acceptances*
2. Mortgage banking*
3. Finance companies*
   a. Consumer
   b. Sales
   c. Commercial
4. Credit card issuance*
5. Factoring company*
6. Industrial banking
7. Servicing loans*
8. Trust company*
9. Investment advising*
10. General economic information*
11. Portfolio investment advice*
12. Full-payout leasing*
    a. Personal property
    b. Real property
13. Community welfare investments*
14. Bookkeeping & data processing services*
15. Insurance agent or broker—credit extensions*
16. Underwriting credit life & credit accident & health insurance
17. Courier service*
18. Management consulting to nonaffiliate banks*
19. Issuance of travelers checks*
20. Bullion broker*
21. Land escrow services*†
22. Issuing money orders and variable denominated payment instruments*†§

**Activities denied by the Board**

1. Equity funding (combined sale of mutual funds & insurance)
2. Underwriting general life insurance
3. Real estate brokerage*
4. Land development
5. Real estate syndication
6. General management consulting
7. Property management
8. Non-full-payout leasing†
9. Commodity trading†
10. Issuance and sale of short-term debt obligations ("thrift notes")†
11. Travel agency*†
12. Savings and loan associations†

**Activities pending before the Board**

1. Armored car service*
2. Underwriting mortgage guarantee insurance‡
3. Underwriting & dealing in U.S. Government and certain municipal securities*‡
4. Underwriting the deductible part of bankers' blanket bond insurance (withdrawn)†
5. Management consulting to nonaffiliated, depository type, financial institutions*†

* Activities permissible to national banks.
† Added to list since January 1, 1975.
‡ These were found to be "closely related to banking," but the proposed acquisitions were denied by the Board of Governors as part of its "go slow" policy.
§ To be decided on a case-by-case basis.
*Source:* D. S. Drum, "Nonbanking Activities of Bank Holding Companies," in Federal Reserve Bank of Chicago, *Economic Perspectives*, 1977, p. 14.

**Correspondent Relationships**

As already emphasized, despite the growing importance of branch and group banking, unit banks still predominate in the United States. Nevertheless, while most unit banks are independent in a legal sense, they are much less so in a practical one. For most banks this dependence takes the form of *correspondent banking,* an arrangement under which some banks hold deposits with other banks and use these banks as agents in various types of transactions, such as check clearing and collection, purchases and sales of securities, purchases and sales of foreign exchange, and participations in large loans.[8] Nations with only a small number of banks, each operating a nationwide system of branches, have no need for such a highly developed domestic correspondent system. In such cases, each bank has an office in the country's major financial center and can reach all parts of the country through its own branches. The importance of correspondent relationships in the United States derives from the structure of our banking system: the facts that most of our thousands of banks operate only one office, that no branch bank is permitted to have branches outside its home state, and that many of our banks are relatively small.

The center of American correspondent banking is New York City, the nation's great financial center. Almost every important bank in the country maintains correspondent relations with at least one large bank in that city. Chicago is the next most important center. Each of its two largest banks has more than 1,000 correspondents. In addition there are many regional centers. The network of correspondent relations is complex, for many banks hold deposits in more than one center, and correspondent banks in one center often have correspondent relations with banks in other centers.

These interbank deposits serve several functions. Among these are the following:

1 TO SERVE AS LEGAL RESERVES. Although members of the Federal Reserve may count as legal reserves only their cash in vault and deposits at the Federal Reserve banks, nonmember banks have more leeway. The relevant state laws permit most nonmember banks to hold at least a part of their legal reserves, usually a large part, in the form of deposit claims against other commercial banks.

2 TO FACILITATE CHECK CLEARING AND COLLECTION. Many banks have their correspondent banks pay at least some of the checks drawn on them and collect checks on other banks that are deposited with them.

---

[8] A loan participation typically occurs when a small bank is unable (for either financial or legal reasons) to satisfy a loan request by a big customer. Through its correspondent relationship the small bank may be able to pass on part of the loan and thus satisfy the customer.

3 TO FACILITATE DOMESTIC AND FOREIGN PAYMENTS. A customer of a New Jersey bank may want to make payments with a draft drawn on a New York bank or on some foreign bank. Holding deposits at Chase Manhattan, the New Jersey bank can draw drafts on that bank or on a foreign correspondent of that bank.

4 TO FACILITATE AGENCY OPERATIONS. The New Jersey bank may use Chase Manhattan as an agent to buy or sell securities, to make loans for it on the Stock Exchange, or to accept or draw drafts. Interbank deposits that can be credited or debited to finance these transactions are helpful.

**THE RATIONALE OF BANK SUPERVISION AND REGULATION**

There is a vast array of ways in which commercial banks are regulated and supervised. We have already encountered many of these, but it will help to focus the discussion if we have a more complete list before us. Any such list would undoubtedly include the following items:

1 Regulation of entry into banking. A related requirement is that banks have an adequate degree of capitalization before a charter is issued.

2 Regulation of bank branching, either through a criterion of community need or through outright legal prohibition of all or particular types of branching.

3 Regulation of bank mergers, either by administrative ruling or via the use of antitrust laws.

4 Regulation and supervision of bank assets. For example, banks are prohibited from directly holding certain types of assets, such as common stock or real estate. Bank portfolios are also examined periodically to ensure that they possess an adequate degree of liquidity.

5 Regulation of the allowable set of bank-related activities that bank holding companies may engage in.

6 Requirements for, and federal provision and regulation of, deposit insurance.

7 Prohibition of interest payments on demand deposits and restrictions on permissible rates of interest payable on time and saving deposits.

As evidenced by this list, regulation covers almost every aspect of commercial banking. Faced with this welter of regulations, one naturally asks why it is so extensive and, more specifically, why it has taken the form it has.

**Basic Goals of Bank Regulation**

An underlying premise of regulation is that commercial banks are of vital importance in the operation of the economy. If banks are to carry out their role successfully, there must be public confidence in the solvency and liquidity of both individual banks and the banking system. As already documented, prior to 1934 public confidence was often severely tried by the instability of the banking system. It is because of this dismal bit of financial history that we find our first theme of modern bank regulation: ensuring the *safety* of banks and the banking system.

Safety, however, is not the only desirable feature of the banking system. It is also of considerable importance that the banking system operate as efficiently as possible. Loosely speaking, in this context efficiency means that banks provide services at as low a cost as possible and that funds are appropriately channeled through banks into their most productive uses. For this to come about, bank regulation must provide an environment in which banks may exercise individual initiative and respond promptly and flexibly to changing economic circumstances. Unfortunately, as we shall see, the goal of fostering efficiency in banking often conflicts with the goal of safety.

A related theme in bank regulation concerns bank competition. Economists have long emphasized the beneficial role of competitive forces in fostering efficiency. In contrast, they have also stressed that monopoly elements and monopolistic practices can hinder efficiency. Thus, it is not surprising to find that the regulatory authorities have been quite concerned with promoting competition in banking. As in the case of safety, however, we shall discover that regulations that are nominally designed to promote competition often have had the unintended effect of reducing efficiency.

We now turn to a more detailed consideration of the issues of safety, efficiency, and competition.

**Safety vs. Efficiency**

In the context of banking, safety has various shades of meaning and consequently can be brought about in a variety of ways. One obvious source of safety is provided by the FDIC, which has made deposits safe and promoted the integrity of the payments mechanism. A host of other regulations also contribute to safety, but in a somewhat different manner. Among these are restrictions on entry, assets, liabilities, and bank activities; ceilings on interest rates; and bank examinations. The philosophy behind most of these regulations is that they promote safety by protecting bankers from themselves. That is, they prevent what some see as the danger of banks' pursuing "excessively" risky strategies in the quest for profits. Or, put another way, these regulations are designed to forestall the possibility of "too much" competition among banks.

Those economists who emphasize the importance of efficiency in banking see many of these regulations as misguided. They argue that the main impact of these restrictions is to stifle competition, innovation, and prudent risk taking, and generally to reduce the efficiency of banking. This conflict between safety and efficiency presents a true dilemma in the design of policies for bank regulation. The issues involved can be illustrated by the regulation that prohibits interest payments on demand deposits, or by the interest rate ceilings ("Regulation Q") that limit the payment of interest on time and savings deposits.

Control over interest rates payable to depositors dates from 1933. The prevailing view at that time was that "excessive" interest rate competition for deposits had undermined the soundness of the banking system. As the story goes, this excessive competition drove deposit rates "too high" and then forced banks to seek out risky high-yielding assets so that they could earn enough to pay depositors. The punch line of this story is that the resultant deterioration in the quality of bank portfolios contributed in an important way to the collapse of the banking system in the 1930s.

The validity of this argument is extremely doubtful. For one, subsequent analysis has not revealed any marked deterioration in the quality of bank assets in the 1920s, when excessive competition was alleged to have occurred. Furthermore, whatever the merits of ceilings might have been in the 1930s, the logic of continuing them today is quite minimal. Given the existence of the FDIC and the expanded role of the Federal Reserve after 1933, it strains reason to credit the post-1934 reduction in bank failures to Regulation Q or to the prohibition of interest on demand deposits.

On the other hand, the undesirable effects of these regulations are all too evident. They constrain efficient, well-managed banks from competing effectively for funds and deprive depositors from reaping the benefits of this competition. Furthermore, since there are currently no ceilings on time deposits over $100,000, Regulation Q discriminates against the small saver. For these and a number of other reasons, ceilings are on the way out (see Chapter 17). These further developments aside, Regulation Q provides a clear example of a restriction designed to promote safety that proved primarily to be a source of inefficiency in banking.

From this and similar episodes many economists have drawn the conclusion that overemphasis on safety can be detrimental to the health and vitality of the banking system. These economists argue that there is an important distinction between protecting a bank's depositors and protecting the bank itself. The former is clearly a necessary prerequisite for securing public confidence. Protecting the bank — that is, protecting its managers and stockholders — is a quite different matter. Indeed some economists, while admitting that safety is of prime concern, have even argued that we may have too *few* bank failures. The logic for this position runs roughly as follows.

While failure of any business is not desirable for its own sake, it can perform a useful role in an economy. Specifically, insofar as business failures are brought about by incompetent management, failures serve the socially useful function of sifting out inefficient managers and businesses. To the extent that we artificially short-circuit this mechanism, we guarantee the continued existence of inefficient enterprises.

Those who argue from this perspective would favor eliminating much of the regulation impinging on commercial banks. Banks would then be freer to innovate and to take prudent risks in search of higher profits. At the same time, these economists argue, it would be possible to improve safety by strengthening our deposit insurance system. For one thing, we could expand coverage so that all deposits are fully insured. For another, the insurance premium paid to the FDIC could be made to depend on the nature of the risks assumed by the bank. Thus, those banks that were more venturesome in assuming risk would pay a higher premium.

While there is considerable food for thought in this general view, bank regulators have been understandably slow in pursuing policies that might be perceived as reducing bank safety. Although some steps in this direction appear in the offing (e.g., those related to interest payments on deposits), the conflict between safety and efficiency is likely to be with us for the forseeable future.

**Competition in Banking**

Taking American banking history as a whole, policy makers have shown a distinctly schizophrenic attitude toward competition in banking. As we have just seen, some regulations designed to promote safety have been specifically aimed at curbing "unhealthy" competition. In other respects, public policy has clearly intended to promote competition, at least insofar as it assured the existence of a large number of competing banks. In particular, there has been a longstanding public concern with the dangers of excessive concentration or monopoly power in banking. And the fear that undue concentration would leave resource allocation in the hands of a relatively small number of large banks undoubtedly accounts for the predominance of unit banking in this country.

At first blush, with nearly 15,000 commercial banks, the United States would appear to have a rather high degree of competition in banking. Numbers alone, however, do not ensure competition. Even with a large number of banks in the nation as a whole, there can be many communities that are served by relatively few banks. In such cases, local borrowers and/or depositors may have very few options for obtaining banking services. To the extent that this is the case, banks in such communities may well possess some degree of local monopoly power. That is, they may be shielded from competition with other banks.

A question naturally arises as to how banks can secure and maintain local monopoly power. The answer in part lies in the nature of bank regulatory policy. For example, limits on bank entry and ceiling interest rates on deposits — policies promulgated to promote safety in banking — have undoubtedly contributed to limiting competition in local banking markets. Somewhat ironically, even those policies aimed at promoting competition may have had anticompetitive effects. In particular, limitations on branching, which were designed to prevent excessive concentration of banking resources, serve to restrict bank competition in local markets. Consequently, policies for avoiding the type of monopoly power traditionally associated with large banks may create opportunities for local monopoly power. While the precise extent of local monopoly power in banking is debatable, it should be clear from this discussion that promoting competition is more complicated than it might seem at first.

There is also another dimension to this issue. As stressed above, limitations on branch banking have fostered the spread of independent unit banks in the United States. A consequence of this is that there are many relatively small banks in this country. Indeed, as Table 5–6 indicates, the vast majority of banks — some 8,445 banks, or 59 percent of all banks — each have fewer than $25 million in deposits. These banks hold less than 9 percent of the total deposits in the banking system. Not surprisingly, most of these small banks are located in unit-banking states.

Many economists see the predominance of small banks as an undesirable consequence of our branching laws. Their concern is that such banks are likely to be too small to be efficient. That is, they are unable to capitalize on economies of scale that would permit larger banks to provide banking services at lower average cost. The empirical evidence

| TABLE 5–6<br><br>*Size distribution of all commercial banks in the United States, June 30, 1978* | Size of banks (in millions of dollars of total deposits) | Number of banks | Percent of number of banks | Total assets (in billions of dollars) | Percent of total assets of all banks |
|---|---|---|---|---|---|
| | Less than $5 | 1,087 | 7.6 | 3.8 | 0.3 |
| | $5–10 | 2,492 | 17.3 | 18.5 | 1.6 |
| | $10–25 | 4,866 | 33.8 | 80.6 | 6.8 |
| | $25–50 | 3,085 | 21.4 | 107.5 | 9.1 |
| | $50–100 | 1,574 | 10.9 | 109.5 | 9.3 |
| | $100–500 | 1,013 | 7.0 | 199.1 | 16.9 |
| | $500–1,000 | 134 | 0.9 | 90.8 | 7.7 |
| | $1,000–5,000 | 123 | 0.9 | 241.5 | 20.5 |
| | More than $5,000 | 21 | 0.1 | 325.4 | 27.7 |
| | Total — all banks | 14,395 | 100.0 | $1,176.7 | 100.0 |

*Source:* Federal Deposit Insurance Corporation, *Assets and Liabilities of Commercial and Mutual Savings Banks*, June 30, 1978.

on this score, although open to interpretation, does seem to suggest that there are substantial economies of scale for banks with up to $15–20 million in deposits and more gradual economies for larger banks. Taken as a whole, these observations provide support for the position that we have many banks that are too small to be efficient. Furthermore, according to this view, these banks can continue their existence because they are somewhat sheltered from the competition of larger banks.

While there is much merit in this line of reasoning, the evidence is not unambiguous. For one thing, empirical studies of economies of scale in banking need to be interpreted with care. The main reason for this is the difficulty in defining precisely what one means by the *output* or *product* of a bank. As department stores of finance, banks produce a variety of outputs, and it is difficult to summarize this variety in a single measure of bank output. But this is precisely what those who produce estimates of scale economies have done.

A second reason for caution is that even if there are economies of scale, it does not follow that, for example, a $60 million branch bank with four branches is more efficient than four $15 million unit banks. This is because the operation of branches is costly, so that we have a trade-off between cost savings due to larger size versus additional costs due to branches. Since it is somewhat difficult to pin this issue down quantitatively, opponents of branch banking have understandably been slow in modifying their position. Nevertheless, as documented earlier, branch banking has expanded markedly and should continue to do so in the forseeable future.

One final question raised by Table 5–6 needs to be addressed. Specifically, at the other extreme from the small unit banks we find 144 very large banks, each with deposits of over $1 billion. In the aggregate these banks, which amount to only 1 percent of the number of banks, account for 48 percent of total deposits. Impressionistically at least, these numbers would appear to raise the specter of the more traditional sort of monopoly power.

While opinions vary on this issue, at the current stage of development most observers of the banking scene tend to regard fears of big-bank monopoly as unfounded. The main reason for this is that there appears to be sufficient competition to keep the big banks "honest." For a particular big bank, this competition stems from other big banks and from the larger number of slightly smaller banks. In addition, large, internationally known corporations have the option of doing business with large foreign banks or of borrowing funds directly from the capital market. Both of these options provide additional competition for large domestic banks.

All of this is not to say that big banks may never present a problem. Technological advances like those that could bring about an electronic funds transfer system may well increase the optimum size of banks in the future. These forces could provide incentives for banks to move into the computer-related activities of data transmission and financial record keeping. What this suggests, then, is that those charged with ensuring the health and vitality of our banking system will need to be alert to changes in the banking environment.

**CONCLUSION** This chapter had the primary objectives of providing some background on the organizational structure of the commercial banking system as it exists in the United States. Among the more important points developed are the following:

1   There are a variety of criteria that can be used to classify commercial banks. Of particular importance are the distinctions between unit and branch banks, between Federal Reserve member and nonmember banks, and between national and state-chartered banks.

2   The total number of commercial banks in the United States has remained relatively constant since 1933 at about 14,500. A significant expansion of the number of banking facilities has taken place through the marked expansion of branch banking.

3   The diversity of forms that banks may take has its counterpart in a varied regulatory structure for the supervision of commercial banks. The Federal Reserve, the FDIC, the Comptroller of the Currency, and the 50 state banking authorities all participate in this process.

4   Bank regulation is concerned with the safety, efficiency, and competitiveness of the banking system. The reconciliation of the potentially conflicting goals of safety and efficiency remains a thorny problem. Nevertheless, one thing is clear: Single-minded pursuit of just one of these goals can produce bad regulation.

While our increased understanding has clarified many issues, controversy continues with debate over such questions as: Should all state banks be required to join the Federal Reserve? Should all be required to join the FDIC? Should states be permitted to issue charters on terms more liberal than those granted by the federal government? Should branching by national banks be limited by the laws of the states in which they are located? Should national banks be permitted to branch across state lines regardless of state laws?

There also continues to be ambivalence and controversy regarding such related issues as bigness and smallness, concentration and decentralization of economic and financial power, and monopoly and competition. Americans have always been divided on such issues and have often been ambivalent. One may at the same time extol the virtues of smallness and the glories of bigness, or the desirability of decentralization of financial power and the advantages of efficiencies achieved only through some degree of concentration. Such controversies appeared at least as early as 1791, when the First Bank of the United States was established; they still persist in debates over group banking, branch banking, and mergers.

**SELECTED READINGS**

American Bankers Association, *The Commercial Banking Industry*, Englewood Cliffs, N.J., Prentice-Hall, 1962.

Benston, G. J., "Economies of Scale in Financial Institutions," *Journal of Money, Credit and Banking*, May 1972, pp. 312–341.

Drum, D. S., "Nonbanking Activities of Bank Holding Companies," *Economic Perspectives*, Federal Reserve Bank of Chicago, 1977, pp. 12–21.

Galbraith, J. K., *Money: Whence It Came, Where It Went*, Boston, Houghton Mifflin, 1975.

Teplitz, P. V., *Trends Affecting the U.S. Banking System*, Cambridge, Mass., Ballinger, 1975.

Tussing, A. D., "The Case for Bank Failures," *Journal of Law and Economics*, October 1967, pp. 129–147.

The preceding chapter examined what might be termed the *industrial organization* of commercial banking. In this chapter we continue our discussion of commercial banking from a different perspective and examine the role of commercial banks in the money supply process. As already noted, commercial bank liabilities in the form of demand deposits constitute the major component of the stock of money. Furthermore, as described in Chapter 2, by acquiring assets banks can "create" demand deposits and, hence, money. Now we consider in more detail the precise nature of this process.

More specifically, the outline of this chapter is as follows. We begin with a brief introduction to balance sheet accounting and then examine an actual balance sheet for the commercial banking system. We next describe the rudimentary mechanics of the creation and destruction of demand deposits. Finally, we consider the factors that determine the actual volume of deposits. As we shall see, the Federal Reserve system, through its provision of bank reserves and the setting of reserve requirements, plays a critical role in this process. While for the most part our focus will be on the banking system as a whole, at the end of the chapter we shall also spell out what happens to individual banks as the banking system expands or contracts.

**BALANCE
SHEET
ACCOUNTING**

A short discussion of some elementary principles of double-entry accounting will not only illuminate the processes through which the commercial banks issue and withdraw their debts that serve as money but also prove useful later, when we discuss the operations of the Treasury and the Federal Reserve.

In drawing up financial statements for any unit, be it a business firm, a government, or any other organization, an accountant considers the unit to be an entity, separate and distinct from its owners. The entity must therefore account to its owners as well as to other claimants against it. There are two principal types of financial statements. One is the *income statement* or *profit and loss statement.* Such statements summarize, for some stated period of time, all the gross income accruing to the entity and the claims against that gross income — claims of owners as well as others. We shall not use income statements at this point, although we shall later refer back to them.

In contrast to income statements, which refer to flows over a stated period of time, the *balance sheet* refers to a stock at a point in time. One side of the balance sheet, the *assets* side, lists the types and values of everything owned by the entity. These things of value may be money itself, debt claims against others, shares of ownership in other firms, inventories, plant and equipment, and so on. The other side of the balance sheet, *liabilities and capital account,* lists the types and amounts of claims against the entity's assets. Since double-entry accounting requires that the entity account for the total value of its assets, no more and no less, the total value of claims against assets must be exactly equal to the value of its assets. Any value of assets in excess of other claims against them accrues to to the owners. Liabilities are all claims against assets other than ownership claims. Under the law, they have priority over ownership claims. They are mostly debt claims of some sort; they may be evidenced by formal documents such as promissory notes or bills of exchange, or they may be evidenced only by book entries. *Capital account,* or *net worth,* is simply the value of ownership claims against the entity. Since owners have only a residual claim, capital account or net worth is equal to the value of assets minus liabilities.

A highly simplified balance sheet might appear as follows:

| ASSETS | | LIABILITIES AND CAPITAL ACCOUNT | |
|---|---|---|---|
| | | Liabilities | $ 85,000 |
| | | Capital account | 15,000 |
| Total | $100,000 | Total | $100,000 |

This necessary equality of assets with the sum of liabilities and capital account permits us to write three simple equations that will be useful:

Assets = liabilities + capital account  (1)
Capital account = assets − liabilities  (2)
Liabilities = assets − capital account  (3)

People are sometimes amazed at the accuracy of accountants, noting that no matter how complex the situation or how great the amounts involved, the accountant still manages to make the sides balance. This becomes less remarkable when we realize how the value of net worth was arrived at.

Since we shall be deeply interested in the behavior of the liabilities of banks in the form of deposits, and especially demand or checking deposits, it will be useful to divide bank liabilities, or debts, into three parts: demand deposits, time and savings deposits, and other liabilities. Thus, we can rewrite our simple equations as follows:

$$\text{Assets} = \text{demand deposits} + \text{time and savings deposits} + \text{other liabilities} + \text{capital accounts} \quad (4)$$
$$\text{Demand deposits} = \text{assets} - \text{time and savings deposits} - \text{other liabilities} - \text{capital accounts} \quad (5)$$

In analyzing the functioning of monetary institutions, we shall emphasize one aspect of the necessary equality of assets and the sum of outstanding claims in the form of liabilities and net worth, namely, that a firm can acquire assets only by creating an equal value of claims against itself. Of course it may change the composition of its assets without changing the other side of its balance sheet at all. For example, it may trade some of its short-term claims against other entities for long-term claims against other entities, and so on. Such exchanges of assets may not disturb either the total value or the composition of outstanding claims against the entity. But an entity can make net additions to its assets only by creating an equal value of claims against itself. And in the process of reducing its total assets, it must withdraw and retire an equal value of claims against itself.

As we proceed, we shall repeatedly find it useful to recall these simple facts:

1　When these monetary institutions make net additions to their assets, they must pay for them by creating and issuing an equal value of claims against themselves.
2　When they make net sales or net reductions in their assets, they must withdraw and retire an equal value of claims against themselves.

**A BALANCE SHEET FOR THE COMMERCIAL BANKING SYSTEM**　Table 6–1 is a simplified consolidated balance sheet for the commercial banking system. It is simplified in the sense that it eliminates or lumps together some minor items in order to concentrate attention on major variables. It is consolidated to eliminate claims of the various commercial banks against each other, leaving only the claims of the commercial banks as a whole against other members of the community, and the claims of other members of the community against commercial banks.

The information in this balance sheet demonstrates several important points, some of which relate to the nature and proportions of the claims issued by banks. One point is that banks have acquired only a very small part, about 8 percent, of their total assets by issuing net worth or capital account claims. Most of the assets of banks were acquired by creating and issuing bank debts in the form of deposit claims. Moreover, for the most part, banks pay for the acquisition of additional assets by creating additional deposit claims against themselves. And when they make net sales of assets, they collect largely by withdrawing and retiring claims against themselves.

Other points relate to the nature and composition of bank assets. It should be emphasized that banks could, if regulations and business prudence permitted, create or withdraw deposit claims by purchasing or selling assets of any kind. One can even imagine their doing this by buying or selling common stocks, real estate, or double-jointed goobers. However, a look at the asset side reveals that, in practice, they restrict their holdings largely to cash, deposits at the Federal Reserve banks, and debt claims against others, mostly the latter. Assets in the form of cash and deposit claims against the Federal Reserve yield no interest and are held largely to meet legal reserve requirements. Loans and securities do yield interest and make up the major part of total bank assets. Loans include the banks' holdings of debt claims against their borrowers, these typically being evidenced by promissory notes. The item "securities," sometimes called "investments," is composed largely of debt obligations of the U.S. Treasury, federal agencies, and state and local government.

As we realize that banks create their own deposit debts primarily by purchasing debt claims against others, we begin to see why these institutions are often referred to as "dealers in debt" and "monetizers of debt."

**TABLE 6–1**

*nsolidated balance et for the commer- al banking system, eptember 30, 1978*

| ASSETS | Amount | Percent of total | LIABILITIES AND CAPITAL ACCOUNT | Amount | Percent of total |
|---|---|---|---|---|---|
| Cash in vault | 12.1 | 1.1% | Demand deposits | $260.3 | 24.1% |
| Deposits at Federal Reserve | 28.0 | 2.6 | Time and savings deposits | 580.9 | 53.7 |
| Loans | 682.9 | 63.1 | Other liabilities | 148.6 | 13.7 |
| Securities | 262.2 | 24.2 | Capital accounts | 91.3 | 8.4 |
| Other | 96.5 | 8.9 | | | |
| Total | $1,081.7 | 100.0% | Total | $1,081.7 | 100.0% |

*Source: Federal Reserve Bulletin,* March 1980, pp. A18–A19.

## THE CREATION OF CHECKING DEPOSITS

Let us start our discussion of the creation of checking deposits with the simple case in which banks issue and withdraw claims only in the form of demand deposits. The purpose of this illustration is to show how commercial banks would operate if they were not in the business of issuing time and savings deposits. This latter function of commercial banks will be reintroduced at a later point.

### Deposits for Cash

The first case to be considered is that in which banks issue deposits in exchange for a net inflow of cash into the banking system. We shall use the term *cash* to include both cash in vault and deposit claims against the Federal Reserve banks. This is justified because banks are free to exchange one of these assets for the other.

Suppose there is a net cash inflow of $1 billion into the commercial banking system resulting from a reduction in the public's holding of currency. The direct effect on the banks' balance sheets will be as follows:

| ASSETS | | LIABILITIES | |
|---|---|---|---|
| Cash | +$1 billion | Demand deposits | +$1 billion |

The banks have bought $1 billion of assets in the form of cash by creating their own debt of $1 billion in the form of demand deposits.

It was perhaps injudicious to begin with this case, for it may reinforce popular misconceptions. The reactions of some may be, "Just as I thought! Deposits are nothing but claims on deposited cash; they arise only from the 'deposit' of cash, and anyone leaving cash on deposit can get back that same cash on demand." Such conclusions would be quite wrong because of the following facts:

1 Only a small part of outstanding deposits was created to pay for net inflows of cash; most deposits were created to pay for other types of assets.
2 The cash holdings of banks are equal to only a small fraction of bank-deposit liabilities.
3 Those who deposit cash with a bank get no preferred claim; they give up title to the cash and take their place with all other depositors as creditors of the bank.

Although deposits created to pay for net cash inflows to the banking system become indistinguishable from all other deposits, two characteristics of the process of creating deposits to pay for net inflows of cash should be noted:

1 In this case, and this case only, the transaction that creates deposits also increases the banks' holdings of cash, the latter

constituting legal reserves for the banks. Such deposits that arise in transactions that also increase the legal reserves of banks are called *primary deposits*. Those created to pay for other assets that will not serve as reserves are called *derivative deposits;* these are derived from the purchase of such things as loans and securities.

2   When the commercial banks create checking deposits to pay for net cash flows to them, they do not increase the total money supply. Since, by assumption, the cash flows in from circulation, the increase of money in the form of checking deposits is offset by the decrease of coin and paper money in circulation. However, we shall see that new flows of cash into the banks have the very important effect of enabling the banks to create more money by purchasing other assets.

**Deposits for Debt Claims**

By far the largest part of outstanding deposits was created to pay for assets in the form of debt claims against others. Suppose the banks increase their loans to customers by $10 billion, giving their customers checking deposits. The effects on the banks' balance sheets are as follows:

| ASSETS | | LIABILITIES | |
|---|---|---|---|
| Loans | +$10 billion | Demand deposits | + $10 billion |

By purchasing debt claims, the banks have created $10 billion of money that did not exist before. In effect, the banks traded debts with their customers, presumably to their mutual satisfaction. The banks acquired debts that are not themselves money but which yield income. The borrowers acquired debt claims (deposits) that usually yield no income but have the advantage of being generally acceptable in payment for all kinds of goods and services. In short, the banks monetized debt.

Banks by no means confine their granting of credit to loans to their customers. They also buy various types of securities in the open market from sellers they do not even know. Among these are such things as government securities. We should not be surprised to find that banks create checking deposits in buying such assets. Suppose the banks purchase $10 billion of securities. The effects on their balance sheets will be as follows:

| ASSETS | | LIABILITIES | |
|---|---|---|---|
| Securities | +$10 billion | Demand deposits | +$10 billion |

The banking system has created $10 billion of money that did not exist before, and has done so by purchasing debt claims against others. Here, again, it has monetized debt.

Two points that are crucial to an understanding of commercial banking should be emphasized:

1   Most checking deposits are derivative deposits, that is, deposits created in the process of bank purchases of debt claims against others.

2   Checking deposits created to pay for such assets are a net addition to the money supply; there is no offsetting decrease of coin and paper money in circulation.

**THE DESTRUCTION OF CHECKING DEPOSITS**

Checking deposits are extinguished by processes just the reverse of those that create deposits. They are destroyed as the banking system decreases its assets in the form of cash, loans, and securities.

**Net Cash Drains**

The banking system as a whole may suffer a net drain of its cash assets. Suppose, for example, that owing to an increase in the demand for currency by the public the cash assets of the banking system are reduced by $500 million. The banks' balance sheets will be affected as follows:

| ASSETS | | LIABILITIES | |
| --- | --- | --- | --- |
| Cash | −$500 million | Demand deposits | −$500 million |

In the process of selling $500 million of cash assets, the banks destroyed $500 million of their outstanding deposit liabilities.

Two aspects of this particular process of reducing the volume of checking deposits should be noted. First, when checking deposits are reduced by net outflows of currency to the public the money supply is unchanged. The decrease in money in the form of checking deposits is offset by the increase of coin and paper money in circulation. Second, the drain of cash from the banks may have very important repercussions, for it may force the banks to decrease the money supply by selling other assets.

**Net Reductions in Bank Assets in the Form of Debt Claims**

Most reductions in the volume of checking deposits are traceable to net reductions of bank assets in the form of debt claims against others. Suppose that the banking system reduces its outstanding loans by $5 billion. The former borrowers usually repay loans by drawing checks against their deposit accounts; bank liabilities are reduced accordingly. The effects on the banks' balance sheets are as follows:

| ASSETS | | LIABILITIES | |
|---|---|---|---|
| Loans | −$5 billion | Demand deposits | −$5 billion |

In this process of reducing their outstanding loans, the banks have destroyed $5 billion of money in the form of checking deposits. This is a net reduction of the money supply; there is no offsetting increase in the coin and paper money in circulation. In effect, those who repay bank loans do so by surrendering an equal value of deposit claims against the banks. Similar results flow from net reductions in bank holdings of securities.

---

**BANK OBJECTIVES**

The preceding sections have traced the processes through which the commercial banking system creates checking deposits by purchasing various types of assets and destroys checking deposits through net sales of assets. However, we have not yet addressed the key issue of what determines the actual volume of deposits. To do this we need first to take a brief look at bank objectives and then to examine the constraints imposed on banks in the form of reserve requirements.

From the owners' viewpoint the primary purpose of a commercial bank is to make profits. We have found that banks earn gross income when they buy debt claims against others by issuing deposit claims on themselves. Why, then, do they not buy up all the debt instruments in the economy and monetize them? Why should banks stop with monetizing all the debts that they could induce governments, business firms, and individuals to issue? Why should they not proceed to buy up great quantities of real goods that yield an income, paying for them with newly created deposits?

It should not be assumed that banks would find it profitable to expand to such lengths if they were free of official regulation. For one thing, banks do not find it costless to create deposit claims and to entice the public to hold very large amounts of them. They must pay interest to get the public to hold large amounts of time deposits, and it would be prohibitively costly for banks to pay interest rates high enough to attract all funds away from competing claims, such as claims against savings and loan associations, credit unions, and investment companies. They could, of course, create more demand deposits, on which they are presently prohibited by law from paying interest. These are not costless, for the bank must provide services to depositors—for example, checkbooks, accounting services, check clearing and collection, and so on. However, the marginal costs of creating additional demand deposits are probably so low relative to the additional income that would be yielded by the additional earning assets that this consideration would not be a strong deterrent to money creation. If banks were free of official control, the most powerful deterrent to an unlimited expansion of deposits would be their obligation to keep their deposits redeemable in currency. In other words, the banks could expand demand deposits only as long as the public exhibited a willingness to hold them.

In discussing the evolution of fractional reserve banking, we noted that banks discovered that they could usually keep their liabilities redeemable in currency if they held cash reserves equal to some fraction, such as one-eighth or one-tenth, of their liabilities. In other words, it was relatively safe for banks to create liabilities equal to 10 or $12\frac{1}{2}$ times their cash reserves. But to increase the ratio of liabilities to reserves beyond some such multiple becomes increasingly dangerous. If a bank attempted to expand its liabilities too far beyond its reserves, it could so damage the public's confidence in its ability to pay currency on demand that the quantity of liabilities it could keep outstanding would actually be reduced. The bank could even be forced into failure by its inability to honor its promises to pay currency on demand. Thus, even if they were free of regulation, banks would not carry out an indefinite expansion of deposits. Of course, as already suggested, the creation of deposits by commercial banks is subject to limitation. This is achieved primarily by regulating the *dollar volume of reserves* available to the commercial banks and by imposing *legal minimum-reserve requirements*.

**RESERVES AND RESERVE REQUIREMENTS**

It must be emphasized that the primary purpose of legal reserve requirements is not to force banks to remain "liquid" enough to be able to meet their obligations to pay. This may indeed have been the original purpose of these requirements. But the purpose now is to serve as a method of regulating the volume of bank deposits and, indirectly, the volume of bank assets.

This involves three steps by the government, central bank, or other monetary authority:

1 Define those particular types of assets that can be counted toward meeting legal reserve requirements. These assets should be of such a type that their dollar value can be regulated by the monetary authority. For commercial banks that are members of the Federal Reserve System, only two types of assets can be counted as legal reserves: cash in vault and deposit claims against Federal Reserve banks.[1]

---

[1] From 1917 to 1959 only deposit claims against the Federal Reserve could be counted as legal reserves by member banks.

2 Regulate the dollar volume of legal reserves available to the banks. This is one of the major functions of the Federal Reserve.

3 Require the banks to hold legal reserves equal to *at least* some stated fraction of their deposit liabilities. We shall see later that the Federal Reserve is empowered to set such minimum fractional-reserve requirements for member banks and to alter within limits the height of these minimum requirements. Note that to fix a minimum ratio of reserves to deposit liabilities is the same as fixing a maximum ratio of deposit liabilities to reserves. For example, to say to a bank, "You must hold reserves equal to at least 20 percent of your deposit liabilities," is the same as saying, "Your deposit liabilities may not exceed five times the volume of your reserves."

Thus, we find that the maximum volume of commercial bank deposit liabilities that may be outstanding depends on (1) the dollar volume of reserves available to the banks and (2) the size of the minimum legal ratio of reserves to deposits. This indicates why dollars in bank reserves are often referred to as *high-powered* money; under a fractional reserve system each dollar of legal reserves can "support" several dollars for checking deposits. And the lower the required reserve ratio, the higher powered each dollar of reserves is.

This also introduces us to the two principal ways in which the Federal Reserve can regulate the behavior of the money supply. Although the Federal Reserve uses a number of instruments, all are aimed at regulating either the dollar volume of reserves available to commercial banks or the height of the minimum legal ratio of reserves to deposit liabilities. The Federal Reserve also indirectly regulates the volume of bank loans and security holdings, because changes in these would affect the volume of deposits.

The combination of the dollar volume of bank reserves and the legal minimum-reserve ratio determines only the *maximum* level of deposit liabilities; it does not force the banks to expand their holdings of loans and securities until this ceiling on their deposit liabilities is reached. The only pressure on banks to reach this maximum comes from the profit motive. Dollars of excess reserves yield no interest; loans and securities do. Usually, therefore, banks are impelled to expand their loans and security holdings close to the maximum limit permitted by their reserve positions. However, some banks do hold reserves in excess of legal requirements, at least occasionally. There are several reasons for this: Forecasts of their average deposits or actual reserves during a reserve period are imperfect; excess reserves are so small and are expected to be retained such a short period that it is not worthwhile to use them to buy other liquid assets; or yields on other liquid assets are extremely low.

We shall return later to the case in which banks elect to hold excess reserves. In the meantime, we shall assume that the banking system expands to the maximum permitted by its reserves.

It should be intuitively plausible that an initial change in the volume of reserves available to a banking system operating on fractional reserves will permit or necessitate a change in bank deposits and assets equal to some multiple of the initial change in reserves. And the size of the multiple will tend to be larger as the functional-reserve requirement is smaller. Thus, each dollar increase in reserves will permit the banking system to expand deposits and earning assets by some multiple of that dollar. If the banks lose a dollar of reserves when they hold no reserves in excess of legal requirements, they will have to reduce their deposit liabilities and assets by some multiple of the dollar lost. This multiple expansion or contraction of the deposits and assets of a banking system in response to an initial change in the volume of its reserves plays a central role in commercial banking theory and is of crucial importance to monetary authorities who are responsible for regulating the volume of bank liabilities and assets.

We shall be interested not in just one multiple but in several: those relating to (1) demand deposits; (2) total deposits, including both demand and time; (3) bank earning assets, including both loans and securities; and (4) the money supply. In some cases the size of these multiples can differ significantly.

Several aspects of our analysis should be noted:

1 For the sake of simplicity we shall make the following assumptions: (a) All commercial banks are subject to reserve requirements imposed by the Federal Reserve, and (b) the money supply is narrowly defined as the sum of demand deposits and currency. Later we consider the minor complications that result from relaxing these assumptions.

2 In the following section we shall be dealing with the banking system as a whole. The multiples that will be developed do not apply to an individual bank experiencing an initial change in its reserves. This case will be treated later.

3 The multiples apply to an *initial* change of reserves because a resulting expansion may induce some loss of reserves and a contraction may induce some gain in reserves. Moreover, the multiples apply to initial changes in excess reserves or to a deficiency of reserves relative to requirements.

4 The multiples apply to derivative deposits only and do not include any initial change that occurs in primary deposits.

The last two points require explanation. The banking system can experience a change in its reserves, either through a change in primary deposits or without a change in primary deposits. An example of the latter would be $100 increase in bank reserves resulting from bank borrowings from the Federal Reserve. The initial effects on the balance sheet of the commercial banks would be as follows:

| ASSETS | | LIABILITIES | |
|--------|--------|-------------|--------|
| Reserves | +$100 | Borrowings from the Federal Reserve | +$100 |

Since banks are not required to hold reserves against liabilities in the form of borrowings from the Federal Reserve, the entire $100 increase in reserves constitutes an increase in excess reserves, and all these serve as a basis for a multiple expansion of derivative deposits and of bank holdings of loans and securities.

Now consider the case in which the banking system receives a $100 initial increase in its reserves through an increase of primary deposits. This could reflect such events as a new inflow of currency from circulation or a Federal Reserve purchase of securities from the public. Suppose further that reserve requirements against demand deposits average 15 percent. The initial effect on the banks' balance sheet will be the following:

| ASSETS | | LIABILITIES | |
|--------|--------|-------------|--------|
| Reserves | +$100 | Demand deposits | +$100 |
| **Addenda** | | | |
| Required reserves | +$ 15 | | |
| Excess reserves | +$ 85 | | |

The $100 of primary deposits have indeed brought a $100 increase in the actual reserves of the banks. But excess reserves are increased only $85 because $15 are required as reserves against the primary deposit. Only this increase of excess reserves can serve as a basis for the multiple increase of derivative deposits and earning assets with which we shall be concerned.

In each of the following cases, we shall assume that the initial change in excess reserves reflects a change in the volume of bank borrowings at the Federal Reserve. This assumption is intended to simplify the accounting and to allow us to deal uniformly with all cases. However, it should be emphasized that the same principles apply to any initial change in excess reserves, regardless of the source.

Before analyzing rigorously the factors determining the size of the various multiples of expansion or contraction, let us consider the subject in more general terms.

Suppose the banks receive an initial increase in their excess reserves. Since these funds yield no interest or other income, the banks will feel impelled to use them as a basis for increasing loans or buying securities, or both. Those members of the public who borrow from or sell securities to the banks will usually receive the proceeds in the form of new checking deposits. But regardless of the form in which the proceeds are initially received, the public is free to change the forms and proportions in which it will hold them. According to its preferences, the public may continue to hold all the proceeds in the form of demand deposits, it may hold some or all in time deposits, or it may take at least some to be held in the form of additional currency outside the banking system. The sizes of the various multiples will be affected substantially by the public's choices as to the forms and proportions in which it will hold the proceeds from new bank loans and security purchases.

If all the proceeds continue to be held as demand deposits, all the initial increase of reserves remains in the banks to serve as a basis for additional demand deposits. The size of the multiples will then depend on the size of the fractional-reserve requirement. For example, if the reserve requirement is 0.15, each $1 initial increase of reserves will support a $1/0.15, or $6.67, increase of demand deposits and also of bank loans and securities.

If the public elects to hold at least some part of the proceeds in time deposits, the sizes of the various multipliers are usually different. This is because reserve requirements against time deposits are usually much lower than those against demand deposits, although these requirements are determined by law and by decision of the monetary authorities. For example, when reserve requirements against demand deposits are 0.15, the requirements against time deposits may be only 0.04. In effect, each dollar of reserves will support more time deposits than demand deposits. Thus, the greater the proportions of the proceeds held in time deposits rather than demand deposits, and the lower the reserve requirement against time deposits relative to those against demand deposits, the greater will be the multiple expansion of *total deposits*, including both demand and time. This is because the greater weight of time deposits with the lower reserve requirement serves to lower the weighted-average reserve requirement against total deposits. Also, the multiple expansion of bank loans and security holdings will be greater, for banks can buy these assets by creating time-deposit claims as well as demand deposits. But the multiple expansion of demand deposits alone will be lower, for the banks must use some part of the initial increase of excess reserves to meet reserve requirements against the increase of time deposits.

All the multiples (those applying to the expansion of demand deposits, total deposits, and bank holdings of loans and securities) will be reduced if some of the proceeds are taken in the form of currency and held as such outside the banking system. We shall call this an *induced cash drain from the banking system.* Each dollar withdrawn to serve as currency in circulation removes a dollar of the initial increase of reserves and leaves the banks with a smaller net increase of reserves to support deposit creation. We shall find that induced cash drains can markedly reduce the sizes of the expansion multiples.

In summary, the sizes of the multiples of expansion of demand deposits, total deposits, and loans and security holdings permitted by each dollar of initial increase of reserves in the banking system depend on several things: the height of legal reserve requirements against demand deposits and time deposits, respectively, and the proportions in which the proceeds from the increased bank loans and security holdings come to be held as demand deposits, time deposits, and currency outside banks.

Consider now the reverse process, that is, the multiple contraction of bank deposits and earning assets required in response to an initial loss of reserves. Suppose the banking system suffers an initial net loss of reserves when it holds no reserves in excess of legal requirements. With their actual reserves now deficient relative to the amounts legally required, the banks will be forced to begin to reduce their outstanding loans or to sell securities, or both, in an effort to remedy their reserve deficiencies. Those who buy securities from the banks or repay loans to the banks must surrender something in payment. These net payments to the banks can occur in various forms and proportions. The public might pay the banks entirely by surrendering demand-deposit claims, or it might pay at least in part by surrendering time-deposit claims or currency formerly held outside the banking system. The sizes of the multiples of contraction of bank deposits and earning assets will be substantially affected by the public's choices among the methods of paying the banks.

Suppose the public pays the banks entirely by relinquishing demand-deposit claims. In this case there is no induced currency flow into the banks to offset any part of the initial loss of reserves. The banks must remedy their reserve deficiency entirely by reducing their loans and security holdings, thus extinguishing demand deposits and lowering the volume of their required reserves. The sizes of the necessary multiples of contraction will then depend on the size of the fractional-reserve requirement. For example, if the reserve requirement is 0.15, each $1 initial loss of reserves will require a contraction of $1/0.15, or $6.67, of demand deposits and also of bank loans and security holdings. As in the case of expansion, the multiples will be different if the public makes at least some of the necessary payments to banks by relinquishing time-deposit claims.

All the multiples of necessary contraction (of demand deposits, time deposits, and bank holdings of loans and securities) will be smaller if the public surrenders in payment to the banks some currency formerly held outside the banking system. We shall call this an *induced cash inflow*. Each dollar of induced cash inflow offsets a dollar of the initial loss of reserves and thus reduces the extent to which the banks must repair their reserve deficiency by contracting their deposit liabilities.

We have now described in general terms the multiples of expansion permitted by an initial increase in the excess reserves of the banking system, and the multiples of contraction required by an initial loss of reserves. We have also noted some of the factors determining the sizes of the multiples. Let us now analyze these more closely, using the following symbols:

$\Delta A$ = the initial change in the volume of excess reserves of the banking system.

$r$ = the fractional-reserve requirement against demand-deposit liabilities.

$b$ = the fractional-reserve requirement against time deposits.

$\Delta D$ = change in the dollar volume of demand deposits.

$\Delta T$ = change in the volume of time deposits. At times it will be convenient to state this as $\Delta T = n \Delta D$, thus stating $\Delta T$ as a fraction or multiple of $\Delta D$.

$\Delta L$ = change in the volume of loans and security holdings of the banking system.

$\Delta C$ = net induced cash drain from the banking system in the case of bank expansion, and net induced cash inflow in the case of bank contraction. This will sometimes be expressed as $\Delta C = s \Delta D$, thus stating $\Delta C$ as a fraction, $s$, of $\Delta D$.

$\Delta M$ = change in the money supply. This is equal to $\Delta D + \Delta C$.

We shall now proceed to develop and compare three different cases of multiple expansion and contraction. In order to compare the sizes of the multiplier, we shall in all cases assume that

$\Delta A$ = $100, reflecting an equal change in bank borrowings from the Federal Reserve

$r$ = 0.15

$b$ = 0.04

The reader should find it useful, however, to work through the various cases, using other values for $r$ and $b$.

<table>
<tr><td>**CASE 1:**<br>$\Delta T = 0, \Delta C = 0$</td><td>We start with the simple case in which expansion or contraction by the banking system involves no change in time deposits and no induced cash drain or cash inflow—otherwise expressed, $n=0$ and $s=0$. Thus, no part of the initial gain or loss of excess reserves comes to be offset by an induced cash drain or cash inflow, and the banks must adjust to the gain or loss of reserves solely by changing the volume of their demand-deposit liabilities.</td></tr>
</table>

**Expansion**

Suppose the banks receive an initial increase in their excess reserves equal to $\Delta A$. With this accretion to their excess reserves, they can proceed to create additional demand deposits ($\Delta D$) by expanding their holdings of loans and securities ($\Delta L$). They will have expanded to the maximum permitted by $\Delta A$ only when they have expanded demand deposits so much that their required reserves ($r\Delta D$) have risen by an amount equal to the initial increase of excess reserves. In other words, maximum expansion has been reached when

$$r \, \Delta D = \Delta A$$

or

$$\Delta D = \Delta A \, \frac{1}{r}$$

Substituting our assumed values of $\Delta A = \$100$ and $r = 0.15$, we get

$$\Delta D = \$100 \, \frac{1}{0.15} = \$666.67$$

The net changes on the balance sheet of the banking system will be as follows:

| ASSETS | | LIABILITIES | |
|---|---|---|---|
| | | Borrowings from the | |
| $\Delta A$ | +$100.00 | Federal Reserve | +$100.00 |
| $\Delta L$ | +$666.67 | $\Delta D$ | +$666.67 |

**Addendum**
Increase of required reserves
= $666.67 × 0.15 = $100

The addendum shows that demand deposits have indeed expanded to the maximum permitted, for required reserves have been increased enough to absorb all of the initial increase of excess reserves. For purposes of comparison with the cases that follow, it should be noted that in this case $\Delta L = \Delta D = \Delta M$. In other words, the expansion of bank loans and security holdings was accompanied by an equal increase in checking deposits and an equal increase in the money supply because the volume of currency outside banks remained unchanged.

**Contraction**     We can deal with contraction briefly because both the process and the reasoning are quite comparable to those above. Suppose that, at a time when they hold no reserves in excess of legal requirements, the banks suffer an initial loss of reserves equal to $\Delta A$. Now that their reserves are deficient, the banks must proceed to reduce their demand-deposit liabilities ($\Delta D$) by reducing their loans and security holdings ($\Delta L$). They will have contracted by the minimum necessary amount only when they have reduced deposit liabilities so much that their required reserves ($r\Delta D$) have decreased by an amount equal to the actual loss of reserves. In short, the minimum required contraction has been reached when

$$r\,\Delta D = \Delta A$$

or

$$\Delta D = \Delta A\,\frac{1}{r}$$

Again substituting our assumed values,

$$\Delta D = -\$100\,\frac{1}{0.15} = -\$666.67$$

The following changes will appear on the balance sheet of the banking system.

| ASSETS | | LIABILITIES | |
|---|---|---|---|
| | | Borrowings from the Federal | |
| $\Delta A$ | −$100.00 | Reserve | −$100.00 |
| $\Delta L$ | −$666.67 | $\Delta D$ | −$666.67 |

**Addendum**
Change in required reserves
  $= -\$666.67 \times 0.15 = -\$100$

The addendum shows that the decrease of demand deposits has decreased required reserves by an amount equal to the initial deficiency of reserves. Note that here again, $\Delta L = \Delta D = \Delta M$. By decreasing their loans and security holdings, the banks have destroyed equal amounts of both checking deposits and the money supply.

---

**CASE II:**
$\Delta C = 0, n > 0$

In this case we shall still assume that in the process of expansion or contraction the banks experience no net cash drain or inflow, but we recognize that there may be induced changes in time deposits ($\Delta T$). Whether or not such changes in $T$ will occur, and how large they will be relative to changes in demand deposits, depend on many things, such as the nature of service charges on demand deposits, the height of interest rates on time deposits, the characteristics of other available claims and the height of their yields, changes in income levels and rates of saving, and so on. Without delving further into the relevant motivations, we shall assume that time deposits do expand and contract as banks expand and contract their earning assets, and that $\Delta T = n \, \Delta D$. In our numerical example we shall let $n = \frac{1}{2}$. That is, every \$1 of $\Delta D$ is accompanied by a 50¢ $\Delta T$.

**Expansion**

Again suppose that excess bank reserves are increased in the amount of $\Delta A$. On the basis of these new excess reserves, the banks can expand their holdings of loans and securities, thereby creating deposit liabilities. The proportions in which these proceeds will come to be held in demand deposits and in time deposits depend on the public's choices between these two types of assets. The expansion will have reached the maximum only when the sum of the increase in reserves required against the increase of demand deposits ($r\Delta D$) plus the increase in reserves required against the increase in time deposits ($b \, \Delta T$ or $nb \, \Delta D$) is equal to the actual increase of reserves, $\Delta A$. In other words, maximum expansion is reached only when

$$r \, \Delta D + nb \, \Delta D = \Delta A$$
$$\Delta D \, (r + nb) = \Delta A$$
$$\Delta D = \Delta A \, \frac{1}{r + nb}$$

By substituting our assumed values of $\Delta A = \$100$, $r = 0.15$, $b = 0.04$, and $n = \frac{1}{2}$, we get

$$\Delta D = \$100 \, \frac{1}{0.15 + 0.02} = \$588.23$$

Since we assumed $n$ to be $\frac{1}{2}$, $\Delta T = \frac{1}{2} \Delta D$, or \$294.12. And since all the proceeds from the increase of bank loans and security holdings came to be held as demand and time deposits, $\Delta L = \Delta D + \Delta T$, or \$882.35. The following balance sheet shows how the changes would appear in the balance sheet of the banking system:

| ASSETS | | | LIABILITIES | |
|---|---|---|---|---|
| | | | Borrowings from the Federal | |
| $\Delta A$ | | +$100.00 | Reserve | +$100.00 |
| $\Delta L$ | | +$882.35 | $\Delta D$ | +$588.23 |
| | | | $\Delta T$ | +$294.12 |

**Addenda**

| Change in reserves required against | |
|---|---|
| Demand deposits = 588.23 × 0.15 | $ 88.24 |
| Time deposits = 294.12 × 0.04 | 11.76 |
| Total | $100.00 |

A glance at the addenda to the table shows that the banks have indeed expanded to the maximum, for the entire $100 initial increase of excess reserves is now "used up" in meeting the $88.24 of reserves required against the expansion of demand deposits and the $11.76 increase of reserves required against the new time deposits.

A comparison of the results in this case with those in Case I highlights some important points. If not all the proceeds from an expansion of bank loans and security holdings are held as demand deposits, but some are instead reflected in an increase of time deposits, the sizes of the various multiples will be affected as follows:

1   The total deposit multiple will be greater. This is because $b$ is lower than $r$. And the size of the multiple will be greater as $n$ is larger and as $b$ is smaller relative to $r$.

2   The multiple of expansion of loans and security holdings will also be greater, for the banks can acquire earning assets by creating both time- and demand-deposit liabilities.

3   The multiple expansion of demand deposits alone will be smaller. This is because some part of the initial increase of reserves is "used up" to meet reserve requirements against the additional time deposits.

4   The multiple expansion of the total money supply, as we define it, will also be smaller, for we exclude time deposits from the money supply.

**Contraction**

Because contraction and expansion are such comparable processes, we ask readers to review the discussion immediately above, and to develop the process of contraction on their own. Assume that at a time when they hold no reserves in excess of legal requirements, the banks suffer an initial loss of reserves equal to $\Delta A$. Then, as the banks decrease their loans and security holdings, the public pays in part by surrendering time-deposit claims. Let $\Delta T = n \Delta D$. Then solve for the minimum necessary contraction of $D, D + T, L,$ and $M$. *Suggestion:* Check your results by computing the changes in the volume of reserves required against $\Delta D$ and $\Delta T$ and comparing the sum with the actual initial change of reserves, $\Delta A$.

<table>
<tr><td>

CASE III:
PANSION AND
CONTRACTION
TH INDUCED
CASH DRAINS
AND INFLOWS

</td><td>

In the first two cases we assumed that, as banks expanded, they induced no net currency drain from the banking system and therefore lost none of the initial increase of reserves. And when they contracted they induced no net currency flow into the banks and were not able to gain reserves in this way to offset some of the initial loss. In a more realistic setting, however, net cash drains or inflows frequently are induced. When these do occur, they can markedly reduce the sizes of the various multiples of expansion or contraction.

</td></tr>
</table>

Why does the public tend to hold more currency as the banks increase the total money supply, and to hold less currency when the banking system contracts? The answers most frequently given are of two general, although not necessarily conflicting, types. One emphasizes that, given the state of institutional arrangements and public preferences, there will be some more-or-less fixed ratio of currency and checking deposits that the public considers to be most advantageous. When the total money supply is increased, the public will elect to hold a major part of it in the form of deposits, but will take some part in additional currency. And when the total supply of money is decreased, the public will give up some currency as well as relinquish deposits.

The other approach emphasizes the behavior of the types of payments for which currency is widely held and used. These include payrolls and consumer expenditures to retail stores, restaurants, transportation companies, nightclubs, parking meters, gasoline stations, and so on. The amounts of currency that the public demands to hold will most likely vary in the same direction as, if not in strict proportion with, these expenditures. When the banking system expands its loans and security holdings to any considerable extent, the result is likely to be an expansion of expenditures in general, including payrolls and spendings of a retail nature. The public is therefore likely to demand more currency. But a sizable contraction of bank credit is likely to bring the opposite results, that is, a decrease of spendings in general, including payrolls and retail trade, and a net relinquishment of currency by the public.

Both these approaches lead to the same qualitative conclusion—that changes in bank deposits and asset holdings are likely to be accompanied by changes in the same direction of the public's demand for currency. For simplicity, we shall assume that there is a proportional relationship between the change in currency ($\Delta C$) and the change in deposits ($\Delta D$). Thus, $\Delta C$ can be expressed as a fraction, $s$, times $\Delta D$. In our numerical example we shall let $s = 0.23$. Thus, $\Delta C = 0.23\ \Delta D$.

**Expansion**      Again we start with the assumption that the banking system enjoys an initial increase in its excess reserves ($\Delta A$) and that it proceeds on this basis to expand its loans and security holdings. The public will hold the proceeds in the desired proportions in the form of additional demand deposits ($\Delta D$), additional time deposits ($n\ \Delta D$), and additional currency ($s\Delta D$). In this case, the initial increase of reserves is "absorbed," or "used up," in three ways: as required reserves against the additional demand deposits ($r\ \Delta D$), as required reserves against the additional time deposits ($bn\ \Delta D$), and to meet the net induced drain of currency from the banking system ($s\ \Delta D$). The banks will have expanded to the maximum only when all the initial increase of reserves has been "absorbed" in these three forms. In short, maximum expansion is reached when

$$r\Delta D + nb\ \Delta D + s\Delta D = \Delta A$$
$$\Delta D\ (r + nb + s) = \Delta A$$
$$\Delta D = \Delta A\ \frac{1}{r + nb + s}$$

Substituting our assumed values of $A = \$100$, $r = 0.15$, $b = 0.04$, $n = 0.5$, and $s = 0.23$, we get

$$\Delta D = \$100\ \frac{1}{0.15 + 0.02 + 0.23} = \$100\ \frac{1}{0.40} = \$250$$

We can also use this formula and our assumed values to compute other magnitudes in which we are interested.

1    $\Delta T$, which is stated as $n\ \Delta D$, is $\frac{1}{2}\ \Delta D$, or \$125.
2    The increase of total deposits, $\Delta D + \Delta T$, may be stated as $(1 + n)\Delta D$. In this case, it is $(1 + 0.5)\ \$250$, or \$375.
3    The net drain of currency into circulation, $\Delta C$, is $s\ \Delta D$. In this case, it is $0.23\ \Delta D$, or \$57.50. Note that this represents both the amount of the initial increase of reserves that the banking system loses through the induced currency drain and the part of the increased money supply that the public elects to hold in the form of increased currency outside the banks.
4    The increase of bank loans and security holdings is equal to the sum of $\Delta D + \Delta T + \Delta C$. This reflects the fact that the banks can buy claims against others by creating demand- and time-deposit claims and also by paying out some of its cash reserves to those who borrow from or sell securities to them. $\Delta L$ may also be expressed as $(1 + n + s)\ \Delta D$. In this case, $\Delta L = (1 + 0.5 + 0.23)\ \$250$, or \$432.50.
5    The increase in the public's money supply ($\Delta M$) is equal to the increase in demand deposits plus the net induced drain of currency from the banks into circulation ($\Delta C$). Since the latter is equal to $s\ \Delta D$, $\Delta M = (1 + s)\ \Delta D$. In this case, it is $(1 + 0.23)\ \$250$, or \$307.50.

The final effects on the balance sheet of the banking system will be as shown in the following table. The addenda indicate that the banks have expanded to the maximum, because the entire $100 initial increase of excess reserves has been "used up" to meet the induced cash drain and to serve as required reserves against the additional demand and time deposits.

| ASSETS | | LIABILITIES | |
|---|---|---|---|
| Initial $\Delta A$ | +$100.00 | Borrowings from the Federal | |
| Less: cash drain | 57.50 | Reserve | +$100.00 |
| Remaining increase of reserves | $ 42.50 | $\Delta D$ | $250.00 |
| $\Delta L$ | $432.50 | $\Delta T$ | $125.00 |

**Addenda**
"Absorption" of the initial $100 increase of reserves:

| | |
|---|---|
| Loss of reserves through cash drain | $ 57.50 |
| Increase of reserve required against new demand deposits | 37.50 |
| Increase of reserve required against new time deposits | 5.00 |
| Total | $100.00 |

Table 6–2 enables us to compare easily the various multiples of expansion in the three cases resulting from a given initial increase of excess reserves and given levels of reserve requirements. The largest multiple of expansion of demand deposits and the money supply is achieved in Case I, in which there is no induced increase in either time deposits or currency outside banks. Case II illustrates the effects when some part of the proceeds of bank net purchases of loans and securities comes to be held in the form of time and savings deposits. The effects are to increase the expansion multiples of total deposits and of loans and security holdings, but to decrease the multiples of expansion of demand deposits and the money supply.

Case III illustrates how sharply an induced currency drain from the banks can decrease all the multiples of expansion. A cash drain has this effect because each dollar it removes from the banks is a dollar of

| **TABLE 6–2** | | **Case I** $n = 0$ $s = 0$ | **Case II** $n = 0.50$ $s = 0$ | **Case III** $n = 0.50$ $s = 0.23$ |
|---|---|---|---|---|
| *Summary of expansion in three cases* $(\Delta A = \$100, r = 0.15,$ $b = 0.04)$ | $\Delta D$ | $666.67 | $588.23 | $250.00 |
| | $\Delta T$ | 0 | 294.12 | 125.00 |
| | $\Delta D + \Delta T$ | 666.67 | 882.35 | 375.00 |
| | $\Delta L$ | 666.67 | 882.35 | 432.50 |
| | $\Delta C$ | 0 | 0 | 57.50 |
| | $\Delta M = \Delta D + \Delta C$ | 666.67 | 588.23 | 307.50 |

reserves which, if it had remained in the banks, would have "supported" several dollars of expansion of bank deposits and of bank holdings of loans and securities. This is a fact of great importance to anyone who would understand banking and also to monetary authorities charged with responsibility for regulating the money supply and the quantity of credit supplied by banks through their acquisition of loans and securities.

**Contraction**     Suppose that the banks suffer an initial loss of reserves, $\Delta A$, at a time when they have no excess reserves, and that the ensuing bank contraction induces a net flow of currency into the banks. You are invited to trace through the process and to calculate the minimum necessary contractions of demand and time deposits, bank loans and security holdings, and the money supply. Test your understanding by considering these questions:

1   Why are all the multiples of minimum necessary contraction so much smaller than in Cases I and II?
2   Why is the contraction in $\Delta L$ greater than that in $\Delta D + \Delta T$?
3   Why is the contraction in $\Delta M$ greater than that in $\Delta D$?
4   How do you know that the banks have contracted by the necessary minimum when they have contracted by the amounts that you calculated?

---

**MULTIPLIERS FOR THE GENERAL CASE**     We developed our analysis through three cases, both to proceed from the simplest to the more complex and also to emphasize the importance of the values of the variables in determining the sizes of the various multiples of expansion and contraction. It should be clear, however, that the formulas used in Case III apply generally. Case I is simply the special case in which $n = 0$ and $s = 0$. Case II is the special case in which $s = 0$. Thus, the general formulas are

$$\Delta D = \Delta A \,\frac{1}{r + nb + s} \tag{6}$$
$$\Delta T = n \,\Delta D \tag{7}$$
$$\Delta D + \Delta T = (1 + n) \,\Delta D \tag{8}$$
$$\Delta C = s \,\Delta D \tag{9}$$
$$\Delta L = \Delta D + \Delta T + \Delta C = (1 + n + s) \,\Delta D \tag{10}$$
$$\Delta M = \Delta D + \Delta C = (1 + s) \,\Delta D \tag{11}$$

Expressions (6) and (11) can be combined in what is called a *money-multiplier* formula. In particular, multiplying both sides of equation (6) by $(1 + s)$ and combining with equation (11) we get

$$\Delta M = \left(\frac{1 + s}{r + nb + s}\right) \Delta A \tag{12}$$

The quantity in parentheses is called the money multiplier because it is the magnitude by which a change in reserves must be multiplied to yield the corresponding change in the supply of money.

From Table 6–2 we see how the numerical value of the multiplier changes as we alter our assumptions. Thus, for example, in case I the money multiplier is roughly 6.7 ($\Delta M = 666.67$ with $\Delta A = 100$), while in case II it is approximately 5.9. The currency drain in the general case (III) serves to sharply reduce the money multiplier, to about 3.1.

We shall shortly consider other aspects of the money multiplier. However, it will be helpful if we first dispose of the fate of the individual bank in the deposit creation process.

**XPANSION AND NTRACTION BY AN INDIVIDUAL BANK N THE SYSTEM**

At several points in the preceding sections, we emphasized that we were dealing with multiple expansion or contraction by *the banking system as a whole* in response to an initial change in its reserves. Although the same analysis can be applied to an individual bank, it can be applied only with very important modifications, because an individual bank is subjected to *induced reserve losses* and *induced reserve gains* that do not apply to the banking system as a whole. An individual bank, like the banking system, may experience an induced drain of currency into circulation or an inflow of currency from circulation. In addition, however, the individual bank is subject to induced reserve losses to make net payments to other banks and to induced reserve gains as other banks make net payments to it. These arise in two principal ways:

1   Through net purchases or sales of other assets by a bank for its own account. For example, a bank may transfer some of its cash reserve (currency or deposits at the Federal Reserve) to buy loans or securities from another bank or from a customer of another bank. Or it may gain cash reserves by selling some of its loans or securities to another bank or a customer of another bank.

2   Through net transfers of deposit claims among banks. Huge amounts of payments are made by transferring, usually by check, deposit claims from payers to payees. Fortunately for banks, only a small fraction of these flows lead to net interbank payments and to net transfers of cash reserves from one bank to another.

For one thing, payers and payees are often depositors at the same bank. For example, both Jones and Whyte may be depositors at bank A. If Jones gives a $1,000 check to Whyte, bank A will simply deduct that amount from its deposit liability to Jones and increase equally its deposit liability to Whyte. The bank's assets and total liabilities remain unchanged. But suppose payer and payee are not depositors in the same bank. Suppose Jones writes a $1,000 check on bank A and gives it to Whyte, who deposits it in bank B. The latter will add $1,000 to its deposit liability to Whyte and send the check to bank A, which will deduct this amount from its deposit liability to Jones. Bank A now owes bank B $1,000, which it will pay by transferring this amount of its cash reserves if there are no offsetting transactions. But there are likely to be some offsetting transactions, which will require bank B or other banks to pay bank A.

In the course of every day, large amounts of checks will be drawn on a bank and deposited in other banks, thus creating large liabilities for it to pay those banks. But at the same time the bank will receive on deposit large amounts of checks drawn on other banks, thus giving it claims for payment by them. Since these will usually be largely offsetting, it would be both confusing and inefficient if each bank had to transfer cash reserves to meet the full value of its liability to pay other banks and to receive cash reserves equal to all its claims for payment by other banks. How much more efficient it would be to offset these flows to the maximum possible extent and transfer cash reserves only to cover net payments or receipts. A complex clearing and collection system has been developed for this purpose. It includes local clearinghouses, correspondent banks, and the Federal Reserve banks. At least once a day, and sometimes oftener, these organizations compare for each bank the flow of checks drawn on it and deposited with other banks, with the flow of checks deposited with it and drawn on other banks. Each bank then receives the net amount due it or pays the net amount owed by it. And these net payments are usually made by transferring cash reserves.

These interbank transfers of funds are significant for several reasons. In the first place, they help to explain why banks seek to attract deposits away from other banks. A bank that succeeds in this can thereby draw reserves from other banks and increase its lending power. In the second place, they make the liquidity problem of an individual bank quite different from that of the commercial banking system as a whole. An individual bank must be able to meet not only its depositors' demands for coin and currency, but also its payments to other banks. And in the third place, because of these interbank transfers, an individual bank that receives an initial addition to its cash reserves usually cannot expand its loans, investments, and deposits by a multiple amount. The bank must recognize that at least some of the deposits that it creates by making loans or buying securities will be checked out to other banks, thereby necessitating transfer of all or some of the initial increase of cash reserves.

**Expansion**

To illustrate this, let us consider an individual bank, which we refer to as "the first bank," and make the following assumptions:

1   The first bank receives a $10 million addition to its reserves through a primary deposit. This may, for example, result from an inflow of currency or a Federal Reserve purchase of securities from the public.

2     All proceeds of bank loans are held in demand deposits; there is no change in time deposits and no induced cash drain.

3     All banks operate under a reserve requirement of 20 percent. The initial effects on the balance sheet of the first bank are these:

| ASSETS | | LIABILITIES | |
|---|---|---|---|
| Reserves | +$10 million | Deposits | +$10 million |
| **Addenda** | | | |
| Requires reserves | +$ 2 million | | |
| Excess reserves | +$ 8 million | | |

Now that it has $8 million of excess reserves, can the first bank proceed to increase its loans and security holdings by $8 million/0.20, or $40 million? It could if all the derivative deposits remained with it. In this case, all of the initial increase of reserves would remain in the first bank, available to support additional derivative deposits. But this is most unlikely to occur in a system with more than 14,000 banks. It is much more likely that a large part of the derivative deposits will be checked out to other banks, thus requiring the first bank to transfer reserves and thereby reducing its ability to expand its own loans and security holdings. Table 6–3 shows the expansion for individual banks and for the banking system as a whole on the extreme assumption that *all* derivative deposits created by one bank are checked out to the next bank and that an equal amount of reserves must be paid over to the transferee bank.

**TABLE 6–3**

*eposit expansion on new reserves by a banking system*

| | Additional deposits received | Additional reserves retained against deposits received (20%) | Additional loans made (80%)* |
|---|---|---|---|
| First bank | $10,000,000 | $ 2,000,000 | $ 8,000,000 |
| Second bank | 8,000,000 | 1,600,000 | 6,400,000 |
| Third bank | 6,400,000 | 1,280,000 | 5,120,000 |
| Fourth bank | 5,120,000 | 1,024,000 | 4,096,000 |
| Fifth bank | 4,096,000 | 819,200 | 3,276,800 |
| Sixth bank | 3,276,800 | 655,360 | 2,621,440 |
| Seventh bank | 2,621,440 | 524,288 | 2,097,152 |
| Eighth bank | 2,097,152 | 419,430 | 1,677,722 |
| Ninth bank | 1,677,722 | 355,544 | 1,342,178 |
| Tenth bank | 1,342,178 | 268,436 | 1,073,742 |
| Total, first ten banks | $44,631,292 | $ 8,926,258 | $35,705,034 |
| Other banks in turn | 5,368,708 | 1,073,742 | 4,294,966 |
| Grand total | $50,000,000 | $10,000,000 | $40,000,000 |

* The deposits created by these loans are all checked out to the next bank.

After receiving the $10 million addition to its deposits and reserves, the first bank "sets aside" the $2 million of additional required reserves, and expands its loans and security holdings by $8 million. These loan-created deposits are checked out to the second bank and an equal amount of reserves transferred to it. (We know that, for the banking system, these are derivative deposits; but to the second bank they will appear as primary deposits, because they brought with them an equal amount of reserves.) The second bank sets aside the $1.6 million of required reserves (20 percent of $8 million) and expands its loans and security holdings by $6.4 million. The resulting derivative deposits and an equal amount of reserves are transferred to the third bank, which continues the expansion, as do the others in turn. Thus, the $50 million expansion of deposits in the system as a whole ($40 million of which was created by bank loans and security purchases) represents increases at many banks.

This example illustrates some important points:

1   Every individual banker could properly say, "I certainly didn't engage in multiple expansion. All I did was to accept deposits, set aside the required reserve, and then lend an amount equal to the remainder." Yet for the system as a whole, there was indeed a multiple expansion of deposits and earning assets, and most of the new deposits were derivative deposits.

2   Most of the expansion occurred not at the bank initially receiving the increase of reserves, but in other banks to which most of the reserves came to be transferred.

3   This illustrates the process through which initial injections of additional reserves in only one or a few banks can lead to increased reserves and credit expansion throughout the banking system.

**Contraction**   Using comparable assumptions, suppose that an individual bank, the first bank, loses $10 million of reserves through a withdrawal of currency. The process, results, and conclusions are symmetrical with those mentioned previously. Table 6–3 can be used to illustrate this if the column headings are changed. Change the first column heading to read, "Decrease in deposits and reserves"; the second to, "Decrease of required reserves because of loss of deposits"; and the third to, "Decrease in loans" (this is equal to 80 percent of deposits lost).

Now that its reserves are deficient, the first bank will decrease its loans and security holdings, receive in payment checks drawn on the second bank, and gain reserves from the latter. The second bank will decrease its loans and security holdings, receive in payment checks on the third bank, and gain reserves from it. And so the contraction process spreads and continues until the system has contracted by the minimum amount required to repair the reserve position of its members.

**The General Case**     In order to emphasize the difference between an individual bank and the banking system as a whole, the preceding examples assumed that when an individual bank experienced an initial increase in its excess reserves and proceeded to expand its holdings of loans and securities, all of the resulting derivative deposits and an equal amount of reserves would be transferred to other banks. Thus, it could expand its loans and securities only by an amount equal to the initial addition to its excess reserves. This is an approximation of what often happens to an individual bank in a system of thousands of banks. However, in some cases a part of the derivative deposits created by an individual bank remains with it, at least for a time, so that its loss of deposits and reserves to other banks is less than depicted above. For example, a borrower from the bank may voluntarily leave some of the proceeds on deposit with the bank, or the bank may require the borrower to do so as a condition for granting the loan. Or the borrower may pay some of the derivative deposits to others who are depositors at the same bank. In such cases an individual bank may expand its loans and securities more than was indicated in the earlier example. However, the distinction between the individual bank and the banking system as a whole remains valid. Failure to make this distinction has in the past led to muddled thinking and policy mistakes and to needless controversies between bankers and economists.

**THE SUPPLY OF MONEY: AN OVERVIEW**     The preceding sections concentrate on the processes through which the commercial banking system creates and destroys deposits by purchasing and selling assets of various kinds. As far as the supply of money is concerned, the net effect of this is summarized in the multiplier formula

$$\Delta M = \frac{(1 + s)\, \Delta A}{r + nb + s}$$

which expresses the change in the money stock, $\Delta M$, as a function of the change in reserves, $\Delta A$, the reserve-requirement ratios, $r$ and $b$, and the two parameters relating to currency and time deposits, $s$ and $n$. One danger with the multiplier approach is that it gives the impression that changes in the quantity of money are brought about by a rather mechanical process. In particular, our formula suggests that, given the reserve-requirement ratios, the Federal Reserve simply picks $\Delta A$ and out pops $\Delta M$. As we shall now see, for a variety of reasons this view is terribly misleading.

**The Behavior of the Public**     Part of the seeming simplicity of the multiplier formula stems from the way in which currency and time deposits appear to affect changes in the supply of money. The influence of these two quantities is captured in the parameters $s$ and $n$, innocently suggesting that these are institutionally determined constants. But nothing could be further from the truth. Currency and time deposits do not move hand in hand with demand deposits. Rather, the quantities of currency and time deposits that the public chooses to hold vary over time in response to economic factors. In determining the quantities that it will demand of currency, time deposits, demand deposits, and other financial assets, the public considers their relative liquidity and safety and their relative yields. Consequently, a change in any one of these factors can alter the willingness of the public to hold currency and time deposits relative to demand deposits (i.e., the parameters $s$ and $n$). For example, the growth of particular kinds of transactions could alter the relative convenience of currency as compared with demand deposits. Variations in bank service charges and yields paid on time deposits could also alter the values of $s$ and $n$. Similar effects could result from changes in yields on savings deposits at nonbank intermediaries.

In short, the parameters $s$ and $n$ are economically determined variables that cannot be expected to remain constant over time. While in some circumstances they may change only slowly, if general economic conditions change rapidly $s$ and $n$ may also exhibit sizable changes in a relatively brief period.

**Commercial Bank Behavior**

Aside from bank-induced variations in the characteristics of their liabilities, the behavior of the commercial banks affects the interpretation of the multiplier formula in another very important way. In deriving the multiplier formula we have assumed that the commercial banks are able and willing to exercise their maximum lending power. Put another way, banks are assumed to utilize fully an injection of new reserves and not to add to their excess reserves. However, throughout many periods of our history this has not been the case. The reason is simple. Excess reserves serve a useful function in keeping a bank liquid so that it may meet adverse clearing balances or the loan demand of its valued customers. The desirability of holding excess reserves for such purposes depends on the cost of holding such reserves—the interest income forgone from holding a nonearning asset—relative to the anticipated costs of meeting a deficient reserve position or new loan demand.

Clearly, as with the case of $s$ and $n$ given previously, this is an economic decision. We would expect that, other things equal, banks would hold more excess reserves the lower the interest rate on relatively liquid securities and hence the lower the opportunity cost on holding such reserves. Evidently then, the implicit assumption in our formula of a maximum expansion of earning assets will not always be met.[2]

---

[2] It is possible to modify the money-multiplier formula to account for excess reserves. See the appendix to this chapter.

**Federal Reserve Influence**

The remaining way in which the multiplier formula somewhat oversimplifies reality is the deceptive appearance of $\Delta A$, the quantity we have identified as the injection of new reserves. While we have suggested that the Federal Reserve can regulate the volume of reserves, it is not endowed with a "reserve dial" that it simply sets to achieve a desired change in reserves. Rather, as we shall see later, it must contend with a significant number of diverse factors that affect bank reserves. Among the various influences on the quantity of reserves are the following: changes in the gold stock, borrowing of reserves by the commercial banks, and the volume of foreign-owned deposits held at the Federal Reserve.[3] Each of these factors can be only imperfectly anticipated by the Federal Reserve, so that the task of regulating the volume of reserves is far from a mechanical one.

**Other Factors**

There are a number of other respects in which the money-multiplier formula presented in equation (12) is somewhat simplified. Here we shall just comment on two possible complications.

First, as noted above, in deriving the money multiplier we have assumed that all commercial banks are subject to the same set of reserve requirements. However, as documented in the previous chapter, about 30 percent of total deposits are at banks that are not members of the Federal Reserve. It is clearly necessary to take this factor into account in any forecast of the change in the money supply stemming from a change in reserves. While we shall not present the algebraic details, it is in fact possible to do this by means of a slight modification of the money multiplier formula.[4] Consequently, the basic money-multiplier approach can be applied even when we recognize the simultaneous existence of both member and nonmember banks.

A second possible complication with the multiplier formula concerns the definition of money. For example, some economists might argue that we should use a broader definition of the money stock, one that includes time deposits. Obviously, the precise form of the money multiplier will change if we adopt this definition. But as shown in the appendix, the money multiplier approach can still be applied in this case. Alternatively, some economists might advance a definition of the money stock that included liabilities of financial intermediaries other than commercial banks (e.g., NOW accounts at savings and loan associations). Once again, for any specific definition we could present an appropriate

---

[3] For a detailed discussion of how these affect reserves, see Chapter 10.

[4] As noted in the previous chapter, recently enacted legislation calls for the gradual imposition of reserve requirements on nonmember banks. As these requirements are phased in, the relevant money multiplier formula will gradually change.

money multiplier.[5] As before, however, one would not use such a formula in a mechanical way. Rather, one would also look at the economic forces that contributed to the development of nonbank liabilities as extremely close substitutes for money as it has traditionally been defined.

CONCLUSION   While we have stressed the fact that the multiplier formula should not be regarded as a mechanical tool, this does not mean that we should minimize the importance of the multiplier approach. The multiplier formula serves an extremely useful role in highlighting how an injection (or withdrawal) of reserves will be translated into a change in the money supply. Indeed, when properly interpreted, it serves to emphasize the importance of asset choices by the public and the commercial banks in the money supply process. Furthermore, it makes clear that the Federal Reserve, should it desire to achieve some specific change in the money supply, must be able to forecast the consequences of the behavior of the public and the commercial banks. Such anticipation is necessary, above and beyond the somewhat more technical problems of controlling the quantity of reserves.

Subsequent chapters consider in more detail the asset choices of both the public and the commercial banks. They also analyze the objectives of the Federal Reserve and spell out more precisely how the Federal Reserve goes about influencing the volume of reserves. Several of the major points in this chapter, however, are essential for our later analysis, especially when we deal with monetary management by the Federal Reserve.

1   Each dollar of bank reserves is indeed "high-powered" money, capable of supporting several dollars of deposits. Thus, by creating an additional dollar of reserves for the banks, the Federal Reserve can enable them to create several dollars of bank credit. And by depriving the banks of a dollar of reserves, the Federal Reserve can force them to reduce bank credit by some multiple.

2   The volume of deposits and also of bank loans and holdings of securities that can be supported by each dollar of reserves depends greatly on the height of legally required reserve ratios. Thus, the Federal Reserve's power to increase and decrease reserve requirements is a potent instrument.

3   The Federal Reserve or any other central bank that wishes to forecast the size of the effects that will flow from its own actions must use the type of analysis presented in this chapter.

---

[5] In many respects, the complications presented by nonbank financial intermediaries are similar in kind to those stemming from the existence of nonmember commercial banks.

| APPENDIX | THE MONEY MULTIPLIER UNDER ALTERNATIVE ASSUMPTIONS |
|---|---|

In the preceding chapter we developed a money multiplier formula that related the change in the money supply ($\Delta M$) to an injection of reserves ($\Delta A$):

$$\Delta M = \left( \frac{1+s}{r+nb+s} \right) \Delta A \qquad (A1)$$

Quite evidently, this is of the general form

$$\Delta M = m \, \Delta A \qquad (A2)$$

where $m$ is the money multiplier. In the case of equation (A1), $m$ depends on the two reserve requirements ($r$ on demand deposits, $D$, and $b$ on time deposits, $T$) and on the parameters $s$ and $n$, which characterize the public's preferences with respect to currency ($\Delta C = s \, \Delta D$) and time deposits ($\Delta T = n \, \Delta D$). However, it was also suggested in the text that the precise form of $m$ would vary if we allowed for the existence of excess reserves or if we altered the definition of money. The purpose of this appendix is to illustrate how these various complications can be introduced.

In what follows we shall, in addition to the notation already introduced, make use of the following symbols:

$\Delta RR =$ the change in required reserves, which can be expressed as $\Delta RR = r \, \Delta D + b \, \Delta T$.

$\Delta E =$ the ultimate change in excess reserves after the banks have responded to initial reserve injection. It will be convenient to express this as a fraction of the change in demand deposits, as in $\Delta E = e \, \Delta D$.

$\Delta M_2 =$ the change in the money stock broadly defined. This is equal to $\Delta C + \Delta D + \Delta T$.

**Excess Reserves**

In deriving equation (A1) we assumed the banks to be fully loaned up. That is, in response to a reserve injection, they were presumed to expand deposits and assets to the maximum. Permitting banks voluntarily to hold excess reserves means that there are now three potential uses of an initial reserve injection: for required reserves, for a currency drain, or for excess reserves. In symbols, we have

$$\Delta A = \Delta RR + \Delta C + \Delta E \qquad (A3)$$

We can manipulate this expression by substituting for $\Delta RR$, $\Delta C$, and $\Delta E$ to yield

$$\Delta A = (r \, \Delta D + b \, \Delta T) + s \, \Delta D + e \, \Delta D$$

Using the fact that $\Delta T = n \, \Delta D$, we can obtain

$$\Delta A = r \, \Delta D + nb \, \Delta D + s \, \Delta D + e \, \Delta D$$

which can be rearranged to yield

$$\Delta D = \frac{\Delta A}{(r + nb + s + e)} \tag{A4}$$

Finally, from

$$\Delta M = \Delta C + \Delta D = s \, \Delta D + \Delta D = (1 + s) \, \Delta D$$

we have

$$\Delta M = \left( \frac{1 + s}{r + nb + s + e} \right) \Delta A \tag{A5}$$

Equation (A5) is the money multiplier formula allowing for excess reserves. Not surprisingly, it is very similar to equation (A1), the only difference being the appearance of the symbol $e$ in the denominator of (A5). What this says, reasonably enough, is that the more banks voluntarily sterilize reserves (i.e., the higher $e$ is), the lower the money multiplier will be. For lower values of $e$ the multiplier rises; in fact, when $e = 0$ equation (A5) collapses to equation (A1).

**The Money Multiplier for $\Delta M_2$**    Given equation (A4), it is quite straightforward to find the multiplier corresponding to the broader definition of the money stock given by $M_2$. In particular, by definition we have

$$\Delta M_2 = \Delta C + \Delta D + \Delta T$$

Substituting for $\Delta C$ and $\Delta T$ yields

$$\begin{aligned} \Delta M_2 &= s \, \Delta D + \Delta D + n \, \Delta D \\ &= (1 + s + n) \, \Delta D \end{aligned} \tag{A6}$$

Finally, combining equations (A4) and (A6), we have

$$\Delta M_2 = \left( \frac{1 + s + n}{r + nb + s + e} \right) \Delta A \tag{A7}$$

The multiplier for $M_2$ given in equation (A7) differs from what we might call the $M_1$ multiplier in equation (A5) in that $n$, the parameter that characterizes time deposit preferences, shows up in the numerator of (A7). While in some respects this is a minor difference, it does have an important policy implication. In particular, an increase in $n$ unambiguously reduces the $M_1$ multiplier. This is so because the increase in time deposits represents a leakage of reserves that could support demand deposits. With the $M_2$ definition, however, things are different. Specifically, as long as reserve requirements on demand deposits exceed those on time deposits, an increase in $n$ leads to an *increase* in the $M_2$ multiplier. In effect, this comes about because the increase in $n$ serves to reduce the average reserve requirement on *total* deposits, and it is *total* deposits that appear in $M_2$.

Overview

We have provided two examples of how the money-multiplier formulas can be modified to take account of alternative assumptions.[1] At the risk of repetition, it needs to be emphasized that whatever formula one derives cannot be used by policy makers in a purely mechanical way. This can be readily illustrated with respect to the two complications introduced in this appendix.

First, with respect to excess reserves, it should be clear that the parameter $e$ is not a constant. Rather, $e$ is a choice variable of the commercial banks, and it will be reduced whenever there are profitable opportunities for the use of bank funds. In its policy making, the Federal Reserve must be alert to variations in $e$.

Time deposits present a similar, and potentially more important, problem for policy makers. Suppose, for example, that, owing to the sort of institutional changes touched on in previous chapters, $n$ tends to increase and $M_2$ becomes the more critical monetary aggregate. This will have two consequences. First, the monetary authorities will have to shift their attention from $M_1$ to $M_2$, or from equation (A5) to equation (A7). Second, and perhaps more problematic, if $n$ increases, the $M_2$ multiplier may rise substantially. Evidently then, the Federal Reserve must keep close tabs on possible changes in $n$. Again, this clearly complicates the policy-making task of the Federal Reserve.

SELECTED READINGS

Burger, A. E., *The Money Supply Process*, Belmont, Calif., Wadsworth, 1971.

Havrilesky, T. M., and J. T. Boorman, *Monetary Macroeconomics*, Arlington Heights, Ill., AHM, 1978.

Nichols, D. M., *Modern Money Mechanics*, Chicago, Federal Reserve Bank of Chicago, 1975.

---

[1] The interested reader might attempt to modify the money multiplier formulas to take account of nonmember banks. *Hint:* Assume that changes in demand deposits of nonmember banks are proportional to changes in those of member banks. Be careful how you treat currency.

# 7

While previous chapters have suggested that portfolio choices of the commercial banks and the money supply process are related, we have yet to provide any detailed treatment of bank portfolio behavior. Furthermore, to this point our discussion of commercial banking has involved primarily the commercial banking system as a whole. Except in a limited way, we have not examined the functioning of an individual bank. Now, however, we shall explore both of these topics. In particular, we shift our attention to the individual bank—to its functions, its problems, its policies, and its portfolio decision making. One result of this approach should be to provide the reader with a better understanding of some basic problems and principles of managing an individual bank. However, by studying the policies of the basic decision-making units— the individual commercial banks—we shall also broaden and deepen our understanding of the system as a whole, because the behavior of the system is a result of the varying degrees and types of competition among the various units, all operating within the broader financial framework.

## A BANK AS A FINANCIAL INTERMEDIARY

The individual banker will probably look at the relationship between bank deposit liabilities and bank assets differently than we looked at the banking system as a whole. In the last chapter we emphasized that the great bulk of deposits were created through bank purchases of assets, although it was also noted that the banking system could not create and keep outstanding a larger volume of deposits than people were willing to acquire and hold. A banker is likely to view the relationship with the roles reversed—that is, the banker may feel that bank deposits give rise to bank acquisitions of assets. The banker might put it this way: "My bank is a member of the family called 'financial intermediaries.' As such, it gathers funds from people by issuing and selling financial claims against itself. It can acquire assets to the extent, and only to the extent, that it is supplied with funds in exchange for financial claims against it."

Thus, a bank participates in financial markets in two principal roles —as a buyer of funds through issues of claims against itself and as a seller of funds or purchaser of financial claims against others.

**Bank Liabilities**   A bank that seeks to attract funds by issuing financial claims against itself realizes that these claims must compete with many other types of financial claims for a place in the portfolios of asset-holders—for example, these claims must compete with currency, with claims against other commercial banks, with claims against other types of financial intermediaries, and with direct securities of varying maturities and varying degrees of safety and liquidity. Thus, the volume of claims against itself that a bank can persuade others to hold depends in part on both its price policy—the yields that it offers—and the characteristics of these claims in terms of safety, liquidity, and conformity to the preferences of various types of asset holders. A banker's freedom in determining the price and characteristics of these claims is to some degree restricted by laws and official regulations, but the banker still has considerable leeway within the regulatory framework. For example, although payment of explicit interest on demand deposits is prohibited by law, bankers have developed many nonprice methods of competing for these deposits. Also, although the Federal Reserve and the FDIC place ceilings on rates that banks may pay on time and savings deposits, these ceilings are sometimes high enough to permit considerable variation of actual rates beneath the ceilings, and, in any case, banks can adjust other characteristics of such deposits to make them more attractive.

For reasons to be discussed later, issues of equity or ownership claims usually provide a bank with only a minor portion of its total funds. Its net worth or capital account is rarely much above 10 percent of its total assets and is usually somewhat less. The bank relies largely on issues of debt claims, the great bulk of which are deposit liabilities of some type. From the mid-1930s until about the mid-1950s, most banks relied largely on demand deposits as sources of funds. However, since the mid-1950s banks have become increasingly aggressive in promoting the issue of time- and savings-deposit claims. This trend has continued to the present; as a result, at the vary majority of commercial banks time and savings deposits exceed demand deposits.

To establish a policy for attracting demand deposits, a bank must first determine the nature and extent of the market from which it can expect to draw such deposits. For example, a small bank in a small or medium-sized town is unlikely to find it feasible to draw demand deposits from long distances or from large corporations; most of its funds of this type are likely to come from households, small and medium-sized business firms, and governmental units within its own locality. To attract deposits of these types the small-town bank must usually compete only against a few local banks. At the other extreme, huge banks located in major financial centers find it feasible to attract demand deposits not only from their own localities but also from all over the nation and even from foreign countries. To attract depositors in such an expansive market these banks must compete against many more banks than does its small-town counterpart.

The characteristics of time- and savings-deposit claims can be varied in many different ways. A major purpose of such differentiation is to tailor the claims to the differing preferences of asset-holders. However, at least an incidental effect is to enable a bank to practice price discrimination—to attach differing yields to the various classes of claims. *Passbook savings deposits* are evidenced only by entries on the bank's books and in the depositor's passbook and bear no stipulated maturity date. The bank is legally empowered to require prior notice for withdrawal—usually at least 30 days—but in practice, banks permit withdrawals at any time, the only penalty being a forfeiture of accrued interest. With the significant growth in the number of banks paying interest on a day-of-deposit to day-of-withdrawal basis, even this possible penalty is rapidly disappearing for most depositors. The interest rate on savings deposits is set by the bank and can be changed at any time, subject, of course, to the prevailing interest ceilings. These deposits are held primarily by individuals and households, as corporations have been legally forbidden to hold such deposits until relatively recently. The principal attraction of these accounts is the immediate availability of the funds; however, their yields are often appreciably below those paid on some types of time deposits.

*Time deposits* have stipulated maturity dates, are evidenced by a written instrument, and bear a rate of interest that remains fixed during the life of the deposit contract. The shortest initial maturity is 30 days, but many have maturities of 60, 90, or 180 days, or even longer. Historically, most maturities have been a year or less, but in recent years many banks have offered longer maturities, some running for 5 or even 10 years. Time deposits are often classified in two categories—consumer type and business type. The consumer type is offered in denominations of less than $100,000 and is meant to appeal primarily to individuals and households. The written instruments representing these deposits are given various names, such as *certificates of deposit and savings certificates*. Holders of these claims are expected to hold them to maturity, but typically banks stand ready to redeem them before maturity, imposing a penalty in the form of a loss of interest, or to make loans to the holders. The business type of time deposit is issued in denominations of at least $100,000, and some may have dollar amounts in the millions. Aside from their larger denominations, most business-type deposits are similar to consumer-type time deposits. However, a major event in commercial banking since the early 1960s has been the rapid development of the large-denomination negotiable certificate of deposit. These are popularly known as *negotiable CDs*. They have fixed denominations, fixed maturity dates, and fixed rates of interest, and they are not payable by the issuing bank before their maturity. However, prior to maturity they can be transferred freely from holder to holder by means of endorsement. If they are made out "to bearer," they do not even require endorsement. A group of dealers and brokers stand ready to facilitate the marketability of these instruments. Thus, while the issuing bank need not redeem the CD before its maturity, any holder can exchange it for money at any time in the secondary market.

The negotiable CD has assumed an important role in short-term money markets. It appeals to many types of investors, including nonfinancial business corporations, as a prime, liquid, earning asset. And for many banks, especially larger banks, it is an important source of funds.

In issuing savings and time-deposit claims, a bank encounters widely differing types and degrees of competition in different segments of the market. For example, some individuals and households have only small amounts of funds, are not sophisticated in their knowledge and appraisal of financial alternatives, and would find it costly and inconvenient to explore distant opportunities. These units may be willing to hold passbook savings accounts even at relatively low yields. At the other extreme are large corporations with millions of dollars of investible funds and expert money managers who are fully aware of all financial alternatives. These corporations are likely to hold time-deposit claims against banks only if their yields are fully competitive with other alternatives. In view of such differences, it is hardly surprising that banks practice price discrimination and attach different yields to claims tailored to appeal to different classes of investors. In this regard, as we shall see, the banks have been aided and abetted by the structure of interest rate ceilings on time and savings deposits imposed by the monetary authorities.

Although deposit liabilities constitute the great bulk of bank debt, banks do create some other types of liabilities. Indeed, in recent years this has been an increasingly important source of bank funds. Some of these nondeposit liabilities are short term in nature, being designed to meet temporary liquidity needs. Others are aimed at longer-term needs. For example, some banks have issued promissory notes or bonds that run for several years. And bank holding companies, or nonbank subsidiaries of these holding companies, have issued commercial paper and transferred the proceeds to subsidiary banks. We shall later discuss the various forms of nondeposit liabilities in more detail.

**Bank Assets**

In its other role as a participant in financial markets, a bank acts as a seller of funds or a purchaser of financial claims against others. In this role it faces various types and degrees of competition from other lenders — such as other commercial banks, other types of financial intermediaries, and individual lenders and purchasers of direct securities. The asset policies of banks will be discussed later in more detail. At this time it is sufficient to indicate that a bank faces difficult policy decisions in determining the composition of its diversified portfolio — how much of its total assets should be allocated to holdings of cash, how much to loan to its various customers, and how much to each of the many other types of earning assets available in financial markets.

**Interrelations Between Asset and Liability Policies**

Although bank asset policies and bank liability policies were separated for expositional purposes, these two sets of policies are interdependent in various ways. For example, the yields that a bank can profitably pay on its deposit liabilities depend in part on the yields realized on its assets, which is influenced by the composition of its portfolio. Disaster may follow if assets and liabilities are seriously mismatched — if, for example, a bank issues liabilities that are denominated in fixed amounts of dollars and acquires assets, such as common stocks, that have values that fluctuate widely. Various other examples could be mentioned. However, at this point we are especially interested in the fact that the terms on which a bank supplies one type of service affects demands for its other types of services. We have all seen bank advertisements extolling the advantages of "one-stop, full-service banking," by which a bank may proclaim, "This bank stands ready to meet all your financial needs; it will supply all your reasonable requests for consumer, housing, and business credit; it provides the best of convenient and cheap checking services; and its savings department offers a wide choice of deposits, all safe and liquid and carrying good returns." Such a bank can offer any one of its services on favorable terms as a means of stimulating demand for its other services. We shall stress a bank's use of its lending policies to customers as a means of attracting deposits.

**International Aspects of Banking**

Although we shall postpone a detailed discussion of the international aspects of commercial banking until Part VI, a brief comment at this juncture may help to keep things in perspective. Up to now we have not distinguished between those assets and liabilities that are held in domestic offices of United States commercial banks and those that are held in foreign branches of those banks. Not too long ago this distinction would have been of minimal importance. However, the marked growth of business in foreign branches of U.S. banks has been an important development in commercial banking during the 1970s. In 1970, there were 61 U.S. banks with foreign offices, and taken as a group, those offices accounted for less than $50 billion in assets. By the end of 1978, 155 banks had foreign offices, and those offices held $260 billion of assets. Taking those banks as a group, this amounted to roughly 30 percent of total assets. Looked at from another perspective, in 1978 U.S. banks with foreign offices earned $2.4 billion before taxes from their international business, out of total pretax income of $7.3 billion.[1] Clearly, then, an increasingly important part of U.S. bank business is conducted abroad. Except in critical cases, however, in the remainder of the chapter we shall make no particular distinction between domestically and foreign-held assets and liabilities. We shall, as already noted, return to this issue in subsequent chapters.

**Bank Earnings, Safety, and Liquidity**

Banks are, of course, profit-seeking institutions. If they operated in a world of perfect certainty, their motive would probably be to maximize their long-run profits. However, as we have already seen, neither a bank nor any other financial intermediary operates under such conditions. It faces uncertainties, and therefore risks, of many kinds—uncertainties as to its future volume and costs of funds and uncertainties as to the future incomes and prices on the various types of earning assets that it may acquire. A bank does not, therefore, consider earnings alone; instead, it seeks some optimum combination of earnings, liquidity, and safety. And to secure more of one the bank must often sacrifice some of the others. For example, to get higher earnings it may have to incur more risk and illiquidity, and to get more safety and liquidity it may have to sacrifice some earnings.

**Safety of Assets**

As noted earlier, the risk that a debt obligation will decline in value takes two forms:

1   The market risk—the risk that the price will decline because of a rise in market rates of interest. On some occasions this risk is estimated to be very small because interest rates are expected to remain stable or even to fall, which would create capital gains.
2   The default risk—the risk that the debtor will not meet promptly and fully the promise to pay interest and to repay principal.

---

[1] For all insured banks, total pretax income in 1978 amounted to $15.1 billion. Thus, the 155 banks with foreign offices accounted for nearly half of total pretax income. Evidently then, banks with foreign offices are among the largest institutions. For details on this see B. N. Oppers, "Insured Commercial Bank Income in 1978," *Federal Reserve Bulletin*, September 1979, pp. 692–706.

Bankers face difficult problems in determining the types and amounts of risk to assume. If they go to the extreme of purchasing and holding only the safest assets, their earnings are likely to be very low. Moreover, they may fail to meet customers' reasonable demands for loans, may acquire the reputation of being an undependable and inadequate source of credit, and may lose customers and their deposits to other banks. On the other hand, there are real dangers in assuming "too much" risk. For one thing, the bank may suffer such large losses on risky assets that its net return will be less than that on safer assets. Moreover, large losses, or even the prospect of such losses, can endanger the future of the bank.

Commercial banks are especially limited in their ability to assume risk because of the very high ratio of their fixed-dollar liabilities to their total assets. As noted earlier, the net worth of banks is equal to only about 8 percent of their total assets. The other 92 percent of claims are liabilities, mostly deposits, that are fixed in terms of dollars. Thus, if the assets of a bank with these ratios depreciated by more than 8 percent, the bank would be insolvent; the value of its assets would be less than its liabilities to depositors and others. The bank might have to be closed. But the bank may face serious consequences long before its assets depreciate enough to wipe out its net worth and make it insolvent. As its net worth shrinks, depositors may become distrustful, and the bank may face problems in attracting deposits and even in retaining existing deposits. This has obvious deleterious effects on the bank's lending power.

A bank can attempt to maintain an adequate degree of solvency in two different ways: (1) by increasing its net worth and (2) by maintaining the safety of its assets. One way to increase net worth is to retain profits. This method has obvious limitations. If profits are low, net worth can be built up only slowly even if the bank pays no dividends to shareholders. And to the extent that a bank reduces dividends in order to retain earnings, it may depress the market price of its outstanding shares. The bank may also increase its net worth by selling additional stock. As it does this, it may feel justified in acquiring a larger proportion of risky assets, thereby increasing its earnings. But there is a limit to the extent that this can be done profitably. Experience indicates that banks can achieve a profit rate on net worth comparable to profit rates in other industries only if they have a large *leverage factor*, that is, only if total earning assets are a large multiple of net worth. At some stage, therefore, a bank finds it unprofitable to expand further its net worth relative to its assets. It must therefore limit the amount of risk that it assumes.

Thus, in determining portfolio composition bankers face difficult problems in balancing safety against earnings. They must estimate the amounts of risks attached to the various types of available assets, compare estimated risk differentials against interest differentials, consider both long-run and short-run consequences, and strike a balance. If they veer too far toward safety, they may face not only inadequate profits in the short run but also charges that aversion to risk prevents them from serving adequately the needs of customers and the economy. But if they veer too far in the direction of risk bearing they may face disaster or at least endanger their ability to attract or even to retain deposits. They must also consider the need for liquidity, a problem to which we now turn.

**Bank Liquidity**

By the *liquidity* of a bank is meant its capacity to meet promptly demands that it pay its obligations. As noted earlier, commercial banks must pay more attention to liquidity than must many other types of financial institutions, such as life insurance companies. This results from the very high ratio of their debt liabilities. A large part of the gross out-payments by a bank is met from current gross receipts of funds in the normal course of business. We have already noted that deposit withdrawals are expected to be offset, at least in large part, by inflows of new deposits. A bank also receives inflows of funds as income on its assets, as repayment of principal on maturing assets, and as weekly or monthly repayments on installment loans. In many cases such gross inflows are at least sufficient to meet gross payments by a bank. Nevertheless, each bank must be prepared to make net payments of two types: (1) payments to meet net withdrawals of currency into circulation, and (2) payments to cover adverse clearing balances with other banks. Some of these are of such regular seasonal or other cyclical nature that they can be predicted with fair accuracy and prepared against. Others are more erratic and less predictable. Inability to meet these drains promptly means failure or at least an impairment of confidence in the bank.

A bank could, of course, elect to "play it safe" and remain completely liquid by holding cash equal to all its liabilities. But the effects on its income would be disastrous. At the other extreme, the bank could select assets solely with an eye to income, ignoring liquidity. This, too, can lead to disaster, perhaps to sudden death rather than slow starvation. Thus, in determining its portfolio composition a bank must balance its desire for income against its desire for liquidity. And it usually tries to buy any given amount of liquidity at the lowest possible cost in terms of sacrifice of net earnings. An individual bank has two principal sources of liquidity: borrowings from others and sales out of its asset-holdings.

How much liquidity a bank will seek in its asset-holdings depends in part on the availability and cost of borrowings. If a bank is assured that it can borrow large amounts at any time without onus and at a low interest cost relative to yields on its assets, it may rely largely on this source for liquidity and hold few liquid assets. But if the availability of borrowings is uncertain or if borrowing carries an onus or if borrowing costs are high relative to yields on the bank's assets, the bank will seek more liquidity on its asset portfolio. We shall explore these two alternative sources more fully when we examine in detail the assets and liabilities of commercial banks.

## A DETAILED COMMERCIAL BANK BALANCE SHEET

In the preceding chapter we encountered a highly consolidated balance sheet for the commercial banking system. Such a balance sheet abstracts from many of the interesting and important features of the determination of commercial bank assets and liabilities. A considerably more detailed balance sheet, suitable for our current purposes, is given in Table 7-1. A glance at this table immediately reveals the extent to which such all-inclusive categories as "loans" or "securities" tend to aggregate over rather diverse components. For example, there are nine different types of loans listed in Table 7-1, and even this degree of detail still involves considerable elements of aggregation.[2]

While the table provides us with a detailed snapshot of the commercial banking *system,* it necessarily conceals differences among the balance sheets of *individual* commercial banks. That such differences exist should hardly be surprising in view of the diversity of banks that we have previously discussed. To examine these differences, however, would take us too far afield. Rather, we shall treat Table 7-1 as though it were the balance sheet of an "average" commercial bank. Our objectives in doing so will be to elucidate the nature of the various assets and liabilities held by banks and, more important, to gain an understanding of the economic reasons that lead to a particular configuration of assets and liabilities. We begin our discussions with the liability side of the balance sheet.

## A SURVEY OF BANK LIABILITIES

As we learned earlier, the bulk of the claims against commercial banks is in the form of deposit liabilities. As we shall see, however, nondeposit liabilities have become an increasingly important source of bank funds.

### Deposit Liabilities

In 1978 deposit liabilities accounted for 80 percent of total assets (or, equivalently, total liabilities plus capital accounts). As of the same date, demand deposits amounted to 38 percent of total deposits while the remaining 62 percent was held in the form of time and savings deposits.

*Demand Deposits*

A glance at Table 7-1 reveals that there are many different types of holders of demand balances at a given commercial bank. These include

---

[2] Another sort of aggregation involved in Table 7-1 stems from the fact that domestic and foreign operations of U.S. banks are consolidated.

individuals; businesses; various governments, both foreign and domestic; and other commercial banks. This latter category of interbank deposits primarily reflects correspondent balances and the fact that, for state banks, such deposits often satisfy reserve requirements.[3]

Banks are currently prohibited from paying interest on demand balances. Not surprisingly, as interest rates on alternative claims have risen over the years, the public has been less willing to hold demand deposits.

---

[3] Interbank deposits were excluded from the consolidated bank balance sheet presented in Table 6–1. This, in part, explains why the figure for total assets in Table 7–1 is larger than the corresponding figure in Table 6–1. However, also see footnote 6.

---

**TABLE 7–1**

*Commercial bank balance sheet, September 30, 1978 in billions of dollars)*

| ASSETS | | LIABILITIES AND CAPITAL ACCOUNT | |
|---|---|---|---|
| **Cash balances** | | **Demand deposits** | |
| Vault cash | 12.1 | Individuals, partnerships, and | |
| Deposits with Federal Reserve | 28.0 | corporations (IPC) | 279.7 |
| Balances with banks | 49.1 | U.S. government | 7.9 |
| Items in process of collection | 69.2 | State and local governments | 17.1 |
| | | Foreign governments and banks | 9.2 |
| | | Domestic banks | 39.6 |
| | | Other | 15.5 |
| Total cash | 158.4 | Total demand deposits | 369.0 |
| **Loans** | | **Time and savings deposits** | |
| Commercial and industrial | 213.1 | Savings deposits | 223.3 |
| Agricultural | 28.1 | Other IPC | 292.1 |
| Real estate | 203.4 | State and local governments | 59.1 |
| Consumer credit | 161.6 | Foreign governments and banks | 8.1 |
| To banks | 10.7 | Domestic banks | 8.0 |
| To other financial institutions | 26.4 | Other | 1.3 |
| Federal funds sold and securities resale agreements | 41.2 | | |
| For purchasing and carrying securities | 15.3 | | |
| Other loans | 17.4 | | |
| Total loans | 717.2 | Total time and savings | 591.9 |
| **Securities** | | | |
| U.S. Treasury | 95.1 | Federal funds purchased and | |
| Other U.S. government agencies | 40.1 | securities sold under repurchase | |
| State and local government | 121.3 | agreements | 92.0 |
| Other securities | 5.7 | Other borrowed funds | 8.7 |
| | | Miscellaneous liabilities | 45.6 |
| | | Capital accounts | 91.3 |
| | | **Total liabilities and capital accounts** | |
| Total securities | 262.2 | | 1,198.5 |
| **Other assets** | 60.7 | | |
| **Total assets** | 1,198.5 | | |

*Source: Federal Reserve Bulletin,* December 1979, pp. A18–A19.

Banks have responded to this by reducing service charges, at least relative to the actual costs of servicing checking accounts, and often in absolute terms as well. This, however, has not been enough to stem the tide. Thus, the fraction of total bank funds raised by demand deposits has declined steadily and markedly in the post-World War II period. For example, from Table 7–2, which gives the percentage of total assets accounted for by various liability categories, we see that demand deposits fell from about 70 percent of total assets in 1947 to about 31 percent in 1978.

*Time and Savings Deposits*

The decline in the relative importance of demand deposits has been offset, to a considerable extent, by the growth in time and savings deposits. In the aggregate such deposits went from 23 percent of total assets in 1947 to nearly 50 percent in 1978 (see Table 7–2). As we have already noted, such deposits come in a variety of forms ranging from passbook savings deposits to negotiable certificates of deposit. While savings deposits have been a relatively stable percentage of total bank assets, time deposits have expanded markedly. Of particular importance in this regard has been the growth in the volume of negotiable CDs. These claims, which only came into existence in 1961, amounted to over $90 billion in 1978.

Unlike the case with demand deposits, banks, of course, pay interest on time and savings deposits. Indeed, the increase in these rates over time has been a significant factor in explaining the growth of such deposits. The rates paid on time and savings deposits vary by type of deposit, with savings deposits earning the lowest yield. Rates on time deposits proper generally increase with maturity (recall the notion of an ascending yield curve discussed earlier), although rates paid on short-term CDs may well exceed those paid on long-term CDs. These various points are illustrated in Table 7–3, which gives average interest rates paid on different types of deposits on January 31, 1979. In interpreting these data it

| TABLE 7–2 | | 1947 | 1960 | 1978 |
|---|---|---|---|---|
| *Various bank liabilities as a percentage of total bank assets: selected dates* | Demand deposits | 69.8 | 60.7 | 30.7 |
| | Savings deposits | 17.7 | 21.6 | 18.6 |
| | Time deposits | 5.2 | 6.9 | 30.8 |
| | Borrowed funds | 0.0 | 0.0 | 8.4 |
| | Other liabilities | 0.8 | 2.6 | 3.8 |
| | Capital accounts | 6.5 | 8.2 | 7.6 |
| | Total | 100.0 | 100.0 | 100.0 |

Source: *Federal Reserve Bulletin* and FDIC Annual Reports, various issues.

should be remembered that interest rates paid on time and savings deposits are subject to ceilings under Regulation Q of the Federal Reserve. Two recent modifications of this regulation are worthy of note. First, as shown in Table 7–3, the yield on six-month money market certificates substantially exceeds yields on comparable time deposits (although not the yield on negotiable CDs). This instrument, which was first permitted in mid-1978, has a ceiling yield that is tied to the yield on six-month Treasury securities. While this represents a considerable softening of the impact of Regulation Q, money market certificates have a minimum denomination of $10,000 and hence do not fully address the problem of the "small saver." This issue was more directly confronted in legislation enacted in early 1980 that provided for a gradual phase out of interest ceilings over a six-year period. We shall examine more fully the consequences of interest rate ceilings, including these recent changes, as we proceed.

**Nondeposit Funds**

Table 7–2 shows that in 1978 nondeposit funds (including capital accounts) amounted to 20 percent of total bank assets. Also evident from this table is the marked expansion that has taken place in recent years in the categories of "borrowed funds" and "other liabilities." In sum, these two sources of funds grew from less than 1 percent of total assets in 1947 to over 12 percent in 1978. In dollar terms the increase was from $1 billion to $146 billion. Clearly, nondeposit liabilities have become a major source of bank funds. The most important items included in the nondeposit category are the following:

*Borrowings from the Federal Reserve*

A Federal Reserve bank rarely refuses to lend to a member bank having deficient reserves, but it does not conceal the fact that this source should be used sparingly. It emphasizes that such borrowing is a privi-

---

**TABLE 7–3**

*erage interest rates
id on time and sav-
zs deposits, January
31, 1979*

| | |
|---|---|
| Savings deposits | 4.94 |
| Time deposits (under $100,000) maturing in | |
| 30–90 days | 4.97 |
| 90–180 days | 5.48 |
| 180 days–1 year | 5.48 |
| 1–2$\frac{1}{2}$ years | 5.99 |
| 2$\frac{1}{2}$–4 years | 6.49 |
| 4–6 years | 7.22 |
| 6–8 years | 7.48 |
| over 8 years | 7.66 |
| Money market certificates (6 months) | 9.44 |
| Negotiable certificate of deposit (3 months) | 10.32 |

*Source: Federal Reserve Bulletin,* May 1979, p. 392.

lege and not a right, reminds banks of the tradition against continuous borrowing, uses moral suasion to discourage "excessive" borrowing and to encourage repayment, and sometimes raises its discount rate to make borrowing more expensive. In recent years, however, there has been a movement in the direction of making such funds available with fewer strings attached, especially for explicitly seasonal needs.

The actual volume of borrowing from the Federal Reserve may vary considerably in a relatively short period of time. For example, such borrowings amounted to $3.4 billion in August 1974, $700 million in December 1974, and only $60 million in May 1975. It should be noted that when a bank borrows from the Federal Reserve it increases its reserves without decreasing the reserves of any other bank. This is not necessarily true of the other types of borrowing described next; in many of these cases the reserves that are borrowed by one bank come out of the reserves of other banks.

### Borrowing Federal Funds

The federal funds market operates through brokers and dealers, including a few very large banks that operate federal funds departments. As originally constituted, the federal funds market was a vehicle for buying and selling, or borrowing and lending, deposits at the Federal Reserve banks. In effect, banks with reserves in excess of legal requirements lend them to other banks. The bulk of these transactions are one-day loans, but they can be renewed if both borrower and lender agree.

Over the years the Federal Reserve has broadened the kinds of transactions that are classified as federal funds transactions. As federal funds transactions are subject neither to basic reserve requirements nor to interest rate ceilings, banks obviously prefer a liberal interpretation of what constitute federal funds. One step in this direction was taken in 1964, when member banks were permitted to borrow deposits, and not just reserves, of any commercial bank—either member or nonmember. Thus, for example, a bank holding a demand deposit with Chemical Bank could lend this deposit to Chemical or, indeed, to another member bank. Permitting member banks to borrow from nonmember banks allowed many smaller banks to lend their excess funds via the federal funds market. A second expansion of the market occurred in 1970, when the Federal Reserve broadened the eligible lenders to include the following: mutual savings banks, savings and loan associations, branches and agencies of foreign banks, securities dealers, and agencies of the federal government. As a consequence of these liberalizations, the volume of borrowing in the federal funds market has risen steadily, from a daily average of $1.5 billion in 1960 to over $60 billion in recent years.

The rate on loans made in the federal funds market has varied markedly over time. This is vividly shown in Figure 7–1. From a low point of about 3 percent in early 1972, the federal funds rate shot up to 13 percent in July 1974 and then fell to below 6 percent by May 1975. Similar gyrations occurred in 1979, when the rate jumped from 11 percent in early September to over 15½ percent in early November and then fell to 12½ percent in early December. Since borrowing from the Federal Reserve and borrowing in the federal funds market are close substitutes for each other, we would expect the rates on these two sources of funds to exhibit similar patterns. This is generally borne out in Figure 7–1, but evidently, in periods of credit restriction some banks are willing to pay a premium to avoid facing Federal Reserve lending officers.

### Borrowing Under Repurchase Agreements (RPs)

A *repurchase agreement* is an arrangement under which a bank sells some asset, typically a Treasury security, to a purchaser with an agreement to repurchase it at some stipulated time at a stipulated price. The bank pays interest in the form of the difference between the repurchase and sale prices.

The RP market is closely related to the federal funds market. The interest rate on RPs typically approximates the federal funds rate but frequently is slightly lower because RPs are collateralized borrowings while federal funds are not. One important difference between the two markets is that, while any person, firm, or government entity may deal in RPs, as we have seen, participation in the federal funds market is limited to certain institutions such as commercial banks, mutual savings banks, savings and loan associations, and federal agencies. Those institutions that are eligible to participate in the federal funds market can, of course, also deal in RPs. In practice, they deal in both markets and are joined in the RP market by state and local governments and business firms, among others. Like the federal funds market, the RP market grew dramatically

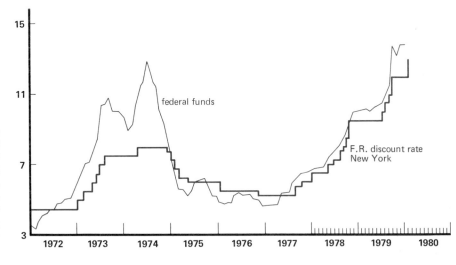

Federal funds interest rate and Federal Reserve discount rate

Source: *Federal Reserve Chart Book*, Washington, D.C., February 1980.

**FIGURE 7–1**

in the 1970s. In particular, in 1970 commercial banks borrowed in the RP market an average of $3–4 billion from the nonbank public, while at the end of 1979 this figure had topped $45 billion. Like the federal funds market, the RP market has permitted member banks to offer a nondeposit liability that bears explicit interest and is exempt from interest rate regulations and reserve requirements. Viewed in this light, it is hardly surprising that this has proved to be such a popular market for borrowers and lenders alike.[4]

### Borrowing Eurodollar Deposits

Eurodollar deposits are dollar-denominated deposit claims against banks domiciled outside the United States. The prefix *Euro* is misleading, since not all the banks issuing these claims are located in Europe. Eurodollar deposits are issued by foreign banks generally in exchange for deposit claims against banks in the United States. For example, if an American or a foreigner transfers a deposit in a U.S. bank to a foreign bank and keeps the new deposit in dollars, Eurodollars are created.

Foreign banks that have issued Eurodollar claims are naturally anxious to lend these balances, and at various times American commercial banks have proved to be willing customers. Commercial banks in the United States typically borrow Eurodollar funds through their foreign branches, receiving in return deposit claims against banks in the United States.[5] Since foreign branches are not subject to interest rate ceilings, this has been a particularly important source of funds (albeit often quite expensive) during periods of domestic credit stringency. For example, they were quite important during the credit crunch of 1969. After that date, owing to developments to be discussed shortly, they declined in importance. Beginning in 1979, however. Eurodollar borrowings once again emerged as an important source of bank funds (see Figure 7–3).

### Borrowing via Promissory Notes and Commercial Paper

Banks began issuing promissory notes in about 1966. A similar and roughly coincident development was the use of commercial paper to raise funds. Such paper was typically issued by a one-bank holding company that passed the funds on to its bank subsidiary by purchasing some of the bank's loans. From the perspective of the individual investor, both commercial paper and promissory notes are quite similar to CDs in that all three types of claims are slightly different forms of unsecured bank debt.

---

[4] At least for large depositors, RPs provide a way of getting around the prohibition on paying interest on demand deposits. The consequences of this fact and of Federal Reserve reaction to these developments are taken up later in this chapter and again in Chapter 11.

[5] The details of this type of transaction are spelled out in Chapter 23.

Our survey of bank liabilities has made clear that in recent years banks did considerably more than passively accept deposits as their sole source of funds. Rather, they both aggressively sold CDs and showed considerable ingenuity in creating marketable nondeposit liabilities. These developments have a number of important implications for bank liquidity practices. We shall return to this issue after we consider the asset side of the balance sheet.

**A SURVEY BANK ASSETS**

Having examined the sources of bank funds, we now turn to the other side of the balance sheet and examine the types and proportions of assets acquired and held by banks. Reference back to Table 7–1 provides us with the composition of total commercial bank assets in 1978. The corresponding proportions or percentage distribution of bank assets are given in Table 7–4. So that we may trace the changing composition of bank assets over time, Table 7–4 provides, in addition to the data for 1978, a snapshot of asset proportions for 1947 and 1960.

A glance at Table 7–1 reveals that several types of assets are conspicuous for their absence or scarcity. Outstanding in this respect are physical assets in the form of land, buildings, and equipment. Few banks own many more assets of this type than are needed for banking purposes. Even smaller are bank holdings of common stock; and most of these are in the form of stock in the Federal Reserve banks, which member banks are required to hold. The most important assets actually held are cash, loans, and securities.

**Cash Assets**

As Table 7–1 shows, there are four types of assets that qualify as "cash"—vault cash, deposits at the Federal Reserve, balances at other banks, and cash items in the process of collection. Vault cash simply refers to the volume of currency and coin held in the vaults of commer-

**TABLE 7–4**

*various bank assets as percentage of total bank assets: selected dates*

| Asset | 1947 | 1960 | 1978 |
|---|---|---|---|
| Cash balances | 24.1 | 20.3 | 13.2 |
| Commercial and industrial loans | 11.7 | 16.7 | 17.8 |
| Real estate loans | 6.0 | 11.1 | 17.0 |
| Consumer loans | 3.7 | 10.2 | 13.5 |
| Other loans | 3.1 | 7.5 | 11.6 |
| U.S. government securities | 44.5 | 23.7 | 7.9 |
| State and local securities | 3.4 | 6.8 | 10.1 |
| Other securities | 2.4 | 1.3 | 3.8 |
| Other assets | 1.0 | 2.3 | 5.1 |
| Total | 100.0 | 100.0 | 100.0 |

*Source: Federal Reserve Bulletin, various issues.*

cial banks. It is needed for transactions purposes but also satisfies, along with deposits at the Federal Reserve, the legal-reserve requirement for member banks. Balances at other banks are generally held as part of the system of correspondent banking relationships described earlier, but they also may be used to satisfy the reserve requirement for many non-member banks. The final category, cash items in the process of collection, is a somewhat esoteric accounting device. Basically, it arises because an economic unit that receives a check may have its account credited before the account of the unit that issued the check is debited. This double counting artificially inflates the volume of demand deposits.[6] Cash items in the process of collection measures the extent of this and is simply a way of making the books balance.

As is clear from Table 7–4, cash assets have declined from about 24 percent of bank assets in 1947 to about 13 percent in 1978. To a large extent this reflects the behavior of required reserves as the mix of deposits shifted more toward time deposits. In particular, the lower required ratio for time deposits meant that banks were permitted to hold a smaller proportion of total assets in the form of required reserves. Banks, of course, were quite happy with this development, since cash assets add nothing, at least explicitly, to bank earnings. Thus, banks were able to devote more of their resources to earning assets, to which we now turn.

**Commercial and Industrial Loans**

Let us start with the type of loan that gave commercial banking its name. The *commercial loan* theory of banking, which has been highly influential but never wholly accepted by either bankers or economists, holds that banks should confine themselves exclusively to this type of credit. They should make only short-term, self-liquidating loans based on the production, distribution, or sale of goods and services. The basic idea is that a bank should lend only on the basis of a specific transaction or process that is short-term in nature and at its termination will provide the borrower with funds that can be used to pay off the loan. For example, it is held that a merchant may properly borrow to buy an inventory of merchandise that can be sold in a few months for enough money to retire the loan. Or a manufacturer may borrow to buy raw materials and components and to meet payrolls in order to turn out a product that can soon be sold and the proceeds used to pay off the loan. Or a farmer may properly borrow to finance the planting, tending, and marketing of a crop that will be sold in a few months. On the negative side, the commercial loan theorists contend that banks should not make long-term loans and should not lend on the basis of a project or process that will bring in proceeds only over a long period. For example, a bank should not lend

---

[6] This is another reason why the balance sheets in Tables 6–1 and 7–1 show different totals. Also see footnote 3.

money to a merchant to buy a store, to a manufacturer to buy plant and durable equipment, or to a farmer to buy land. Virtually all economists now reject the commercial loan theory, and few bankers are seriously guided by it.

Some of the loans included in "Commercial and industrial" in Table 7–1 conform to the commercial loan theory, but many do not. For one thing, a sizable percentage are not short term (their original maturity exceeded one year) but are *term loans* that may run for three to five years or even longer. Perhaps more important, many of these loans, short-term as well as term loans, are not based on a specific transaction or process. Rather, they are based on the general credit rating of the borrower as reflected by past and prospective income and expenses; the ratio of assets to total liabilities; and the ratio of short-term assets to short-term liabilities. A borrower whose rating in these respects is satisfactory may get a short-term or term loan from a bank without specifying any particular project, mix the proceeds with his other funds, and use the funds as he or she sees fit, including perhaps the purchase of real estate or durable equipment.

The term *commercial banks* is appropriate in the sense that these institutions are by far the largest source of short-term, and even of term, commercial and industrial loans. In many areas and for many business firms, there is no other source of short-term loans that can compare in convenience, adequacy, and cheapness. But it remains true that these loans represent only a fraction of total commercial bank credit. This fraction, however, has grown over time. In recent years commercial and industrial loans have accounted for about 20 percent of total bank assets, or nearly twice the fraction they represented in the early post-World War II period.

**Other Loans**

Aside from business loans, the most important types of loans made by banks are for consumer credit, real estate, and securities transactions.

*Consumer Loans*

Commercial banks constitute one of the largest sources of installment consumer credit, providing nearly 50 percent of all such funds. Banks extend much of this credit directly to consumers. From Table 7–4 we see that this has been an increasingly important part of bank assets. However, banks also provide such credit indirectly through sales finance companies, consumer finance companies, and others who lend to consumers. Banks do this by lending directly to these institutions and by purchasing in the open market the short-term or longer-term promissory notes that these institutions issue to get funds.

A smaller but rapidly growing amount of consumer credit is extended through bank credit cards and arangements given such names as "instant credit" or "check credit." These credit systems became economically feasible as computers became available to handle the large amounts of record keeping involved. Some banks issue their own individual credit cards, but the trend is toward cards that are also issued by many other banks and are acceptable over wide geographic areas. Two of the most widely used are Visa and Mastercard. A bank customer who establishes creditworthiness receives, in effect, a line of credit that can be used to purchase goods and services from merchants who have joined the plan or to get cash advances from any bank that is a member of the plan. Instant credit or check credit is, in effect, an arrangement for overdrafts. After establishing a line of credit at his bank, the customer can get credit automatically by writing checks in excess of his or her deposit balance. Such methods of extending consumer credit will probably become increasingly important in the future.

### Real Estate Loans

Loans for real estate have also been a growing component of bank assets, amounting to about 17 percent of total assets in recent years. Some of the loans on real estate are short-term construction loans, which are paid off when a building is finished and sold. But most of them are long-term mortgages on farms, on residential properties, and less often on commercial and industrial properties. Banks feel justified in holding these long-term mortgages primarily because of their time and savings deposits.

### Security Loans

Loans on securities are for various purposes, but have the common characteristic that securities are used as collateral. Some are a type of business loan to enable security dealers to carry inventories. For example, dealers in U.S. government securities have to carry large inventories relative to their net worth and borrow heavily for this purpose, usually on a very short-term basis. Banks are an important source of such credit and also lend to dealers who hold inventories of other types of securities. Loans to brokers are primarily for the account of the brokers' customers who buy securities *on margin*. In effect, the broker gets a loan on the basis of the customer's securities and uses the proceeds to pay the sellers of the securities. Individuals and others sometimes borrow directly from banks on the basis of securities and clearly use the proceeds for purchasing or carrying securities. But the proceeds from loans backed by securities are often used for other purposes, securities being used as collateral simply because the lending bank finds them acceptable. For example, you might pledge as collateral some shares of General Motors and use the proceeds to buy a car, finance a marriage, or buy business inventory. In many cases there is no relation between the nature of the collateral and the use of loan proceeds. This is well expressed in the observation, "I once knew a fellow who pawned his overcoat to buy beer."

We need not discuss the other types of bank loans to establish the fact that commercial banks lend to many types of borrowers, for widely varying lengths of time, on many bases, and for a wide variety of stated purposes.

**U.S. Government Obligations**

For several years after World War II, these securities made up 40 percent or more of total commercial bank assets. More recently they have declined in absolute amount and even more as a percentage of total assets as banks have increased their holdings of private debt. Indeed, in 1978 they accounted for merely 8 percent of total bank assets. Historically, such obligations played an important role as bearers of safety and liquidity. They still serve this function, but the extent of this is limited by the relatively small volume of such securities held by the banks.

Owing both to the nature of the securities themselves and to the efficiency and cheapness of the market mechanism, these securities, and especially Treasury bills and other short-term issues, have been a highly important instrument for adjusting cash, liquidity, and portfolio positions. We shall later see how commercial banks buy these securities when they have excess reserves or wish to shift funds from other uses, and how they sell these securities to repair reserve deficiencies or to get funds for other purposes. Other financial institutions and nonfinancial holders act in comparable ways.

**Other Securities**

Among the other types of securities held by commercial banks, obligations of the states and their subdivisions are by far the largest. Some of these are acquired directly from their issuers, others in the open market. Their special attraction to banks is the exemption of their income from the federal income tax.

In summary, banks hold a wide variety of earning assets. Far from restricting themselves to short-term business loans, banks hold debt claims of widely varying maturities against other financial institutions, governments at all levels, consumers, and others. Thus, they are involved in many branches of the markets for savings and financial claims and can bring about widespread effects as they expand or contract their credit.

Yet we must not overstate the point. We do find differences when we compare bank portfolios with those of other important financial institutions. Perhaps most obvious, they are on balance in shorter maturities. And they tend to be more liquid and less risky. Certainly commercial banks contrast sharply with mutual savings banks (which hold largely long-term mortgages and bonds), with mutual investment companies (which are mostly in common stocks), and with life insurance companies (which are largely in mortgages, long-term bonds, and some real estate and common stock).

**OPEN-MARKET AND CUSTOMER RELATIONSHIPS**

As a further step in explaining the behavior of bank portfolios, it will be useful to distinguish between customer loans and earning assets acquired and sold in the open market. Like most classifications, this one presents troublesome borderline cases, but it does highlight some motivations and market differences that strongly influence a banker's decisions relative to his portfolio.

The very term *customer* suggests a relationship that is usually of a continuing nature and that at least one of the parties involved would be reluctant to break. *Open market* suggests a quite different sort of relationship: impersonal, not necessarily continuing, and "open to all comers."

**Open-Market Assets**

The clearest examples of open-market relationships are those in which the bank that buys or sells a debt claim does not deal directly with the ultimate debtor. Thus, a bank may buy or sell, through a broker or dealer, U.S. government securities, state and municipal obligations, acceptances, open-market commercial paper, brokers' loans, and so on. In many cases the banker knows the debtor only by reputation and the debtor does not know who holds the claims.

Open-market relationships usually have the following characteristics:

1   The bank decides whether to buy or sell a particular debt claim solely on the basis of the asset's attractiveness relative to other available open-market assets, and is not influenced by considerations concerning other possible relations with the debtor. For example, it does not assume that by purchasing a particular debt claim, it will attract deposits from the debtor.

2   The bank is not impelled to buy or is not constrained from selling a particular debt claim by any feeling of "loyalty" or "responsibility" to the debtor.

3   The individual bank has no significant monopoly power in the open market as a whole, or even in the market for the particular type of debt claim. From the individual banker's point of view, conditions in the open market approach the "purely competitive." Each bank controls only such a small part of the total demand that its own actions in buying or selling an open-market asset is assumed to have no significant effect on the price of the asset. Bankers assume that they can buy or sell as much of the asset as they wish at the going price.

This is not to say that conditions in the open market conform completely to those required for pure competition. But they come much closer than do conditions in customer-loan markets.

**Customer Loans**

Relations between a bank and its borrowing customers are quite different in several respects. For one thing, the lender-borrower relationship is intertwined with other bank–customer relationships. The customer usually holds checking deposits, and sometimes time deposits, at the bank, and may also be a customer of the trust or foreign exchange departments. Customers are made fully aware that the amount of loans they can get depends in part on the bank's experience with them as depositors. And bankers are equally aware that the amount of deposits they can attract and retain, and therefore their lending power, depends in part on their reputation for taking care of the legitimate credit needs of customers, even in periods of credit tightness. This is important partly because of the limited degree of price competition among banks in a local market. Banks are legally prohibited from paying interest on demand deposits, and they are reluctant to compete aggressively on rates charged on loans. Where price competition is thus restricted, nonprice competition comes to the fore. This takes many forms: reputation for soundness, convenience of location, decor, courtesy, and so on. Not the least of these is the bank's reliability as a loan source. The advertising slogan, "You have a friend at Chase Manhattan," referred to a loan officer, but it was not meant to be ignored by potential depositors.

As already implied, there are many imperfections of competition in customer-loan markets, and each bank has some degree of monopoly power relative to its customers. The amount of this power depends on many things, including the nature of the customers. No bank may have much monopoly power relative to a huge corporation with a well-known credit rating that has access to banks all over the country and can easily secure funds by selling short- or long-term claims in the open market. In fact, a huge corporation can often dominate even a very large bank by threatening, in effect, "If you do not give us the money we need at a rate of interest as low as that charged your most-favored customer, we shall find it necessary to move our multi-millions of deposits to banks that are more sympathetic." At the other extreme is the small firm that is virtually unknown to any bank other than its own and that could issue securities in the open market only at prohibitive cost. For such reasons, there are wide differences among customers' price elasticities of demand for loans at an individual bank. It is not surprising, therefore, that banks practice price discrimination.

To illustrate our points let us consider the intermediate case of a small or medium-sized business firm that is a good credit risk but whose credit rating is not widely known. Such a firm finds it costly and inconvenient to shift its banking business to distant banks. To hold all its deposits at distant banks is possible but usually costly in time and convenience. To borrow at distant banks is even more costly because of the time and expense incurred by those banks in investigating its creditworthiness. Thus, there are strong forces tending to confine the firm's borrowing to banks in its own area, but as it surveys the local banking structure, the firm finds a situation of banking oligopoly (few sellers) of customer credit. There are only a few local banks, all charging about the same rate of interest, and afraid to compete aggresively for loans by lowering interest rates. Each bank knows that if it lowers its rates its competitors will soon do the same, so it will gain a differential advantage for no more than a short period. If the firm tries to "shop around" at the various banks, it is likely to meet responses of this sort: "Why don't you borrow at your own bank, where you do your other banking business? They know you, understand your credit needs, and are in a position to take care of you. It isn't sound policy to change frequently from one bank to another. Of course, if you decide to switch banks and bring all your banking business here, we can talk about the loan. Our first obligation is to meet the borrowing needs of our own customers." Such imperfections of competition give each bank some degree of monopoly power over its customers. But the attachment of customers to other banks works to the disadvantage of a given bank, for that bank finds it harder to attract the business of those customers.

**Comparison of Open Market and Customer-Loan Market**

Much can be learned from observing differences between conditions in the open market and those in customer-loan markets. For one thing, this comparison helps to explain differences in the behavior of interest rates and yields in the two branches of the market. Like prices in most other highly competitive markets, interest rates in the open market change frequently and quickly in response to changes in supply–demand relations. They often change every day and even several times during a day. In contrast, rates on customer loans change less frequently and more slowly. Like other "administered prices," they often go unchanged for a considerable period, even though supply–demand relationships have clearly changed. In recent years the rate on customer loans has been somewhat more flexible than in the past. This is due to some institutional changes to be described shortly. However, let us first consider the situation as it prevailed through the early 1970s.

The basic rate on bank loans to business customers is called the *prime rate*. This is the rate charged to "prime" customers, usually very large customers with an unquestioned credit rating and a favorable competitive position. Rates to other customers range upward from the prime, those to customers who are almost prime being only a little higher, and so on. Historically, the prime rate was changed only infrequently. The most extreme illustration of this is provided by the fact that when, in December 1947, the prime rate was moved from $1\frac{1}{2}$ percent to $1\frac{3}{4}$ percent (indeed, interest rates were once that low), this was the *first* change in the prime rate since its inception in 1933. Subsequent changes in the prime rate were, by this standard, considerably more frequent. Such changes were typically initiated by a very large bank, usually in New

York City but sometimes in another major financial center, which assumed the role of price leadership.

For the most part, changes in the prime rate occurred only after considerable pressure for change had accumulated. For example, suppose bank lending power had increased markedly relative to the demand for loans. Instead of lowering the prime rate quickly, banks sought to expand their credit in other ways. For one thing, they increased their holdings of open-market paper. In the customer-loan market they became more generous in meeting loan requests, gave some nonprime customers rates closer to the prime rate, and so on. Only after a delay, when downward pressures had already lowered rates in the open market, did they lower the prime rate. Suppose, on the other hand, that the supply of credit had decreased relative to the demand for it and that this was reflected in rate increases in the open market. Here again banks often delayed in raising the prime rate, perhaps partly because each bank feared that if it raised the rate, other banks would not follow suit. For some time they would ration loans to customers, not by raising the interest rate but by scaling down loan requests and otherwise limiting the availability of credit. Only after pressures for rate increases had accumulated and open-market rates had already risen was the prime rate increased.

As noted previously, a number of recent developments have led to more frequent changes in the prime rate. The most important of these was an innovation, introduced in October 1971, called a *floating formula prime rate.* At that time one of the largest banks announced that in the future it would adjust its prime rate weekly, floating it $\frac{1}{2}$ percent above the average yield on prime open-market commercial paper during the preceding week. A number of other banks quickly followed suit and also introduced a floating prime rate, although the specific formula varied from bank to bank. Part of the banks' motivation for a floating prime rate was undoubtedly to try to insulate themselves from the political criticism that often resulted from a change in the prime rate. In this respect the innovation was not really successful. In particular, in 1973 the banks came into direct conflict with the governmental Committee on Interest and Dividends (CID), established as part of the then-prevailing program of economic controls. Under pressure from the CID the banks were forced to suspend the floating prime rate temporarily and to roll back some announced increases in the prime rate. The floating rate was subsequently reintroduced and the CID eventually dismantled. However, at present only a small fraction of banks have explicitly adopted floating rates. Even those that have adopted them tend to use the formula more as a guide rather than as a rigid device. Nevertheless, the legacy of this recent episode will unquestionably be a greater flexibility in the prime rate.

Differences in conditions in the open market and in customer-loan markets also help to explain why, other things equal, a bank is likely to prefer customers' loans over assets acquired in the open market. One reason for this preference is that a given initial amount of excess reserves is likely to enable a bank to lend more to customers than it could lend in the open market. If a bank lends in the open market, the entire amount of the loan is likely to be deposited in other banks, thereby draining off an equal amount of reserves. But if the bank lends to customers, some of the proceeds are likely to be kept on deposit with it, thereby lessening its loss of reserves. Customers may hold some of the deposits voluntarily; the lending bank also has ways of encouraging the customer to be a depositor. For example, it may require what are termed *compensating deposit* balances from its borrowers, and let them know that the availability of loans will depend on the amount of their deposits. Indeed, this relationship is often formalized in that a business may be required to hold a compensating deposit balance in order to obtain a *line of credit* under which, at the firms' initiative, it can borrow from the bank in the future.

Perhaps more important, a banker knows that total lending power is not independent of lending policies to customers. If the bank acquires a reputation of meeting all reasonable loan demands of customers, it will be able to attract and retain more deposits, and thus to lend more. But if it becomes known as niggardly in meeting customers' needs, it will be able to attract and retain only a smaller volume of deposits, and the bank's total lending power will shrink. The extent to which this consideration will influence the composition of a bank's portfolio depends in part on the size of customers' loan demands relative to the total lending power of the bank. If customers' demands are relatively small, the bank can feel free to hold a large fraction of its portfolio in open-market assets. But if customers' demands for loans are very large relative to its total lending power, the bank is under heavy pressures to hold most of its portfolio in this form. The extent of these pressures vary from bank to bank, and they can also change markedly at a given bank as customers' loan demands rise and fall.

Thus, other things equal, a bank is strongly impelled to meet customers' loan demands rather than acquire open-market assets. But "other things," such as interest rates and degrees of safety and liquidity, may not be equal. For example, open-market assets may be safer, more liquid, or higher yielding. The bank's desire to make customer loans must therefore be balanced against its demand for safety, liquidity, and, in some cases, earnings. It should be emphasized, however, that what a bank considers to be an optimum portfolio composition in one set of circumstances may not be optimum under other circumstances. The optimum can be shifted by such things as changes in the banker's estimates of the amount of safety and liquidity needed, changes in the general level of interest rates and in the relative heights of the various types of interest rates, and changes in customers' demands for loans. Let us illustrate some of these with two examples.

**Increase
in Customers'
Demands
for Loans**

Assume that we start from a situation in which bankers in general consider their portfolios to be close to their optimum composition under existing conditions. Suppose now that there occurs a sharp increase in customers' demands for bank loans, and that the Federal Reserve does not supply additional reserves and does not provide excess reserves by reducing reserve requirements. The banks will be strongly impelled to supply at least a part of the increase in customers' demands for loans, but to do so they will need funds to meet the increased reserves required against the newly created deposits and perhaps also to cover induced cash drains. They can seek these funds from a variety of sources: any excess reserves they may have, new CDs, borrowings, or sales of assets. With a substantial increase in loan demand, excess reserves are likely to be depleted quickly. Furthermore, if the rise of demand for customers' loans is general, many banks will simultaneously be trying to tap the other sources of funds. This will tend to raise interest rates in the open market and cause an increase in the cost of acquiring funds to lend to customers. Banks are thereby impelled to raise interest rates on customer loans, although perhaps only after a delay.

Thus, the banks do indeed increase the proportion of customers' loans in their portfolios in response to marked increases in customers' demands for loans. But as the process continues, the banks become increasingly reluctant to make further increases in their loans to customers. This is because of the impairment of their liquidity and perhaps also their safety. They become less liquid as they increase their borrowings and sell off their most liquid assets. And they become less safe to the extent that customers' loans are riskier than the assets sold. The banks may seek to reduce the impairment of their liquidity and safety by selling off not their most liquid and safe assets but some of their longer-term, riskier, open-market assets such as long-term bonds. This usually involves capital losses, for the rise of interest rates will have lowered the market prices of longer-term securities.[7] Increasingly, therefore, banks will resist further increases of customers' loans. They will ration loans to some extent by raising interest rates. They may also reduce the availability of credit by nonprice rationing methods, that is, by trying to convince customers that they should reduce their loan requests, by granting only a fraction of the loans requested, and by outright denial of loan applications. Such methods of nonprice rationing of loans are likely to have quite uneven impacts on borrowers, with the most generous treatment

---

[7] The tax laws make it more palatable for banks to take capital losses because, unlike other businesses and individuals, in calculating their tax liability commercial banks are allowed to deduct all losses on securities from normal operating income. Thus, for a bank in the 50 percent tax bracket the Treasury absorbs one-half of the loss the bank experiences in selling securities to meet loan demand. See P. S. Nadler, *Commercial Banking in the Economy*, 3rd ed., New York, Random House, 1979, chap. 6.

being accorded to customers considered by the bank to be most valuable.

**Increase in Bank Reserves**

Alternatively, suppose that the Federal Reserve provides banks with considerable amounts of additional reserves at a time when customers' loan demands are not rising and may be falling. The immediate effect is to increase bank liquidity in the form of excess reserves, which yield no income. These funds may be used to pay off bank borrowings from the Federal Reserve and others, to purchase open-market assets, and to expand loans to customers. How the funds will be distributed among these uses will depend on existing conditions, such as the liquidity of the banks and the amount of unsatisfied demands for customers' loans. If the banks have been rationing loans, they may relax their restrictions and expand customers' loans at an early stage. But they are most unlikely to lower interest rates on these loans at an early stage. Rather, they will pay off borrowings and purchase assets—especially highly liquid assets—in the open market. As they do this, interest rates in the open market will fall. At first, the decline of interest rates may be largely limited to short-term maturities; but as these yields decline relative to yields on longer-term obligations, both banks and other buyers will be impelled to switch their purchases to the longer maturities, thereby tending to lower their yields.

Thus, the initial response of banks to an increase of their excess reserves may be to purchase assets in the open market and to lower interest rates there. But as the banks become more liquid and face lower yields in the open market, they will try to expand their loans to customers. At first they may try to do this solely by relaxing restrictions and encouraging customers to borrow, but at some stage interest rates on customers' loans will be reduced.

**The Story in Pictures**

Figure 7–2 illustrates the banks' shares of loans and securities, as a fraction of total assets, for the period since 1961. The long-term trend in bank assets away from securities and toward loans is evident in this figure. What is equally apparent, however, is that during periods characterized by a restrictive monetary policy—indicated by the shaded areas in Figure 7–2—the long-term trends were disrupted.[8] In particular, during each of the tight-money periods the loan share of bank assets slowed its upward trend and then declined as the economy entered a sluggish

---

[8] See D. P. Eastburn and W. L. Hoskins, "The Influence of Monetary Policy on Commercial Banking," *Business Review*, Federal Reserve Bank of Philadelphia, July-August 1978, pp. 12–13. This article also explains the dating of the periods of tight money in Figure 7–2: May 1966–February 1967, April–November 1969, and September 1973–September 1974.

phase. The share of securities in total assets declined during tight-money periods as banks continued to try and satisfy customer loan demand. For many banks this undoubtedly involved accepting capital losses on securities. After the end of each period of tight money, as the economy and the demand for business loans turned sluggish, banks countered the long-term trend by increasing the share of securities. Aside from providing an outlet for funds in the face of weakened loan demand, this had the effect of repairing bank liquidity positions.

**Overview**     This discussion has served to illustrate some of the forces that influence the composition of bank portfolios. It also indicates the critical role that bank liquidity plays in the process of choosing an optimal bank portfolio. Although we have already touched on the subject of bank liquidity, our discussion was somewhat incomplete. Now, having sur-

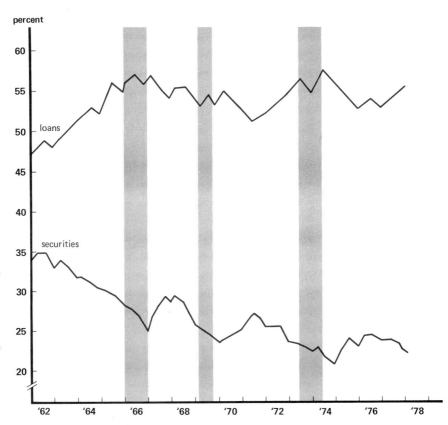

*Holdings of loans and securities as share of total assets, commercial banks, 1961–1978*

Source: *Business Review*, Federal Reserve Bank of Philadelphia, July-August 1978, p. 13.

**FIGURE 7–2**

Note: Shaded areas indicate tight money periods.

veyed both the assets and liabilities of commercial banks, we are in a better position to finish our examination of bank liquidity.

**BANK LIQUIDITY RECONSIDERED**

As has already been pointed out, banks have a variety of ways in which to solve their liquidity problems. Less clear, perhaps, is the fact that there have been marked changes over time in bank liquidity practices. And as we shall see, the Federal Reserve has been an important influence in this process. Since banking tradition typically placed primary emphasis on using the asset side of the balance sheet as a source of liquidity, it is there that we shall begin our discussion.

**Assets as a Source of Liquidity**

Available to banks are many types of assets with varying degrees of liquidity. Among the most liquid are vault cash; deposits at the Federal Reserve; call loans to other banks, brokers, dealers in government securities, and others; Treasury bills and other short-term obligations of the federal government; and open-market commercial paper issued by large firms. Among the less liquid are loans to customers, long-term bonds, and mortgages.

It is somewhat paradoxical that vault cash and deposits at the Federal Reserve, which are the most liquid assets in the sense of being closest to cash, do not provide a bank with a great deal of liquidity. The reason is a simple one. Such assets are held largely as required reserves and hence are not generally available to make payments to others. Only so-called *excess reserves* are available for this purpose. Banks held substantial quantities of excess reserves in the 1930s and 1940s but have kept their holdings quite small in recent years.

One should not, however, leap to the conclusion that required reserves, even in the absence of excess reserves, provide no liquidity. That they do so stems from the fact that a bank need not meet its legal-reserve requirement every day but only on the average over a *reserve period*, which is one week. Thus, a bank can indeed use some of its legally required reserves to make net payments for a few days in a reserve period, as long as it balances out for the period as a whole.

In recent years banks have gained another degree of flexibility in using vault cash as a source of liquidity. In particular, since late 1968 the vault cash used in satisfying the legal-reserve requirement for the *current* reserve period is the vault cash that was held in the reserve period two weeks *prior* to the current one. Consequently, at least as far as its current reserve position is concerned, a bank could, in principle, use all its vault cash for transactions purposes. This would, however, have important consequences for the quantity of deposits it would need to hold at the Federal Reserve two weeks hence.

In summary, a bank has the ability to use its reserves as a source of liquidity in a variety of ways. Nevertheless, it should be clear that this provides liquidity only on a very short-term basis. To balance out it must acquire additional reserves in the near future, and to do so requires other sources of liquidity.

Historically, the assets that provided the bulk of this liquidity were U.S. government securities, particularly short-term obligations. Banks would typically sell such securities when economic activity was on the upswing and loan demand was strong. Conversely, they would buy some of these back when opportunities for making loans deteriorated in a downswing of the business cycle. While this general pattern still prevails, as already noted, banks currently hold only a relatively small quantity of such obligations. In fact, even this limited quantity is not fully available for liquidity needs. This is because many of these potentially liquid securities are *pledged assets*. Pledged assets arise from the fact that banks are required to hold U.S. government (or high-quality municipal) bonds as collateral against deposits of federal, state, and local governments. Sales of pledged assets would entail loss of a corresponding quantity of deposits, hardly the way to solve liquidity problems.

In short, when judged from the asset side of the balance sheet, it seems clear that banks are considerably less liquid at present than they have been in the past. One quantitative indication of this can be seen from the percentage of total assets held in the form of loans. In the aggregate this figure has risen from 25 percent in 1947 to 45 percent in 1960 and then to 60 percent in 1978 (see Figure 7–2). Although only a rough measure, this steady increase in the loan share clearly points to reduced liquidity for bank assets over time. To offset this, banks have relied to a great extent on the liability side of the ledger.

**Liability Management and Liquidity**

As was brought out by our survey of bank liabilities, in the past twenty years or so banks have greatly expanded the nature and scope of their liabilities. This development became so fashionable and widespread that it was dubbed, somewhat pretentiously, the doctrine of *liability management*. In its boldest form this doctrine suggested to bankers that liquidity problems were passé. In particular, so the story went, funds could always be raised by borrowing from one source or another. Banks, thus, had as much latent liquidity as they needed. They could, therefore, turn in their lower-yielding liquid assets for more profitable alternatives, and as we have seen most banks did so. Bankers, however, came to rue this simplistic view — but we are getting ahead of ourselves.

Liability management began in earnest with the development of the CD market in the early 1960s. Throughout the first half of the decade the volume of CDs outstanding grew steadily and stood at $18.6 billion in August 1966. This growth was greatly facilitated by the Federal Reserve, which raised interest ceilings on such deposits whenever a rise in market rates threatened to impair the ability of the banks to tap this source of funds for liquidity. Such increases in ceilings were effected in 1962, 1963, 1964, and 1965. So far, so good. Then, in the credit crunch of 1966, the banks experienced a rude shock when the Federal Reserve not only refused to raise ceilings as market rates of interest rose but actually reduced some ceilings. As a consequence, the banks were unable to "roll over" CDs as they matured and their volume declined to $15.5 billion in November 1966.

Faced with this dilemma, banks turned to the various sources of funds examined previously. In so doing, they were exploiting the fact that the line between deposits and nondeposit liabilities was a fuzzy one. Indeed, as suggested earlier, such borrowed funds are quite similar to CDs from the point of the holder of the claim. From the viewpoint of the issuing bank, however, there was an important difference. In particular, borrowing sources such as promissory notes, commercial paper, and Eurodollars were not legally regarded as deposits. Hence they were not subject to reserve requirements or interest rate ceilings.

The next time a credit crunch materialized, which took place in 1969, banks again experienced a substantial decline in CDs, a decline of roughly $13 billion. However, they were able to offset these runoffs by raising large quantities of funds via repurchase agreements, Eurodollars, and the like. Needless to say, the Federal Reserve, which had created tight monetary conditions in the first place, did not look too kindly on bank efforts to blunt the restrictive effects of monetary policy. Thus began a cat-and-mouse game in which each "creative" act of bank liability management was countered by a series of regulatory changes. The most important of these was the imposition of reserve requirements on commercial paper, promissory notes, and Eurodollar borrowings. By forcing part of the funds raised from these sources to remain idle, this necessarily made such funds considerably more expensive to the banks.

With the advent of the 1970s some more order returned to liability management. In two stages (in 1970 and 1973) the Federal Reserve removed the interest ceiling on large ($100,000 or more) time deposits. Banks once again were free to raise funds by the use of CDs in times of credit stringency. Furthermore, the reserve requirements on nondeposit liabilities were modified until the cost of funds from alternative sources was comparable to the cost of CD funds. As a consequence, in the next period of credit stringency, which took place in 1973–1974, there was no runoff of CDs. In fact, in marked contrast to 1966 and 1969, CD volume grew throughout this period. As a result, other forms of borrowing were of less importance in 1973–1974. For example, Eurodollar borrowings, which had exceeded $15 billion in 1969, remained under $5 billion in 1973–1974.

Since the mid-1970s liability management has taken on a new character with the marked expansion of the markets for federal funds and repurchase agreements (RPs). This can be seen in Figure 7–3, which provides an overall picture of managed liabilities since 1973. Shown are the outstanding volume of large time deposits, which includes negotiable CDs as well as other large time deposits with denominations over $100,000, and total nondeposit liabilities of commercial banks. The latter consist primarily of borrowing from nonbank sources via the federal funds and RP markets, and Eurodollar borrowings.[9]

What accounts for the remarkable growth of nondeposit managed liabilities in recent years? As hinted at earlier, the regulations of the Federal Reserve are an important part of the answer. One factor is that the interest rates on federal funds, RPs, and Eurodollar borrowings are all market-determined rates—not subject to interest rate ceilings. The same, of course, is true of large time deposits, since the Regulation Q

---

[9] Total nondeposit liabilities also includes another relatively minor item of loans sold by banks to their affiliates. It does not, however, include funds raised via federal funds or RPs from *within* the banking system. While some $50 billion of such loans were outstanding at the end of 1979, these funds, since they come from within the banking system, are not a net addition of funds to the banks. For individual banks, of course, this remains an important source of funds.

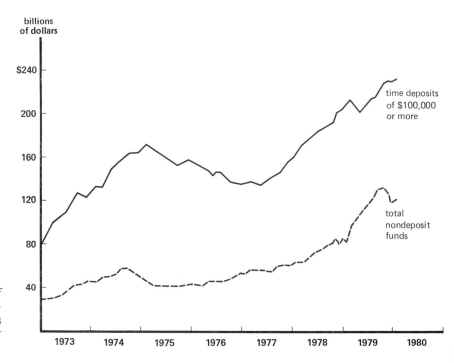

*...naged liabilities of commercial banks.*

**FIGURE 7–3**

ceiling was lifted on these deposits in 1973. Large time deposits, however, are subject to a basic reserve requirement of 1–6 percent (depending on maturity), and, since November 1978, to a supplemental reserve requirement of 2 percent. Nondeposit liabilities, until quite recently, have had no reserve requirements.[10] An additional advantage of nondeposit liabilities is that the transactors have greater flexibility in setting maturities than they do with CDs, which must have at least a 30-day maturity. In contrast, for nondeposit liabilities, maturities can be negotiated from one day up. This feature has proved particularly attractive to corporations and other holders of large cash balances, which have used the RP market as a way of earning a secured rate of return on these balances until they are needed for payments. In view of all these factors, the growth of managed liabilities documented in Figure 7–3 is much more understandable.

In keeping with the cat-and-mouse game alluded to above, in a recent move to tighten monetary policy the Federal Reserve finally decided to do something about the situation. Specifically, in October 1979 it imposed an 8 percent marginal reserve requirement on managed liabilities, where managed liabilities were defined to include large time deposits, Eurodollar borrowings, RPs, and federal funds borrowings from nonmember institutions. Because the reserve requirement was a marginal one, it applied only to managed liabilities in excess of some base amount. Or, put another way, it applied to additions to managed liabilities. The consequence of this move was to increase the effective cost of additional managed liabilities to the banks, and, the Federal Reserve hoped, to slow the growth in managed liabilities.

Taken as a whole, our discussion makes clear that liability management, in its various guises, has become a permanent feature of bank behavior. Nevertheless, it should also be apparent that the possibility of regulatory response makes exclusive reliance on liability management for bank liquidity a somewhat risky strategy. Our discussion has also suggested that bank liability management has tended to complicate the life of the Federal Reserve in its conduct of monetary policy. We shall return to this theme when we delve more deeply into issues of monetary policy.

CONCLUSION In this chapter we focused on some of the basic issues involved in the management of a commercial bank. Our emphasis has been on the bank as a financial intermediary and, hence, on the nature of the sources and

---

[10] This is not strictly accurate, since there was a reserve requirement on one component of nondeposit liabilities, Eurodollar borrowings. In August 1978 this requirement was set at zero, and soon thereafter Eurodollar borrowing mushroomed.

uses of bank funds. Banks seek to choose an optimal mix of assets and liabilities that is consistent with reconciling the conflicting objectives of safety and earnings or, as it is sometimes termed, risk and return. Banks, of course, must operate in the face of uncertainty as to the future course of the economy and of financial markets. This makes for a complex interaction between their assets and liabilities, especially as it works through the bank–customer relationship. It also means that banks must be prepared to make relatively rapid adjustments in their portfolios, which in turn requires ready access to new funds.

As a consequence, we analyzed the various liquidity practices by which banks could secure such funds. On this score, it became clear that a diversified approach to liquidity was the most prudent course of action for a bank. However, our discussion of bank liquidity also hinted at one final point that needs to be made explicit. In particular, in the last analysis the liquidity of an individual bank, or indeed of the banking system as a whole, is not fully within its own control. As we have suggested, the Federal Reserve, should it be so inclined, has a variety of tools for sopping up a considerable volume of bank liquidity. Precisely why it might want to do this and how it could accomplish this are questions we shall explore in subsequent discussions of Federal Reserve policy.

**SELECTED READINGS**

Bowsher, N. N., "Repurchase Agreements," *Review*, Federal Reserve Bank of St. Louis, September 1979, pp. 17–22.

Havrilesky, T. M., and J. T. Boorman, *Current Perspectives in Banking*, Arlington Heights, Ill., AHM, 1976.

Mason, J. M., *Financial Management of Commercial Banks*, Boston, Warren, Gorham, and Lamont, 1979.

Mayer, M., *The Bankers*, New York, Ballantine Books, 1976.

Nadler, P. S., *Commercial Banking in the Economy*, 3rd ed., New York, Random House, 1979.

# CENTRAL BANKING

Visitors to the United States are often puzzled by the complexity of the American banking system. In most countries there is a single central bank to perform the functions of monetary management; power to charter and regulate commercial banks is usually concentrated in the central government; and the commercial banking system typically consists of no more than 20, and in many cases no more than 10, banks with numerous branches. Against such a background, the American system inevitably seems complex, if not confused and confusing. Here, there is not a single central bank but a central banking system composed of the Board of Governors of the Federal Reserve System located in Washington, D.C., and 12 separately incorporated Federal Reserve banks located in as many regions. Even at the federal level, jurisdiction over commercial banks is not concentrated in a single agency but divided among three—the Federal Reserve, the Comptroller of the Currency, and the Federal Deposit Insurance Corporation. Moreover, power to charter and regulate commercial banks is shared in complex and often overlapping ways among federal agencies and the various state governments. The result is the American *dual banking* system.

No wonder the visitor asks in bewilderment, "How did it get that way, and why?" No one can understand this system without a knowledge of American banking history, which is closely interlinked with old and continuing political and economic controversies over such issues as the relative roles of the central and state governments in a federal system, concentration of economic and financial power, and conflicts between creditor and debtor areas. Our purpose in this chapter is not to present a complete history of American banking, but rather to concentrate on those episodes, events, and forces that contribute most to an understanding of the present system of commercial and central banking.

**BANKING FROM
1781 TO 1863**

In banking, as in most other aspects of American life, this early period from 1781 to 1863 was one of rapid development and widespread controversy. Having gained its independence, the new nation was struggling to determine its social, political, economic, and financial patterns. On all these matters there were important differences of opinion. By far the largest part of the population lived on farms, most of which were largely self-sufficient; all except a few of the cities were small; manufacturing was still in its infancy; and trade occupied a far less important position than it does today. The nation had virtually no experience with banking of modern types, and there were wide disagreements concerning the contributions that banks could make. Some people were perhaps too laudatory, overestimating the extent to which banks could stimulate capital formation and promote productivity and trade by providing credit and a more generous supply of money in the form of bank notes and deposits. Others denied that banks were productive at all; instead, they insisted that banks merely lowered the quality of the nation's money because issues of bank notes and deposits drove out, or kept out, an equal value of good metallic coins. Alexander Hamilton and others who shared his goal of developing an industrial and commercial type of economy were generally favorably disposed toward banking, believing that banks were an essential part of such an economy. Thomas Jefferson and his sympathizers, who believed that the country should remain largely agricultural, were generally opposed to banks, at least partly because banking was closely related to industry and commerce. The Federalists and others who favored centralization of political power believed that the power to charter and supervise banks should be exclusively federal. They questioned the constitutionality of state activities in this field. On the other hand, the anti-Federalists and their friends, who opposed centralization of political power and championed states' rights, insisted that only the states had the power to create and supervise banks and that such federal activities were unconstitutional. Much of the banking controversy of the period is understandable only as a part of the broader controversy over industrialization versus agrarianism and centralization of political power versus states' rights.

It is important to remember also that bank notes were more important than deposits as means of payment until about the time of the Civil War. Checking deposits were used, especially in the cities, but they were not well suited to a predominantly agricultural country with few towns and slow travel and communication. In fact, during the Colonial period the word *bank* meant "a batch of paper money." The first bank of a modern type in this country was the Bank of North America, which was established in Philadelphia in 1782 to aid in financing the Revolutionary War. The Bank of New York and the Bank of Massachusetts were established in 1784. These three were the only incorporated banks in the United States in 1790. There were, however, a few unincorporated or private banks, for under the common law everyone had a right to engage in banking as well as in other types of business. Only later, after 1800, did the states begin to limit banking by unincorporated firms.

**The First Bank of the United States, 1791–1811**

The First Bank of the United States, the first to be authorized by the federal government, received a 20-year charter in 1791. It had a capital stock of $10 million, of which $2 million was subscribed by the federal government with funds borrowed from the bank; the remainder was subscribed by private individuals, some of them residents of foreign countries. By today's standards it was a small bank; in its day it was huge. It was not only by far the largest bank of its day, but also the largest corporation in America. It established its head office in Philadelphia and branches in the other principal cities of the country. Thus, the first federally chartered bank was a nationwide branch bank jointly owned by the federal government and private investors.

The bank made loans and purchased securities; issued both deposits and bank notes; transferred loan funds and payments from one end of the country to the other; and performed useful functions for the government in lending to it, acting as its depository, and transferring funds for it. It also performed some central banking functions, for it regulated the lending and note-issuing powers of state banks. As the largest bank in the system, its own lending policies greatly affected the reserves of other banks. When it expanded its loans, some of the proceeds flowed to other banks, thereby augmenting their reserves in the form of deposits at the First Bank, or gold and silver specie. When the First Bank contracted its loans, it drained reserves from the other banks and limited their lending ability. It could greatly affect their specie reserves and lending power by its disposal of their bank notes that came into its possession. By simply holding these notes or paying them out into circulation, it could permit the banks to retain their species reserves. But by presenting their notes to the issuing banks for redemption, the First Bank could decrease their specie reserves. It was in the exercise of its central banking power, and especially in limiting the loans and note issues of state banks, that the First Bank made some of its bitterest enemies.

The First Bank seems to have functioned well, especially when compared with other banks during the first half of the nineteenth century. Nevertheless, Congress refused to renew its charter when it expired in 1811. Several arguments against recharter were advanced:

1 Much of the bank stock was owned by foreigners. Some people feared that foreigners would exercise excessive control over our economy through the bank, although foreign stockholders had no

vote; it was also argued that money was drained out of the country by the payment of dividends to foreign stockholders.

2   Only "hard money" was good money. A large part of the community was still opposed to paper money of any sort, whether issued by banks or by government.

3   The bank was unconstitutional. The Constitution contained no express provision for bank charters. The anti-Federalists contended that no such power was even implied and hence the bank had been unconstitutional from the beginning. Moreover, they feared that it would tend to centralize power in the federal government at the expense of the states, as its foremost proponent, Alexander Hamilton, hoped it would. It was frequently charged, apparently with some justice, that the bank was dominated by Federalists and that it discriminated against anti-Federalists in making loans.

4   The bank discouraged the growth of state banks. It is clear that the First Bank curbed the issue of state bank notes by presenting them regularly for redemption. Some elements of the community, including the owners and officers of state banks as well as other proponents of "easy money," wanted to eliminate the curbing effects of the bank.

Whatever the deciding motives of Congress in refusing its recharter, the First Bank of the United States expired in 1811.

**State Banking,**
**1811–1816**

Freed from the restraining influence of the First Bank and favored by inflationary financing of the War of 1812, state banks went on a spree. They grew in number from 88 in 1811 to 246 in 1816, and their note issues rose from $45 million in 1812 to at least $100 million in 1817. Virtually all ceased to redeem their notes in gold or silver, and their notes depreciated by varying amounts; the notes of many banks became virtually worthless. All the banking abuses that we shall study later appeared during this period. It was largely because of these gross abuses of the banking privilege by state banks and because of the extreme disorder of the monetary system that the Second Bank of the United States was established in 1816.

**The Second Bank of**
**the United States,**
**1816–1836**

The Second Bank of the United States received a 20-year charter from the federal government in 1816. In many respects it resembled the First Bank, but it was much larger and some of its charter provisions were different. Its capital was fixed at $35 million, of which one-fifth was to be subscribed by the federal government and paid for with its bonds. The remaining $28 million was subscribed by individuals, corporations, companies, and states. The bank was governed by a board of directors, of whom 5 were appointed by the President of the United States and 20 were elected by the private stockholders. It established 25 branches to serve all the settled parts of the country.

Like the First Bank, the Second Bank performed both commercial and central banking functions. Moreover, it acted as a regulator of state banks, presenting their notes for redemption, insisting that they redeem their obligations promptly in specie, and limiting in general the amount of credit they created. This was one of the principal purposes for which the Second Bank was created. This regulatory function, which constrained the operation of the state banks, naturally proved to be a source of considerable tension between the Second Bank and the state banks. In addition, state banks did not take kindly to competition from the Second Bank in the areas of loans and deposits, and hence generally were a major source of opposition to the continued existence of the Second Bank. As with the First Bank, there were also other sources of opposition. Once again questions of constitutionality emerged, as did challenges from those who doubted the wisdom, in a political democracy, of concentrating financial and economic power in the hands of a small group.

The Second Bank might have survived this opposition, and even the charges of mismanagement leveled against it, were it not for its political activity. This became particularly troublesome with the election of Andrew Jackson to the presidency in 1828. A large majority of those in control of the Second Bank were opposed to Jackson and his party. Moreover, they were often aggressive in their political activities, with at least some of the Bank's branch managers using their lending power to influence votes. The fate of the Bank was sealed when its president, Nicholas Biddle, openly but vainly opposed Jackson's reelection in 1832 and made recharter of the Bank one of the issues of the presidential campaign. After his reelection Jackson saw to it that federal deposits were withdrawn from the Bank and placed with selected state banks, and the charter of the Bank was allowed to expire in 1836. The country was to see no more federally chartered banks until 1863 and was not to have another central banking system until 1914. The clash between Biddle and Jackson thus may well have altered the course of our banking history.

Was President Jackson right in refusing to recharter the Second Bank in 1836? A full answer to this question would require far more space than we can devote to it. Two facts now seem clear, however. In the first place, it is questionable public policy to grant central banking powers to a corporation, which is largely owned and controlled by private individuals and corporations, is operated by its owners primarily for profit, and as a profit-seeking enterprise has interests in conflict with those of the banks that it regulates. We now recognize that central banking is a governmental function that can be properly exercised only by institutions with a primary motive that is not profit but financial and economic stabilization. A properly managed central bank must often follow policies that will decrease its profits. In the second place, it is quite clear that the abolition of the Second Bank without establishing another institution to assume its functions was a major blunder. It ushered in a generation of banking anarchy and monetary disorder.

**State Banking, 1836–1863**

From the lapse of the Second Bank's charter in 1836 until the establishment of the National Banking System in 1863, our banking system was made up exclusively of private (unincorporated) banks and of banks operating under corporate charters granted by the various states. We shall not discuss the unincorporated banks except to say that, as a group, they seem to have been neither significantly better nor significantly worse than the incorporated banks. The incorporated banks, operating under widely diverse state laws, varied from those that performed their functions satisfactorily to those that engaged in practically all known banking abuses.

Prior to 1837 a bank could secure a corporate charter from a state only by a special legislative act. This method of granting bank charters gradually fell into disfavor for several reasons. It injected banks into politics and politics into banks. Loyal members of the political party in power might receive a bank charter, whereas members of the minority party had little chance of success. The controversy over bank charters threatened to corrupt state governments. Legislators were offered large sums of money to grant new charters and other large sums by existing banks to reject the applications of potential competitors. Furthermore, this method of granting charters often gave monopoly power to the favored banks.

To remedy this situation, Michigan in 1837 and New York in 1838 enacted *free-banking* laws. Most of the other states later enacted laws of the same general type. These laws ended the practice of granting charters by special legislative act and provided that anyone might secure a corporate charter and engage in banking by complying with the provisions of a general bank-incorporation law. Banking was made "free" to all enterprisers who met the specified general requirements. The quality of state banks came to depend on how appropriate these general requirements were and on how well they were enforced. In some states the requirements were strict; banks could issue notes only by depositing with a state official an equivalent amount of high-quality bonds and by meeting adequate capital and reserve requirements. But in the majority of states the collateral requirements for notes were hopelessly inadequate and capital and reserve requirements were virtually meaningless.

The relationships between banks and the states varied widely. At one extreme, the banks merely received their charters from the state;

they secured all their capital from private sources and made any loans that were permitted within the broad framework of the banking laws. At the other extreme, many banks were wholly owned and operated by states. There were several variations between these two extremes. Thus, some banks were owned jointly by a state and private investors. Others had to pay large sums to the state for the privilege of banking. And still others were permitted to act as banks only if they would lend stipulated amounts to canal companies, railroads, or other enterprises considered meritorious by the state legislature. In a period when "capital" was still scarce, states encouraged and even forced banks to lend large amounts for the financing of selected projects.

With the transfer of federal deposits from the Second Bank to selected state banks and the removal of the moderating hand of the Second Bank, both the number of state banks and the volume of their credit increased. This growth was far from steady, and there were often violent fluctuations in the amount of money created by the banks. The principal expansions and contractions during this period are shown in Table 8–1. Business activity and prices fluctuated widely as banks alternated between (a) inflationary periods of increased money supplies and liberal loans and (b) periods of shrinking money supplies and reduced loans. The banks' policies were not the sole causes of these fluctuations, but they were unquestionably contributory factors.

**Abuses by the State-Chartered Banks Before the Civil War**

Without inferring that all the banks were guilty, we shall now investigate the principal banking abuses during this period. These abuses were so widespread that they greatly influenced both public attitudes toward banks and subsequent banking legislation. Some of the most serious abuses were the following:

**TABLE 8–1**

*Principal expansions and contractions of the state bank notes and deposits, 1834–1860*

| | PERCENTAGE EXPANSION (+) OR CONTRACTION (−) | | |
|---|---|---|---|
| Period | Bank notes | Bank deposits | Total notes and deposits |
| 1834–1837 | + 56 | + 67 | + 61 |
| 1837–1843 | − 60 | − 56 | − 58 |
| 1843–1848 | +119 | + 84 | +102 |
| 1848–1849 | − 11 | − 12 | − 11 |
| 1849–1854 | + 78 | +107 | + 91 |
| 1854–1855 | − 9 | + 2 | − 4 |
| 1855–1857 | + 15 | + 21 | + 18 |
| 1857–1858 | − 28 | − 19 | − 24 |
| 1858–1860 | + 36 | + 37 | + 36 |

*Source:* Board of Governors of the Federal Reserve System, *Banking Studies*, Washington, D.C., 1941, pp. 417–418.

1   INADEQUATE BANK CAPITAL. Many banks failed to maintain large enough capital accounts to protect their creditors. Some made no pretense of having adequate capital. Others had a large enough nominal capital, but it was paid for with the promissory notes of the stockholders, many of whom were unable to meet their obligations. Even when bank stocks were initially paid for with gold or silver, stockholders often borrowed back the coin, giving in return their doubtful paper. Furthermore, bank capital was frequently dissipated by excessive dividend payments.

2   RISKY AND ILLIQUID LOANS. Many of the banks made highly risky, illiquid, and speculative loans without regard for the safety of their creditors, and some lent excessively to their own stockholders and officers. This combination of inadequate bank capital and highly risky and illiquid loans could lead to but one result: numerous bank failures and serious losses to note-holders and depositors.

3   INADEQUATE RESERVES AGAINST NOTES AND DEPOSITS. In certain of the state banking laws the reserve requirements were either wholly absent or very inadequate, and evasions of existing requirements were widespread.

As a result of all these abuses—excessive issues of bank notes, inadequate bank capital, risky and illiquid bank assets, and highly inadequate reserves—bank notes had widely differing values. The notes of some banks were freely redeemed in gold and silver and circulated at their face value. Others circulated at small but varying discounts; still others circulated at only a small percentage of their face value; and many became completely worthless.

The period was a counterfeiter's paradise. Each of the hundreds of banks issued notes of its own design and in many denominations; the notes were made of many kinds of paper, mostly of low quality; the workmanship on the genuine notes was usually poor; and no one could be familiar with all the bank notes outstanding. Under these conditions it was easy to raise the denomination of genuine notes and to issue counterfeits on existent or even nonexistent banks. "Bicknall's Counterfeit Detector and Bank-Note List" of January 1, 1839, contains the names of "54 banks that had failed at different times; of 20 fictitious banks, the pretended notes of which are in circulation; of 43 banks besides, for the notes of which there is no sale; of 254 banks, the notes of which have been counterfeited or altered; and 1,395 descriptions of counterfeited or altered notes [then] supposed to be in circulation, from one dollar to five hundred."[1] That these conditions had not been remedied by 1858 is in-

---

[1] Raguet, quoted by Horace White, *Money and Banking*, Boston, Ginn, 1896, pp. 403–404.

dicated by the fact that Nicholas's *Bank Note Reporter* gave 5,400 separate descriptions of counterfeit, altered, and spurious notes. There were 30 different counterfeit issues of the Bank of Delaware notes.[2]

The numerous counterfeit detectors and bank-note reporters that attempted to warn against counterfeits and to indicate the current values of the various bank notes were of only limited assistance. Even with their supplements they were often out of date, they were beyond the reach of small businesses and individuals, and they could not remove the confusion in trade resulting from the fact that the price charged for an article depended on the type of bank note with which payment was to be made.

Although banking abuses during this period were widespread, we must not leave the impression that all state banks were unsound. Some states, notably New York, Massachusetts, and Louisiana, enacted highly protective banking laws and implemented them with bank supervision and examinations. In fact, some of these laws, especially those of New York, contributed much to the legislation establishing the national banking system.

Moreover, it should not be concluded without investigation and analysis that banks that "play it safe" are always more socially beneficial than those that assume large risks in both the types and amounts of their loans. On the one hand, we want banks to be safe, we do not want them to fail, and we want them to keep their bank notes and deposits continuously at parity with other types of money. On the other hand, we want banks to stand ready to finance productive projects, some of which are inherently risky. It may well be that some of the banks that made highly risky loans contributed more to American economic development and growth than some that were overly concerned with safety. It is not always easy to find an optimum balance of these objectives.

**THE NATIONAL BANKING SYSTEM, 1863–1914**

In 1863, just 27 years after the expiration of the Second Bank of the United States, the federal government again entered the banking field by passing "An Act to provide a national currency, secured by a pledge of United States Stocks, and to provide for the Circulation and Redemption thereof." The 1863 law, which contained a large number of imperfections, was replaced by a new law in 1864. The latter is usually referred to as the National Banking Act.

**Principal Provisions of the National Banking Act**

We have already said that the National Banking Act owed much to earlier state banking laws, especially those of New York. The new law provided for "free banking." Anyone meeting the general requirements of the Act was to receive a charter and permission to engage in banking.

[2] Ibid., p. 398.

A new office, the Comptroller of the Currency, was created in the Treasury Department to grant charters and to administer all laws relating to national banks. Among its principal provisions, in order to provide for the safety and liquidity of the banking system, the Act imposed several sorts of capital requirements, elaborated many restrictions on the kinds of assets banks could hold, and introduced minimum reserve requirements for both circulating bank notes and deposits. Furthermore, remembering the sorry record of state bank notes, the Act set forth a detailed set of regulations concerning the issuance of bank notes. Finally, in order to ensure compliance with both the letter and the spirit of the Act, national banks were required to supply the Comptroller of the Currency with periodic reports on their financial condition and were made subject to examination by the Comptroller's representatives.

Thus, every effort was made to ensure the safety and parity of value of national bank notes. In these respects the Act was successful.

**State Banks**

It was hoped that the authorization of national banks would induce state banks to take out federal charters and comply with the requirements of the National Banking Act. When it became evident that few state banks were going to do this, Congress decided to force the issue by levying a 10 percent tax on any bank or individual paying out or using state bank notes. The purpose was to end the issuance of circulating notes by state banks and to force all or most of these banks to become national banks or to cease doing a general banking business. As shown in Table 8–2, the Act did succeed in reducing the number of state banks from 1,089 in 1864 to 247 in 1868. After 1868, however, the number of state banks again began to expand, and by 1914 they outnumbered national banks by more than two to one.

How were state banks able not only to survive but even to expand greatly in spite of the prohibitive tax on their notes? The first and

**TABLE 8–2**

*State and national banks in the United States, 1864–1914*

| Year | State banks | National banks |
|------|------------|----------------|
| 1864 | 1,089 | 467 |
| 1868 | 247 | 1,640 |
| 1870 | 325 | 1,612 |
| 1880 | 650 | 2,076 |
| 1890 | 2,250 | 3,484 |
| 1900 | 5,007 | 3,731 |
| 1910 | 14,348 | 7,138 |
| 1914 | 17,498 | 7,518 |

*Source:* Board of Governors of the Federal Reserve System, *Banking Studies*, Washington, D.C., 1941, p. 418.

foremost reason was that note issue had become of much less importance in banking. With the growth of cities and more rapid transportation and communication, people used checking deposits more and more as a means of payment. With the privilege of creating checking deposits, a bank could now operate successfully without issuing notes. But why did many banks prefer to operate under state rather than federal charters when national banks also had the right to create circulating notes? The answer is to be found largely in the fact that many states imposed less rigid restrictions and granted more liberal powers than those contained in the National Banking Act. In general, state banking laws provided lower capital requirements, lower reserve requirements, less supervision by the government, and more liberal powers to lend.

**Shortcomings of the National Banking System**     Although the national banking system unquestionably greatly improved the general quality of banking, the system became subject to increasing criticism. Demands for further bank reform swelled during the late years of the nineteenth century and grew still more in the first years of the twentieth, finally ushering in the Federal Reserve System in 1914. Although many aspects of national banks were criticized, the greatest complaint was against their "inflexibility," or "inelasticity." The keynote of the National Banking Act was safety, especially safety of national bank notes. Less attention was paid to the safety of deposits. Critics now complained that the system was too inflexible and that it must be given a greater degree of elasticity. The meaning of this term was often unclear, but we can discover its general import as we proceed.

Although national bank notes were safe, there was no provision for appropriate variations in their quantity over the long run, in response to seasonal variations in the need for them, and during crisis periods. One reason for this was a provision of the National Banking Act that tied the allowable quantity of national bank notes to the quantity of federal bonds owned by the banks. The effect of the Act was to restrict the volume of bank notes to at most 90 percent of the eligible bonds outstanding. Critics maintained that a note system of this type, which was subject to the vagaries of the supply of government bonds, could never provide a properly elastic currency that would respond to the needs of the economy.

National bank notes were also criticized for their lack of seasonal elasticity. The demand for currency for hand-to-hand use showed marked seasonal variations, yet the volume of outstanding national bank notes remained relatively constant throughout the year. Hence, banks could meet seasonal peak demands for currency only by draining funds from their reserves, and the inflow of currency to the banks during slack seasons increased their reserves. Critics complained that this led to seasonal credit stringencies and demanded the creation of a currency that would increase and decrease with seasonal demands for coin and currency and would leave bank reserves unaffected.

Critics also complained of the inelasticity of national bank notes during banking crises. They pointed out that there was no existing way in which new currency could be created to satisfy general demands on the banks for cash, and that banks could not meet these demands out of the limited cash in their vaults.

The disturbing effects of an inelastic bank note system were intensified by another feature of the National Banking Act—a defective system of reserve requirements. This reserve system had three principal weaknesses. The first drawback was that a large part of the nominal reserve was fictitious in the sense that it was not available for meeting actual cash drains from the banking system. This was because such a large part of the reserves was in the form of deposit claims against other banks, which in turn held only a small percentage of actual cash as a reserve against their deposit obligations. The second weakness of the system was that reserve requirements were very inflexible. Each bank was ordered to meet its reserve requirements at all times; it could not legally make any new loans while its reserves were deficient. There arose a general demand that reserve requirements be relaxed by being suspended in periods of crisis or at least by banks' being allowed to meet these requirements on the average over a period of time, deficiencies at one time being balanced by overages at another. The latter method is employed for banks that are members of the Federal Reserve System.

The third shortcoming, which was widely criticized, was the "parcelation of reserves" resulting from the lack of any orderly way of pooling the reserves of individual banks to meet drains of cash from any segment of the banking system. Some compared existing reserve requirements with attempts to fight fires by placing a pail of water in each house; the greater effectiveness of pooling the water and providing a system of pipes to concentrate it at the point of need is obvious. Advocates of bank reform proposed the establishment of a similar system of pooling individual bank reserves so that they could be concentrated at the points of greatest need in time of emergency. This was another purpose of the Federal Reserve Act of 1914.

The inelasticity of national bank notes and the defects, or at least the inadequacy, of bank reserve requirements were dramatized by the recurrent banking panics that occurred under the national banking system before 1914. There were full-fledged panics in 1873, 1884, 1893, and 1907; and serious credit stringencies threatened at other times. Unable to meet their obligations to pay cash on demand, most banks suspended payments for periods of varying lengths; some of them never reopened, a mad scramble to call loans ensued, and business activity suffered. The panic of 1907 was the last straw; popular disgust with recurrent panics made the Federal Reserve Act politically possible, although the Act had objectives beyond the prevention of panics. As Carter Glass told the House of Representatives:

> *Financial textbook writers in Europe have characterized our banking as "barbarous," and eminent bankers of this country . . . have not hesitated to confess that the criticism is merited. . . . The failure of the system in acute exigencies has caused widespread business demoralization and almost universal distress. Five times within the last thirty years financial catastrophe has overtaken the country under this system; and it would be difficult to compute the enormous losses sustained by all classes of society — by the banks immediately involved; by the merchants whose credits were curtailed; by the industries whose shops were closed; by the railroads whose cars were stopped; by the farmers whose crops rotted in the fields; by the laborer who was deprived of his wage. The system literally has no reserve force. The currency based upon the nation's debt is absolutely unresponsive to the nation's business needs. The lack of cooperation and coordination among the more than 7,300 national banks produces a curtailment of facilities at all periods of exceptional demand for credit. This peculiar defect renders disaster inevitable.*[3]

Many other observers agreed with Glass that the primary problem was that the existing system had no "reserve force," no "elasticity" in time of strain. No existing institution was motivated to hold large excess reserves for use in time of strain, none had the power to create new bank reserves in such periods, and none was empowered to create additional currency in time of need. The remedy followed from the diagnosis; new institutions should be created that would be empowered to create new currency and new bank reserves "as needed." *Elasticity* was the central theme of the new reserve system.

Even among those who favored banking reform, and many did not, there were widely differing opinions as to the proper control and structure of any new institutions that might be established. Some thought they should be regarded as cooperative or mutual aid societies formed privately by banks, while others argued that this was properly a function of the government or its appointees. Opinions as to the proper structure of the new system also differed. Some insisted that the United States, like most other countries, should have a single central bank with centralized control. Others thought such centralization both unnecessary and undesirable. It would bring a dangerous concentration of financial power, invite domination of the entire country by Wall Street or Wash-

---

[3] *The Congressional Record*, September 10, 1913, p. 4642.

ington, and ignore regional differences in economic and financial conditions. One congressman thought that fifty such regional institutions would be about the right number.

The Federal Reserve Act represented a compromise among such conflicting views. The country was divided into a number of districts, each with its own Federal Reserve Bank, and a central authority was established in Washington to supervise the various Reserve banks and to coordinate their policies while permitting some degree of regional autonomy.

**BANKING UNDER THE FEDERAL RESERVE SYSTEM**

The establishment of the Federal Reserve System in 1914 is one of the great landmarks in American banking history.[4] Then, more than 75 years after the demise of the Second Bank of the United States, the nation again had a set of institutions capable of exercising central banking powers. We shall discuss the details of the structure of the Federal Reserve System in the next chapter. For the present, let us focus on the initial objectives of the newly established central bank, on how these objectives were modified over time, and on the important legislative developments subsequent to the passage of the Federal Reserve Act.

As we have suggested, the Federal Reserve began with the primary objectives of using its power to create currency and bank reserves, to provide "elasticity," and to prevent or deal with banking crises and panics. In addition, the Federal Reserve Act sought to replace the slow and expensive system of check clearing and collection with one that would be faster and more efficient; to provide a more satisfactory fiscal agent for the federal government; to achieve a better coordination of state and national banks, and especially to secure more effective supervision of state banks; and to provide more liberal powers for national banks, such as those of establishing trust departments and lending on real estate, to enable them to compete more effectively with state banks and trust companies, many of which enjoyed more freedom of action. These reforms were important, but they were secondary. The primary purpose of the new banking reform was to end recurrent banking panics and crises.

To accomplish this primary objective the Federal Reserve, judged by present-day standards, had only limited discretionary powers. The new, supposedly elastic, currency provided by the Federal Reserve Act

---

[4] Despite their "landmark" status, in the early years Federal Reserve Board members were rather low on the Washington protocol list. President Wilson, to whom they complained, is reputed to have said, "They might come right after the fire department." The press, rather more sympathetically, referred to the Board as "the new Supreme Court of finance." Cited in J. K. Galbraith, *Money*, Boston, Houghton Mifflin, 1975, p. 135.

was in fact tied to supplies of gold and eligible paper, with no possibility of modifying this in times of crisis. Furthermore, changes in the reserves of member banks were determined largely at the initiative of the member banks rather than by policy response of the Federal Reserve. The major point to be emphasized is that the purposes of the Federal Reserve System as conceived by its originators were far different from those of today. Now, the belief is widespread that the primary purpose of the Federal Reserve is to manage money deliberately and continuously so as to promote the achievement of desired economic objectives. Despite the desire for an "elastic" currency, such an idea was alien and unacceptable to those who established the Federal Reserve System. They were well pleased with the international gold standard that was then in operation, and did not want a "managed money." Indeed, there would almost certainly have been no Federal Reserve System if its advocates had heralded it as an instrument of monetary management.

With the benefit of hindsight, this view certainly seems short-sighted. As was the case with the National Banking Act, the restructuring of the banking system in 1914, despite good intentions, did not go far enough. In particular, the limited scope of the Federal Reserve, as initially constituted, was not up to handling the financial shocks created by the stock market crash of 1929 and its aftermath. As already noted there were nearly 8,000 bank failures in the period 1930–1933. This period culminated in the major banking crisis of 1933, during which President Roosevelt was forced to declare a banking holiday closing all the banks. The result of these developments was a number of basic changes in the regulation of the banking industry. This was accomplished in large part, by a significant reorganization of the Federal Reserve that led to a much greater degree of centralization in monetary affairs. In particular, the central bank was given responsibility for implementing monetary policies that would promote economic stability and growth. Toward this end, the mechanism for borrowing from the Federal Reserve was altered to give less discretion to member banks, and the Federal Reserve was given the authority to set maximum rates of interest paid on time and savings deposits and to vary reserve-requirement ratios on demand and time deposits. Although we shall discuss the details of these developments later, the important point to emphasize is that as a result of the changes introduced in 1933 and soon thereafter, the Federal Reserve evolved into a full-fledged modern central bank.

CONCLUSION   This excursion into American banking history, brief and incomplete as it has been, should have contributed to the reader's understanding of banking structure, public policies toward banks, and current controversies over banking policies and structures. Through our banking history run two themes—change and continuity. Change there has certainly been—changes of many types, sometimes in one direction, sometimes in another. But there has also been continuity, at least in attitudes and in the nature of controversies.

A most important instance of continuity has been the persistence of controversy over the relative powers and responsibilities of the federal and state governments in the banking field. This was illustrated most dramatically in the creation and demise of the First and Second Banks of the United States; in the establishment of the national banking system, which might have been rejected if some of the strongest supporters of states' rights had not seceded; and in the establishment and determination of the structure and powers of the Federal Reserve.

Against this historical background it becomes easier to see why we have a dual banking system, with both national and state banks; why we have so many banks; and why government responsibilities for chartering and regulating banks are so diffused.

**SELECTED READINGS**

Board of Governors of the Federal Reserve System, *Banking Studies*, Washington, D.C., 1941.

Dewey, D. R., *Financial History of the United States*, 11th ed., New York, McKay, 1931.

Hammond, Bray, *Banks and Politics in America from the Revolution to the Civil War*, Princeton, N.J., Princeton University Press, 1957.

Sprague, O. M. W., *History of Crises Under the National Banking System*, Senate Document No. 538, Washington, D.C., Government Printing Office, 1910.

Taus, E. R., *Central Banking Function of the U S. Treasury, 1789–1941*, New York, Columbia University Press, 1943.

Trescott, P. B., *Financing American Enterprise*, New York, Harper & Row, 1963.

In passing the Federal Reserve Act in late 1913 and actually establishing the Federal Reserve banks in November 1914, the United States was one of the last of the great economic powers to provide itself with a central bank. The Bank of Sweden was founded in 1656, the Bank of England in 1694, the Bank of France in 1800, the Netherlands Bank in 1814, and the Bank of Belgium in 1835. In general outline, the functions of the Federal Reserve are similar to those of central banks in other countries. Like other central banks, its primary function is to regulate monetary and credit conditions. To this end it creates and destroys money and regulates the creation and destruction of money by commercial banks. It also performs many other functions, including check clearing and collection, acting as fiscal agent for the government, engaging in operations in the foreign exchange market, and so on. This chapter will focus on these subsidiary functions as well as on the structure of the Federal Reserve System and on the question of who controls (or should control) the Federal Reserve. The role of the Federal Reserve in the regulation of money and credit will be taken up in the next two chapters.

**HE STRUCTURE OF THE FEDERAL SERVE SYSTEM**
**The 12 Federal Reserve Banks**

The Federal Reserve Act provided that the continental United States should be divided into no fewer than 8 nor more than 12 Federal Reserve districts, each to have a Federal Reserve bank. The maximum number of districts and Reserve banks was established at the outset. The boundaries of these districts are shown on the map in Figure 9–1. Each Federal Reserve bank is named after the city in which it is located; thus, there is the Federal Reserve Bank of Boston, the Federal Reserve Bank of New York, and so on. To facilitate their operations some of the Federal Reserve banks have established branches in their districts. There are now 25 of these branches distributed unequally among the various Federal Reserve districts.

To outsiders, the existence of the various district banks sometimes give the appearance of the United States' having 12 central banks. In the early years of the Federal Reserve, there was an element of truth in this view. Indeed, to the designers of the Federal Reserve System it was at least plausible to argue in 1913 that each broad region should have its own central bank, which could adapt its policies to the specific conditions of the region.[1] This strategy, however, inevitably gave rise to a number of complications. In particular, as originally passed, the Federal Reserve Act was rather vague as to the precise relationship among the 12 regional banks and between the 12 banks as a group and the Federal Reserve Board in Washington. As events developed, at first the district banks played a dominant role in the system, with the Federal Reserve

---

[1] According to one waggish economist, the multiplicity of district banks—each of which resided in a building of "somber fiduciary classic"—had the side benefit of contributing "an impression of solid substance to such otherwise secondary financial centers as Cleveland or St. Louis." See J. K. Galbraith, *Money*, Boston, Houghton Mifflin, 1975, p. 119.

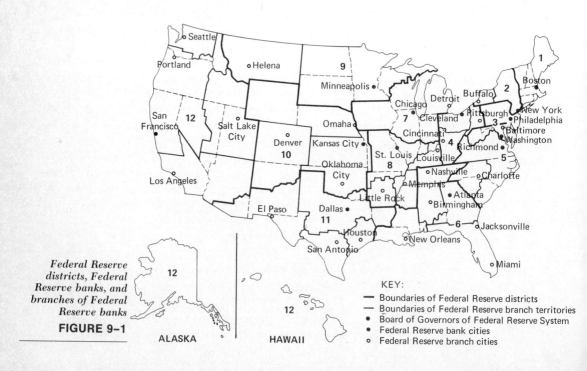

*Federal Reserve districts, Federal Reserve banks, and branches of Federal Reserve banks*

**FIGURE 9–1**

KEY:
— Boundaries of Federal Reserve districts
— Boundaries of Federal Reserve branch territories
• Board of Governors of Federal Reserve System
• Federal Reserve bank cities
○ Federal Reserve branch cities

Bank of New York assuming particular importance. The role of the New York bank reflected its size (even today it holds about 25 percent of the total assets of all the Reserve banks); the forceful leadership of its president, Benjamin Strong; and its critical location at the hub of the domestic and international financial markets. Overall, the relative importance of the district banks vis-à-vis Washington in the early years is illustrated by the fact that on several occasions the chairman of the Federal Reserve Board moved on (at a doubled salary) to head a Federal Reserve Bank.[2] The struggle for power between the Federal Reserve Board in Washington and the 12 district banks continued for roughly two decades. It was not until the reorganization of the Federal Reserve System by the Banking Act of 1935 that Washington (and the newly renamed Board of Governors) finally achieved ascendancy. Thus, today, despite appearances, the United States does have a single central bank.

**Member Banks**    Each of the twelve Federal Reserve banks has many *member banks*, which are those commercial banks in the district that have met at least the minimum requirements and have been accepted for membership in the Federal Reserve System. As a member of the Federal Reserve, a commercial bank has both obligations and privileges. It must continue to meet various requirements for membership, submit to supervision and examination by Federal Reserve authorities, subscribe to stock in its Federal Reserve bank, and hold all its legal reserves in the form of cash in vault or deposits at its Federal Reserve bank. On the other hand, it enjoys the privilege of borrowing from its Federal Reserve bank and of using the other facilities of the System.

Before the establishment of the Federal Reserve System, there were wide differences of opinion as to which commercial banks should be required or permitted to become members. At one extreme, those who were opposed to further "regimentation" of banks would have made membership in the system optional with each bank. At the other extreme, some would have forced every commercial bank in the country to become a member or cease to perform commercial banking functions. Here again, the issue was settled by compromise. Every national bank must become and remain a member of its Federal Reserve bank or forfeit its federal charter. Each state bank may, at its option, become a member if it can meet the minimum requirements for membership.

---

[2] These days the salary structure is the same but movement is the other way. For example, Paul Volcker left the presidency of the Federal Reserve Bank of New York to assume his current position as chairman of the Board of Governors in 1979. For his pains, Volcker was rewarded with a pay cut of more than $50,000. Evidently, members of the Board of Governors are perceived as civil servants while the heads of the district banks are viewed as bankers—and paid accordingly.

Table 9–1 shows the number of members and nonmembers of the Federal Reserve System on various dates. In mid-1978 there were 5,621 member banks, of which 4,616 were national banks and 1,005 were state banks. Thus, 38.2 percent of all commercial banks, holding 71.9 percent of total deposits in commercial banks, were members. Some 9,077 state banks, or 90 percent of all state banks, were nonmembers. However, most of these institutions are relatively small, as is indicated by the fact that although they constitute more than 60 percent of all commercial banks, they account for less than 30 percent of total bank deposits.

In the early years of the Federal Reserve, optimists hoped that a large percentage of state banks would find membership so attractive that they would join voluntarily. As the data in Table 9–1 show, this hope has been largely disappointed. At no time have as many as 25 percent of all state banks been members of the Federal Reserve. Indeed, since 1945, the percentage of all commercial banks that are members has declined steadily from 48.8 percent to 38.2 percent (see Table 9–1). This has come about because new state banks refuse to join the system and some existing members leave the system.

There are several reasons why many state banks have either left or failed to become members of the Federal Reserve System. Many of them cannot qualify for membership because of their inability to meet its minimum-capital requirements. But there are other reasons as well.

1  LOWER RESERVE REQUIREMENTS UNDER STATE LAWS. The fact that reserve requirements for member banks are higher than those

**TABLE 9–1**

*Member and non-member commercial banks*

| Data as of June 30 | Number of commercial banks | MEMBER BANKS | | | Non-member state banks | Number of member banks as a percentage of all commercial banks | Deposits at member banks as a percentage of total deposits |
|---|---|---|---|---|---|---|---|
| | | Total | National | State | | | |
| 1915 | 25,875 | 7,715 | 7,598 | 17 | 18,260 | 29.4 | 49.4 |
| 1925 | 27,858 | 9,538 | 8,006 | 1,472 | 18,320 | 34.2 | 72.8 |
| 1935 | 15,478 | 6,410 | 5,425 | 985 | 9,068 | 41.4 | 84.5 |
| 1945 | 14,003 | 6,840 | 5,015 | 1,825 | 7,163 | 48.8 | 86.6 |
| 1950* | 14,121 | 6,873 | 4,958 | 1,915 | 7,248 | 48.7 | 85.7 |
| 1955* | 13,719 | 6,543 | 4,692 | 1,851 | 7,176 | 47.7 | 85.2 |
| 1962* | 13,429 | 6,049 | 4,505 | 1,544 | 7,380 | 45.0 | 83.7 |
| 1970* | 13,686 | 5,767 | 4,620 | 1,147 | 7,919 | 42.1 | 80.0 |
| 1975 | 14,570 | 5,796 | 4,732 | 1,064 | 8,874 | 39.8 | 76.1 |
| 1978 | 14,698 | 5,621 | 4,616 | 1,005 | 9,007 | 38.2 | 71.9 |

* Data as of end of the year.
Source: *Federal Reserve Bulletin,* various issues.

prescribed by some state laws makes some banks unwilling to join. Furthermore, in many states reserve requirements can be met by the holding of interest-bearing assets. This is in contrast to the zero yield on vault cash or deposits with the Federal Reserve.

2 UNWILLINGNESS TO COMPLY WITH OTHER REGULATIONS APPLICABLE TO MEMBER BANKS. Many state banks operating under more lenient state banking laws are unwilling to comply with member bank regulations, such as the Clayton Anti-Trust Act prohibitions against interlocking bank officers, directors, and employees; restrictions on affiliates of member banks; limitations as to the types of assets acquired; limitations on a bank's loans to its executive officers; and reports required.

3 AVAILABILITY OF FEDERAL RESERVE SERVICES WITHOUT MEMBERSHIP. With certain limitations, nonmember banks may use the Federal Reserve clearing system and various other Federal Reserve facilities. A less generous policy toward nonmembers might force more banks into the System.

Somewhat understandably, Federal Reserve officials have been disturbed by declining membership in the system. We shall shortly consider some recently enacted remedies for this situation.

**Ownership of the Federal Reserve Banks**

Another controversial question prior to the passage of the Federal Reserve Act was, "Who shall provide the capital for the Federal Reserve banks?" Some wanted government ownership. Others wanted the stock to be sold to the general public, and still others wanted all stock to be sold to member banks. The solution was a compromise. Each member bank is required to subscribe to the stock of its Federal Reserve bank in an amount equal to 6 percent of its own paid-up capital and surplus, although in practice member banks have been required to pay in only half of their subscriptions. Thus, the Federal Reserve banks are wholly owned by their member banks.

It is important to note, however, that in this case, ownership does not carry with it control of the corporation and enjoyment of all its earnings. (The distribution of control is discussed in the next section.) Annual dividends to stockholders of the Reserve banks are limited to 6 percent of the paid-in capital stock. The remainder of Reserve-bank earnings has been used to build up the surplus accounts of the Reserve banks and to provide revenue for the Treasury. Since 1947 the Board of Governors has voluntarily operated under a plan whereby it channels into the Treasury most of the Reserve-bank earnings in excess of their dividend requirements. In 1977 this amounted to $5.9 billion, in 1978 the sum transferred was $7 billion, and in 1979 a hefty $9.3 billion.

**CONTROL OF THE FEDERAL RESERVE SYSTEM**

Closely related to the heated controversies over the structure of the Federal Reserve System were those concerning its control. The most widely debated questions were: (1) Who should control the Federal Reserve? (2) Should control be centralized or decentralized? Three principal groups wanted a voice in control — the federal government, member banks, and businesses that were customers of member banks. Some, arguing that central banking is essentially a governmental function and that one of its principal objectives is the regulation of member banks, demanded full government control. On the other hand, many bankers who considered the new Reserve banks to be essentially cooperative institutions for member banks demanded that full control be placed in the hands of bankers, although small banks feared domination by their larger competitors. Others argued that business customers of banks should be given a voice. No less heated were the discussions concerning the degree of centralization of control. Some wanted almost complete centralization, whereas others demanded a large degree of regional autonomy.

Here, too, the issue was settled by compromise. All the competing groups were given representation, and control was divided between a central authority in Washington, D.C., and the regional Federal Reserve banks. In the succeeding sections we shall describe the present system of control, which is summarized in Figure 9–2. It should be remem-

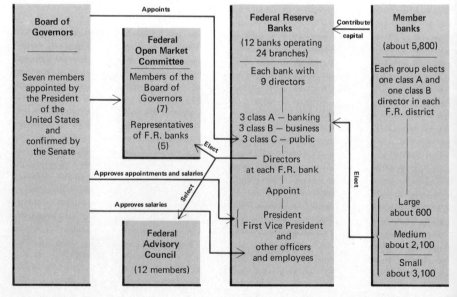

*Organization of the Federal Reserve System*

Source: Board of Governors of the Federal Reserve System, *The Federal Reserve System: Purposes and Functions*, 6th ed., Washington, D.C., 1974, p. 18.

**FIGURE 9–2**

bered, however, that the original division of authority proved unsatisfactory in many respects and has been changed in several ways since 1914. In general, the evolution has been toward greater centralization of authority and a greater degree of control by the federal government.

**The Board of Governors of the Federal Reserve System**

The central controlling authority, which has its offices in Washington, D.C., is the Board of Governors of the Federal Reserve System. This Board is composed of seven members (called governors) appointed by the President of the United States with the advice and consent of the Senate. Each member devotes full time to the Board, is appointed for a term of 14 years, and is ineligible for reappointment after serving a full term. No more than one member of the Board may be selected from any one Federal Reserve district, and in making appointments the President is to "have due regard to a fair representation of the financial, agricultural, industrial, and commercial interests, and geographical divisions of the country." The President designates one of the members as chairman of the Board and another as vice-chairman.

Although the actual location of control has in the past depended greatly on economic and political conditions and on the forcefulness of the various personalities involved, the Board of Governors is now clearly the most powerful controlling force in the entire Federal Reserve System. Among its most important powers are the following:

1   To exercise general supervision over the Federal Reserve banks, to examine their accounts and affairs, and to require reports by them.
2   To approve or disapprove appointments to the positions of president and first vice-president of each Federal Reserve bank and to suspend or remove any officer or director of any Federal Reserve bank.
3   To supervise the issue and retirement of Federal Reserve notes by each Federal Reserve bank.
4   To serve as a majority of the members of the Federal Open Market Committee.
5   To permit one Reserve bank to lend to another and, by a vote of at least five members of the Board, to require it to do so.
6   To determine, within the broad limits prescribed by law, the types of loans that the Reserve banks may make.
7   To approve or disapprove discount rates established by the Reserve banks.
8   To fix, within the limits established by law, member bank reserve requirements.
9   To regulate loans on securities.

Although this list is far from complete, it indicates the general scope of the Board's authority.

The Federal
Open Market
Committee

As we shall see later, one of the most powerful instruments of control in the hands of the Federal Reserve System is its power to buy and sell government securities, acceptances, and other obligations in the open market. The Reserve banks can create additional member bank reserves by purchasing obligations in the open market and can contract member bank reserves by selling securities. The original Federal Reserve Act was vague as to who should control this function, with the result that the individual Reserve banks sometimes followed conflicting policies, and sharp controversies arose within the system. Attempts were made to solve the problem in the 1920s by creating an informal open-market committee made up of representatives of the Federal Reserve banks, but these efforts were only partially successful. Some Reserve banks complained that they were not adequately represented; others ignored the decisions of the informal committee; and the Board in Washington, D.C., felt that it should have more control of this function.

The Federal Open Market Committee was created by amendments to the Federal Reserve Act in order to clarify the location of authority and to centralize the control of Federal Reserve open-market operations. It is composed of 12 members; 7 of these (a majority) are members of the Board of Governors of the Federal Reserve System and 5 are representatives of the Reserve banks. The latter are elected annually, must be either presidents or vice-presidents of Reserve banks, and are elected by the boards of directors of the various Reserve banks, each board having one vote. The distribution of the five Reserve bank representatives is as follows:

One from the Federal Reserve Bank of New York
One from the Federal Reserve Banks of Boston, Philadelphia, and
    Richmond
One from the Federal Reserve Banks of Atlanta, Dallas, and St.
    Louis
One from the Federal Reserve Banks of Minneapolis, Kansas City,
    and San Francisco
One from the Federal Reserve Banks of Cleveland and Chicago

Because of its key position, the New York Bank is always represented on the Committee.

*The Federal Reserve Bank of New York occupies a unique position with respect to the Federal Reserve System, the Treasury, and the banking system of the country. Its resources total approximately 40 percent of the aggregate of the twelve Federal Reserve Banks. It is located at the central money market and at the principal market for Government securities; its operations as fiscal agent of the United States and its transactions with foreign governments, foreign central banks and bankers, as well as its operations in foreign exchange, are in far greater volume than those of any other Federal Reserve Bank. It is clearly in the public interest that the Federal Open Market Committee be given at all times the benefit of counsel of the Federal Reserve Bank which is in constant touch with the domestic and international money and capital markets and has had long experience in these fields.[3]*

The Federal Open Market Committee has full control of all open-market purchases and sales by the Reserve banks. No reserve bank may engage in or decline to engage in open-market operations except in accordance with the regulations adopted by the Committee. The Committee was also given jurisdiction over Federal Reserve purchases and sales of foreign exchange soon after these began in the early 1960s.

**The Federal Advisory Council**

The Federal Advisory Council is composed of 12 members, one selected by the board of directors of each Reserve bank. The sole function of this Council is to act in an advisory capacity to the Board of Governors. The only sources of its power are its eloquence and the prestige of its members, most of whom are prominent individuals.

**Control of Individual Federal Reserve Banks**

Control of each of the 12 Federal Reserve banks is divided among the member banks in the district, businesspeople in the district, and the Board of Governors of the Federal Reserve System. Each Reserve bank has a board of directors with nine members. Three of these are known as Class A directors, three as Class B directors, and three as Class C directors. The Class A directors represent the member banks of the district and are chosen by them. To prevent domination of the Reserve bank by any one banking group, the member banks of the district are divided into three groups based on size, and each group elects one Class A director. The Class B directors represent industry, commerce, and agriculture in the district and must be actively engaged in one of these pursuits at the time of their election. They may not be officers, directors, or employees of any bank. They are, however, elected by the member banks of the district in the same way as the Class A directors. All three of the Class C directors are appointed by the Board of Governors. One of these, who must be "a person of tested banking experience," is chairman of the board of directors and Federal Reserve agent at the bank. As such, that person acts as official representative of the Board of Governors in carrying out its legal functions. Another Class C director at each Reserve bank acts as deputy chairman of the board of directors.

The chief executive officer of each Reserve bank is its president, who is appointed by its board of directors with the approval of the Board

---

[3] *Federal Reserve Bulletin*, August 1942, pp. 740–741.

of Governors. The first vice-president of each Reserve bank is appointed in the same way. Other Reserve bank officers and employees are appointed by the bank's board of directors, although they may, of course, be removed by the Board of Governors.

After a long period of doubt as to the proper location of authority in the Federal Reserve System, it is now clear that the Board of Governors occupies the dominant position. Some power still rests with the representatives chosen by member banks, but the Board of Governors has many sources of power:

1 Exclusive regulation of many Federal Reserve and commercial bank functions is in the hands of the Board.
2 Its members make up a majority of the members of the powerful Federal Open Market Committee.
3 The Board appoints three members of the board of directors of each Reserve bank, one of its appointees at each bank being chairman of the board of directors and Federal Reserve agent.
4 The Board may disapprove appointments of presidents and first vice-presidents of the Reserve banks and may remove directors, officers, and employees.

## FEDERAL RESERVE "CHORES"

Having examined the structure and control of the Federal Reserve System, we can now begin to study its functions. We shall look first at its functions other than those of monetary and credit management. For brevity these will be called chores. But these chores are not merely incidental or unimportant functions. Collectively, they account for the great bulk of work within the Federal Reserve. And in performing these chores, the Federal Reserve has contributed greatly to the efficiency and convenience of the banking system.

### Banking Supervision

As noted earlier, the supervision and examination of banking in this country are not exclusively a Federal Reserve function, but are shared with several other authorities. The Comptroller of the Currency has jurisdiction over all national banks. State banking authorities have jurisdiction over state banks. And the Federal Deposit Insurance Corporation has jurisdiction over all banks with deposit insurance, which includes all members of the Federal Reserve System and most nonmembers. Each Reserve bank has its staff of bank examiners, and member banks must periodically report their condition. In addition to requiring reports and examining member banks, the Federal Reserve exercises other important supervisory powers, among which are the powers to:

1 Remove officers and directors of member banks for continued violation of banking laws or for continued unsafe or unsound banking practices.

2  Suspend a member bank's borrowing privileges at the Federal Reserve if it is found to be making undue use of bank credit for speculation in securities, real estate, or commodities.

3  Permit national banks, where appropriate, to exercise trust powers.

4  Evaluate applications and rule on mergers between banks.

5  Establish allowable lines of business for bank holding companies.

6  Permit member banks to establish branches in foreign countries.

Overlapping jurisdictions of the chartering, supervisory, and examining authorities remain a problem despite the degree of cooperation achieved. These agencies sometimes conflict with each other, differ in their administrative interpretations if not in basic principles, and enable banks to "play off one agency against another." To eliminate the overlapping of federal and state jurisdictions may be politically infeasible. But many think it desirable, and perhaps politically possible, to eliminate at the federal level the overlapping jurisdictions of the Comptroller of the Currency, the Federal Reserve, and the Federal Deposit Insurance Corporation. Some suggest that all supervisory and examination powers should be vested in one of the existing agencies. Others think they should be concentrated in a newly created agency, which might also have jurisdiction over other types of financial institutions.

**Clearing and Collection of Checks**

The Federal Reserve System has greatly enhanced the speed, convenience, and cheapness of clearing and collecting checks and other similar items. Before 1914, a check might spend two weeks or more in the process of being cleared and collected, especially if it had to move long distances. The maximum time now required is only a few days, and banks that clear checks through the Federal Reserve receive payment in two days or less. The whole process is completed with virtually no shipment of coin or currency. Deposit accounts at the Federal Reserve banks play a central role in this process. All member banks hold deposit claims against their Federal Reserve banks to meet their legal reserve requirements, although cash in vault also counts as legal reserves. Many nonmember banks have deposits at the Federal Reserve for clearing purposes. This permits banks to make or receive net payments through the transfer of deposit credits on the books of the Federal Reserve.

To illustrate the development of the clearance and collection system for checks and similar instruments, let us look at the process in a few typical situations. The processes often vary in detail from those described below, but the principles involved are similar. Let us suppose that Smith deposits with the First Hartford Bank in Connecticut a check for $100 given him by Jones. If Jones's check is drawn on the First Hartford Bank, the clearance process is simple; the bank merely adds $100 to Smith's deposit account and deducts $100 from Jones's account.

Suppose, however, that Jones had written the check on another bank in the same city, the Second Hartford Bank. After Smith has deposited the check with the First Hartford Bank, it may be cleared in either of two general ways. The two banks may informally exchange their claims against each other at the end of the day, the net debtor then paying the other bank with a check drawn on another bank, probably the Federal Reserve bank of the district. Final payment is thus made by transferring a deposit credit at the Federal Reserve from the account of the Second Hartford Bank to that of the First Hartford Bank. Or the banks may clear and collect checks through a local clearinghouse. At an appointed time each day, each bank in the area takes to the clearinghouse all the checks and other matured claims that it has against the other members of the clearinghouse. There, clearinghouse officials compare the total amounts of checks presented by each bank against all other banks with the total amount of checks presented by all other banks against it, and then pay each bank the net amount due it or collect the net amount owed by it. These net payments are usually made with checks, often with checks drawn on the Reserve bank of the district. Actual coin or currency is almost never used to pay net differences at a clearinghouse.

If the check Jones gives to Smith is drawn on a bank located in another city in the same Federal Reserve district (say, in Springfield, Massachusetts), the clearance and collection procedure is somewhat as follows: Smith deposits the check with the First Hartford Bank, which credits his account and sends the check along with others to the Federal Reserve Bank of Boston for clearance and collection. The Boston Reserve bank then sends the check to Springfield, and the Springfield bank deducts the amount of the check from Jones's deposit account. After the lapse of sufficient time for notification if the check is not good, the Boston Reserve bank deducts the amount of the check from the Springfield bank's reserve account with it and adds the same amount to the Hartford bank's reserve account. Payment of the check has been achieved quickly and with no shipment of coin or currency.

The procedure is only slightly more complicated if Jones's check is drawn on a bank in another Federal Reserve district, say, on the Los Angeles Commercial Bank. Smith deposits the check with the Hartford bank, which credits his deposit account and sends the check along with others to the Federal Reserve Bank of Boston. The latter then sends the check along with others via air mail to the Federal Reserve Bank of San Francisco, which then sends it to the Los Angeles Commercial Bank. If the San Francisco bank is not notified within an appointed time that the check is bad, it deducts the amount of the check from the Los Angeles bank's reserve account with it. At or about the same time, the Boston Reserve bank adds the amount of the check to the Hartford bank's reserve account. At this point Smith has been paid, Jones has paid, Smith's bank has been paid, and Jones's bank has paid. But the San Francisco bank still owes the Boston bank the amount of the check, if it has not been offset by counterclaims. How is a net balance paid between Reserve banks? This is accomplished without any shipment of coin or currency by the simple expedient of book entries in the Interdistrict Settlement Fund, which is maintained by the Board of Governors in Washington, D.C. Each Reserve bank establishes a credit in the Interdistrict Settlement Fund. Any net balance due a Federal Reserve bank at the end of a day is added to its account in the Fund, and any net claim of another Reserve bank against it is deducted from its account.

It is through arrangements of this type that payments can be made to all points within the country quickly and without the inconvenience and expense of shipping coin or currency. Federal Reserve facilities for clearing and collection are available without charge to all member banks and to virtually all nonmembers.

**Wire Transfers**

In addition to providing a rapid and efficient system for clearing and collecting checks, the Federal Reserve transfers funds and certain types of securities by wire. Until the early 1970s the wire transfer system consisted of telegraphic linkages among the Board of Governors, the 12 Federal Reserve banks, and the 25 branches of the latter. This system was replaced in the early 1970s by a system of interconnected computers. The new system has far greater capacity than the old one and can accomplish in minutes what might earlier have required hours. Partly because of the rapidly rising burden of handling checks and other paper instruments, the Board of Governors encourages the use of wire transfers. To this end it has lowered charges for such transfers, lowered the minimum amounts that may be transferred by wire, and requested the Reserve banks to promote uses of the system. Almost all large payments are now transferred by wire.

Through the wire transfer system, the federal government, banks, and customers of banks can transfer funds from one end of the country to another almost instantaneously. Suppose, for example, that Jones in Los Angeles wishes to transfer by wire $1 million to Smith in Hartford, Connecticut. Jones gives her bank a check for that amount, and the bank wires the Federal Reserve Bank of San Francisco, asking it to transfer the funds. The San Francisco Reserve bank deducts the amount from the reserve account of the Los Angeles bank and wires the Federal Reserve Bank of Boston, telling the latter to transfer the funds to Smith at the First Hartford Bank. The Boston Reserve bank adds the amount to the First Hartford Bank's reserve account and wires the Hartford bank to credit Smith's account. The whole process is completed within minutes. The San Francisco Reserve bank settled with the Boston Reserve bank through a transfer on the books of the Interdistrict Settlement Fund at the Board of Governors.

Through its wire transfer system the Federal Reserve can also transfer federal government securities over long distances within a few minutes. Suppose, for example, that a bank in Seattle wishes to transfer $10 million of Treasury obligations to a New York dealer in government securities. The bank will take the securities to the Seattle branch of the Federal Reserve Bank of San Francisco, indicating the identity of the dealer to whom they are to be delivered. The Seattle branch will retire the $10 million of certificates and wire the Federal Reserve Bank of New York to issue and deliver to the buyer new Treasury obligations of the same issue and in the same amount. After the dealer has sold these securities, the Seattle bank may be paid through the wire transfer system.

In some cases such transfers of claims against the government debt are even simpler than the process just described. This is because at least some of the member bank's debt claims against the Treasury may not be evidenced by certificates or any other paper document, but only by book entries at its Federal Reserve bank. This claim at the Federal Reserve indicates the particular Treasury issues against which the bank has claims, and the amounts of each. If a bank wishes to sell some of these claims, it simply sends the relevant information to the Federal Reserve, which makes the transfer on its books.

Overall, some see the growing use of wire transfers, facilitated by advances in computer technology, as leading to the development of a nationwide electronic payments system. However, even if a fully integrated electronic payments system does not emerge in the near future, its encouragement of wire transfers shows that the Federal Reserve is committed to promoting a more efficient payments system.

**Truth in Consumer Lending**

In 1968 Congress passed the Truth in Lending Act and gave the Board of Governors responsibility for formulating and issuing regulations to carry out the intent of the Act—namely, to promote the informed use of credit. This responsibility has been fulfilled by the issuance of Regulation Z and the preparation of an annual report to Congress. Among other things, the report assesses the extent to which compliance is being achieved and suggests changes in the Act.

**Data Gathering and Economic Research**

Through its supervision of many aspects of banking, the Federal Reserve has also become a major source of economic data. These data are analyzed by economic researchers both in and out of government to help improve our understanding of monetary phenomena. In particular, the various Reserve banks and the Board of Governors all maintain sizable research staffs whose findings serve as inputs to the policy-making process. Both the economic data and the Federal Reserve analyses of these data are frequently communicated to the public. The Board of Governors, for example, publishes the extremely useful *Federal Reserve*

*Bulletin* on a monthly basis and even has weekly releases of monetary data. The Reserve banks also issue publications, typically in the form of a monthly review, which present analyses of both national and regional economic developments.

## FISCAL-AGENCY FUNCTIONS

As noted earlier, one purpose of the Federal Reserve Act was to provide the U.S. Treasury with a more satisfactory fiscal agent. Before that time the Treasury relied on commercial banks and on the so-called independent treasury system, which consisted of a number of regional suboffices of the Treasury. Both were unsatisfactory. Banks were unsatisfactory because some were unsafe, check clearing and collection were slow, and the limited geographic scope of each bank was not conducive to rapid regional transfers of government funds. The independent treasury system was unsatisfactory partly because its offices were so expensive to operate. Much more serious was that net movements of coin and paper money into and out of its vaults sometimes had undesirable effects on general credit conditions. Net collections of coin and currency from the public served to reduce bank reserves and restrict bank credit, whether or not this was desirable. And net outpayments of coin and currency tended to increase bank reserves and ease credit, sometimes when such results were not wanted. Treasury officials gradually learned how to avoid such undesirable results and even to use these powers in a stabilizing way. Nevertheless, it became clear that a more efficient mechanism was needed.

In acting as a fiscal agent, the Federal Reserve banks do an enormous amount of work for the federal government and its various offices and corporations. At some of the Reserve banks, the amount of work done for the government is comparable to, and even greater than, that done for the bank itself as principal. Among the functions performed by the Federal Reserve as principal banker to the government are the following:

1. Financial adviser
2. Depository and receiving and paying agent
3. Agent for issuing and retiring Treasury securities
4. Agent in other transactions involving purchases and sales of securities for Treasury account
5. Agent for the government in purchasing and selling gold and foreign exchange
6. Lender to the Treasury

### Financial Adviser

The Treasury and other government departments do not, of course, rely solely on the Federal Reserve for financial information and advice; they have their own staffs and many other sources. Yet the Federal

Reserve, which is so intimately and continuously in contact with the money, securities, and foreign exchange markets, is in a position to be especially helpful to the government in its debt management and foreign exchange transactions.

**Depository**    The Federal Reserve banks, collectively, are in one sense the principal depository of federal government funds, for most government payments are made out of the Treasury's deposit accounts at the Federal Reserve. Yet the Treasury ordinarily holds only a part of its deposit balances at the Federal Reserve; the remainder are held in thousands of commercial banks. This system was evolved to minimize disturbances to bank reserves and the general credit situation that would otherwise result as the government had large net receipts or made large net payments. During some periods, especially at the peak of tax collections or when the Treasury has sold a large issue of securities, the Treasury has large net receipts, mostly in the form of checks. If all these were put into deposits at the Federal Reserve banks, the Federal Reserve would add them to its deposit liability to the Treasury and deduct them from its deposit liabilities to the banks on which the checks were drawn. Thus the banks would lose reserves and the supply of money and credit would tend to be restricted, whether or not this was desired. At other times, especially when tax collections are small relative to expenditures, the reverse would happen. We shall see later that the Federal Reserve can attempt to offset such disturbances by sales and purchases of government securities in the open market. But to do this smoothly and effectively when the disturbances are large presents difficulties.

It is largely to avoid such difficulties that the Treasury holds deposits in tax and loan accounts at qualified commercial banks. These banks are those that want to hold Treasury deposits, have pledged government securities to assure the safety of these deposits, and have met certain other requirements. The system works as follows: A bank or customers of a bank send checks to the Treasury to pay taxes or to pay for securities purchased from the Treasury. The Treasury records the amounts received and routes the checks back through the Federal Reserve to the bank on which they are drawn, and the latter adds the amounts of the checks to its deposit liability to the Treasury. Note that at this stage the bank has lost no reserves; it has merely increased its deposit liability to the Treasury and, if the checks were written by customers, has reduced its deposit liabilities to the public. In the meantime, the Federal Reserve maintains complete records of the amounts of Treasury deposits at every bank. Later, a few days before the Treasury wishes to use the deposits for payment, the Federal Reserve in its capacity as fiscal agent announces the date when a stated percentage of Treasury deposits will be called. The call states, in effect, "On the specified date, X percent of

Treasury deposits will be withdrawn from your bank. On this date we shall deduct this amount from your reserve account at the Federal Reserve and you shall deduct this amount from your deposit liability to the Treasury." This tends, of course, to reduce bank reserves. However, meanwhile the Treasury checks drawn on the Federal Reserve will have been sent to payees. As these are deposited with banks and sent by banks to the Federal Reserve, the effect is to restore bank reserves. If the timing is perfect, there will be no net change in the total volume of bank reserves, although there may be some redistribution of reserves among the banks.

In the last few years there have been some changes in these procedures. A 1974 Treasury study concluded that revenues lost by the Treasury in holding balances in non-interest-bearing tax and loan accounts were not justified by offsetting cost savings in bank services. As a result, a sizable volume of Treasury deposit balances was shifted to the Federal Reserve. This permitted the Federal Reserve to hold a larger volume of securities and thus increase its earnings. Since, as we have seen, the Federal Reserve returns the bulk of its earnings to the Treasury, the Treasury was thus better off. More recently there has been a shift back toward the old system, but with more explicit compensation of the Treasury for the value of its deposits.[4]

**Agent for the Treasury in Securities Transactions**

The Federal Reserve does a tremendous amount of work for the Treasury in issuing and retiring securities and in purchasing and selling securities for trust funds and other accounts controlled by the government. When the Treasury offers new securities for sale, the Federal Reserve publicizes the issue, receives bids and subscriptions, decides which to accept and which to reject in accordance with Treasury instructions, and collects on behalf of the Treasury. As paying agent for the Treasury, it pays interest on the federal debt and redeems maturing securities. When, as sometimes happens, the Treasury offers an issue through an investment-banking syndicate, the Federal Reserve serves as agent for the Treasury in making arrangements.

**Agent for the Treasury in Gold and Foreign Exchange Transactions**

As already indicated, and as will be discussed more fully at a later point, the Treasury is sole custodian of the nation's monetary gold and buys and sells gold for monetary purposes. In almost all these transactions the Federal Reserve acts as agent for the Treasury. The Federal Reserve also buys and sells foreign exchange (claims against foreign moneys) both on its own account and as agent for the Treasury. Many of

---

[4] For a description of the current system, see Joan Lovett, "Treasury Tax and Loan Accounts and Federal Reserve Open Market Operations," Federal Reserve Bank of New York, *Quarterly Review*, Summer 1978, pp. 41–46.

these transactions are for the purpose of influencing the behavior of the exchange rate on the dollar. Others are merely to assist the Treasury in making or receiving international payments.

**Lender to the Government**

To be able to borrow directly from the central bank is a great convenience to the Treasury. But it is also dangerous, for the Treasury may insist on borrowing unduly large amounts from the central bank, thereby increasing bank reserves, despite potentially inflationary consequences. It is largely because of this danger that the power of the Federal Reserve to lend directly to the Treasury is limited by law. The Federal Reserve may not at any time hold more than $5 billion of federal securities acquired directly from the Treasury, and even this authorization is extended by Congress only on a year-to-year basis. However, this limitation removes neither the danger of undue Treasury pressure nor the power of the Federal Reserve to facilitate Treasury finance, for the Federal Reserve can purchase federal debt that has been sold to others and can otherwise create a liberal supply of credit that will be favorable to Treasury borrowing.

**PROPOSALS FOR CHANGE**

While we have spelled out the structure and duties of the Federal Reserve as they now stand, it would be rash indeed to assume that the evolutionary development of the system has ended. Even today, there are still heated controversies over the structure and control of the Federal Reserve. Three issues of concern are the independence of the Federal Reserve, the location of control in the Federal Reserve, and the problem of declining commercial bank membership in the system.

**Independence**

The Federal Reserve is based on the principle of independent central banking. It is, of course, responsible to Congress: It was created by Congress and must make reports to Congress. Nevertheless, there are a number of features that tend to insulate the Federal Reserve from Congress. These include long and staggered terms for members of the Board of Governors and the fact that the Federal Reserve neither is subject to conventional government audits nor depends on congressional appropriations for operating funds. One should not, however, overemphasize the Federal Reserve's insulation, since Congress can at any time change its basic legislation, give it directives, or even abolish it.

There is another aspect of "independence" that is perhaps more controversial, since in the nature of things the Federal Reserve is free to follow monetary policies that may be at odds with the wishes of Congress or the administration. This can result either from different readings of the economic tea leaves as to appropriate policies or from the fact that the Federal Reserve may be pursuing somewhat different goals than Congress or the administration. Those who defend the current system of independence — especially from the executive branch — base their views on the following types of considerations:

1   The administration in power is likely to have an easy-money inflationary bias, partly because easy money and mild inflation tend to be popular and to increase the ability of the incumbent political party to remain in power, and partly because the Treasury is likely to insist on easy money and low interest rates to keep down interest charges on the national debt and to facilitate its refunding and new-borrowing operations.

2   Control of the central bank is likely to inject "politics" into the bank's operations: patronage, discrimination on the basis of party affiliation, and so on.

3   Successful monetary management requires greater continuity among top officials than would be likely to result from responsibility to the President, whose tenure will be only four to eight years.

4   The existing arrangement elicits more confidence and cooperation from the commercial banks than they would give to a politically dominated institution.

On the other hand, several arguments are advanced for terminating the independence of the Federal Reserve and to making it responsible to the executive branch:

1   Monetary policy, like other governmental policies, should be controlled by people responsible to the electorate.

2   The present arrangement makes the appropriate coordination of monetary policy with the other economic policies of the government difficult. It is intolerable that the Federal Reserve should follow policies in conflict with those determined by the elected representatives of the people.

While this controversy has not been officially resolved, a number of developments have tended to reduce the level of conflict. For one, in recent years there has been considerable consultation between Federal Reserve and administration officials on economic policy. There are, for example, regular meetings involving the chairman of the Federal Reserve Board, the Secretary of the Treasury, and the chairman of the Council of Economic Advisers. In addition, since 1975 the Federal Reserve has regularly consulted with Congress as to the Board's overall economic objectives and its specific targets for the growth of the various measures of the money supply. Consultation, of course, does not imply agreement, so it should not be surprising that we can still find evidence of acrimonious debate prominently displayed in the financial press.[5]

**Control Within the Federal Reserve**

Less intense, but nevertheless important, are the continuing controversies over the location of control within the Federal Reserve System. Some who believe that centralization has gone too far would transfer some power back to the Reserve banks, or at least from the Board to the Federal Open Market Committee, on which the Reserve banks are represented. Others would concentrate still more power in the Board.

Proposals such as the following have been advanced in recent years:

1   Reduce the number of members of the Board of Governors from seven to no more than five. The primary purpose of this would be to increase the prestige of the Board and attract more able people to it. Other possible benefits are a greater concentration of responsibility and more flexible decision making.

2   Abolish the Federal Open Market Committee, remove from the Reserve banks their last vestige of control over the discount policy, and vest in the Board of Governors complete authority over discount policy, open-market policy, foreign exchange policy, and member bank reserve requirements. The boards of directors and executive officers of the 12 Reserve banks would then be responsible for carrying out the policies laid down by the Board of Governors, but their role in policy making would be purely advisory.

3   Retire the Federal Reserve stock now held by member banks, and with it, all the power of member banks to elect members of the boards of directors of the Reserve banks. This, it is expected, would leave the banks with no more control over monetary policy than they could achieve as members of the community.

None of these proposals has been adopted, and all remain controversial. If all were adopted, we should have in fact, if not in form, a single central bank.

**Federal Reserve Membership**

As already noted, commercial bank membership in the Federal Reserve System has been declining in recent years. Indeed, since 1945 the fraction of total deposits accounted for by member banks has declined from 87 percent to about 70 percent. The primary reason for this

---

[5] One proposal for reform that has often been advanced stems from the nature of the term of the chairman of the Federal Reserve. In particular, the chairman serves for four years, but the term is not matched up with the term of the President. Thus, for example, the term of the current chairman expires in March 1982, nearly one and one-half years after a presidential election. Those in favor of reducing Federal Reserve independence have argued for matching the chairman's tenure to that of the President.

decline lies in the nature of member bank reserve requirements. The current chairman of the Board of Governors, Paul Volcker, has expressed the issue as follows:

> *Members of the Federal Reserve System are currently subject to a special burden—from their point of view, the equivalent of a special tax—because they must maintain substantial levels of reserves in non-interest-bearing balances at Federal Reserve Banks. Nonmember commercial banks or other depository institutions—even when their business overlaps—have no comparable requirement. Member banks receive some offset to this burden because of their access to System services, but all studies indicate that the value of these services is, for the bulk of members, not sufficient to compensate for the earnings foregone on required sterile balances. In these circumstances, members leave the System, narrowing our base of control.*[6]

As this statement implies, the Federal Reserve is quite concerned with ensuring its continued ability to conduct an effective monetary policy—an ability it sees being undermined by declining commercial bank membership. To remedy this situation the Federal Reserve has advocated instituting homogeneous reserve requirements on all commercial banks and indeed, most recently, on all depository institutions. As perceived by the Federal Reserve, comprehensive reserve requirements covering commercial banks, savings and loan associations, mutual savings banks, and credit unions would solve both the membership problem and the problem created by the growing similarity of the liabilities of the various depository intermediaries. This similarity, of course, has precipitated a need for rethinking how we define the money stock. Since, as indicated in earlier chapters, it no longer seems possible to ignore nonbank intermediaries in defining the money stock, it is understandable that the Federal Reserve would prefer to have a comprehensive set of reserve requirements to improve control over such an expanded concept of money.

Not surprisingly, there was considerable opposition to any attempt to reform the structure of reserve requirements, especially from those who might face newly imposed requirements. These opponents bolstered their position with several arguments.

1   The Federal Reserve already has adequate credit-control powers, since its members hold over 70 percent of total commercial bank assets and deposits. Moreover, the presence of nonmembers is disadvantageous only when the Federal Reserve tries to increase reserve requirements of members to excessive levels, and this should not be done anyway.

---

[6] *Federal Reserve Bulletin*, October 1979, p. 823.

2   Such an extension of federal power would violate states' rights, in this case the right of states to regulate the banks that they charter.
3   The ability of banks to abstain from Federal Reserve membership or to withdraw from the system is a desirable part of our governmental system of "checks and balances"; it acts as a check on the severity of Federal Reserve actions.
4   A requirement that all banks hold their reserves in the form of deposits at the Federal Reserve would cause some of the bigger banks to lose at least part of their profitable interbank deposits.

Despite these arguments, in the face of declining Federal Reserve membership and the growing "moneyness" of the liabilities of all depository institutions, on March 31, 1980, a bill was signed into law calling for the gradual imposition (over an eight-year period) of reserve requirements on both nonmember commercial banks and the thrift institutions. Over the longer run, at least, this should largely solve the "membership problem."[7]

**SELECTED READINGS**

Bach, G. L., *Making Monetary and Fiscal Policy*, Washington, D.C., Brookings Institution, 1971.

Board of Governors of the Federal Reserve System, *The Federal Reserve System, Purposes and Functions*, 6th ed., Washington, D.C., 1974.

Chandler, L. V., *Benjamin Strong, Central Banker*, Washington, D.C., Brookings Institution, 1958.

Commission on Money and Credit, *Money and Credit*, Englewood Cliffs, N.J., Prentice-Hall, 1961.

Maisel, S. J., *Managing the Dollar*, New York, Norton, 1973.

*Report of the Committee on Financial Structure and Regulation*, Washington, D.C., Government Printing Office, 1971.

---

[7] The new legislation does not force any financial institutions to become members of the Federal Reserve. Rather it imposes reserve requirements on certain liabilities that are identical to those faced by member banks. In partial compensation, the legislation does extend the full range of Federal Reserve services, including discount privileges, to these newly affected institutions. For details of the legislation see Chapter 18.

Although its service functions are highly useful, the primary function of the Federal Reserve, as well as other central banks, is monetary management, that is, regulation of the supply of money and of the supply and availability of loan funds for business, consumer, and government spending. In an earlier chapter we found that the volume of deposits that commercial banks can create and have outstanding, and also the volume of earning assets that they can acquire and hold, depend on (1) the dollar volume of legal reserves available to the banks and (2) the height of their legal fractional-reserve requirements against deposits. Every dollar of legal reserves is high-powered money in the sense that each dollar of reserves can support several dollars of commercial bank deposits. But how high powered each dollar of reserves is depends on the height of legal-reserve requirements.

To carry out its function of general monetary and credit management, the Federal Reserve has powers to control both the height of reserve requirements and the volume and cost of bank reserves. As we have already seen, the Federal Reserve Act provides that only two types of assets can be counted as legal reserves for member banks: deposits at the Federal Reserve and cash in vault. Moreover, it empowers the Board of Governors to alter, within specified limits, the percentage reserve requirements against deposits in member banks. By raising the level of these requirements, the Board can inhibit the creation of money by the banking system and exert an antiexpansionary or even a contractionary influence. By lowering these requirements, the Board can permit and even encourage an expansion of money and credit. We shall see later that this is a powerful instrument, which the Board sometimes uses.

However, the Federal Reserve relies more continuously on its power to regulate the volume and cost of reserves available to the commercial banking system. This chapter will discuss the factors determining the volume of bank reserves and the processes through which the Federal Reserve creates and destroys these reserves. We shall emphasize Federal Reserve control of the money-creating and money-destroying activities of the commercial banks. However, it should be noted that in this process the Federal Reserve can itself create and destroy money. For example, when the Federal Reserve makes net purchases of assets it creates and issues funds that usually appear somewhere in the money supply. And when it makes net sales of assets it can directly decrease the money supply.

**FEDERAL RESERVE BALANCE SHEETS**

An analysis of the consolidated balance sheets of the 12 Federal Reserve banks will help us understand the processes through which the Federal Reserve increases or decreases the reserves of the commercial banking system. We start with basic balance sheet equations of the type developed in Chapter 6:

Assets = liabilities + capital accounts                        (1)
Liabilities = assets − capital accounts                      (2)

*Assets* include everything of value owned by the Federal Reserve banks at the stated point in time. *Liabilities* are debt claims against the Federal Reserve banks. *Capital accounts,* or net worth, are the ownership claims against the Federal Reserve banks. At any point in time the Federal Reserve banks must have outstanding a total of debt claims and ownership claims exactly equal to the value of their assets. If they make net increases in their assets, they must pay for these assets by creating and issuing an equal net increase in debt and ownership claims against themselves. And if they decrease their total asset holdings, they must withdraw and retire an equal amount of outstanding debt and ownership claims against themselves.

An examination of the Federal Reserve balance sheet in Table 10–1 reveals that the Reserve banks have paid for only a very small fraction, about 2 percent, of their assets by issuing capital account, or net worth, claims. Thus, the Reserve banks pay for their assets largely by issuing debt claims against themselves, and they withdraw and retire debt claims when they decrease their total assets. It is precisely through this mechanism that the Federal Reserve balance sheet provides the key ingredient in understanding how member bank reserves are determined. The essentials of this process can be seen as follows.

We first observe that the most important component of member bank reserves — namely, member bank deposits with the Federal Reserve — is an entry in the Federal Reserve's balance sheet. By rearranging the balance sheet, we can therefore express these deposits as the difference between total Federal Reserve assets and the Federal Reserve liabilities *other than* member bank deposits. Since elementary arithmetic and standard accounting procedures assure us that the balance sheet must balance, we inescapably come to the following conclusion: Unless it is offset elsewhere in the balance sheet, any change in an asset or liability *other than* member bank deposits has to affect member bank deposits. For example, if total Federal Reserve assets rise because of, say, a purchase of government securities, and if no other balance sheet item changes, then member bank deposits at the Federal Reserve must increase. Similarly, an increase in a Federal Reserve liability, say, in foreign deposits held with the Federal Reserve, if not counteracted elsewhere, necessarily leads to a decrease in member bank reserves.

Evidently then, it is changes in the various items in the Federal Reserve's balance sheet that contribute to the determination of member bank reserves. This suggests that it will be worthwhile to take a closer look at the major components of the balance sheet in Table 10–1. In the process we shall be able to go beyond what may seem, to some, accounting gimmickry, and gain a firmer understanding of the mechanics of *how*

**TABLE 10–1**

*Balance sheet of the Federal Reserve ~~Ban~~ks, August 31, 1979 ~~in~~ millions of dollars)*

| ASSETS | | LIABILITIES AND CAPITAL ACCOUNT | |
|---|---:|---|---:|
| Gold certificates | $ 11,259 | Federal Reserve notes | $106,900 |
| SDR certificates | 1,800 | Deposits due to Member banks | 29,493 |
| Coin | 441 | U.S. Treasury | 3,542 |
| Loans | 1,572 | Foreign | 325 |
| Acceptances | 475 | Other | 663 |
| Federal agency obligations | 8,395 | Deferred availability | |
| U.S. government securities | 113,027 | Cash items | 5,729 |
| Cash items in process of | | Other liabilities | 1,813 |
| collection | 9,938 | Total liabilities | $148,465 |
| Foreign exchange | 2,213 | Capital accounts | 3,063 |
| All other | 2,408 | **Total liabilities and** | |
| **Total assets** | $151,528 | **capital accounts** | $151,528 |

**Addenda**

| | |
|---|---:|
| Cash items in process of collection | $9,938 |
| **Minus:** Deferred availability cash items | 5,729 |
| **Equals:** float | $4,209 |

*Source: Federal Reserve Bulletin, October 1979, p. A12.*

changes in Federal Reserve assets and liabilities result in movements in member bank reserves.

**FEDERAL RESERVE NOTES AND DEPOSITS**

Federal Reserve liabilities are largely of two types: Federal Reserve notes and deposit liabilities. As indicated earlier, Federal Reserve notes make up the great bulk of paper money in the United States. Although they are impressively engraved and endowed by law with full legal-tender powers, they are nothing but debt claims against the Federal Reserve banks. Deposits at the Federal Reserve banks are also merely debts owed by the Federal Reserve. They are evidenced by book entries. Table 10–1 indicates that the Federal Reserve issued deposit claims against itself to only a few types of holders. It will not accept deposits from individuals, businesses, or state and local goverments. Most of its deposit liabilities are to member banks. These serve both as legal reserves for member banks and as a medium for clearing and collection, as noted earlier. Smaller deposit liabilities are owed to the federal government, to nonmember banks for check-clearing purposes, and to foreign central banks and the International Monetary Fund. It should be evident that member bank deposits at the Federal Reserve may be decreased as these deposits are shifted to the ownership of other depositors at the Federal Reserve, and that member bank deposits at the Federal Reserve may be increased as other deposits at the Federal Reserve are transferred to the ownership of member banks.

Changes in the volume of Federal Reserve notes outstanding reflect changes in the demand for paper money to be held in commercial bank vaults or to be used as currency in circulation, predominantly the latter. Whenever the public wants more currency, the commercial banks are the first to feel the impact. Customers write checks on their deposit accounts and withdraw cash. The banks may supply the currency out of their cash in vault, thereby losing legal reserves in this form, or they may get it by drawing down their deposits at the Federal Reserve. In the latter case, the increase in Federal Reserve notes outstanding is at the expense of member bank deposits at the Federal Reserve. On the other hand, when the public wishes to hold less paper money, it deposits the excess at commercial banks, which may either add it to their legal reserves in the form of cash in vault or send it along to the Federal Reserve. In the latter case, the Federal Reserve retires the net inflow of Federal Reserve notes and adds an equal amount to its deposit liabilities to banks.

This demonstrates several important points. First, it indicates how the volume of Federal Reserve notes is made responsive to the public's demand for paper money. Second, it shows that increases in Federal

Reserve notes outstanding tend initially to be at the expense of bank deposits at the Federal Reserve, and that decreases in Federal Reserve notes outstanding tend initially to increase the volume of bank deposits at the Federal Reserve. Third, it suggests why we are justified in assuming that when the Federal Reserve makes net purchases of assets, it initially pays for them by creating deposit claims against itself; and when it makes net sales of assets, it initially collects by withdrawing an equal value of its deposit liabilities. For simplicity of exposition we shall assume in the succeeding sections that when the Federal Reserve purchases assets, it makes payment by adding to the reserves of commercial banks; and that when it sells assets, it collects by deducting from the reserve balances of commercial banks.

**FEDERAL RESERVE ASSETS**

It should be emphasized that the Federal Reserve banks can create or destroy their own deposit liabilities by purchasing or selling any kind of asset whatsoever. Thus, they can create deposit liabilities to pay for land, buildings, equipment, services, or any type of claim against others. Or they can withdraw their deposit liabilities by making net sales of any kind of asset. This point should be borne in mind, because even now the Federal Reserve makes several kinds of purchases and sales, and in the future it might broaden the categories of assets in which it deals.

It will be useful to distinguish between two types of Federal Reserve purchases and sales of assets:

1  TRANSACTIONS WITH MEMBER BANKS. When the Federal Reserve purchases assets from a member bank, it pays that bank by adding to its reserve account. When it sells an asset to a member bank, it collects payment by reducing the bank's reserve account.

2  TRANSACTIONS WITH THE "PUBLIC." When the Federal Reserve buys an asset from the public—from an individual, business firm, or state or local government—it usually pays with a check drawn on a Federal Reserve bank. The seller of the asset usually deposits the check at a commercial bank, receiving in return a deposit credit there, and the commercial bank then sends the check to its Federal Reserve bank, which adds the amount of the check to the commercial bank's reserve account. Thus, Federal Reserve purchases of assets from the "public" tend to increase directly both the public's money supply and commercial bank reserves. Federal Reserve sales of assets to the public have the reverse effects. When a member of the public buys an asset from the Federal Reserve, he usually pays with a check drawn on a commercial bank. The Federal Reserve deducts the amount of the check from the commercial bank's reserve account and sends the

check to the commercial bank, which deducts its amount from the customer's deposit account. Thus, a Federal Reserve sale of an asset to the public tends to reduce directly both the public's money supply and commercial bank reserves. The effect on commercial bank reserves is, of course, more important, for each dollar of change in commercial bank reserves may induce, or even force, several dollars of change in the commercial banks' loans, investments, and deposit liabilities.

Although the Federal Reserve can create or destroy commercial bank reserves by buying or selling assets of any kind, Table 10–1 indicates that, in practice, Federal Reserve purchases and sales are largely confined to a few types of assets. We shall now examine these assets, and the ways in which they are acquired and sold by the Federal Reserve.

**United States Government Obligations**

By far the largest volume of Federal Reserve assets is in the form of debt claims against the U.S. government, including fully guaranteed obligations of federal agencies. Table 10–1 showed that in August 1979 these amounted to about $121 billion, or 80 percent of total Federal Reserve assets. This asset is of special importance not only because it is so large but also because it has become the principal medium through which the Federal Reserve regulates the volume and cost of bank reserves. The Federal Reserve creates bank reserves by purchasing government securities, and it destroys bank reserves by selling government securities. It buys and sells very frequently, sometimes almost continuously, and its purchases or sales are often very large.

As already indicated, Federal Reserve purchases and sales of government securities are under the jurisdiction of the Federal Open Market Committee and are executed for the system account through the Federal Reserve Bank of New York. The manager of the account buys and sells through government security dealers, of which there are about two dozen. These, in turn, deal with every type of investor that buys and sells government securities — commercial banks, all other types of financial institutions, nonfinancial business firms, individuals, foreign central banks, and others. The manager of the open-market account usually does not know the ultimate source of the securities bought or the ultimate buyers of the securities sold. It will further our analysis, however, to distinguish two types of transactions: (1) Federal Reserve purchases from, and sales to, commercial banks; and (2) Federal Reserve purchases from, and sales to, nonbank investors.

Consider first the case in which the Federal Reserve purchases $500 million of government securities from commercial banks. As shown in case I, the effect is to increase bank reserves by $500 million. The Federal Reserve pays for its additional assets by creating additional deposit liabilities to the selling banks.

|  | FEDERAL RESERVE | | COMMERCIAL BANKS | |
|  | ASSETS | LIABILITIES | ASSETS | LIABILITIES |
|---|---|---|---|---|
| se I | Government securities +$500 million | Deposits due banks +$500 million | Reserves +$500 million<br>Government securities −$500 million | |
| se II | Government securities −$700 million | Deposits due banks −$700 million | Reserves −$700 million<br>Government securities +$700 million | |

The total assets of commercial banks are not directly changed; the banks have simply exchanged $500 million of earning assets for an equal amount of legal reserves. The public's money supply is not directly affected. However, with the addition of $500 million to the excess reserves of banks, an expansion of bank credit and deposits becomes likely. Case II shows that a Federal Reserve sale of $700 million of government securities to banks will decrease bank reserves by that amount. In effect, the Federal Reserve collects from the buying banks by subtracting from their reserve accounts. There is no direct effect on the public's money supply, but a reduction may be induced by the decrease in bank reserves.

|  | FEDERAL RESERVE | | COMMERCIAL BANKS | | PUBLIC | |
|  | ASSETS | LIABILITIES | ASSETS | LIABILITIES | ASSETS | LIABILITIES |
|---|---|---|---|---|---|---|
| ase III | Government securities +$500 million | Deposits due banks +$500 million | Reserves +$500 million | Deposits +$500 million | Deposits +$500 million<br>Government securities −$500 million | |
| ase IV | Government securities −$700 million | Deposits due banks −$700 million | Reserves −$700 million | Deposits −$700 million | Deposits −$700 million<br>Government securities −$700 million | |

Let us now consider the case of Federal Reserve purchases of securities from any ultimate seller other than a bank. Case III assumes that you, as an insurance company executive, a manufacturer, or an individual, sell $500 million of government securities to the Federal Reserve. As shown in the balance sheets, the direct effect is to increase by $500 million both the public's money supply and bank reserves. When you, as the seller of securities, receive the $500 million check, you deposit it in your bank, which adds this amount to your deposit account and then sends the check to the Federal Reserve, which adds the amount to your bank's reserve account.

A comparison of cases I and III shows that all Federal Reserve purchases of securities add to the volume of bank reserves, but that only purchases from nonbank sellers add directly to the public's money supply. The total effects on the public's money supply and on the supply of credit may be the same in the two cases when both the direct effects and the induced expansion of commercial banks loans and security holdings are taken into account. In case I, where the banks receive increased reserves without any increase in primary deposits, the entire $500 million is added to excess bank reserves and becomes the basis for creating new derivative deposits through an expansion of commercial bank loans and security holdings. In case III, however, the banks receive the $500 million of reserves in a transaction that increases their primary deposits. some part of the increase of reserves must therefore be used to meet reserve requirements against the primary deposits, and only the remainder becomes excess reserves that can serve as a basis for creating derivative deposits.

Separation of cases I and III nevertheless serves to emphasize some important points.

1   The Federal Reserve can buy securities even when commercial banks do not want to sell; it can buy them from nonbank sellers who are depositors at banks.

2   The Federal Reserve can itself directly increase the public's money supply and need not rely solely on the willingness of banks to expand their loans and security holdings. Quantitatively, this direct effect of Federal Reserve purchases is usually much smaller than the expansion of commercial bank credit induced by the increase in their reserves. At times, however, it is important.

3   The Federal Reserve can directly contribute to the supply of lendable and spendable funds. Nonbank financial institutions, business firms, and others who sell securities to the Federal Reserve are provided with funds that they can lend, spend, or use in any other way they wish.

We shall emphasize the effects of Federal Reserve purchases and sales on the volume of commercial bank reserves, and thus on the ability of the banks to create credit and money, because these are usually so much larger. But the other effects should not be forgotten.

The effects of Federal Reserve sales of securities to purchasers other than commercial banks are exactly the reverse of those in case III. As shown in case IV, Federal Reserve sales of $700 million of securities to you, a nonbank, would reduce by that amount both the public's money supply and commercial bank reserves. When the Federal Reserve received your check, it would deduct its amount from the reserve balance of your bank and send the check to your bank, which can be relied on to deduct it from your deposit account. You and other nonbank purchasers of securities from the Federal Reserve would have less funds to lend to others, to spend, or to use otherwise.

Later sections will discuss at length the policy problems faced by the Federal Reserve as it must decide when, to what extent, and on what terms it will purchase or sell acceptances and government securities in the open market.

**Federal Reserve Loans**

This category consists almost exclusively of loans to member banks or, as this is sometimes called, *member-bank borrowing.* On rare occasions the Federal Reserve has made direct loans to the Treasury, nonmember banks, foreign central banks, and businesses. For example, loans to nonmember banks have been limited largely to periods of war and national crisis. It is felt that in more normal times these banks should not have the privilege of borrowing if they will not assume the obligations involved in becoming members of the Federal Reserve.[1]

Although the distinction has little economic significance, Federal Reserve loans to member banks are of two principal types: discounts (sometimes called rediscounts) and advances. When a bank secures Federal Reserve credit by discounting, or rediscounting, it simply endorses some of its customers' paper and sends it to a Reserve bank for *discount.* In effect, the Federal Reserve subtracts interest at its prevailing discount rate and credits the remainder to the borrowing bank's reserve account. Advances are simply loans to a bank on its own promissory note, although some sort of acceptable collateral is required. In recent years most Federal Reserve loans have been in the form of advances. Despite this fact, the facility for carrying out member-bank borrowing is still known as the *discount window.*

As is the case with purchases or sales of government securities, it should be clear that the Federal Reserve can create or destroy bank reserves by increasing or decreasing its outstanding loans. This is illustrated in the following table.

---

[1] As noted in the previous chapter, with the extension of reserve requirements to nonmember banks and to the thrift institutions, borrowing privileges were similarly extended. See Chapter 11.

| FEDERAL RESERVE | | | | COMMERCIAL BANKS | | | |
|---|---|---|---|---|---|---|---|
| ASSETS | | | LIABILITIES | ASSETS | | | LIABILITIES |
| Case I | Loans | +$100 | Deposits due banks +$100 | Reserves | +$100 | | Borrowings from the Federal Reserve +$100 |
| Case II | Loans | −$ 50 | Deposits due banks −$ 50 | Reserves | −$ 50 | | Borrowings from the Federal Reserve −$ 50 |

Case I indicates that when the Federal Reserve expands its loans to banks, it creates for them an equal increase in their reserves. Case II shows that when the Federal Reserve decreases its outstanding loans, it collects by reducing bank reserves.

**Acceptances**

A banker's acceptance arises out of a draft on a bank, typically drawn by or for the benefit of one of its customers, ordering the bank to pay to a stated party a specific sum of money on some well-defined future date. By writing "accepted" on the draft, the bank commits itself unconditionally to pay as ordered. It anticipates that the customer will provide the necessary funds to pay the acceptance when it is due. An acceptance is thus a way of substituting the credit of the bank for that of the customer. As with other securities, there is a market for bankers' acceptances. Consequently, Federal Reserve purchases and sales of acceptances have the same effects on bank reserves and the money supply as do similar transactions in government securities.

The importance of Federal Reserve open-market operations in acceptances has varied widely. During the period prior to the Great Depression, Federal Reserve holdings of this paper were often large, sometimes larger than its holdings of government securities. The volume of outstanding acceptances declined sharply during the Great Depression and remained very low until after the end of World War II. Federal Reserve operations in acceptances were negligible during this period. More recently, however, there has been a renewed increase in the volume of acceptances and the Federal Reserve has resumed its purchases and sales of them. These operations are still very small, but they could grow in the future.

**International Reserve Assets**

The next three types of Federal Reserve assets we consider — gold certificates, SDR certificates, and foreign exchange — are closely related to international monetary transactions. In particular, they are all components of, or claims against components of, the nation's international monetary reserves. As such, purchases and sales of these assets are not made for the primary purposes of affecting the reserve positions of domestic banks and domestic monetary conditions. Instead, the primary purpose is to influence the behavior of the exchange rates between the dollar and foreign moneys. Furthermore, to an important extent the Federal Reserve does not have complete control over its holdings of these assets. This can present a problem in the conduct of monetary policy since, as we shall see, changes in these assets can affect the supply of bank reserves. Fortunately, the Federal Reserve can prevent such increases or decreases of bank reserves, if they are undesired, by making offsetting sales or purchases of other types of assets, such as securities of the U.S. Treasury.

In the aggregate, gold certificates, SDR certificates, and foreign exchange assets account for about 10 percent of Federal Reserve assets (see Table 10–1). Gold certificates are by far the most quantitatively important of these three.

### Gold Certificates

Gold certificates are Federal Reserve claims against monetary gold held by the Treasury. For all practical purposes, the value of these claims is equal to the value of the nation's monetary gold stock. This is so because the Treasury generally *monetizes* the gold stock by issuing a dollar's worth of gold certificates for each dollar of gold it holds.[2] To see how this Federal Reserve asset arises, we consider the following example.

Suppose that an American gold miner or melter of scrap offers $10 million of gold, which is purchased by the Federal Reserve for the account of the Treasury. Let us trace the direct effects in two steps.

Step 1: The gold becomes an asset of the Treasury, which issues $10 million of gold certificates to the Federal Reserve, which adds $10 million to the Treasury's deposit account at the Federal Reserve. At this stage the gold purchase has not yet affected either the volume of bank reserves or the money supply.

Step 2: The Treasury write a check for $10 million on its deposit at the Federal Reserve and sends the check to the gold seller; the latter deposits the check in a commercial bank, which sends it to the Federal Reserve, which deducts $10 million from the Treasury's deposit and adds it to the bank's deposit account at the Federal Reserve. All this appears on the various balance sheets as follows:

---

[2] For purposes of valuing the gold stock the Treasury uses the official price of gold, currently $42.22 per ounce.

| | TREASURY | | FEDERAL RESERVE BANKS | | COMMERCIAL BANKS | |
| STEP | ASSETS | LIABILITIES | ASSETS | LIABILITIES | ASSETS | LIABILITIES |
| --- | --- | --- | --- | --- | --- | --- |
| 1 | Gold stock +$10 | Gold cert. +$10 | Gold cert. +$10 | Treas. dep. +$10 | | |
| 2 | | | | Treas. dep. −$10 Due banks +$10 | Reserves +$10 | Deposits due public +$10 |
| Net direct effects | Gold stock +$10 | Gold cert. +$10 | Gold cert. +$10 | Deposits due banks +$10 | Reserves +$10 | Deposits due public +$10 |

Thus, the normal direct effects of a net purchase of gold by the Treasury are to increase by equal amounts (1) the public's money supply, (2) commercial bank reserves, and (3) Federal Reserve holdings of gold certificates. Note that these are only the direct effects; further effects may be induced by the increase of commercial bank reserves. Net sales of gold by the Treasury to Americans normally have exactly the opposite direct effects.

The mechanics of gold certificates are slightly different when the transaction is between the Treasury and an official foreign or international institution. Suppose, for example, that the Federal Reserve, acting as agent for the Treasury, purchases $100 million of gold from a foreign central bank. The Treasury adds the gold to its assets. It then creates and issues an equal amount of gold certificates to the Federal Reserve, and the latter adds $100 million to its deposit liabilities to the foreign central bank. Thus, as long as the foreign central bank continues to hold the proceeds as a deposit at the Federal Reserve, there will be no effect on either the public's money supply or on the volume of bank reserves. Only when the foreign central bank withdraws these funds from the Federal Reserve will there be an effect.

Historically speaking, the size of the nation's monetary gold stock has varied over a wide range, thereby tending to have large direct effects on the volume of bank reserves and the money supply. In recent years, especially since the final demise of the gold standard in 1971, variations in the gold stock have been of considerably less importance. Those variations that have occurred stemmed from regular monthly gold sales by the Treasury.

### SDR Certificates

SDR certificates are Federal Reserve claims against Special Drawing Rights (SDRs) that are created by the International Monetary Fund and held by the Treasury. These are quite similar to gold certificates except that they are issued against "paper gold."[3] Thus, the normal effects of issuing SDR certificates are virtually identical to the effects of gold purchases. Similarly, the direct effects of a decrease of Federal Reserve holdings of SDR certificates are like those of gold sales — decreasing both bank reserves and the money supply.

*Foreign Exchange Holdings*

Federal Reserve assets in the form of foreign exchange are claims denominated in foreign currencies. These are in various forms — such as deposit claims against foreign, central, and commercial banks; short-term claims against foreign governments; and so on. When the Federal Reserve makes net purchases or sales of foreign exchange, the effects are almost exactly the same as those resulting from net purchases or sales of gold. When the Federal Reserve buys foreign exchange, it pays with checks on itself, and these are added to the money supply of the seller and to bank reserves. When it sells foreign exchange, it withdraws funds from both the money supply and bank reserves.

**Federal Reserve Float**

Only one other Federal Reserve asset requires consideration here. This is Federal Reserve float. This is actually a net-asset item arrived at by subtracting a liability called *deferred availability cash items* from an asset called *cash items in process of collection*. Both arise out of the Federal Reserve function of clearing and collecting checks and other such claims. Checks worth billions of dollars flow into the Federal Reserve banks every day and require some time to be cleared, paid to the reserve accounts of the banks that deposited them, and deducted from the reserve accounts of the banks on which they are drawn. As a result, at any point in time the Federal Reserve owns a great volume of checks that it has not yet collected and has not yet paid. The asset "cash items in process of collection" indicates the value of checks in its possession on which it has not yet collected by deducting from its deposit liabilities to banks. The liability "deferred availability cash items" indicates the value of checks it has not yet paid by adding to its deposit liabilities to the banks that sent the checks to it.

If the Federal Reserve paying and collection schedule were to work out perfectly, these asset and liability items would balance out exactly, because the Federal Reserve attempts to pay banks depositing checks at the same time that it collects from the banks on which the checks are drawn. As checks flow into the Reserve banks, they are classified as payable "today," "tomorrow," or "the day after tomorrow," the date depend-

---

[3] In contrast to its normal practice with respect to gold and gold certificates, the Treasury does not issue to the Federal Reserve a volume of SDR certificates equal to all its holdings of SDRs; instead it holds some of its SDRs inactive or unmonetized.

ing on the estimated time required for the checks to reach the banks on which they are drawn. On the appointed day the amounts of the checks are credited to the reserve accounts of the depositing banks. Ideally, they would on the same day be deducted from the reserve accounts of the banks on which they are drawn. In this case "deferred availability cash items" would be exactly equal to "cash items in process of collection"; the Federal Reserve would not have paid depositing banks before it collected from others. In the process of clearing and collection, it would have neither created nor destroyed bank reserves but would have only shifted reserves from some banks to others.

In practice, however, the Federal Reserve sometimes pays depositing banks before it collects from the banks on which checks are drawn. To this extent, it contributes to total bank reserves. This source of bank reserves is called *Federal Reserve float*. At any point in time it measures the net amount the Federal Reserve has contributed to bank reserves because it has paid some banks before it collected from others. For example, on the date to which Table 10–1 refers, Federal Reserve float amounted to $4,209 million. In most of the Federal Reserve balance sheets that we shall use later, we shall enter float as a net asset item and omit the two items from which it has been derived.

Several factors account for the existence of Federal Reserve float:

1   UNREALISTIC COLLECTION SCHEDULES. In at least a few cases, checks could not reach the banks on which they are drawn within the appointed time even if their flow were unimpeded. For example, checks drawn on banks located in remote sections of Utah and Nevada and deposited at the Federal Reserve Bank of Boston are credited two days later to the reserve accounts of the banks that deposited them, even though the checks cannot within that time reach the bank on which they are drawn.

2   DELAYS IN THE TRANSIT DEPARTMENTS OF THE FEDERAL RESERVE BANKS. The time of paying a check is determined at the time of its receipt at a Federal Reserve bank. If the process of clearing is delayed because of inadequate staff or an unusually heavy flow of work, or for any other reason, the collection of checks may be delayed.

3   DELAYS IN TRANSPORTATION. Anything that delays the transportation of checks after they have been received by a Reserve bank and their dates of payment have been determined can increase float. For example, a heavy fog over the eastern half of the United States could delay air mail and the collection of checks from the banks on which they are drawn and thereby increase Federal Reserve float and bank reserves by several hundred million dollars.

Once the Federal Reserve has determined its schedules for clearing any collection, it has no direct control over the volume of float. It must passively pay and collect checks in accordance with its announced schedules. Unfortunately, Federal Reserve float fluctuates widely over short periods. For example, for the week ending September 12, 1979, the float rose by nearly $2\frac{1}{2}$ billion. If nothing had been done about this, it would have led to a substantial increase in bank reserves. However, as a result of offsetting sales of government securities by the Federal Reserve, bank reserves for the week in question actually declined. This illustrates the general point that one function of the Federal Reserve is to prevent fluctuations in the volume of float, and in other things that might alter the reserve positions of the banks, from exerting unwanted influences on monetary and credit conditions.

**LIMITS ON FEDERAL RESERVE LIABILITIES**

What, if anything, limits the extent to which the Federal Reserve can create Federal Reserve note and deposit liabilities by purchasing assets of various kinds? One type of limit has been in the form of legal-reserve requirements. The precise nature and extent of these have varied over time, but the requirements have typically specified that some fraction of Federal Reserve deposit liabilities and of outstanding Federal Reserve notes be backed by gold certificates. However, as it appeared that these reserve requirements might limit Federal Reserve expansionary policies or even require restrictive action, Congress first reduced them and then eliminated them completely. Since March 1968 the Federal Reserve has not been subject to any reserve requirements related to gold. It is, however, still true that each Federal Reserve bank must maintain collateral to match the volume of its outstanding Federal Reserve notes.[4] Thus far, at least, ample collateral has been readily available,[5] so that for all practical purposes the volume of Federal Reserve notes and deposit liabilities now depends solely on discretionary management.

**DETERMINANTS OF MEMBER BANK RESERVES**

In the words of the Federal Reserve itself, bank reserves function as "a fulcrum for the operation of monetary policy." This, indeed, was the primary motivation for setting ourselves the objective of analyzing the factors determining the volume of bank reserves and the process through

---

[4] In case you never noticed, paper currency in the form of Federal Reserve notes does indeed bear the imprint of an individual Federal Reserve bank. Next time you have a dollar bill, look closely at the circular design on the left-hand side over the serial number.

[5] Eligible collateral includes U.S. government securities, gold certificates, SDR certificates, and collateral received in making loans.

which the Federal Reserve creates and destroys these reserves. Having examined the important components of the Federal Reserve's balance sheet, we are now in good position to be able to complete this task. In particular, as suggested earlier, we can now explicitly rearrange the Federal Reserve balance sheet so as to focus on member bank reserves. In so doing, we will arrive at what is commonly called the member bank reserve equation.

**Member Bank Reserve Equation**

The *member bank reserve equation* is derived from a set of satistical series, developed by the Federal Reserve, entitled "Factors Affecting Member Bank Reserves." These statistics, which are issued in a weekly statement by the Board of Governors, are carried in the major newspapers on Thursday afternoon and Friday morning, and in the monthly *Federal Reserve Bulletin*. Table 10–2 presents such a statement for the end of August 1979.

As anticipated, Table 10–2 bears a striking similarity to the Federal Reserve balance sheet, an example of which was provided for the same date in Table 10–1, but there are a number of differences. These arise from the fact that Table 10–2 has consolidated the balance sheets of both the Federal Reserve and the monetary section of the Treasury. This accounts for the appearance of items such as "Treasury currency outstanding" and "Treasury cash holdings" in Table 10–2.[6]

The column on the left side of Table 10–2, labeled "Factors supplying reserve funds," includes all the sources of funds that are capable of being used as member bank reserves. For the most part, the entries arise from the asset side of the Federal Reserve balance sheet. If there were no competing uses for these funds, the volume of member bank reserves at any time would be equal to the sum of these sources. The first principal source is what is known as *Federal Reserve credit*. This is simply the volume of funds that have been created by the Federal Reserve in the process of acquiring and holding assets in the form of United States government securities, acceptances, loans, float, and other Federal Reserve assets. This source accounted for about 84 percent of all these funds. The second major source is the monetary gold stock, which represents the volume of funds supplied as the Treasury bought and held

---

[6] A number of other minor differences also result from consolidation. For example, gold shows up in Table 10–2 under "Gold stock" and in Table 10–1 as "Gold certificates." The difference, if any — there actually was none for the date shown — reflects unmonetized gold held by the Treasury, and this would be included in Treasury cash holdings. For a detailed discussion of the Federal Reserve's balance sheet and member bank reserves, see D. M. Nichols, *Modern Money Mechanics*, Federal Reserve Bank of Chicago, 1975, or D. H. Friedman, *Glossary: Weekly Federal Reserve Statements*, Federal Reserve Bank of New York, 1976.

gold. The third source is the amount of SDRs monetized by the Treasury. The fourth source, Treasury currency outstanding, indicates the amount of funds supplied by the outstanding coin and paper money issued by the Treasury.

The right-hand column of Table 10–2 labeled "Factors absorbing reserve funds," shows the various uses of the total funds provided by the sources, and the amounts absorbed in each use. It is immediately apparent that large amounts of the funds supplied by the sources are not available for use as member bank reserves because they are absorbed in competing uses. The volume of member bank deposits at the Federal Reserve at any time is equal to the total volume of funds absorbed by the sources in the left-hand column minus the amounts of these funds absorbed in competing uses, shown in the column on the right. Thus, Table 10–2 shows member bank reserves with Federal Reserve banks of $29,493 million. These are equal to the $158,082 million supplied by the various sources, minus the $128,589 million absorbed by competing uses.

Total reserves, of course, consist of both deposits of member banks at the Federal Reserve and vault cash. As indicated in Table 10–2, cash in the vaults of member banks amounted to over $10 billion in August 1979, so that total reserves were slightly over $40 billion. All of this can

**TABLE 10–2**

*Factors affecting nber bank reserves end-of-month data for August 1979 in millions of dollars)*

| Factors supplying reserve funds | | Factors absorbing reserve funds | |
|---|---|---|---|
| Federal Reserve credit | | Currency in circulation | $118,914 |
| U.S. government securities | $113,027 | Treasury cash holdings | 268 |
| Federal agency securities | 8,395 | Deposits at Federal Reserve other than | |
| Acceptances | 475 | member bank reserves | |
| Loans | 1,572 | Treasury | 3,542 |
| Float | 4,209 | Foreign | 325 |
| Other Federal Reserve assets | 4,621 | Other | 663 |
| Total F.R. credit | $132,299 | Other Federal Reserve liabilities | |
| Gold stock | 11,259 | and capital | 4,877 |
| SDR certificates | 1,800 | Subtotal | $128,589 |
| Treasury currency outstanding | 12,724 | Member bank reserves with | |
| Total | $158,082 | Federal Reserve Banks | 29,493 |
| | | Total | $158,082 |

**Addenda: Member bank reserves**

| | |
|---|---|
| Member bank deposits at the Federal Reserve | $ 29,493 |
| **Plus:** cash in vault | 10,523 |
| **Equals:** Total reserves | $ 40,016 |

*Source: Federal Reserve Bulletin, October 1979, p. A4.*

be expressed in equation form in the so-called member bank reserve equation:

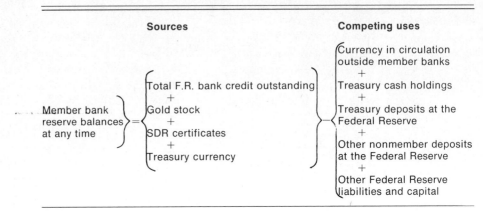

As we have already examined the various sources in some detail, no further description of these should be needed. However, in order to understand better the workings of the member bank reserve equation, some of the items under "Competing uses" require comment.

*Currency in Circulation*

**Competing Uses of Funds**    Of all the competing uses of funds supplied by the sources, currency in circulation outside member banks is by far the largest. It also shows substantial changes from one period to another. As noted earlier, when the public wishes to hold more coin and paper money, it withdraws these forms of money from the banks, which thereby lose reserves in the form of cash in vault or deposits at the Federal Reserve. On the other hand, when the public surrenders some of its holdings of coin and paper money to the banks, the latter receive an addition to their legal reserves. As indicated in Table 10–2, the official Federal Reserve tables handle this item in a somewhat clumsy way. They first include as a factor absorbing reserve funds (or a competing use) all currency outside the Federal Reserve and the Treasury, including the cash held in member bank vaults. Then, at the end, they add back as a component of member bank reserves the amount of currency held by the member banks. Accordingly, in writing our member bank reserve equation we have adjusted the competing uses of currency so as to be equivalent to currency in circulation outside the member banks (and, of course, outside the Federal Reserve and Treasury as well). It is this substitution that allows us to put *total* member bank reserves on the left-hand side of the reserve equation.[7]

*Treasury Cash Holdings and Treasury Deposits at the Reserve Banks*

Because they are so closely related and because their fluctuations have the same effects on the general monetary and credit situation, we shall consider the Treasury cash holdings and Treasury deposits at the Federal Reserve banks together. Both compete with member bank reserves for funds supplied by the sources. Increases in both tend to decrease bank reserves, and decreases in both tend to add to bank reserves.

The Treasury can alter both the size of its money balance and the form in which it is held. It holds its money balance in three principal forms: (1) as cash in its own vaults, (2) as deposits at the Reserve banks, and (3) as deposits with commercial banks. As noted earlier, the last are usually called "tax and loan accounts." To illustrate the process through which increases in Treasury cash holdings or in Treasury deposits at the Federal Reserve tend to reduce member bank reserves, let us consider two cases.

1   The Treasury deposits at the Federal Reserve $100 million of checks it has received from the public. These checks may represent payments of taxes or payments for securities bought by the public. On receiving the checks, the Federal Reserve will add $100 million to Treasury deposits and deduct the same amount from the reserve accounts of the banks on which they are drawn. The checks will then go to the banks on which they are drawn, which will deduct them from the public's deposit accounts. Thus, the effects are to decrease by $100 million both the public's money supply and member bank reserves.

2   The Treasury increases its deposits at the Federal Reserve by withdrawing $100 million of deposits from commercial banks. On receiving the checks, the Federal Reserve will add them to Treasury deposits and subtract them from member bank reserves.

When the Treasury draws down its cash in vault or its deposits at the Federal Reserve, it produces the reverse effects. We have already noted that fluctuations in the size of Treasury holdings of cash and deposits at the Federal Reserve often tend to have important effects on the reserve positions of commercial banks, especially in periods of large net receipts or net payments by the Treasury, and the Federal Reserve often takes action to prevent their having undesired effects on the general credit situa-

---

[7] This apparent sleight of hand involves nothing more than subtracting vault cash from currency in circulation in Table 10–2 and, so as to keep the books balanced, adding it to member bank deposits, yielding total reserves.

tion. In addition, as discussed previously, the Treasury assists in minimizing these effects by the use of tax and loan accounts.

*Foreign Deposits at the Federal Reserve*

These are largely deposits owed by the Federal Reserve to foreign central banks. Like Treasury deposits at the Federal Reserve, foreign deposits compete with member bank reserves for funds supplied by the sources. Increases in this item tend to decrease member bank reserves, and decreases in it tend to add to member bank reserves. Suppose, for example, that foreign central banks pay out to the U.S. public $100 million of checks drawn on the Reserve banks. This will tend to increase by $100 million both the public's money supply and member bank reserves, because the public will deposit the checks at commercial banks, which will send them to the Federal Reserve to be added to their reserve accounts. If foreign central banks deposit at the Federal Reserve $100 million of checks received from the U.S. public, the effects will be just the reverse: decreases in both the public's money supply and member bank reserves.

*Other Deposits at the Federal Reserve*

These are largely deposits that nonmember banks maintain at the Federal Reserve to facilitate check clearing and collection. They are usually relatively small and fluctuate narrowly. Nevertheless, they are competitive with member bank reserves for funds supplied by the sources. Increases in this term tend to reduce member bank reserves, largely because they reflect net losses of reserves by member banks to nonmembers. On the other hand, decreases in this item, usually reflecting gains of reserves by members from nonmembers, tend to increase member bank reserves.

*Other Federal Reserve Liabilities and Capital*

This item is made up largely of the Federal Reserve net worth or capital account, with adjustments for minor liability items not accounted for elsewhere, and competes with member bank reserves for funds supplied by the sources. To the extent that the Federal Reserve acquires assets by issuing ownership claims, it does not have to issue liability claims. This item usually fluctuates only narrowly over short periods.

*Changes in Member Bank Reserves Over Time*

The preceding discussion relates to the factors that determine the size of member bank reserves as of a given date. Changes in these factors over any stated period of time determine the change in the volume of member bank reserves during that period. Increases or decreases in the source items tend to increase or decrease member bank reserves.

On the other hand, increases in the amounts of funds absorbed in competing uses tend to reduce bank reserves, and decreases in the amounts of funds employed in competing uses tend to increase bank reserves. This is illustrated in Table 10–3, which compares the factors affecting member bank reserves in August 1979 and August 1977. Some factors tended to increase and some to decrease bank reserves during this period, but the net effect was an increase of $3,042 million. The factors tending to decrease bank reserves were decreases in the gold stock (a source) and increases in competing uses in the forms of currency in circulation and other Federal Reserve liabilities.and capital. All of the

**TABLE 10–3**

*Factors affecting member bank reserves, August 1977 and August 1979 end-of-month data (millions of dollars)*

| Bank reserves and related items | August 1977 | August 1979 | Increase bank reserves | Decrease bank reserves |
|---|---|---|---|---|
| **Sources** | | | | |
| Federal Reserve credit: | | | | |
| U.S. government securities | 98,436 | 113,027 | + 14,591 | |
| Federal agency securities | 7,505 | 8,395 | + 890 | |
| Acceptances | 131 | 475 | + 344 | |
| Loans | 1,265 | 1,572 | + 307 | |
| Float | 3,842 | 4,209 | + 367 | |
| Other Federal Reserve assets | 2,462 | 4,621 | + 2,159 | |
| Gold stock | 11,595 | 11,259 | | − 336 |
| SDR certificates | 1,200 | 1,800 | + 600 | |
| Treasury currency | 11,161 | 12,724 | + 1,563 | |
| Total sources | 137,597 | 158,082 | | |
| **Minus:** | | | | |
| Competing uses | | | | |
| Currency in circulation | 97,943 | 118,914 | | +20,971 |
| Treasury cash holdings | 440 | 268 | − 172 | |
| Treasury deposits at Federal Reserve | 6,115 | 3,542 | − 2,573 | |
| Foreign and other nonmember deposits at Federal Reserve | 1,214 | 988 | − 226 | |
| Other Federal Reserve liabilities and capital | 3,623 | 4,876 | | + 1,253 |
| Total competing uses | 109,335 | 128,588 | | |
| **Equals:** | | | | |
| Member bank deposits at Federal Reserve | 28,262 | 29,494 | | |
| **Plus:** | | | | |
| Member bank cash in vault | 8,712 | 10,523 | | |
| **Equals:** | | | | |
| Total member bank reserves | 36,974 | 40,017 | | |

Source: Federal Reserve Bulletin, October 1977, October 1979.

remaining items listed in Table 10–3, be they sources or uses, tended to change in such a way so as to increase bank reserves.

As Table 10–3 reveals, the single most important factor tending to change reserves during the period in question was the rise of currency in circulation. For changes in reserves taken over long periods of time, this is typically the case. In the short run, however — say, for a week or a month or even several months — the other sources and uses are often of greater importance in contributing to potential reserve movements.

While it is informative simply to list the factors tending to increase and decrease reserves, this does not convey the true nature of the problem faced by the Federal Reserve, should it want to achieve a given volume of member bank reserves. This stems from the fact that only a small number of items in the reserve equation are under the direct control of the Federal Reserve. The items under direct control of the Federal Reserve include Federal Reserve holdings of government securities and acceptances and, to a lesser extent, loans to member banks.[8]

The remaining items either fall under the control of "outsiders" or result from technical or external factors, such as the weather in the case of the float. Items controlled by outsiders include the public's holding of currency, Treasury deposits, and foreign central-bank deposits with the Federal Reserve. This is not to suggest that the Federal Reserve cannot offset, if it wishes, these factors to a considerable extent. Indeed, the large net purchases of government securities shown in Table 10–3 were for the purpose of offsetting all the factors that tended to decrease bank reserves and to achieve a net increase. In the next chapter we shall consider in more detail how open-market operations are used for this purpose.

CONCLUSION   In carrying out its monetary policy, and especially its open-market operations in acceptances and government securities, the Federal Reserve relies heavily on the type of analysis developed previously. As Robert V. Roosa has pointed out, Federal Reserve open-market purchases and sales are of two principal types: dynamic and defensive. *Dynamic purchases* or sales are those undertaken to effect net increases or net decreases in member bank reserves. *Defensive purchases* or sales are those undertaken to prevent other factors from bringing about unwanted changes in bank reserves. In effect, they are offsetting operations. These defensive operations can be in the right direction and in the right magnitude only to the extent that the Federal Reserve can forecast the behav-

---

[8] Member bank borrowings are determined jointly by the demand for such loans by the commercial banks and the willingness of the Federal Reserve to supply these loans. The precise nature of this interaction is spelled out in the following chapter.

ior of the various determinants of member bank reserves. The manager of the open-market account therefore seeks not only to detect changes as they occur but also to forecast future changes.

For this purpose, the manager has several sources of information. To help in forecasting the behavior of Federal Reserve float, there are elaborate studies of its seasonal behavior in the past and reports from the various Reserve banks concerning any unusual conditions that might cause it to rise or fall. Nevertheless, the behavior of float has proved difficult to forecast with accuracy. The Treasury reports any significant changes that it plans in the volume of its outstanding currency and in the size and location of its money balance. Studies of past seasonal patterns are used in predicting the volume of currency in circulation. Instructions from foreign central banks assist in forecasting the behavior of foreign deposits at the Federal Reserve. The Reserve banks also report changes in their deposit liabilities to nonmember banks and any large transactions that would affect significantly the size of other Federal Reserve accounts.

In short, an understanding of the nature and behavior of the various determinants of member bank reserves is esential for both the student and the practioner of monetary management.

**SELECTED READINGS**

Board of Governors of the Federal Reserve System, *The Federal Reserve System, Purposes and Functions*, 6th ed., Washington, D.C., 1974.

Friedman, D. H., *Glossary: Weekly Federal Reserve Statements*, New York, Federal Reserve Bank of New York, 1975.

Nichols, D. M., *Modern Money Mechanics*, Chicago, Federal Reserve Bank of Chicago, 1975.

# INSTRUMENTS OF MONETARY MANAGEMENT

In this chapter we shall analyze the various instruments of monetary management in the hands of the Federal Reserve. General monetary or credit controls—those directed toward regulating the total supply of money or credit without necessarily regulating the allocation of credit among its various possible borrowers or uses—will be discussed first. Selective controls, those intended to regulate or influence the allocation of credit, will be considered later.

As already indicated, the Federal Reserve's powers to regulate the total volume of money and bank credit are of two broad types: (1) various powers to regulate the magnitude and cost of member bank reserves, and (2) power to determine and alter member bank reserve requirements. These will be discussed in order.

## OPEN-MARKET OPERATIONS

Open-market operations constitute the most important tool of the Federal Reserve in regulating the cost and dollar volume of member bank reserves. Operations are conducted primarily through purchases and sales of U.S. Treasury obligations, but the Federal Reserve also buys and sells bankers' acceptances and securities issued by federal agencies such as the Federal National Mortgage Association.

### Some Mechanics

As noted earlier, Federal Reserve open-market operations are controlled by the Federal Open Market Committee (hereafter referred to as the FOMC), which is composed of the seven members of the Board of Governors, the president of the Federal Reserve Bank of New York, and four other presidents of Reserve banks. The FOMC meets in Washington, D.C., approximately once a month. These meetings typically begin with a review of recent and prospective economic and financial developments, in both words and pictures (via what is known as the "chart show"). Following a discussion of the objectives of monetary policy for the near-term future, the meeting culminates with the issuance of a domestic policy *directive* aimed at spelling out the broad nature of the actions to be taken. Actual purchases and sales are made by the manager of the open-market account, who is a vice-president of the Federal Reserve Bank of New York but is accountable to the FOMC. In addition to the directive, which is rather general, the FOMC provides some operating guides for the manager by specifying acceptable ranges for certain key financial variables. We shall later discuss the choice of these variables and specific nature of the directive. For the present it suffices to note that the FOMC does not set the actual quantity and nature of future open-market operations at its monthly meeting. This is left to the discretion of the manager, who, however, confers daily by telephone with some of the FOMC members. In buying and selling, the manager deals with about two dozen government security dealers, who, as noted earlier, are at the center of a national and even international market for government securities. The manager of the open-market account is thus in a position to use open-market operations in a highly timely and flexible manner. The account manager can buy or sell quickly, change the rate of purchases or sales quickly, and shift quickly from buying to selling, or vice versa.

When the manager of the open-market account purchases government securities from a dealer, the dealer is paid with a check on the Federal Reserve Bank of New York. The dealer must, of course, pay these funds to the seller of the securities. If the seller is a commercial bank, the immediate effect is to increase the volume of bank reserves. If the seller is someone other than a bank, the effect is to increase directly both the public's money supply and the dollar volume of bank reserves, because the seller will deposit the check with his or her bank, which will deposit it at a Reserve bank.

Sales of government securities by the manager of the open-market account have the opposite effect. If the buyer is a commercial bank, the effect is to reduce bank reserves. If the buyer is someone other than a bank, the effect is to reduce directly both bank reserves and the public's money supply. In effect, the dealer pays the Federal Reserve with a check received from a customer of some bank, the Federal Reserve deducts the check from the bank's reserve account and sends the check to the bank, which deducts it from the customer's deposit account.

In actual practice, such transactions typically do not even require a check, since the process is accelerated by a computer linking the Reserve banks and the banks that act as clearing agents for the dealers. Dealer payments and debits or credits to member bank reserves are thus made simultaneously, and the transaction is fully cleared during the day specified for delivery, which is often the same as the day of purchase.

Although these transactions typically occur in New York City, their effects are by no means confined to that area. Those who sell the government securities purchased by the Federal Reserve, and thereby gain Federal Reserve funds, may be located at any place within the country. So may those who buy the government securities from the Federal Reserve and thereby lose Federal Reserve funds. Moreover, the effects will be spread throughout the banking system and the financial markets regardless of the geographic location of the institution or person selling securities to, or buying securities from, the Federal Reserve. This happens because the banks that receive the reserves created by Federal Reserve purchases will lose reserves to other banks as they expand their own loans and security holdings. And banks that lose reserves because of Federal Reserve sales will draw reserves from other banks as they contract their credit. These processes may, of course, require some time.

Federal Reserve open-market operations are of two principal types: (1) outright purchases and sales, and (2) purchases under repurchase agreements and sales under matched sale–purchase arrangements. *Outright purchases and sales* are ordinary transactions in which neither the buyer nor seller makes a commitment to resell or rebuy. The transaction is final. In contrast, under a *repurchase agreement* the Federal Reserve buys securities from a dealer, with an agreement that the dealer will repurchase the securities within a stipulated period, which never exceeds 15 days and is typically less than 7 days. This is much like a short-term loan to the dealer, and the effective rate of interest is set by an auction among dealers. A *matched sale–purchase* transaction is simply the other side of the coin, in which the Federal Reserve sells securities to a dealer and agrees subsequently to buy the securities back, usually in less than 7 days.

Federal Reserve officials regard money created by repurchase agreements as "dollars with strings on them," for the very purchases that involve the issue of the dollars make provision for return of the dollars on a stipulated date. Such acquisitions are a useful instrument for at least two purposes. For one thing, they are a convenient way of supplying funds to meet a temporary need, and of withdrawing funds when the need has passed. For example, the Federal Reserve may acquire securities under repurchase agreements during the week before Christmas, when currency is being drained from the banks, arranging for dealers to repurchase the securities just after Christmas, when large amounts of currency flow back into the banking system. This device is also useful for avoiding disorderly changes in the market price of government securities. Dealers in these securities ordinarily hold inventories far larger than they can finance with their own capital funds. They rely heavily on borrowed money. If at some time they could not borrow sufficient funds, or could do so only at very high rates of interest, they might dump large amounts of their inventory on the market, thereby seriously disturbing not only government security prices but also money market conditions in general. Judicious Federal Reserve acquisitions under repurchase agreements can help prevent such occurrences.

Matched sale–purchase transactions work in an analogous way, except, of course, that their effects are restrictive. In particular, the initial sale causes reserves to flow from banks through the dealers to the Federal Reserve. Later, when the Federal Reserve purchase is made, the flow of reserves is reversed. Quite obviously, such arrangements are ideally suited to situations in which the Federal Reserve wishes to absorb a temporary surplus of reserves created by some external factor.

Table 11–1 contains data pertaining to open-market transactions for two years, 1974 and 1978. In particular, it shows both the extent of the various types of transactions and the securities in which these transactions were made. In regard to these data, the following points are worth emphasizing:

**TABLE 11–1**

*Transactions of the open-market account, selected years (in millions of dollars)*

| Type of transaction | 1974 | 1978 |
|---|---|---|
| **U.S. government securities** | | |
| Outright transactions | | |
|   Gross purchases | 13,537 | 24,591 |
|   Gross sales | 5,830 | 13,725 |
|   Redemptions | 4,682 | 2,033 |
| Matched sale–purchase transactions | | |
|   Gross sales | 64,229 | 511,126 |
|   Gross purchases | 62,801 | 510,854 |
| Repurchase agreements | | |
|   Gross purchases | 71,333 | 151,618 |
|   Gross sales | 70,947 | 152,436 |
| **Federal agency obligations** | | |
| Outright transactions | | |
|   Gross purchases | 3,087 | 301 |
|   Gross sales | 0 | 173 |
|   Redemptions | 322 | 235 |
| Repurchase agreements | | |
|   Gross purchases | 23,204 | 40,567 |
|   Gross sales | 22,735 | 40,885 |
| **Bankers acceptances** | | |
| Outright transactions, net | 511 | 0 |
| Repurchase agreements, net | 420 | −366 |
| **Total net change (all categories)** | 6,149 | 6,951 |

1   The bulk of open-market transactions are now made via repurchase agreements or matched sale–purchase arrangements and not through outright purchases and sales.[1] A comparison of the data for the two years shown reveals that this tendency has been more marked in recent years.
2   Most open-market transactions are in Treasury securities. Furthermore, although not detailed in the table, the bulk of these are in relatively short-term Treasury bills.
3   The *gross* volume of transactions is huge when compared with the *net* change in Federal Reserve holdings of Treasury securities, agency obligations, and acceptances. It is even large when compared with the stock of Federal Reserve holdings of these assets, which amounted to some $120,000 million in mid-1979.

**Defensive and Dynamic Open-Market Operations**

As noted earlier, *defensive open-market operations* are those undertaken by the Federal Reserve to prevent other factors, such as changes in the gold stock or in currency in circulation outside the banks, from bringing about unwanted changes in the reserve positions of banks. *Dynamic operations* are those aimed at altering the reserve positions of banks. This distinction is useful in emphasizing that not all Federal Reserve purchases and sales are designed to bring about net increases or decreases in bank reserves. In fact, as one might suspect from the statistics in Table 11–1, the great majority of open-market transactions are purely defensive. Consider for a moment the data for 1978. As Table 11–1 reveals, gross purchases (outright or otherwise) of Treasury securities alone amounted to over $685 billion in 1978. The net increase in Federal Reserve holding of government securities and acceptances was a much smaller $7 billion. But even this overstates the change in member bank reserves. In particular, because of other factors in the bank reserve equation that tended to absorb reserves, actual member bank reserves increased by about $5 billion during 1978. It should be quite evident that the manager of the open-market account would have to earn his or her salary even if the FOMC wanted reserves to stay constant.[2]

While we have stressed the prevalance of defensive open-market

---

[1] The astute reader may be puzzled as to why, in Table 11–1, gross sales and purchases are not identical for repurchase agreements and matched sales–purchases. The reason is that some transactions that are initiated near the end of the year may not be completed until the following year.

[2] Some economists have argued that part of the explanation for the substantial volume of open-market operations displayed in Table 11–1 is that the Federal Reserve Board has tried to keep short-term interest rates from moving very much in a short period of time. This is considered briefly in the next sections and will be taken up again in a subsequent chapter.

operations, we should not lose sight of the importance of dynamic operations. After all, it is through dynamic changes, which purposively alter member bank reserves, that monetary policy has its impact on the financial sector and thus on the economy. From this perspective defensive operations are a technical detail from which one might well abstract. Indeed, this is precisely the tack we shall take in all subsequent discussion of monetary policy. That is, whenever we talk about the impact of an open-market transaction, we shall always have in mind an operation designed to change member bank reserves. Let us turn now to the effects of such operations.

**Effects of Federal Reserve Purchases or Sales**

Federal Reserve purchases or sales of government securities may have three types of direct effects: (1) effects on the dollar volume of bank reserves, (2) impact effects on the price and yield of the particular type of security bought or sold, and (3) effects on expectations concerning the future behavior of security prices and yields. In some cases one or more of these effects may fail to appear, but when they do, they may be powerful or weak, desired or undesired, anticipated or unanticipated.

Effects on the volume of bank reserves appear in every case and are usually the most powerful, for every change of one dollar in bank reserves is the basis for a change of several dollars in the money supply and bank credit. It is for this reason that throughout we shall stress the effect of open-market operations on the reserve position of the banking system. However, it would in some cases be a mistake to ignore the other effects.

When the Federal Reserve buys or sells a particular type of government security, the impact or initial tendency is to change the price and yield of that particular security. This effect may be negligible if the amount purchased or sold is very small relative to the total supply, but it may be significant if the operation is larger relative to the supply. Suppose, for example, that the Federal Reserve purchases a large amount of government securities in the ten-year maturity range. This may be described as an increase in the demand for that type of security. Or it may be described as a decrease in the supply available to meet private demands. In any case, the initial tendency is to raise the price of the security and lower its yield. This impact effect is likely to be moderated and spread to other securities through private arbitrage. Private investors will tend to shun this security, and even to sell it, until its yield is as attractive as yields on other securities. However, this process may be time-consuming and imperfect, especially if the impact effects were very large. Comparable processes may be involved if the Federal Reserve sells large amounts of a particular security.

Federal Reserve attitudes toward the impact effects of its purchases and sales on the prices and yields of particular securities or groups of securities have varied widely. During much of its history the Federal Reserve has sought to avoid, or at least to minimize, them. To this end, it has often confined its operations to short maturities, where the impact effects are expected to be small, and has spread its purchases or sales over time. At other times it has consciously used this power to influence directly the prices of particular securities or groups of securities. For example, it has often bought or sold to prevent or ameliorate "disorderly movements" of security prices. From 1942 to 1951 it even went so far as to "peg" the prices and yields on long-term government securities within narrow limits. It has also engaged in "swap operations," sales of securities in one maturity range offset by purchases of securities in another maturity range. For example, in the early 1960s it sold Treasury bills and other short-term securities in order to hold down their prices and support their yields, at the same time buying long-term securities in order to support their prices and hold down their yields. We shall see later that some Federal Reserve efforts to affect directly the behavior of the prices and yields of securities have jeopardized its ability to control the volume of bank reserves.

Federal Reserve open-market operations may also influence the behavior of security prices and yields by influencing private expectations. These are often called "announcement" effects. Suppose, for example, that private investors see that the Federal Reserve has begun to purchase large amounts of securities with the apparent purpose of easing credit. If they come to believe that the policy will continue and will succeed, private investors will be impelled to increase their demands for securities, thereby increasing the flow of loanable funds, supporting the rise of security prices, and reinforcing the decline of yields. On the other hand, large Federal Reserve sales of securities may create expectations of higher interest rates in the future, which will tend to decrease private demands for securities and tighten credit further.

**Treasury Financings and Open-Market Operations**

We have already seen that flows of funds into and out of the coffers of the Treasury may require offsetting open-market operations to minimize the impact on bank reserves. There is, however, another way in which the operations of the Treasury impinge on the conduct of open-market operations. More specifically, large-scale Treasury debt financings—especially those involving intermediate- and longer-term debt—are regarded as having the potential to create "disorderly" financial markets. To avoid such problems, during a period of major Treasury financing the Federal Reserve resorts to a policy of keeping an *even keel* in the bond markets. For example, if it is pursuing a tight-money policy, the Federal Reserve will be somewhat less aggressive in carrying out its open-market operations. The Federal Reserve is somewhat sensitive about this policy and is quick to point out that "in no way does even keel provide a guarantee that the Federal Reserve will stabilize securities markets for Treasury financings at the expense of reserve objectives." Nevertheless, it seems clear that for a period of from one to three weeks the Federal Reserve partially gives up its freedom to maneuver in the conduct of monetary policy.

**Patterns of Open-Market Operations**

The Federal Reserve can use its powers to buy and sell in the open market in many different ways, with quite different consequences for financial markets and the economy. We shall explore only a few of the possible patterns. The first is one in which the Federal Reserve retains precise control of the amount of securities held. Members of the FOMC might describe it this way: "We shall determine the amount of securities that we hold, the types and amounts that we buy and sell, and when we buy and sell. We retain the initiative and will not buy or sell simply because others wish to sell to us or buy from us." Under such a policy, the Federal Reserve can accurately control both the volume of its holdings and the volume of bank reserves, but the prices and yields on securities can fluctuate in response to changes in demand-and-supply relationships in the market.

Another and very different pattern is the one in which the Federal Reserve passively buys and sells some security or group of securities at a fixed price and yield. For example, the FOMC might say, "At this price and yield on long-term government securities we shall buy all offered to us and shall sell all demanded from us." While such a policy is in effect, the price of the selected security or group of securities obviously cannot fall below the price at which the Federal Reserve will buy, nor can it rise above the price at which it will sell. However, the Federal Reserve, in adopting such a policy, loses control over both the volume of its security holdings and the volume of bank reserves. It must hold all the securities that others issue and what others do not want to hold at the fixed price and yield levels. As passive buyer and seller, it surrenders control over the volume of its holdings.

We shall later consider other patterns of open-market operations and some of the problems faced by the Federal Reserve in determining which pattern to follow. However, two points should be emphasized here.

1   The system must choose between accurate control of the volume of its holdings of government securities on the one hand and stabilization of interest rates on the other. If it is to control accurately the volume of its holdings, it must allow the prices and yields of government securities to fluctuate in response to changes in the supply of, and demand for, these obligations. If it is to stabilize their prices and yields, it must abandon accurate control of the volume of its holdings and passively buy or sell all the

securities offered to it, or demanded from it, at the selected level of prices and yields. In this case, the initiative is with other investors, for it is they who determine the volume of securities offered to, or demanded from, the Federal Reserve. This means, of course, that they also determine the volume of bank reserves.

2    As long as investors can shift freely between government securities and other obligations, the Federal Reserve can dominate the entire structure of interest rates by regulating yields on the federal debt. This debt now makes up a sizable fraction of all the outstanding interest-bearing debt of the country, and is equal to many times the annual increase in total debt. If the Federal Reserve buys and sells these securities freely in such a way as to maintain a certain structure of yields on them, it also establishes, within narrow limits, the structure of yields on other debts. The reason for this is that private investors are free to arbitrage among the various branches of the debt market, to sell in one and buy in another until they see no further advantage in shifting their funds. This applies not only to banks but to other investors as well. In short, Federal Reserve operations in the government securities market can dominate the entire money market. However, we shall see later that if this power is used to stabilize interest rates, the effect may be to destabilize the rest of the economy.

**DISCOUNT POLICY AND DISCOUNT RATES**

We have already noted that the Federal Reserve can create bank reserves by increasing its loans to member banks and can destroy bank reserves by decreasing its outstanding loans. Indeed, this Federal Reserve lending mechanism was originally conceived of as the focal point of central banking operations in the United States. Although the Federal Reserve now relies primarily on open-market operations to regulate the volume of bank reserves, its discount policy, which refers to the terms and conditions on which it will lend, remains of considerable importance.

**Types of Borrowings**

As noted previously, member banks may borrow funds by means of either discounts or advances. Discounting entails the sale (rediscount) of "eligible paper" to a Reserve bank. An advance is a loan to a bank on its own promissory note, secured by adequate collateral. The original notion in setting up the Federal Reserve System was that most borrowing would take the form of rediscounting of short-term self-liquidating commercial paper. This was evidently a direct result of the then-prevailing commercial loan theory of banking. With the demise of the commercial loan theory, this form of borrowing has fallen into disuse. In modern times virtually all borrowing, facilitated by the marked growth in the public debt, takes the form of advances secured by government securities (although such borrowing is still loosely referred to as discounting). In addition, the Federal Reserve Act has been amended to permit advances on collateral other than government securities or eligible paper. In short, the trend has been toward greater freedom for the Federal Reserve to determine the types of loans it will make.

**Administration of the Discount Window**

Unlike the case with open-market operations, where the impetus lies with the Federal Reserve, the initiative for discounting resides with the member commercial banks. As we have seen, borrowing from the Federal Reserve is but one way in which banks can seek to augment their liquidity. Other methods include the sale of securities, the issuance of CDs, and borrowing in either the federal funds or Eurodollar markets. The extent to which a bank relies on discounting depends on its opportunities with respect to these other sources, the duration of its needs, and the relative price and availability of advances from the Federal Reserve. Indeed, it is through these latter two factors that the Federal Reserve influences the volume of advances. In particular, the administration of the discount window has two major components:

1   DISCOUNT RATE POLICY. As noted earlier, the discount rate is simply the interest rate charged by the Reserve banks on their loans. Increases in discount rates raise the cost of acquiring reserves by borrowing, whereas decreases in discount rates make it cheaper for banks to acquire reserves in this way.

2   NONPRICE METHODS. A wide array of "nonprice" methods is used to influence the amount of discounting. These range from moral suasion to quantitative rationing and even to outright denial of loans.

Central banks differ greatly in the extent to which they rely on discount rates and on other methods to regulate the volume of their loans and discounts. Also, the role of the discount rate and the effects of discount-rate changes are strongly influenced by the extent to which other methods of control are used.

Under certain conditions a central bank's discount rate could regulate with accuracy the level of market rates of interest, or at least of short-term interest rates. Suppose, for example, that two conditions obtain: (1) The central bank stands ready to lend freely at its established discount rate; it uses no other rationing methods and relies on the discount rate alone to regulate the volume of its loans. (2) Commercial banks have no inhibitions against borrowing from the central bank. Intent on maximizing their profits, they borrow from the central bank and lend whenever market rates of interest exceed the discount rate by an amount sufficient to cover the cost of risk bearing and loan administration. They also withdraw loans from the market and repay their borrowings at the central bank whenever market rates of interest are not sufficiently higher than the discount rate. Under such conditions the central-bank discount rate could dominate market rates of interest. Increases and decreases in the discount rate would almost automatically raise or lower market rates of interest. Moreover, discount rates would be the central bank's sole method of regulating the volume of bank reserves that it created by lending.

These are not the conditions in American banking, and the Federal Reserve discount rate is not the only method used to regulate the volume of bank borrowing. Many observers have pointed out that even before the establishment of the Federal Reserve there was, among American banks, a "tradition against continuous borrowing," a feeling that it was unsound for a bank to borrow continuously or excessively. Although such a tradition undoubtedly did exist, it would probably be far weaker and less powerful as a deterrent to borrowing if Federal Reserve officials had not worked so hard and continuously to strengthen it. Perhaps it would be more accurate to say that the Federal Reserve developed "a tradition against continuous and excessive lending to an individual bank," and that the banks are well aware of this. Federal Reserve officials have repeatedly stated that borrowing is a privilege and not a right, that a member bank should not borrow simply because it is profitable to do so, and that a bank should borrow only to meet the drains it could not foresee, and even then only for short periods except under "unusual and exceptional circumstances."

A Reserve bank rarely refuses to lend to a member bank that is facing an actual or prospective deficiency in its reserves. But after making a short-term loan to a bank, it studies the situation carefully. If it finds that the bank has borrowed too often, too continuously, too much, or for improper reasons, it may advise the bank to contract its loans or sell securities in order to reduce or retire its borrowings. It may even go as far as to refuse to renew the loan, and in extreme cases it may suspend the bank's borrowing privilege.

Federal Reserve officials could, of course, attempt to regulate the volume of member bank borrowing by varying their own attitudes toward lending — being very strict on some occasions and more liberal on others. Although this method is used to some extent, it is not a very flexible or effective instrument.

This combination of member bank inhibitions against large and continuous borrowing from the Federal Reserve and the latter's unwillingness to make such loans to a member helps to explain several aspects of monetary policy in the United States.

1　When member bank borrowings from the Federal Reserve are large, credit is usually "tight." Credit is, of course, less tight than it would have been if the banks had not been able to borrow and secure reserves, but it is tighter than it could have been if the banks had had the same volume of reserves without borrowing.

2   The role of discount rates in regulating the volume of bank reserves is reduced in importance. The Federal Reserve does not rely solely on increased discount rates to limit member bank borrowing. And because of the tradition against continuous borrowing, decreases in discount rates may not be very effective in inducing larger member bank borrowings.

It would be a mistake to dismiss changes in discount rates as ineffective and useless and to rely solely on the tradition against continuous borrowing and on Federal Reserve admonitions to regulate the amount of member bank borrowing. Changes in discount rates remain important and influence the economy in several ways.[3]

1.  They do have some effect on the volume of member bank borrowings from the Federal Reserve. A member bank faced with the question of how to deal with an actual or prospective deficiency in its reserves is tempted, despite the tradition against continuous borrowing, to repair its reserves in the cheapest way. If the Federal Reserve discount rate is lower than the yield it would have to sacrifice by selling some of its earning assets, a member bank may elect to borrow from the Federal Reserve and may be in no hurry to repay its borrowings. This is especially true of banks that have not been borrowing continuously and therefore fear no early chastisement by Federal Reserve officials. The result can be a significant increase in member bank borrowings and reserves and a minimum of pressure toward credit restriction. However, if the discount rate is higher than the yields on assets that the banks might sell to repair their reserve positions, many banks will not borrow and will repay their borrowings quickly. They will attempt to repair their reserve positions by calling loans or selling securities. The result may be to decrease member bank borrowings and to enhance restrictive pressures.

2.  Changes in discount rates can be an effective way of announcing to both the banks and the public the direction of Federal Reserve policy. Open-market operations are not well suited to this purpose, partly because they are not widely understood and partly because dynamic operations are often obscured for some time by defensive operations. On the other hand, changes in discount rates are widely publicized as soon as they occur, and are generally believed to be important. In fact, many people exaggerate their importance. An increase in discount rates is generally interpreted as meaning that the Federal Reserve is moving toward tighter credit and higher interest rates. This may induce some lenders to

---

[3] For data on actual discount rate changes in recent years, the reader is referred back to Figure 7–1.

restrict their loans in anticipation of higher interest rates in the future. A reduction of discount rates, presaging an easier monetary policy and lower interest rates, may induce some lenders to increase immediately their willingness to lend. Of course, there is the possibility that changes in discount rates will have perverse announcement effects. For example, if an increase in discount rates is interpreted to mean that Federal Reserve officials believe inflation is coming, such an action might encourage people to borrow and spend, thereby increasing the danger of inflation. If a decrease in discount rates is taken as a forecast of business recession, it could encourage a reduction of spending and hasten a business decline. However, such perverse announcement effects are likely to occur only if changes in discount rates create expectations about the trend of business that the public would not have had anyway, and if the public believes the Federal Reserve will not be able to achieve its objectives. The public has so many other sources of information that it would usually know about dangers of inflation or recession even if the Federal Reserve did nothing to announce its intention of combating such disturbances.

3. Changes in discount rates affect market rates of interest in various ways. We have already noted that increases or decreases in this rate may affect lenders' expectations about future rates and immediately cause them to lend less liberally or more liberally. There are other effects as well. A few (but only a few) long-term debt contracts escalate their interest rates with the Federal Reserve discount rate. The other principal effects are less direct, but nevertheless important. For example, an increase in the discount rate increases the bargaining power of lenders relative to borrowers. A bank can argue, "I have to charge you more because I have to pay more when I borrow." Nonbank lenders may insist that "even the Federal Reserve recognizes that credit is scarcer and interest rates should go up." Reductions in discount rates generally increase the bargaining power of borrowers and tend to bring down "sticky" rates of interest, such as those on loans by banks to their large and medium-sized customers. They are less effective in reducing rates to small borrowers.

**Some Recent Developments**    In recent years, there has been a tendency toward liberalization of the discount mechanism, albeit for rather specific purposes. One development along these lines resulted from a decision, made in 1973, to introduce a more formal mechanism for the extension of seasonal credit to member banks that lacked access to national money markets. To be eligible for this new borrowing privilege, a member bank must exhibit a seasonal pattern in loans and deposits that persists for at least eight weeks. It must also arrange for the seasonal credit prior to the need for funds. For some banks this new feature can provide funds for a period of several months. The primary beneficiaries of the seasonal borrowing privilege are smaller banks, especially those that do a substantial volume of loan business in agricultural or resort areas.

The Federal Reserve discount mechanism can also be used to provide emergency credit to individual banks or groups of banks facing financial stringency. Two examples of this have received widespread attention in the press in recent years. The first instance took place in 1970 following the bankruptcy of the Penn Central Railroad. Penn Central defaulted on its outstanding commercial paper, and this had a rather chilling effect on the commercial paper market in general. As a consequence, many firms found themselves unable to reissue their maturing commercial paper and turned quickly, and with substantial need, to their backup lines of credit at banks. To ease the crisis atmosphere, the Federal Reserve allowed the banks involved to cover some of their added needs for funds through special borrowings at the discount window. A more recent use of emergency credit involved the Franklin National Bank, which ran into serious financial difficulties in 1974. It was allowed to borrow a quite substantial volume of funds for a relatively long period while plans for reorganizing the bank were being formulated. In short, through emergency credit the Federal Reserve is able to fulfill its traditional role as the ultimate provider of liquidity or, as it is called, "the lender of last resort."

Finally, in early 1980 there were two further important developments in the evolution of the discount mechanism. In mid-March, for the first time the Federal Reserve established a split discount rate with a basic rate of 13 percent and a *surcharge* of 3 percent. The surcharge potentially applied only to the 270 large banks with deposits of $500 million or more and came into play when one of these large banks borrowed for more than a week consecutively or for more than four weeks in a calendar quarter. This surchage, which came as a part of a general package to tighten monetary policy, remained in effect for about two months. Despite this brief span, the Federal Reserve clearly signaled its intention to make more active use of the discount window in the conduct of monetary policy. This is particularly noteworthy in view of the other major development of early 1980 — the extension of borrowing privileges to nonmember banks and thrift institutions via the Depository Institutions Deregulation and Monetary Control Act of 1980. While as of this writing the practical details of these expanded discount privileges are in the process of being worked out, it should be readily apparent that the discount window could play a still larger role in future monetary policy.

**Overview**     Borrowing from the Federal Reserve takes place at the initiative of the commercial banks but is subject to administrative oversight by the Federal Reserve. Such borrowing provides banks with a simple way of meeting unexpected temporary needs for liquidity, for dealing with recurring seasonal needs, and for coping with more serious emergency situations. Nevertheless, some economists have criticized the discounting privilege since it permits banks temporarily to escape the effects of monetary restraint. In particular, these critics argue that discounting, by introducing "slippage" into Federal Reserve control of bank reserves, necessarily diminishes the effectiveness of monetary policy. While there is an element of truth in this, most economists do not regard this as a serious problem, certainly not one that warrants dismantling the discount mechanism. Indeed, it is generally accepted that open-market operations and administration of the discount window provide the Federal Reserve with ample flexibility to achieve its objectives, even in the face of the safety valve provided by discounting.

## MEMBER BANK RESERVE REQUIREMENTS

Having discussed the two major tools for regulating the volume and cost of member bank reserves, we now turn to the powers of the Federal Reserve to determine member bank reserve requirements.

### Structure of Reserve Requirements

Prior to 1935 member bank reserve requirements were rigidly set by the Federal Reserve Act and could not be altered by Federal Reserve officials. This legislation provided that nothing other than deposits at Reserve banks would count as legal reserves. Minimum-reserve requirements against time and savings deposits were set at 3 percent for all member banks. In fixing reserve requirements against demand deposits at member banks, the Federal Reserve Act carried over the classifications used in the National Banking Act. Central reserve city banks are those located in New York and Chicago; reserve city banks are those located in about 60 other specified large cities; country banks are those located elsewhere. The minimum percentages of reserves required against demand deposits were fixed at 13 percent for central reserve city banks, 10 percent for reserve city banks, and 7 percent for country banks.

The Banking Act of 1935 empowered the Board of Governors to alter the reserve requirements of any class or of all classes of member banks. However, it placed limits on these alterations, providing that the percentages required should not be fixed below those already prevailing or at more than twice those already prevailing. Thus, the Board of Governors could vary member bank reserve requirements as shown in Table 11–2.

Legislation enacted in 1959 and the 1960s changed these arrangements in four principal ways:

1  It empowered the Board of Governors to allow member banks to count cash in vault as legal reserves. Since November 24, 1960,

all member bank cash in vault has been included in legal reserves.

2   It ordered the Federal Reserve to discontinue the category of central reserve city and to apply to member banks in those cities (New York and Chicago) the reserve requirements applicable to member banks in reserve cities. This was done on July 28, 1962.

3   It provided that the Board of Governors should set reserve requirements against demand deposits in banks in reserve cities at not less than 10 percent nor more than 22 percent.

4   Legislation in September 1966 empowered the Board to set and change requirements against time and savings deposits within a range of 3 to 10 percent.

The ranges within which the Board is legally enpowered to set and alter reserve requirements against the various types of deposits at the different classes of member banks are indicated in Table 11–3. As this table shows, when compared with the pre-1935 rigidity of reserve requirements, the range of options available to the Board in setting reserve requirements was considerable. Despite this, the Board was still not content with the structure of reserve requirements. Over time it had become increasingly unhappy with the historical legacy that made for differential reserve requirements based on the location of a member bank, and it strongly advocated a system in which reserve requirements would be graduated on the basis of the amount of deposits in a bank re-

| TABLE 11–2 *Member bank reserve requirements, 1935* | | PERCENTAGE AT WHICH REQUIREMENTS COULD BE SET | |
|---|---|---|---|
| | **Reserves required against** | **Lowest level** | **Highest level** |
| | Net demand deposits at | | |
| |   Central reserve city banks | 13 | 26 |
| |   Reserve city banks | 10 | 20 |
| |   Country banks | 7 | 14 |
| | Time deposits at all member banks | 3 | 6 |

| TABLE 11–3 *Member bank reserve requirements since 1966* | | PERCENTAGE AT WHICH REQUIREMENTS COULD BE SET | |
|---|---|---|---|
| | **Reserves required against** | **Lowest level** | **Highest level** |
| | Net demand deposits at | | |
| |   Central reserve and reserve city banks | 10 | 22 |
| |   Country banks | 7 | 14 |
| | Time deposits at all member banks | 3 | 10 |

gardless of the bank's location. After Congress had ignored several recommendations that such changes be enacted into law, the Board began to initiate the principle within the percentage limits embodied in the existing law. In particular, it amended its regulations so as to interpret "reserve city" not as a geographic concept but as one that was related to bank size. Specifically, it declared that any bank with net demand deposits of $400 million or more was "considered to have the character of business of a reserve city bank." By this bit of ledgerdemain, which took effect in November 1972, the Board moved to a system of reserve requirements in which bank size, not geographic location, was the critical element.

The reserve requirements prevailing against net demand deposits on September 30, 1979, are given in Table 11-4.[4] These requirements were last changed on December 30, 1976. Also shown are the requirements previously prevailing. As a comparison of the columns reveals, the last change reduced reserve requirements by one-fourth or one-half of a percentage point, depending on the category of demand deposits.

The reserve requirements on time and savings deposits that were in force on the same date are given in Table 11-5. As can be seen, the requirements against savings deposits are the same at all banks, whereas those against time deposits vary by both deposit size and the maturity of the deposit. In addition, it should be noted that the average level of reserve requirements against time and savings deposits is distinctly lower than those against demand deposits.

**Use as a Policy Instrument**

Changes in member bank reserve requirements are a powerful instrument for monetary management. A change of even a fraction of a percentage point can have a marked effect on monetary and credit conditions. To illustrate this, let us start with a situation in which member banks have neither excess reserves nor a deficiency of reserves, their deposits subject to reserve requirement total $800 billion, their average

---

[4] Demand deposits subject to reserve requirements are known as *net* demand deposits. These are defined as gross (total) demand deposits less cash items in the process of collection and demand balances due from domestic banks.

**TABLE 11-4**

*Reserve requirements against net demand deposits at member banks, September 30, 1979 (in percentages)*

| Amount of net demand deposits | Reserve requirement | Previous requirement |
|---|---|---|
| First $2 million or less | 7 | $7\frac{1}{2}$ |
| Over $2 million to $10 million | $9\frac{1}{2}$ | 10 |
| Over $10 million to $100 million | $11\frac{3}{4}$ | 12 |
| Over $100 million to $400 million | $12\frac{3}{4}$ | 13 |
| Over $400 million | $16\frac{1}{4}$ | $16\frac{1}{2}$ |

reserve requirement is 5 percent, and their actual reserve balances are $40 billion. This is, in fact, approximately the situation that prevailed in mid-1979. Suppose now that the Board lowers average reserve requirements to $4\frac{3}{4}$ percent. This does not affect the total amount of reserve balances held by member banks. Rather, it changes the volume of deposits and the volume of loans and investments that member banks can support with existing reserves. In the present example the action by the Federal Reserve will reduce required reserves by $2 billion, thereby initially creating that amount of excess reserves. The latter will serve as a basis for multiple expansion by the banking system, which will tend to lower interest rates and increase the availability of bank credit.

Suppose, on the other hand, that the Board raises average reserve requirements from 5 to $5\frac{1}{4}$ percent. This will raise required reserves by $2 billion, thus creating a reserve deficiency of that amount. If the banks are unable to secure additional reserves, they will have to reduce by some multiple both their earning assets and their deposits. This would decrease the availability of bank credit and raise market rates of interest.

Consequently, we see that although they do not directly alter the volume of reserves available, changes in reserve requirements have ultimate effects that are quite similar to those of open-market operations. This should hardly be surprising when we recall the money-multiplier formula developed in Chapter 6. Despite this equivalence, until the advent of the 1970s the Federal Reserve employed changes in reserve requirements relatively infrequently. This was consistent with the commonly held view that changes in reserve requirements were well adapted only to two limited purposes:

1   Absorbing large excess reserves or offsetting large losses of reserves by the banking system. For example, in the late 1930s, owing largely to huge gold inflows, member banks accumulated several billions of excess reserves, far more than the Federal

| | |
|---|---|
| **TABLE 11–5** | **Type of deposit** |

| Type of deposit | Reserve requirement |
|---|---|
| Savings deposits | 3 |
| Time deposits under $5 million maturing in | |
|    30–179 days | 3 |
|    180 days–4 years | $2\frac{1}{2}$ |
|    4 years or more | 1 |
| Time deposits over $5 million maturing in | |
|    30–179 days | 6 |
|    180 days–4 years | $2\frac{1}{2}$ |
|    4 years or more | 1 |

*Reserve requirements on time and savings its at member banks, September 30, 1979 (in percentages)*

*Note:* Effective November 2, 1978, a supplementary reserve requirement of 2 percent was imposed on time deposits of $100,000 or more.

Reserve could have eliminated by selling all its government securities and other earning assets. Large increases in member bank reserve requirements absorbed most of these excess reserves and reduced the potential expansion of bank credit on the basis of the excess reserves that remained. Reductions of reserve requirements might be similarly useful if the banks should at some time suffer large losses of reserves.

2   Announcing important policy decisions to both the public and the banks. Changes in reserve requirements are overt and well-publicized actions that the public can understand and that immediately affect the reserve positions of thousands of banks. They are, therefore, an effective way in which the Board of Governors can in effect say, "This is the direction our policy is taking, and we really mean it!"

Evidently then, the prevailing view was that variations in reserve requirements should be used to bring about relatively large changes in the reserve positions of banks; not for day-to-day or week-to-week adjustments. In part, this is because it has acquired the reputation of being "more like an ax than a scalpel." This reputation, which dates largely from the late 1930s, when requirements were changed several percentage points at a time, is not wholly justified. Indeed, as already suggested, in the last decade or so the Federal Reserve has increasingly resorted to reserve requirement changes as a policy tool. But these changes have not been directed primarily toward the conventional liabilities of demand and time deposits. Rather, they have focused on nondeposit liabilities.

**Reserve Requirements on Nondeposit Liabilities**

We saw earlier that in the 1960s, when banks were faced with needs for funds, they turned in a significant way to certain nondeposit liabilities such as Eurodollar borrowings. Such liabilities were not originally covered by reserve requirements, but in a series of moves beginning in 1969 the Federal Reserve imposed reserve requirements on these sources of funds as well. In particular, reserves now must be held against the following: net balances due from domestic offices to their foreign branches; foreign branch loans to U.S. residents; and borrowings from foreign banks by domestic offices of a member bank.

For each of these categories reserve requirements were initially imposed by exempting certain base amounts outstanding. In effect, this introduced a *marginal reserve requirement* that penalized banks only for increases in these categories. This was done largely to minimize the shock to banks that would have occurred had requirements been imposed on the substantial existing volume of these liabilities. Gradually, however, these exemptions were eliminated, and reserve requirements were applied to the full amounts of these categories. The percentage reserve requirement has been varied substantially over time. The applicable reserve percentage, which was originally 10 percent, was increased to 20 percent in 1971 and reduced to 8 percent in 1973, to 4 percent in 1975, and to zero in 1978. As described below, in October 1979 a marginal reserve requirement was reinstituted on these liabilities.

Aside from the liabilities already discussed, other nondeposit liabilities have also been subjected to reserve requirements. In 1973 and 1974 marginal reserve requirements were applied to the issuance of commercial paper by a bank's affiliates. In addition, a marginal reserve requirement was introduced—on top of the basic requirement—on time deposits of $100,000 or more. This lapsed in 1974 and was reintroduced in 1978 as a supplementary reserve requirement.

The most recent changes in reserve requirements on nondeposit liabilities occurred in October 1979 and in March 1980 as part of major monetary policy moves involving all three tools: open-market operations, a discount rate change, and a revision of reserve requirements. More specifically, as far as reserve requirements are concerned, in October 1979 the Federal Reserve introduced a marginal requirement of 8 percent on all *managed liabilities* above a base amount. Managed liabilities were defined to include the following: large time deposits ($100,000 and over with maturities of less than a year); Eurodollar borrowings; repurchase agreements; and federal funds borrowing from nonmember institutions. Since the marginal requirement applied to the *aggregate* level of managed liabilities, an increase in one component could be offset with a decrease in another without an increase in required reserves. As the Federal Reserve described it: "This action is directed toward sources of funds that have been actively used by banks in recent months to finance the expansion of bank credit."[5] It was clearly the hope of the Federal Reserve that the action, which increased the effective cost of nondeposit liabilities to banks, would lead to slower growth of bank credit. When the resulting growth did not prove slow enough for its liking, in March 1980 the Federal Reserve increased the reserve requirement on managed liabilities to 10 percent and expanded the base to which the reserve requirement applied.

**Overview**     As should be apparent from this bit of recent history, changes in reserve requirements have become increasingly common. Furthermore, the introduction of marginal reserve requirement changes has added a new dimension to monetary policy. The Federal Reserve can, for example, impose an extra reserve requirement on a liability when that liability grows beyond some base period amount. This would have no immediate impact on a bank. Rather, it only affects the expansion of the bank at the margin. The additional flexibility resulting from these vari-

---

[5] *Federal Reserve Bulletin*, October 1979, p. 831.

ous developments may well lead the Federal Reserve to use variations in reserve requirements in a more active way. Nevertheless, it is still likely to rely largely on open-market operations and discount policy for its finer short-term adjustments.

**COORDINATION OF THE INSTRUMENTS OF GENERAL MONETARY MANAGEMENT**

We have now discussed the three major Federal Reserve instruments of general monetary management: changes in member bank reserve requirements, open-market operations, and discount policy. We now consider the interrelationships of these instruments and the coordination of their use.

**Methods of Coordination**

If one looks only at the legal provisions of the Federal Reserve Act, one may fear that these instruments will not be used in a coordinated way, for authority over them is not fully centralized. Member bank reserve requirements are set by the Board of Governors alone. Open-market operations are controlled by the FOMC. Discount-rate changes are usually initiated by the 12 Federal Reserve banks, subject to approval by the Board of Governors. Loan offices at the 12 Reserve banks decide whether or not to make specific loans to member banks, although they operate under general regulations prescribed by the Board of Governors. In practice, there is far more coordination than this dispersion of legal authority suggests, and it is achieved in many ways, both formal and informal. In this process the Board of Governors plays a central role. With full authority over member bank reserve requirements, a majority of the members of the FOMC, power to approve or disapprove discount rates, and authority to prescribe regulations for lending to member banks, its legal powers are formidable. It is also in a position to persuade other Federal Reserve officials to cooperate.

In this process the meetings of the FOMC are very important. These meetings are attended not only by the members of the FOMC but also by the seven presidents of Reserve banks who are not currently members of the FOMC, by the principal economists on the Board's staff, and by an economist from each of the Reserve banks. The presidents who are not members of the FOMC are free to participate in the meeting, but not to vote. Those assembled analyze current and prospective financial and economic conditions and discuss various policy alternatives. By the end of the meeting they all know what the open-market policy will be, as well as the Board's intentions with respect to member bank reserve requirements and the Board's attitude toward discount rates.

**The Importance of Coordination**

The various instruments of monetary policy may be used singly or in various combinations, and they may supplement each other or tend to weaken each other. For example, if the Federal Reserve wishes to restrict credit, it may take one or various combinations of the following actions: raising reserve requirements, selling securities in the open market, and increasing discount rates. The net effects of using one instrument depend in part on current policies with respect to the others. Suppose the Federal Reserve increases member bank reserve requirements enough to absorb existing excess reserves and put many banks in a deficient reserve position. Banks may be forced to restrict credit sharply if the Federal Reserve refuses to create additional reserves by purchasing securities and if it raises discount rates to discourage borrowing. However, the restrictive effects may be largely negated if the Federal Reserve stands ready to buy at fixed prices and yields all the government securities offered to it. And the degree of restriction will be lessened if the Federal Reserve fails to raise discount rates or to take other actions to restrict member bank borrowing.

This example indicates the importance of proper coordination in the use of the various instruments. Proper coordination does not require that all the instruments be used in every case. It requires only that the instruments not be used in such a way as to prevent the achievement of desired results. In many cases the Federal Reserve can achieve its objectives by using only one or two of these instruments. Open-market operations are often used alone, especially for defensive purposes or where only small dynamic effects are desired. For larger operations, they are ordinarily combined with changes in discount rates. In some cases, as for example in the policy action of October 1979, both are combined with changes in member bank reserve requirements.

In a later chapter we shall describe the purposes for which the Federal Reserve has used its powers and the ways it has used its instruments. The succeeding examples will illustrate a few of the patterns of Federal Reserve restrictive and expansionary policies.

**Restrictive Policies**

Suppose that to avoid an actual or threatened inflation—due to an excessive rate of increase in the total of government and private money demands for output—the Federal Reserve decides to implement a *restrictive* monetary policy. Such a policy has the purpose of restricting the rate of growth of spending for output and, to this end, restricting the rates of growth of the stock of money and the stock of bank credit in the face of rising demands for them.

Suppose, for example, that the Federal Reserve decides that for some time it will permit no increase whatsoever in the money supply. Sometimes it can achieve this by simply refraining from further purchases of securities. At other times it will actually sell some government securities to reduce bank reserves and force banks to borrow or to sell assets in order to repair their reserve positions. On some occasions, it may raise reserve requirements for the same purpose. Commercial banks, facing shortages in their reserves and probably also continued increases in customers' demands for loans, try in various ways to adjust. One way that a bank can improve its position is by seeking more loans from the Federal Reserve. At this stage, if not before, the Federal Reserve will raise its discount rates and may also admonish banks that seek to "borrow too much or too frequently." Banks also try to borrow more from others—in the federal funds market, from correspondent banks, in the Eurodollar market, and so on. Moreover, they sell earning assets, such as Treasury bills and commercial paper, to repair their reserve positions and meet customers' demands for loans. Both the banks' increased demands for borrowings and their sales of assets tend to raise interest rates. At first the rise of yields may be largely confined to short-term assets, but the rise spreads to longer maturities as banks make few, if any, net purchases of them and may be net sellers. Eventually banks will restrict their loans to customers by raising interest rates and through various types of nonprice rationing.

It is through such processes that restrictive Federal Reserve policies control the growth of credit supplies, raise interest rates, and slow down the rate of increase of spending for output.

**Expansionary Policies**
Suppose now that the country is slipping into a recession following a prosperity period in which interest rates, including discount rates, were relatively high and member bank borrowings were large. Such recession periods are usually characterized not only by declining business activity and rising unemployment, but also by declining demand for credit, which tends to lower market rates of interest. If the Federal Reserve neither lowers discount rates nor takes other positive action, it will encourage decreases in the money supply. Faced with declining demand for credit and falling interest rates, banks that were willing to borrow and lend when interest rates were high relative to discount rates will now seek to repay their debts to the Federal Reserve. Some banks may also want to hold some excess reserves if they think lending is becoming riskier. Thus, the Federal Reserve must take some positive liberalizing action if it is to prevent an actual decrease in the volume of money and bank credit, and still more positive action if it is to induce an expansion.

Which instruments the Federal Reserve will use, the sequence in which it will use them, and the scope of its actions will depend on its estimate of the strength and probable duration of the depressive forces. If it fears that the recession will be serious and prolonged, it may at an early stage reduce reserve requirements. If it does, the banks will add some of the released reserves to their excess reserves and use some to repay borrowings at the Federal Reserve. Usually, however, the Federal Reserve "leads off" with either decreases in discount rates or open-market purchases. As their reserve positions improve, and especially as they receive excess reserves, banks seek to put the money to work. At first they may buy short-term government securities and other open-market assets, thereby depressing short-term interest rates. Gradually, however, interest rates will fall in almost all parts of the market. At some point, usually early, the Federal Reserve will begin to lower discount rates. In a prolonged recession these are usually decreased several times as market rates decline.

**SELECTIVE CREDIT CONTROLS**

We have emphasized that the purpose of general monetary management is to regulate the total supply of money and bank credit and the general level of interest rates; it is not to determine the allocation of credit among its many possible users and uses. This allocative or rationing function is left to the private market. Those who believe in a predominantly free-market economy generally favor primary reliance on general monetary management because the allocation of credit helps to allocate real resources, which they believe should be allocated through competition in the marketplace. However, many persons, including some who favor primary reliance on general measures, believe that these measures should be supplemented by *selective controls*, that is, by measures that would influence the allocation of credit, at least to the point of decreasing the volume of credit used for selected purposes without the necessity of decreasing the total supply and raising the cost of credit for all purposes.

Selective credit controls can be either negative or positive. *Negative controls* seek to decrease the supply or increase the cost of credit for certain specified purposes. *Positive controls* seek to increase the supply or lower the cost of credit for specified purposes. Although our central interest is in selective controls by the Federal Reserve, it should be noted that many actions by other government agencies significantly affect the allocation of credit among its potential uses and users. A few examples will suggest the range of these policies.

1 Low-cost government loans to rural electric and telephone cooperatives, to finance exports, and for certain types of housing.
2 Limitations on types of assets that may be acquired by savings and loan associations. A major purpose of this action is to increase the supply of credit for housing.
3 Government guarantees of loans for such purposes as storing farm products or housing.
4 Tax policies, such as exemption from the federal income tax, which lower the rates that state and local governments must pay on their borrowings.

These examples suggest that even when selective credit controls are justified, it does not necessarily follow that they should be wielded by the Federal Reserve.

We now turn our attention to some of the forms of selective credit controls that have been administered by the Federal Reserve.

**Moral
Suasion**

The Federal Reserve sometimes employs moral suasion as an instrument of general monetary management—to influence total borrowings at the Federal Reserve and the behavior of the total supply of money and bank credit. Moral suasion is also used for selective purposes, especially with banks currently borrowing from the Federal Reserve. For example, in the late 1920s, and especially in early 1929, the Federal Reserve urged banks to curb their "speculative loans on securities" and to favor "loans for legitimate business purposes." In the spring of 1951, during the Korean conflict, the Federal Reserve sponsored a "voluntary credit-restraint program," which encouraged banks and some other financial institutions to restrict "nonessential, nonproductive loans" while continuing to make "essential productive loans." In 1966, the Federal Reserve urged banks to curb the rate of expansion of business loans and to reduce their sales of government securities. This encouragement came in the form of a letter sent by each Federal Reserve bank president to all the member banks in the district. The letter contained a suggestion that a bank's ability to borrow at the discount window might depend on its cooperation. Also, in the mid-1960s, as a part of a program to improve the nation's balance of payments, banks were first urged, and then legally required, to refrain from increasing their total loans to foreigners.

A recent example of moral suasion was contained in a 1973 letter from the chairman of the Board of Governors to all banks with deposits exceeding $100 million. The letter suggested that banks should be more cautious in extending lines of credit for commercial loans and warned them that more stringent bank examination procedures would be employed to enforce this suggestion. The most recent attempt at moral suasion occurred in March 1980 when, with bank credit growing at 18 percent per year, the Federal Reserve introduced a voluntary program to restrain bank credit to a rate of increase of 6 to 9 percent. This voluntary program was part of a more comprehensive attempt to tighten monetary policy. To demonstrate its seriousness of purpose, the Federal Reserve summoned leading bankers to Washington and, although there is no official account of the meeting, apparently read them the riot act. After the meeting the bankers, who are notoriously not shy about getting their names in print, all refused to be quoted. Anonymously, however, they hinted at Federal Reserve threats designed to assure compliance, and they generally expressed the view that the voluntary program was tantamount to formal credit controls. Soon after the program was announced, bank credit growth slowed substantially. However, a weakening economy and the 20 percent prime loan rate undoubtedly also had something to do with the reduced demand for loans.

From these examples it is evident that the Federal Reserve regards moral suasion as a useful supplement to its other policy tools. It should be noted, however, that many economists do not agree with this view.[6]

Let us now look at some of the more formal types of selective controls.

**Margin Requirements on Security Loans**

This selective control arose out of the Federal Reserve's unhappy experience with stock market speculation in the late 1920s. At that time there was nothing in the basic economic situation that called for a policy of very tight money. Employment was not overly full, commodity prices were steady, and the objective of promoting recovery and prosperity abroad called for easy money. However, the stock market was booming, and the rapid rise of prices was supported in part by large increases of loans on stock collateral. Federal Reserve officials were convinced that this was unsound and that less credit should be available for stock purposes. However, they then had only two methods of dealing with the situation — moral suasion and general credit restriction. They attempted moral suasion, exhorting banks not to make speculative loans on stocks while borrowing at the Federal Reserve. This did not work, partly because most of the banks were not in debt to the Federal Reserve and partly because of the huge and rising volume of nonbank loans on stock. They also invoked general credit restriction, which seemed to damp business activity more than stock market speculation. The outcome is now famous; stock speculation climbed until the great crash in October 1929, and the Federal Reserve's policy of general credit restriction came to be blamed in part for the ensuing Great Depression.

In 1934, largely because of this experience, Congress gave the Board of Governors power to fix, and to alter at its discretion, minimum margin requirements on security loans. These apply where two conditions are met. (1) The loan is collateraled by a security listed on a national securities exchange and not exempted — government obligations and some others are exempted. And (2) the purpose of the loan is for purchasing or carrying such securities. Minimum margin requirements are, in effect, minimum down payments stated as a percentage of the market value of the security. Setting a minimum margin requirement is an indirect way of setting a maximum loan value.

Several aspects of this selective control are worth noting.

1 It applies to borrowers as well as to lenders. It is just as illegal for

---

[6] See, for example, Edward Kane, "The Central Bank as Big Brother," *Journal of Money, Credit, and Banking*, November 1973, pp. 979–981.

a borrower to borrow in excess of the maximum loan value as it is for a lender to make such loans. Thus, this control limits the demand for such credit as well as limiting the supply for this purpose.

2   It applies not only to member banks but also to lenders of every type. Thus, for this purpose it extended the jurisdiction of the Board of Governors. This precedent was followed in later selective controls.

3   It not only enables the Federal Reserve to restrict the volume of credit used for this purpose without restricting the supply or raising the cost of credit for other purposes, but it may actually ease credit for other purposes. To the extent that less credit is demanded or supplied for this purpose, more credit tends to be made available for other uses.

Since early 1974 margin requirements have stood at 50 percent. However, the Board of Governors had changed margin requirements numerous times between their inception (in 1934) and 1974. Sometimes it has increased margin requirements to discourage borrowing and lending for these purposes (including one occasion in 1946 when the margin requirement was 100 percent). Other times it has decreased margin requirements to lessen the degree of restriction.

It is very difficult to assess precisely the effectiveness of this regulation in curbing the amount of credit used for purchasing and carrying securities. It certainly has some overall effect, and is especially effective in curbing such borrowing by those persons who could borrow little without pledging the securities as collateral. However, many people have found ways of evading the intent of the regulation. For example, they buy and carry these securities with funds acquired by borrowing on their general credit standing, on exempt securities, on their houses, on their businesses, and so on.

**Consumer-Credit Controls**

Selective controls of consumer credit, which were administered under Federal Reserve Regulation W, had a checkered career. They were first instituted in the autumn of 1941 under an executive order, and remained in effect until 1947, when they were withdrawn. They were reinstated in September 1948 under a temporary authorization by Congress, and expired in June 1949. After the outbreak of war in Korea, they were imposed again, but they were withdrawn in 1952. Since that time the Federal Reserve has not been empowered to use this type of control.

This selective control employed two devices: minimum down payments and maximum periods of repayment. Both applied to consumer loans on listed articles. Raising the required down payment tended to reduce the demand for credit for this purpose as well as to reduce the amount that could be legally supplied for it. Shortening the maximum period of repayment, which increased required monthly payments, also tended to reduce the demand for such loans. Only the latter device applied to consumer loans for unlisted purposes.

Consumer-credit control proved to be almost impossible to administer and enforce. Since this control applied not only to banks but also to other providers of consumer credit, a very large number of lenders had to be kept under surveillance, and the Federal Reserve was not adequately staffed for the job. Consumers who were offered credit terms more liberal than those permitted by the regulations were not inclined to file complaints, and many suppliers of consumer credit, especially those who sold goods and services on credit, either ignored the regulations or violated them frequently.

A different sort of consumer credit control was implemented in March 1980 when President Carter invoked the Credit Control Act of 1969. Given the authorization, the Federal Reserve introduced a 15 percent "deposit requirement" for all lenders on increases of certain types of consumer credit including credit cards, check credit overdraft plans, and unsecured personal loans. In effect this action amounted to a marginal reserve requirement with two novel features: (1) reserve requirements typically apply to liabilities of lenders such as bank deposits, but this applied to the asset side of the balance sheet; and (2) the requirement applied to all lenders, not just commercial banks. In addition to banks, those affected included finance companies, credit unions, savings and loans, mutual savings banks, retail establishments, gasoline companies, and firms offering travel and entertainment cards. The intent of the 15 percent requirement was to increase the cost of funds to lenders and, since these cost increases were likely to be passed on to the consumer, to reduce the demand for consumer credit. While the demand for consumer credit did moderate after this action, the quantitative role of the 15 percent requirement in contributing to this slowdown has yet to be precisely analyzed.

**Real Estate Credit Controls**

From 1950 until 1952, as a part of the anti-inflation program initiated after the outbreak of war in Korea, Congress authorized the Board of Governors to exercise selective control over credit extended to finance new residential construction. This it did under Regulation X. It utilized the same devices as Regulation W: minimum down payments and maximum periods of repayment. Also, its terms, like those of Regulation W, were not uniform for all loans of this general type. Instead, Regulation X was designed to favor lost-cost housing and housing for veterans. It therefore required larger down payments and shorter periods of repayment for higher-cost housing and on loans to nonveterans. This regulation was in effect for only a short time, and even then it did not apply to many construction projects that were already in progress or in the planning stage. For these reasons, it is difficult to predict its effectiveness over a longer period. However, there are reasons to expect that it would be difficult to enforce.

**Interest Rate Ceilings**        As we have already seen, interest rate ceilings only emerged with the restructuring of the Federal Reserve in the mid-1930s. In particular, the Banking Act of 1935 prohibited the payment of interest on demand deposits and ordered the Federal Reserve and the FDIC to impose ceilings on the rates that their members might pay on time and savings deposits. It was alleged, without persuasive evidence, that in competing for funds banks had driven interest rates on deposits to excessive levels, which tempted them into risky and unsound loans. Another reason for these provisions of the Banking Act was undoubtedly the desire of many banks to enlist the help of government in keeping down their operating costs by limiting price competition among banks for deposits.

With the passage of this legislation, the Federal Reserve potentially gained another monetary instrument, since it was permitted to adjust the ceilings on time and savings deposits.[7] From 1935 to 1956, this tool was not used at all as these ceilings were kept constant at low levels, none above $2\frac{1}{2}$ percent. Over the subsequent ten years, upward adjustments were made to the ceiling rates whenever they threatened to become binding. Consequently, over the period 1935 to 1965 ceilings were not used as a selective credit control. Then, first in 1966 and again in 1969, a major change took place and interest rate ceilings became an important component of monetary policy.

Both 1966 and 1969 were years of price inflation, highly restrictive Federal Reserve policies, and the highest interest rates in over 100 years. In fact, general credit restriction was so severe that some feared a credit crunch or crisis. Two special aspects of the situation led to consideration of some type of selective controls. One was the rapid expansion of bank loans to business. The other was the plight of savings and loan associations and some other types of financial intermediaries. They could not afford to pay much higher rates for savings because the average rate of earnings on their existing assets was dominated by the lower levels of long-term interest rates that had prevailed in earlier years. Yet yields on competing open-market assets, such as Treasury bills, rose to historically high levels, and it was clear that banks would also raise their rates on time and savings deposits to high levels if the Federal Reserve would raise the ceilings. Savings and loan associations first suffered a decrease in the flow of funds to them, and then the danger of large net withdrawals. The effects would be not only a shortage of mortgage funds,

---

[7] The prohibition of interest payments on demand deposits was absolute in the sense that the Federal Reserve had no discretionary authority to adjust this zero ceiling.

with further depressing effects on housing, but perhaps also wide distress among these financial institutions.

Several actions were taken to deal with these special situations.

1   The Board refused to raise rate ceilings on time and savings deposits even though rates on competing assets in the open market rose to much higher levels. This action was effective in checking flows of funds into time and savings deposits at banks; in fact, some banks suffered large net withdrawals, especially in the form of large-denomination CDs. In addition, in September 1966 Congress empowered the various regulatory agencies to extend interest rate ceilings to nonbank financial intermediaries such as savings and loan associations and mutual savings banks. The primary argument advanced for this was that these institutions, like commercial banks, needed protection from their own overly aggressive competitive tendencies, which might have impaired their solvency.

2   The Federal Home Loan Banks sold very large amounts of their own bonds, which carried a government guarantee, and loaned the proceeds to savings and loan associations to help them meet withdrawals and purchase some mortgages. This positive selective control was very helpful to the savings and loan associations, but it did not, of course, serve to slow down the expansion of bank loans to business.

3   The Board of Governors raised the legal-reserve requirements from 4 to 6 percent against time deposits at each bank in excess of $5 million. One purpose of this action was general credit restriction. The other was to decrease bank demands for time-deposit funds. It was believed that banks would compete less aggressively for funds and pay lower interest rates if they could lend an amount equal to only 94 percent instead of 96 percent of such time deposits. It is very doubtful that this small increase in required reserves appreciably reduced bank demands for time deposits. After all, the banks were by this time paying much more for funds from other sources.

The refusal to raise ceilings on rates that banks might pay only partially achieved its basic objectives. It did not stop withdrawals from other financial intermediaries. It did inhibit shifts of funds to commercial banks, but it did not stop customers of other intermediaries from withdrawing funds in order to buy Treasury bills and other high-yielding assets in the open market. These effects were exacerbated by the ceilings placed on nonbank intermediaries, and the effects on the housing and mortgage markets were only partially cushioned by the actions of the Federal Home Loan Banks. Also, the refusal to raise ceiling rates was only partially successful in slowing the expansion of bank loans to business. As we have seen in our discussion of commercial banking, banks, and large banks especially, showed great ingenuity in devising other ways of getting funds for this purpose—by selling government securities, selling participations in their portfolios, issuing commercial paper through holding companies or their subsidiaries, borrowing federal funds, borrowing Eurodollars, and so on. As the Federal Reserve itself has described it:

> *The result of these developments was a great deal of churning in financial markets, a loss to some degree of the stability in financial flows and risk-taking associated with financial intermediation, and perhaps a disproportionate credit squeeze on those bank customers unable to shift to open-market sources of funds.*

Understandably, these experiences somewhat diminished the enthusiasm of the Federal Reserve toward the use of ceilings as a credit-control device. In June 1970, following the bankruptcy of the Penn Central Railroad, ceiling interest rates on short-maturity (30 to 89 days) CDs were suspended. And in May 1973, when advances in market interest rates threatened a runoff of longer-term CDs, the ceilings on these were also suspended. As long as these ceilings remain suspended, monetary policy cannot operate as it did in 1966 and 1969. It is still debatable whether interest rate ceilings can be used effectively to create selective credit control in periods of unusual financial stress. There is general agreement, however, that they should not be regarded as a substitute for basic reforms that would make real estate credit less vulnerable in periods of high interest rates.

The status of interest rate ceilings as of September 1979 is given in Table 11–6. As the table reveals, while large CDs are exempted, there remains a fairly intricate set of ceiling rates on other time and savings deposits. Of particular note are the two most recent additions to the list— the special variable ceiling rates. The first of these, the 6-month money market rate, was introduced in June 1978, while the special rate on 4-year certificates dates from July 1979. The special rates were introduced to permit commercial banks, and other financial intermediaries,[8] to compete effectively for deposits. Without these, as market interest rates rose above ceiling levels, the fear was that funds would be bid away from banks and other intermediaries. This process, which has been dubbed *disintermediation*, could result as depositors moved their funds directly

---

[8] Interest rate ceilings like those listed in Table 11–6 also apply to savings and loan associations and mutual savings banks. Generally speaking, these two types of institutions are allowed to pay up to ¼ percent more than commercial banks on corresponding categories.

into the Treasury bill market or into the so-called money market mutual funds whose phenomenal growth was documented in an earlier chapter. The special money market certificate rate, which roughly permits banks to match the Treasury bill rate, has been quite successful in stemming the tide of disintermediation. Indeed, as of February 1980 there were $124 billion of these certificates outstanding at commercial banks and a whopping $183 billion outstanding at thrift institutions.

While special variable rates have served to remove some of the inflexibility of ceilings, many economists and bankers remain critical of the present system. As noted earlier, ceilings impair the efficiency of the financial system by inhibiting the growth of the most efficient financial institutions and practices. Furthermore, the remaining ceilings tend to discriminate against small savers who lack information or ready access to higher-yielding assets.[9] For these reasons, many serious students of the financial system have long proposed that all ceilings (including the prohibition of interest on demand deposits) should be abolished. This is precisely the intent of the recently enacted Depository Institutions

---

[9] Small savers have not always been able to take advantage of money market certificates because of the $10,000 minimum deposit. However, see "Loophole Certificates: Regular and Jumbo."

---

| | | Maximum rate (percent) |
|---|---|---|
| **TABLE 11–6** | **Type and maturity of deposit** | |
| *Maximum interest es payable on time nd savings deposits commercial banks, September 1979* | Savings | $5\frac{1}{4}$ |
| | Negotiable order of withdrawal (NOW)* | 5 |
| | Time accounts in amounts less than $100,000 maturing in | |
| | 30–89 days | $5\frac{1}{4}$ |
| | 90 days–1 year | $5\frac{1}{2}$ |
| | 1–2 years | 6 |
| | 2–$2\frac{1}{2}$ years | 6 |
| | $2\frac{1}{2}$–4 years | $6\frac{1}{2}$ |
| | 4–6 years | $7\frac{1}{4}$ |
| | 6–8 years | $7\frac{1}{2}$ |
| | 8 years or more | $7\frac{3}{4}$ |
| | Issued to governmental units (all maturities) | 8 |
| | Special variable ceiling rates, by maturity | |
| | 6 months (money market time deposits) | † |
| | 4 years or more | ‡ |
| | Time deposits over $100,000 | no ceiling |

\* For authorized states only. As of September 1979 these included the New England States and New York.
† The ceiling rate is the rate prevailing on the most recently issued 6-month Treasury bills. Certificates must have a minimum denomination of $10,000.
‡ The ceiling rate is $1\frac{1}{4}$ percentage points below the yield on 4-year U.S. Treasury securities.
*Source: Federal Reserve Bulletin*, October 1979, p. A10.

Deregulation Act of 1980 that provides for a six-year phase out of interest rate ceilings. We shall discuss this Act in more detail in Chapter 17.

**Attitudes Toward Selective Controls**

Attitudes toward selective controls differ widely. Few people object to their use in time of war or rapid military mobilization, when the government will in any case intervene heavily to regulate the allocation of resources and output. At such times selective credit controls may serve a useful purpose, both in diverting resources away from nonessential uses and in inhibiting inflation. But their use in noncrisis peacetime periods is another matter. As might be expected, they are often opposed by those whose economic interests may be diversely affected. Thus, some stock exchange members and officers are not friendly toward margin requirements on security loans, automobile manufacturers and dealers have criticized regulation of consumer credit, and the construction industry and realtors have opposed restrictions on credit for residential purposes.

Many economists have opposed selective controls on several grounds: (1) that they may interefere unduly with the freedom of borrowers and lenders, (2) that they prevent an allocation of resources

---

**LOOPHOLE CERTIFICATES: REGULAR AND JUMBO**

While the new six-month money market certificates (MMCs) nominally require a minimum deposit of $10,000, financial intermediaries have found a way around this as well. To do so they have introduced the aptly named *loophole certificate* that works as follows. Suppose a potential purchaser of an MMC has $5,000 and therefore needs an additional $5,000 to acquire the certificate. No problem—the bank or thrift institution can simply and legally lend the customer the additional funds and, presto, an MMC is born. In such transactions the loan rate is typically set so as to yield the depositor about one percentage point below the going rate on a $10,000 certificate. In other words, if MMCs are paying 13 percent, our depositor will realize about 12 percent on his or her $5,000. Some banks have even proved willing to lend as much as $8,000 to attract depositors.

Seeing the success of the regular loophole certificate, some financial institutions have recently introduced the *jumbo loophole* certificate. The basic idea is the same as before, but the jumbo loophole applies to large ($100,000) certificates of deposit (CDs) that are free from all interest ceilings. With jumbo loophole certificates, the depositor puts up $50,000 and the banks lend the difference. After deducting the cost of the loan, the depositor typically realizes a return about one percentage point below the going rate on large CDs.

and output in line with buyers' wishes, (3) that they are unnecessary because general monetary management and fiscal policies are sufficient, (4) that they may come to be looked upon as a substitute for more general and more widely effective measures, and (5) that they are likely to become unenforceable or enforceable only with a very large staff. Other economists contend that selective controls can be a useful supplement to general monetary controls, especially when the misbehavior of credit is limited to only one or a few sectors of the economy.

## FEDERAL RESERVE POLICY: THE EARLY YEARS

Previous sections of this chapter have spelled out the various tools of monetary policy as they have evolved to the present day. In its early years, however, the Federal Reserve did not have such a complete set of tools. Open-market operations in government securities were unknown, and reserve requirement changes were prohibited by law. Further hampering early monetary policy was the fact that the Federal Reserve had not yet evolved a clear understanding of its policy objectives. This section briefly traces some of the growing pains experienced by the Federal Reserve, and the country, in the years preceding World War II. The aim is to provide an appreciation of some of the complexities of monetary policy and an understanding of how we got where we are.

### World War I and Its Aftermath

The war had already been declared (in August) before the Federal Reserve banks first opened for business in November 1914. By the late spring of 1915, the United States was enjoying an export boom as neutrals turned to it for products formerly purchased in Europe and as the Allied Powers bought heavily to meet their needs. Between August 1914 and April 1917, the United States had an export surplus of over $6 billion. Foreign buyers paid for these huge net purchases in three principal ways: reselling U.S. securities, borrowing, and shipping over $1 billion of gold. Since the U.S. gold stock had been only $1½ billion at the beginning of the war these imports increased it by nearly 70 percent. No one had ever anticipated such gold inflows. Both the great increase in the foreign demand for U.S. exports and the flow of gold into bank reserves created strong inflationary pressures.

During the period between the opening of the Reserve banks in late 1914 and the entrance of the United States into the war in April 1917, Federal Reserve officials had no opportunity either to develop meaningful objectives or to use their instruments of control effectively. It was obvious to them that they should not, in response to the gold inflow, follow expansionary policies and enhance inflationary pressures. Yet they could do nothing to offset or to sterilize the expansionary effects of gold inflows. They had almost no assets to sell, and they had no power to raise member bank reserve requirements. They had to stand by while the money supply rose from $11.6 billion in mid-1914 to $15.8 billion in mid-1917. Wholesale prices had already risen more than 50 percent when the United States entered the war.

With this country's entrance into the war, the Federal Reserve entered a new phase, "accommodating" the Treasury. The government's fiscal policy was the one common to periods of major war — large deficits representing increases in expenditures far in excess of increases in tax collections. For the three years ending in June 1919, the cumulative deficit amounted to over $23 billion.

The Federal Reserve played a central role in this process by meeting the greatly increased demand for currency in circulation, and by supplying the banking system with sufficient reserves to enable it to buy Treasury obligations, to lend to others for the purchase of Treasury securities, and to meet essential private demands for productive purposes. In sharp contrast to its policies during World War II, it did this to only a very small extent by purchasing government securities itself. It supplied the funds largely by lending to commercial banks.

The government's highly expansionary fiscal policy and the Federal Reserve's accommodating monetary policy were accompanied by inflation and monetary expansion. The nation's total money supply, which had been $11.6 billion in mid-1914 and $15.8 billion three years later, had risen to $21.2 billion by mid-1919. The wholesale price level was 25 percent higher than it was just before the entrance of the United States into the war. Inflation continued unabated, even after the end of hostilities, and by May 1920 wholesale prices were 140 percent above their prewar level. Thus, over the six-year period from 1914 to 1920 the annual inflation rate averaged 15.7 percent.

The period of inflation came to an abrupt halt in May 1920. The end was signaled by a worldwide break in the prices of basic commodities. The ensuing depression, which ran into early 1922, was relatively short, but sharp and painful. The unemployment rate more than doubled, reaching 12 percent, and wholesale prices fell 45 percent. Both the solvency and the liquidity of the economy were seriously weakened. And the commercial banks, which owed the Federal Reserve about $2.5 billion, were in no position to offer easier credit.

Not until April 1921, about a year after the depression started, did the Federal Reserve take a single action to ease monetary and credit conditions. The Reserve banks did refrain from putting pressure on member banks to repay their borrowings. But they did not buy either government securities or acceptances to provide the banks with reserves and enable them to reduce their borrowings, and they did not reduce discount rates. Such a policy now seems incomprehensible.

This episode was extremely painful both for the country and for the

Federal Reserve. A question arises as to why the Federal Reserve followed the policies it did in the depression of 1920–1921. A complete answer to this question would take us far afield, but a basic point is that the Federal Reserve had not yet come to believe it had the responsibility of using its powers aggressively to promote economic stability. Also important was the fact that the Federal Reserve had not yet learned how to use open-market operations for general monetary management. Prompted by its poor performance in 1920–1921, the Federal Reserve gradually achieved both a clearer understanding of its policy objectives and an appreciation of the potential usefulness of open-market operations. Indeed, in 1924 and again in 1927 it pursued aggressively easy monetary policies to combat recessionary tendencies in the economy. While this was a first step toward becoming a force for stability, the decade of the 1930s revealed that the Federal Reserve still had much to learn.

**The Great Depression**

At the time of the stock market crash in October 1929, and even in 1930, no one could foresee that the depression into which the world was sliding would be the most devastating in its entire history and would be a major contribution to political and economic upheavals and even to the outbreak of a second world war. This depression lasted more than a decade and ended only in World War II. At its depth in the United States, the depression reduced money national income by 50 percent and real output and income by 25 percent. One worker in four was jobless, and many others worked only part time. Business firms failed by the tens of thousands, farmers lost their farms, and families their homes. Amidst falling incomes and price levels, the monetary and financial system virtually collapsed. The gold standard system largely disappeared by 1932. The U.S. banking system, weakened earlier, collapsed in 1933. Many other financial institutions closed their doors, or at least ceased to function effectively in the saving–investment process. International lending came to a standstill. With hindsight, it is clear that many of the problems of the 1930s were aggravated by an ineffective performance by the Federal Reserve.

*Monetary Policies: 1929–1933*

From October 1929 to the autumn of 1931, the Federal Reserve began to gradually relax its previously restrictive credit policy. In particular, it reduced the discount rate several times and also engaged in expansionary purchases of government securities. Despite these steps, critics have justifiably attacked Federal Reserve policies during this period as too slow and too timid. Furthermore, starting about September 1931 the Federal Reserve allowed credit conditions to tighten significantly. A major development that was responsible for this was an upsurge of bank failures, which damaged confidence in banks and induced large withdrawals of cash from the banking system. At the same time, banks began accumulating sizable pools of excess reserves. As might be expected from the money-multiplier formulas developed in Chapter 6, in the absence of vigorous expansionary policies by the Federal Reserve, the money supply declined dramatically. Indeed, from the peak in the fall of 1929 to the trough in March 1933 the money supply dropped by over 35 percent.

At the same time, real incomes were declining precipitously; unemployment was rising dramatically; and the solvency of individuals, businesses, and financial institutions was seriously undermined. With thousands of banks illiquid, if not insolvent, any sharp decline in confidence could topple the entire structure. The storm broke in Detroit with the failure of the Union Guardian Trust Company, which was one of the largest banks in Michigan and was also closely connected with many other banks. So great was the blow to public confidence and so panicky were withdrawals from other banks that on February 14, 1933, the governor of Michigan declared an eight-day banking holiday. The panic quickly spread to other states. By March 4, every state in the Union had declared bank holidays, and bank deposits were no longer redeemable in cash. President Roosevelt's decree of a four-day nationwide banking holiday beginning on March 6 merely recognized the existing situation.

While there has been much debate about the extent to which the Federal Reserve "caused" the Great Depression, there is little doubt that prompter and more vigorous use of monetary policy in the early 1930s might well have prevented the buildup of deflationary momentum. Similarly, policy measures to shore up the liquidity of the banking system may well have cushioned its collapse in 1933. Once again we see that, even after nearly twenty years of operation, the Federal Reserve still had much to learn.

### Monetary Policy in the Late 1930s

Following the banking debacle of 1933, although gradually improving, the economy limped along for several years. By mid-1936 about 15 percent of the labor force was still unemployed (down from a high of 25 percent) and real national output was about 5 percent below its level in 1929. During the same period commercial banks had accumulated a substantial volume of excess reserves, which stood at $2.9 billion in mid-1936 (see Table 11–7).

To a large extent, the growth in both actual and excess reserves came about as a result of the huge volume of gold inflows (review Chapter 10 for how this works). For their part, the banks were content to hold this increased volume of excess reserves. For one thing, in view of the recent history of bank failures they were quite concerned with maintaining adequate liquidity. Furthermore, in the midst of the depression there were precious few opportunities to make sound loans to business.

As the economy kept up its gradual improvement, Federal Reserve and Treasury officials became increasingly concerned with the possibility that inflationary pressures would reemerge. To prevent this, they decided to take some slack out of the system by mopping up excess reserves. They took two actions to achieve this end. For one thing, the Board of Governors for the first time used its recently acquired power to change member bank reserve requirements. In three steps—the first on August 16, 1936, and the last on May 1, 1937—it doubled all these requirements, thereby setting them at the maximum level permitted by law. In addition, the Treasury embarked on a policy of sterilizing all gold imports, thereby preventing them from augmenting the public's money supply, commercial bank reserves, and Federal Reserve bank reserves. It did this by selling government securities to get the funds with which to pay for the gold and then adding the gold to its own cash holdings without issuing gold certificates against it. In effect, it engaged in an offsetting open-market operation.

As a result of these actions, excess reserves were substantially reduced. Consequently, interest rates rose rather sharply. While, once again, it is debatable whether what followed was caused by the Federal Reserve, there ensued a sharp downturn in economic activity—a recession amidst a depression. The unemployment rate rose to about 20 percent and real output declined.

In the face of these developments, the Federal Reserve and the Treasury reversed directions, and in fact, excess reserves advanced to

| | | Actual reserve balances | Required reserves | Excess reserves |
|---|---|---|---|---|
| **TABLE 11–7** | **Period** | | | |
| *Member bank reserve* | Last quarter 1933 | 2,612 | 1,839 | 773 |
| *positions on selected* | February 1934 | 2,822 | 1,931 | 891 |
| *dates, 1933–1941* | June 1934 | 3,790 | 2,105 | 1,685 |
| *(Averages of daily* | June 1935 | 4,979 | 2,541 | 2,438 |
| *figures, in millions* | June 1936 | 5,484 | 2,891 | 2,593 |
| *of dollars)* | July 1936 | 5,861 | 2,954 | 2,907 |
| | May 1937 | 6,932 | 6,005 | 927 |
| | August 1937 | 6,701 | 5,951 | 750 |
| | May 1938 | 7,587 | 5,062 | 2,525 |
| | June 1939 | 10,085 | 5,839 | 4,246 |
| | June 1940 | 13,596 | 6,900 | 6,696 |
| | December 1940 | 14,049 | 7,403 | 6,646 |
| | June 1941 | 13,201 | 7,850 | 5,351 |
| | December 1941 | 12,812 | 9,422 | 3,390 |

*Source:* Board of Governors of the Federal Reserve System, *Banking and Monetary Statistics,* Washington, D.C., 1943, pp. 371–373.

new heights (see Table 11–7). Nevertheless, it was not until 1940 that the economy reattained its 1937 level. The Federal Reserve, and the country, learned the hard way that excess reserves and superfluous reserves are not the same thing.

**Overview**

As should be apparent from this brief excursion into the history of monetary policy, there is much to criticize in early Federal Reserve actions. Indeed, to a large extent this early lackluster performance ushered in a period in which monetary policy was regarded with extreme disfavor by many economists. It was not until well after the conclusion of World War II that the monetary authorities once again played a prominent role in policy making.

**CONCLUSION**

This chapter completes, at least for the time being, a lengthy excursion into the functioning of the Federal Reserve System. We have examined both the structure of the Federal Reserve and the tools it possesses for the conduct of monetary policy. Since it is largely through variations in the cost and volume of bank reserves that the monetary authorities exert their influence on the economy, we have examined in detail the three principal instruments for affecting reserves available to the Federal Reserve—open-market operations, discount operations, and changes of reserve requirements.

The discussion of the past few chapters—taken in conjunction with our earlier analysis of the commercial banking system—should have provided the reader with an understanding of how the money supply is determined and the process of increasing and decreasing it. The essential ingredients of this are as follows: (1) the provision or removal of reserves by the Federal Reserve and (2) the behavior of the commercial banks in adjusting to the new level of reserves by expanding or contracting their assets and liabilities. This latter process typically leads to an expansion or a contraction of the money supply that is a multiple of any change in bank reserves. As noted earlier, however, this multiplier is not a fixed constant but rather varies with, among other things, the height of reserve requirements, the willingness of the banks to expand their portfolios, and the attitudes of the public toward holding currency, demand deposits, and time deposits. All of these factors must be taken into consideration by the Federal Reserve in the conduct of monetary policy. On several occasions in subsequent chapters, it will be convenient to assume that the Federal Reserve simply fixes the money supply. While this will make the exposition easier, it should be borne in mind that this assumption abstracts from all the complexities that underlie the determination of the money supply.

To this point, our discussion of the Federal Reserve has focused largely on what might be termed the mechanics of monetary policy. That is, we have examined *how* the Federal Reserve can affect bank reserves and the money supply. But we have not yet addressed the broader issues of *why* the Federal Reserve might pursue one policy or another. While this will be discussed later, it may help to motivate the next several chapters if we briefly anticipate some of the relevant issues.

Rational policy making must begin with the selection of objectives or ends. This is both difficult and controversial because there are many different objectives toward which monetary actions can be directed and not all of these objectives are likely to be compatible with each other. It is therefore necessary not only to identify the possible objectives but also to have some preferences about the various objectives and to make choices among them. Since all individuals are unlikely to have the same view as to what the Federal Reserve should be doing, such choices inevitably leave the Federal Reserve open to potential criticism.

The second important component of rational policy making is a theory of the relationship among economic variables. As a guide to the appropriate use of the instruments of policy making to promote its selected objectives, the Federal Reserve must have some theory—implicit or explicit, but preferably explicit—concerning relationships among the relevant economic variables, and especially of relationships among the actions that might be taken and the effects that would flow from them. By sheer coincidence and rare good luck, a policy maker might do the thing most conducive to the promotion of the chosen objectives, even if his or her actions were not guided by an explicit valid theory. But such a happy outcome would indeed be sheer coincidence and rare good luck, unlikely to be often repeated.

Some of the many ways in which theory is inescapably involved in policy making can be illustrated by an example. Suppose the Federal Reserve has selected as its dominant objectives the simultaneous promotion of continuously high levels of employment and output, the highest sustainable rate of economic growth, stability of price levels, and stability of the exchange rate on the dollar. The Federal Reserve is not empowered to control or regulate directly any of these important variables. Its powers are largely limited to actions relating to discounting, open-market operations, and reserve requirements of the banks. It is immediately involved in important theoretical questions on several levels. If it takes, or fails to take, some specific action, what will be the effects on the stock of money? On the supply of credit? On interest rates? On the behavior of aggregate money demands for output? On the responses of employment, real output, money wage rates, and prices?

It would indeed be misleading to claim that either central bankers or economists have developed fully satisfactory answers to these and many other important theoretical questions. Yet it is clear that rational policy must be guided by some type of theory. And it is unlikely that policy can for long be better than the theory on which it is based. It is partly for this reason that we shall devote so much attention to monetary theory.

Much of our theory will deal with the effects of money and monetary policy on other economic variables in which we are interested. In effect, we shall ask: How will this specific monetary action affect such things as the aggregate demand for output, employment, real output, interest rates, and prices? How will the results differ from those that would have prevailed if this action had not been taken or if some other action had been taken? This type of analysis is highly important to the monetary authority, which must be concerned with, and responsible for, the effects attributable to its own action or inaction.

However, monetary theory has another related but broader function, which is to analyze all the determinants, or at least the most powerful determinants, of the behavior of the economic variables in which we are interested. It is clear that the behavior of such measures as employment, output, and prices is determined not by money and monetary policy alone, but also by many other forces. The monetary authority needs to understand these if its policy actions are to be appropriate. Much of monetary policy is of a defensive nature, designed to offset or compensate disturbances from other sources. If the roles of these other determinants of economic behavior are not understood, the monetary authority is not in a position to prescribe the appropriate compensating or offsetting action. More generally, we need to analyze all important determinants in order to view monetary policy in an overall context and to assess realistically the role that it can play.

**SELECTED READINGS**

Board of Governors of the Federal Reserve System, *The Federal Reserve System: Purposes and Functions*, 6th ed., Washington, D.C., 1974.

Chandler, L. V., *American Monetary Policy, 1928–1941*, New York, Harper & Row, 1971.

Friedman, M., and A. J. Schwartz, *A Monetary History of the United States, 1867–1960*, Princeton, N.J., Princeton University Press, 1963.

Kaminow, Ira, and J. M. O'Brien, "Selective Credit Policies: Should Their Role Be Expanded," *Business Review*, Federal Reserve Bank of Philadelphia, 1975, pp. 3–22.

Meck, Paul, *Open Market Operations*, Federal Reserve Bank of New York, 1969.

# IV MONETARY THEORY

With this chapter we begin an extended discussion of monetary theory—
that is, an analysis of the relationships between money and the behavior
of other economic variables such as real output and income, employment
and unemployment, interest rates, and the price level. The output and
income measures that will receive much attention in this and subsequent chapters are variables known as *money flows*. They measure rates
of expenditure and income per unit of time, which is typically taken to
be a year. Two important examples of money flow variables are gross national product (GNP) and disposable income.

   While output and income are money flow measures, they should not
be confused with the concept of money itself. Of course, in everyday language the terms *income* and *money* are sometimes used interchange-
ably. It should be stressed, however, that this is not how economists view
the matter. Furthermore, measures of the money supply, however defined, are *stock* concepts. That is, as we saw earlier, data on the money
supply tell us how much money is outstanding at a *point of time*. In this
regard, the stock of money is analogous to other stocks encountered in
economics, such as the stock of automobiles or the stock of houses. While
they are different concepts, money flows and the stock of money are, of
course, related. In fact, according to a simple version of what is known as
the quantity theory, money flows vary proportionately with the stock of
money. However, as we shall see, this simple relationship does not hold
in all circumstances.

   Our objective, then, in the following chapters will be the development of a theory or economic model explaining the determination of key
macroeconomic variables such as income, interest rates, and prices. The

building blocks of our analysis will be the markets for money balances, goods, and labor. We shall first consider the conditions for equilibrium of supply and demand in each of the markets separately and then provide an integrated view of all three markets. Since the preceding chapters were largely concerned with the supply of money balances, we begin our excursion into monetary theory with the demand side of the market for money balances.

**SOME PRELIMINARIES**

What determines the community's demand for money balances? How is this demand equated with the supply of money? What effect does the process of equilibration have on the economy? These are the kinds of questions we shall address in this chapter. As we shall see, many of the controversies in both monetary theory and monetary policy stem from the fact that different economists have given different answers to these questions.

The theory of the demand for money balances is best viewed as but one part of the theory of choice in the allocation of scarce resources. All members of the community have at their command only limited resources in the form of current income and total accumulated assets. They must, therefore, make choices concerning their allocation. If they choose more consumption, they must hold fewer total assets. And if they choose to hold more of one type of asset, they must hold less of others. They must constantly balance the advantage of holding more of one against the disadvantage of holding less of others. Putting the matter this way raises the question of why people elect to hold any money balances at all. Money usually yields no explicit income, or at most, only a low rate of return relative to yields on other assets. But holding money costs something; the cost is the satisfaction or income forgone by holding money rather than devoting this amount of resources to other uses.

The fact that people do choose to hold some money balances at the cost of attractive alternatives suggests that holding money must yield some sort of advantage or provide some sort of service to the individual. It does, and these result from the qualities of money—its general acceptability in payments, its perfect liquidity, and its safety in the sense that it does not depreciate in terms of money. Indeed, as we shall see, these properties of money give rise to several distinct reasons for holding money.

A final point concerns the definition of money. As we have seen, money can and has been defined in various ways. This issue is of considerable importance for both empirical researchers and policy makers, and we shall return to it later. For our present purposes, however, beyond reminding the reader that we prefer a relatively narrow definition of money, the only explicit assumption we shall make is that money yields no interest return. While this assumption, which accords with current practice, serves to simplify the exposition, it should be emphasized that the various theories to be discussed continue to have validity if this assumption is relaxed. We now turn directly to some explicit theories of the demand for money.

**HE CLASSICAL QUANTITY THEORIES**

Quantity theories have had a long history and a widespread use in economics. Not surprisingly, such theories have appeared in many versions, differing in terminology and in degree of sophistication. As originally formulated, quantity theories were not explicitly designed as theories of the demand for money, although, as we shall see, they can be so interpreted. Rather, they began from the assumption that the quantity (stock) of money is a significant determinant of the rate of flow of money expenditures, and focused on the problem of explaining the linkage between the stock of money on the one hand and the rate of money flows on the other. Some versions of the quantity theory have been concerned with expenditure flows in the most comprehensive sense, including in their purview all money expenditures or transactions. Others have utilized a narrower concept of expenditures restricting attention to money expenditures for output. We shall adopt this latter approach, sometimes called the income variant, and represent expenditures by GNP at current prices.[1]

Two principal techniques have been used to express the linkage between the stock of money and the flow of money expenditures. The first employs the concept of the *velocity of money* — in this case the *income velocity of money*. This is the average number of times each dollar of the money stock is spent for output during a year. To facilitate exposition, those who employ this approach often begin with an identity:

$$MV = OP = Y \tag{1}$$

where

$M =$ the stock of money
$V =$ the income velocity of money, or the average number of times per year that each dollar of $M$ is spent for output
$O =$ real output, stated at an annual rate
$P =$ average price per unit of output or the price level of output
$Y = OP =$ GNP at current prices

This is often called a *Fisherine* type of equation because a similar type

---

[1] The distinction arises because GNP is a measure of "final" output excluding many intermediate economic transactions. Such transactions would be included in a more comprehensive measure of money flows.

was used by Irving Fisher, the great Yale economist. Note that this is not a theory; it is only an identity asserting the necessary *ex post* equality between the flow of expenditures for output ($MV$) and the money value of output purchased by that flow ($OP$ or $Y$).

The other technique used to express the linkage between the stock of money and the flow of money expenditures is the *Cambridge approach*, so called because it was used by Alfred Marshall and other economists at Cambridge University. Users of this approach also employ an identity to facilitate exposition:

$$M = KOP = KY \qquad (2)$$

where

$M$, $O$, $P$, and $Y$ are defined as in equation (1)
$K =$ the fraction of $OP$ that the community holds in the form of money balances

Like the Fisherine equation, the Cambridge equation is only an identity; it expresses the necessary *ex post* equality between the left and right sides of equation (2). As a consequence, arithmetically $V$ and $K$ are reciprocals; that is, $V = 1/K$ and $K = 1/V$. For example, if $V = 4$, $K = \frac{1}{4}$. If we divide the Fisherine equation by $V$, we get the Cambridge equation, $M = (1/V)Y$, or $M = KY$. And if we divide the Cambridge equation by $K$, we get the Fisherine equation, $M(1/K) = Y$, or $MV = Y$.

As indicated earlier, the quantity theory can be transformed into a framework for the demand for money. Indeed, the Cambridge identity is already seemingly cast in the form of equating the supply of money to the demand for money. With the aid of few new symbols, we can make this more explicit. In particular, if we denote the quantity of money balances demanded by $M^D$ and the quantity supplied (assumed fixed by the monetary authorities) by $M^S$, we can rewrite our earlier equations as follows:

$$M^D = KY = KOP \qquad (3)$$
$$M^D = M^S \qquad (4)$$

Equation (3) is a demand function for money, albeit an extremely simple one. It makes the demand for money balances, $M^D$, a proportion of GNP in current prices (or, as it is sometimes called, *nominal* GNP). Alternatively, dividing both sides of (3) by $P$ we get:

$$\frac{M^D}{P} = \frac{KY}{P} = KO \qquad (5)$$

Equation (5) indicates that the demand for *real*-money balances, $M^D/P$, is a proportion of real output or real GNP. Equations (3) and (5) are simply two ways of saying the same thing.

At this juncture the reader may be puzzled, since, beginning from the quantity theory *identify*, we have seemingly manufactured a theory of the demand for money. The proverbial catch lies in the apparently innocuous symbol $K$ (or $V$). To see this, let us consider equation (3) a bit more carefully. On the left side of (3) we have the symbol $M^D$ denoting the community's demand for money balances. In other words, $M^D$ is the quantity of money balances that the community *desires* to hold, *given* the level of income, $Y$. Of course, in equilibrium the community's desired money balances must equal the quantity of money supplied. Equation (4), in fact, expresses this equilibrium condition. Now let us ask what happens if, at some initial level of $Y$, $M^D$ is not equal to $M^S$. Assuming that equilibrium is ultimately established and that the authorities maintain a fixed supply of money, then clearly either $Y$ or $K$ (or both) must change to produce this equilibrium. Which of these occurs is naturally of considerable consequence for both the economy and the operation of monetary policy. It should be evident by now that to answer this latter question and to rescue equation (3) from the status of an identity we must examine the determinants of $K$ more closely.

In general, quantity theorists before the 1930s considered $V$ and $K$ to be relatively stable. In fact, in the short run at least, they tended to treat $V$ and $K$ as constants. The underlying basis for this was the view that $V$ and $K$ were determined by institutional considerations such as credit practices among various firms or between firms and households, and by technological factors such as the nature of communications. We shall examine these factors in more detail shortly. For our present purposes we only need note that the early quantity theorists tended to perceive these factors as changing only slowly over time. Consequently, it seemed quite plausible to regard $V$ or $K$ as relatively constant. Before evaluating the validity of this view, it is worthwhile briefly to pursue its implications.

From equations (3) and (4) we see that a constant $K$ implies that the stock of money is the major determinant of aggregate demand, or, expressed another way, the level of $Y$ can be managed precisely through control of $M$.[2] Evidently, if the demand and supply for money are unequal at some initial level of income, since $K$ is constant, then income must change if equilibrium is to be restored. This is clearly a strong conclusion, but unfortunately it is based on an oversimplification— namely, the assumed constancy of $K$. To see this, let us look at some data.

Table 12–1 shows the behavior of $V$ and $K$ during recent decades.

---

[2] It should be noted that just using equation (3) we are unable to say how a change in $Y$, induced by a change in $M$, will be split up between $P$ and $O$, that is, between the price level and real output. We shall return to this issue in a later chapter.

Column (3) shows the behavior of income velocity, which is simply GNP/M. Column (4) shows the behavior of K, which is M/GNP, or 1/V. This equation assumes that in each year the public had adjusted its money balances to desired levels relative to GNP. During the Great Depression and World War II, V had fallen by nearly half from its level in the late 1920s; it was still low by historical standards in 1947. Since that time it has shown a marked upward trend, rising from about 2.1 in 1947 to 6.6 in 1979. Consistent with this, K has shown a marked downward trend, falling from about 48 percent of GNP in 1947 to 15 percent of GNP in 1979. Clearly, V and K are not constant through time and indeed can change substantially within a period of several years. But what about changes from one year to the next? Judged on this basis the changes in velocity appear relatively small. Indeed, since 1947 the average arithmetic change in V is of the order of 0.14 per year, while no change exceeds .35 (see the third column of Table 12–1). However,

**TABLE 12–1**

*The income velocity of money and the ratio of the money supply to GNP (money values in billions of dollars)*

| Calendar year | (1) GNP at current prices | (2) Average money supply* | (3) Income velocity of money [(1) ÷ (2)] | (4) Ratio of money supply to GNP [(2) ÷ (1)] |
|---|---|---|---|---|
| 1959 | $ 486.5 | $141.0 | 3.45 | .290 |
| 1960 | 506.0 | 141.0 | 3.59 | .279 |
| 1961 | 523.3 | 143.9 | 3.64 | .275 |
| 1962 | 563.8 | 147.4 | 3.82 | .261 |
| 1963 | 594.7 | 151.9 | 3.92 | .255 |
| 1964 | 635.7 | 157.8 | 4.03 | .248 |
| 1965 | 688.1 | 164.5 | 4.18 | .239 |
| 1966 | 753.0 | 172.0 | 4.38 | .228 |
| 1967 | 796.3 | 178.7 | 4.46 | .224 |
| 1968 | 868.5 | 191.2 | 4.54 | .220 |
| 1969 | 935.5 | 202.6 | 4.62 | .217 |
| 1970 | 982.4 | 210.2 | 4.67 | .214 |
| 1971 | 1,063.4 | 224.3 | 4.74 | .211 |
| 1972 | 1,171.1 | 240.3 | 4.87 | .205 |
| 1973 | 1,306.6 | 257.6 | 5.07 | .197 |
| 1974 | 1,412.9 | 270.2 | 5.23 | .191 |
| 1975 | 1,528.8 | 282.1 | 5.42 | .185 |
| 1976 | 1,702.2 | 296.8 | 5.74 | .174 |
| 1977 | 1,899.5 | 317.7 | 5.98 | .167 |
| 1978 | 2,127.6 | 342.1 | 6.22 | .161 |
| 1979 | 2,368.8 | 360.8 | 6.57 | .152 |

* Annual average daily figures; money supply concept is M-1A.
*Source:* Board of Governors of the Federal Reserve System, *Economic Report of the President, 1980,* Washington, D.C., Government Printing Office.

while in some loose sense the numbers seem small, this is quite mislead-ing. The reason for this can best be illustrated by use of an example.

Let us consider a year in which $Y = 600$, $M = 150$, and consequently, $V = 4$ and $K = \frac{1}{4}$. Now assume that the monetary authorities would like $Y$ to grow by 6 percent, so that during the next year they would like to have $Y = 636 = 1.06 \times 600$. How much $M$ should they supply? The answer ob-viously depends on their estimate of $V$ or $K$. If $V$ is expected to remain constant at $V = 4$, then clearly the appropriate quantity of money to sup-ply is $M = 636/4 = 159$. That is, with a constant $V$ they would let $M$ also grow at 6 percent. But what if the actual value of $V$ turns out to be 4.2? The value of $Y$ that would then result would be $Y = 4.2 \times 159 = 667.8$. In other words, $Y$ would grow at over 11 percent per year rather than the in-tended 6 percent. If the economy were already near full employment, this could produce a considerable amount of unwanted inflation. While the example could be done with many other assumptions, they would not change the basic message: Seemingly small fluctuations in $V$ or $K$ can have substantial repercussions on the level of economic activity.

Given that $V$ and $K$ are not constants and do fluctuate in the short run, can we say anything about the reasons for these fluctuations? In the first instance it is important to recognize that the behavior of $V$ and $K$ is determined by the choices of the community, not by the monetary au-thority. Even if the latter has firm control of the stock of money, the com-munity is free to decide its rate of expenditures relative to $M$. In terms of the velocity approach, members of the community may elect to hold money balances only briefly before spending them, in which case $V$ will be high. Or they may elect to hold money balances longer before spend-ing, which will be reflected in a lower $V$. In terms of the $K$ approach, members of the community may choose to hold only small balances rela-tive to their rate of expenditures, which will be reflected in a high rate of expenditures relative to the stock of money. Or they may choose to hold larger balances relative to their expenditures, in which case $Y$ will be smaller relative to $M$. Moreover, the choices of the community do not fluctuate in a haphazard manner, but rather are systematically related to the state of the economy.

A closer look at Table 12–1, or the corresponding velocity data that have been plotted in Figure 12–1, shows that the sharpest increases in velocity tend to occur during periods of prosperity. On the other hand, during periods of recession, indicated in Figure 12–1 by the shaded areas, velocity declines or rises less rapidly.[3] Clearly, a theory of the

---

[3] The 1974–1975 recession is obviously an exception. Indeed, the rapid increase in velocity after 1974 deserves particular attention. We shall have more to say about this in later chapters.

demand for money should capture these effects, and to do so we shall rely on another variable we have encountered earlier—the interest rate.

In general, classical quantity theorists tended to assume that demands for money balances were not affected significantly by the level of interest rates. Since the 1930s this view has been strongly challenged. Most monetary economists, including modern quantity theorists, now believe that demands for money balances are sensitive to the level of interest rates, tending to fall as interest rates rise and to rise as interest rates fall.

In explaining why demands for money balances should be negatively related to the level of interest rates, economists stress the fact that an interest rate is both a cost of holding money balances and a reward for holding earning assets. Therefore, increased interest rates encourage the community to economize on money balances and to hold a larger fraction of its total assets in the form of earning assets. Reduced interest rates have the opposite effect. Since interest rates tend to rise in periods of

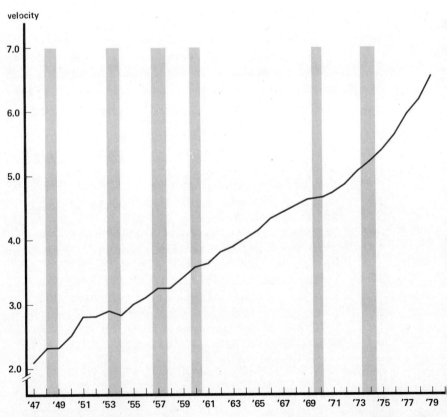

*Income velocity of money, 1947–1979*

**FIGURE 12–1**

Note: Velocity is based on M-1A.

prosperity and to fall in recessions, this belief is certainly consistent with the data in Figure 12–1.

To recapitulate, the quantity theory in its simplest form does not provide a fully satisfactory theory of the demand for money. To construct such a theory we must explicitly introduce interest rates into the determination of the demand for money. One of the first economists to do this in a systematic and coherent way was John Maynard Keynes, in his monumental 1936 work, *General Theory of Employment, Interest, and Money.*

## IE KEYNESIAN APPROACH

Two of the functions of money discussed in the first chapter were (1) to serve as a medium of exchange or means of payment and (2) to serve as a store of value. Roughly paralleling these functions, Keynes, in his writings on the demand for money, distinguished between two primary motives for holding money—the *transactions motive* and the *speculative motive.*

## The Transactions Motive

Households and business firms hold money balances for transactions purposes because they think they will, or may, want to make expenditures before they enjoy a sufficient inflow of money receipts. They might hold little or no money if they were assured that money would flow to them in sufficient volume just a moment before they wanted to spend. Usually they have no such assurance. Therefore, they elect to hold some money to cover the excess of their expenditures over their receipts during some period.

It should be noted that households and business firms would hold money balances even if they could forecast perfectly and confidently both the amounts and timing of their expenditures and receipts. Realistically speaking, of course, forecasts of cash receipts and expenditures can rarely be made with such precision and confidence. Expected receipts may fail to materialize, or highly important expenditures may be earlier or larger than anticipated, or unusually attractive bargains may become available. Such contingencies provide an additional motivation for holding transactions balances.[4]

Keynes posited that the demand for money balances for transactions purposes was a function of income. This dependence is illustrated in Figure 12–2, where $L_1$ denotes the quantity of real money balances

---

[4] Keynes actually introduced a third motive, the *precautionary* one, to apply to money holdings that stemmed from the community's desire to protect itself against the possibility of unforeseen contingencies. However, this did not play a major part in his formulation of the demand for money, and we shall not make use of the distinction between the precautionary motive and the other motives.

demanded for transactions purposes. Although the relationship between transactions balances and income is shown as a straight line—$L_1L_1$ in Figure 12–2—the actual relationship need not be a linear one.

It should be evident that, at least in regard to the transactions motive, Keynes was following in the quantity theory tradition of his colleagues at Cambridge. Where he departed from this tradition was in his emphasis on the speculative motive and the role of the interest rate in determining speculative balances.

**The Speculative Motive**

Keynes recognized that the community may elect to hold balances in excess of its needs for transactions purposes because of its desire to hold assets that are perfectly liquid and perfectly free from risk of depreciation in terms of money. Balances that fulfill the *store-of-value* function constitute the speculative demand for money. In more modern terminology, this is sometimes called the *asset demand for money.*

The speculative demand for money was conceived by Keynes as primarily determined by the rate of interest. In particular, Keynes posited that higher interest rates would lead to smaller speculative balances and lower interest rates would produce larger demands for speculative balances. Keynes offered two reasons for this. First, when interest rates are high, other things equal, this is a way of saying that the opportunity cost of holding money is high. But the second part of Keynes' argument was that other things would not be equal. In particular, he argued that capital gains on earning assets are likely when interest rates are high and capital losses are likely when interest rates are low. Since, as we saw in Chapter 4, the relevant opportunity cost is the effective rate of interest taking into account capital gains or losses, this view serves to bolster the case that the speculative demand for money is inversely related to the interest rate.

But on what did Keynes base his view that capital gains (losses) are likely when interest rates are high (low)? Essentially, he reasoned as follows: First, he cited the familiar fact that increases of interest rates

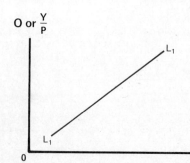

*Transactions demand for money*

**FIGURE 12–2**

lower prices of outstanding debt obligations, and decreases of interest rates increase such prices. Second, he hypothesized that members of the community have some concept of "a normal level" of interest rates, which is based on experience, and especially on recent experience. This level is normal in the sense that the interest rates are expected to return to this level after each significant departure from it. Thus, if actual rates are well above the normal level, the community will consider further increases of rates less likely than future declines and capital losses less likely than capital gains. It will therefore demand to hold more earning assets and thus smaller money balances. However, as actual interest rates fall well below the normal level, the community considers future rate increases to be more likely than rate decreases and capital losses more likely than capital gains. It therefore demands larger money balances and less earning assets.

The dependence of the speculative demand for money, denoted by $L_2$, on the interest rate is shown in Figure 12–3. The $L_2L_2$ curve slopes downward, reflecting the *inverse* relationship between the speculative demand for money and the interest rate. Part (*a*) of the figure corresponds to what might be called the "standard" case; in (*b*) we have drawn the $L_2L_2$ curve to illustrate the Keynesian concept of the liquidity trap. The *liquidity trap* reflects the notion that at some positive rate of interest that is low by historical standards, the demand for money balances becomes infinitely elastic. In (*b*) the liquidity trap is represented by the flat section of the curve $L_2L_2$ to the right of point A. At the low level of the interest rate, $r_L$, the demand for money balances is infinitely elastic. The community will not hold any bonds at yield rates below $r_L$ because it expects that income from holding bonds will be more than offset by capital losses resulting from future increases in interest rates.

The liquidity trap hypothesis has pessimistic implications for the

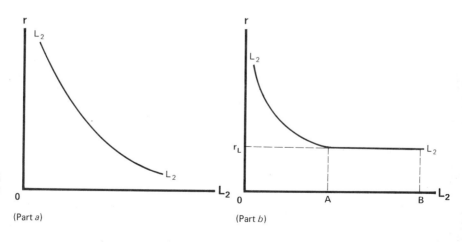

Speculative demand for money

**FIGURE 12–3**

(Part *a*)          (Part *b*)

adjustability of interest rates and for the efficacy of monetary policy. Interest rates could not fall below $r_L$, but that level of interest rates may at times be too high to be consistent with establishing a full-employment level of income. Under such conditions output and employment would be "trapped" at levels below full employment. Moreover, increases of the money supply could not lower interest rates below $r_L$ or stimulate spending.

Few economists now accept the liquidity trap hypothesis in the extreme form just described. For one thing, it is based on a model having only two types of financial instruments—money itself and perpetual bonds—and this bears little resemblance to a modern economy with a wide array of earning assets of all maturities. In such an economy people who are unwilling to hold long-term bonds because they fear a rise of interest rates need not increase their holdings of money balances. Instead, they can buy earning assets of short maturities, which have prices that would be affected but little by a rise of interest rates. Such shifts to short maturities tend to lower at least short-term interest rates. Also, expectations concerning the future behavior of interest rates are neither so homogeneous nor so unalterable as is implied by the horizontal section of the $L_2$ curve. Some members of the community are likely to expect lower rates than others; this would give some negative slope to the $L_2$ curve. Moreover, the $L_2$ curve can be shifted upward or downward to some extent. For example, the monetary authority may shift the community's expectations downward by adopting an aggressive easy-money policy and by announcing their determination to lower interest rates.

While economists have generally rejected the extreme version of the liquidity trap, the more basic Keynesian contribution of introducing the interest rate into the theory of the demand for money has remained to the present day.[5] Indeed, the importance of the interest rate is now even more widely accepted since the realization that the interest rate may also be an important influence in the transactions demand for money.

**THE TRANSACTIONS MOTIVE RECONSIDERED**

One of the primary contributions of post-Keynesian work on the transactions demand for money has been to emphasize the importance of the interest rate in determining the amount of transactions balances demanded. Keynes acknowledged the existence of this effect; yet, as we have just seen, he largely confined the role of the interest rate to the

[5] However, it should be noted that the precise rationale on which the speculative motive is based has changed somewhat since Keynes first introduced the concept. The appendix to this chapter discusses some of the difficulties with the Keynesian approach and sketches the later developments.

speculative motive. In order to see why it is relevant for the transactions motive as well, let us consider a simple example.

Imagine a hypothetical individual whose annual income is $9600 and who spends all his income evenly over the year. In the first instance, let us further posit that he is paid $800 on the first day of each month. Under these assumptions his money holdings will have the sawtooth pattern shown in Figure 12–4. At the beginning of each month he has money balances of $800. These money balances are used up uniformly over the month; just when they are exhausted, he receives his paycheck for the following month; and thus the pattern is repeated. Since he begins the month with $800 and ends with zero, quite evidently his *average* money balances over the month must be half his paycheck, or $800/2 = $400. Since each month is representative of all months, his average money balance over the year is also $400. The income velocity of circulation of his money balances is the ratio of his annual income to his average money holdings, or a rate of 24 per year ($9600/$400).

Now let us ask how the situation would change if our hypothetical individual were paid $400 twice a month rather than $800 once a month. Pictorially, the situation would be as in Figure 12–5. As contrasted with Figure 12–4, the sawtooth pattern in Figure 12–5 is clearly finer. Over each half-month period and, consequently, over the year as a whole, the individual's average money balances are now $200, or half as large as before. Income velocity is now 48 per year ($9600/$200).

To this point we have simply assumed that the individual responds passively to whatever frequency of payment he is presented with, but this need not be the case. In particular, an individual who is paid monthly and whom we have characterized by the pattern in Figure 12–4 could readily achieve the pattern of Figure 12–5. He can do this by putting one-half of his monthly paycheck ($400) into an earning asset such as a bond or savings deposit and leaving the remaining $400 in the form

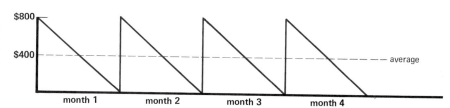

*Transactions balances: monthly payments*

**FIGURE 12–4**

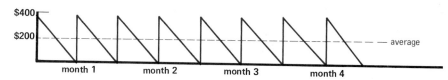

*Transactions balances: semimonthly payments*

**FIGURE 12–5**

of money balances. Then, in the middle of the month when his cash has run down, he can convert his earning asset to cash. Thus, even though he is paid once a month, his cash holdings would have the pattern shown in Figure 12–5. That is, his average cash holdings would be $200, and his average holdings of the earning asset would also be $200.[6]

Indeed, should the individual so desire, he could make even more frequent conversions to cash and further lower his average cash holdings. For example, he could take $600 of each paycheck and place it in an earning asset, leaving himself with $200 in cash. Since he makes expenditures at the rate of $800 per month, he will run out of cash after one quarter of the month has elapsed. He could then convert an additional $200 into cash, leaving $400 of his balances in earning assets. This pattern would be repeated until all balances are exhausted and he is paid again at the beginning of the new month. Clearly, this would result in average money balances of only $100, average holdings of the earning asset of $300, and an income velocity of 96 per year ($9600/100).[7]

It should be evident from these illustrations that our hypothetical individual is not necessarily constrained by the frequency with which he is paid in determining his average transactions balances.[8] But how is he to decide the optimal amount of money to hold? Or, putting the question in an equivalent way, how often should he convert from earning assets into cash during the payment period? These questions have been addressed directly in the work of W. J. Baumol and James Tobin.[9] Their formulation of the problem has two basic ingredients: (1) the rate of interest on earning assets and (2) the brokerage fee or *transactions cost* of converting an earning asset into money. When we speak of the rate of interest here, we refer to a short-term rate, such as the rate on savings deposits or on Treasury bills, which is not subject to fluctuation over the

---

[6] He holds $400 of earning assets for the first half of the month and zero for the second half, yielding an average over the month of $200.

[7] The individual's average holding of the earning asset is computed as follows: For the first quarter of the month he holds $600 of earning assets; for the second quarter, $400; for the third quarter, $200; and for the last quarter, zero. Consequently, for the month as a whole we have $\frac{1}{4} \times$ ($600 + $400 + $200 + $0) = $300 as his average balance of earning assets.

[8] In some extreme situations this need not be true. For instance, during hyperinflations, workers generally wish to get paid extremely frequently so as to avoid holding any liquid assets. Indeed, during the German hyperinflation of the 1920s, workers were paid daily or twice daily. There are, in fact, many stories of workers who were met at the factory gates at noon by a family member so that the family could shop immediately, thus beating the *afternoon* inflation.

[9] See W. J. Baumol, "The Transactions Demand for Cash—An Inventory Theoretic Approach," *Quarterly Journal of Economics*, November 1952, pp. 545–556, and James Tobin, "The Interest Elasticity of Transactions Demand for Cash," *Review of Economics and Statistics*, August 1956, pp. 241–247.

payment period. By transactions costs we mean any cost, either explicit or implicit, incurred in converting from earning assets to money. Examples of these costs might be fees and commissions paid to brokers or dealers for such a conversion. But to restrict attention to these types of costs is to take too narrow a view of the matter. Transactions costs are also meant to cover the value of time and trouble taken by an individual in converting an asset to money. As a simple illustration, if it involves an element of inconvenience to go to a savings bank to obtain cash for one's deposits there, then qualitatively this should be treated no differently than a brokerage fee for selling stocks or bonds. Judged in this light, transactions costs are really a quite general concept.

In a frictionless world—that is, one without any transactions costs— individuals would hold no money for transactions purposes. As long as the rate of interest was positive, individuals would hold earning assets until the last instant before a transaction, only converting their assets into money as they were needed. In any realistic setting, however, transactions costs are not zero. As a consequence, the rational individual is faced with a trade-off between interest earnings on the one hand and transactions costs on the other. Lower average money balances permit higher average balances of earning assets and thus greater interest income. However, as we have seen, lower money balances also mean more frequent conversions from earning assets into money and hence higher transactions costs. Conversely, higher average money balances reduce both transactions costs and interest earnings. Clearly, somewhere in the middle there must be an optimum money holding that just balances these two considerations. The precise nature of this solution need not concern us, although the interested reader is referred to the appendix of this chapter for the details. For our present purposes we only need stress the following properties of the optimal solution:

1  The optimal level of average money balances increases with the total volume of expenditures (income) during the payment period.
2  Optimal average money holdings increase with the level of transactions costs and decrease with the level of interest rates on earning assets.

The first conclusion is, of course, reminiscent of both the quantity theory and the Keynesian approaches.[10] The second conclusion is the novel one. It states, in part, than individual's demands for transactions balances—and consequently aggregate demands as well—will vary inversely with the interest rate. Higher interest rates will encourage

---

[10] One important difference is that the results obtained by Baumol and Tobin suggest that the transactions demand for money will rise less than proportionately with income, thus indicating that there are economies of scale in holding transactions balances (see the appendix).

economizing on cash balances, thereby increasing income velocity. Lower interest rates will yield higher average cash balances and will reduce velocity.

In summary, in more modern treatments the interest rate is given a prominent place in the transactions view of the demand for money. The direction of the effect is the same as in the speculative motive discussed earlier. Consequently, taken together these two motives provide a convincing rationale for the importance of the interest rate in the demand for money.

**OTHER FACTORS IN THE DEMAND FOR MONEY**

To this point we have focused on the level of real output or income and the interest rate as the primary determinants of the demand for money. Restricting our attention to a few key variables is naturally of considerable analytic convenience, and we shall continue to adopt this approach in subsequent discussions. Nevertheless, it is important to emphasize that other factors can influence the demand for money. While it is generally possible to identify these factors with either the transactions or asset motives, for our present purposes this is not of critical importance. Consequently, we can simply list some of these other factors as follows:

1   THE WEALTH OF THE COMMUNITY. One would expect that the richer the community, the greater will be the quantity of money that it will demand. However, with such a wide variety of highly liquid and safe earning assets available, there is no logical reason why any large part of any increase of wealth should come to be reflected in an increase of demand for money balances.

2   THE EASE AND CERTAINTY OF SECURING CREDIT. If credit were unavailable, or were available only uncertainly and on onerous terms, both households and business firms would find it advantageous to hold larger money balances relative to their expenditures. However, as financial institutions and the use of credit become more highly developed, the community finds it advantageous to hold smaller balances relative to expenditures. Consumers need not accumulate large balances to pay for an expensive item, such as a car or a TV set; they buy it on credit and pay so much each payday. They need not hold balances to cover their expenditures between paydays; they can charge it and pay when they receive income. This also applies to business; it need not hold so much money relative to expenditures if it is assured of credit to meet excesses of expenditures over receipts. Thus, such developments as credit cards, instant credit, and confirmed lines of credit serve to reduce the demand for money balances.

3   EXPECTATIONS AS TO FUTURE INCOME RECEIPTS. The demand for

money is also affected by the community's expectations as to the certainty and size of its future income receipts. Suppose, for example, that at some time the community comes to fear that its future income receipts will be less certain and may decline seriously. Community members may try to build up their money balances to tide them over the feared or expected lean period. But if they come to believe that the flow of income receipts will rise markedly in the future, they may decrease their money holdings relative to their current rate of expenditure; that is, they may increase their current rate of expenditure relative to their money balances.

4 EXPECTATIONS AS TO PRICES. Expectations concerning the future behavior of prices are also relevant. If the members of a community believe that the prices of the things they intend to buy will remain stable, that a dollar will buy in the future just what it will buy today, they may elect to hold one quantity of money relative to their expenditures. They are likely to increase this quantity if they expect prices to fall. Both businesses and consumers may postpone purchases and hold larger balances relative to expenditures. They may elect to hold money, which they expect to increase in purchasing power, rather than hold inventories of goods that they expect to depreciate relative to money. They try to do this by decreasing their expenditures. Expectations of higher prices have the reverse effects; the members of the community are likely to try to hold smaller balances relative to their expenditures. They try to buy before prices rise. In hyperinflations, such as that in Germany after World War I, the quantity of money demanded relative to expenditures falls to very low levels. When members of the community come to fear that each monetary unit will lose half or more of its purchasing power in a day or two, they try to avoid holding money. They refuse to accept money for their goods and services, resorting to barter instead, or if they sell for money, they race to get rid of it immediately.

5 THE NATURE AND VARIETY OF SUBSTITUTE ASSETS. The demand for money is likely to be high if the only other assets available for holding are highly illiquid and risky. However, the demand for money is reduced as more liquid and safer substitutes become available. We have seen that a wide variety of highly liquid and safe substitutes are available in American financial markets. These include short-term Treasury obligations, open-market commercial paper, bankers' acceptances, time and savings deposits at commercial banks, and claims against a wide variety of nonbank financial intermediaries. This also suggests that the use of a single

interest rate to characterize the effects of interest rates on the demand for money is necessarily an oversimplification. Consequently, it should hardly be surprising that empirical studies of the demand for money tend to use several interest rates in explaining aggregate money holdings.

6   THE SYSTEM OF PAYMENTS IN THE COMMUNITY. We have already examined one aspect of this in our discussion of the frequency of income receipts. Another aspect concerns the structure of the production process. The more often that currently produced goods and services are sold for money in the process of production and distribution, the larger the demand for money is likely to be. Suppose, for example, that in producing a certain product all the processes of producing the raw material, fabricating, jobbing, wholesaling, and retailing are carried out by different firms, and that all payments among them are made with money. The demand for money relative to the final value of output is likely to be large. But the demand for money is likely to be smaller if all these processes are combined within vertically integrated firms with no money payments among the departments of each firm.

Such, then, are some of the factors, in addition to real income and the interest rate, that influence the behavior of the demand for money balances. This multiplicity of factors raises a question as to how predictable or stable is the demand for money. We address this briefly here and more extensively in Chapter 18.

THE STABILITY OF THE DEMAND FOR MONEY

In principle, each of the numerous factors listed above must be taken into account in predicting or explaining actual money demand. In practice, both in empirical work and in policy analysis, a number of these factors tend to be ignored. This is especially true of some of the more institutional factors—the nature and variety of substitute assets and the system of payments in the community—which are viewed as changing only slowly.

While this convenient simplification seemed to work well for many years, in the mid-1970s difficulties began appearing. Specifically, such things as NOW accounts, money market mutual funds, and convenient transfers from savings to checking accounts served simultaneously to expand the menu of assets, alter the nature of payments, and reduce the transactions costs of going from earning assets to money as conventionally defined. As a consequence, observers found that the community was demanding a lower volume of money balances, given their income, interest rates, and past behavior patterns. In addition, as noted earlier, these developments raised fundamental questions about the definition of money.

While we shall leave the policy implications of these developments until a later point, these events should alert us to the fact that there may be periods during which we shall observe shifts in the community's money demand function.

EQUILIBRIUM
N THE MONEY
MARKET

Having discussed the demand for money in some detail, we are now in position to examine the nature of the equilibrium between supply and demand in the market for money balances. This equilibrium condition will provide us with one of the important building blocks—the so-called *LM* curve—necessary for a complete theory of the determination of income, interest rates, and prices.

**Money
Supply**

Since the money supply has already been discussed at some length, only a few comments will be added here. Unless otherwise indicated, the following sections will assume that the size of the stock of money is firmly and precisely controlled by the monetary authority and that $M$ is not allowed to respond passively to increases or decreases in demands for money balances. In short, $M$ is a policy-determined independent variable. One consequence of this assumption is that to achieve equilibrium the demand for money must be brought into equality with the available supply by means of adjustments in the quantities demanded. Excesses of the supply of money over the demand for it must be eradicated by developments that increase the quantity demanded. And excesses of quantities demanded over the available supply must be corrected by some sort of development lowering the quantity demanded.

It should be recognized, however, that the assumption that the monetary authority has and exercises precise control over the size of $M$ is in some cases unrealistic. For one thing, the Federal Reserve may be unable to control the size of $M$ precisely, even if it tries to do so. There may be slippages between the instruments under its control—open-market operations, discount policy, and member bank reserve requirements—and the size of $M$. Also, the intermediate policy guide that dominates Federal Reserve actions may not be that of achieving a certain size or rate of change of $M$, but rather a specified behavior of some other economic variable, such as interest rates.[11] For example, the objective may be to stabilize interest rates, or to achieve some other pattern of behavior of interest rates. In such cases the Federal Reserve would have to allow $M$ to respond to the extent necessary to achieve its other intermediate objectives, and $M$ would itself be determined, at least in part, by factors determining the behavior of demands for money balances. Some cases in which $M$ is allowed to respond passively will be treated later.

[11] See Chapter 18.

**Money Demand**    In examining equilibrium in the money market, we shall confine our attention to a formulation of the demand for money that focuses only on the two key variables — real income and the interest rates. We can write our demand function for money in a general way as

$$\frac{M^D}{P} = f\left(\frac{Y}{P}, r\right) = f(O, r) \tag{6}$$

This equation states that the demand for real-money balances, $M^D/P$, is a function of real income or output, $Y/P$ or $O$, and the interest rate, $r$. It should be noted that in writing equation (6) we have made no distinction between money balances demanded for transactions purposes and those demanded for asset or speculative purposes. The reason we have not done so is that despite the analytical convenience of distinguishing among motives for holding money, the distinctions are really fuzzy ones. This is certainly true empirically, but it is true conceptually as well. For example, even if a dollar is to be spent for output in the near future, it serves as a store of value while it is held. Similarly, considerations of transactions costs should, strictly speaking, be introduced into the speculative or asset motive as well. Thus, for the time being at least, we shall work with a single demand function for money.

Equilibrium in the money market requires the equality of supply and demand, or

$$\overline{M}^S = M^D \tag{7}$$

where the bar over $\overline{M}^S$ is meant to indicate that the monetary authorities fix the supply of money at some given level. Combining equations (6) and (7), we can rewrite the condition for equilibrium as

$$\frac{\overline{M}^S}{P} = f\left(\frac{Y}{P}, r\right) \tag{8}$$

For the present we take the price level, $P$, as given. Consequently, (8) defines a single equation in two variables, $Y$ and $r$. The equation is thus not capable of determining values for both of the variables. Rather, it defines *combinations* of pairs of values for $r$ and $Y$ that keep the money market in equilibrium, given the supply of money and the price level. If we were to plot the values of these equilibrium pairs, we would have the *LM* curve.

**Construction of the *LM* Curve**    Although we have just indicated how one might construct an *LM* curve, actually carrying out this procedure would seem to require some specific numerical examples. We shall, in fact, shortly do this by way of illustration. But in reality one can deduce the *qualitative* nature of the *LM* curve without resorting to numbers.

To do this we must first plot the demand for real money balances as a function of the interest rate alone. Since equation (6) tells us that the demand depends on both real income and the interest rate, at first sight it may not be clear how to do this. The way around this difficulty is to plot the demand for money *given* the level of real income. Of course, this will give us a different curve for each level of income. Figure 12–6 plots two such curves for two different levels of real income, $O_1$ and $O_2$, where by assumption $O_2$ is larger than $O_1$. The first of these curves, labeled $f(O_1)$ in the figure, shows how the demand for real balances varies as a function of the interest when real income is fixed at $O_1$. It is downward sloping to reflect the inverse relationship between the demand for money and the interest rate. The second curve, labeled $f(O_2)$, has the same general shape as the first but is displaced to the right. This happens because at any given interest rate, since $O_2$ is larger than $O_1$, the demand for money must be larger at $O_2$ than at $O_1$. For example, at the interest rate $r_0$ shown in the diagram, the demand for real balances is $(M^D/P)_1$ when income is $O_1$ and $(M^D/P)_2$ when income is $O_2$, where $(M^D/P)_2$ exceeds $(M^D/P)_1$.

We are now virtually finished. To establish the general shape of the *LM* curve we must simply examine the condition for equilibrium in the money market. This is done in Figure 12–7, where we have superimposed the fixed money supply on a slightly expanded version of Figure 12–6. The vertical line in Figure 12–7 is drawn at the level of the money supply that is fixed by the authorities, $\overline{M}^S/P$. (It should be recalled that the price level is fixed throughout.) The points labeled $A$, $B$, and $C$ in the figure are precisely the points where the demand for money equals the fixed supply. At point $A$ the value of the interest rate is given by $r_1$ and the value of real income is $O_1$. Point $B$ corresponds to both a higher level of real income, $O_2$, and a higher interest rate, $r_2$, while point $C$ corresponds to still higher levels of both variables. If we plot these various combinations of the interest rate and real income, we shall have our *LM* curve. This is done in Figure 12–8.

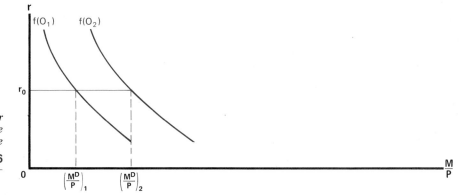

*The demand for money and the interest rate*

**FIGURE 12–6**

While the precise shape of the *LM* curve will, of course, depend on the slope of the money-demand function, the important thing to note about the *LM* curve is that it is upward sloping. This follows directly from the fact that as we move from *A* to *B* to *C* in Figure 12–7, we are increasing *both* the interest rate and real income. A moment's thought will reveal that this upward slope could easily have been anticipated. As we raise the level of real income, the demand for money (largely for transactions purposes) must increase. However, with a fixed supply of money, equilibrium in the money market requires that the interest rate must increase to choke off this additional demand — hence the upward slope of the *LM* curve.

**A Specific Example** To clarify further the nature of the *LM* curve, it may be helpful to consider a specific example. In constructing our example it will be helpful if we make the following simplifying assumptions:

1    The total demand function for money can be decomposed into

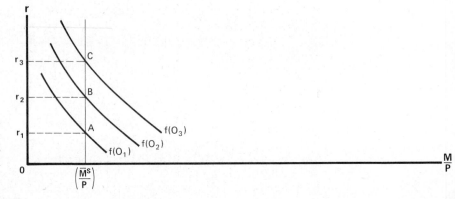

*Equilibrium in the money market*

**FIGURE 12–7**

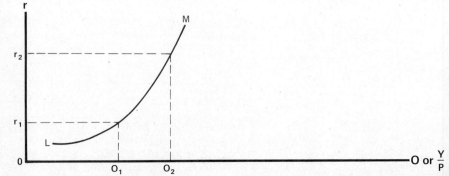

*The* LM *curve*

**FIGURE 12–8**

separate parts corresponding to the transactions and asset or speculative demand for money.

2  Transactions demand will be taken to be a function of income alone, whereas asset demand will be assumed to be a function of the interest rate alone.

3  Both the transactions and the asset demand will be taken to be linear functions; that is, we assume that they have constant slopes.

Thus, we can write

$$M^D = L_1 + L_2 \tag{9}$$

where

$M^D$ = the total demand function for (nominal) money balances
 $L_1$ = the demand function for transactions purposes
 $L_2$ = the demand function for asset or speculative purposes
We further assume that

$$L_1 = JOP = JY \tag{10}$$

where

$J$ = a constant giving the fraction of $OP$ or $Y$ demanded for transactions purposes

and that

$$L_2 = P(A - er) \tag{11}$$

where

$A$ = a positive constant, stated in billions of dollars of constant purchasing power

$e = \dfrac{\Delta L_2}{\Delta r}$ = the "slope," stated as the number of billions of change in $L_2$ with each change of 1 percentage point in $r$

Inserting equations (10) and (11) into equation (9), we get

$$M^D = JOP + P(A - er) \tag{12}$$

Dividing both sides of equation (12) by the price level, $P$, yields

$$\frac{M^D}{P} = JO + (A - er) \tag{13}$$

which states that total real money balances depend linearly on real income, $O$, and interest rate, $r$. Equation (13) is thus nothing other than a linear version of our general demand for money function, equation (6).

To obtain the $LM$ curve we must now use the equilibrium condition, equation (7), which, combined with equation (12), gives

$$\overline{M}^S = JOP + P(A - er)$$
$$= JY + P(A - er)$$

To use this algebraic expression to trace out an *LM* curve, we must, of course, put in some numbers, for example:

$\overline{M}^S = \$250$ billion
$J = \frac{1}{5}$
$A = \$110$ billion
$e = \$10$ billion
$P = 1$

Equation (13) then simplifies to

$$250 = \frac{1}{5}Y + (110 - 10r) \tag{15}$$

Table 12–2 shows nine of the many combinations of *r* and *Y* for which equation (15) is satisfied. This occurs at $Y = \$1,150$ billion and $r = 9$ percent; at $Y = \$1,000$ billion and $r = 6$ percent; and so on. This *LM* curve is depicted graphically in Figure 12–9.[12]

The fact that the *LM* curve is a straight line stems from the assumption of linearity in equations (10) and (11). The constant slope of the *LM* curve can be calculated by rewriting equation (15) with *r* on the left-hand side, as in

$$r = \frac{1}{50}Y - 14 \tag{16}$$

Thus, the slope is given by

$$\frac{\Delta r}{\Delta Y} = \frac{1}{50}$$

---

[12] Since we have assumed that $P = 1$, the horizontal axis in Figure 12–9 can either be regarded as measuring nominal income, *Y*, or real income, *O*.

---

| TABLE 12–2 | (1) | (2) | (3) | (4) | (5) | (6) |
|---|---|---|---|---|---|---|
| *A numerical LM example (amounts in billions of dollars)* | **M** | **Y** | $L_1 = 1/5Y$ | **r (in percent)** | $L_2 = 110 - 10r$ | Total $M^D$ [(3) + (5)] |
| | $250 | $ 750 | $150 | 1 | $100 | $250 |
| | 250 | 800 | 160 | 2 | 90 | 250 |
| | 250 | 850 | 170 | 3 | 80 | 250 |
| | 250 | 900 | 180 | 4 | 70 | 250 |
| | 250 | 950 | 190 | 5 | 60 | 250 |
| | 250 | 1,000 | 200 | 6 | 50 | 250 |
| | 250 | 1,050 | 210 | 7 | 40 | 250 |
| | 250 | 1,100 | 220 | 8 | 30 | 250 |
| | 250 | 1,150 | 230 | 9 | 20 | 250 |

In summary, the *LM* curve in Figure 12–9 represents all combinations of $Y$ and $r$ that satisfy the condition for equilibrium in the money market, equation (15). Any combination off the line will be one of disequilibrium, which will create pressures for adjustment. Any combination above the *LM* curve, such as point $A$, is one at which the supply of money exceeds the demand for money. We know this because there is a point on the *LM* curve vertically below $A$, at the same level of income at which equilibrium is established. At the same level of $Y$ and a higher $r$, demand will be smaller and the excess supply of money will create pressure for a decrease of $r$, thus moving us from a point like $A$ to the *LM* curve.

On the other hand, at any combination below the *LM* curve, such as point $B$, demand exceeds supply. This excess demand for money will bring pressure for an increase of $r$, again moving us to the *LM* curve.

**Shifting the LM Curve**

Before temporarily leaving the discussion of the *LM* curve, we should note that anything that shifts the demand function or the supply of money will shift the *LM* curve. For example, an increase in the supply of money shifts the *LM* curve to the right, and a decrease in the supply of money shifts the *LM* curve to the left. The reason is really quite simple. Consider first an increase in the supply of money. This creates excess supply in the money market. Reestablishing equilibrium thus requires a fall in $r$, a rise in $Y$, or both. Consequently, following an increase in the supply of money the new *LM* curve must lie down from and to the right of the original *LM* curve. This is illustrated in Figure 12–10. The original *LM* curve is labeled $L_1M_1$. Consider for a moment point $A$ on $L_1M_1$, which corresponds to the combination $r_1$ and $Y_1$. Now let us ask what value of $Y$ will put us on the new *LM* curve *if* the interest rate stays at $r_1$. With the interest rate constant, only way in which a new equilibrium can be established is if income rises so as to make individuals *want* to

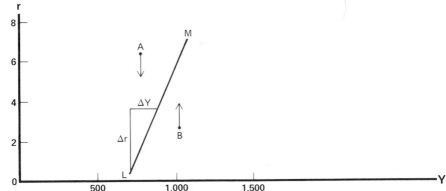

*An **LM** curve*

**FIGURE 12–9**

hold the new higher stock of money. Thus, we know that at the interest rate $r_1$ the value of income that puts us on the new LM curve $L_2M_2$ must be some higher level, like $Y_2$, in Figure 12–10.

Conversely, a decrease in the stock of money creates excess demand in the money market, leading to an increase of $r$, a decrease of $Y$, or both. Diagramatically, in Figure 12–10 this amounts to beginning with $L_2M_2$ and moving left toward $L_1M_1$.

In examining the effects of monetary policy in subsequent chapters, we shall frequently encounter such shifts in the LM curve. It is important, therefore, that the logic behind these shifts be well understood.[13]

**CONCLUSION**    This chapter has considered the nature of the demand for money in some detail. Tracing through the simple quantity theory, the Keynesian approach in terms of speculative and transactions motives, and the more modern view of the transactions approach, we have concluded that the level of real income and the interest rate are the primary determinants of the demand for real-money balances. We have also explored the nature of the LM curve, which gives the combinations of interest rates and real income that produce equality between demand and supply in the money market. As has been emphasized, however, this curve is not sufficient to determine unique equilibrium levels of income and the interest rate. To determine the unique point of equilibrium on the LM curve, we need further information. That will be supplied by the consumption, saving, and investment functions to be developed in the next chapter.

---

[13] We should note that an increase in the *real* quantity of money supplied can be brought about by either a *rise* in the nominal quality supplied, $\overline{M}^s$, or a *decline* in the price level, $P$. Since it is actually variations in the real quantity of money that shift the LM curve, we see that either a decline in the price level or a rise in $M^s$ shifts the LM curve to the right. Similarly, a rise in the price level or a decrease in $M^s$ shifts the LM curve to the left.

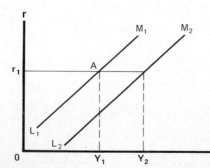

*Shifting the*
*LM curve*

**FIGURE 12–10**

## SOME NOTES ON THE TRANSACTIONS AND SPECULATIVE DEMANDS FOR MONEY

In the preceding chapter we discussed both the transactions and the speculative demands for money. At several points we touched on some of the post-Keynesian developments in these areas, but we did not spell out any of the arguments in detail. The purpose of this appendix is to close this gap.

**Transactions Demand**

As noted earlier, the problem faced by the individual transactor is to decide on his optimal holdings of money and an earning asset that we shall call bonds. The givens of the problem are as follows:

$Y$ = the real value of the individual's income per payment period (e.g., a month), which by assumption also equals the real value of expenditures to be made during the period

$r$ = the rate of interest per payment period, assumed constant over the period

$b$ = the real brokerage fee or transactions cost incurred each time the individual sells bonds[1]

The individual is assumed to sell bonds in equal-lot-size units of $D$, evenly spaced over the period. For example, if $Y$ is $800 per month, $D$ could be $800 once a month or $400 twice a month, and so on.[2] It is, of course, the optimal value of the variable $D$ that our analysis must determine. The problem is to choose $D$ so as to maximize total interest earnings less total transactions costs.

Since expenditures are made at a constant rate, the individual's average balances of *both* money and bonds must be one-half his income or $Y/2$. Similarly, his average money holdings must be $D/2$. Consequently, his average bond holding over the period is the difference between these two or $(Y/2 - D/2)$. The income he receives on this will be equal to the interest rate times his average bond holdings or $r(Y/2 - D/2)$. On the cost side, if each conversion of bonds into money is in the amount $D$, since all balances must eventually be converted, the individual must

---

[1] Note that this is a fixed cost per conversion of bonds into money. One can also introduce a cost that varies with the amount converted, but this would not change the results. See Baumol, op. cit.

[2] The reader will observe that we are implicitly assuming that the individual is paid in bonds. This could arise, for example, if the employer deposits the employee's paycheck directly into a savings account. This assumption makes the analysis simpler but does not change the qualitative nature of the conclusions.

engage in $Y/D$ conversions during the period. Since the brokerage charge is $\$b$ per conversion, his total conversion costs are $\$b(Y/D)$.

These two elements can be combined in a total net-revenue expression:

$$N = r\left(\frac{Y}{2} - \frac{D}{2}\right) - b\left(\frac{Y}{D}\right) \tag{A1}$$

where the first term in equation (A1) corresponds to interest earnings and the second to conversion costs. To find the value of $D$ that maximizes net revenue we must take the derivative of (A1) with respect to $D$, equate it with zero, and solve for $D$. The solution to this is[3]

$$D = \sqrt{\frac{2bY}{r}} \tag{A2}$$

Since average money holdings, here denoted by $M$, have been observed to equal $D/2$, from equation (A2) we derive

$$M = \sqrt{\frac{bY}{2r}} = kY^{1/2}r^{-1/2} \tag{A3}$$

where

$$k = \sqrt{\frac{b}{2}}$$

Equation (A3) is then our desired result. For obvious reasons it is sometimes called the *square-root law* of money demand.

While we have spelled out several of the implications of this result in the preceding chapter, it is worth emphasizing the following points:

1   Both the level of interest rates and transactions costs influence optimal money holdings, with larger money holdings stemming from either lower interest rates or higher transactions costs.

2   Technological or legal developments that reduce transactions costs will yield lower average money holdings. Thus, for example, if telephone or computer terminal transfers between savings and demand deposits become widespread, we would expect individuals to economize further on money balances.

3   The way in which income enters equation (A3) implies that there are economies of scale in individual money holdings. For

---

[3] The appropriate condition is $dN/dD = (-r/2) + (bY/D^2) = 0$, which when solved yields (A2). The astute reader may observe that the optimal value of $D$ may imply a number of transactions that is not an integer. This difficulty is more apparent than real. In this regard see Tobin, op. cit.

example, if the income of an individual goes up fourfold, (A3) predicts that money balances will only rise by a factor of 2.

4   While this last result cannot be directly carried over to the aggregate economy, it certainly suggests that aggregate money holdings may rise less than proportionately with aggregate income. It further suggests that aggregate money holdings may be sensitive to the distribution of income. In particular, (A3) implies that the more highly concentrated is a fixed level of aggregate income, the lower will be the demand for money.

**Speculative Demand**

As with the transactions motive, subsequent developments in monetary theory have served to clarify the concept of the speculative motive introduced by Keynes. In order to see why these developments were necessary, we shall first provide a brief critical review of the Keynesian approach to the speculative motive. We shall then outline some more recent work whose emphasis has been on providing a firm theoretical foundation for the speculative motive.[4]

As noted earlier, Keynes analyzed a world in which two assets were available—money and perpetual bonds or consols. Money yields no return, nor does it depreciate in terms of money. Bonds, of course, do yield a return made up of two components: (1) the interest payment received and (2) the change in capital value of the bond stemming from a change in the rate of interest. As we saw in Chapter 3, the formula for the price of a perpetual bond is

$$P = \frac{A}{r} \tag{A4}$$

where

$P$ = the price of the bond
$A$ = the dollar amount of interest paid per year to the bondholder
$r$ = the annual rate of interest

Thus, an individual who anticipates that in the future the interest rate will be $r^e$ must necessarily expect a bond price of $P^e$ given by

$$P^e = \frac{A}{r^e} \tag{A5}$$

Consequently, the expected percentage capital gain (or loss if it is negative), which we will denote by $g$, is given by

---

[4] For a more complete exposition of the material in this section, see James Tobin, "Liquidity Preference as Behavior Towards Risk," *Review of Economic Studies*, February 1958, pp. 65–86.

$$g \equiv \frac{P^e - P}{P} = \frac{A/r^e - A/r}{A/r} \tag{A6}$$

The second part of equation (A6) is derived by substituting equations (A4) and (A5) into the definition of $g$. This can be simplified by canceling the $A$ terms and multiplying the numerator and denominator of (A6) by $r$ to give

$$g = \frac{r}{r^e} - 1 \tag{A7}$$

This expresses $g$ in terms of the current and expected rate of interest. For example, if $r^e = r$, then $g$ is zero, so that no capital gain or loss is expected. Alternatively, if the current interest rate is 6 percent and is expected to fall to 5 percent, then

$$g = \frac{0.06}{0.05} - 1 = 0.2, \text{ or } 20 \text{ percent}$$

The total return from holding bonds from one year to the next is simply the sum of the interest rate and the expected capital gain. That is, we have

$$e = r + g = r + \frac{r}{r^e} - 1 \tag{A8}$$

where

$e =$ the one-year expected holding period yield[5]

Given equation (A8), according to Keynes the individual investor now has a simple choice. If the expected holding period yield is greater than zero — which is the expected holding period yield on money — then the individual should keep his assets in bonds. If the expected yield is less than zero, he should hold money. Since expectations were perceived by Keynes as being determined by some kind of normal rate, quite evidently the lower the current interest rate, the more likely it is that $e$ will be negative and that money will be held. Conversely, the higher $r$ is, the more likely it is that $e$ will be positive and bonds will be held. Thus, the demand for speculative balances will be inversely related to the current interest rate. In essence, this is a simple restatement of the Keynesian speculative motive developed earlier.

This analysis has, however, at least three troublesome aspects:

---

[5] This concept, it will be recalled, was discussed in Chapter 4. It should also be noted that there is nothing special about our use of the time unit of one year. Any other period would work equally well.

1   The analysis implies that each individual will hold all his assets in either the form of bonds or the form of money. However, it is more reasonable to suppose that individuals tend to hold *diversified* portfolios of both bonds and money, a result that does not follow from the Keynesian analysis.

2   To explain why both bonds and money are held in the *aggregate*, we must appeal to the existence of different expectations on the part of different individuals. Some of these individuals would be exclusively in bonds, others exclusively in money. However, if the market for money balances is in equilibrium for a sufficient length of time, the expectations of different individuals should tend to converge to a common expectation. When this happens, we are back to the all-or-nothing situation described previously and, consequently, cannot explain how both money and bonds will be held in the aggregate.

3   Despite the obvious element of uncertainty faced by the individual in making his portfolio choices, the Keynesian analysis proceeds as if the individual's beliefs were held with certainty. In other words, the individual investor pays no attention to any risks associated with his portfolio choice.

It was to overcome these various difficulties that the portfolio balance approach was developed.

**The Portfolio Balance Approach**

The *portfolio balance approach* begins from the relatively simple notion that individuals like to earn high rates of return on their assets but that they dislike risk. Put in terms of utility, the rate of return (or the wealth that it brings) is a "good," but risk is a "bad." To gain some perspective on this consider an individual who is presented with the following three options:

Option 1: $1,000 offered with certainty
Option 2: a 50:50 chance of getting $750 or $1,250
Option 3: a 50:50 chance of getting $250 or $1,750

All three options offer the same average or expected return of $1,000, but only the first does so with certainty. Both the second and third options have some risk attached to them; and the third option, since it has a greater dispersion of outcomes, is, in some intuitive sense, riskier than the second. To postulate that individuals like return but dislike risk, or are *risk averse*, is to argue that option 1 would be chosen by most people. Indeed, an individual might well continue to choose option 1 even if she were allowed to pick

Option 4: a 50:50 chance of getting $252 or $1,750

which has an expected return of $1,001.

However, it is clearly possible to modify option 4 further so that we raise the expected return by just enough to compensate the individual for the risk involved; that is, by sufficiently raising the expected return of a risky option, we can make the individual *indifferent* between a certain option and a risky one. This discussion is not meant to suggest that all individuals are *necessarily* risk averse, but rather that this is a reasonable assumption on which to base a theory of portfolio behavior. Let us now see how this would work in the case of the speculative motive.

As earlier, we consider an individual who wishes to divide her assets between money and perpetual bonds. Abstracting from any change in the general price level, money is a riskless asset with a zero rate of return. Bonds have an *expected* rate of return, which we previously denoted by $e = r + g$, where $r$ was the interest component and $g$ was the expected capital gain or loss. In contrast to $e$, however, the *actual* rate of return on bonds is uncertain, so that individuals holding bonds must bear some risk.

The problem faced by the individual is to choose a portfolio so as to maximize her utility. We first observe that negative values of $e$ will definitely lead to an all-money portfolio, since, in this case, bonds offer both less return and more risk as compared with money. As a consequence, we might as well restrict our attention to positive values of $e$. For such values, holding more bonds increases expected interest income and hence tends to increase utility. However, this also increases the dispersion of possible outcomes, since the future value of an individual's assets can fluctuate over a greater range the higher the fraction of assets held in bonds. Viewed from this perspective, higher bond holdings tend to increase risk and thus decrease utility. The problem is clearly one of striking an optimal balance between risk and return. Even without exhibiting a specific solution to this problem, it should be intuitively clear that this will lead to an inverse relationship between speculative money holdings and the interest rate. In particular, higher current interest rates, *other things being equal*, will lead to higher expected returns from bonds. With no change in the inherent riskiness of bonds, individuals will, at the margin, find bonds more attractive than money and thus reduce their money holdings somewhat. In other words, higher current interest rates lead to lower money balances and vice versa. The plausibility of this conclusion can be buttressed by the use of some diagrams.

In Figure 12A–1 we have plotted a typical individual's *indifference curves*. Each curve corresponds to a given level of utility and thus portrays the combinations of expected return and risk between which the individual is indifferent. The curves slope up to the right, since, as we have noted earlier, increased risk must be associated with increased return to leave the individual equally well off. Similarly, indifference curve $I_2$ corresponds to a higher level of utility than $I_1$, which is in turn more desirable than $I_0$. This can be seen by comparing points $A$, $B$, and $C$ in Figure 12A–1. Each point has the same riskiness, but expected return increases as we move from $A$ to $B$ to $C$. Clearly, then, the individual will prefer being on $I_2$ rather than on $I_1$ and on $I_1$ rather than on $I_0$.

To complete the givens of the problem, we must specify the set of possible combinations of expected return and risk that are available to the individual. The quantity of bonds the individual can hold ranges from zero to the total size of her assets, which we assume fixed. Denoting the quantity of bonds held by the symbol $H$, we have the following:

$$E = He = H(r + g) \qquad \text{(A9)}$$
$$R = H\sigma \qquad \text{(A10)}$$

where

$E$ = expected return
$R$ = total risk
$\sigma$ = a measure of risk associated with \$1 bonds

Equation (A9) simply says that the expected return in dollars is equal to the expected *rate* of return times the dollar value of bonds held. Equation (A10) states that total risk is given by the product of the dollar volume of bonds and the riskiness of a single bond.[6] If we divide (A9) by (A10), we can eliminate $H$ and simplify to obtain

$$E = \left(\frac{r + g}{\sigma}\right)R \qquad \text{(A11)}$$

---

[6] Those familiar with elementary statistics will recognize the symbol $\sigma$ as a standard deviation, which is a conventional measure of dispersion. For a more detailed justification of its use as a measure of risk, see Tobin, op. cit.

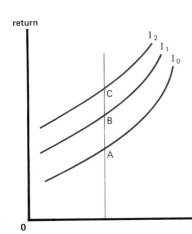

return

$I_2$
$I_1$
$I_0$

C

B

A

*Indifference curves*

**FIGURE 12A–1**

0

risk

Expression (A11) is the desired relationship between expected return and risk. It is the opportunity locus available to the individual, and it is analogous to the budget line in the conventional theory of the consumer. We have plotted several possible loci in Figure 12A–2.

The following observations on Figure 12A–2 should be noted:

1   Since (A11) expresses a linear relationship between $E$ and $R$, the loci are all straight lines.

2   Again from (A11), we see that the slope of the straight lines depends on the market rate of interest, $r$. In particular, higher rates of interest correspond to steeper loci (that is, $r_2 > r_1 > r_0$).

3   All the loci go through the origin. The origin corresponds to the portfolio consisting entirely of money for which both the expected return and risk are zero.

We are now in a position to indicate diagrammatically the nature of the individual's portfolio choice. Given the interest rate, the expected

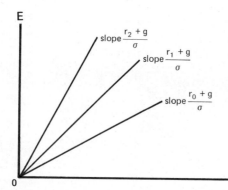

*Opportunity curves*
**FIGURE 12A–2**

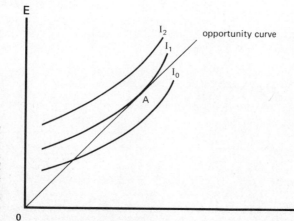

*Individual equilibrium: tangency between indifference and opportunity curves*
**FIGURE 12A–3**

capital gain or loss, and the riskiness of bonds (that is, $r$, $g$, and $\sigma$), the individual is constrained to choose along some particular opportunity locus. Her objective is to get onto the highest indifference curve, and this obviously is at a point where the opportunity locus is just tangent to an indifference curve. Figure 12A–3 indicates the nature of this tangency, with point $A$ being the optimal point for the individual.

Let us now consider how an individual's portfolio will change as the interest rate changes. In figure 12A–4 we have plotted the loci corresponding to two different interest rates. When the interest rate is $r_0$, the individual is in equilibrium at point $A$. However, if the interest rate should be at the higher level $r_1$, equilibrium would occur at point $B$. At this latter point the individual has a higher expected return and a higher risk as compared with point $A$.[7] Increased return and risk can only come about because the individual has more bonds. Consequently, the portfolio corresponding to point $B$ contains more bonds and therefore less money than the portfolio corresponding to point $A$.

We now have obtained the desired result. That is, we see that higher interest rates lead to lower speculative money balances and, conversely, that lower interest rates lead to higher money balances. While this has been developed as a theory of individual behavior, it is reasonable to assume that the same general properties carry over to the aggregate demand for money. In other words, the aggregate speculative demand

---

[7] In Figure 12A–4 we have ignored the possibility that the individual, feeling wealthier because of a higher interest rate, may actually assume less risk. This possible perversity of what is known as the "income effect" is discussed in D. E. W. Laidler, *The Demand for Money: Theories and Evidence*, 2nd ed., New York, Dun-Donnelley, 1977, pp. 93–95.

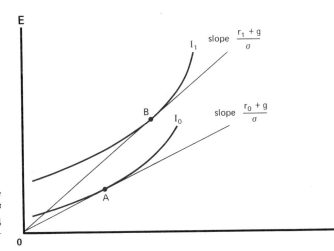

*The effect of a change in interest rates*

**FIGURE 12A–4**

for money has the downward-sloping shape we have seen in Figure 12–4.

In summary, the portfolio balance approach leads to the same result as that obtained by Keynes, but it does so under somewhat more appealing assumptions. In particular, it both directly confronts the problem of uncertainty and allows for the possibility that individuals will hold diversified portfolios.

Branson, W. H., *Macroeconomic Theory and Policy*, 2nd ed., New York, Harper & Row, 1979.

Friedman, M., "The Quantity of Money—A Restatement," in M. Friedman (ed.), *Studies in the Quantity Theory of Money*, Chicago, University of Chicago Press, 1956.

Goldfeld, S. M., "The Demand for Money Revisited," *Brookings Papers on Economic Activity*, No. 3, 1973, pp. 577–638.

Laidler, D. E. W., *The Demand for Money: Theories and Evidence*, New York, Dun-Donnelley, 1977.

# 13

In this chapter we continue our development of the building blocks of a theory for determining the levels of income and interest rates. We saw in the previous chapter that equilibrium between the supply of money and the demand for money yields a relationship between income and interest rates—the *LM* curve—but this was not sufficient to determine the levels of these variables. Obviously, we must find another relationship between these two variables. To accomplish this, we turn now from the money market to the market for goods or commodities. In particular, we shall focus on the "income and expenditure approach," which utilizes concepts such as the consumption and saving functions and the investment function. As we shall see, the income approach emphasizes that a necessary condition for equilibrium of income and interest rates is that the supply of saving be equal to the investment demand for output. It is precisely this condition that will give us the additional relationship we are seeking and thus permit us to develop a complete model of the determination of income and interest rates. That is, the establishment of *joint equilibrium* in the money market and the goods market will determine both the levels of aggregate output and the interest rate.

The concept of aggregate income, measured by GNP, played a critical role in the explanation of the behavior of the aggregate demand for money. Aggregate income will receive an equally prominent role in explaining the behavior of consumption, saving, and investment. Therefore, prior to launching into the theory of saving and investment behavior, it will be extremely helpful if we understand how the concepts of income, output, saving, and investment are actually measured in practice.

**NATIONAL INCOME CONCEPTS**   As just indicated, one concept that we need to make precise is the notion of *gross national product* or *expenditure*, popularly known as GNP. As we shall see, there are a number of equivalent ways of measuring GNP. We begin with the most common approach, that of viewing GNP as the market value of the output of goods and services produced by the nation during some time period. Subsequently we exploit the wonders of double-entry balance sheet accounting to show that GNP can be equivalently defined as the sum of all factor incomes (e.g., wages, profits, etc.) generated in the economy.[1]

**GNP as Expenditure for Output**   GNP is composed of three main categories of expenditures for output:[2] (1) personal consumption expenditures, (2) gross private domestic investment, and (3) government purchases of goods and services. We shall consider each in turn.

*Personal Consumption*

Personal consumption expenditures include all purchases of current output by consumers. These include durable consumer's goods, nondurable consumer's goods, and consumer's services. The durables include such things as new automobiles, TV sets, refrigerators, and furniture. The nondurables include food, beverages, clothing, tobacco, and so on. Consumer's services embrace a wide variety of services such as shelter, medical care, and transportation.

*Gross Private Domestic Investment*

Every word in this title is important. The term *investment*, as used here, has nothing directly to do with buying stocks, bonds, or any other type of financial instrument. We use it here and in the succeeding sections to mean simply expenditures for the current output of goods and services for the purpose of maintaining and increasing the stock of capital goods. The term *domestic* indicates that we include here only expenditures for the purpose of maintaining or increasing the stock of capital goods at home, not those for maintaining or building up capital abroad.

---

[1] Our discussion of national income accounting will be quite brief. For a more detailed treatment see T. F. Dernburg and D. M. McDougall, *Macroeconomics*, New York, McGraw-Hill, 1976. The most recent national income data are contained in the *Survey of Current Business* published by the Department of Commerce, especially the July issue.

[2] A fourth category, net exports of goods and services, is also included in GNP. Net exports, which is defined as exports minus imports, is typically only a very small fraction of GNP. As a consequence, to simplify matters we postpone international considerations until Part VI.

*Private* means that only private expenditures for these purposes are included, not those by the government. The term *gross* indicates that we include expenditures for output to offset the depreciation of capital goods as well as to make net additions to the stock. If we deduct from gross private domestic investment for any period the depreciation or "using up" of capital during the period, we arrive at net private domestic investment, the net increase in the stock of these goods during the period.

Gross private domestic investment is actually made up of three broad types of investment: new construction, both residential and nonresidential; producers' durable equipment such as individual machinery, computers, and railroad cars; and *net changes in business inventories.* The last term, which perhaps requires a bit of clarification, refers to changes in the stock of business inventories from one period to another. These inventories, which may be raw materials, goods in process, or finished goods, are clearly part of the community's stock of capital goods. Hence, a net increase in business inventories is investment because it is an addition to the stock of capital goods. Historically, changes in the volume of output used to increase or decrease inventories have been an important source of fluctuations in GNP and employment.

### Government Purchases of Goods and Services

Government purchases consist of the expenditures of the federal, state, and local governments for the current output of goods and services. These include expenditures both for the services of productive factors, primarily labor, and for the output of business firms. Government transfer payments, such as social security or welfare payments, are excluded from government purchases because they are not payments for productive services. As we shall see shortly, however, government transfer payments can indirectly affect GNP by altering household disposable income and, hence, personal consumption expenditures.

### Transactions Excluded from GNP

We have just seen that government transfer payments are not directly included in the calculation of GNP. This is just one example of the fact that only transactions that represent payments for currently produced goods and services are included in GNP. Other transactions excluded by this principle are the following: purchases of existing houses or used cars, and financial transactions such as purchases of corporate stock or government bonds (regardless of whether they are "new" or "used"). A second general class of excluded transactions are those stemming from *intermediate* sales, that is, sales from one producer to another. The purchase of flour by a baker is an example. It would be double counting to include in GNP both the value of flour sold to the baker and the full value of bread sold by the baker to the consumer. As a consequence, only the *final sale* to the consumer is counted in GNP.

### The Accounting Identity and Some Data

We find, then, that GNP for any period is the sum of expenditures for output in the form of personal consumption, gross private domestic investment, and government purchases of goods and services.

For convenience, we shall denote these expenditures by the following symbols:

$C$ = personal consumption
$I$ = gross private domestic investment
$G$ = government purchases of goods and services
$Y$ = GNP, or gross national product

Thus, for any period,

$$Y = C + I + G \tag{1}$$

Table 13–1 gives some actual data on GNP and its components for several recent years. For each year, GNP is measured in terms of the average level of prices prevailing during that year. This is sometimes called *current-dollar* GNP or *nominal* GNP. As an addendum, Table 13–1 also shows the value of GNP for each year at constant (1972) prices, and the corresponding price index. GNP in constant prices is called either *real* GNP or *constant-dollar* GNP. The price index shown is called the *implicit GNP price deflator.* It is an index of average prices of all goods and services included in GNP, with the index constructed so as to have the value of unity in 1972.[3]

---

[3] In the previous chapter we denoted real GNP and the price index by $O$ and $P$, respectively. Using these symbols, the relationship between real and nominal GNP is given by $Y = O \times P$ or $O = Y/P$.

| TABLE 13–1 | | 1973 | 1976 | 1979 |
|---|---|---|---|---|
| *Gross national product and its components (in billions of dollars)* | Consumption | $ 809.9 | $1,089.9 | $1,510.0 |
| | Investment | 220.0 | 243.0 | 387.2 |
| | Government purchases | 269.5 | 361.3 | 476.4 |
| | Net exports | 7.1 | 8.0 | −4.2 |
| | GNP | $1,306.6 | $1,702.2 | $2,369.4 |
| | **Addendum** | | | |
| | Implicit GNP price deflator (1972 = 1.00) | 1.058 | 1.337 | 1.655 |
| | Real GNP in constant (1972) prices | $1,235.0 | $1,273.0 | $1,431.7 |

*Source:* U.S. Department of Commerce, *Survey of Current Business*, Washington, D.C., various issues.

**he Circular Flow**
**of Income**

We noted earlier that GNP may be viewed not only as the value of output or expenditures for output but also as the sum of gross national income shares accruing to the members of the community, including the government. We also noted that the sum of these shares accruing to the community during any period must be exactly equal to the value of output or expenditures. On reflection, this becomes almost obvious. Value created must accrue to someone; it cannot disappear in thin air. Nor can the community as a whole receive values that are not created. To state this observation in another way, expenditures made must be received by someone, but no one can receive expenditures that are not made.

A pictorial representation of this circular flow is given in Figure 13–1. It shows total aggregate demand, $C + I + G$, arriving at firms where actual production takes place. The circular flow emerges from firms as payments to the various factors of production. We have relabeled this flow "Gross national income," but as just indicated, gross national income and gross national product must be equal.

Another way to see this is to consider what happens to a firm that produces and sells some dollar value of output. The bulk of these revenues must be used to pay its workers (wages), people who have lent it money (interest payments), and perhaps landlords who own the firm's

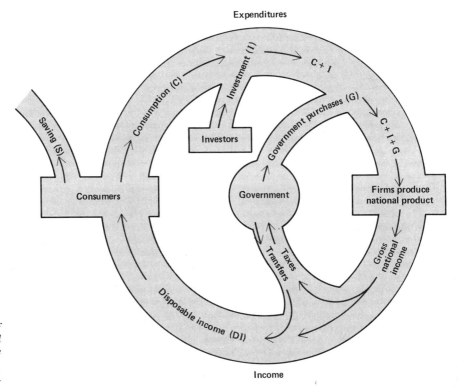

*The circular flow of*
*expenditure and*
*income*

**FIGURE 13–1**

building (rents). What is left over is received by the owners of the firm in the form of *profits*. But the income of these owners also counts in national income. Hence, when we add up all the factor payments, including profits, to obtain gross national income, we must also obtain the dollar value of expenditures, or GNP.

**Disposable Income, Saving, and Investment**

If we follow the circular flow past firms, we see that there are both some additions and some leakages in the income stream before it gets to consumers. The major leakage takes the form of taxes — on both individual and corporate incomes — collected by the government sector.[4] Partially offsetting this are government transfer payments, which may be thought of as "negative" taxes. Subtracting transfer payments from taxes yields *net taxes*. Net taxes thus represent the overall leakage in going from gross national income to what is known as consumer *disposable income*. In symbols, if we let DI = disposable income and $T$ = net taxes, we have

$$DI = Y - T \tag{2}$$

As Figure 13–1 illustrates, disposable income flows to consumers, where it has two uses — it is either consumed or saved.[5] We already have a symbol for consumption expenditures, namely, $C$. If we denote *saving* by $S$, we can then express these two uses of disposable income by

$$DI = C + S \tag{3}$$

Combining equations (2) and (3), we have

$$Y - T = C + S$$

or

$$Y = C + S + T \tag{4}$$

Thus, we see that a third way to measure $Y$ or GNP is by the various ways it can be disposed of — by either consuming, saving, or paying taxes.

Finally, we can combine equations (1) and (5) to get

$$C + I + G = C + S + T$$

Eliminating $C$ from both sides yields

---

[4] As regards potential leakages, Figure 13–1 embodies a number of simplifications. For example, it assumes that all profits are paid out to owners of firms. In actual fact, some profits are retained by firms and contribute to business saving.

[5] While the saving flow appears to hit a dead end, as we saw in Chapter 3 it is recycled via financial markets or intermediaries to finance investment. This relationship between saving and investment is made more explicit in equation (6).

$$I + G = S + T \qquad (5)$$

Or, bringing $G$ to the left-hand side of (5), we get

$$I = S + (T - G) \qquad (6)$$

What equation (6) tells us is that there is an identity between investment on the one hand and saving plus the difference between net taxes and government expenditures on the other. The latter difference, $(T - G)$, is nothing other than the government surplus, if it is positive, or the government deficit, if it is negative. Another way to interpret $(T - G)$ is that it measures *government saving*, that is, government income $(T)$ less government spending $(G)$. Thus, the right-hand side of equation (6) can be interpreted as total saving, consisting of private saving, $S$, and government saving, $(T - G)$. In these terms, equation (6) simply expresses the accounting identity between saving and investment. We shall put this identity to good use as we proceed.

---

**SOME SIMPLIFYING ASSUMPTIONS**

For the remainder of this chapter we shall concentrate on consumption, saving, and investment. Several characteristics of the following analysis should be borne in mind:

1  It is essentially short run in nature. That is, it does not attempt to analyze changes in the productive capacity of the economy through time; instead, it is concerned with the behavior of income and output within given capacity levels.

2  Unless otherwise indicated, it assumes that price levels of output are constant, so that the money value of output is an index of the behavior of real output.

3  It assumes that there are no foreign transactions, so that exports and imports need not concern us for the present.

4  For the first part of the chapter, it assumes that the government engages in no economic activity, so that there are no taxes, government transfer payments, or government purchases. Thus, private disposable income is equal to GNP. From equations (1), (4), and (6), with government spending $(G)$ and net taxes $(T)$ by assumption equal to zero, we have

$$Y = C + I = C + S$$
and
$$I = S$$

Hence, by temporarily ignoring the government sector we can decrease the number of variables. Consequently, we can describe the principles involved more clearly. The government will be restored to the picture toward the end of the chapter. Our first task will be to develop consumption and saving functions.

## CONSUMPTION AND SAVING

We now move from the accounting or definitional aspects of consumption and saving to the more interesting question of the determinants of consumer behavior.

### The Functions

The most powerful determinant of private consumption and saving is the level of private disposable income, which in the absence of government is equal to total income. Both consumption and saving are positive functions of the level of income. That is, at higher levels of income, the private sectors will both consume more and save more; at lower levels of income, they will both consume less and save less. This is shown schematically in Figure 13–2. The level of income created $(C + I)$ is measured on the horizontal axis. The amount of private disposable income $(C + S)$ is measured on the vertical axis in part $(a)$. As an expositional device we draw a line at a 45° angle through the origin. If a line is dropped vertically from any point on the 45° line, the vertical distance to the base is exactly equal to the horizontal distance from the origin to the point of intersection on the base. This illustrates the fact that the amount of disposable income $(C + S)$ must be exactly equal to the amount of income created $(C + I)$.

The $CC$ line represents the *consumption function*. That is, it states consumption as a function of the level of income. The consumption function can also be stated algebraically:

$$C = B + \left(\frac{\Delta C}{\Delta Y}\right)Y \tag{7}$$

$B =$ a positive constant, stated in billions of dollars. It is the height of the intercept on the vertical axis, and its size establishes the height of the consumption function

$\dfrac{\Delta C}{\Delta Y} =$ the "slope" of the consumption function

= the marginal propensity to consume

= MPC

The slope of the consumption function $(\Delta C / \Delta Y)$ indicates the marginal responsiveness of consumption to changes in the level of income. This is called the *marginal propensity to consume,* or MPC. A basic hypothesis of income theory is that the marginal propensity to consume $(\Delta C / \Delta Y)$ is greater than zero but less than one. That is, in response to a rise (or fall) of disposable income, the community will increase (or decrease) its consumption, but by an amount less than the change in income. For example, a $\Delta C/\Delta Y$ of 0.8 indicates that a given change of disposable income will change consumption by an amount equal to eight-tenths of the income change.[6]

The saving-supply function is shown in part (*a*) of Figure 13–2 as the vertical distance from the 45° line to the amount of consumption at that level of income. This necessarily follows from the fact that $S = Y - C$. For convenience, the saving-supply function, represented by the line SS, is shown separately in part (*b*) of Figure 13–2. It, too, is a positive function of income. Its slope ($\Delta S/\Delta Y$) measures the marginal responsiveness of saving to income. This is called the *marginal propensity to save*, or MPS. The value of MPS is obviously related to the value of MPC. In fact, since $Y \equiv C + S$,

$$\Delta Y = \Delta C + \Delta S$$

and, dividing both sides of the equation by $\Delta Y$, we get

$$1 = \frac{\Delta C}{\Delta Y} + \frac{\Delta S}{\Delta Y} \quad \text{or} \quad \frac{\Delta S}{\Delta Y} = 1 - \frac{\Delta C}{\Delta Y}$$

Thus, if $\Delta C/\Delta Y = 0.8$, then $\Delta S/\Delta Y = 0.2$. Any change in income must be equal to the changes in consumption and saving; any part that is not used to change consumption must be reflected in a change in saving.

It is important to remember that when we define either the consumption function or the saving-supply function, we are actually defin-

---

[6] It is, of course, possible that the value of $\Delta C/\Delta Y$ will be different at different levels of income. We use a linear consumption function partly because of its simplicity and partly because empirical studies suggest that linear functions fit the data as well as other types of functions.

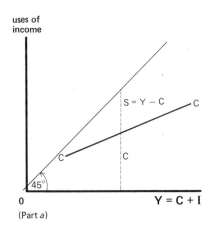

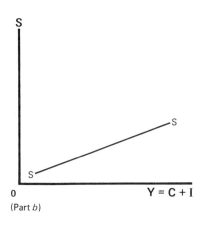

*Private disposable income and its disposal*

**FIGURE 13–2**

ing both functions because each function is simply $Y$ minus the other function. For example, we obtain the saving-supply function by subtracting the consumption function from $Y$:

$$S = Y - (B + \frac{\Delta C}{\Delta Y}Y) \qquad (8)$$

$$= Y - \frac{\Delta C}{\Delta Y}Y - B$$

$$= Y \left(1 - \frac{\Delta C}{\Delta Y}\right) - B$$

Since $1 - \Delta C/\Delta Y = \Delta S/\Delta Y$, we can also express the saving-supply function as

$$S = Y \frac{\Delta S}{\Delta Y} - B$$

**Other Factors**    Thus far we have concentrated on the effects of income on the level of consumption and saving. We did this because both a priori reasoning and empirical investigations indicate that income is the most powerful determinant of these variables.

This is not to say that the amounts of consumption and saving depend solely on the level of disposable income; many other factors help determine how any given level of disposable income will be divided between consumption and saving. Moreover, changes in these other factors can shift the consumption function up or down; that is, they can lead to more or less consumption at each level of income. Some of the more important of these factors are the following:

1    Social attitudes toward current consumption versus saving for the future.

2    Distribution of total household income by size of household income. For example, total saving out of a given level of total household income is likely to be higher if a greater part of the total income accrues to high-income classes, rather than to low-income groups.

3    Age composition of the population. Both elderly and young families have higher propensities to consume than families in their middle years. A shift in age composition could shift consumption and saving functions.

4    The stock of wealth. Other things equal, a wealthy community might be expected to consume a larger part of its income than a population with the same income but less wealth. "Windfall" capital gains or losses can increase or decrease the consumption function.

5    Expectations concerning future levels of income relative to

current income levels. When future levels of income are expected to be higher than present levels, the community is likely to consume more out of its current income.

These are some of the factors that determine the height and shape of the consumption and saving functions. When we state consumption and personal saving as functions of disposable income, we implicitly assume that such other factors are constant in their effects.

**TERMINATION EQUILIBRIUM INCOME: SPECIAL CASE**

We can gain some insight into the workings of the consumption and saving functions by examining the determination of equilibrium income in the special case of an exogenously determined level of investment, that is, where investment is given from the outside. The major point to be made here is that income and output can be at an equilibrium level only when investment expenditure is exactly equal to the supply of saving. We have already encountered the *identity*, $I \equiv S$. This indicates that as a matter of national income accounting, saving always equals investment. Since this is always true, our equilibrium condition must be referring to a different kind of equality between saving and investment. This is indeed the case, and to see this we must distinguish between intended and unintended investment.

*Intended investment* is that part of investment stemming from business plans. That is, it is planned or "desired" investment. *Unintended investment* refers to the unforeseen changes in inventories arising because of unexpected changes in the level of demand or sales. Obviously, equilibrium requires that unintended investment be zero, so that we must have: Intended investment= saving. This latter equality is clearly not an identity, but rather an equilibrium condition. The working of this condition is illustrated in Figure 13–3, where we have plotted a saving function, SS, and a line indicating the intended level of investment, II.

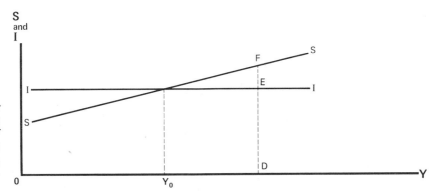

*The equality of investment demand and the supply of saving*

**FIGURE 13–3**

Given the $II$ and $SS$ functions, the only equilibrium level of $Y$ is $Y_0$. Only at this level of $Y$ is the investment demand for output exactly equal to the supply of output represented by the supply of saving, that is, to the supply of output in excess of the amount taken off the market by $C$. Only at this level of $Y$ is the market just cleared of output, with neither excess demand nor excess supply. Any level of $Y$ greater than $Y_0$ would be a level of disequilibrium, because the supply of output represented by saving would exceed investment demand; some part of the supply would not be cleared from the market. Consider, for example, point $D$ in Figure 13–3, which corresponds to some level of income greater than $Y_0$. At this level of income, saving is given by $DF$. Actual or realized investment will, of course, equal actual saving, $DF$, and this clearly exceeds intended investment which is $DE$. Indeed, the difference, $EF$, represents the amount of unintended investment. Clearly, point $D$ is one of disequilibrium. Producers of goods are not selling all they would like, and some of their output is piling up in unintended inventories. When such a situation occurs, producers will respond by reducing their rate of output, thus lowering $Y$. In this process they might temporarily reduce their output below $Y_0$ until their excess inventories had been sold off.

Any level of output below $Y_0$ would be a level of disequilibrium, because at lower levels of $Y$ the investment demand for output would exceed the supply of output represented by saving. Faced by such a situation of excess demand, producers might immediately increase their rate of output, thereby raising the level of $Y$. If they did not increase the output rate fast enough, they would experience an "unwanted" depletion of their inventories, which would lead them to accelerate production in order to rebuild their stocks. In this process they might temporarily raise their rate of output above $Y_0$ until their inventories had been replenished.

Thus, we see that equality of intended investment demand and saving supply is always a necessary condition for an equilibrium level of $Y$. We now turn to the question of what happens to the level of income as a result of changes in the level of intended investment. To help answer this we shall introduce the notion of the multiplier.

**THE MULTIPLIER**

The multiplier is one of the key concepts in Keynesian models of income determination. It refers to the fact that an autonomous increase or decrease of expenditures for output can increase or decrease total expenditures for output by some multiple by inducing a change of consumption expenditures in the same direction. This effect results from the positive slope of the consumption function, which posits that the community will increase its consumption expenditures by a fraction, equal to

$\Delta C/\Delta Y$, or MPC, of each increase in its disposable income. The total effect on the level of expenditures for output $(\Delta Y)$ is equal to the autonomous rise of expenditure (designated by $\Delta E$) plus the induced change of consumption $(\Delta C)$. In symbols, we have

$$\Delta Y = \Delta C + \Delta E \tag{9}$$

An autonomous change in expenditures can take any one of several forms. For example, an autonomous increase can be in the form of a rise of investment demand $(\Delta I)$ or an upward shift of the consumption function, which is the same as a downward shift of the saving-supply function.[7] To illustrate the principles involved, let us assume that the autonomous change is an increase of investment demand $(\Delta I)$, that $\Delta I = \$100$, and that investment demand remains at this higher level. Thus, in terms of our previous notation we have $\Delta E = \Delta I = 100$.

What we are interested in finding is the *investment multiplier*, which is the ratio of the change in $Y$ to the change in $I$, or $\Delta Y/\Delta I$. We can do this either algebraically or diagramatically. We begin with some simple algebra.

Since $\Delta E = \Delta I$, we can write equation (9) as

$$\Delta Y = \Delta C + \Delta I \tag{10}$$

Now, from the definition of the marginal propensity to consume, we have $\Delta C/\Delta Y = \text{MPC}$ or $\Delta C = \text{MPC} \times \Delta Y$. Thus, we have

$$\Delta Y = \text{MPC} \times \Delta Y + \Delta I$$

or

$$(1 - \text{MPC}) \times \Delta Y = \Delta I$$

The outcome is then

$$\frac{\Delta Y}{\Delta I} = \frac{1}{1 - \text{MPC}} \tag{11}$$

What equation (11) tells us that the investment multiplier is $1/(1 - \text{MPC})$. Alternatively, since $1 - \dfrac{\Delta C}{\Delta Y} = \dfrac{\Delta S}{\Delta Y}$, we have $1 - \text{MPC} = \text{MPS}$. We can then also write the multiplier as

$$\frac{\Delta Y}{\Delta I} = \frac{1}{\text{MPS}} = \frac{1}{\Delta S/\Delta Y} \tag{12}$$

To illustrate this numerically, suppose that $\Delta C/\Delta Y = 0.8$ and $\Delta S/\Delta Y$

---

[7] Although we are temporarily exluding the government and foreign sectors from our consideration, it should be noted that an autonomous increase in expenditures can also take the form of a rise of government purchases of goods and services or a rise of foreign demand for American exports.

$= .2$. The multipler is then $1/.2$ or 5. Thus, if, as assumed, $\Delta I = 100$, then $\Delta Y = 5 \times 100 = 500$.

It should be clear that as $\Delta C/\Delta Y$ increases (that is, as $\Delta S/\Delta Y$ grows smaller), the multiplier will become larger. It should also be clear that the multiplier operates downward in response to an autonomous decline of expenditures. For example, trace the effects on $Y$ if investment falls by \$50 and remains at the lower level, and $\Delta C/\Delta Y = 0.8$.

As indicated, the multiplier process can also be explained diagrammatically in terms of saving–investment relationships. For example, suppose that, starting from the equilibrum income level, $Y_0$ at which $I = S$, $I$ rises by \$100 and remains at this higher level (see Figure 13–4). $Y_0$ is no longer an equilibrium level, because of that level of income there will now be a \$100 excess of $I$ over $S$, which will drive income upward. If $I$ remains at its new higher level, a new equilibrium will be reached only when $S$ is also increased by \$100. But with a given saving-supply function, $S$ can be increased only by an increase of $Y$. How much $Y$ will have to rise to increase $S$ by \$100 varies reciprocally with the marginal responsiveness of $S$ to $Y$. Suppose $\Delta S/\Delta Y = 0.2$. In this case $Y$ must rise by \$500 to increase $S$ by \$100.

Let us consider this in steps:

1 Since $I$ has risen \$100 and remains at the new level, $S$ must rise by the same amount if a new equilibrium is to be established.

2 With a given saving-supply function, only a rise of $Y$ can increase $S$, and each rise of $Y$ will increase $S$ by an amount equal to $\Delta S/\Delta Y$.

3 Since the required rise of $S = \$100$, we can write

$$\$100 = \Delta Y \frac{\Delta S}{\Delta Y}$$

Dividing both sides of the equation by $\Delta S/\Delta Y$ to find the required increase of $Y$, we get

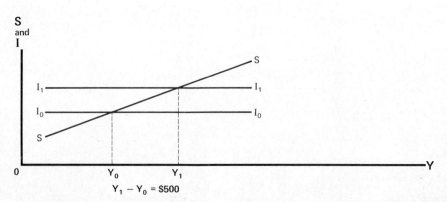

*Multiplier effects of an increase in investment*

**FIGURE 13–4**

$$\Delta Y = \$100 \times \frac{1}{\Delta S/\Delta Y}$$

*If* $\Delta S/\Delta Y = 0.2$,

$$\Delta Y = 100 \, \frac{1}{0.2} = \$500$$

Only if $Y$ rises by this amount can it be in equilibrium with $I = S$. Any smaller rise of $Y$ would leave $S$ smaller than $I$, and the excess demand for output would continue to increase $Y$. On the other hand, any larger rise of $Y$ would make $S$ larger than $I$, and excess supply of output over the total demand for output would serve to depress $Y$.

The multiplier approach, then, provides a direct answer to the question of how equilibrium income will change following a change in autonomous investment. To clarify the multiplier principle, we have employed an elementary model and made some simplifying assumptions. One of the latter is that investment is determined autonomously and thus does not respond to economic forces. This, of course, is rather implausible, and we must now modify this assumption. We shall do so by introducing the interest rate as a determinant of investment spending. As we shall see later, this will have important consequences for the interpretation of the multiplier approach.

---

**INVESTMENT DEMAND FUNCTIONS**

An investment demand function indicates the values of output demanded for investment purposes at each possible rate of interest. The latter will be denoted by $r$. Note that because we are interested in determining an equilibrium level of $Y$, we include in investment demand only intended or desired changes in business inventories. The investment demand function thus corresponds to the notion of intended investment introduced earlier.

Most of the components of investment demand ($I$) are demands by business for output with which to maintain or increase stocks of capital goods. These demander are presumably motivated by a desire for profits, perhaps a desire to maximize their profits. For this purpose they compare the expected returns from new investment with the costs involved. However, some of investment demand, notably expenditures by homeowners for new residential construction, may not be profit motivated. However, even these demanders presumably arrive at decisions by balancing expected benefits and costs; and, other conditions being constant, they will presumably buy less when the cost to them is higher. Interest costs are an important part of the carrying charges of a house.

An investment demand function, such as that illustrated in Figure

13–5, is a typical demand curve showing the relation of quantity demanded to price. In this case the price of loan funds, or the interest rate on investable funds, is measured along the horizontal axis. The values of output demanded for investment are measured along the vertical axis. The $II$ curve depicts the size of investment demand at the various possible levels of $r$. From the point of view of spenders for investment, $r$ is the cost. If they get the money to finance investment by borrowing from others, $r$ is the annual interest rate they must pay to lenders. If they finance their investment spending by using their own money, $r$ is their opportunity cost; it is the interest rate they sacrifice by using the money rather than by lending it to someone else. It is therefore plausible to assume that, other things remaining the same, a rise of interest rates will decrease the actual investment demand for output and a fall of interest rates will stimulate it.

The investment demand function can also be stated in algebraic terms:

$$I = D - \frac{\Delta I}{\Delta r}\, r \tag{13}$$

where

> $D =$ a positive constant in billions of dollars. It is the intercept on the vertical axis and establishes the location of the $I$ function
> $r =$ the interest rate
> $\Delta I/\Delta r =$ the marginal responsiveness of investment to the interest rate. $\Delta I/\Delta r$ is to be interpreted as a positive number so that the negative slope to Figure 13–5 stems from the minus sign in equation (13)

We are engaging in oversimplification in assuming a single interest rate in the market. There are, of course, many rates. Moreover, other

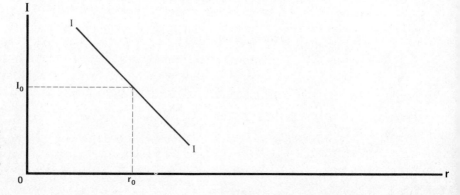

*An investment demand function*

**FIGURE 13–5**

terms of lending and borrowing may change: the length of time for which lenders will make funds available, the risks that they will take at any given interest rate, the amount of security demanded for loans, and so on. Nevertheless, it will be convenient to let *r* represent the height of the structure of interest rates and the annual cost per dollar of borrowed funds.

In drawing any demand curve, we have to assume that all other conditions affecting demand are given and unchanged. But it is important to know what determines the position of the demand curve. We need to answer questions such as: Why is the demand curve neither higher nor lower at each level of interest rates? What forces can shift *I* upward at each rate of interest? What forces can shift the curve downward? To answer such questions we need to know the motivations of those who spend for investment, and the nature of the benefits they balance against interest costs in arriving at decisions as to whether and how much to spend for investment.

**Marginal Efficiency of Investment**

The great bulk of investment expenditures are made by business firms intent on making net profits. Hence, in determining whether or not to make a capital expenditure, they ask: "Will the acquisition of this capital good add at least as much to my revenues as it adds to my costs?" This applies to purchases for replacement as well as to net additions to capital. Decisions as to the amount of new investment therefore depend on a comparison of interest costs and the expected annual rate of return on new investment. The latter has been given many names, including *marginal revenue product of capital* and *marginal efficiency of investment*. We shall use the latter term and define it as the annual amount (stated as a percentage of the cost of the capital goods) that the acquisitions of the new capital goods is expected to add to the enterprise's net revenues after deduction of all additional costs of operation except interest costs on the money used. For our purposes, we shall view the marginal efficiency of investment as a schedule or function showing the various amounts of new investment that are expected to yield at least various rates of return. The demand for investment is derived from the marginal-efficiency-of-investment schedule. Enterprisers intent on maximizing their profits tend to buy those types and amounts of capital that they expect to yield a rate of return in excess of the interest cost of the money used to purchase them. Presumably, they will not buy capital whose expected rate of return is below the interest rate.

Note that we have emphasized that the *expected* annual rate of return is a prime consideration in the selection of a new investment. Enterprisers select their investments on the basis of their expectations as to future yields—their decisions are based on the best forecasts they can make. They cannot be certain that the returns will meet their expectations because many types of capital yield their returns only over a long period and much can change in the interim. But they must make decisions, even if they recognize the fallibility of their forecasts.

Of the many factors that affect the schedule of the marginal efficiency of investment, some of the more important are listed below.

1  SIZE AND COMPOSITION OF STOCK. If the existing stock of capital goods is largely obsolete and too small to produce most economically the rate of output currently demanded, large amounts of new investment may.be expected to yield high rates of return. But if the existing stock of capital goods is efficient and very large relative to the current demand for output, only small amounts of new investment will be profitable. If there is already excess capacity, business firms may refrain from replacing some of their equipment when it wears out.

2  RATE OF INNOVATION. If the rate of innovation is high, it may be profitable to undertake much new investment in order to produce the new types of products or to use new and more economical processes of production.

3  EXPECTED FUTURE BEHAVIOR OF DEMANDS FOR OUTPUT. If demands for output are expected to rise rapidly, much new investment may be expected to yield high profits. If demands for output are expected to remain at existing levels and the present stock of capital goods is adequate, the demand for new capital goods may be largely a replacement demand. And if demands for output are expected to decline, potential spenders for investment may not replace their capital equipment when it wears out.

4  COST EXPECTATIONS. Expectations as to future wages, other costs, taxes, and government policies also determine investment efficiency. Estimates of the profitability of new investment may be greatly affected by expectations regarding the future course of these factors.

As should be evident from this list, there are many factors that are capable of altering the marginal efficiency of investment. This should be borne in mind for two reasons:

1  When we draw an investment demand schedule to show the effects of interest rates on investment demand, we are assuming that the schedule of the marginal efficiency of investment is given and constant.

2  We shall later want to deal with upward and downward shifts of the investment demand schedule and their effects on $Y$. An upward shift of the $II$ curve, an increase of investment demand at each interest rate, may be brought about by any force that raises the marginal efficiency of investment schedule. The $II$ curve may be shifted downward at each level of interest rates by anything that lowers the marginal-efficiency-of-investment schedule.

**Marginal Responsiveness of Investment Demand to Interest Rates**

Let us now return to the investment-demand curve that is drawn on the assumption that the marginal efficiency of investment is given and constant, and which therefore enables us to consider the effects of interest rates on the size of the investment demand for output. In determining the equilibrium level of $Y$, it is sometimes sufficient to know that $I$ tends to be larger when $r$ is lower, and lower when $r$ is higher. For some purposes, however, it is useful to try to quantify this relationship, to ask how much a given change of interest rates would alter the size of the investment demand. We shall call this the *marginal responsiveness of investment to interest rates*. By this we shall mean the dollar change in the annual rate of investment expenditure for output in response to a change of 1 percent in the interest rate. As in equation (13) this will be denoted by $\Delta I/\Delta r$, the slope of the investment demand function. In Figure 13–6, $\Delta I/\Delta r$ is clearly larger on the $I_0 I_0$ investment demand curve than it is on the $I_1 I_1$ curve.[8]

**THE *IS* CURVE**

In an earlier model, which assumed that investment demand is unaffected by the level of interest rates, we found not only that equality of $I$ and $S$ is a necessary condition for equilibrium, but also that $I$ and $S$ functions alone were sufficient to determine a unique equilibrium level of $Y$. The latter conclusion is not valid when $I$ is responsive to the level of $r$. In this case, there are many combinations of $Y$ and $r$ that satisfy the necessary condition for equilibrium, $I = S$. This is shown graphically in Figure 13–7.

The vertical scales in parts (*a*) and (*b*) of Figure 13–7 are the same, so that the same vertical heights indicate equal amounts of $S$ and $I$. Even

---

[8] An investment demand curve need not, of course, be a straight line, and the value of $\Delta I/\Delta r$ may be different at different ranges of interest rates.

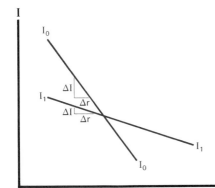

*The marginal responsiveness of investment to the interest rate*

**FIGURE 13–6**

a casual inspection of the two upper graphs reveals that there are various combinations of interest rates and income levels that will produce the condition $I = S$. For example, $S = I$ at the low vertical level $I_0 S_0$ if $r$ is at the high level $r_0$, thereby holding $I$ to a low level, and if $Y$ is at the low level $Y_0$, thereby generating only a low supply of $S$. $I = S$ at the somewhat higher level $I_1 S_1$ if the rate of interest is at the lower level $r_1$, thereby stimulating $I$, and if $Y$ is at the higher level $Y_1$, thereby generating a larger supply of saving. $I = S$ at the very high level $I_2 S_2$ if the rate of interest is at the very low level $r_2$ and income is at the high level $Y_2$. We might thus note all the possible combinations of interest rate levels and income levels that would produce the condition $I = S$.

This is done in part (c) of Figure 13–7. The line $I = S$ plots out all those combinations of $r$, measured on the vertical axis, and $Y$, measured on the horizontal axis, at which $S$ and $I$ would be equal. The $IS$ curve slopes downward to the right because the supply of $S$ would be larger at higher levels of income, and with a given investment demand function, $I$ can be made correspondingly larger only by a fall of $r$.

The same conclusions emerge from the numerical example in Table 13–2. This table is based on the types of consumption, saving, and investment functions presented earlier in equations (7), (8), and (13). The following values are assumed.

$$C = 130 + 0.8Y$$
$$S = 0.2Y - 130$$
$$I = 130 - 10r$$

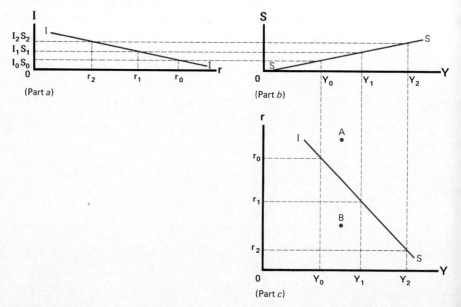

*Investment demand and the supply of saving*

**FIGURE 13–7**

It will be noted that $I = S$ at every combination of $Y$ and $r$ shown in the table. For example, $I = S = \$120$ at $Y = \$1,250$ and $r = 1$ percent; $I = S = \$70$ at $Y = \$1,000$ and $r = 6$ percent; and so on. Note also that when $I = S$, $Y = C + I$. Thus, we could also analyze total demand for output by adding together the consumption and investment demand functions.

Let us return to part (c) of Figure 13–7. No point representing a combination of $r$ and $Y$ that is off the $IS$ curve can represent equilibrium conditions. For example, consider any point $A$ that lies above the $IS$ curve. At any such point, $I$ would be less than $S$. We know this because at the same level of $Y$ there is some lower rate of interest directly below $A$ on the $IS$ curve at which $I$ is exactly equal to $S$. If, by some chance, the combination of $r$ and $Y$ represented by point $A$ should occur, the excess of $S$ over $I$ could be remedied only by a fall of interest rates to stimulate $I$, a decline of $Y$ to reduce $S$, or some combination of changes of $r$ and $Y$ to a point on the $IS$ curve. On the other hand, at any point such as $B$, below the $IS$ curve, $I$ would be greater than $S$. We know this because at the same level of $Y$ there is some higher rate of interest directly above $B$ on the $IS$ curve at which $I$ is exactly equal to $S$. A disequilibrium combination such as $B$ could be remedied only by a rise of $r$ to reduce $I$, an increase of $Y$ to increase $S$, or a combination of changes of $r$ and $Y$ to a point on the $IS$ curve.

Any combination of $Y$ and $r$ that is off the $IS$ curve is not only one of disequilibrium but also creates pressure serving to return the level of $Y$ to some point on the $IS$ curve. For example, a combination above the line with saving supply exceeding investment demand indicates that there is an excess of the total supply of output over the total demand for output $(C + I)$. This deficiency of demand will lead producers to reduce output and employment. On the other hand, a combination below the line with $I$ exceeding $S$ indicates an excess of total demand for output $(C + I)$ over the total supply of output, thus inducing producers to expand output and employment. However, the point on the $IS$ curve to which $Y$ returns need not to be a point of full employment.

| | r (percent) | Y | C | S | I |
|---|---|---|---|---|---|
| **TABLE 13–2**<br>*Equality of I and S with I responsive to r* | 1 | 1,250 | 1,130 | 120 | 120 |
| | 2 | 1,200 | 1,090 | 110 | 110 |
| | 3 | 1,150 | 1,050 | 100 | 100 |
| | 4 | 1,100 | 1,010 | 90 | 90 |
| | 5 | 1,050 | 970 | 80 | 80 |
| | 6 | 1,000 | 930 | 70 | 70 |
| | 7 | 950 | 890 | 60 | 60 |
| | 8 | 900 | 850 | 50 | 50 |
| | 9 | 850 | 810 | 40 | 40 |

**Shifting the IS Curve**

As we have seen, the *IS* curve represents the pairs of *r* and *Y* that are consistent with equality between intended investment and saving, or in other words, that are consistent with equilibrium in the market for commodities or goods. The precise location and shape of the *IS* curve is determined jointly by the saving and investment functions. This suggests that anything that changes either of these underlying functions will shift the *IS* curve. A particular example of this, the case of an upward shift in the investment demand function, is illustrated in Figure 13–8.

Assume that the initial situation from which we begin is represented by the *IS* curve labeled $I_0S_0$, which is derived from the investment demand function $I_0I_0$ and the saving-supply function $S_0S_0$. Assume further that the equilibrium level of interest rates is $r_0$ and the equilibrium level of income of $Y_0$. Suppose now that the investment demand function shifts upward at each level of interest rates by $100, rising to $I_1I_1$, while the saving-supply function remains unchanged. The various combinations of *Y* and *r* that formerly equated *S* and *I* will no longer do so; at each such combination *I* now exceeds *S* by $100. At any given level of interest

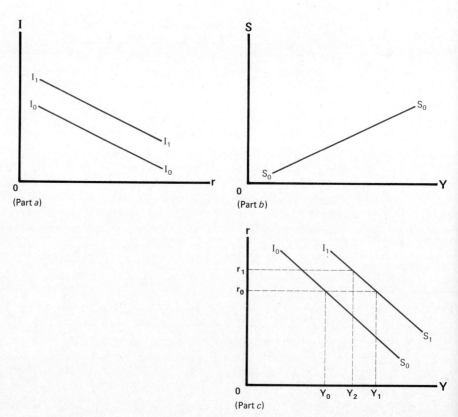

*Shift of investment demand*

**FIGURE 13–8**

rates, $S$ can be raised to the level of $I$ only by a rise of $Y$. As before, the amount by which $Y$ must rise to increase $S$ by $100 varies reciprocally with $\Delta S/\Delta Y$. If $\Delta S/\Delta Y = 0.2$,

$$\Delta Y = \$100 \; \frac{1}{0.2} = \$500$$

The new $IS$ curve, labeled $I_1 S_1$, lies to the right of the initial curve $I_0 S_0$ at each level of interest rates by the amount $500. In other words, the amount by which the $IS$ curve has shifted to the right depends directly on the size of the multiplier, that is, on the reciprocal of $\Delta S/\Delta Y$.

Unlike the case previously considered, in the present instance, where $I$ is responsive to the level of interest rates, the multiplier analysis in its simplest form is not sufficient to determine the new equilibrium level of $Y$. Without introducing other information, all we can say is that the new equilibrium level of $Y$ must lie on $I_1 S_1$, for this includes all combinations of $Y$ and $r$ that equate $I$ and $S$. If interest rates remain unchanged at the level $r_0$, the full multiplier effect on income will be realized, with income rising from $Y_0$ to $Y_1$. Suppose, however, that in this process interest rates are increased, perhaps from $r_0$ to $r_1$. As will be seen in the next chapter, this is quite likely to happen if monetary policy is not such as to prevent a rise of rates. In this case the full multiplier effect will not be realized. Some of the rise of investment expenditures that would have occurred if interest rates had remained constant will be "snubbed" by the rise of interest rates.

We have illustrated in detail the effects on the $IS$ curve of an upward shift in the investment demand function. However, as indicated earlier, the $IS$ curve can shift in other ways as well. For example, a downward shift of the $I$ function at each level of $r$ will shift the $IS$ curve to the left by an amount equal to the downward shift of $I$ times the multiplier. Similarly, an upward shift of the saving function (which is equivalent to a downward shift in the consumption function) will also shift the $IS$ curve to the left. We shall have some more opportunities to gain familiarity with these types of shifts as we proceed.

---

**INTRODUCING THE GOVERNMENT**

To this point we have deliberately ignored the activities of the government, assuming in effect that both government receipts and expenditures were zero. This was done so that the number of variables could be reduced and the reader could concentrate on the behavior of private consumption, saving, and investment. Now we shall add the government to the picture. Specifically, we shall consider government expenditures for goods and services (designated by $G$), and net taxes (designated by $T$).

**Government
Purchases
of Goods and
Services (G)**

As already indicated, G includes all expenditures by federal, state, and local governments for currently produced goods and services. Like any other form of expenditure for output, G is both a part of the aggregate demand for output and a contributor to the total of national income shares.

We shall assume that G is exogenously determined by the government and is not responsive to changes in the level of Y. The government can, of course, increase or decrease the level of G. Our earlier analysis suggests immediately that upward or downward shifts of G will serve to induce upward or downward multiplier effects, just as would similar shifts of the I or C functions.

**Net Taxes (T)**

As noted above, net taxes are defined as taxes minus transfers. As we shall see, both taxes and transfers are responsive to the level of income, with taxes increasing as income rises and transfers decreasing as income rises. Consequently, for both reasons, net taxes tend to increase as income increases and decrease as income decreases. This is illustrated in Figure 13–9, where the net tax function, TT, is shown as a positively sloped function of Y. In keeping with our earlier assumption, government spending is shown as unresponsive to Y (i.e., the level of GG does not vary with Y). We now briefly explore the reasons for the upward slope of the TT curve, beginning with taxes.

Taxes include all receipts by federal, state, and local governments on income and product account. Thus, they include not only taxes in the narrow sense of the term but also various types of license fees and contributions by employers and employees to governmentally sponsored social insurance programs.

Total yields of the American tax system are highly responsive to changes in the level of GNP. With a given tax program on the books,

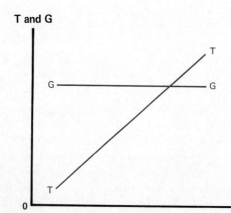

T *and* G

**FIGURE 13–9**

defining both the things subject to tax and applicable tax rates, total yields rise and fall sharply with increases and decreases of $Y$. This is not true of all types of taxes. For example, total yields of property taxes and certain types of fees do not respond automatically to changes in $Y$ in the absence of action by the tax authorities. It is, however, true of taxes that account for the great bulk of government receipts. Corporate profits usually vary directly with $Y$, and in recent years these have been subject to marginal tax rates fluctuating around 50 percent. Yields of personal income taxes, which exempt certain amounts of household income and tax the remainder at graduate rates, are highly sensitive to changes in $Y$. So are total contributions for social insurance, which are based on payrolls. Total revenues from various taxes on production and sales, included in indirect business taxes, also vary with $Y$.

We turn now to government transfers. These, it will be recalled, are payments for which the government does not receive goods or services in return. At least some of these payments are responsive to the level of $Y$ and tend to rise when $Y$ falls and to decline when $Y$ rises, especially to the extent that changes in $Y$ are accompanied by changes of unemployment in the opposite direction. This is clearest in the case of unemployment benefits. A rise of unemployment increases total unemployment benefit payments, which serve to cushion the decline of private incomes; and a decline of unemployment reduces these payments. Some other transfer payments are also responsive to changes in income levels and employment opportunities. For example, when employment opportunities are scarce for the elderly, some retire earlier and draw old-age benefits. Direct relief payments also tend to vary directly with the amount of unemployment.

As should be apparent by now, there are ample reasons to assert that taxes and transfers depend positively on the level of $Y$ as portrayed in Figure 13–9. What this also suggests is that net tax receipts will fluctuate "automatically" as the level of $Y$ changes. This fact is of great significance for the behavior of private disposable income and for the stability of the economy as a whole.

**Net Taxes as an Automatic Stabilizer**

As we saw earlier, total private disposable income at any level of GNP is equal to $Y - T$. Thus, the higher the level of $Y$, the greater will be the difference between $Y$ and private disposable incomes. This is often referred to as an *automatic stabilizer effect*, although automatic *snubber* effect would be a more accurate description. These are the effects that follow automatically from an initial decline of $Y$ even if the government makes no change in $G$, in its tax system or in its transfer payment program. If there is an initial decline of $Y$ and no change at all in total $T$, the full impact of the decline of $Y$ will fall on private disposable incomes. However, to the extent that the decline of $Y$ is reflected in a decrease of

$T$, the impact on private disposable incomes is reduced, with a corresponding decrease of pressures for further reductions of private spending. The decline of $Y$ is snubbed.

On the other hand, an increase of expenditures for output may occur when the economy is already operating at virtually full-employment levels and an undesirable rate of price inflation threatens. If total $T$ remained constant, the full increase of $Y$ would be reflected in private disposable incomes. To the extent that the rise of $Y$ is absorbed by an increase of $T$, the rise of private disposable incomes is snubbed.

Such automatic stabilizer or snubber effects can be quite powerful. Their strength is determined by what might be called the *marginal responsiveness of net tax receipts to Y*. Pictorially, this marginal responsiveness is nothing other than the slope of the $TT$ function in Figure 13–9, which we can denote by $\Delta T/\Delta Y$. The value of $\Delta T/\Delta Y$ depends on the nature and rates of taxes. Currently, $\Delta T/\Delta Y$ appears to be at least 30 percent. That is, each $1 increase or decrease of GNP raises or lowers $T$ by at least 30 cents.

While such strong automatic snubber effects often contribute to the stability of the economy, they sometimes militate against recovery of economic activity. For example, in the early 1960s, when unemployment remained excessive, the large increases of $T$ with each rise of $Y$ snubbed the rise of aggregate private demands for output and slowed recovery. There was an automatic fiscal drag. This was remedied by a tax reduction in 1964 – a downward shift of the $TT$ function in Figure 13–9. On other occasions, when it becomes desirable to curb aggregate demand, the government can shift its net tax function upwards. For example, by broadening tax bases or raising tax rates or both, it can increase $T$ at each level of $Y$, thus serving to lower private disposable incomes at each level of $Y$. In subsequent chapters we shall explore such policy actions more fully.

**THE *IS* CURVE, INCLUDING GOVERNMENT**

Having investigated the basic ingredients of the government's fiscal operations, we are now in a position to modify the $IS$ curve so as to allow for the effect of government activity. Introduction of the government requires several important changes. For one thing, we introduce another type of expenditure for output, $G$, so that total demand for output becomes $C + I + G$. Also, the introduction of taxes and government transfer payments alters the relationship between GNP and total private disposable income; these two items would be the same in a system without taxes or government transfer programs. Finally, allowance for the government introduces government saving into the analysis, so that total saving is now given by the sum of government saving and private saving. Based on this observation, in fact, we can directly proceed to modify the *IS* curve to take account of the government.

This *IS* curve is, of course, defined by the condition that investment equals saving. In the absence of the government, this was algebraically expressed by $I = S$. As we saw previously, however, in the presence of the government the algebraic expression for investment equals saving is slightly more complicated. This is due to the existence of government saving, $(T - G)$. The precise condition is given by equation (5) or, equivalently, equation (6). For convenience, these equations are repeated here.

$$I + G = S + T \tag{5}$$
$$I = S + (T - G) \tag{6}$$

Equation (6) reminds us that equilibrium in the goods market requires that investment equal private saving plus government saving. The equivalent equation (5) is actually more useful for constructing the new *IS* curve.

We have graphed the two sides of equation (5) in Figure 13–10. The line labeled $I + G$ in part (*a*) shows how the left-hand side of equation (5) varies with the interest rate. This line is derived from our familiar investment demand function, which is shown as *II* in part (*a*). In particular, since *G* is exogenously determined by the government, the line $I + G$ is simply obtained by uniformly shifting up the investment demand function by the amount *G*.

In part (*b*) we have graphed the right-hand side of equation (5). The *SS* curve is the saving-supply function we have encountered earlier and corresponds to private saving. The *TT* curve, which is taken from Figure

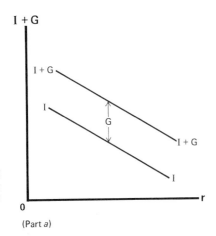

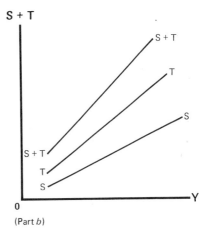

*Investment and saving, including government*

**FIGURE 13–10**

(Part *a*)        (Part *b*)

13–9, shows how taxes less transfers depend on $Y$. Ths sum of the $SS$ and $TT$ curves, labeled $S + T$ in part (b), thus corresponds to the right-hand side of equation (5).

The alert reader may have noted that in drawing $S$ and $S + T$ as functions of $Y$ in Figure 13–10 we have glossed over one step. As emphasized earlier, both consumption and saving are functions of disposable income, $Y - T$. How then did we get rid of the $T$? The trick is to recognize that net taxes, $T$, is itself a function of $Y$ (see Figure 13–9). Consequently, we can use this relationship to eliminate $T$ and express $S$ as a function of $Y$ rather than $Y - T$. A numerical example may help illustrate the point. Consider the following consumption and saving functions:

$$C = 100 + .8DI = 100 + .8(Y - T)$$
$$S = -100 + .2DI = -100 + .2(Y - T)$$

which clearly satisfy $C + S = DI = Y - T$. Now suppose that $T = .25Y$; that is, there is a flat 25 percent tax rate on $Y$. We then have

$$S = -100 + .2(Y - .25Y)$$
$$= -100 + .15Y$$

We have thus expressed $S$ as a function of $Y$. This in turn can be used to express $S + T$ as a function of $Y$, thus fully justifying part (b) of Figure 13–10.[9] With this little detail out of the way, we are ready to proceed.

Armed with the two curves in Figure 13–10, we can now construct an $IS$ curve. This is shown diagrammatically in Figure 13–11. The vertical scales in parts (a) and (b) of Figure 13–11 are the same, so that the same vertical heights indicate equal amounts of $(I + G)$ and $(S + T)$. The resulting $IS$ curve, giving the combinations of pairs of $r$ and $Y$ that satisfy equation (5), is shown in part (c). The reader will immediately recognize that we are following the same procedure used earlier, that is, in the absence of the government. Indeed, the only difference between our earlier derivation in Figure 13–7 and the present one in Figure 13–11 is that the curve labeled $I + G$ has replaced the $II$ curve in part (a) and the curve labeled $S + T$ has replaced the $SS$ schedule in part (b). Conceptually at least, this is really a minor modification.

While the $IS$ curve is conceptually the same with or without the government, the actual shape and location of the $IS$ curve will, of course, depend on the level of government expenditures and the nature of the $TT$ function. Furthermore, shifts in the level of $G$ or in the tax or transfer functions will induce corresponding shifts in the $IS$ curve.

---

[9] Since $T = .25Y$, we have $S + T = -100 + .4Y$. Substituting for $T$ in the consumption function also gives $C = 100 + .6Y$. Hence, we see that $C + S + T = 100 + .6Y - 100 + .4Y = Y$, as it should. This numerical example is taken up again in the appendix to the next chapter.

As an example, let us first consider how the *IS* curve would shift as a result of an increase in government expenditures. The effects of this are illustrated in Figure 13–12. The direct effect of an increase in G is to shift the curve for *I + G* upward. That is, at any given level of interest rates, *I + G* is now higher. This is shown in part (*a*) as a movement from $(I + G)_0$ to $(I + G)_1$. The $(S + T)$ function in part (*b*) is unchanged by the increase in G. To see what happens to the *IS* curve let us trace our way around Figure 13–12 beginning at $r_0$ in part (*a*). Before the increase in G, $r_0$ was associated with the income level $Y_0$. This is shown as point *D* on $I_0S_0$, the original *IS* curve. After the increase in G, we see from part (*b*) that a higher income level, $Y_1$, now corresponds to $r_0$. This is shown as point *E* on the new *IS* curve, labeled $I_1S_1$ in part (*c*). By choosing alternative starting values for the interest rate one can trace out the entire curve $I_1S_1$.

Quite evidently, an increase in G serves to shift the *IS* curve to the right. In this respect, an increase in government expenditures is analo-

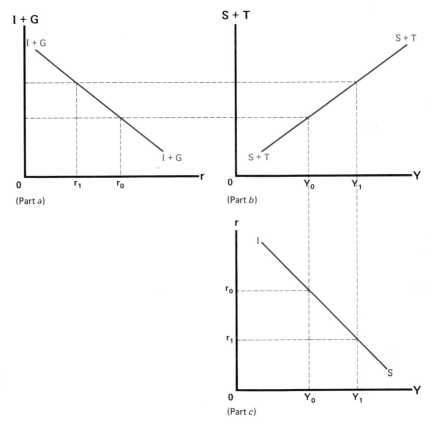

gous to any other increase in autonomous spending which would also shift the *IS* curve to the right. Such increases could arise, for example, from upward shifts in the investment demand or consumption functions. It should be equally clear that a decrease in government spending will shift the *IS* curve to the left.

**Shifting the IS Curve: a Change in T**     As a final example, let us consider how the *IS* curve would shift as a result of a reduction in taxes or an increase in transfer payments. Either of these actions would serve to produce a downward shift in the *TT* function, and this in turn would lead to a downward shift in the $(S + T)$ function.[10] This is illustrated in part (*b*) of Figure 13–13, where the initial state of affairs is given by the curve labeled $(S + T)_0$ and the relevant curve after this shift is given by $(S + T)_1$. Again, by tracing our way around the figure we see that the end result is to shift the *IS* curve to the right. Thus, we see that a decrease in taxes tends to have the same impact on the *IS* curve as an increase in government spending, a result that makes good

---

[10] The shift in the $(S + T)$ function will be less than the shift in the *TT* function. This is because there will be a partially offsetting rise of $S$ at each level of $Y$ as private disposable income is increased.

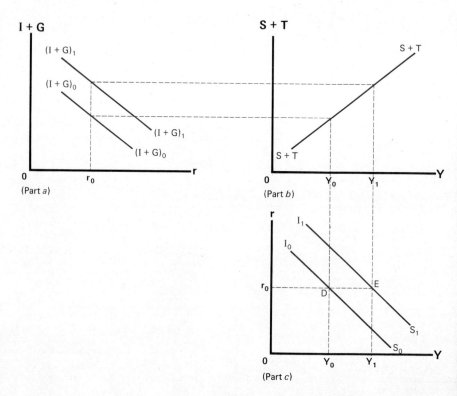

*Shift of government expenditures*

**FIGURE 13–12**

intuitive sense. There are, however, important economic differences between the tax cuts and expenditure increases, and these will be explored
in a later chapter.

CONCLUSION    This chapter has presented several functions that will be essential elements in the equilibrium determination of income and interest rates to
be presented in the next chapter. In particular, we considered the consumption function, the saving-supply function, the investment demand
function, and the government net-tax function. The various functions
were combined in constructing the *IS* curve, which is defined as the
combination of pairs of $r$ and $Y$ that produces equilibrium in the product
market. We also investigated the ways in which the *IS* curve could be
shifted. In particular, we found that rightward or expansionary shifts in
the *IS* curve could be brought about by any of the following: an increase
in government spending, an increase in autonomous investment or con-

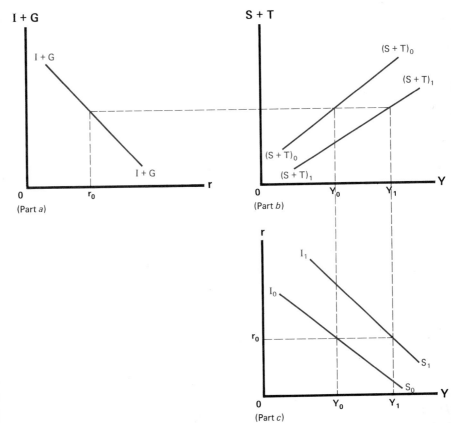

*Shift of tax or
transfer function*

**FIGURE 13–13**

sumption expenditures, a decrease in the saving-supply function, and a decrease in the net tax function.

Although the various functions introduced in this chapter are necessary elements in explaining equilibrium levels of $Y$ and $r$, they are not by themselves sufficient to determine unique equilibrium levels of $Y$ and $r$. To do this we must supplement the *IS* curve with the *LM* curve, the latter, of course, being based on our old friends—the money supply function and the demand function for money balances.

Allen, R. G. D., *Macroeconomic Theory: A Mathematical Treatment*, London, Macmillan, 1968.

Branson, W. H., *Macroeconomic Theory and Policy*, 2nd ed., New York, Harper & Row, 1979.

Dornbusch, R., and S. Fisher, *Macroeconomics*, New York, McGraw-Hill, 1978.

Gordon, R. J., *Macroeconomics*, Boston, Little, Brown, 1978.

THE
TERMINATION
EQUILIBRIUM
INCOME

In previous chapters we investigated the markets for money balances and for commodities, and we analyzed the conditions for equilibrium in each market separately. In the money market, this involved equating the demand and supply for money balances; in the commodity market, we saw that equilibrium occurs when investment equals saving. Out of this process emerged the *LM* and *IS* curves, which give the pairs of $r$ and $Y$ consistent with equilibrium in the money and commodity markets, respectively. Neither the *LM* curve nor the *IS* curve, taken by itself, is capable of determining an *overall* equilibrium combination of $Y$ and $r$. Rather, as we shall see, unique equilibrium levels of $Y$ and $r$ must be determined by two curves simultaneously. That is, overall equilibrium can exist when we have equilibrium in both the money and the commodity markets simultaneously.

In this chapter we shall analyze the nature of this overall equilibrium in some detail. We shall first do this with given and constant supply and demand functions that underlie the *LM* and *IS* curves. This type of analysis is often referred to as *statics:* It involves those equilibrium conditions that tend to be established and maintained with given underlying supply and demand functions. The bulk of this chapter, however, will be concerned with what is called *comparative statics.* This type of analysis compares two sets of equilibrium conditions: those existing before and after a shift of a demand or supply function. It attempts to determine how equilibrium will be changed if a demand function or a supply function shifts in a specified way. This kind of analysis will be used to examine the consequences of shifts in the investment demand and saving-supply functions. Somewhat more interestingly, it will also enable us to analyze the workings of monetary and fiscal policy.

It should be noted that throughout this chapter we shall continue to assume that the price level remains constant, so that money values also indicate the behavior of real values. Complications accompanying changes in price levels will be taken up in the following chapter.

**REVIEW OF BASIC FUNCTIONS**

Before we proceed to analyze the determination of equilibrium $Y$ and $r$, it may be helpful to list briefly the basic supply and demand functions that underlie the $LM$ and $IS$ curves. As we have seen, the $LM$ and $IS$ curves are defined by the two conditions

$$M^D = M^S \tag{1}$$
$$I + G = S + T \tag{2}$$

Corresponding to these conditions are the following underlying supply and demand functions:

1   MONEY SUPPLY. The supply of money ($M^S$) is assumed to be a policy-determined variable set by the monetary authority. The quantity of money supplied will be denoted by $\overline{M}$.

2   MONEY DEMAND. The demand function for money balances ($M^D$) is a function of income and interest rates. For expositional purposes it will sometimes be convenient to think of $M^D$ as sum of the demand function for money for transactions purposes ($L_1$) and the demand function for money balances for speculative or asset purposes ($L_2$). It will be convenient further to assume that $L_1$ is a positive function of $Y$, such that $L_1 = JOP = JY$, and $L_2$ is a negative function of interest rates, such that $L_2 = P(A - er)$. Thus,

$$M^D = L_1 + L_2 = JOP + P\,(A - er)$$

or

$$M^D = P\,(JO + A - er) \tag{3}$$

Since we are assuming that the price level is constant, we can simply set $P = 1$. This, of course, makes real and nominal income equal; that is, $Y = O$. We can thus rewrite (3) as

$$M^D = JY + A - er \tag{4}$$

3   INVESTMENT DEMAND. Investment demand ($I$) is a negative function of interest rates, such that

$$I = D - \frac{\Delta I}{\Delta r}\,r \tag{5}$$

4   SAVING SUPPLY. Saving and consumption are positive functions of disposable income. Net taxes, in turn, are a positive function of total income, $Y$. As we have seen, this means that saving plus

taxes, $S + T$, can be regarded as a function of $Y$. We shall write this as[1]

$$S + T = Y \frac{\Delta S}{\Delta Y} - B \qquad (6)$$

As before, the basic *multiplier* for changes in autonomous spending is given by $1 \div (\Delta S/\Delta Y)$.

5    GOVERNMENT SPENDING. Government purchases of goods and services are assumed to be fixed by the fiscal authorities and do not vary with the level of income.

COMPLE STATICS

We begin with the determination of equilibrium levels of income and interest rates with four given and constant functions: saving-supply, investment demand, money supply, and demand-for-money balances. Equilibrium does not necessarily signify a full employment level or a desirable level; it indicates only the levels that will tend to be established and maintained by the given and constant functions.

Given these functions, interest rates and income can be in equilibrium only at the point of intersection $(r_e, Y_e)$ of the $IS$ and $LM$ curves. Only this combination satisfies simultaneously the two necessary conditions for equilibrium. Any other combination of $r$ and $Y$ would be a disequilibrium combination and would create pressures for change. We found earlier that at any combination above the $LM$ curve, $M^S$ would exceed $M^D$, and the excess supply of money would serve to lower interest rates. This pressure toward lower interest rates is indicated in Figure 14–1 by the downward-pointing arrows from points $A$ and $B$, both of which lie above the $LM$ curve. On the other hand, at any combination of $Y$ and $r$ below the $LM$ curve, $M^D$ would exceed $M^S$, and the excess demand for money balances would serve to raise interest rates. This is indicated in Figure 14–1 by the upward-pointing arrows from points $C$ and $D$. We also found that at any combination of $Y$ and $r$ above the $IS$ curve, there would be an excess of supply of output over total demands for it, and this would induce reductions of output and employment. This is indicated in Figure 14–1 by the left-pointing arrows from points $A$ and $D$, both of which lie above the $IS$ curve. However, at any combination below the $IS$ curve, the excess of total demand over the supply of output would lead producers to increase output and employment. This is

---

[1] For an illustration derivation of equation (6), see p. 350 in the previous chapter. It should be noted that the symbol $\Delta S/\Delta Y$ in the present context is slightly broader than the marginal propensity to save. As equation (6) indicates, here it is the marginal responsiveness of both saving *and* taxes to a change in income. We use the same symbol because, as the text states, with the government included the basic multiplier remains $1 \div (\Delta S/\Delta Y)$.

indicated in Figure 14–1 by the right-pointing arrows from points $B$ and $C$. Only at the point of intersection of the $LM$ and $IS$ curves $(Y_e, r_e)$ is there no pressure for change.

**COMPARATIVE STATICS**

Let us now use comparative statics to analyze the effects of shifts of the investment demand and saving-supply functions. We shall shift the functions one at a time and compare equilibrium conditions before and after the shift.

**Increase of the Investment Demand Function**

Suppose that, starting from the equilibrium situation illustrated in Figure 14–1, there occurs an upward shift of the investment demand function, and that the function remains at the higher level. For example, investment expenditures might be increased by $10 billion at each level of interest rates. The combination $r_e$, $Y_e$ is no longer an equilibrium combination because at those levels of $r$ and $Y$, investment demand now exceeds saving supply by $10 billion. The rise of investment spending increases directly the total demand for output and also increases the community's disposable income, which will induce a rise of consumption spending. This is the multiplier process discussed earlier. A new equilibrium can be established only when $I + G$ and $S + T$ are again equated. Given the constant saving-supply function and the new investment demand function, these can be equated only by a rise of $Y$ that will increase $S + T$, a rise of $r$ that will decrease $I$, or some combination of the two. $S + T$ can be raised by $10 billion to match the rise of $I$ at each level of interest rates only by an increase of $Y$, such that

$$\Delta Y \frac{\Delta S}{\Delta Y} = \$10 \text{ billion}$$

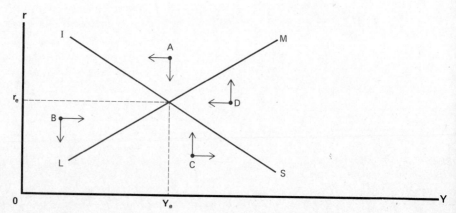

LM *and* IS *curves*

**FIGURE 14–1**

If we assume that $\Delta S/\Delta Y = 0.2$,

$$\Delta Y = \frac{\$10\ \text{billion}}{0.2} = \$50\ \text{billion}$$

This is illustrated by the horizontal shift to the right of the *IS* curve from $I_0S_0$ to $I_1S_1$ in Figure 14–2. The new equilibrium must be somewhere on this line.

Figure 14–2 indicates that *if interest rates remain unchanged* at the old equilibrium level, $r_e$, the full multiplier effect on income levels can be achieved. Actual investment expenditures will increase by an amount equal to the upward shift of the function, $10 billion, and the multiplier effect will be

$$\Delta Y = \$10\ \text{billion} \frac{1}{0.2} = \$50\ \text{billion}$$

so that income would rise from $Y_e$ to $Y_1$.

However, as Figure 14–2 demonstrates, if the money supply remains constant and the $M^D$ function is of the type assumed here, the full basic multiplier effect on income will not be realized. In particular, instead of increasing to $Y_1$, the new equilibrium level of income will be at $Y_2$, which is less than $Y_1$. Thus, the actual increase in income is less than the full basic multiplier effect. This is because the use of $Y$ serves to increase the quantity of money demanded, so that the total demand for money can be equated to the constant supply only if interest rates rise, and the rise of interest rates will "snub" the increase of investment. How much the rise of actual investment will be snubbed depends on the extent of the rise of $r$ and on the marginal responsiveness of investment to interest rates ($\Delta I/\Delta r$).

It is clear, therefore, that the consequences of the upward shift of the $I$ function depends in part on the slope of the *LM* curve ($\Delta r/\Delta Y$). If the

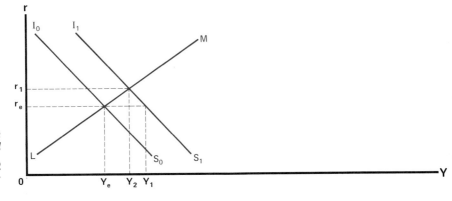

*Shift of investment demand*

**FIGURE 14–2**

$LM$ curve is nearly vertical—that is, if $\Delta r/\Delta Y$ approaches infinity—the outcome will be a large rise of $r$ and virtually no increase of actual investment or income. However, if the $LM$ curve approaches a horizontal position—that is, if $\Delta r/\Delta Y$ approaches zero—there will be virtually no rise of $r$ and almost the full multiplier effect will be realized.

The value of $\Delta r/\Delta Y$ depends on both the size of $J$ and the degree of responsiveness of $L_2$ to $r$, or $\Delta L_2/\Delta r$. This can be seen by examining equation (4). The reasoning is as follows: Each rise of $Y$ will increase the quantity of money demanded for $L_1$ purposes by an amount equal to $J\Delta Y$. With total $\overline{M}$ constant, the quantity of money demanded for $L_2$ purposes must decline by an offsetting amount to maintain the necessary equilibrium condition, $M^D = M^S$. But with $L_2$ a constant negative function of $r$, the quantity of money demanded for $L_2$ purposes can be reduced only by a rise of $r$. If the responsiveness of $L_2$ to $r$ approaches zero, very large increases of $r$ will be required to reduce $L_2$ demands enough to offset each increase of $L_1$ demands, and the $LM$ curve will be nearly vertical. This is illustrated by the curve labeled $L_0M_0$ in Figure 14–3. However, if $L_2$ demands for money are almost infinitely responsive to $r$, only a very small rise of $r$ will be required to offset each increase of $L_1$ demands, and the $LM$ curve will be almost horizontal. This is illustrated by the curve labeled $L_1M_1$ in Figure 14–3.

Two extreme cases will be instructive.

1   The marginal responsiveness of $M^D$ to $r$ is so small as to approach zero. That is, a rise of interest rates brings no decrease in the quantity of money demanded, so none is freed to satisfy the increased demand for money that would be generated by a rise of $Y$. In this extreme case, the upward shift of the investment demand function increases neither actual investment nor the level of income; it is reflected solely in a rise of interest rates.

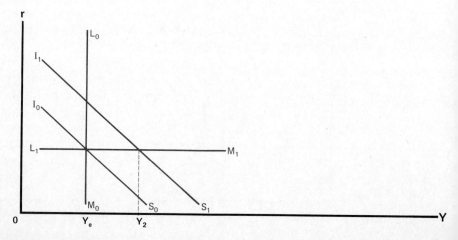

*Some slopes of the*
*LM curve*

**FIGURE 14–3**

2   The responsiveness of $M^D$ to $r$ approaches infinity; that is, even a minute rise of $r$ will decrease by huge amounts the quantity of money demanded, and this will be available to meet the increased demand for money generated by a rise of $Y$; the $LM$ curve will be virtually horizontal. In this extreme case, there will be no rise of interest rates, investment will rise by the full amount of the upward shift of the investment function, and the full multiplier effects on $Y$ will be achieved.

In the usual case, the $LM$ curve will be neither vertical nor horizontal; it will have a positive slope between these two extremes. From this case of an upward shift of the investment demand function we can draw several conclusions:

1   The very process of increasing the level of income generates an increase in the quantity of money demanded, which, in the absence of a compensating increase of the money supply, will tend to raise interest rates and snub the increases of investment and income. Put another way, in the case of an intermediately sloped LM curve, *the relevant multiplier is smaller than what we have been calling the full basic multiplier*, $1 \div \Delta S/\Delta Y$. As we shall see, this conclusion applies to all types of shifts in autonomous spending.[2]

2   To hold the money supply constant in the face of an upward shift of the investment function will usually not suffice to prevent some rise of total expenditures for output. The ensuing rise of $r$ will free some part of the money stock to satisfy the increased demands for money generated by the rise of the money value of output.

We need not trace in detail the effects of a downward shift of the investment demand function. In brief, at the old equilibrium levels of $r$ and $Y$, the supply of saving will exceed investment demand, and a downward multiplier process will begin. This can be represented by a shift to the left by the $IS$ curve. However, the very decline of $Y$ will serve to reduce the quantity of money demanded, and the excess supply of money will tend to reduce $r$, which will snub the decline of $I$ and $Y$. Here again, the extent of the actual changes of $I$ and $Y$ will depend in part on the shape of the $LM$ curve in the relevant range. If $L_2$ demands for money are very highly responsive to each reduction of $r$, the $LM$ curve will be nearly horizontal, interest rates will fall but little, and nearly the full downward multiplier effects will result. But if $L_2$ demands for money are less responsive to each decline of interest rates, a larger decrease of $r$ will result and the declines of $I$ and $Y$ will be snubbed.

---

[2] The appendix to this chapter provides a numerical illustration of the difference between the multiplier pictured in Figure 14–2 and the basic multiplier.

**Decrease of the Saving-Supply Function**

Suppose now that, starting from the initial equilibrium situation with $Y = Y_e$ and $r = r_e$, there occurs what may be viewed as either an upward shift of the consumption function or a decrease of the saving-supply function. For example, consumption demand may rise by $10 billion at each level of income, which is the same as saying that the supply of saving declines by $10 billion at each level of income. In many respects, although not all, the process and the results are the same as those following an upward shift of the investment demand function. At the old equilibrium levels of $Y$ and $r$, investment demand will exceed saving supply and the total demand for output (including the rise of consumption) will exceed the total supply of output by $10 billion. Thus, an upward multiplier process is initiated. $S + T$ and $I + G$ can again be equated only by a rise of $Y$ that will increase $S + T$, a rise of $r$ that will reduce $I$, or some combination of the two. In other words, as we have seen before, a decrease of the saving-supply function serves to shift the $IS$ curve out to the right. This means that the effects in the present case are analogous to those already portrayed in Figure 14–2. That is, a decrease in the saving-supply function leads to a new equilibrium with both a higher $Y$ and a higher $r$.

Up to this point we have stressed the similarities of the case in which the investment demand function shifted upward and the present case, in which the consumption function shifted upward or the saving-supply function shifted downward. In both cases there is an upward multiplier effect on income; and in both cases the actual outcome depends on the slopes of the $IS$ and $LM$ curves. However, there is an important difference between the two cases, and this relates to the composition of the increased output. In the general case in which the investment demand function shifted upward, the resulting increase of output is composed in part of increased investment and in part of increased consumption. Only in the extreme case in which the $LM$ curve is vertical is there no rise of I and C. In all other cases there is some rise of $Y$, and this includes both some rise of $I$ and an induced rise of $C$. However, if the upward thrust on income emanates from an upward shift of the consumption function (a decline of the saving-supply function), there will occur no rise of investment if investment remains a constant function of interest rates. In the extreme case in which the $LM$ cure is completely horizontal, so that there is no rise of interest rates, investment remains unchanged and the entire increase in output is in the form of consumption goods. However, to the extent that $r$ rises and $I$ is responsive to interest rates, $I$ will actually decline.[3] This serves, of course, to reduce the extent of the rise of $Y$.

---

[3] These conclusions depend heavily on the assumption, followed throughout this chapter, that changes in the level of income do not shift the investment demand function in the same direction.

The reader is invited to trace the effects of a downward shift of the consumption function or upward shift of the saving-supply function. Note the initial autonomous decline of consumption demand, the downward multiplier effect on income illustrated by a shift to the left of the *IS* curve, and the relevance of the slope of the *LM* curve to the outcome. The outcome is, of course, some decline of output and income. This is often referred to as "the paradox of thrift"; an increase in the thriftiness of a community, in the sense of an upward shift of its saving function, can make it less prosperous. The outcome seems less paradoxical when we remember that this is a downward shift of the consumption function and note the implicit assumption that there is neither an offsetting rise of the investment demand function nor a fall of interest rates sufficient to stimulate *I* enough to offset the fall of *C*.

Having gained some familiarity with manipulating the *IS-LM* apparatus, we shall now use the tool of comparative statics to study the effects that monetary and fiscal policy can have on the equilibrium levels of income and interest rates.

## MONETARY POLICY: AN INTRODUCTION

In the context of the *IS-LM* model we have developed, the only tool of monetary policy is the supply of money. Thus far we have treated the money supply as fixed. Now we investigate the consequences of altering it. For the present, we leave aside the questions of why the monetary authorities might want to change the money supply and how they would actually accomplish this. Hence, our only purpose here is to understand the consequences for $Y$ and $r$ of a change in the money supply. We focus first on an increase of the money supply.

## Increase of the Money Supply

Again starting from an initial equilibrium situation in which $Y = Y_e$ and $r = r_e$, suppose that the money supply is increased by some amount, such as $10 billion, with all the other functions remaining constant. At the old equilibrium levels of $Y$ and $r$, $M^S$ will now exceed $M^D$, and the excess supply of money will serve to raise demands for securities and to lower interest rates. With the demand function for money constant, $M^D$ can again be equated to $M^S$ only when it is increased by $10 billion by a rise of $Y$, a decline of $r$, or some combination of the two. At a constant level of interest rates, $M^D$ could be increased $10 billion by some increase of $Y$ such that

$$\Delta Y \, \frac{\Delta M^D}{\Delta Y} = \$10 \text{ billion}$$

where $\Delta M^D / \Delta Y$ is the marginal responsiveness of the demand for money to $Y$ and $\Delta M^D / \Delta Y = J$ for the special case of the linear demand function of equation (4). For example, if $J = 1/5$, the rise of $Y$ required to equate $M^D$ and $M^S$ would be

$$\frac{\$10 \text{ billion}}{1/5} \quad \text{or} \quad \$50 \text{ billion}$$

This is shown in Figure 14–4 as a horizontal shift to the right of the *LM* curve from $L_0 M_0$ to $L_1 M_1$. $M^D$ could also be increased \$10 billion by some decrease of *r* such that

$$\Delta r \ \frac{\Delta M^D}{\Delta r} = \$10 \text{ billion}$$

where $\Delta M^D / \Delta r$ is the marginal responsiveness of money demand to *r*. The quantity $\Delta M^D / \Delta r$ is, of course, negative, since a decline in *r* increases the demand for money. In equation (4), we have $\Delta M^D / \Delta r = -e$. This is a special case. Suppose, for example, that $\Delta M^D / \Delta r = -5$; that is, each decline of *r* by 1 percent increases $M^D$ by \$5 billion. In this case, the decline in *r* required to equate $M^D$ and $M^S$ would be

$$\frac{\$10 \text{ billion}}{\$5 \text{ billion}} = 2 \text{ percent}$$

In Figure 14–4 this is shown as a vertical downward shift of the *LM* curve from $L_0 M_0$ to $L_1 M_1$. Thus, we see that an increase in the money supply may equivalently be regarded as shifting the *LM* curve either to the right or downward.

In any event, the new equilibrium for *Y* and *r* must be somewhere on $L_1 M_1$. At any combination lying below and to the right of this line, $M^D$ would exceed $M^S$ and the excess demand for money balances would serve to reduce demands for securities and to raise interest rates. At any combination lying above and to the left of the *LM* curve, $M^S$ would exceed $M^D$, and the excess supply of money would serve to increase demands for securities and to lower interest rates.

As pictured in Figure 14–4, the new equilibrium occurs at $Y = Y_1$ and

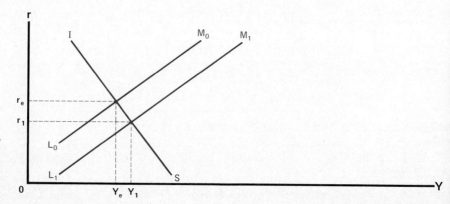

*Shift of the money supply*

**FIGURE 14–4**

$r = r_1$ where the new $LM$ curve, $L_1M_1$, intersects the unchanged $IS$ curve. That is, as a result of the increase in the money supply (denoted by $\Delta M$), income increases (by $\Delta Y$) and interest rates decline (by $\Delta r$).

**Effectiveness of Monetary Policy**

We have just seen that an increase in the supply of money is *qualitatively* an expansionary action as far as output or income is concerned. But it seems natural to ask how *quantitatively* effective it is in this regard. One common measure of the effectiveness of monetary policy is $\Delta Y / \Delta M$. This quantity, which is a monetary analogue of the multiplier concept introduced earlier, tells us the extent to which a given change in the money supply succeeds in altering $Y$. In this sense, larger values of $\Delta Y / \Delta M$ correspond to a more effective monetary policy. It should be emphasized that *effective* in this context has no connotation of success or desirability. It simply refers to what is also sometimes called the *bang-for-a-buck* concept of monetary policy. However, what one calls $\Delta Y / \Delta M$ is of little consequence. What is important is that we understand the factors that make for larger or smaller values of $\Delta Y / \Delta M$, and it is to this issue that we now turn.

One factor that determines the effect of a given increase of the money supply is the location and shape of the $IS$ curve. Beginning from an initial equilibrium of $Y = Y_e$ and $r = r_e$, we consider an increase in the money supply that shifts the $LM$ curve from $L_0M_0$ to $L_1M_1$. As is illustrated in Figure 14–5, where $Y$ and $r$ end up depends directly on the slope of the $IS$ curve. Two possible curves are shown in Figure 14–5 — $I_0S_0$, which is relatively flat, and $I_1S_1$, which is relatively steep. If the relevant curve is $I_0S_0$, then we shall move from $Y = Y_e$ and $r = r_e$ to $Y = Y_1$ and $r = r_1$. If, however, the somewhat steeper curve, $I_1S_1$, is the appropriate one, we see that the interest rate will decline more (to $r_2$ as opposed

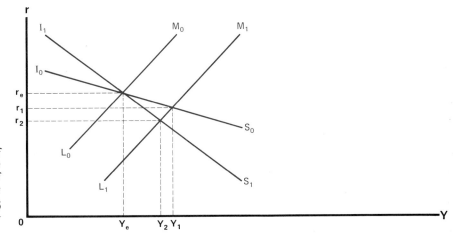

*The effectiveness of monetary policy: the influence of the IS curve*

**FIGURE 14–5**

to $r_1$) and income will increase less (to $Y_2$ instead of $Y_1$). In the extreme case, when the *IS* curve is virtually horizontal, there will be little change of $r$ but an increase of $Y$ approximating the shift to the right of the *LM* curve. However, if the *IS* curve is virtually vertical, the principal effect will be to lower $r$, with little increase of $Y$. It is imperative, therefore, to investigate the determinants of the shape of the *IS* curve. For this purpose, it will be convenient to deal not with the slope of the line, but rather with its reciprocal, $\Delta Y/\Delta r$. This is a measure of the flatness of the line.

If, from some point on the *IS* curve, $r$ is lowered by some amount, $\Delta r$, this will increase $I$ by an amount equal to $\Delta r(\Delta I/\Delta r)$. Thus, $I + G$ will exceed $S + T$. With a constant saving-supply function, $S + T$ can be increased to match the increase of $I + G$ only by some rise of $Y$ such that

$$\Delta Y \frac{\Delta S}{\Delta Y} = \Delta r \frac{\Delta I}{\Delta r}$$

Dividing both sides of the equation by $\Delta r$ and $\Delta S/\Delta Y$, we get

$$\frac{\Delta Y}{\Delta r} = \frac{\Delta I}{\Delta r} \times \frac{1}{\Delta S/\Delta Y}$$

Thus, the flatness of the *IS* curve ($\Delta Y/\Delta r$) varies directly with the marginal responsiveness of investment to interest rates ($\Delta I/\Delta r$) and with $1 \div \Delta S/\Delta Y$), our old friend the multiplier. For example, if investment is completely unresponsive to interest rates—if $\Delta I/\Delta r = 0$—an increase of the money supply will not increase $Y$. However, the more responsive investment is to interest rates, the greater will be the response of $Y$.

In summary, a flatter *IS* curve makes for a more effective monetary policy; and, in turn, the *IS* curve will be flatter the larger $\Delta I/\Delta r$ is and the smaller $\Delta S/\Delta Y$ is.

In addition to the slope of the *IS* curve, the effectiveness of a given change in the money supply also depends on the nature of the money demand function. In particular, it is the money-demand function that determines how far the *LM* curve will shift as a result of a given change in the money supply. To see how this works, consider the *LM* curve labeled $L_0M_0$ in Figure 14–6. Unlike the previous examples of this chapter, $L_0M_0$ is a "curved" *LM* curve. As indicated earlier, however, this is really the general case. One consequence of the curved feature of $L_0M_0$ is that the slope of $L_0M_0$, $\Delta r/\Delta Y$, is not constant. Indeed, as drawn, $L_0M_0$ is much flatter at lower values of $Y$ and $r$ and much steeper at higher values of $Y$ and $r$. As a result of this, an increase in the money supply will produce a shift of the kind illustrated in Figure 14–6—that is, from $L_0M_0$ to $L_1M_1$. We shall shortly explain why this kind of shift results, but first let us examine its consequences for the effectiveness of monetary policy. The main point is illustrated in Figure 14–7, where we have superimposed two different *IS* curves — with the same slope — on the *LM* curves of Figure 14–6. If the relevant *IS* curve is $I_0S_0$, we see that monetary policy will induce only a small change in Y, from $Y_1$ to $Y_2$. On the other hand, if the relevant *IS* curve is $I_1S_1$, then a much larger change in income will result, with Y going from $Y_3$ to $Y_4$. Evidently then, the effectiveness of monetary policy also depends on the nature of the *LM* curve. Before examining the consequences of this further, however, we must understand why the *LM* curve shifts in the manner portrayed in Figures 14–6 and 14–7.

As indicated earlier, the answer lies in the slope of the *LM* curve. This suggests, as was done for the *IS* curve, that it will be instructive to disentangle the underlying components of the slope of the *LM* curve. To

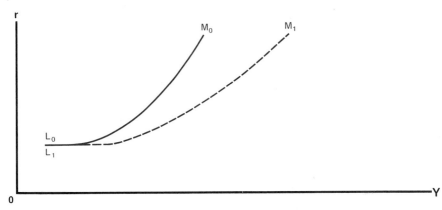

*Shifting the* LM *curve*

**FIGURE 14–6**

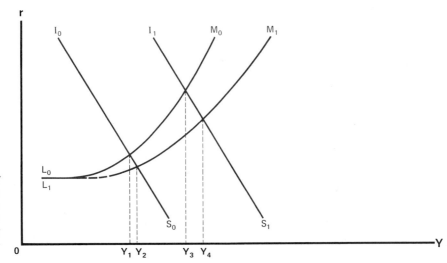

*The effectiveness of monetary policy: the influence of the* LM *curve*

**FIGURE 14–7**

determine this slope we consider some point on the *LM* curve and lower *r* by some amount, $\Delta r$. This will increase the demand for money, $M^D$, by an amount equal to $\Delta r \, (\Delta M^D/\Delta r)$, and thus $M^D$ will exceed $M^S$. With a given $M^S$, $M^D$ can be restored to its equality with $M^S$ only by some rise of $Y$ such that[4]

$$\Delta Y \frac{\Delta M^D}{\Delta Y} + \Delta r \frac{\Delta M^D}{\Delta r} = 0 \tag{7}$$

or

$$\Delta Y \frac{\Delta M^D}{\Delta Y} = -\Delta r \frac{\Delta M^D}{\Delta r} \tag{8}$$

Dividing both sides of equation (8) by $\Delta r$ and $\Delta M^D/\Delta Y$, we get

$$\frac{\Delta Y}{\Delta r} = -\frac{\Delta M^D}{\Delta r} \times \frac{1}{\Delta M^D/\Delta Y}$$

The quantity $\Delta Y/\Delta r$ is, of course, the flatness of the *LM* curve. Thus, we see that the flatness varies directly with the responsiveness of money demand to interest rates $(\Delta M^D/\Delta r)$ and inversely with the responsiveness of money demand to income $(\Delta M^D/\Delta Y)$. Thus, if money demand is extremely responsive to the interest rate, $\Delta M^D/\Delta r$ will be a large negative number and the *LM* curve will be quite flat. In the extreme, when $\Delta M^D/\Delta r$ approaches negative infinity—this is the case of the liquidity trap discussed earlier—the *LM* curve becomes perfectly flat. At the other extreme, when $\Delta M^D/\Delta r$ approaches zero, then so does $\Delta Y/\Delta r$ and the *LM* curve becomes vertical.

Armed with this, we can readily see why the type of *LM* shift pictured in Figure 14–6 results. At low levels of *r* the *LM* curve is flat because $\Delta M^D/\Delta r$ is large in absolute value and the people are willing to absorb substantial increases in the stock of money into speculative balances. As a consequence, equilibrium can be maintained in the money market with only small changes in *r* and *Y*, so that the *LM* curve shifts only slightly. On the other hand, for high values of *r* the *LM* curve is steep because $\Delta M^D/\Delta r$ is relatively small in absolute value. This means that most of the increase in the money stock can be used to finance transactions, so that the effect on *Y* will be substantial. That is, the *LM* curve will shift farther to the right at high levels of *r*.

Figure 14–7 has sometimes been interpreted as demonstrating that the effectiveness of monetary policy varies with the cyclical state of the economy. The reason is that periods of economic slack are likely to be ones with low *r* and *Y*, putting us on the relatively flat side of the *LM*

---

[4] If we are to remain on the *LM* curve, with a given supply of money, then the change in $M^D$ must be zero along the *LM* curve. This is the condition expressed by equation (7).

curve. Similarly, boom periods are likely to be ones with high $r$ and $Y$, corresponding to the relatively steep part of the $LM$ curve. In this view, monetary policy is seen to be its most effective in a period of relatively full employment and least effective during a recession or a depression. While these results are certainly quite plausible, as we shall see later they need to be qualified somewhat.

**The Adjustment Process**
We are now in a position to summarize the process through which a given increase of the money supply influences interest rate and income levels and some of the factors that determine the nature and extent of the effects. We shall assume that the monetary authority increases the money supply by purchasing securities of various types from the public, and that spending for output is affected only through effects on the prices and yields on securities. The following processes are involved.

1.  In creating the additional money, the monetary institutions — the central bank and the commercial banks — increase their demands for securities and loans. This increase of their demands tends to raise the prices of debt obligations and to lower their yields. As the public sells debt obligations to the monetary institutions and acquires more money, it finds that money constitutes a larger fraction of its total assets and is impelled to buy more debt obligations, which tends to decrease interest rates still more.

2.  As interest rates fall, the public demands larger quantities of money balances. How much a given increase of the money supply can depress interest rates varies inversely with the marginal responsive of the demand for money to interest rates $(\Delta M^D/\Delta r)$. If $\Delta M^D/\Delta r$ is large — if each fall of interest rates greatly increases the quantity of money demanded — the increase of the money supply can lower interest rates but little. However, if $\Delta M^D/\Delta r$ is very small, interest rates can be lowered more.

3.  The size of the increase of investment demand depends not only on the size of the decrease of interest rates but also on the marginal responsiveness of investment to interest rates $(\Delta I/\Delta r)$. The greater $\Delta I/\Delta r$ is, the greater will be the expansionary effects on $I$.

4.  The size of the expansion of $Y$ depends not only on the rise of $I$ but also on the value of the multiplier, which varies directly with the marginal propensity to consume.

5.  The rise of $Y$ increases the quantity of money demanded; and as the expansion of $Y$ continues, interest rates will rise. At some point the rise of $r$ will bring the expansion to an end. This is the point of intersection of the $IS$ curve and the new $LM$ curve. How large this expansion will be depends in part on $\Delta M^D/\Delta Y$.

We find, then, that the effects on $Y$ of a given increase in the money supply depend on a number of factors: on $\Delta M^D/\Delta r$, which determines how much interest rates can be lowered; on $\Delta I/\Delta r$, which determines how much each decline of interest rates will stimulate investment; on $\Delta C/\Delta Y$, which determines the size of the multiplier; and on $\Delta M^D/\Delta Y$, which reflects the amount by which the demand for money balances will be increased by each increase of $Y$. The smaller $\Delta M^D/\Delta Y$ is, the larger will be the increase of income that can occur before a rise of interest rates ends the expansion.

The case of a decrease of the money supply is symmetrical with that of an increase of the money supply. With the decrease of $\overline{M}$, $M^D$ exceeds $M^S$ and the excess demand for money balances decreases demands for securities and raises interest rates. The effects of $Y$ and $r$ depend on all of the factors described previously. The reader is invited to trace out the effects, noting that the decrease in $\overline{M}$ will be evidenced by a horizontal leftward shift of the $LM$ curve.

**Overview**      This section has provided an introduction to the workings of monetary policy. We have seen that an increase in the money supply will increase $Y$ and decrease $r$. We have also discussed the various factors influencing the quantitative extent of these changes. Although we have focused on an increase of the money supply, the case of a decrease is really quite analogous. In particular, a decrease serves to shift the $LM$ curve leftward and upward, and in the new equilibrium we shall have a higher value of $r$ and a lower value of $Y$. The quantitative effect on $Y$ and $r$ depends on all the factors just described. We shall have a great deal more to say about monetary policy as we proceed, but now let us turn to fiscal policy.

---

**FISCAL POLICY:**      We shall now investigate the government's principal instruments of fis-
**AN INTRODUCTION**   cal policy—its expenditures for goods and services ($G$) and its net taxes ($T$). To conserve space, we shall only elaborate on expansionary fiscal policies, that is, increases in $G$ or reductions in $T$. The effects of restrictive policies will simply be the reverse of those considered below.

Before discussing the details, it may be helpful if we utilize our previous discussion to anticipate the results. The following two points should be borne in mind.

1    We saw in the previous chapter (especially Figures 13–12 and 13–13) that the effect of an increase in $G$ *or* a reduction in $T$ is to shift the $IS$ curve upward and to the right.

2    From our discussion of increases in investment demand—which also shifts the $IS$ curve upward and to the right (see Figure 14–2) —we know that such shifts generally produce an increase in both income and interest rates. Expansionary fiscal policy therefore will do likewise.

We now consider a few of the more important details, beginning with an increase in the government's demand for output, $G$.

**Increase of G**   Suppose that the government raises $G$ and maintains this higher level of expenditures while leaving its tax and transfer programs unchanged. The direct impact effect is to increase both aggregate demand for output in the form of $C + I + G$ and also the total of gross income shares accruing to the nation. As just noted, the increase in $G$ shifts the $IS$ curve upward and to the right. This is illustrated in Figure 14–8, where the $IS$ curve shifts from $I_0 S_0$ to $I_1 S_1$.

The original equilibrium levels of income and the interest rate, before the rise of $G$, are again represented by $Y_e$, $r_e$. After the rise of $G$ this is no longer an equilibrium. A new equilibrium can be established only by a rise in the interest rate, which reduces $I$; a rise in income, which would raise $S + T$; or some combination of the two. As Figure 14–8 shows, with a conventionally sloped $LM$ curve, $r$ and $Y$ will both rise, with the new equilibrium being established at $Y_1$, $r_1$. As before, the interest rate rises because increased $Y$ increases the quantity of money demanded while the supply of money is unchanged by assumption. This rise in $r$ tends to reduce $I$ and thus to snub somewhat the rise of $Y$.

The foregoing discussion assumes that the increase of $G$ and the ensuing rise of $Y$ left the investment demand function unchanged. This may occur, especially if the economy is operating significantly below capacity levels. However, the rise of $Y$ may increase the expected profitability of investment and shift the investment demand function upward at each level of interest rates. In such cases a rise of interest rates may reduce $I$ less or not at all; in fact, the upward shift of $I$ could be so large that $I$ would be increased despite the rise of interest rates.

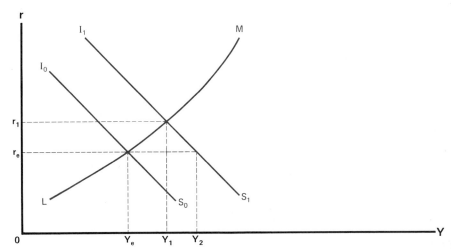

*An increase of* G

**FIGURE 14–8**

**Reduction**
**in _T_**      We now explore the case in which the government lowers its net tax collections at each level of _Y_, leaving its rate of expenditures for output unchanged. This result could be achieved in either or both of two ways: (1) by decreasing tax yields at each level of _Y_ by reducing tax bases, tax rates, or both; or (2) by increasing transfer payments at each level of _Y_. A reduction of _T_ does not directly affect aggregate demand for output; it does, however, increase disposable income at each level of _Y_. With greater disposable incomes, the private sector could be expected to consume more at each level of GNP.

As we have seen before (especially in Figure 13–13), the decrease of _T_ shifts the _S_ + _T_ function rightward and consequently shifts the _IS_ curve up and to the right. Both of these shifts are shown in Figure 14–9.

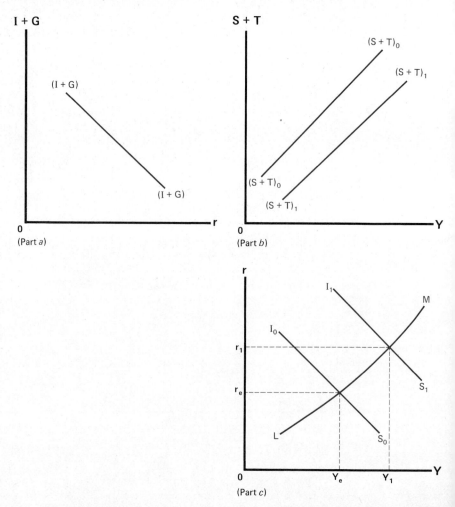

_A tax decrease_

**FIGURE 14–9**

The end result, as in the case of an increase in $G$, is a higher level for both income and the interest rate.

**Increase of $G$ vs. Decrease of $T$**

We find, then, that the government can raise $Y$ by increasing $G$ or by lowering its $T$ function through reducing taxes or raising its transfer payment function. A comparison of the effects of a given increase of $G$ and an equal reduction of $T$ brings out some interesting similarities and contrasts.

1   Both serve to increase $Y$. However, the rise of $Y$ resulting from a given increase of $G$ will be greater than that resulting from an equal decrease of $T$. This is because all of an increase of $G$ is reflected in an exogenous rise of demand for output whereas an equal decrease of $T$ will not increase the consumption function by the full amount; some of the tax rebate will be used to increase $S$.

2   Both are likely to increase interest rates if the money supply is not increased. This will inhibit investment if the rise of $G$, the decrease of the $T$ function, and the ensuing rise of $Y$ do not raise the investment demand function sufficiently to offset the rise of interest rates.

3   Effects on the composition of the increased output are different. If the expansion results from a decrease of the $T$ function, all of the increased output is in the form of consumer goods. If it results from an increase of $G$, the increased output is partly in the form of additional goods and services for the government and partly in the form of additional consumer goods.

**The Effectiveness of Fiscal Policy**

We have just seen that an increase of $G$ or a decrease of $T$ is an expansionary action in that it tends to increase the equilibrium value of $Y$. As we did for monetary policy, it is possible to examine the factors that determine the quantitative extent of this—that is, the effectiveness of fiscal policy. In fact, however, our discussion of this can be quite brief, since we have already touched on many of the issues. In particular, as stressed earlier, both a shift in $G$ and a shift in the investment demand function are examples of shifts in autonomous demand and have essentially the same kinds of effects. Thus, since we have already discussed the factors that determine the size of the change in $Y$ resulting from a shift in the investment demand function, we can simply apply those findings to the present case. In particular, we note that fiscal policy will be more effective—in the sense that a given increase in $G$ or decrease in $T$ will produce a larger increase in $Y$—under the following conditions:

1   THE SMALLER $\Delta S / \Delta Y$ IS. The reciprocal of $\Delta S / \Delta Y$ is, of course, the simple multiplier, and this determines how far to the right the $IS$ curve shifts.

2    THE SMALLER $\Delta I/\Delta r$ IS. The smaller this quantity is, the less the
    increase in $r$ will tend to decrease $I$ and thus to snub the increase
    in $Y$.

3    THE FLATTER THE $LM$ CURVE IS. With a flat $LM$ curve, the
    induced rise in $r$ will be relatively small; consequently, the
    decline in $I$ will be smaller, thus lessening the extent to which
    the increase in $Y$ is snubbed.

This last point is illustrated in Figure 14–10, where we are again utiliz-
ing a "curved" $LM$ curve. If the $IS$ curve crosses the $LM$ curve in its relatively flat part, we see that income will increase from $Y_0$ to $Y_1$. If, on the
other hand, the $LM$ curve is steeper, the *same* increase of $G$ will produce
a much smaller increase in $Y$ (from $Y_2$ to $Y_3$ in Figure 14–10).

As earlier, we may interpret this as saying that the effectiveness of
fiscal policy depends on the cyclical state of the economy. In particular,
fiscal policy is seen to work best in relatively slack economic conditions,
when we are likely to be on the flat part of the $LM$ curve. Fiscal policy
will be less effective under conditions more closely approximating full
employment, since the $LM$ curve is likely to be steeper at such times. In
this respect we see that the cyclical effectiveness of fiscal policy is exactly the opposite of monetary policy, which we had earlier characterized as working best during boom periods and least well during times of
economic slack. While these considerations provide one element in
deciding between the use of monetary and fiscal policies for stabilization
purposes, there are other important elements involved in this choice.

**COMPOSITION
OF OUTPUT AND
THE POLICY MIX**

As we have seen, beginning from some initial position of equilibrium,
either monetary or fiscal policy can be used to achieve some desired
change in the level of $Y$. Or, for that matter, some combination or *mix* of

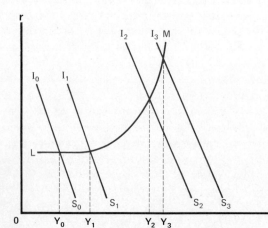

*The effectiveness of
fiscal policy*

**FIGURE 14–10**

monetary and fiscal policies could be used to produce some desired level of $Y$. Which policy mix is chosen may, of course, be affected by the cyclical state of the economy, since this influences the relative effectiveness of monetary and fiscal policy. This issue aside, however, there is another element in the choice, namely, the resulting composition of total output.

By the *composition* of output we mean the distribution of some given level of $Y$ between $C$, $I$, and $G$. We have touched on this issue in comparing policies involving $G$ and $T$, and we now expand on this. In particular, beginning from some level of $Y$, let us consider the following three policies: an increase of $G$, a decrease of $T$, and an increase in the supply of money, $M^S$. Let us further assume that each of these policies is quantitatively chosen so as to produce the *same* increase in $Y$. Then, drawing on the results of the previous sections we have the following:

1    AN INCREASE OF $G$. This induces an increase in $C$ and a decrease in $I$ because $r$ rises. By assumption, of course, $G$ increases.

2    A DECREASE OF $T$. Here $G$ is unchanged, $C$ increases, and again $I$ declines because $r$ rises.

3    AN INCREASE OF $M^S$. $G$ again remains the same, but because $r$ decreases both $C$ and $I$ rise.

Since each of these three policies is assumed to lead to the same $Y$, by looking at the identity $Y = C + I + G$ we see that the increase in consumption is biggest when we cut taxes and smallest when monetary policy is used to increase $Y$. Furthermore, monetary policy is the only policy that leads to an increase of investment.[5] This suggests that if policy makers care about the composition of output, and there is certainly evidence to this effect, this will have a direct influence on the mix of policies pursued.

As an illustration of this, let us consider the case in which the monetary and fiscal authorities are both quite happy with the aggregate level of output but feel that the level of investment is too low. To rectify the situation we need a change in the mix of policy designed to produce an interest rate that is low enough to yield the desired level of investment while keeping the level of $Y$ unchanged. Such a mix shift is illustrated in Figure 14-11.

By expanding the money supply, the monetary authorities shift the $LM$ curve down and to the right, moving from $L_0M_0$ to $L_1M_1$. This must be balanced by a tighter fiscal policy that shifts the $IS$ curve from $I_0S_0$ to $I_1S_1$. This could be accomplished by either a tax increase, a decrease of transfer payments, or a decrease in $G$. As shown, the net effect of these two policy changes is to move the interest rate down from $r_0$ to $r_1$ but to leave income unchanged at $Y_0$.

---

[5] See footnote 1.

Thus, we see how an easier monetary policy used in conjunction with a tighter fiscal policy can bring about a shift in the composition of output while leaving total aggregate demand unchanged. Such a policy mix obviously requires a considerable amount of coordination between the monetary and fiscal authorities. As might be suspected, this is easier said than done. We shall return in subsequent chapters to the problem of coordinating monetary and fiscal policies and to the question of the optimal mix of policies.

**DEBT MANAGEMENT AND DEFICIT FINANCING**

In earlier chapters we discussed the outstanding stock of government debt, while in the present chapter we have analyzed the role of taxes and government expenditures. As should be apparent, there is a direct relation between these two subjects. The connection, of course, stems from the possibility of an imbalance in the federal budget. For example, if government spending exceeds taxes, there will be a *budget deficit* that has to be *financed*. That is, if the government is going to be able to spend more than it takes in, it must somehow gain command of the necessary resources. Typically, this is accomplished by issuing Treasury securities to raise the required funds. This, in turn, adds to the outstanding stock of government debt. Alternatively, if tax revenues exceed government expenditures, the government has a *budget surplus*, which can be used to retire Treasury securities and reduce the outstanding stock of government debt.

In the light of this discussion, two questions immediately arise: (1) How does the government decide what *kinds* of debt to issue or retire? (2) What happens if, rather than altering the stock of interest-bearing government debt, the government resorts to changes in the stock of

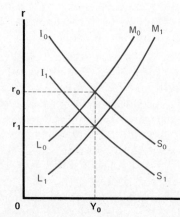

*A policy mix shift*

**FIGURE 14–11**

money to accommodate a surplus or a deficit? We consider each of these questions in turn.

**Debt Management**

*Debt management* refers to the government's policies concerning the *composition* of its debt—the characteristics of financial claims against it. In determining the characteristics of its debt instruments and the proportions in which the various type of instruments will be issued, debt managers have a wide range of choice as to maturities, coupon rates of interest, and other technical features. These choices must be faced whenever the government issues securities. Such issues will be required if the government makes net additions to the outstanding stock of debt. Even in the absence of such net additions, however, debt issue will be called for as outstanding securities mature and have to be *refunded* or *refinanced*.

What principles typically govern debt management? One objective that is sometimes espoused is that the Treasury should generally issue long-term debt so as to minimize the frequency with which it has to market its securities. For a variety of reasons, this principle is not often followed. One reason is that it can conflict with a second, and more plausible, objective, namely, managing the debt so as to minimize the interest cost to the Treasury. Even if one accepts this principle, it is easier stated than carried out. To see this, consider a simple example in which the Treasury wants to decide between issuing a two-year security or a sequence of two one-year securities. At the time that it makes its decision, it knows the currently prevailing market interest rates on both one- and two-year securities, but it does not know what the rate of interest on one-year securities will be one year from now. Hence, it cannot with certainty choose a least-cost option. It can, of course, make a forecast of future interest rates and act accordingly. This practice is, in fact, quite common in debt management.

A third principle is to manage the debt so as to be consistent with stabilization policies being pursued by the Federal Reserve or the fiscal-policy arm of the Treasury. To see what this entails, we must briefly consider what effects debt management could have on the economy.

The effects of debt management policies on financial markets and on the economy can be illustrated by shifts in the composition of a government debt of constant size. Suppose that the government creates and issues a large amount of long-term debt, retiring an equal amount of short-term debt. At least initially, this will tend to lower the prices and raise the yields on long-term bonds and to raise the prices and lower the yields on short maturities. Such a differential may persist if investors do not consider long and short maturities to be close substitutes, but it will later narrow to the extent that the differing maturities are considered to be close substitutes. Such a shift of maturities is likely to have more important and persistent effects by means of its altering the overall liquidity and safety of the public's portfolios. Longer maturities are less liquid and more susceptible to loss because of the chance of future increases of interest rates. Thus, the shift from short to long maturities reduces the overall liquidity and safety of investors' portfolios. To restore its liquidity and safety, the public is likely to demand larger money balances and to reduce its demands for other risky assets. In the absence of an increase in the money supply, interest rates tend to be raised; this is especially true of the interest rates on less safe and less liquid assets. An increase of short-term debt offset by a decrease of long-term debt has the opposite effects.

What this discussion suggests is that the countercyclical debt management would involve issuing long maturities during economic booms and short maturities in recessions. While such a practice is likely to be consistent with Federal Reserve policy, it tends to increase the interest cost on the debt, since the Treasury would prefer to borrow long in recessions, when long-term interest rates are low. At various times the conflict between these objectives has been resolved in different ways. As a consequence, there have been many instances in which the debt managers and Federal Reserve officials have worked at cross-purposes.[6]

**Alternative Methods of Deficit Financing**

We have thus far assumed that budget deficits are financed by issuing government securities. There is, however, another possibility in that the government may issue money (non-interest-bearing debt) to cover its deficit. This has been a popular method of finance in some countries, especially those in which the market for government securities is not well developed. This is clearly not the case in the United States, where, furthermore, the stock of money is under the control of an independent Federal Reserve. Thus, the Treasury cannot simply "print money" to finance deficits. If the Federal Reserve is willing, however, the Treasury can accomplish the same thing by selling its securities to the Federal Reserve. In the process of paying for the securities, the Federal Reserve will create bank reserves, enabling the banking system to expand bank credit and the money supply by some multiple. In other words, this method of finance, which is sometimes called *monetization of the debt*, is nothing other than an expansionary open-market operation by the Federal Reserve. Hence, money finance of a deficit, since it combines expansionary fiscal policy with an expansionary monetary policy, should provide a greater stimulus to income than a bond-financed increase in government spending.

This can be readily illustrated by use of the *IS-LM* framework. We start in Figure 14–12 from the position of the equilibrium given by $(r_1, Y_1)$,

---

[6] For one example of this, see the description of Operation Nudge in Chapter 20.

which, to keep matters simple, we assume corresponds to a balanced budget. Now suppose, because of an increase in government spending or a cut in taxes, the $IS$ curve shifts upward from $I_1S_1$ to $I_2S_2$. If the resulting deficit is financed solely by issuing bonds, the $LM$ curve remains at $LM$ curve will shift to the right (to $L_2M_2$) and yield the equilibrium $(r_3, Y_3)$. nance that we have implicitly assumed throughout this chapter. However, if the deficit is partly or solely financed by monetizing the debt, the $LM$ curve will shift to the right (to $L_2M_2$) and yield the equilibrium $(r_3, Y_3)$. Quite evidently, money finance is more expansionary than bond finance. Thus, whether money or bond finance is appropriate depends on the degree of stimulus that is desired.

One conclusion, which is strongly suggested by all of this discussion, is that an efficient overall stabilization policy requires coordination of fiscal, debt management and monetary policy. We shall have more to say about this in later chapters.

**CONCLUSION**  This chapter has made extensive use of the $IS$–$LM$ apparatus to study the behavior of the interest rate and the level of income or output. As we have seen, equilibrium levels of $Y$ and $r$ depend on many factors. These can be summarized in the following functions:

1    The saving-supply function
2    The investment demand function
3    The money supply function
4    The demand function for money

Equilibrium levels of $Y$ and $r$ depend not just on one or two of these functions but on all of them together. This was illustrated in the case of

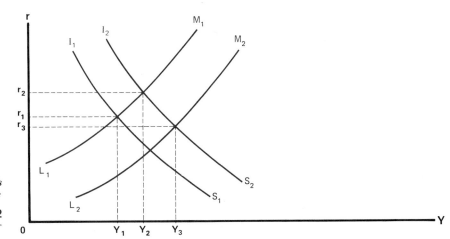

*Alternative methods of deficit finance*

**FIGURE 14–12**

static equilibrium; the equilibrium would have been different if any one of the functions had been different. It became clearer in the cases of comparative statics, in which we shifted the functions one at a time, leaving all other functions constant. The outcome depended not only on the function that was shifted but also on its interactions with the other functions.

This chapter has also provided an introduction to the workings of monetary and fiscal policy, although on this score we have just scratched the surface. Subsequent chapters will consider a variety of other aspects of the policy-making process. Before doing this, however, we must modify one important feature of the model we have been using. In particular, we must now relax the assumption that the price level is fixed.

---

**APPENDIX** | **ALGEBRAIC APPROACH TO EQUILIBRIUM LEVELS OF INCOME AND THE INTEREST RATE**

---

The preceding chapter relied primarily on a graphic approach to explain the determination of equilibrium levels of $Y$ and $r$ that would simultaneously satisfy the necessary conditions that $I + G = S + T$ and $M^D = M^S$. This can also be done by using simultaneous equations, and some readers may find it useful to have the foregoing parts of the analysis stated in algebraic terms. For the sake of simplicity, we shall assume that all the functions are linear. To simplify further, we shall largely work with some specific numerical assumptions.

With respect to the product market, personal consumption expenditures and saving are assumed to be linear functions of disposable income, DI, such that

$$C = 130 + 0.8 \text{ DI} \tag{A1}$$
$$S = -130 + 0.2 \text{ DI} \tag{A2}$$

Disposable income, it will be recalled, is defined as

$$\text{DI} = Y - T \tag{A3}$$

Assuming that net taxes are given by

$$T = 0.25Y \tag{A4}$$

we can substitute equation (A4) into equation (A3) to obtain

$$\text{DI} = Y - 0.25Y = 0.75Y$$

This in turn can be substituted in the consumption and saving functions, (A1) and (A2), to yield

$$C = 130 + 0.8\,(0.75Y) = 130 + 0.6Y \tag{A5}$$
$$S = -130 + 0.2\,(0.75Y) = -130 + 0.15Y \tag{A6}$$

which, as before, express $C$ and $S$ as a function of $Y$ or total income.

To complete the product market we need a specific investment demand function, which we take to be

$$I = 130 - 10r \tag{A7}$$

$G$, of course, is exogenously determined by the government. We shall shortly assume some specific numerical values for $G$, but for the present it will be more informative to keep it general.

We now have all the ingredients for the $IS$ curve, which is defined by the condition

$$I + G = S + T \tag{A8}$$

Equations (A7), (A6), and (A4) give us $I$, $S$, and $T$. These can be substituted into equation (A8) to give

$$130 - 10r + G = -130 + 0.15Y + 0.25Y$$

which can be solved for $r$ to yield

$$r = 26 + 0.1G - 0.04Y \tag{A9}$$

Equation (A9) is the algebraic expression for the $IS$ curve giving all $Y$, $r$ combinations that clear the product market.[1] The negative coefficient on $Y$ indicates that the $IS$ curve is downward sloping. Furthermore, the positive coefficient on $G$ indicates that an increase in $G$ will shift the $IS$ curve up and to the right.

With the $IS$ curve in hand, we now turn to the $LM$ curve. The demand for money is assumed to be given by

$$M^D = 0.2Y + (110 - 10r) \tag{A10}$$

The supply of money will be denoted by

$$M^S = \overline{M} \tag{A11}$$

As with $G$, we shall shortly assume some specific numerical values for $\overline{M}$. Since the $LM$ curve is defined by

$$M^S = M^D \tag{A12}$$

we can combine equations (A10), (A11), and (A12) to yield

$$\overline{M} = 0.2Y + (110 - 10r)$$

---

[1] The reader may readily verify the equation for the $IS$ curve can also be obtained by solving $Y = C + I + G$ with $C$ and $I$ given by equations (A5) and (A7), respectively.

This can be solved for $r$ to give

$$r = 0.02Y + 11 - 0.1\overline{M} \qquad \text{(A13)}$$

Equation (A13) is the algebraic expression for the $LM$ curve. The negative way in which $\overline{M}$ enters the equation shows that an increase of $\overline{M}$ will shift the $LM$ curve down and to the right. This is so because at any given level of $Y$ a larger value for $\overline{M}$ will yield a lower value for $r$—and this is algebraically what one means by a downward shift.

Overall equilibrium is achieved at the intersection of the $IS$ and $LM$ equations, which algebraically amounts to solving equations (A9) and (A13) simultaneously. That is, we have

$$0.02Y + 11 - 0.1\overline{M} = 25 + 0.1G - 0.04Y$$

After some arithmetic this can be rearranged to yield

$$Y = 250 + \frac{5}{3}G + \frac{5}{3}\overline{M} \qquad \text{(A14)}$$

Equation (A14) is actually a most useful result because it permits us to calculate the equilibrium value of $Y$ corresponding to any combination of values for $G$ and $\overline{M}$. For example, if $G = 200$ and $\overline{M} = 250$ we see that

$$Y = 250 + \frac{5}{3}200 + \frac{5}{3}250 = 1{,}000$$

From either (A9) or (A13) we can then calculate that

$$r = 6$$

Thus, the equilibrium corresponding to $G = 200$, $M = 250$ is $Y = 1{,}000$, $r = 6$.

Equation (A14) can, of course, be used to produce the equilibrium values of $Y$ corresponding to other values of $G$ and $\overline{M}$. Table 14A–1 gives the equilibrium values for $Y$, $C$, $I$, and $r$ corresponding to the values just assumed and to two other sets of assumptions for $G$ and $\overline{M}$.

**TABLE 14A–1**

*Some numerical examples*

| | | EQUILIBRIUM VALUES | | | |
|---|---|---|---|---|---|
| | | Y | C | I | r |
| Case I | $G = 200$ $M = 250$ | 1,000 | 730 | 70 | 6 |
| Case II | $G = 230$ $M = 250$ | 1,050 | 760 | 60 | 7 |
| Case III | $G = 200$ $M = 280$ | 1,050 | 760 | 90 | 4 |

Case I is the one used originally. Cases II and III both result in the same higher level of income ($Y = 1,050$), but in case II this is achieved by an increase of $G$, whereas in case III this comes about from an increase of $\overline{M}$. The effects on the composition of output discussed earlier are quite evident in Table 14A–1. An expansionary monetary policy is seen to result in an increase of $I$ and a decrease of $r$ relative to case I, while the reverse is true for an expansionary fiscal policy.

The reader is invited to shift some of the functions and solve for the results. For example, assume that

1.  $G$ is reduced from $G = 200$ to $G = 180$ and $\overline{M}$ is simultaneously increased from $\overline{M} = 200$ to $\overline{M} = 220$.
2.  The consumption function is shifted to $C = 160 + 0.8DI$.
3.  Taxes are increased, so that $T = 0.30Y$.

Finally, we can also use our example to illustrate numerically how the full basic multiplier or $1 \div (\Delta S/\Delta Y)$ tends to be snubbed by a rise in interest rates. From equation (6) in the text of this chapter, we recall that $\Delta S/\Delta Y$ stands for the marginal responsiveness of saving and taxes to a change in income. In the present example, combining (A6) and (A4) we get

$$S + T = -130 + 0.4Y$$

Thus, $\Delta S/\Delta Y = 0.4$ and the basic multiplier is $1/0.4 = 2.5$. This means, for example, if $r$ were to remain unchanged, an increase in $G$ of 30 ($\Delta G = 30$) would raise $Y$ by $30 \times 2.5 = 75$. Of course, as we have already seen in comparing cases I and II in Table 14A-1, when $\Delta G = 30$, $r$ is driven up from 6 percent to 7 percent. As a consequence, the actual increase in $Y$ is held to 50. Hence, the actual multiplier is $\Delta Y/\Delta G = 50/30 = 5/3$.[2] This is a numerical illustration of the effect pictured in Figure 14–8.

**SELECTED READINGS**

Branson, W. H., *Macroeconomic Theory and Policy*, 2nd ed., New York, Harper & Row, 1979.

Dornbusch, R., and S. Fischer, *Macroeconomics*, New York, McGraw-Hill, 1978.

Gordon, R. J., *Macroeconomics*, Boston, Little, Brown, 1978.

---

[2] As should be apparent, the relevant multiplier for a change in $G$ is the coefficient of $G$ in equation (A14). Similarly, the relevant multiplier for changing $\overline{M}$ is its coefficient in equation (A14). The fact that the two numbers are the same in the present case is merely a coincidence. This will not be true in general.

**AGGREGATE DEMAND AND AGGREGATE SUPPLY**

# 15

In previous chapters we have made extensive use of the *IS–LM* framework to explore the determination of equilibrium values for income and the interest rate. Two important assumptions were made in the development of the *IS–LM* model. First, the price level was assumed to be constant, so that changes in real and nominal quantities were equivalent. Second, the notion of overall equilibrium for the economy was confined to simultaneous equilibrium in the commodity market (*IS*) and the money market (*LM*). No attention was paid to the labor market or to the production side of things. In other words, the *IS–LM* framework focuses exclusively on questions of aggregate demand but neglects issues concerning aggregate supply.

The purpose of this chapter is to relax both of the assumptions just cited. In particular, we shall be concerned with questions such as: "Suppose that nominal aggregate demand increases or decreases by some specified amount. To what extent will this be reflected in price changes? In changes in money wage rates? In the rate of real output? In the level of employment?" Answers to these questions are important because effects on economic welfare depend heavily on the nature of the response. For example, it does matter whether a decline of money demands for output is reflected almost entirely in decreased price levels or largely in decreased real output and employment. And it does matter whether an increase in money demands for output is reflected solely in price inflation or in large increases in real output and employment.

DEMAND AND SUPPLY

As a first step toward understanding the responses of output, employment, and prices to demand conditions and to changes in demand condi-

384

tions, it will be useful to recall some aspects of general economic theory relating to the demand and supply of a commodity that is produced and sold under conditions approximating those of pure competition. Suppose, for example, that the demand and supply conditions for this commodity are represented by the demand function (DD) and the supply function (SS) in Figure 15–1. Price (denoted by P) is measured along the vertical axis. The quantities demanded and supplied per period of time, such as per year, are measured along the horizontal axis (designated by Q). We find that as long as demand and supply conditions for this commodity continue to be those represented by the DD and SS curves, the market for this commodity can be in equilibrium only if the quantities actually supplied and demanded are at $Q_0$ and the price is $P_0$. Only this combination of P and Q will exactly clear the market, leaving no excess supply or excess demand.

This example illustrates at least two simple points that will be useful for our later analysis. First, market equilibrium is not determined by demand conditions alone, nor by supply conditions alone, but by a combination of both. Second, both price and the actual rate of output and sales are determined simultaneously.

As before, we can use comparative statics to compare two sets of equilibrium conditions: those existing before and after a shift of a demand or supply function. We can thus determine how equilibrium will be changed if the demand function or the supply function shifts in a specified way. Suppose, as in Figure 15–2, that for some reason the demand function increases from DD to $D_1D_1$. That is, the community demands more of the commodity at each price or will pay a higher price for each quantity. This increase of the demand function will tend to raise the price, to increase the quantities actually supplied and purchased, or to raise both prices and quantities produced and sold. The actual effects of any given increase of demand will depend on supply conditions, and

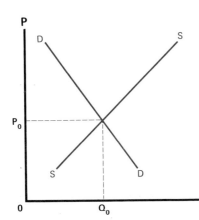

*Demand for, and supply of, a commodity*

**FIGURE 15–1**

more specifically on the responsiveness of quantities supplied to changes in price.

Suppose supply is completely unresponsive or inelastic to price, as indicated by the supply curve $S_1S_1$ (Figure 15–2). In this case the entire effect of the increase in demand is to raise the price from $P_0$ to $P_1$. The quantities produced and sold and the quantities of productive factors employed in producing the commodity remain unchanged. Suppose, to go to the other extreme, that supply is completely responsive or elastic to price, as indicated by the supply function $S_2S_2$. That is, suppliers stand ready to supply at price $P_0$ any quantity that may be demanded, but will supply nothing at a lower price. In this case the increase of demand will not raise price at all; its entire effect will be to increase quantities produced and sold and to increase the quantity of productive factors employed in producing the commodity. Usually, the responsiveness of supply to price will lie somewhere between these extremes. This is illustrated by the supply function $SS$. In these situations an increase of demand will increase price, quantities actually produced and sold, and the quantities of productive factors employed in producing the good. The more responsive supply is to price, the less a given increase of demand will raise price, and the more it will increase quantities.

In the remainder of this chapter, we shall adapt this type of analysis, which was originally developed to explain the prices and output of individual commodities, to the economy as a whole. Our supply function will relate to the economy's aggregate output of goods and services, and our demand function will relate to the quantities of that output demanded at various levels of prices. If we are to study the aggregate economy by analogy to the demand-supply framework, we must next focus on how one arrives at the aggregate versions of the demand and supply function.

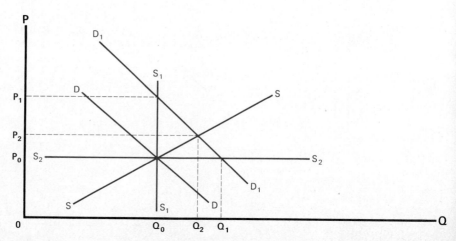

*Shifts in demand*

**FIGURE 15–2**

**THE AGGREGATE DEMAND FUNCTION**

In Figure 15–1 we saw that the demand function for an individual commodity is a relationship between the price of the commodity and the quantity of the commodity demanded. By analogy then, the *aggregate demand function* or, as it is sometimes called, the *economy's demand curve*, is a relationship between the general price level, $P$, and the level of real output, which we previously have denoted by $O$. But how are we to arrive at such a relationship? As implied earlier, we must reconsider the *IS–LM* framework when the price level is no longer required to be a constant. This introduces an important distinction that was glossed over before. In particular, when the price level was being treated as a constant, we could afford to be casual as to the differences between nominal and real magnitudes. However, this is no longer the case. Thus, it is important for our present purposes that the reader carefully distinguish between the following: $M^D$, which is the quantity of *nominal* balances demanded, and $M^D/P$, which is the quantity of *real* balances demanded; and between *nominal* income, $Y$, and *real* income, $O = Y/P$. With these distinctions in mind, we now turn first to a reconsideration of the *LM* curve.

**The *LM* Curve**

The *LM* curve is defined by the condition

$$M^D = M^S \tag{1}$$

where, as before, we shall assume that the money supply is exogenously fixed by the monetary authorities at $\overline{M}$. Thus, we have

$$M^S = \overline{M} \tag{2}$$

It will be recalled from Chapter 12 that the general form of our money-demand function is

$$\frac{M^D}{P} = F\left(\frac{Y}{P}, r\right) = F(O, r) \tag{3}$$

which says that the demand for real balances is a function of real income ($Y/P$ or $O$) and the interest rate. We have also seen a special case of equation (3) given by

$$\frac{M^D}{P} = J\frac{Y}{P} + (A - er) = JO + (A - er) \tag{4}$$

Equations (1), (2), and (3) can be combined to give

$$\frac{\overline{M}}{P} = F\left(\frac{Y}{P}, r\right) = F(O, r) \tag{5}$$

while (1), (2), and (4) yield

$$\frac{\overline{M}}{P} = J\frac{Y}{P} + (A - er) = JO + (A - er) \tag{6}$$

As earlier, equation (5) or (6) defines the *LM* curve. But there is now one important difference. With $P$ taken as a constant, (5) is an equation in two variables, $Y/P$ (or $O$) and $r$. And the pairs of $r$ and $Y/P$ that satisfy this equation give the *LM* curve. However, when $P$ is free to vary, equation (5) contains three variables, $Y/P$, $r$, and $P$. Consequently, when $P$ is variable, it is no longer true that (5) defines a *single LM* curve relating $r$ and $Y/P$. However, it is still true that for any *given* value of $P$, (5) does define a conventional *LM* curve. Thus, we see that what (5) really does is to define a *family* of *LM* curves, one for each possible value for $P$. This is illustrated in Figure 15–3.

As drawn, the curve $L_1M_1$ corresponds to an assumed value for the price level of $P_1$. Now let us ask what *LM* curve will correspond to some lower price level, $P_2$. From equation (5) we see that lowering the price level raises the left-hand side of (5). That is, it increases the supply of real-money balances. To achieve equilibrium with this new higher supply of real-money balances requires that the demand for real-money balances also increase. This can be brought about either by an increase in $O$, or a decrease in $r$, or both. Consider, for example, point $A$ on $L_1M_1$, which has $r = r_1$ and $O = O_1$. With a lower price level such as $P_2$, if the interest rate stays at $r_1$, real output must increase, say, to $O_2$, to reestablish equilibrium. Thus, we see that the *LM* curve corresponding to $P_2$ must lie to the right of $L_1M_1$, as shown by $L_2M_2$ in Figure 15–3. Similarly, if the price level was at an even lower value such as $P_3$, we know that the corresponding *LM* curve, $L_3M_3$, must lie still farther to the right of $L_1M_1$.

A moment's thought should reveal that this result could have been readily anticipated. Inspecting equation (5), we see that a decrease in $P$ has the same effect on $\overline{M}/P$ as an increase in $\overline{M}$. But we have already seen

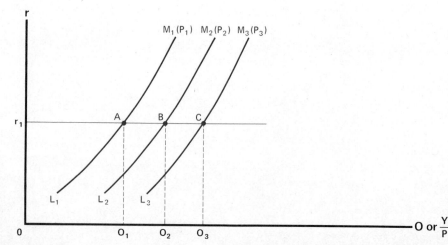

*LM curves corresponding to alternative price levels*

**FIGURE 15–3**

that increasing the money supply shifts the *LM* curve out to the right. It is thus hardly surprising that a decrease in *P* should do the same.

In summary then, permitting the price level to vary forces us to replace a single *LM* curve with a family of *LM* curves such as is pictured in Figure 15–3. We now turn to a reexamination of the *IS* curve.

**The *IS* Curve**

Here the situation is, fortunately, quite simple, since there remains a single *IS* curve, even when *P* is variable. The only difference is that the *IS* curve must now be regarded as a relationship between *r* and *Y/P* (or *O*) rather than between *r* and *Y*. The reason for a single such *IS* curve is as follows.

Although we were not explicit on this point earlier (it did not matter with a constant *P*), the expenditure functions underlying the *IS* curve should be regarded as expressing relationships between real or constant dollar magnitudes. Thus, for example, the proper way to think of the consumption function is that it makes real consumption expenditures depend on real income. Similarly, the investment demand function is properly specified with real investment expenditures depending on the interest rate. In each case the reason is straightforward. What lies behind a consumption function is some kind of utility-maximizing behavior by individuals. But utility can only sensibly be regarded as a function of the real quantity of goods consumed. Consequently, the process of utility maximization must lead to a consumption function expressed in real terms. As for the investment demand function, as we have seen, it results from the desire of firms to achieve an optimal quantity of capital goods for production. But clearly it is only the quantity of capital goods measured in real terms that is relevant for production. As a consequence, the investment demand function itself must be specified in real terms.

The thrust of this argument can be summarized quite briefly. With the consumption function in real terms we must have the saving function in real terms. Thus, real saving, $S/P$, is a positive function of real income, $Y/P$, and real investment, $I/P$, is a negative function of the interest rate. Equilibrium is now characterized by[1]

$$\frac{I}{P} + \frac{G}{P} = \frac{S}{P} + \frac{T}{P}$$

or, equivalently, by

$$\frac{Y}{P} = \frac{C}{P} + \frac{I}{P} + \frac{G}{P}$$

---

[1] We are implicitly assuming here that government expenditures are set in real terms and that the tax functions are also similarly expressed. These assumptions considerably simplify the exposition but, at best are only approximately true.

Consequently, the *IS* curve can be derived exactly as we did before. As already indicated, the only difference is that the *IS* curve now relates *r* and *Y/P*. A typical *IS* curve is shown in Figure 15–4 where we again have drawn a family of *LM* curves corresponding to different price levels.

As Figure 15–4 shows, when the price level is $P_1$, the equilibrium value of real output is $O_1$. At $P_2$, which is less than $P_1$, output is $O_2$, while at $P_3$ it is $O_3$. At each intersection, of course, there is a different equilibrium value for the interest rate. We thus see that, as far as the demand side of the economy is concerned, varying the price level produces opposite variations in the equilibrium level of output demanded. This inverse relationship between *P* and *O* is precisely the aggregate demand curve we have been seeking.

**The *DD* Curve**

In other words, to obtain the aggregate demand curve we must simply plot the equilibrium values of *P* in Figure 15–4 against the corresponding values for *O*. This is done in Figure 15–5, where the resulting

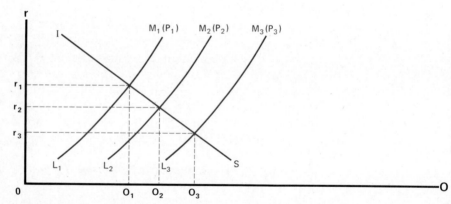

**IS and LM curves for alternative price levels**

**FIGURE 15–4**

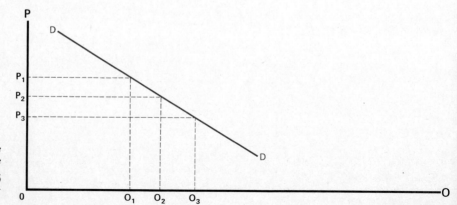

**The aggregate demand curve**

**FIGURE 15–5**

curve is labeled $DD$. Thus, for example, the equilibrium pairs $(P_1, O_1)$, $(P_2, O_2)$, and $(P_3, O_3)$ of Figure 15–4 all lie on the $DD$ curve in Figure 15–5. We thus see that the $DD$ curve, like a conventional demand curve, is downward sloping, so that as the price level increases, the equilibrium output demanded decreases. The explanation of the downward slope is not, however, the ordinary substitution effect of a rising price reducing demand. Rather, an increase in $P$ reduces output demanded, $O$, by tightening the money market, increasing the interest rate, and consequently reducing investment. As this reemphasizes, as we move along the $DD$ curve, the interest rate is constantly adjusting in the background to its new equilibrium level.

**Shifting the $DD$ Curve**

We have earlier studied how shifts in government purchases of goods and services, in the tax and transfer functions, and in the investment and saving functions can induce shifts in the $IS$ curve. Similarly, we have seen how changes in the money supply can shift the $LM$ curve. As we shall now see, precisely these factors will shift the $DD$ curve. Let us first consider an exogenous change, perhaps an expansionary fiscal policy of some kind, which shifts the $IS$ curve to the right.

This is illustrated in part $(a)$ of Figure 15–6 as a shift from $I_0S_0$ to $I_1S_1$. When the relevant $IS$ curve is $I_0S_0$, we see that points like $(P_1, O_1)$ and $(P_2, O_2)$ lie on the initial $DD$ curve, labeled $D_0D_0$ in part $(b)$. After the shift to $I_1S_1$, we see from part $(a)$ that equilibrium comes about at pairs like $(P_1, O_3)$ and $(P_2, O_4)$, where $O_3$ exceeds $O_1$ and $O_4$ exceeds $O_2$. Thus, we see that anything that shifts the $IS$ curve to the right will also shift the $DD$ curve to the right. This is shown in part $(b)$ as a shift from $D_0D_0$ to $D_1D_1$. Similarly, anything that shifts the $LM$ curve will also shift the $DD$ curve in the same direction. Consider, for example, an increase in the money supply. We know that at any *given* price level this must shift the

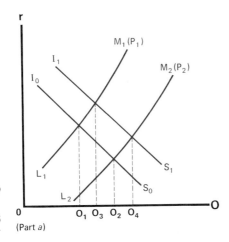
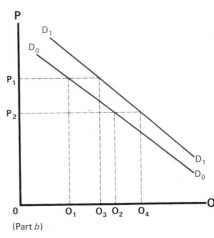

*Shifting the* **DD** *curve: An IS shift*

**FIGURE 15–6**

(Part *a*)

(Part *b*)

*LM* curve to the right. This is shown in part (*a*) of Figure 15–7, where *both* $L_1M_1$ and $L_2M_2$ are drawn on the assumption that the price level is $P_1$. $L_1M_1$, of course, shifts to $L_2M_2$ as a result of the increased money supply. We thus see that $(P_1, O_1)$ must be on the initial *DD* curve, labeled $D_0D_0$ in Part (*b*), and that $(P_1, O_2)$ must be on the new *DD* curve. This is labeled $D_1D_1$ in Part (*b*). Consequently, we see that an increase in $M^S$ serves to shift the *DD* curve to the right.

Overview      This section has introduced the notion of the aggregate demand or *DD* curve, which gives the combinations of *P* and *O* that equilibrate the aggregate demand sector. We have also seen that anything that shifts the *IS* and *LM* curves will shift the *DD* curve in the same direction. As should be readily apparent, however, the *DD* curve is not itself sufficient to determine the overall equilibrium of the price level and real income. This is because we have added a new variable, the price level, to our *IS–LM* framework, but we have added no new equations. As indicated earlier, this new equation, the aggregate supply curve, will come from the labor market, and it is to this that we now turn.

AGGREGATE
SUPPLY:
THE CLASSICAL
CASE

We begin our discussion of the supply side of the economy with what is known as the *classical* or *real-wage* model. John Maynard Keynes applied the term *classical* to those economists who dominated economic thought, at least in England and the United States, from the latter part of the nineteenth century until the early 1930s. Three basic assumptions are essential for the operation of the classical model:

1   All markets for output and labor are purely competitive and all enterprises seek to maximize their profits.

2   Decisions relating to output and employment are not based on

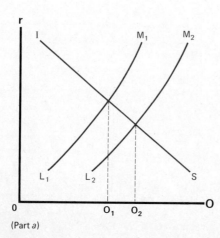
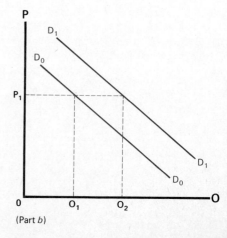

*Shifting the* DD
*curve; an* LM *shift*

**FIGURE 15–7**

(Part a)                                                    (Part b)

absolute levels of prices and money wage rates; instead, they are based on relative wages and prices. Thus, each producer bases output decisions not on the absolute price of the product, but on its price relative to its cost. In equilibrium, production is such that the price of the product is equal to marginal cost. Equiproportionate changes of price and of the marginal-cost function will not alter the equilibrium rate of output. The quantity of labor demanded by an employer does not depend on the absolute money wage rate, but on the level of wages relative to the marginal value product of labor. Equiproportionate changes of money wage rates and of the marginal value product of labor will not affect the quantity of labor demanded. Similarly, the quantities of labor supplied depend not on the absolute level of money wage rates, but on real wages or real money wage rates. We shall designate the real wage by $W/P$. The supply of labor was assumed to be a positive function of $W/P$. Note that the quantity of labor supplied is assumed to be unaffected by equiproportionate changes of money wage rates, $W$, and the price level, $P$.

3    Both the prices of output and the money wage rates are perfectly flexible, and they can fluctuate both upward and downward. They change to the extent necessary in order to secure equilibrium levels of relative prices and wages.

    The consequences of these assumptions can best be illustrated with a few diagrams. We begin in Figure 15–8 with the labor market and the production of output. Part ($a$) shows aggregate output or the *production function* of the economy ($OO$) stated as a function of the amount of labor employed. This function assumes a given state of technology and given endowments of capital and natural resources. The decreasing slope of

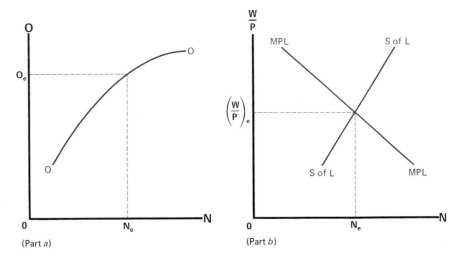

*The production function and labor market equilibrium*

**FIGURE 15–8**

(Part $a$)                (Part $b$)

the total output function as larger amounts of labor are used reflects the operation of the law of diminishing returns.

Demand and supply conditions in the labor market are shown in part (b). The marginal product of labor function (MPL) is derived from the aggregate production function; it is the amount by which total output is changed by a change of one unit in the amount of labor used. This is the demand function for labor, for under pure competition each enterprise will demand all labor whose marginal product is at least as great as its real wage.[2] The supply function of labor (S of L) is a positive function of the real wage rate (W/P), not of the money wage rate alone. Workers do not suffer from money illusion.

Figure 15–8 shows the simultaneous determination of the equilibrium levels for total output $(O_e)$, employment $(N_e)$, and the real-wage rate $(W/P)_e$. Only at the real-wage rate $(W/P)_e$ are the supply of labor and the demand for labor equated. At any higher real wage, the supply of labor would exceed the demand for labor and the excess supply of labor would serve to drive down the real wage. But at any real wage below $(W/P)_e$ the demand for labor would exceed its supply and the excess demand would serve to drive up the real wage. The equilibrium amount of employment $(N_e)$ is full employment, in the sense that all labor that is offered at the real wage $(W/P)_e$ finds employment. And the level of real output $(O_e)$ is the *full-employment level of income*.

The important thing to note from this discussion—and from Figure 15–8—is that under the classical model the equilibrium levels of real output, the real wage, and employment are determined *independently* of the aggregate demand side of things. While this has important implications for policy that we shall examine shortly, for the present the force of this observation is that the supply of output is fixed at the level $O_e$. As a consequence, in the classical case the aggregate supply curve is simply a vertical line at the level $O_e$. This is illustrated in Figure 15–9, where the aggregate supply curve is labeled SS. In order to explore the consequences of this, we turn directly to an examination of the workings of the full classical model.

**THE FULL CLASSICAL MODEL**

The full classical model is summarized by the aggregate supply curve just developed and the aggregate demand curve as previously derived. These curves are both illustrated in Figure 15–9, which shows the joint

---

[2] The comparison will, of course, be made in money terms, with each enterprise hiring all labor whose marginal value product is at least equal to its money wage. That is, equilibrium requires that $W = P(MPL)$. But if we divide both sides by the price level $(P)$, we get $W/P = MPL$.

determination of $O$ and $P$. It must be recalled, however, that behind these two summary curves lie the following functions: saving supply, investment demand, the demand for and the supply of money, the production function, and the demand for and the supply of labor. As a consequence, while Figure 15–9 only determines $O$ and P, the full classical system determines all of the following variables:

$O$ = real output
$P$ = price level
$N$ = employment
$W/P$ = real wage
$r$ = interest rate
$W$ = money wage
$Y$ = nominal output

To see how the classical model works, we again rely on the tool of comparative statics. We first consider an increase in the demand for output.

**Increase in the Demand for Output**

Suppose we begin from the situation illustrated in Figure 15–9, in which the aggregate demand curve is $D_0D_0$ and the aggregate supply curve is vertical at $O_e$. At the initial equilibrium the price level is $P_0$ and nominal income is $P_0 \times O_e$. Suppose now that, because of an autonomous increase in investment demand, the aggregate function shifts up from $D_0D_0$ to $D_1D_1$. That is, at any given level of output the community becomes willing to pay a higher price for that level of output. At the initially prevailing price level, $P_0$, we now have a situation of excess demand, which puts upward pressure on the price level. Since the supply of output is unresponsive to the rise of demand and prices, equilibrium will be reestablished only when the price level has risen to $P_1$, thus eliminating the excess demand.

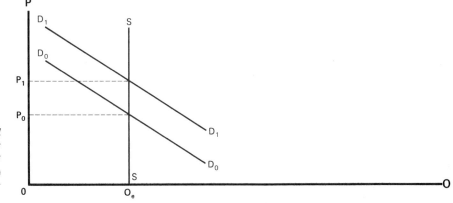

*Aggregate demand and supply: the classical case*

**FIGURE 15–9**

We may be sure that such a rise in demands for output and in the prices of output will be accompanied by increases in money wage rates. The rise of money wages will occur as employers, enjoying an increase in the prices of their output, bid against each other for labor. Indeed we know that in the new equilibrium money wages and prices will have risen exactly in proportion. This is because, with output unchanged at $O_e$, from Figure 15–8 we know that employment and the real wage must be unchanged. Since the real wage, $W/P$, is unchanged, $W$ and $P$ must increase proportionately.

The final variable of importance is the interest rate, $r$, and it is easy to see that $r$ must increase. Since real output is unchanged, saving, and therefore investment, must also be unchanged in the new equilibrium. But we began from the assumption that an upward shift in the investment demand function had caused the shift in the $DD$ function. It should be obvious, then, that with actual investment unchanged, the interest rate must rise to choke off this potential addition to investment. This point is illustrated in the $IS–LM$ diagram of Figure 15–10. The initial equilibrium is at the intersection of $I_0S_0$ and $L_0M_0$ or at $r = r_0$ and $O = O_e$. The shift of the investment demand function in turn shifts the $IS$ curve to $I_1S_1$. This creates excess demand, and the resulting upward movement in prices shifts the $LM$ curve up and to the left—recall that an increase of the price level is like a decrease of the money supply. As we know from Figure 15–9, a new equilibrium will be established only when the $LM$ curve has shifted to $L_1M_1$, which corresponds to a price level of $P_1$. When this happens, the level of output is maintained at $O_e$ but the equilibrium interest rate rises from $r_0$ to $r_1$.

In summary then, an upward shift in investment demand in the classical model increases the interest rate and raises wages and prices proportionately. It thus also raises nominal income. But it leaves unchanged real output, employment, and the real wage.

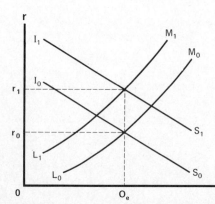

*An IS shift*

**FIGURE 15–10**

**Decrease in Demand for Output**

Let us turn now to the reverse case, in which the demand function for output shifts downward. We can again use figure 15–9 for this purpose, assuming that we start from a situation in which the demand function for output is $D_1D_1$, the rate of real output is at the capacity level $O_e$, and the price level is $P_1$. Suppose now that the demand function shifts downward because of a decline in the investment demand function. This is shown in Figure 15–9 as a shift of the $DD$ curve from $D_1D_1$ to $D_0D_0$. The initial equilibrium price level, $P_1$, is now one of disequilibrium. At this price level the amount of output demanded is below the full-employment level, $O_e$. With flexible prices and competitive markets, this will tend to lower prices. The fall of prices also lowers the marginal value product of labor, leading employers to decrease the quantity of labor demanded at the old level of money wage rates. Some unemployment will occur, at least initially. However, the unemployed will bid against each other for jobs, thereby lowering money wage rates. Such decreases of money wage rates lower money costs of production, including marginal costs, and with each decrease of their marginal costs, producers lower the prices of their output. Such declines of money wage rates and prices will continue so long as unemployment persists.

Is it inevitable that decreases in money wage rates and prices will again make it profitable for producers to employ the entire labor supply? A decrease of money wage rates has at least two types of effects. On the one hand, as we have already seen, it serves to lower costs of production. This appears favorable to an expansion of output and employment. On the other hand, it lowers the amount of money income received by labor for each hour of work. Thus, it is possible, at least in principle, that the favorable effects of reductions in money costs of production will be offset by reductions of money demands for output. The classical economists contended that this would not occur; the deflationary spiral of money wage rates and prices would be stopped and recovery of real output and employment would be induced by a phenomenon that has been called variously the *Pigou effect*, the *real-balance effect*, and the *real-wealth effect*. The real-wealth effect is based on two propositions:

1   Real demands for output depend not only on real income but also on real wealth. The latter is defined as (*money value of assets/* price level). In general, the greater the community's real wealth, the greater will be the level of its real consumption relative to its real income.

2   A fall of the price level raises the real wealth or purchasing power of the community's assets that are fixed in terms of monetary units. Members of the private sector, feeling richer in real terms because of the increased purchasing power of their debt claims against the government, increase their real demands for output,

thereby pushing output and employment back toward full-employment levels.

The net result of this process is the restoration of the equilibrium pictured in Figure 15–9 by the intersection of $D_0 D_0$ and SS. That is, the shift in investment demand yields proportionately lower levels of prices and money wage rates but leaves unchanged equilibrium levels of real output, employment, and real wages.

**Policy in the Classical Model**

In the classical model, as we have just seen, shifts of the aggregate demand curve ultimately produce no changes in the level of real output, employment, and the real wage rate. Since both monetary and fiscal policy operate by shifting the $DD$ curve, we know immediately that neither policy can affect any real magnitudes. While the operation of policy in the classical model is thus somewhat dull, it will nevertheless be instructive to sketch quickly the main points.

*Monetary Policy*

Consider a decrease in the money supply. This shifts the $LM$ curve to the left and creates excess demand in the money market. This tends to push up the interest rate, which in turn tends to reduce investment demand. As a consequence, excess supply is created in the commodity market and prices start falling. The fall in prices raises the real-money supply, moving the $LM$ curve back down toward its initial position. Equilibrium will be restored when the fall in prices exactly balances the decrease in the money supply. This is illustrated in Figure 15–11.

Thus, a decrease in the money supply leaves $O$, $N$, $r$, and $W/P$ unchanged and merely changes $W$ and $P$. Both $W$ and $P$, in fact, decrease *exactly in proportion* to the decrease in the money supply. This can be seen by examining the condition for equilibrium in the money market—equation (5)—which is reproduced below:

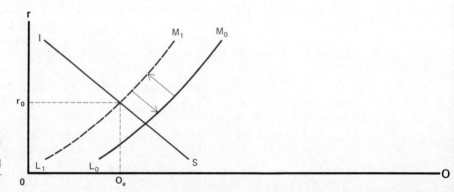

*An LM shift*

**FIGURE 15–11**

$$\frac{\overline{M}}{P} = F\,(O,\,r)$$

From this equation we see that a 5 percent reduction of $\overline{M}$, for example, which leaves $O$ and $r$ unchanged, must produce a 5 percent reduction of the price level, $P$, for this is the only way in which equilibrium in the money market can be maintained.

We thus see that in the classical model there is a complete dichotomy between the real economy and nominal or money values. The only effect of a change in the money supply is to change nominal values proportionately.

*Fiscal Policy*

Suppose we are dealing with a contractionary fiscal policy such as a reduction in government spending. The decline in $G$ creates an excess supply of goods and puts downward pressure on prices. As prices fall, the real money money supply increases, interest rates fall, and investment is stimulated. The details of this can, in fact, be traced with the help of Figures 15–9 and 15–10. In the new equilibrium $W$ and $P$ are lower but $O$, $N$, and $W/P$ remain unchanged. The interest rate, however, will decrease. This serves to stimulate investment in an amount exactly equal to the decline in government spending. Thus, fiscal policy does have an allocative effect: Resources are shifted from government spending to investment with a given level of total real output.

Overview    Having analyzed the operation of the classical model, we see that a fair characterization of the classical school is the following: "A free-enterprise economy contains within itself strong forces toward the achievement and maintenance of full employment. These forces serve to prevent departures from full employment, and any unemployment that may occur invokes automatic adjustments that restore full employment. Equilibrium at less than full employment is impossible."

It is worth emphasizing again the crucial role played in this model by the absence of money illusion and by the perfect downward flexibility of prices and money wage rates. It was the fall of prices that restored the community's real-money balances and raised real demand for output enough to absorb the full-employment supply of output. And the perfect downward flexibility of money wage rates served both to lower labor costs of production in money terms, thus rendering possible the required fall of prices, and to adjust real wage rates to the level necessary to restore full employment.

While the logic of the classical model is impeccable, its characterization of the economy has often seemed wide of the mark. This was certainly true during the 1930s, when many countries suffered extended periods of substantial unemployment. In the minds of many it is also true of the behavior of the U.S. economy in recent years. Those who are disaffected with the conclusions of the classical model have sought to reconcile economic theory and economic experience in two different ways. One way has been to accept the premises of the classical model but to argue that the process of adjustment to a downward shift in aggregate demand—what is sometimes called the *dynamics*—is such that the economy may experience difficulties in attaining a new equilibrium. Among the reasons that have been advanced in this regard are the following:

1   The real-wealth effect may be too weak to overcome unfavorable forces. Small declines of prices and wages are likely to generate only weak expansionary effects, and very large declines may generate depressing effects that outweigh their expansionary effects.

2   Price declines may generate price expectations that are unfavorable to recovery of demands for output. Effects will be unfavorable if each price decline creates expectations of still further price decreases in the future, because potential buyers will be encouraged to postpone their purchases. This applies especially to consumer's durable goods and to capital goods.

3   The process of price deflation decreases the net worth and creditworthiness of business firms and may discourage investment.

In summary, it may well be that even in an economy conforming to all the assumptions of the classical model, there would be no assurance that automatic forces would restore full employment reliably, quickly, and at minimum social cost. Under such circumstances prompt action by policy makers could well have desirable effects.

The second way in which economists have attempted to reconcile theory and experience has been to challenge the assumptions of the classical model. In particular, many writers have found that actual conditions in markets for labor and output depart significantly from those assumed in the classical model. We shall now examine some of these criticisms, as well as the consequences of departing from the classical model.

**DEPARTURES FROM THE CLASSICAL MODEL**

**Lack of Price Flexibility**

Among the assumptions of the classical model, those relating to the flexibility of prices and wages have received the most critical attention.

We have seen that one of the important facets of the classical model is the flexibility of prices, which, in turn, is related to the assumption that all output markets are purely competitive. If, on the other hand, we recognize various types and degrees of *imperfect competition*, we may find limitations on price flexibility. It is often argued, for example, that firms set prices with respect to longer-run or *normal standard* costs, rather than varying their prices in response to temporary shifts, either up or down, in costs. One rationale for this is that, as in commercial banking, there is often a "customer relationship" between firms and those who buy from them. In particular, customers prefer to avoid costly searching for the best price and firms have an incentive to maintain a degree of price stability to encourage customers to return.

As a consequence of this behavior, prices may not immediately or fully respond to shifts in aggregate demand. For example, in response to a decline in nominal aggregate demand, prices may decline only slowly. This is not to say that prices will remain inflexible in such situations, especially if the decline in demand is large and prolonged. Nevertheless, the description of the economy that emerges from this view is quite different from the classical one. In particular, for some considerable period of time much of the effect of a decline in aggregate demand may be translated into a decline in real output or employment. Similar departures from the classical model may occur in response to increases in aggregate demand.

While it would be possible to allow directly for limitations on price flexibility in the classical model, it is somewhat more standard to introduce such rigidities via wages. We shall follow this practice.

**Rigid Money Wages**
It will be remembered that the classical model assumed that the supply of labor was a function of real wages rather than money wage rates, and that wage rates were freely flexible both upward and downward. As one looks at labor markets in the United States and other industrialized countries, one is forced to conclude that these conditions are not always met. Money wage rates are often rigid, sometimes for long periods. For example, when unemployment appears or increases in amount, money wage rates do not fall, or they begin to fall only after a long delay.

The possibility that the money wage rate is rigid or "sticky," especially downward, was introduced by Keynes as an explanation for unemployment in the context of the classical model. Following this, we shall assume that once the money wage rate rises to an equilibrium level, it cannot fall from that level. This assumption is based on the presumption of institutional imperfections in the labor market. Obviously, it is not meant to imply any kind of permanent rigidity to the money wage. Rather, it is meant to suggest that the wage rigidity lasts sufficiently long to produce a substantial observable impact on the economy.

To see how this works, we must first examine the behavior of the labor market if we drop the classical assumption of wage flexibility and assume that money wages are rigid, at least during the period under consideration. We will continue to assume, however, that all markets for output are purely competitive and that firms attempt to maximize their profits. As a consequence, each firm hires labor up to the point where the marginal value product of labor is equal to its wage rate. The marginal value product of labor, $(MPL)\,P$, is the marginal product of labor $(MPL)$ *times* the price of the unit of output produced by this labor $(P)$. Thus, firms equate

$$W = (MPL)\,P \tag{7}$$

or, dividing both sides by $P$,

$$\frac{W}{P} = MPL \tag{8}$$

This gives precisely the kind of labor demand curve we used in Figure 15–8.

In part $(a)$ of Figure 15–12 we have reproduced from Figure 15–8 the demand and supply curves characterizing equilibrium in the labor market. A similar picture is shown in part $(b)$ of Figure 15–12, but the reader will note that we have relabeled the vertical axis so that it measures the nominal or money wage rate, $W$, rather than the real wage, $W/P$. This amounts, in the case of the demand for labor, to using equation (7), instead of (8), as the demand curve. As a consequence, the curves in $(b)$ now have a price level attached to them and will vary as the price level varies.

Suppose we begin from the initial equilibrium position indicated in Figure 15–12. That is, the price level is $P_1$, the money wage $W_1$, and the real wage is $W_1/P_1$. The amount of labor employed is $N_1$, which will produce some level of total output (not shown) $O_1$. Suppose now that for some reason, such as a collapse in investment demand or a reduction in the nominal money supply, the aggregate demand for output declines and the price level falls to $P_2$. In the classical model this would shift down both the demand and supply curves in part $(b)$—those in part $(a)$ are, of course, unchanged. The resulting curves—the dashed ones in the figure—intersect at the initial level of employment, $N_1$, indicating that in the absence of wage rigidity the classical result would hold. The money wage, however, is assumed to remain rigid at $W_1$. This means that relevant supply curve is not the dashed one shown in part $(b)$ but the horizontal line at the level $W_1$. The effect of this will be to lower the level of employment from $N_1$ to $N_2$ and to reduce the level of real output. The reason for this can be stated two ways. Stating it in real terms, we can say that the fall of the price level from $P_1$ to $P_2$, while the money wage rate remained rigid, increased the real wage from $W_1/P_1$ to $W_1/P_2$, which reduced the quantity of labor demanded. Or, stating it in money terms, we can say that the fall of prices shifted downward and to the left the $(MPL)P$ function, which is the demand function for labor. With the money wage rate rigid, less labor is demanded. Thus, the amount of labor employed can be read off either part of Figure 15–12. We are, of course, assuming that employers cannot be forced to hire more laborers than they desire. That is, the amount of labor actually utilized is the quantity, $N_2$, implied by the demand-for-labor function. Associated with this level of employment is some reduced level of output, $O_2$.

This entire process is perhaps best summarized by the aggregate demand and supply diagram in Figure 15–13. Initial equilibrium is at $P = P_1$ and $O = O_1$, where the demand curve $D_1D_1$ intersects the classical vertical supply curve $SS$. The decline in aggregate demand is shown as the downward shift of $D_1D_1$ to $D_2D_2$. In the classical model the new equilibrium would be at $P = P_3$ and $O = O_1$. That is, the level of real output

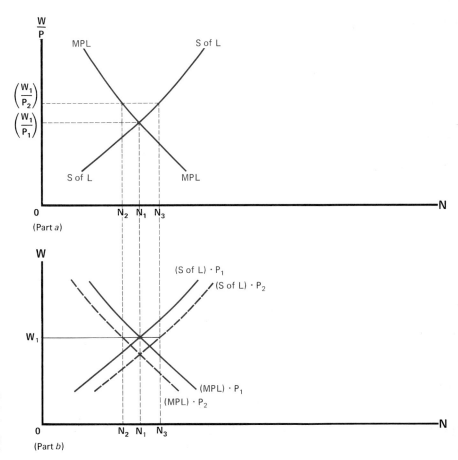

*Labor market equilibrium: the rigid wage case*

**FIGURE 15–12**

would be unchanged and the price level would decline. In contrast, in the case of a rigid money wage, as we have just seen, *both* output and prices would decline. Thus, we would move along a supply curve such as *ss* in Figure 15–13 to the new equilibrium $P = P_2$ and $O = O_2$. In other words, the effect of a rigid wage is to turn the vertical supply curve of the classical model into one that, below $P_1$, has an upward-sloping but less than vertical slope. On the other hand, if we assume that money wages are flexible in an upward direction, the classical model holds above $P_1$ and the relevant supply curve is again vertical above $P_1$.

Thus, the effects in the model with rigid wage rates differ markedly from those in the classical model. A shift of the aggregate demand function for output, stated in terms of money, can indeed change the level of employment and real output. Moreover, once a decline of output and employment has been induced by a decrease of the aggregate demand for output, there are in this model no forces that automatically tend to restore output and employment to their full-employment levels. The result is what Keynes called an **underemployment equilibrium.** That is, at the prevailing real wage, workers would like to supply more labor than firms wish to demand. This indicated in Figure 15–12, part (*a*), where the quantity of labor supplied is $N_3$ and that demanded is $N_2$. The difference between these quantities is an aggregate measure of what is sometimes called **involuntary unemployment.** One important features of this situation is that, unlike the classical model, the shape of the supply curve means that monetary and fiscal policy can have some effect on aggregate output. We shall explore this shortly, but we first consider one other aspect of the labor market.

**The Supply of Labor**     As we have just seen, the primary effect of introducing a rigid wage was to change the vertical character of the aggregate supply curve, thus making aggregate supply responsive to changes in aggregate demand

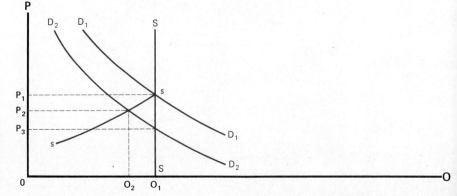

*Aggregate demand and supply: the rigid wage case*

**FIGURE 15–13**

and price. It is important to note that this can also be accomplished, without resort to a rigid wage, by relaxing the assumption that workers respond to the real wage in their labor supply decisions. In particular, if we assume that workers primarily respond to the money wage, the same kind of aggregate supply curve results. This is illustrated in Figure 15–14.

Initial equilibrium is at the intersection of the demand for labor, $(MPL) P_1$, and the supply of labor, $(S \text{ of } L)_1$, giving a volume of employment equal to $N_1$. For variety's sake, let us suppose that an outward shift in aggregate demand *increases* the price level from $P_1$ to $P_2$. At any given money wage rate, the demand for labor increases, and this is shown as a rightward shift from $(MPL) P_1$ to $(MPL) P_2$. What happens to employment depends on the precise assumption we make concerning the behavior of workers. If we assume that workers have an extreme version of *money illusion* and respond only to the money wage, then the supply of labor function remains at $(S \text{ of } L)_1$. In this case employment increases from $N_1$ to $N_2$.

But we need not assume extreme money illusion to get an expansion of employment. We can allow some response to the real wage as long as the labor supply curve shifts by less than would occur in the classical case. In the classical case, the higher price level ($P_2$ as opposed to $P_1$) makes workers supply less labor at any given money wage. This corresponds to a leftward shift of the labor supply function. In fact, in the classical case the supply curve must shift to $(S \text{ of } L)_3$ in Figure 15–14, which intersects the new labor demand curve at the original level of employment, $N_1$. Consequently, any smaller shift to the left will permit employment to expand. Thus, for example, the labor supply curve could shift from $(S \text{ of } L)_1$ to $(S \text{ of } L)_2$, as illustrated in Figure 15–14, and increase

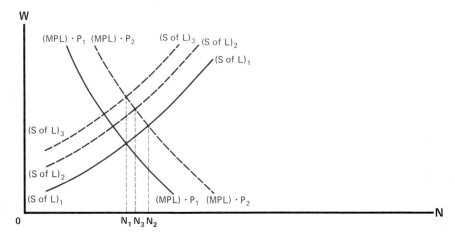

*Labor market equilibrium: the money wage case*

**FIGURE 15–14**

employment from $N_1$ to $N_3$. This would correspond to somewhat less money illusion than the first case considered.[3]

What we see is that relaxing the assumption that the supply of labor is a function of the real wage means that an increase of the price level yields more employment and consequently more output. Similarly, a decrease in the price level will be associated with both lower employment and output. Simply put, what this means is that the aggregate supply curve is once again not vertical, but rather has the upward-sloping shape seen before. This is pictured in Figure 15–15 (for the moment ignore the $DD$ curves), where we have drawn the aggregate supply curve so that it becomes vertical at high values of $P$. Loosely speaking, what this is meant to reflect is that for high $P$, workers shed their money illusion and behave more in accord with the assumptions of the classical model.

In summary then, we have now examined two alternative ways of departing from the classical model and its vertical aggregate supply curve. It is now time to explore the consequences of this for the operation of monetary and fiscal policy.

---

[3] The reader will note that we have omitted the multiplicative price label from the supply curves in Figure 15–14. This is because in the presence of money illusion it is not true that $S$ of $L = W/P$, so that one cannot simply multiply through by $P$. Of course, as is made clear in the text, even under money illusion the supply curve may shift with the price level. Thus, the supply curves in Figure 15–14 may depend on $P$, and this should be borne in mind, despite the simple way in which we have labeled the curves.

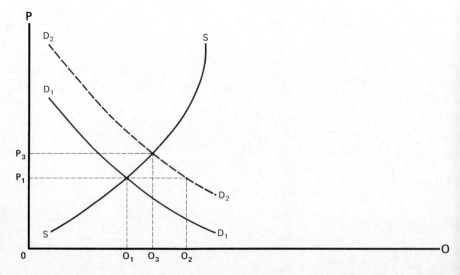

*Aggregate demand and supply: the money wage case*

**FIGURE 15–15**

POLICY IN THE
EXTENDED
MODEL

If actual conditions in the economy corresponded to those assumed in the classical model, it would not be wholly unreasonable to argue that monetary policies, fiscal policies, and other deliberate measures to control the behavior of aggregate money demands for output are of relatively little importance. Fluctuations of aggregate demands for output would change price levels and money wage rates but not employment and real output. The complete flexibility of wages and prices might be relied on to restore full employment. However, even under these conditions, measures to regulate aggregate money demands for output could improve the functioning of the economic system. For one thing, the required adjustments of prices and money wage rates could not be achieved instantaneously; they would require time. Monetary and fiscal policies might do the job faster.

The case for deliberate management of aggregate money demands for output becomes compelling in an economy with money wage rates that are rigid or adjust only after a long delay and then to only a limited extent, and with incompletely flexible prices. In such an economy fluctuations of aggregate money demands for output affect not only prices and money wage rates but also employment and output. In addition, it cannot be expected that a departure from full employment will be corrected automatically, quickly, and effectively by quick and complete flexibility of prices and money wage rates.

In such an economy monetary, fiscal, and other policies that regulate aggregate money demand for output can indeed be used to regulate total employment and output. For example, an increase of aggregate demand can increase total employment and output if the economy is operating below capacity levels. As a part of the process of adjustment, it can adjust real wage rates to equilibrium levels; to the extent that money wage rates are rigid, real wages can be lowered by increases of demand that raise prices.

While there are no essential differences between the effects of policy in the rigid wage and money illusion cases, to make matters concrete let us focus on the case in which the supply of labor is only a function of the money wage. In particular, let us assume that we start from the position of equilibrium indicated in Figure 15–15, where $P = P_1$ and $O = O_1$. We next assume that the policy authorities are unhappy with the level of employment and output at the initial position and wish to increase both of these. As before, we shall examine separately fiscal and monetary policies aimed at bringing about the desired expansion.

Fiscal
Policy

Suppose that the fiscal authorities attempt to bring about the expansion by increasing real government purchases of goods and services, $G/P$. The immediate effect of this, shown in Figure 15–16, is to shift the *IS* curve from $I_1S_1$ to $I_2S_2$. This is because the increase in $G/P$ increases GNP both directly and indirectly through the multiplier process on consumption. At the initial price level this increase in output raises the demand for money, putting upward pressure on the interest rate. Thus, with the price level at $P_1$, we see in Figure 15–16 that equilibrium on the demand side moves us to $r = r_2$ and $O = O_2$. But of course the price level cannot remain unchanged, since at $P_1$ the supply of output is $O_1$ but the demand is greater ($O_2$). Hence, prices start to rise.

This has two effects, one illustrated in Figure 15–16 and the other in Figure 15–17. In the first instance, the rise in $P$ reduces the real supply of money, shifting the $LM$ curve back to the left toward $L_2M_2$. This raises interest rates further, tending to reduce investment and hence total aggregate demand. On the aggregate supply side, the increasing price level raises the demand for labor, shifting the demand curve in Figure 15–17 up toward $(MPL)\,P_3$. By assumption of the strict money wage case, the supply curve for labor remains unchanged.

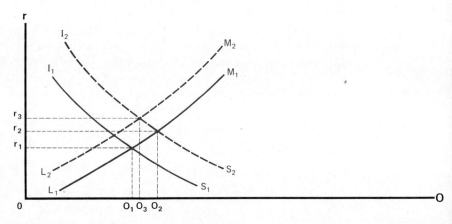

*A fiscal policy shift*

**FIGURE 15–16**

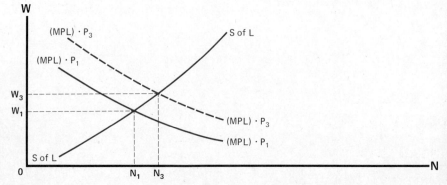

*Effects of a policy shift on the labor market*

**FIGURE 15–17**

The rise in prices continues until the excess demand has been eliminated — at $P = P_3$ and $O = O_3$ in Figure 15–15. At this price level the IS and LM curves intersect at $O_3$ and the labor demand and supply curves intersect at $N_3$, the amount of employment it takes to produce $O_3$. In short, we have equilibrium in all markets.

We thus see that fiscal policy is quite capable of bringing about an expansion of employment and real output in the present case. As for the other variables, we see that $r$ increases and both $W$ and $P$ increase as well. We do know, however, that the real wage must fall if firms are to be induced to hire the additional labor.

**Monetary Policy**    The same expansion of output and employment can also be brought about by an increase in the nominal supply of money. As we have seen before, however, the composition of output will differ from that obtained by fiscal policy. The detailed effects of a money supply increase on the IS–LM curves are shown in Figure 15–18. As far as the aggregate picture is concerned, Figure 15–15 will again suffice, with the understanding that the DD shift now originates with the monetary authorities. Similarly, Figure 15–17 can again be used in the present case.[4]

The increase in the money supply shifts the LM curve to the right from $L_1M_1$ to $L_2M_2$ in Figure 15–18. This puts downward pressure on the interest rate, which in turn stimulates investment. This tends to increase GNP and thus increase the quantity of money demanded. As a consequence, the interest rate does not fall as far as it would if output

---

[4] In using Figures 15–15 and 15–17 for both monetary and fiscal policies, we are implicitly assuming that the magnitude of each policy is chosen so as to produce the same level of real output and, hence, employment.

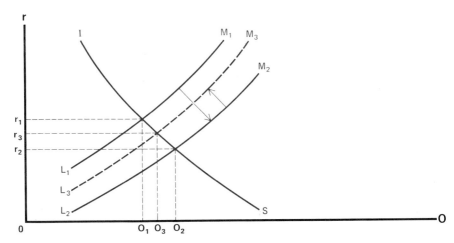

*A monetary policy shift*

**FIGURE 15–18**

remained unchanged. With the price level fixed at $P_1$, equilibrium on the demand side occurs at $r = r_2$ and $O = O_2$. But once again, this is a situation of excess demand, and the price level begins rising, setting up the same kinds of adjustments in labor, commodity, and money markets described for fiscal policy.

New equilibrium again occurs at $P = P_3$ and $O = O_3$, where the LM curve has moved part of the way back toward the original curve, $L_1M_1$. We thus see that the major difference between fiscal and monetary policies in the present case is that $r$ falls with expansionary monetary policy and rises with fiscal policy. Clearly, then, investment will be a greater fraction of GNP in the case of monetary expansion.

INFLATION
At the start of the 1980s, *inflation*, the increase in the general price level over time, was solidly entrenched as public enemy number one. While we shall examine the attempts of policy makers to "do something" about inflation in a later chapter, for the present we can put our model of aggregate demand and supply to good use and shed some light on the nature of inflation. We begin with the oldest and simplest explanation of inflation.

Money and
Inflation
The classical explanation of inflation is accurately described by the phrase "too much money chasing too few goods." This diagnosis naturally suggests the appropriate medicine to cure inflation, namely, bringing the rate of money creation under strict control.

The accuracy of this diagnosis and the curative nature of the medicine have been illustrated most vividly during periods of runaway inflation, which are known as *hyperinflation*. One case of this disease was exhibited by Germany after World War I. Prices increased about 80 percent in 1920, over 140 percent in 1921, and an astronomical 4100 percent in 1922. If this was not impressive enough, it was at this point that things got wildly out of hand—prices rose by over 100 million percent from December 1922 to November 1923. But even this was dwarfed by the greatest of all hyperinflations, which was experienced by Hungary in 1945–1946. For a period of one year, the rate of inflation averaged about 20,000 percent *per month*, while in the final month the price level advanced by an unbelievable 42 *quadrillion* percent. Overall, in the space of 13 months the price level rose more than one *octillion* times ($5.2 \times 10^{27}$).

Now comes the punch line. In each of these episodes the inflation was fueled by new injections of money in larger and larger amounts. Thus, for example, during the Hungarian hyperinflation the outstanding stock of money also rose by more than one octillion times ($3.8 \times 10^{27}$), closely matching the increase in prices. Furthermore, it was only when the monetary brakes were slammed on that the hyperinflation came to end. At least in such pathological episodes, the relation between money and inflation is all too painfully clear.

Hyperinflation, of course, is relatively rare. Most of our bouts of inflation are considerably more tranquil and indeed are sometimes given the benign-sounding label *creeping inflation* Is excessive money creation the cause of creeping inflation as well? Here the answer is considerably less clear-cut, and many economists deny that there is a mechanical one-to-one connection between money and prices, at least in the short run. To see what is involved, it will be helpful to turn to a demand–supply analysis of inflation.

**Demand–Supply Interpretation**

Up to this point we have used the framework of aggregate demand and aggregate supply to analyze the determination of aggregate real output and the price level. Since inflation is simply an increase in the price level, we can use the same framework to shed some light on the nature of inflation. We start from the observation that in a healthy, growing economy there will normally be systematic outward shifts in the aggregate demand and supply curves. Increases in population, for example, tend to expand aggregate demand. At the same time, by contributing to a larger labor force, such increases can also shift the aggregate supply curve outward. Outward shifts in aggregate supply can also come about as an economy adds to the stock of physical capital or accumulates advances in technical knowledge. Ideally, of course, shifts in demand and supply would be "balanced" so as to produce a growth in real output with little or no increase in the price level.

Such a situation is portrayed in Figure 15–19, where the economy's demand curve for various years shifts to the right at the same rate as the supply curve. As a result, real output increases each year but the price

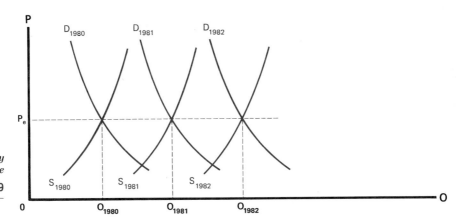

*Demand–supply shifts over time*

**FIGURE 15–19**

level remains at $P_e$. Unfortunately, as the reader is well aware, the idyllic pattern eshibited in Figure 15–19 has only infrequently been realized. One way in which historical experience has departed from this pattern is that the aggregate demand curve has often shifted outward too rapidly, thus putting upward pressure on prices. This case is illustrated most simply if we assume that we are dealing with a short period in which the supply curve is fixed and the demand curve shifts outward.

### Demand Inflation

Suppose, as in Figure 15–20, the economy starts at some initial price level, $P_1$, and level of real output, $O_1$, where $(P_1, O_1)$ lies at the intersection of the aggregate demand and supply curves, $D_1D_1$ and $SS$, respectively. Now assume that the aggregate demand curve shifts out to $D_2D_2$. Such a shift could come about from a variety of factors, such as a war-induced expansion of government spending or an outward shift in the consumption or investment functions of the private sector. Whatever the source, as Figure 15–20 indicates, the shift of the aggregate demand curve serves to raise both the level of real output (from $O_1$ to $O_2$) and the price level (from $P_1$ to $P_2$). This then provides an example of what is called *demand pull* inflation, that is, a situation in which a shift of the demand curve "pulls up" the price level and leads to inflation. The actual amount of inflation will, of course, depend both on how far the demand curve shifts and on the shape of the supply curve. If the supply curve is steep, as it is likely to be at close to full employment, there will be a larger increase in prices and a smaller response in real output than if the supply curve were less steep.

Conventional stabilization policy is well equipped to fight a demand pull inflation. In particular, through restrictive monetary or fiscal actions policy makers can offset any outward shift in the aggregate demand curve. In Figure 15–20, for example, restrictive policy would be used to

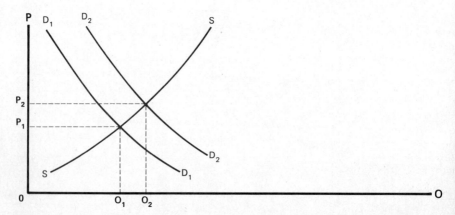

*Demand pull inflation*

**FIGURE 15–20**

reshift the demand curve from $D_2D_2$ back to $D_1D_1$. This would curb the inflationary pressures and prevent the rise in the price level. At the same time, however, this would choke off the possible increase in real output. How one regards this policy depends on the state of the economy. If the economy were already operating at its full employment or potential level of output, then any increase in real output would likely be temporary, In such circumstances policy makers need not seriously worry about retarding the increase in output.

Things are not so nice, however, if the economy is operating below full employment. Such a situation is portrayed in Figure 15–21. The economy is initially in short-run equilibrium at point $E$, which lies at the intersection of the initial aggregate demand curve, $D_1D_1$, and the short-run supply curve, $ss$. The level of real output at $E$ is $O_1$, which is clearly less than the full-employment level, $O_F$. A shift in the aggregate demand curve from $D_1D_1$ to $D_2D_2$ would tend to move the economy to point $A$, raising both prices and output and thereby decreasing unemployment. A policy response that shifted the economy back to point $E$ would thus prevent the economy from moving closer to full employment. At least in this sense, there is clearly a short-run trade-off between inflation and unemployment. Of course, in the long run, as the self-correcting mechanism emphasized by the classical economists came into play, the economy could reestablish equilibrium at a point like $B$ or $C$ on the long-run supply curve, $SS$. However, if this self-correcting mechanism were to take a substantial amount of time and, correspondingly, involve a significantly long spell of unemployment, policy makers might welcome a rightward shift of the aggregate demand curve to $D_2D_2$. Indeed, one could well imagine, if such a shift did not arise in the natural course of things, that policy makers might well think about engineering such a

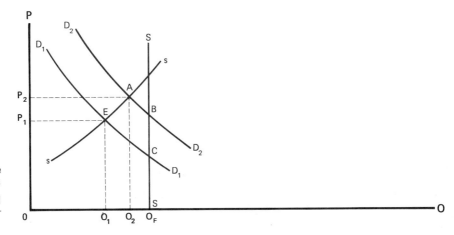

*policy trade-offs with
demand pull inflation*

**FIGURE 15–21**

shift, accepting a bit more inflation as the cost of driving down the unemployment rate more quickly. We shall come back to the issue of such trade-offs in a subsequent chapter.

*Supply Inflation*

While shifts in aggregate demand can create inflation, inflation may arise even with a fixed demand curve. For this to come about, it is necessary that the aggregate supply curve shift upward and to the left, as shown in Figure 15–22. Since we have suggested that, under "normal" conditions, over time the supply curve shifts down and to the right (see Figure 15–19), how can such a perverse shift come about? Unfortunately, as history has revealed, there are far too many ways. Basically, any development that restricts supply or autonomously pushes up prices will cause an upward shift in aggregate supply. Real-world events that have produced such shifts include crop failures, autonomous oil price increases imposed by OPEC, and declines in productivity.

The effects of a perverse supply shift are readily illustrated in Figure 15–22. As the supply curve shifts from $S_1S_1$ to $S_2S_2$, prices clearly increase—that is sometimes called *cost push* inflation, but unlike the case of demand pull pictured in Figure 15–20, real output *declines* (from $O_1$ to $O_2$). This unhappy constellation of events—rising prices and falling output—is often dubbed *stagflation* (from stagnation and inflation).

Cost push or supply inflation presents policy makers with a singularly unpleasant dilemma. As we have seen, both fiscal and monetary policy work through shifts of the aggregate demand curve. But as should be apparent from Figure 15–22, aggregate demand management cannot really solve the problem. This is perhaps illustrated more clearly in Fig-

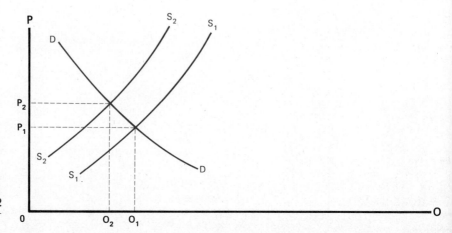

*Cost push inflation*

**FIGURE 15–22**

ure 15–23, where the initial equilibrium is at point $E$. As in Figure 15–22, the supply curve is assumed to shift from $S_1S_1$ to $S_2S_2$. A "do-nothing" policy, which leaves the aggregate demand curve alone, will yield an equilibrium at point $A$, with higher prices and lower output. The decline in output and the rise in unemployment could be prevented by an expansionary policy that shifted out the demand curve to $d_ud_u$ so as to establish point $B$ as an equilibrium. This keeps output at its original level ($O_1$), but unhappily, this policy creates even more inflation than experienced at point $A$ ($P_3$ vs. $P_2$). Alternatively, policy makers could decide to fight inflation. For example, a restrictive policy that shifted the demand curve down to $d_pd_p$ would yield point $C$. This restores the initial price level ($P_1$), but reduces output even further (to $O_3$) and creates additional unemployment. There is, thus, a trade-off of sorts, but not a very appealing one. In view of this discussion it should hardly be surprising that cost push inflation has proved to be a most frustrating problem for policy makers. Unhappily, as we shall see when we review recent economic events below, the jury is still out on the proper policy for combating supply inflation.

**Money Again**   Milton Friedman has written that "inflation is always and everywhere a monetary phenomenon." All economists agree with this statement as applied to periods of hyperinflation, and nearly all would agree that long, extended bouts of inflation have a monetary source. For shorter periods, however, the connection between money and prices is viewed by many economists as considerably looser. For example, from the end of 1930 to the end of 1940 the money supply grew by 70 percent, but prices, rather than rising, fell 15 percent. From 1953 to 1973 the

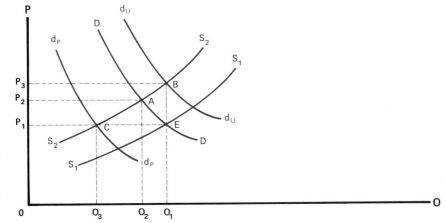

*he dismal trade-offs with cost push inflation*

**FIGURE 15–23**

increases in the money supply and prices were 110 percent and 80 percent, respectively. Thus, over this period the increase in the money supply was substantially more than the increase in the price level. Finally, in our most recent experience the money supply advanced 40 percent from 1973 to 1979, while prices, reflecting a variety of cost push influences, rose substantially more—56 percent. To many, this experience suggests that inflation is considerably more complex than a simple "monetary phenomenon." Unfortunately, as our previous discussion suggests, there is as yet no widespread agreement on the exact nature of the inflationary process. The problems this creates will become apparent as we turn to a closer examination of the policy process in the next part of the book.

CONCLUSION   This chapter has completed the model begun several chapters ago. In particular, by adding a production and labor sector we were able to use the expanded model to determine equilibrium levels of output, employment, and interest rate, the price level, and the money wage rate. One particular way of doing this—the so-called classical case—led to a model in which there was a vertical aggregate supply curve. This meant that equilibrium output was determined independently of demand factors and, consequently, that monetary and fiscal policy were unable to alter equilibrium employment and output.

We subsequently argued, however, that for purposes of short-run analysis a number of the assumptions of the classical model were too restrictive. We then saw how relaxing one of these assumptions—either by introducing the notion of a downwardly rigid money wage or by allowing for money illusion in labor supply—moved us away from a vertical aggregate supply curve. As a consequence, monetary and fiscal policy was once again capable of altering equilibrium output and employment. Indeed, the working of policy in this modified model was seen to be quite similar to its operation in the *IS–LM* framework with a fixed price level. The primary difference in the present case is that expansionary policy, by increasing $P$, yields a somewhat smaller increase in real output than would occur with a fixed $P$.

We also utilized the framework of aggregate demand and supply to examine briefly the nature of demand pull and cost push inflation. Cost push inflation was found to be particularly nasty, since it tended to result in a poor performance on both the inflation and unemployment fronts—a performance denoted by the sinister-sounding term *stagflation*.

One theme that ran throughout this chapter is that policy makers, through the use of fiscal and monetary tools, are capable of influencing the levels of output, employment, and prices. To say this, however, is not to suggest that policy makers can necessarily achieve optimum behavior of output, employment, and prices. For one thing, as we have seen, policy makers may be faced with trade-offs between price and output performance. Also of considerable importance is that, for many practical, technical, and political reasons, the job of the policy maker is not as simple as we have thus far made it out to be. Therefore, in the following chapters we shall examine the policy process in considerable detail.

**SELECTED READINGS**

Branson, W. H., *Macroeconomic Theory and Policy*, 2nd ed., New York, Harper & Row, 1979.

Dornbusch, R., and S. Fischer, *Macroeconomics*, New York, McGraw-Hill, 1978.

Gordon, R. J., *Macroeconomics*, Boston, Little, Brown, 1978.

# V MONETARY POLICY IN THEORY AND PRACTICE

In previous chapters we provided a framework for analyzing the effects of monetary and fiscal policy on aggregate variables such as output, employment, and prices. However, in order to keep the discussion manageable we omitted a number of the complexities of the policy process. Furthermore, except for selected instances, we have yet to examine the actual record of policy making in any detail. In this and succeeding chapters we attempt to fill this gap. In this chapter we analyze some general issues in policy making. In subsequent chapters we take a closer look at the evolution of financial intermediaries and their growing similarities. We also examine the consequences of this evolution for the regulation of financial institutions and the conduct of monetary policy. The final chapters of this part review the historical record of monetary policy in the United States.

More specifically, in the present chapter we consider the following sorts of questions: What goals do policy makers pursue, and are they all attainable? What complications are presented by imperfect knowledge and the explicit allowance for lags in the policy process? What prescriptions for policy makers emerge from the monetarist view, and are these plausible? We begin our discussion by considering the goals of economic policy.

## GOALS OF POLICY

In a general way we are all familiar with the goals of macroeconomic policy. Simply put, the primary objective of policy is to avoid the economic ills that have often beset us — namely, inflation, unemployment, lackluster economic growth, and difficulties with our international payments.

Stated more positively, these goals would be price stability, high or "full" employment, satisfactory economic growth, and equilibrium in our balance of payments. While there is now fairly widespread agreement about the desirability of these policy goals, at least in the abstract, this has not always been the case. For example, as previously discussed, in its early years the Federal Reserve had an extremely limited scope. In particular, it was largely concerned with providing an elastic currency, with avoiding bank crises and financial panics, and with the maintenance of a smoothly functioning gold standard. It was only after the experience of the 1930s that policy, both monetary and fiscal, became increasingly sensitive to the overall quality of our economic performance. This concern, coupled with the growth of our economic understanding as to what policy could accomplish, gradually led to a more activist approach to policy. This was partially reflected in the reorganization of the Federal Reserve in the mid-1930s, but it was not until the passage of the Employment Act of 1946 that the responsibility of government policy for the quality of economic performance was formalized.

**Some Specific Goals**    The Employment Act declared "that it is the continuing policy and responsibility of the Federal Government to use all practicable means . . . to promote maximum employment, production, and purchasing power." While in many ways this was an immense step, the act left many questions unanswered. For example, it did not distinguish between the roles of monetary and fiscal policy in carrying out the stated objectives. As a consequence, it did not offer any mechanism to achieve coordination between the monetary and fiscal authorities. Furthermore, despite the explicit statement of responsibility, the act did not provide an unambiguous set of goals. In particular, it left vague the notions of "maximum employment" and "maximum purchasing power" and certainly did not provide any specific numerical targets for unemployment or inflation. This vagueness is, perhaps, understandable. The reasons for this will be more apparent if we briefly consider some of the ambiguities in making these goals more precise.

*Full Employment*
    Taken by itself, economists generally agree that a high rate of unemployment is an undesirable state of affairs. But what is a reasonable goal for the unemployment rate? While an idealist might argue that the only acceptable level is zero unemployment, this is somewhat implausible. At the very least, "full" employment is consistent with some *frictional* unemployment as potential workers (either those who have left their jobs or new entrants into the labor force) search for employment. Furthermore, some economists argue that we must accept a certain amount of *structural* unemployment, at least in the short run, since individuals without jobs may not have the skills needed by employers. But

whether these considerations translate into an unemployment rate goal of 3 percent, 4 percent, 5 percent, or some other number is certainly unclear. Not surprisingly, there has been considerable dispute, among both economists and policy makers, as to what our unemployment goal should be.

*Price Stability*

By and large, the problem of price stability, at least in the post-World War II era, has been the problem of avoiding inflation. Unlike the case of unemployment, it is perhaps less clear who is hurt by inflation. Nevertheless, there are costs of inflation, especially if it is **unanticipated**. For one thing, unanticipated inflation can redistribute income among individuals and groups in the economy. While gainers and losers may somewhat balance out in the aggregate, this redistribution can be an arbitrary and capricious thing. A second problem is created by the fact that unanticipated inflation adds a considerable degree of uncertainty to decision making and may have depressing effects on the willingness of individuals and firms to save and invest. Furthermore, unanticipated inflation erodes the usefulness of many institutional features of the economy, and consequently, individuals devote additional resources to protecting themselves against inflation—resources that could be put to better use elsewhere. Consider, for example, the institutional arrangements in which workers enter multiyear labor contracts that call for payment every two weeks. Such arrangements become less useful in an inflationary environment and tend to be eroded. An extreme case of this occurs during hyperinflations, when individuals may be paid several times a day at wage rates that must be renegotiated almost continuously. Indeed, under such extreme conditions individuals often resort to barter, with all its attendant inefficiencies. While unanticipated inflation of a mild sort does not involve such extreme costs, even in a mildly inflationary environment individuals may become less willing to enter into long-term contracts, and the need for more frequent negotiations can waste resources.

It should be evident, then, that unanticipated inflation entails some very real costs. Many of these costs would not be present if the inflation were of the fully anticipated variety. This is so because a fully anticipated inflation, which entails no surprises, could be much more readily accounted for in individual and firm decision making.[1] While this may

---

[1] Even a fully anticipated inflation may entail some costs, especially if the economic system is not "neutral" with respect to inflation. Examples of nonneutralities include the progressive income tax rate structure, whereby inflation pushes taxpayers into a higher tax bracket even without an increase in real income. In addition, inflation leads individuals to use resources economizing on cash balances as a result of the prohibition of interest on demand deposits.

suggest that we could learn to live with, say, a steady 10 percent inflation rate, the historical record indicates that steady inflation is difficult to achieve at anything other than low rates of inflation. As a consequence, many would argue that, in principle at least, we should strive for zero inflation. But there are some practical problems with this. First, there are at least three prominent price indexes—the consumer price index, the

---

## INFLATION AND INTEREST RATES: NOMINAL VS. REAL RATES

The text suggests that, unlike unanticipated inflation, inflation of the fully anticipated variety could be accounted for in individual and business decision making. One way in which this comes about is through adjustments of interest rates in response to inflation. To see how this works, let us consider a simple example.

Suppose Mr. Consumer wants to borrow $1,000 from Ms. Lender and both agree that, in the absence of inflation, a fair rate of interest would be 3 percent on a one-year loan. Thus, for the right to $1,000 currently, Mr. Consumer will pay $1,030 one year hence. In the absence of inflation, when received this sum will provide Ms. Lender with a 3 percent increase in the purchasing power of her funds.

Now assume that, instead of zero inflation, both parties expect prices to increase by 7 percent over the course of the year. While Mr. Consumer would be delighted to still borrow money at 3 percent, Ms. Lender is likely to be rather disenchanted with this prospect. As she reasons, the $1,030 she would get back on the deal actually represents a loss of purchasing power of about 4 percent (the 3 percent she receives less the 7 percent loss of purchasing power due to inflation).

The jargon used to describe this situation is that the *nominal rate of interest* is 3 percent whereas the *real rate of interest* is negative 4 percent. The difference between the two rates is the 7 percent *anticipated* or *expected rate of inflation.* That is, the nominal rate equals the real rate plus the anticipated rate of inflation.

Of course, in the present example Ms. Lender is hardly going to be willing to make the loan at a nominal interest rate of 3 percent. What is likely to happen, if the market for loans is a competitive one, is that the market nominal interest rate will rise to 10 percent. This will restore the real rate of interest to 3 percent and neither partly will be made better or worse off than it was originally.

What this suggests is that nominal interest rates tend to reflect fully anticipated inflation. Of course, if the actual realized inflation rate deviates from the anticipated inflation rate, then one party will be made better off and the other worse off. It is in this sense that unanticipated inflation may induce capricious redistribution of income—an effect that is absent when inflation is fully anticipated.

wholesale price index, and the GNP deflator—and these do not always tell the same story. Second, it has been argued that all of the price indexes suffer from an upward bias because they do not properly reflect quality improvements. These considerations might lead to a goal for inflation of 1 or 2 percent per year. However, we clearly have done nowhere near this well in recent years. As we shall see, the problem of price stability is not in setting a goal but in achieving that goal.

*Other Goals*

In addition to high employment and price stability, we can briefly identify a number of other goals. One is economic growth, which is typically measured by the rate of increase of real GNP. As a goal for economic growth, policy makers tend to think in terms of sustainable rate of growth—that is, one that allows demand to grow at the same rate that the capacity of the economy is expanding. Precisely what rate this is has been the subject of dispute, and this has been complicated by the fact that the rate of growth of capacity may itself be influenced by policy.

Several other goals stem from international considerations. One of these is the maintenance of equilibrium in our balance of payments. This is complicated by the difficulty of making precise the notion of equilibrium that results, in part, from the many definitions of the balance of payments. Another related goal is the one of exchange rate stability, which often requires the intervention of policy makers in the foreign exchange market.

A final set of goals, largely pursued by the Federal Reserve, concern financial markets. Among these are the prevention of financial panics, the facilitation of sales of government securities, the maintenance of orderly financial markets, and the promotion of a sound banking system. While some of these might be regarded as a *means* to achieve the previous goals, at least at some times these considerations appear to be independent goals.

**Compatibility of Goals**

The existence of multiple goals immediately gives rise to the question of whether these objectives are compatible. To desire price stability, full employment, satisfactory economic growth, and balance-of-payments equilibrium is one thing, but to achieve them simultaneously is another. Indeed, there are many ways in which these various goals come into conflict. For example, economic growth and full employment, which tend to be complementary, may not be compatible with either balance-of-payments considerations or price stability. Rapid economic growth, for instance, tends to increase our imports and worsen the balance of payments. Similarly, a monetary policy designed to bring us out of a recession is likely to be associated with lower interest rates. But as a result, foreigners may reduce their holdings of U.S. assets. The consequent outflow of capital could lead to a deterioration in our balance of payments.

However, by far the most important conflict of goals concerns the reconciliation of price stability and full employment. As we saw in the previous chapter, attempts to achieve, simultaneously, low levels of unemployment and a high degree of price stability by regulating aggregate demand for output present serious policy problems. A higher rate of increase of aggregate demand to promote output and employment brings a higher rate of increase of money wages and prices, while a lower rate of increase of aggregate demand to promote price stability has its cost in terms of a lower rate of increase of employment and real output.

Unhappiness about such trade-offs has led to widespread interest in measures to improve behavior patterns in labor and output markets. In particular, many economists now believe that control of aggregate demand needs to be supplemented by measures aimed at improving the supply function of output—measures that will increase the extent to which a given increase of demand will increase real output rather than prices. Various measures for this purpose have been proposed. One such program aims at improving the mobility of labor by means of improved employment exchanges and more widely disseminated information about employment opportunities, assistance in moving to areas where employment opportunities exist, job training and retraining, elimination of racial discrimination in employment, lowering of barriers to entry, and so on. Among the objectives of this program are to open "labor bottlenecks," to lessen the extent to which unemployment and excess demand for labor can coexist, and to lower the rate of wage increases while considerable amounts of unemployment persist.[2]

Although, over time, these programs may well contribute to improving the trade-offs between price stability and full employment, the fact remains that in the short run the monetary and fiscal authorities are faced with the problem of reconciling these conflicting objectives. One way of going about this would be to assign weights to the various objectives so that we could rank alternative combinations of unemployment and inflation. This would be akin to defining a *national utility function*, with price stability and full employment as the "goods." While there is some indirect evidence that policy makers may do this implicitly, they are naturally reluctant to make explicit their priorities and value judgments. As

---

[2] Other measures are aimed at compelling or persuading those in labor and output markets to use their monopoly power more responsibly. These measures have been given various names, such as *wage-price guidelines* in the United States and *incomes policy* in Great Britain. To date at least, such policies have had questionable success. The reasons for this will be discussed in a subsequent chapter.

a result, outsiders have been forced to infer these priorities from the observable actions of the policy makers. And many have not liked what they have found. As a consequence, there has been much criticism of the policy makers in regard to their perceived choices of relative priorities.

It is not fully clear what the answer to this dilemma is. As long as there are conflicts among objectives, some hard choices will have to be made. To do so intelligently requires that we increase our understanding of the costs and benefits of inflation and unemployment. It may also require that we make such choices openly and explicitly, and perhaps in a more democratic way. However, this is easier said than done, especially in view of the independence of the Federal Reserve.

**Recent Developments**

For over 30 years the Employment Act of 1946 was the major statement of goals and obligations of economic policy. However, as noted previously, the Act was vague in several respects. For one thing, it did not spell out the precise role of monetary and fiscal policy in achieving the various economic goals. For another, although some would say this was wise, it omitted specific numerical targets for unemployment and inflation. These perceived shortcomings eventually led to the Full Employment and Balanced Growth Act of 1978 (the so-called Humphrey-Hawkins bill). This Act generally amplified and extended the goals of the earlier Employment Act. Indeed, the 1978 Act contained a litany of economic goals, including the following: full employment, reasonable price stability, more capital formation, a balanced budget, reduced government spending, an improved trade balance, freer international trade, and a sound and stable international monetary system. In addition to this shopping list, the 1978 Act spelled out the following procedural reforms.

1   The administration must set annual numerical goals over five years for key indicators such as employment, unemployment, real income, productivity, and prices. Furthermore, the administration must present to Congress fiscal policies that are consistent with these goals.

2   The Federal Reserve is required to report to Congress twice a year on its objectives and plans for monetary policy and to comment on the plans of the Administration.

3   The Act stipulates that the 1983 goal for the unemployment rate shall be 4 percent for workers over the age of 16 and 3 percent for workers over 20 years of age. On the price front, the goal for 1983 was specified as a 3 percent rate of inflation in the consumer price index. Beginning in 1980 the President was permitted to change the timetable for reaching these specific numerical goals, but not without indicating when they would be achieved. In fact, in the 1980 *Economic Report of the President* the unemployment and inflation goals were delayed until 1985 and 1988, respectively.

Taken as a whole, the 1978 Act may well improve the level of economic discussion among Congress and other policy makers. Nevertheless, despite the list of objectives, the bill itself provided little in the way of real means to achieve or reconcile these objectives. Indeed, some have suggested that the specification of unrealistic numerical goals may turn out to be counterproductive. For the time being at least, the jury is still out on whether the 1978 Act will lead to an actual improvement in the performance of the U.S. economy.

**Overview**

Despite general agreement on the desirability of full employment and price stability, the choice of specific goals is not a simple matter. Furthermore, goals that are incompatible need to be reconciled. As a practical matter, the process by which this happens is certainly a murky one. It is, therefore, hardly surprising that policy makers have been criticized for either (1) a poor choice of goals or (2) having a socially undesirable set of priorities. But if—and this is a big if—policy makers are consistent and intelligent in the pursuit of their chosen goals, they at least deserve our sympathy for the problems they face. Put another way, except insofar as there are policies that can be pursued to improve the trade-offs, policy makers cannot be faulted for economic problems that result simply because there are trade-offs. This suggests that we need to move beyond the issue of goals. In particular, we shall assume that the choice of goals and the reconciliation of conflicts have been accomplished, and we shall now examine some further details of the policy process.

**LAGS IN THE OPERATION OF POLICY**

Our earlier discussion of monetary and fiscal policy was essentially static, or timeless, in character. Specifically, we relied on comparative statics to contrast the nature of equilibrium prevailing before and after some policy change. As a consequence, we disregarded the entire set of questions concerning the timing of policy. In other words, we have made it appear that policy makers could diagnose the state of the economy, prescribe and administer the appropriate medicine, and cure the patient all in an instant. In the real world, however, each of these steps takes time.

**Alternative Types of Lags**

It is convenient to decompose the total lag between the need for policy and the final effect of policy into three parts.

The first, the *recognition lag*, refers to the elapsed time between the actual need for a policy action (such as the onset of a recession) and the realization that such a need has occurred. In terms of our medical analogy, the recognition lag thus corresponds to the time it takes to realize the patient is sick and to diagnose the specific ailment. One reason for the existence of this lag is that economic data take time to collect, so that an accurate measurement of where the economy is on some specific date will only be available some time after that date. Another reason is that, even with accurate data, reasonable individuals may take some time to arrive at a common diagnosis.

A second kind of lag, the *policy lag*, refers to the period of time it takes to produce a new policy after the need for a change in policy has been recognized. For fiscal policy this lag may be rather long, especially if congressional approval is required (as it is in most instances). For example, the income tax reduction first called for by President Kennedy in the summer of 1962 was not enacted until early 1964. And the income tax surcharge of 1968 took nearly two years before its passage was secured. Monetary policy, on the other hand, gets distinctly better marks on this score, and this, of course, stems from the fact that monetary policy is made by a relatively small group of politically independent individuals.

The final lag, termed the *outside lag*, is the period of time that elapses between the policy change and its effect on the economy. This lag arises because individual decision makers in the economy will take time to adjust to new economic conditions. Thus, for example, households will generally only gradually adjust their consumption expenditures when their disposable income changes. This may come from a certain amount of habit persistence or may reflect a desire to see whether the change in income is temporary or permanent. Similarly, if the interest rate declines, firms may not immediately increase their investment. And even if they do, it will typically take some time to produce the capital goods that the firms desire.

As a consequence, the effect of a policy change will be distributed over time, and it can take a significant period before a substantial fraction of the full policy effect is felt. Comparing monetary and fiscal policy in this regard, many writers have argued that monetary policy, because it affects the economy less directly, will have a longer outside lag. Another way of looking at this is that, relative to fiscal policy, monetary policy tends to work by influencing investment. And the lags in the physical process of building plants and heavy equipment are undoubtedly longer than the lags in producing consumer goods. Overall, then, the longer outside lag of monetary policy must be balanced against the shorter policy lag in deciding the optimal mix of policy.

**Lags and Forecasting**    The existence of lags in the policy process, especially the outside lag, means that to prescribe the proper dosage of policy the authorities must consider both the current state of the economy as well as what the economic situation will be in the future. That is, successful policy will require accurate forecasts of the macroeconomic conditions six months, one year, or perhaps even two years into the future. To make such forecasts economists rely on a variety of techniques.

1   LEADING INDICATORS. This technique attempts to make predictions by exploiting the existence of various lead–lag relationships between economic series. For example, it may have been found that, in the past, downturns in the stock market always preceded declines in economic activity, say, as measured by industrial production, by a number of months. If such a relationship could be counted on to persist into the future, this would be an extremely useful aid in forecasting. Of course, reliance on any particular leading indicator may be somewhat risky, since it can give false signals or fail to signal a change in economic conditions. To minimize these problems, those who use this technique tend to rely on an average index based on a large set of leading indicators. Although this does improve the quality of the signal, it is hardly a foolproof technique. Furthermore, the actual lead time is often considerably shorter than would be ideal.

2   SURVEYS OF INTENTIONS. This approach is based on the plausible assumption that if you want to know what aggregate demand will be you should go to the "horse's mouth." That is, you should survey the spending intentions of businesses and consumers. There are, in fact, a number of such surveys regularly undertaken by both governmental and private groups. For example, the Commerce Department, in conjunction with the Securities and Exchange Commission, surveys firms as to how much they expect to invest in plant and equipment over the next one to four quarters. The McGraw-Hill Company also conducts a similar survey. As for consumers, the Bureau of the Census has collected expectations of future purchases of durable goods such as automobiles. The main difficulty with intentions or anticipations data is that they need not be realized. Thus, should economic conditions in the future change markedly from these conditions that are implicit in the intentions data, actual spending can deviate substantially from intentions. Nevertheless, such data are an important tool in the forecasting kit of most economists.

3   ECONOMETRIC MODELS. An econometric model is a set of empirical relationships, statistically fit to historical data. Typical components of a model would be relationships such as the consumption function, the investment function, and the money-demand function. Once estimated, an econometric model is like the numerical *IS–LM* example considered earlier, albeit with many more equations (sometimes several hundred). Like the leading indicator approach, the use of an econometric model for

forecasting generally requires that the structure of the economy remain fairly stable over time. This is necessary to assure that historically estimated relationships continue to be good guides to the operation of the economy in the future. However, even this condition is not sufficient to guarantee the reliability of forecasts based on an econometric model. The reason is that in using an econometric model one is required to make assumptions (forecasts) of the values of the exogenous variables that drive the model but are determined outside the model. These might include the foreign demand for our products, the weather, or the incidence of strikes. Only if our model is correct *and* our forecasts of exogenous variables are also accurate can we be confident that our forecasts of the endogenous variables—GNP, prices, employment, and so on—will be accurate. Clearly, this is a difficult state of affairs to achieve in practice.

It should be evident from this discussion that forecasting is as much an art as a science. As a consequence, no single method of forecasting is likely to be unambiguously the best. Most practitioners look at the advice proffered by advocates of all three techniques discussed and then tend to make some judgmental compromise. However this is done, one can be sure that forecasts will generally be subject to error. And the magnitude of these errors is likely to increase the further ahead one attempts to forecast. The consequences of this for policy deserve to be stressed.

Given the lag in the operation of policy, we need accurate forecasts to accomplish successful stabilization policy. If our forecasts are highly inaccurate, our policy record is likely to be undistinguished, no matter how well we understand the workings of the economy. This suggests that, if the outside lag of policy is long, we must be cautious in our policy because our recommendations are likely to be based on relatively inaccurate forecasts. Indeed, it is even possible that policy actions aimed at stabilizing economic activity may inadvertently succeed in destabilizing it. The difficulties inherent in conducting a successful stabilization policy have, in fact, led some economists to conclude that we should abandon all attempts at discretionary stabilization policy. We shall examine this view shortly, but we must first consider some of the other complexities of the policy process.

## UNCERTAINTY AND POLICY

Another respect in which our treatment of monetary and fiscal policy in previous chapters was oversimplified was in ignoring the issue of uncertainty. In particular, our discussion proceeded as if the policy maker were precisely sure of what would happen as a result of a policy action. Under this simple view of the world, the analogy is sometimes drawn between a policy maker and a technician fine-tuning a precision instrument. This, however, is rather misleading. As one economist has expressed it:

> A *better analogy might be to a novice sailor trying to steer a sailboat through a windy and shallow channel. He knows basically where he is going; but he is not sure how far away from the shoals he is. He knows in which direction the boat will respond to manipulations of the sail; but he does not know how strongly, and he does not know how fast. It all depends on such uncontrollable — and perhaps unpredictable — factors as wind, weather and currents.*[3]

The appropriateness of this analogy should be readily apparent. Policy makers have a number of instruments under their control and generally have a good idea as to the direction in which each instrument will push the economy. However, they are not necessarily able to predict precisely the magnitude or timing of the effect of their policies. And even if they could, exogenous developments could always lead to an undesired outcome.

Where do these uncertainties come from? We have already touched on three sources of uncertainty in discussing the problem of lags:

1   The inability to assess perfectly the current state of the economy.
2   The uncertainty associated with the timing of monetary and fiscal policy effects.
3   The inevitable imprecision of the forecasts of future values of exogenous variables that impinge on the economy.

There is, in addition, another source of uncertainty that deserves to be stressed. In particular, the policy maker will not have a terribly precise model of the economy with which to work. This should hardly be surprising in view of the lack of unanimity among economists as to the underlying structure of the economy. Thus, for example, economists and policy makers may have only rough estimates of critical parameters such as the marginal propensity to consume and the marginal responsiveness of both investment demand and money demand to the interest rate. Since, as we have seen, such parameters are the essential building blocks in determining the quantitative effectiveness of both monetary and fiscal policy, uncertainty over these means that policy makers "will not know their own strength." As a consequence, *even in a fully static world*, they will be unable to carry out policy in a precise way.

Few economists would argue with the existence and even the importance of these various uncertainties. There has, however, been considerable debate over the proper moral to be drawn for policy making.

---

[3] A. S. Blinder, *Fiscal Policy in Theory and Practice*, Morristown, N.J., General Learning Press, 1973, p. 25.

Much of this debate has taken place in the context of a longstanding feud between the so-called *monetarist* and *nonmonetarist* economists. It is to this that we now turn. Our discussion will follow the actual historical pattern of the debate. Thus, we first examine the monetarist view that fiscal policy is ineffective and monetary policy is all-powerful. Subsequently we consider the monetarist position that even monetary policy should not be used as part of an activist stabilization policy.

**THE MONETARIST DEBATE: FISCAL VS. MONETARY POLICY**

As just noted, there are substantial disagreements among economists as to the effects of monetary and fiscal policy. Disputes in this area have focused both on the mechanisms by which each type of policy works and on their ultimate effectiveness in influencing macroeconomic activity. Views on the importance of monetary and fiscal factors, like clothing fashions, have come and gone and then come again. Prior to the 1930s, economists tended to follow the quantity theory approach, and this, of course, stressed the importance of monetary factors. With the advent of the Depression and the publication of Keynes' *General Theory*, attention focused more on fiscal factors. Indeed, for a period of over 15 years monetary policy fell somewhat into disrepute. To some extent this was due to the kinds of problems raised by the Keynesian liquidity trap. But it also reflected the view that interest rates were not a terribly important component of investment decisions. With the further passage of time, a more balanced view of policy emerged, stressing the importance of both monetary and fiscal factors. In the past 15 or so years, however, at least part of the economics profession has come full circle with the development of monetarism.

**Tenets of Monetarism**

Monetarism is prominently associated with the name of the distinguished monetary economist Milton Friedman. However, other economists have made important contributions to the evolution of the monetarist position. And not all of these share precisely the same views. There are, thus, both "hard" and "soft" monetarists. While this makes it difficult to define precisely, the following propositions should at least serve to give the flavor of the first phase of the monetarist debate.

1   Money matters in the determination of aggregate income. Few economists, of any persuasion, would disagree with this statement, but what distinguishes monetarism is the emphasis given to monetary considerations. As Friedman has put it:

   *I regard the description of our position as "money is all that matters for changes in* nominal *income and* short-run *changes in real income" as an exaggeration but one that gives the right flavor of our conclusions. I regard the statement that "money is all that matters," period, as a basic misrepresentation of our conclusions.*[4]

2    Fiscal policy is impotent in that it is unable to affect real income or the price level, unless it is accompanied by an accommodating monetary policy. That is, a change in taxes or government spending with no change in the money supply is of minuscule importance in influencing aggregate demand. However, where such changes are financed by changes in the money supply, aggregate demand will be affected. Of course, then it is called monetary policy.

In summary then, monetarism both denies the effectiveness of fiscal policy and elevates money to a singular and an exalted position. A natural question to ask is how all this might come about.

**Workings of a Monetarist Model**    We can gain some insight into this issue by use of the model developed in the previous chapters. In fact, under suitable assumptions that model is perfectly capable of generating monetarist conclusions. In particular, this will be true if the money-demand function is assumed to be insensitive to the interest rate. This can be seen as follows.

The general form of the money-demand function we have used is

$$\frac{M^D}{P} = F(O, r) = F(Y/P, r) \tag{1}$$

while for illustrative purposes we have sometimes relied on a linear version of this given by

$$\frac{M^D}{P} = JO + (A - er) \tag{2}$$

If the demand for money is insensitive to the interest rate, then the variable $r$ should be omitted from (1) and (2). For our present purposes we can just as well work with (2), so that we now have[5]

$$\frac{M^D}{P} = JO \text{ or } M^D = JOP \tag{3}$$

With the money supply fixed exogenously, as $M^S = \overline{M}$, we can write the condition for equilibrium in the money market as

$$\overline{M} = JOP \tag{4}$$

---

[4] M. Friedman, "A Theoretical Framework of Monetary Analysis," *Journal of Political Economy,* 78 (March/April 1970), p. 217.

[5] In going from (2) to (3) we have also dropped the constant $A$, but this is inconsequential.

Equation (4) says that, given $\overline{M}$, the level of money output, $OP$, is determined in the money market *independently* of the interest rate. In our previous terminology this means that the $LM$ curve is vertical. This is illustrated in Figure 16–1. The curve $L_1M_1$ is drawn on the assumption that $P = P_1$, while the curve $L_2M_2$ corresponds to some lower level, $P = P_2$.

As before, we can summarize the complete model by the aggregate demand and supply diagram, as in Figure 16–2. The initial $DD$ curve is labeled $D_1D_1$. To keep matters general, we have drawn two possible aggregate supply curves — $S_1S_1$, corresponding to the classical case, and $S_2S_2$, corresponding to our modified money wage model. We can now quickly see how the monetarist propositions emerge.

Let us turn first to fiscal policy. An increase of government spending or a decrease in taxes will shift the $IS$ curve up as in the movement from $I_1S_1$ to $I_2S_2$ illustrated in Figure 16–1. However, with the money supply unchanged, the family of $LM$ curves also remains fixed, and thus the $DD$ curve stays at $D_1D_1$. This comes about because interest rates rise (from $r_1$ to $r_2$ in Figure 16–1), reducing investment just enough to offset the increase in government spending or the induced rise in consumption expenditures. Thus, equilibrium remains at $(P_1, O_1)$ in Figure 16–2. It should be noted that this result comes about no matter which aggregate supply curve is used.

On the other hand, an increase of $\overline{M}$ will shift the $LM$ curve to the right. Figure 16–1 also illustrates this if we now regard $L_2M_2$ as emerging from the increase of $\overline{M}$ and not from a lower price level. Unlike fiscal policy, this will succeed in shifting the $DD$ curve — shown as the movement from $D_1D_1$ to $D_2D_2$ in Figure 16–2. If the relevant supply curve is $S_1S_1$, both prices and real output will increase, bringing us to $(P_2, O_2)$. On the other hand, in the classical case of $S_2S_2$ real output stays at $O_1$ but the price level rises to $P_3$. Thus, we see that in either case the increase in $\overline{M}$

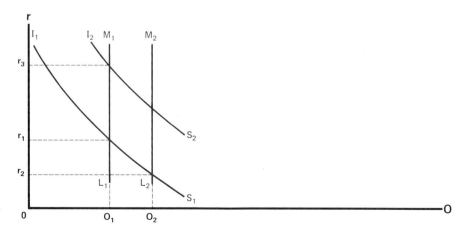

IS–LM: *the monetarist case*

**FIGURE 16–1**

will raise nominal GNP, $Y = OP$. It is the labor market assumption that determines whether this will serve only to increase $P$ or will be split between $P$ and $O$.

This discussion would seem to suggest that a relatively simple test of the validity of the monetarist view would be to settle the empirical question of whether or not the demand for money is sensitive to the interest rate. However, we have already indicated that virtually all economists (monetarists included) now accept the proposition the interest rate does influence the demand for money. Does this mean we can summarily dismiss the monetarist position? The answer, of course, is not quite. Indeed, there could hardly be an ongoing debate if the matter were so simple. There are at least two reasons why this is the case.

In the first instance, some monetarists have offered some "direct" empirical evidence to support their views. Second, as we have seen before, the effectiveness of monetary and fiscal policy depends on several factors, of which the interest sensitivity of money demand is only one. Consequently, even though the demand for money responds in a "significant" way to changes in interest rates, it is possible that these other factors offset this in such a way so as to make the economy "almost" monetarist in character. Both of these questions need to be examined a bit further.

**Some Monetarist Evidence**    Monetarists are not impressed with existing evidence on the effectiveness of monetary and fiscal policy. To a large extent, this is because they feel we do not know enough about how the economy operates and therefore we cannot sensibly specify how policy works. To try to circumvent this problem they have adopted a rather simple bare-bones approach to the question of policy effectiveness.

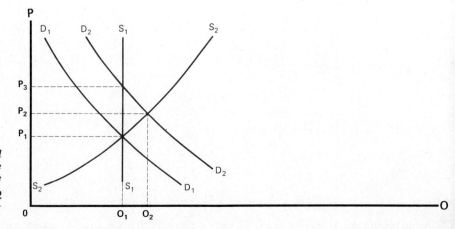

*Aggregate demand and supply: the monetarist case*

**FIGURE 16–2**

They begin from an assumption that income is influenced (some-how) by monetary and fiscal policy as well as by other factors. This means that the changes in nominal income ($\Delta Y$) from one time period to the next ought to be explained by the change in fiscal policy ($\Delta F$), the change in monetary policy ($\Delta M$), and changes in the remaining other fac-tors. If we assume that changes in these other factors (1) either exert a constant influence on $\Delta Y$ and/or (2) can be represented by a random fac-tor, we then have

$$\Delta Y = a_1 + a_2 \Delta F + a_3 \Delta M + \text{a random factor} \tag{5}$$

We should be able to fit this equation to actual data by standard statis-tical procedures. And in fact, this has been done many times, most prominently by economists at the Federal Reserve Bank of St. Louis, but also by others as well. The results have varied somewhat depending on, for example, the choice of time periods, the precise definitions of the policy variables, and the statistical techniques used. Nevertheless, one finding that seemed to emerge from many of these studies is that the ef-fectiveness of fiscal policy (measured by $a_2$) is very small. Indeed, not in-frequently $a_2$ has turned out to be a small negative number, suggesting that an expansionary fiscal policy actually decreases nominal GNP. In contrast, the effectiveness of monetary policy ($a_3$) is always positive and typically quite large.

While seemingly offering strong support for the monetarist position, this evidence is not nearly as persuasive as might be thought at first blush. There are, in fact, three major problems with the simple approach embodied in equation (5).

1    OMITTED VARIABLES. It is a rather marked oversimplification to assume that the other factors influencing GNP can be adequately characterized by a constant ($a_1$) and/or a random term. There are obviously other systematic factors influencing GNP (e.g., exports), and their omission from (5) can bias the results.

2    IMPERFECT POLICY MEASURES. Typically, monetary policy is represented by the stock of money or the monetary base, while fiscal policy is summarized by government spending (ignoring taxes) or by what is called the *full-employment surplus*, that is, what the budget surplus or deficit would be if the economy were at full employment. Ignoring taxes is certainly inappropriate, but even use of the full-employment surplus is incorrect. This measure weights government spending and taxes equally, but this is inappropriate, since, as we have seen, they do not have identical effects on GNP. A further difficulty is that a fiscal measure calculated as if we were at full employment may not give an accurate guide to the effect of fiscal policy at less than full employment.

3   REVERSE CAUSATION. This difficulty can best be illustrated with an example. Suppose the following assumptions are true: We can ignore the first two difficulties; monetary policy is behaving erratically; fiscal policy is systematically trying to stabilize GNP by offsetting the random forces in (5). The fiscal authorities would thus set fiscal policy, $\Delta F$, so that the fiscal impact, given by $a_2\Delta F$, was equal and opposite to the random forces. In this event, equation (5) would reduce to

$$\Delta Y = a_1 + a_3\Delta M \tag{6}$$

In other words, we would find that monetary policy explained changes in GNP perfectly but that fiscal policy did not matter. Of course, the reverse would occur if the monetary authorities were successful stabilizers and the fiscal authorities were erratic. As this example makes clear, a smart policy maker will look impotent, and this effect has generally not been allowed for in estimating equation (5).

In summary then, monetarist empirical studies suffer from a number of difficulties that render the results quite suspect. Furthermore, various writers have shown that alternative definitions of the fiscal variable or the use of more recent data tend to produce results that imply a positive and significant role for fiscal policy.[6] However, even these more recent results suffer from difficulties of omitted variables. This suggests that we ought to look at some additional empirical evidence.

**Other Empirical Evidence**

As noted earlier, while investigators have found that the demand for money is sensitive to the interest rate, we still must look at a complete model to assess the effectiveness of monetary and fiscal policy. Fortunately, there are several econometric models available for this purpose. Although it would take us too far afield to analyze these models in any detail, even a cursory examination of these models suggests that the monetarist conclusions are not borne out. Rather, these models suggest that *both* monetary and fiscal policy are quite capable of altering GNP. For fiscal policy, this is illustrated in Figure 16–3, which exhibits the effectiveness of fiscal policy as calculated from seven different models. Effectiveness in this context is defined as the change in nominal GNP induced by a permanent $1 billion change in nominal government spending. Six of the models give qualitatively similar results leading to GNP changes of between $2 and $3 billion after three years.[7] Only the

---

[6] See, for example, B. M. Friedman, "Even the St. Louis Model Now Believes in Fiscal Policy," *Journal of Money, Credit and Banking*, May 1977, pp. 365–367.

[7] Figure 16–3, also illustrated a point made earlier. In particular, it shows that effects of a policy change take time to build up. In some cases these effects may even cycle somewhat.

monetarist St. Louis model, which is based on an equation like (5), suggests that fiscal policy is impotent.

In short, while the precise quantitative effectiveness of fiscal policy is still an open question, the monetarists' contention that fiscal policy is totally ineffective seems to be inconsistent with a substantial body of evidence.

**Overview**

One of the main tenets of monetarism is that monetary policy works but fiscal policy does not. We have little quarrel with the first part of this statement, but it seems to us that the majority of the evidence runs counter to the second part. That is, money matters, but so does fiscal policy. As suggested earlier, in recent years this aspect of the debate between monetarists and nonmonetarists has died down somewhat,[8] and the battle is now being fought in another arena.

---

[8] This is not to suggest that the debate on this subject has ended. See, for example, the monetarist counterattack in K. M. Carlson and R. W. Spencer, "Crowding Out and Its Critics," *Review*, Federal Reserve Bank of St. Louis, December 1975, pp. 2–17.

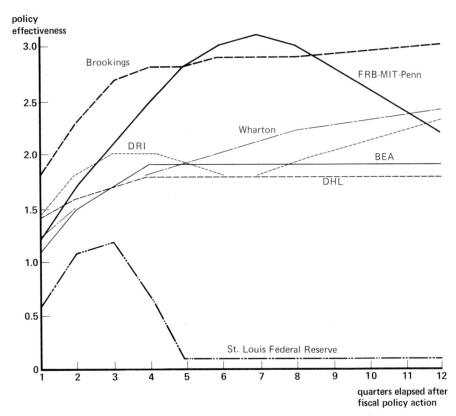

*...fectiveness of fiscal policy: selected ...conometric models ...f the United States*
Source: Alan S. Blinder and Robert Solow, "Analytical ...undations of Fiscal Policy," in *The ...conomics of Public Finance*, © 1974, Washington, D.C.: ...ookings Institution.

**FIGURE 16–3**

THE
MONETARIST
DEBATE:
RULES VS.
DISCRETION

Earlier we touched on some of the problems created by uncertainty and lags in the policy process. A number of economists, after taking stock of these difficulties, have concluded that we would be better off if we did not use discretionary policy at all. In place of discretion, these economists would have rules to govern the behavior of monetary and fiscal policy. Aside from the alleged superiority of the rules from the viewpoint of stabilization, the proponents of rules argue that they are to be preferred on philosophical grounds as well. This view is based on the belief that economic freedom is best served when we are governed by laws, not by people who may misuse their power.

The best known of these rules is one advanced by Milton Friedman. Friedman has proposed that the Federal Reserve adopt a rule of letting the money supply steadily increase at some fixed rate of growth. That is, the same rate of growth should be followed week in, week out, month in, month out, and year in, year out. While the specific rate chosen would depend on which concept of the money supply was used, the numbers generally advanced have been in the range of 3 to 4 percent per year. Friedman, however, has been quick to point out that the specific rate is less critical than the need to keep the money supply growing *steadily* at whatever rate is selected.

The rules that have been proposed for fiscal policy have generally involved the notion that the government budget ought, in some sense, to be balanced. In the past this has often been translated into the view that the budget ought to be balanced annually. There is a basic difficulty with this view, stemming from the fact that taxes endogenously or automatically respond to changes in income. Because of this, if private demand autonomously declines, tax revenues will fall. Any attempt to balance the budget would require raising tax rates in the face of a weak economy. Judged by modern standards this would be a rather perverse policy, and in fact this rule is no longer advocated by any serious economist. A less rigid version of this rule, however, still maintains some currency. This would involve determining the level of government spending on its own merits, independent of stabilization policy, and then setting tax rates so as to yield a balanced budget *if* the economy were at full employment. That is, the so-called *full-employment surplus* should be zero. This rule does not suffer from the gross defects of the simple budget rule, but it would take us too far afield to discuss its specific merits and demerits in any detail.[9] We turn, instead, to the more general question of whether rules should replace discretionary policy.

As already suggested, economists of the monetarist persuasion have

[9] For a discussion of this specific rule see A. S. Blinder and R. M. Solow, "Analytical Foundations of Fiscal Policy," in *The Economics of Public Finance*, Washington, D.C., Brookings Institution, 1974.

been in the forefront of those advocating rules over discretion. The essence of this debate has been well summed up in the following statement by Franco Modigliani (a prominent nonmonetarist), taken from this 1976 presidential address to the American Economic Association:

> *In reality the distinguishing feature of the monetarist school and the real issues of disagreement with nonmonetarists is . . . the role that should probably be assigned to stabilization policies. Nonmonetarists accept what I regard to be the fundamental practical message of* The General Theory; *that a private enterprise economy using an intangible money* needs *to be stabilized,* can *be stabilized, and therefore* should *be stabilized by appropriate monetary and fiscal policies. Monetarists by contrast take the view that there is no serious need to stabilize the economy; that even if there were a need, it could not be done, for stabilization would be more likely to increase than to decrease instability.*[10]

Several key points implicit in Modigliani's statement deserve to be stressed: (1) Monetarists emphasize the basic stability of the economy; (2) as such, they view the economy as able to adapt readily to shocks and to return to a position of long-run equilibrium; and (3) monetarists, pointing to the actual historical record, infer from the evidence that policy makers have generally been a destabilizing force in the economy. Naturally, nonmonetarists have something to say about each of these points. For one thing, they regard it as self-evident that the economy is subject to numerous shocks. Moreover, they argue that while there is certainly a tendency, after a shock, for the economy to return to its long-run equilibrium, this does not happen quickly enough. As a consequence, nonmonetarists see ample opportunity for discretionary policy to improve our economic performance. Reliance on rules, thus, removes a needed degree of flexibility.

This point can be illustrated by considering the full-employment fiscal rule given previously. That rule requires policy makers to offset any "surprises" that arise within the federal budget. Thus, if expenditures fall short of budget plans because Congress rejects some presidential spending proposals, there would be a call for a tax cut. Or if uncontrollable expenditures take a sharp jump, a tax increase would be needed. At the same time, however, advocates of this rule are determined not to respond to surprises in private demand. This seems somewhat illogical. If surprises in government demand require attention, then why not apply the same standard to unexpected shocks emanating from the private sector? Although the Friedman rule has no such problems of in-

---

[10] F. Modigliani, "The Monetarist Controversy or, Should We Forsake Stabilization Policies?" *American Economic Review*, March 1977, p. 1.

consistency, since the money supply would grow steadily no matter what economic conditions were, under this rule we would still give up the ability to respond to any shocks to the economy.[11]

If one accepts the view that there is scope for discretionary stabilization policy, there remains the empirical issue of whether stabilization policies have worked in the past and whether they will work in the future. We are thus reduced to this seemingly simple question: Would the actual path of the economy be more stable and would we be able to sustain higher average levels of output and employment if we abandoned discretion and followed a set of policy rules? Despite the apparent simplicity of the question, no readily agreed-upon answer has yet emerged. In particular, various investigators have reached quite different conclusions from an empirical examination of the same historical evidence. A major part of the difficulty in securing a consensus on this issue is that, as we have seen, there is less than full agreement as to the ways in which monetary and fiscal policy affect the economy. As a result, neither camp — neither those advocating rules nor those advocating discretion — has managed to interpret the historical evidence to the satisfaction of the other.

But even if the historical evidence is somewhat mixed, this is not sufficient cause to abandon discretionary stabilization. Policy makers are certainly permitted to (and, it is hoped, do) learn from their past mistakes. Errors committed in the formative years of both our macroeconomic understanding and practical policy making should not be permanently held against discretionary policy.

On balance, the adoption of a set of fixed rules for monetary and fiscal policy does not appear to be a panacea for our economic ills. Discretionary policy, for better or for worse, still seems to us to have the edge. Nevertheless, there certainly remains considerable room for improvement in the conduct of discretionary policy, and efforts designed to bring this about deserve a high priority.[12]

---

[11] Modigliani (*ibid.*, p. 13) has characterized the Friedman rule as follows: *Friedman's logical argument against stabilization policies and in favor of a constant money growth rule is, I submit, much like arguing to a man from St. Paul wishing to go to New Orleans on important business that he would be a fool to drive and should instead get himself a tub and drift down the Mississippi; that way he can be pretty sure that the current will eventually get him to his destination; whereas if he drives, he might make a wrong turn and, before he notices, he will be going further and further away from his destination and pretty soon he may end up in Alaska, where he will surely catch pneumonia and he may never get to New Orleans!*

[12] For a detailed discussion of all the issues raised in this section, see A. M. Okun, "Fiscal–Monetary Activism: Some Analytical Issues," *Brookings Papers on Economic Activity*, vol. 1, 1972, pp. 23–64.

**CONCLUSION** A naive interpretation of the framework presented in previous chapters might suggest that policy makers could readily achieve desirable economic outcomes. But a glance at our concerns of recent years — inflation, unemployment, and difficulties with our international payments — indicates that there is a substantial gap between the promise of the textbook and actual economic performance. One could explain this gap by casting aspersions on the intentions of policy makers or even on their intelligence. And economists have not been above doing this — even, in some instances, justifiably. But as we have seen, there are many other reasons why economic policy may be less than fully successful. These include basic incompatibilities among goals and lags and uncertainties that necessarily complicate the policy process. At the very least, this suggests the need to improve both the trade-offs among conflicting goals and our understanding of the way in which the economy operates. While we have come a long way on this score, there is still much to be done.

We have also examined various aspects of the monetarist debate, agreeing with the monetarist position that "money matters," but taking issue with the monetarists' dismissal of fiscal policy as ineffective. In addition, we reviewed the issues in the debate over rules versus discretion. In so doing, we may have appeared to draw a very sharp line between rules and discretion, but, at least in some instances, the distinction is not all that precise. As Paul Samuelson has observed, a set of rules "is set up by discretion, is abandoned by discretion, and is interfered with by discretion." In other words, there is no assurance that political considerations will lead to any less tinkering in a world of rules. While this consideration is undoubtedly more relevant for fiscal policy, it carries some force for monetary policy as well.

One final point raised by the monetarist debate deserves comment. As noted above, led by Friedman, the monetarists have advocated that the money supply should be made to grow at some constant rate. While this rule has not been explicitly adopted by the monetary authorities, the monetarist argument has had a strong impact on the nature of discretionary policy. In particular, as we shall see later, in recent years the Federal Reserve has paid important attention to the growth rate of the money stock. There is more than a bit of irony in all this, because soon after the Federal Reserve tilted toward monetarism a variety of developments in the nature of financial intermediaries served to cast serious doubt on the proper definition of money. Thus, even if one wanted to follow a Friedman-type rule, it became rather unclear as to how best to carry this out. Furthermore, the same developments that created ambiguity as to the proper definition of money also served to make it more difficult, as a practical matter, for the Federal Reserve actually to control any particular definition of the money supply. As Samuelson warned us, the Federal Reserve was thus forced to use discretion in the application of a rule.

It should be apparent from this discussion that the next item of business should be an examination of recent developments in financial intermediaries and the definition of money. These and related items, in fact, are the substance of the next chapter.

**SELECTED READINGS**

Blinder, A. S., *Fiscal Policy in Theory and Practice*, Morristown, N.J., General Learning Press, 1973.

Okun, A. M., "Fiscal–Monetary Activism: Some Analytic Issues," *Brookings Papers on Economic Activity*, vol. 1, 1972, pp. 23–64.

Friedman, M., "A Theoretical Framework for Monetary Analysis," *Journal of Political Economy*, 78 (March/April 1970), pp. 193–238.

Mayer, T., *Monetary Policy in the United States*, New York, Random House, 1968.

Modigliani, F., "The Monetarist Controversy or, Should We Forsake Stabilization of Policies?" *American Economic Review*, 67 (March 1977), pp. 1–19.

The money market was a key feature of the theoretical framework developed in Part 4. Indeed, it was through the interplay of the demand and supply for money that we modeled the way in which Federal Reserve policy works. Since our previous concern was with the general principles of monetary policy, we could afford the luxury of being somewhat imprecise as to the exact definition of money. As our present aim is to move to more realistic policy questions, somewhat greater precision is needed. One object of this chapter, then, is to consider more closely the definition of money. In so doing, however, we shall seemingly range far afield into a reexamination of the nature of financial intermediaries. The necessity for this can be sketched briefly.

The general issues in defining money were spelled out in the first chapter. There, we expressed a preference for a narrow, transactions-based definition of money. We also indicated, however, that what constitutes a medium of payments cannot be settled once and for all. Rather, those assets which are used in transactions may change with advances in technology and the evolution of institutional practices. Thus, at an early stage of monetary development a narrow definition of money might have included only currency. Then, as commercial banking gained in importance, the commonly accepted definition of money came to include demand deposits at commercial banks. With the continuing evolution of the financial system, especially in the last decade, still other financial instruments have appeared that might plausibly be incorporated into money, even narrowly defined. Many of these instruments (e.g., NOW accounts)—and this is a key point—are available at financial intermediaries such as savings and loan associations and mutual savings banks.

Furthermore, there appears every prospect that such nonbank intermediaries will play an expanding role in the provision of transactions balances. These developments clearly suggest that both the definition of money and, even more generally, the understanding of monetary policy require us to examine the evolving nature of financial intermediaries.

More specifically, the outline of this chapter is as follows. We first review the major types of financial intermediaries and examine some structural problems in our financial system. Then, after considering some proposals for reform, we trace the evolution of financial intermediaries in the 1970s. As we shall see, one result of this process has been the growing similarity between commercial banks and other financial intermediaries—a similarity that emerged without any comprehensive legislative reform. We then examine the Depository Institutions Deregulation Act of 1980. With this Act, Congress formally acknowledged the need for continuing the process of structural reform and removed many of the legal impediments to reform. Over the long run, this Act should have a profound impact on the shape of the financial system. In the final section of the chapter, we consider the implications of the past and prospective evolution of financial intermediaries for the definition of money and for monetary policy.

## DEPOSITORY FINANCIAL INTERMEDIARIES

In an earlier chapter we discussed the important role served by financial intermediaries in channeling funds from lenders to borrowers. We also indicated that they are outstanding manufacturers of liquidity, creating and issuing claims against themselves that are much more liquid than the direct securities that they acquire. Indeed, it is precisely some of these liquid claims that are candidates for being counted in the money supply. Before getting to this, however, we need briefly to review the major types of depository financial intermediaries and indicate the general nature of the environment in which they operate.

### Types of Intermediaries

As we have already seen, commercial banks constitute the most significant type of financial intermediary. As we have discussed these institutions in detail, they need no further introduction. We turn instead to the remaining intermediaries.

#### Savings and Loan Associations

Once called building and loan associations, these institutions are legally of two types. Stock savings and loan associations issue at least two types of claims against themselves—equity claims to their owners and deposit-debt claims to their creditors. In most cases, however, equity claims are very small relative to deposit claims. The other major type—the mutual savings and loan association—is a form of cooperative;

it is owned by those who acquire claims against it. Legally, therefore, these claims are equity claims and are often called "shares." In practice, however, they are the equivalent of deposit-debt claims. Claims against most of the savings and loan associations are now insured up to $100,000 per account. As of the end of 1979, there were about 4,700 savings and loan associations, which, in the aggregate, had assets of $580 billion.

The primary sources of funds for savings and loan associations are savings and time deposits. Interest rates payable on savings and time deposits are subject to ceilings like those in Regulation Q. These are slightly higher for savings and loan associations than for commercial banks. Since their introduction in mid-1978, money market certificates (a form of time deposit, discussed below) have been a particularly important source of funds. Prior to 1981, NOW accounts (also discussed below) were only permitted in selected states. While this has thus far limited their importance, they represent a significant potential source of funds. The major use of funds by savings and loan associations is to issue mortgages on residential real estate, and at year-end 1979 mortgages accounted for over 80 percent of total assets. Many of these mortgages are of very long maturity.

### Mutual Savings Banks

In many respects mutual savings banks are similar to mutual savings and loan associations: They obtain funds from the same types of sources, subject to similar interest rate ceilings; their deposits are comparably insured; and they invest primarily in mortgages. There are, however, some significant differences. For one, mutual savings banks can only be chartered by a state agency, and only in selected states at that. Currently, about 500 mutual savings banks exist in 18 states, primarily in the Northeast, and at year-end 1979 these institutions had $163 billion in assets. Savings and loan associations are thus more numerous and have a wider geographic distribution. A second difference is that mutual savings banks have been permitted to invest their funds more broadly than savings and loan associations. Hence, while mortgages are the largest component (accounting for 60 percent of total assets in 1979), mutual savings banks also hold significant quantities of corporate bonds and equities and U.S. government securities.

### Credit Unions

Credit unions are mutual institutions whose depositors have some common affiliation, such as employment at Princeton University. There are approximately 23,000 credit unions, which by 1980 had amassed total assets of $65 billion. Their primary source of funds is savings accounts. These accounts are insured and are subject to interest ceilings. However, the maximum rate payable on these accounts (7 percent) is above the corresponding rate at other thrift institutions (5½ percent). As a consequence, credit unions have grown relatively rapidly in the past decade. A recent innovation at credit unions is the *share draft*, which is similar in function to the NOW account. That is, it provides an interest-bearing medium of exchange. The primary use of funds by credit unions is for consumer loans to their members. In addition, credit unions also hold U.S. government securities and home mortgages.

### Money Market Mutual Funds

One of the most interesting and significant financial developments in the past decade has been the emergence and recent phenomenal growth of money market mutual funds. These funds provide shareholders with an interest return that varies with short-term money-market rates of interest, and their growth has been closely tied to interest rate movements. These money market funds first emerged in 1971, but remained insignificant until 1974. When interest rates began their upward march in early 1974, the money market funds experienced their first period of substantial growth, expanding more than twenty-fold as total assets grew from under $200 million to about $4 billion in early 1975. Growth slowed as interest rates moderated, and in fact, over the next several years money market funds declined slightly in size. As interest rates rose in 1978, these funds expanded from about $4 billion at the start of the year to $10 billion at year-end. With interest rates continuing to soar upward in 1979, the money market funds experienced a period of phenomenal growth, and by mid-1980 they had amassed about $70 billion in assets.

Money market funds generally invest in short-term financial instruments that are issued in large denominations such as Treasury bills, CDs, commercial paper, and bankers acceptances. Shareholders usually invest much smaller amounts, although there are minimum initial investments, which typically have ranged from $500 to $10,000. Most funds calculate and pay dividents on a daily basis, and shares can easily be redeemed at any time by either wire transfer or check. The check feature is of particular significance and works roughly as follows. The fund, after making arrangements with a commercial bank, provides the shareholder with a book of checks. These can be used to make ordinary payments, although a minimum check size, such as $500, is often specified. When the check clears, the shareholder's account is reduced by the amount of the check, thus allowing the shareholder to earn interest on transactions balances.

As should be apparent from this discussion, shares in money market funds provide a highly liquid asset that, because management fees and transactions costs are kept relatively low, yield a virtual market rate of return as well. Despite the fact that these shares, unlike deposits at banks and thrift institutions, are uninsured, money market funds have proved to be an attractive substitute for both demand and savings deposits offered by depository institutions.

This completes our rundown of the major depository financial intermediaries. There are, of course, other types of financial intermediaries that do not issue deposit-type claims but do issue indirect securities with characteristics that differ significantly from those of the direct securities that they hold. Examples include insurance companies, finance companies, and private pension funds. There are also government-sponsored financial intermediaries such as the Federal National Mortgage Association, commonly dubbed Fanny Mae, which issues its own debt and purchases mortgages on residential real estate.[1] However, since our present focus is the evolving role of depository intermediaries and the definition of money, we shall say little more about these other types of intermediaries. Rather, we turn to the role of the government in regulating the depository institutions.

**Government Regulation**

By their very nature, depository financial intermediaries present problems of management and regulation. As we have seen, they generally issue claims against themselves that are fixed in terms of dollars and have maturities shorter than those of the direct securities that they hold. They "borrow short and lend long." This inevitably creates problems of maintaining solvency and liquidity without undue sacrifice of net income. There is risk that the intermediary will become insolvent—that the value of its assets will fall below the value of its liabilities. And there is risk of illiquidity, or inability to pay promptly and in full, even though the intermediary may be solvent if given a longer period in which to sell its assets.

Because of problems such as these, the government has intervened in many ways to regulate and otherwise influence the creation and functioning of financial intermediaries. We saw numerous examples of this in our discussion of commercial banking. Here it will be sufficient to list briefly the major types of regulation.

*Asset Regulation*

In their choice of assets, financial intermediaries are limited in various ways. For one, they may be prohibited from holding certain assets such as common stock. At the other extreme, they may be required to

---

[1] Fanny Mae has a number of "friends" with the same function, namely, Ginny Mae (the Government National Mortgage Association) and Freddie Mac (the Federal Home Loan Mortgage Corporation).

hold other types of assets. Such requirements are typically aimed at improving the liquidity of the intermediary. However, reserve requirements also fall into this category.

### Liability Regulation

There are two kinds of regulations affecting liabilities issued by financial intermediaries. One type prohibits the issuance of certain forms of claims. For example, savings and loan associations are not permitted to issue demand (checking) deposits. The second type controls the maximum amount of interest that can be paid on various forms of deposits. The prohibition of interest payments on demand deposits is an example of this.

### Regulation of Service and Structure

There is a wide range of potential customer services that are either explicitly prohibited to certain financial intermediaries and/or specifically allowed to others. In addition, there exists a set of complex regulations that control, among other things, chartering, branching, and audit and supervision of each type of intermediary.

### Insurance of Claims Against Financial Intermediaries

As already indicated, individual accounts are insured up to $100,000 at most commercial banks, mutual savings banks, credit unions, and savings and loan associations. This has increased the safety and liquidity of these claims, made them more attractive to holders, and enhanced the ability of these institutions to compete for funds. It has also enhanced the geographic mobility of funds.

### Provision of Rediscount Facilities

Because of the very nature of their operations, involving the issue of claims more liquid than most of their assets, it is almost inevitable that financial intermediaries will, at least occasionally, encounter liquidity difficulties. It is because of such experiences that we now have federally sponsored institutions to provide liquidity to financial intermediaries by lending to them or by purchasing assets from them. Recent legislation, described below, has expanded the role of the Federal Reserve discount window as a source of funds for all depository institutions.

**Overview**     As should be apparent from this brief list, regulation has a pervasive influence on the structure of financial intermediaries. Via regulation, the government has tried to produce a safe-and-sound financial system—one that would be immune from the financial panics so prevalent in our early history. However, as we saw in Chapter 5, financial regulation must also promote an efficient financial system—one that channels funds from lenders to borrowers at the least cost possible. Toward that end, it should seek to promote competition among financial intermediaries, since competition itself encourages efficiency and innovation. Furthermore, regulation must provide an environment in which financial intermediaries can flexibly adapt to changing economic conditions. Unfortunately, at various times in the 1960s and 1970s when interest rates rose rapidly, the financial system experienced serious difficulties precisely because regulations hindered a smooth adjustment to altered economic conditions.

In many respects it is not surprising that difficulties should emerge over time as a result of regulations. For one thing, through the years financial regulation has often been introduced in piecemeal fashion, coping with the problems of a particular type of institution in isolation. This approach has tended to create artificial differences among the various kinds of financial intermediaries, and these differences have made the system as a whole less able to respond flexibly to new economic conditions. Second, the impetus for financial regulation has often been a financial crisis. The most obvious example of this is the extensive legislation of the 1930s. Regulations produced during a crisis often suffer from several defects. In particular, they tend to overemphasize safety at the expense of efficiency. In addition, in a crisis rarely is sufficient time devoted to careful thought about the long-run consequences of a proposed solution. As we proceed, we shall see ample illustration of shortcomings in the way the financial system has been regulated.

## REGULATION: PROBLEMS AND PROPOSALS

In the previous section we suggested that there have been, and indeed still are, substantial structural problems in the financial system. These problems have arisen in various ways, but many economists have identified ceiling restrictions on interest rates as the single most important source of difficulties. Such restrictions are of three types: maximum interest rates payable on time and savings deposits; prohibition of interest payable on demand deposits; and usury ceilings on various loan rates. For the present we shall only be concerned with the first two types.

### Ceilings on Deposit Rates

As we saw earlier, deposit rate ceilings were imposed on commercial banks in the 1930s to prevent "overly vigorous" competition for funds by banks. This competition, it was thought, would lead to excessively risky asset choice and an unsound banking system. Regulation Q ceilings on savings and time deposits were later extended to savings and loan associations and mutual savings banks under a similar rationale. Policy makers were particularly worried about these thrift institutions, as they play a vital role in financing housing. Since the bulk of the thrifts' assets were tied up in long-term mortgages, as interest rates rose, their earnings only changed slowly. Hence, it was argued, they would not be able to "afford" to pay higher rates on time and savings deposits, so ceilings were necessary. These were first applied to the thrifts in 1966. To further bolster the housing market, ceilings on thrifts were generally set $\frac{1}{4}$ percent higher than those on commercial banks. This was designed to make it somewhat easier for the thrifts to compete with commercial banks.

So much for intentions. What actually happened is another matter, especially after 1965. Prior to that year Regulation Q had little visible impact on the financial system, as market rates of interest rarely rose markedly above ceilings on time and savings deposits. This is illustrated in Figure 17–1, where we have displayed the *differential* between the yield on Treasury bills and the ceilings rate on passbook savings accounts at commercial banks. Then, as shown, in 1966, again in 1969, and still again in the mid-1970s there were extended episodes in which market rates of interest exceeded ceiling rates. What resulted, of course, was what we have previously termed *disintermediation*. That is, as market rates on such instruments as Treasury bills and commercial paper rose to a point at which they substantially exceeded interest rate ceilings, depositors transferred funds out of demand, time, and savings accounts to these higher-yielding instruments. In some time periods, this produced an actual decline in deposits at commercial banks and the thrift institutions; in others, deposits grew at an extremely slow rate. This process of disintermediation seriously disrupted the flow of funds to consumer and mortgage credit and put banks and thrift institutions in a rather precarious position. This undoubtedly gave the Federal Reserve pause in its pursuit of tighter monetary conditions, and in several instances may well have led to a premature easing of monetary policy. After several bouts of disintermediation it became apparent to many that interest rate ceilings created more problems than they solved. The Federal Reserve itself became disillusioned with ceilings. Critics of ceilings further bolstered their case with the following points:

1   Ceilings impair the efficiency of the financial system by inhibiting the growth of the most efficient financial institutions and practices. That is, ceilings do not permit efficient institutions to

*Yield spread: Treasury bill rate minus ceiling rate on passbook savings accounts*

Source: *Federal Reserve Bulletin,* February 1980, Washington, D.C., p. 106.

**FIGURE 17–1**

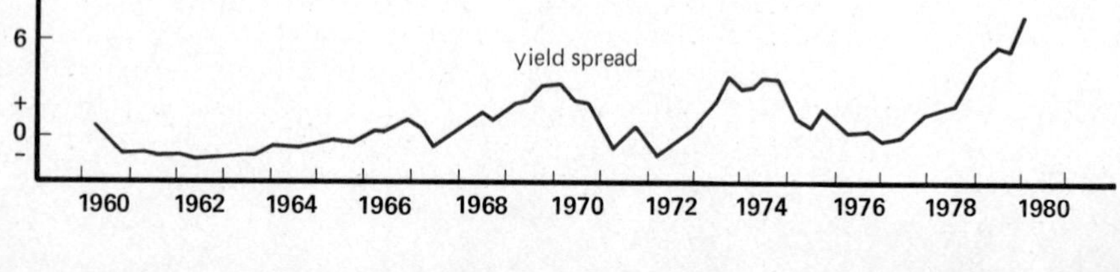

pay a higher rate of interest to attract funds, which is precisely what would happen in a competitive environment.[2]

2   Ceilings tend to discriminate against small savers who lack information or whose limited supply of funds does not permit them to purchase higher-yielding assets.

**Proposals for Reform**

In response to widespread dissatisfaction with structural problems in the financial system, a presidential Commission on Financial Structure and Regulation (called the Hunt Commission after its chairman) was established in 1970. The Commission undertook a thorough analysis of the financial system and in its report, issued at the end of 1971, made a number of sweeping proposals for the reform of the financial system. These proposals provided the foundation for the Financial Institutions Act (FIA) of 1973, which was, however, not enacted into law. A second attempt, the FIA of 1975, also failed, despite the fact that the subsequent Financial Institutions and the Nation's Economy (FINE) study by Congress generally agreed with the Hunt report. While these various attempts at comprehensive reform failed, it is nevertheless instructive to consider briefly the nature of the recommendations.

Generally speaking, the Hunt report advocated establishing a financial system in which competitive forces were allowed a much freer rein. As expressed in the Report:

> The Commission's objective, then, is to move as far as possible toward freedom of financial markets and equip all institutions with the powers necessary to compete in such markets. Once these powers and services have been authorized and a suitable time allowed for implementation, each institution will be free to determine its own course. The public will be better served by such competition. Markets will work more efficiently in the allocation of funds and total savings will expand to meet private and public needs.[3]

Toward this end, the Commission made eighty-nine recommendations. While it would obviously take us too far afield to discuss these in any detail, the flavor of the report can be gauged from the following selected recommendations.

---

[2] In response to ceilings on time and savings deposits and the prohibition of interest on demand deposits, financial institutions tend to offer "free gifts" (e.g., toasters, TVs, and the like) and provide services to customers below cost. In effect this compensates depositors with *implicit interest*, but it still involves a waste of resources. Both depositors and financial institutions would be better served by a system in which competition could take the form of *explicit interest*.

[3] *Report of the President's Commission on Financial Structure and Regulation,* Washington, D.C., Government Printing Office, 1971, p. 9.

1   All Regulation Q ceilings should be gradually removed. While the Hunt report advocated the retention of the zero ceiling on demand deposits, subsequent groups have urged the abolition of this restriction.
2   All deposit institutions should be permitted to offer third-party payment services, but with identical reserve requirements and equal tax and regulatory burdens. In effect this would extend checking accounts or their equivalent to the thrift institutions.
3   Thrift institutions should be permitted a far wider range of loan and investment powers and should be allowed to offer a wider menu of time and savings deposits.
4   Restrictions on entry into banking and other financial markets should be reduced. Financial institutions should be given more flexibility in converting from federal to state charter and vice versa. In addition, reductions of restrictions on intrastate and interstate branching are encouraged.

Taken as a group, as the Report states, "the recommendations authorize depository institutions to engage in a wider range of financial services. At the same time, the recommendations require that after a transitional period, all institutions competing in the same markets do so on an equal basis."[4]

As should be apparent from this discussion, were the recommendations of the Hunt report implemented into law, they would have a profound and, most economists would agree, beneficial impact on the structure of the financial system. Why then throughout the 1970s did they fail to secure passage? Here of course we are in the realm of political speculation, but several plausible hypotheses have been offered. For one, given the comprehensive nature of the proposed reforms, each constituency in the financial community found something to be unhappy about and registered opposition. Compromise in such situations, especially in the absence of a glaring crisis, is difficult to achieve. The fact that we had a small and growing crisis proved insufficient to spur action.

A second reason for legislative inaction is that many individuals, including politicians, are basically distrustful of financial institutions and how they would behave in a freer competitive environment. As a result, they are much more comfortable with interest rate ceilings and the use of tax incentives to shape flows of funds. Related to this view is the populist notion that high interest rates are somehow sinful. Indeed, public figures have frequently championed usury ceilings as a way of defending the poor little consumer from big bad financial lenders. In so doing, they seem willing to ignore the fact that when usury ceilings are binding there tends to be a shortage of funds relative to demand so that

[4] Ibid., p. 8.

many borrowers come away empty-handed. In any event, it should be clear that many individuals are skeptical of freely determined interest rates, be they on deposits or loans.

Whatever the reasons, the fact remains that, despite reasonably widespread agreement as to need, no comprehensive reform of the financial system emerged in the 1970s. This is not to suggest that important changes did not occur, for in many ways the character of the financial system was dramatically altered by events of the 1970s. Indeed, it was precisely these events and the crisis they created that led to the passage of the Depository Institutions Deregulation Act of 1980. Thus, rather than coming about in an orderly fashion, it was with kicking and screaming and fits and starts that we gradually groped our way toward a world not unlike that envisaged by the Hunt report. The events and players in this continuing saga are spelled out in the next section.

**FINANCIAL INNOVATION AND REGULATORY CHANGE**

Financial reformers, as we have seen, have advocated the following actions: (1) removal of ceiling interest rates on time and savings deposits; (2) extension of checking-like accounts to thrift institutions; and (3) ending the prohibition of the payment of interest on demand deposits. Developments in the past decade have produced progress on each of these fronts. In many respects the events that unfolded resembled a soap opera. The major characters, at least as innovators, were the private financial institutions themselves, with an occasional big assist from the regulatory authorities and some state legislatures. The courts too have had a role to play, although as we shall see, they both helped and hindered progress. The final actor—Congress—had only a cameo role in the 1970s, in which, to a large extent, it grudgingly reacted to events. With the passage of the Deregulation Act of 1980, however, Congress abandoned its bit part and jumped to center stage. This section focuses on events leading up to the 1980 Act, while the Act itself is examined in the next section.

As already noted, there was a certain theatrical quality to the evolution of the financial system in the 1970s. In any drama there are a number of "forces" that move the participants. Lust, power, greed, and progress often rank high on such a list. In the present context greed is replaced by the more genteel-sounding profit motive, which, as interest rates rose, provided incentives to find ways to evade the shackles imposed by interest rate ceilings. Furthermore, the thrifts, in order to gain a more equal footing vis-à-vis the commercial banks, sought ways to improve their competitive position. In so doing, they were abetted by the force of progress, represented here by computer-related technological advances. Overall, as we shall see, these various forces have

| TABLE 17-1 | Date | Change |
|---|---|---|
| *Selected innovations and regulatory changes since 1970* | June 1970 | Regulation Q ceilings on time deposits of $100,000 or more with maturities of 30–89 days are suspended. |
| | September 1970 | Federally chartered savings and loan associations are permitted to make preauthorized nonnegotiable transfers from savings accounts for household-related expenditures. |
| | June 1972 | State-chartered mutual savings banks in Massachusetts, led by the Consumer's Savings Bank of Worcester, begin offering NOW accounts. |
| | May 1973 | Regulation Q ceilings on time deposits of $100,000 or more with maturities exceeding 90 days are suspended. |
| | January 1974 | All depository institutions in Massachusetts and New Hampshire are authorized by Congress to offer NOW accounts. Accounts similar to NOWs but non-interest bearing (NINOWs) are offered by state-chartered thrifts in additional states throughout the year. |
| | January 1974 | Under new authorization, the First Federal Savings and Loan of Lincoln, Nebraska, places electronic terminals in two Hinky Dinky supermarkets, allowing its customers to pay for groceries and make deposits to or withdrawals from their savings accounts. |
| | Early 1974 | Money market mutual funds come into existence on a large-scale basis. |
| | August 1974 | Under an experimental program selected Federal credit unions are permitted to issue credit union share drafts, which are check-like instruments payable through a commercial bank. |
| | November 1974 | Commercial banks are permitted to offer savings accounts to state and local government units. |
| | April 1975 | Member banks are authorized by the Federal Reserve to make transfers from a customer's savings account to a demand deposit account upon telephone order from the customer. |
| | April 1975 | The 1970 action is broadened to allow savings and loan associations to make preauthorized third-party nonnegotiable transfers from savings accounts for any purpose. This authority is extended to commercial banks in September 1975. |
| | November 1975 | Commercial banks are authorized to offer savings accounts to business. |
| | February 1976 | Congress extends NOW accounts to all New England states. |
| | May 1976 | New York permits checking accounts at state-chartered mutual savings banks and savings and loans. |
| | June 1978 | Six-month money market certificates (MMCs) are introduced at banks and thrifts. The ceiling rate on these fluctuates weekly and is tied to the six-month Treasury bill rate. |
| | October 1978 | Congress extends NOW account authority to New York State |
| | November 1978 | Commercial banks and mutual savings banks are authorized to offer automatic transfers (ATS) from a savings account to a checking account or other type of transaction account. |
| | April 1979 | U.S. Court of Appeals rules that share drafts, ATS, and remote-service computer terminals are illegal and must be discontinued by January 1, 1980, unless Congress acts to legalize them. |
| | July 1979 | A floating ceiling for time deposits at banks and thrifts with a maturity of four years or more is established. |
| | December 1979 | Unable to cope in time with the Court ruling, Congress temporarily extends authority for ATS and share drafts March 31, 1980. It also extends NOW accounts to New Jersey. |
| | January 1980 | The floating ceiling is extended to time deposits with a maturity of $2\frac{1}{2}$ years or more. |

produced much drama,[5] but the final scene is still in the process of un-folding.

We turn now to the events themselves. A relatively complete chro-nological list of the major changes in the evolution of the financial struc-ture is given in Table 17–1. It will, however, lead to a more instructive discussion if we group these events topically. We begin with develop-ments related to Regulation Q.

Ceilings on Time and Savings Deposits

As noted earlier, after two bouts of disintermediation (in 1966 and 1969) the Federal Reserve became somewhat disenchanted with certain aspects of the ceilings. In both these periods the ceilings had applied to large ($100,000 or more) negotiable certificates of deposit (CDs), and as market rates exceeded the ceiling rate, outstanding CDs had declined. Banks, having embraced the strategy of liability management, had scrambled to raise lendable funds in the Eurodollar and commercial paper markets. In June 1970 the Federal Reserve grew tired of this cat-and-mouse game and lifted the ceilings on large CDs with maturities of 30–89 days.

A glance at Figure 17–1 suggests that the next potential period of disintermediation was 1973–1974, as market interest rates again rose above ceiling rates. However, several events helped to moderate disin-termediation during this period. For one, in May 1973 the Federal Reserve removed the remaining ceilings on large CDs so that commer-cial banks, at least, had much greater flexibility than they had had in 1966 or 1969. Furthermore, from July until November 1973 ceiling rates were suspended on time deposits of $1,000 or more with maturities of at least four years. These so-called wild-card deposits were available at both commercial banks and thrift institutions. As a result of these ac-tions, time and savings deposits at commercial banks maintained their rapid growth during 1973–1974. The thrift institutions suffered some disintermediation, but this took the form of slower growth in time and savings deposits rather than an absolute decline in these deposits. Overall, then, disintermediation was relatively mild during this period.

With the withdrawal of the wild-card deposits, the thrifts lost a degree of flexibility that they were not to regain until 1978. In addition, individual savers lost the chance for a competitive rate of interest on time deposits. It was partly in response to this situation that in early 1974 money market funds first appeared on the scene in a major way. Since they were not subject to interest ceilings, these funds could purchase open-market financial instruments and, after deducting a fee for manage-ment and transactions, offer shareholders a near-market rate of return.

---

[5] The alert reader will have noted that we provided no analogies for the forces of lust and power. In the interests of decency these are left to the imagination.

These funds grew rapidly until early 1975 and then stagnated for a while as interest rates declined somewhat.

As Figure 17–1 shows, for a roughly three-year period beginning in 1975 the pattern of interest rates created little pressure for disinter-mediation. In the absence of a crisis, there was, correspondingly, no major development pertaining to ceilings during this period. In the beginning of 1978, as Figure 17–1 shows, market interest rates began to diverge steadily from ceiling interest rates. Deposit growth at thrift institutions slowed in early 1978 and the authorities, fearing a new serious bout of disintermediation, felt compelled by the potential crisis to once again take action. In June 1978 they introduced the so-called six-month money market certificate (MMC). MMCs require a $10,000 minimum deposit and are available at both commercial banks and thrift institutions. Commercial banks are permitted to pay an interest rate on MMCs equal to the six-month Treasury bill rate.[6] Initially thrift institutions were able to pay $\frac{1}{4}$ percent more, but in March 1979 that differential was eliminated whenever the six-month bill rate was 9 percent or higher.

MMCs proved to be a significant innovation for both commercial banks and thrift institutions. While from mid-1978 to year-end 1979 savings deposits and small time deposits other than MMCs declined at both banks and thrifts, the growth of MMCs was quite remarkable. By the end of 1979 commercial banks had issued more than $100 billion of MMCs, while the thrifts held about $160 billion, which amounted to roughly one quarter of their total deposits. The thrifts also issued a substantial amount of large time deposits. These actions, as a group, served to keep thrift deposits growing at a healthy 8.2 percent clip from mid-1978 to the end of 1979. Overall then, a serious bout of disintermediation was averted, at least temporarily, and with the MMCs a partial dent was made in the Regulation Q ceilings.

These developments, however, were not sufficient to take us out of the woods. Indeed, toward the end of 1979 signs of strain appeared at thrift institutions as deposit growth slowed noticeably. In part this was due to fierce competition from the money market funds, which grew by nearly 30 percent from September to December of 1979. To bolster the menu of deposit offerings by the thrifts, on January 1, 1980, Regulation Q was further eroded as a floating ceiling was introduced on time deposits with a maturity of $2\frac{1}{2}$ years or more. On this new certificate thrifts are permitted to offer a yield $\frac{1}{2}$ percent below the yield on $2\frac{1}{2}$ year Treasury

---

[6] The regulation actually only permits payment of the "discount" yield on Treasury bills, which is lower than the true yield. To illustrate the difference consider a one-year Treasury bill with a face value of $10,000 that is sold at a discount yield of 10 percent. This means the buyer would pay $9,000 for the bill and receive the face value of $10,000 at maturity. The true bond yield is thus 11.1 percent ($1,000 as a percentage of $9,000).

securities, while commercial banks are limited to a rate of $\frac{3}{4}$ percent less than the Treasury yield. Whether these new certificates will be anywhere near as popular as the six-month MMCs remains to be seen.

A second problem for the thrifts cropped up as the rate on MMCs rose to the point at which it exceeded the usury ceilings in a number of states. This threatened to make it unprofitable to lend mortgage funds even if thrift institutions could acquire the deposits. To cope with this crisis, at the end of 1979 Congress enacted legislation temporarily suspending state ceilings for mortgage rates during the first quarter of 1980.

As should be clear from our discussion, even prior to 1980 various events had forced the monetary authorities to partially relax Regulation Q ceilings. However, as the decade came to an end we were still some considerable way from a system unfettered by ceilings.

**Checking Accounts<br>for Nonbank<br>Intermediaries**

Historically speaking, one of the major distinguishing features of commercial banks, in contrast with other financial intermediaries, has been their ability to offer demand deposit or checking accounts. The Hunt report, it will be recalled, proposed that such powers be extended to thrift institutions. As with ceilings, events of the 1970s have inexorably moved us toward this outcome.

### Preauthorized Transfers

The first step in this direction was in 1970, when some thrifts were permitted to make preauthorized nonnegotiable transfers from savings accounts for household-related expenditures. In 1975 this was extended to allow such transfers for any purpose. Although this approach offers thrifts a way to make third-party payments, the necessity of preauthorization makes it rather inconvenient for the depositor except for such things as utility and telephone bills.

### NOW Accounts

A more significant step toward giving the thrifts checking privileges occurred in June 1972, when the NOW account was born. A NOW account is a savings deposit that permits the depositor to withdraw funds by writing a negotiable order of withdrawal — hence the acronym NOW. NOWs were first proposed in 1970 by a state-chartered mutual savings bank in Worcester, Massachusetts, and were introduced in 1972 after the Massachusetts State Supreme Court found there was no legal basis for prohibiting NOWs. Hence, even though the holder of such an account writes a NOW exactly as he or she would write a check, NOW accounts were deemed to be distinct from checking accounts. The legal niceties are preserved by pointing to the fact that a NOW account is technically a savings account and that financial institutions therefore have the right to thirty days' notice before they are required to make payments. Needless to say, no case of such a delay has ever been reported.

Once the NOW account had been legally blessed, other state-chartered mutual savings banks in Massachusetts jumped onto the NOW bandwagon. In September 1972 a New Hampshire savings bank joined in the fun, and others soon followed. The result of all this was that state-chartered mutual savings banks held a competitive advantage over federally chartered savings institutions and all commercial banks. As a result, commercial banks, regulators, and some members of Congress opposed NOWs and tried to have them banned. However, the reverse occurred. As of January 1974, all depository institutions in Massachusetts and New Hampshire (except credit unions) were permitted to offer NOW accounts.

While it was perhaps the hope of Congress that NOWs could be "contained" in New Hampshire and Massachusetts, other states knew a good thing when they saw it. A few states discovered that existing laws permitted checklike instruments for thrifts, while in other states the legislatures proved willing to act. For example, toward the end of 1975 legislatures in both Maine and Connecticut permitted state-chartered thrifts to offer personal checking accounts. These actions, in conjunction with the ever-present example of NOWs in New Hampshire and Massachusetts, led Congress to extend NOWs to all six New England states in February 1976. Shortly thereafter New York passed legislation permitting checking accounts, including overdraft privileges, at state-chartered mutual savings banks and savings and loans. Congress responded in October 1978 by authorizing NOWs in New York. Then, in January 1980, NOWs continued their southward trickle as Congress extended NOW accounts to New Jersey.

To many observers, the only logical outcome of this process was for NOW accounts to be authorized on a nationwide basis and, as already indicated, the Deregulation Act of 1980 did precisely that. In some respects this episode provides a vindication for those who defend the curious patchwork quilt of regulation governing financial institutions. As may be recalled, one argument in favor of the chartering of financial institutions by individual states is that it encourages financial innovation by providing fifty "experimental laboratories." At least in the case of NOW accounts, it seems clear that we have gotten to the present state of affairs only because of innovation at the state level, which has forced action at the federal level. Indeed, it was the momentum of this process that served to give us NOWs on a nationwide basis.

### Electronic Money Once Again

While Congressional action has dictated that nationwide NOWs should serve as the solution to the problem of providing checklike powers to the thrifts, as events were unfolding in the 1970s this was less than evident. Consequently, the thrifts pursued other strategies aimed at eroding the checking advantage of the commercial banks. One of these developments is worthy of note, since it may well have a role to play in conjunction with universal NOW accounts. In particular, we are referring to the use of electronic terminals to make transactions. Such terminals, which go by the name of *remote service units* (RSUs) or *point of sale* (POS) terminals, were first utitilized by a savings and loan association in Nebraska that placed several RSUs in Hinky Dinky supermarkets. Account holders could thus withdraw cash, make deposits, make charge account and loan payments, and transfer funds from one account to another while shopping. Other savings and loans soon followed suit, locating terminals in such convenient places as airports, factories, and student centers at colleges and universities.

While it is apparent that RSUs are not a perfect substitute for checking accounts, they clearly make savings accounts at thrifts more useful for transactions purposes.[7] Indeed, it should be apparent that even with nationwide NOWs, RSUs could well be a critical component in the financial system of the future. The status of the RSUs was temporarily clouded by an April 1979 court order declaring them illegal under existing law. However, a grace period was provided before RSUs actually had to be withdrawn, and as we shall see, the legal issue was subsequently settled by Congress.[8]

As should be apparent from our discussion, in the 1970s savings and loans and mutual savings banks came a long way toward acquiring check-like powers. Via share drafts, which function much like NOW accounts, some credit unions had also acquired checklike powers.[9] As far as customers are concerned, these new deposit services at nonbank intermediaries are quite similar to demand deposits at commercial banks. There is, of course, one important difference in that NOWs pay explicit interest. This brings us to the last reform that we shall consider—the payment of interest on demand deposits.

**Payment of Interest on Transaction Accounts**   Like ceilings on time and savings deposits, the prohibition of payment of interest on demand deposits had its origin in the tumultuous period of the 1930s. However, unlike Regulation Q ceilings, which have undergone some erosion, the zero ceiling on demand deposits has

---

[7] Some thrifts have also introduced telephone transfers to third parties.

[8] Another interesting legal aspect of RSUs is that, before they had been challenged, RSUs were not considered branch offices of the thrifts. In contrast, as we saw in Chapter 5, similar terminals introduced by commercial banks (CBCTs) had been judged to be subject to branch banking laws.

[9] Thus far share drafts have been of relatively limited quantitative importance. The legal status of share drafts was temporarily cast into doubt by the April 1979 court order cited above.

remained intact. Instead, there have been a series of end runs around this prohibition. An early form of this technique was the payment of implicit interest via gifts to depositors or the provision of services below cost (e.g., "free checking"). The most recent end runs have involved moving away, either directly or indirectly, from sole reliance on the use of demand deposits as a medium of transactions. There are four key developments of this sort that deserve mention.

1   NOW ACCOUNTS. As we have noted, NOWs look, feel, and smell like checks but pay interest (currently subject to a ceiling of 5 percent). Consequently, when nationwide NOWs come into being, this will represent a significant step toward circumventing the payment of interest on demand deposits. This action would not, however, make demand deposits obsolete. For one, only individuals and certain nonprofit organizations can hold NOW accounts, so businesses would still make use of demand deposits. Second, there is the issue of service charges on NOWs. With NOWs available on a nationwide basis, financial institutions will undoubtedly charge for various services that are currently provided free. Especially if the ceiling on NOW accounts remains at 5 percent, some individual depositors might still find demand deposits attractive relative to NOW.[10] Nevertheless, nationwide NOWs could contribute to making zero-yielding demand deposits an endangered species.

2   MONEY MARKET FUNDS. As previously described, money market funds pay a near-market rate of return on shares but also permit, subject to a minimum check size, shareholders to withdraw funds by writing a check. While evidence on the use of these funds for transactions purposes is a bit sketchy, in at least a limited sense these funds contribute to the circumvention of the interest prohibition on demand deposits.

3   REPURCHASE AGREEMENTS. In our discussion of commercial banking, we noted that repurchase agreements (RPs) have grown dramatically in recent years. An RP, it will be recalled, is an acquisition of funds via the sale of securities, with a simultaneous agreement by the seller to *repurchase* them at a specified later time. RPs are frequently made for one business day (i.e., overnight).[11] The repurchase price is naturally higher than the sale price, this being the way in which interest is paid. Suppose,

---

[10] Some economists have estimated the implicit interest payment on demand deposit accounts of individuals to be only slightly below 5 percent.

[11] For an informative and readable analysis of repurchase agreements, on which much of our discussion is based, see N. N. Bowsher, "Repurchase Agreements," *Review*, Federal Reserve Bank of St. Louis, September 1979, pp. 17–22.

for example, a corporation has cash in a demand deposit account that is not needed today but is likely to be required to meet anticipated expenditures tomorrow.[12] The corporation would naturally like to earn interest on these temporarily excess funds, and can do so by use of an RP. More specifically, it can arrange to buy a government security from a commercial bank, at the same time obtaining an agreement that the bank will repurchase the security on the following day. The net effect of this is temporarily to reduce the corporation's holding of demand deposits while at the same time earning a secured market rate of return. When the RP matures, the corporation's demand deposit is restored. While the RP itself is not a medium of exchange, from the corporation's viewpoint the overnight RP and the demand deposit are virtually indistinguishable. Indeed, the corporation may even write checks on the funds, since the RPs will be available as deposits before the check clears. As should be apparent from this discussion, the use of overnight RPs allows the bank to pay interest on funds that are effectively demand deposits.[13] Thus, for the large corporations that participate in the market (most RP transactions are in amounts of $1 million or more), the RP market offers a way of circumventing the zero ceiling on demand deposits.

4 TRANSFERS FROM SAVINGS TO CHECKING DEPOSITS. It would be possible to avoid the prohibition of the payment of interest on demand deposits if funds were kept in an interest-bearing account until the very last moment before they were needed, and only then transferred to a checking account. To a large extent, both individuals and corporations try to accomplish precisely this through their cash management practices. Transactions costs, however, have frequently made it uneconomical to achieve a perfect synchronization in the transfer of funds. For example, for the individual such transactions costs might reflect the effort of carefully monitoring receipts and payments as well as the cost of a "trip to the bank" to effect the transfer to a checking account. Quite evidently, any development that reduces transactions costs will enable the depositor to achieve a closer synchronization.

One such development was introduced in April 1975, when the Federal Reserve authorized member banks to accept

---

[12] In recent years, spurred by high interest rates, virtually all large corporations have undertaken to manage their cash balances on a daily basis. A number of other techniques for accomplishing this are discussed in the next chapter.

[13] Some economists prefer to think of RPs as more like time deposits even though they start out and end up as demand deposits. For longer-maturity RPs, this seems quite plausible. For overnight RPs, the situation is admittedly ambiguous.

telephone orders for transferring funds from a savings account to a checking account. This reduced the cost of a "trip to the bank" and meant that individuals could wait to transfer funds until they actually wrote a check. Indeed, if they wanted to be gutsy they could even delay a day or two after writing a check, hoping to earn additional interest until the check actually cleared.[14] Of course, there were still some transactions costs involved, stemming from the need to monitor receipts and expenditures and from the telephone call itself. This was all carried to its logical conclusion in November 1978, when commercial and mutual savings banks were authorized to offer *automatic transfer services* (ATS) from a savings account to a checking account or other type of transaction account.

Under ATS the customer need not keep any funds in a checking account. Transactions balances are kept in savings accounts, earning the passbook rate of interest, and funds are transferred as checks clear. In effect ATS functions much like a NOW account, and in fact it was congressional slowness in approving nationwide NOWs that led the Federal Reserve to introduce ATS. Unfortunately, in April 1979, in the court decision referred to earlier, the U.S. Court of Appeals ruled that ATS were illegal and could not be maintained after January 1, 1980, unless Congress enacted appropriate legislation. At the end of 1979 Congress provided temporary authorization of ATS until March 31, 1980, and planned to use the time to sort out the whole ATS–NOW issue. We now turn to the end result of this process.

**DEPOSITORY INSTITUTIONS DEREGULATION ACT OF 1980**

As should be apparent from the previous section, at the start of 1980 Congress found itself under considerable pressure to undertake reform of the financial system. The immediate source of this pressure arose from the court decision that had invalidated ATS, RSUs, and credit union share drafts. In addition, however, with the spread of NOW accounts to New York, New Jersey, and the six New England states, it became increasingly evident that "containment" of NOWs was no longer a viable strategy. Finally, there was the long-standing pressure to "do some-

---

[14] The consequences of waiting too long depend on the type of demand deposit account one has. For some accounts, waiting too long to transfer funds could involve the embarrassment of a bounced check and the subsequent payment of a penalty. If the account has overdraft privileges, the check will clear but the bank will, in effect, lend the funds to the depositor to cover the check. Since the loan rate exceeds the savings deposit rate, the depositor could lose in this way as well.

thing" about the Regulation Q ceilings, and, relatedly to expand the scope of activities permitted to the thrift institutions. It was in the face of all these pressures that Congress undertook a comprehensive reexamination of the financial system and ultimately passed the Deregulation Act of 1980.[15] The Act contained many important provisions with the following among the most noteworthy:

*NOW Accounts.* Authorizes NOW accounts nationwide at all depository institutions, effective year-end 1980. NOW accounts are avaialable to individuals and nonprofit organizations.

*ATS.* Permits banks to provide automatic transfer services from savings to checking accounts.

*RSUs.* Permits the establishment of remote service units by savings and loan associations for such purposes as crediting and debiting savings accounts and credit payment on loans.

*Share Drafts.* Authorizes all federally insured credit unions to offer share draft accounts, thus extending checking-like power to credit unions.

*Mortgage Usury Ceilings.* Eliminates State mortgage usury ceilings unless a State adopts a new usury ceiling prior to April 1, 1983.

Quite evidently these actions are far-reaching and should have a marked and relatively immediate impact on the nature of the financial system. Other provisions of the Act, specifically those dealing with interest rate ceilings on deposits, will have their effects felt only gradually.

**Regulation Q Ceilings**

In the introduction to the Deregulation Act it states the following:

*The Congress hereby finds that*
*(1) limitations on the interest rates which are payable on deposits and accounts discourage persons from saving money, create inequities for depositors, impede the ability of depository institutions to compete for funds, and have not achieved their purpose of providing an even flow of funds for home mortgage lending; and*
*(2) all depositors, and particularly those with modest savings, are entitled to receive a market rate of return on their savings as soon as it is economically feasible for depository institutions to pay such rate.*

---

[15] Strictly speaking the Deregulation Act pertains to interest rate ceilings, while such things as NOW accounts were authorized by the formidable-sounding Consumer Checking Account Equity Act of 1980. For simplicity we shall merely refer to the Deregulation Act. Another part of the legislation, the Monetary Control Act of 1980, was designed to improve the ability of the Federal Reserve to conduct monetary policy. This Act is discussed in the next chapter.

The introduction then goes on to indicate that it is the purpose of the Act to provide for an "orderly phase-out and the ultimate elimination of the limitations on the maximum rates of interest and dividends which may be paid on deposits."

To accomplish this phase-out of interest ceilings, the Act established a Deregulation Committee consisting of the Secretary of the Treasury and the Chairmen of the Federal Reserve, the FDIC, the Federal Home Loan Bank Board, and the National Credit Union Administration Board. The Deregulation Committee is charged with bringing about the phase-out over a six-year period and with making regular reports on how the deregulation process is working. Other than providing a self-destruct mechanism for the Committee and for repealing all authority to impose interest ceilings after six years, the Act sets no specific timetable for the phase-out. As of this writing, it is too early to tell how fast the phase-out is likely to proceed. The question of speed aside, however, it should be apparent that in the longer run this provision of the Act will initiate marked changes in the nature of financial intermediation.

**Expanding the Powers of the Thrifts**

As suggested earlier, piecemeal tinkering with the financial system is potentially dangerous in that it can sometimes upset a delicate balance. It was with this in mind that the Hunt Commission, while proposing the elimination of interest rate ceilings, simultaneously proposed expanding the powers of the thrift institutions to enable them to compete effectively with the commercial banks. In shaping the Deregulation Act of 1980, Congress was also mindful of this issue and took several steps to enrich the menu of asset choices available to the thrifts. In particular, the Act contained the following provisions:

1   Authorization for savings and loans to invest up to 20 percent of assets in consumer loans, commercial paper, and corporate securities.
2   Expansion of the authority of savings and loans to make real estate loans by removing the geographic restrictions on lending.
3   Permission for savings and loans to issue credit cards and extend credit in connection with such cards.
4   Authorization for savings and loans to offer trust services.
5   Permission for mutual savings banks to make commercial and business loans up to 5 percent of their assets.

These steps, in conjunction with NOW accounts and the elimination of mortgage usury ceilings, should improve the competitive position of the thrifts. Nevertheless, it is not clear whether these steps go far enough. Doubts on this score are explicitly recognized in the Deregulation Act itself, which calls for the President to convene a task force to study and make recommendations regarding options available to improve the balance between assets and liabilities in thrift portfolios.

Similarly, the Act provides for the Deregulation Committee phasing out interest ceilings to pay due regard to the viability of the thrift institutions. What this all suggests is that over the longer run further legislative actions may be necessary to assure the health of the thrift institutions. However, for the moment, at least, a wait-and-see attitude seems in order.

**Overview**

At the start of the 1970s, the Hunt Commission advocated a restructuring of the financial system that would eliminate the distinction among various intermediaries and make the system more responsive to market forces. Events of the 1970s inexorably moved the financial system in the directions prescribed by the Hunt Report, and the process culminated with the Deregulation Act of 1980. Over the longer run the Act should have a far-reaching impact on the financial system. In the short run, the effects of the Act will be more limited, but the Act nevertheless has profound immediate implications for the definition of money and the conduct of monetary policy. It is to this issue that we now turn.

**E DEFINITION OF MONEY ECONSIDERED**

As we have seen, even prior to the Deregulation Act, more and more financial instruments began serving the function of a medium of transactions. As a consequence, by the late 1970s it had become evident that the traditional narrow definition of money as the sum of currency and demand deposits would no longer suffice. Of course, the passage of the Deregulation Act and the authorization of nationwide NOW accounts made it even more imperative to adopt a modernized definition of money.

In recognition of the fundamental changes that were occurring in the financial system, in February 1980—just prior to the passage of the Deregulation Act—the Federal Reserve introduced a new set of definitions of the monetary aggregates. This set runs the gamut from the traditional narrow definition to an extremely broad measure of liquidity. The full set of definitions, with corresponding data as of year-end 1979, is given in Table 17–2. The organizing principle underlying the redefined monetary aggregates was the functional one that at each level of aggregation one should combine similar kinds of monetary assets. To see how this principle was applied, we shall examine the narrow and broad measures in turn.

**Money, Narrowly Defined**

The traditional narrow definition of money has been the sum of currency and demand deposits at commercial banks, generally denoted by M-1. With a minor modification, this series will continue to be reported, although designated by the symbol M-1A. The minor modification is that

M-1A, unlike M-1, excludes demand deposits held by foreign commercial banks and foreign official institutions.

The new "modern" narrow definition is denoted by M-1B and consists of M-1A *plus* what are termed "other checkable deposits." In this category the Federal Reserve has included NOW and ATS balances as well as share drafts held at credit unions and demand deposits at thrift institutions. Thus, M-1B includes transaction-type balances at thrift institutions as well as commercial bank balances other than demand deposits that also function as media of payments. As Table 17–2 shows, at the end of 1979 these "other checkable deposits" amounted to some $16 billion. Clearly, however, there is a rather dramatic potential for growth in this category, especially when nationwide NOWs come into existence. It is precisely because of this possibility that the Federal Reserve retained, for the time being, two narrow measures of money, M-1A and M-1B.

**TABLE 17–2**

*Various money stock measures and components (in billions of dollars, not seasonally adjusted, November 1979)*

| Aggregate and component | Amount |
|---|---|
| M-1A | 372.2 |
|   Currency | 106.6 |
|   Demand deposits | 265.6 |
| M-1B | 387.9 |
|   M-1A | 372.2 |
|   Other checkable deposits* | 15.7 |
| M-2 | 1,510.0 |
|   M-1B | 387.9 |
|   Overnight RPs issued by commercial banks | 20.3 |
|   Overnight Eurodollar deposits held by U.S. nonbank residents at Caribbean branches of U.S. banks | 3.2 |
|   Money market mutual fund shares | 40.4 |
|   Savings deposits at all depository institutions | 420.0 |
|   Small time deposits at all depository institutions† | 640.8 |
| M-3 | 1,759.1 |
|   M-2 | 1,510.0 |
|   Large time deposits at all depository institutions‡ | 219.5 |
|   Term RPs issued by commercial banks | 21.5 |
|   Term RPs issued by savings and loan associations | 8.2 |
| L | 2,123.8 |
|   M-3 | 1,759.1 |
|   Other Eurodollar deposits of U.S. residents other than banks | 34.5 |
|   Banker acceptances | 27.6 |
|   Commercial paper | 97.1 |
|   Savings bonds | 80.0 |
|   Liquid Treasury obligations | 125.4 |

* Includes NOW, ATS, and credit union share draft balances and demand deposits at thrift institutions.
† Time deposits issued in denominations of less than $100,000.
‡ Time deposits issued in denominations of $100,000 or more.
*Source: Federal Reserve Bulletin,* February 1980, p. 98.

Consider, for example, what might happen when NOWs exist on a nationwide basis. Evidence based on the NOW account experience in New England and New York indicates that during the transition period, when the majority of NOW accounts were opened, growth in total NOW balances was buoyed by shifts from demand deposits, savings balances, and other liquid assets. As the Federal Reserve has put it:

> *This suggests that during a conversion period associated with nationwide NOW accounts, growth in M-1B could significantly overstate underlying growth in the public's transactions balances. M-1A, by contrast, would tend to understate such growth, as households converted demand deposit balances into NOW accounts. In practice, since the extent of shifting from demand deposits or other accounts to NOW accounts is uncertain, the availability of both M-1 measures is expected to help in the interpretation of narrow money stock growth during the transition period, should NOW accounts be offered nationwide.*[16]

In view of our previous discussion, the question naturally arises as to whether the Federal Reserve has included all relevant assets in the category "other checkable deposits." The Federal Reserve has already acknowledged one such omission, which it plans to remedy as soon as data availability permits. In particular, it intends to include in M-1B the volume of travelers checks of nonbank issuers. But as we have seen, there are other potential candidates as well. These would include shares in money market funds and overnight RPs. While admitting that a case could be made for including these assets in M-1B, for the present the Federal Reserve has not done this. Rather, it has argued that money market funds are more like savings deposits, and hence has included them in a broader definition of money. As for overnight RPs, the Federal Reserve has noted that "professional opinion is currently divided over whether RPs are mainly liquid investments or transaction-type balances," and has opted for only including them in a broader aggregate. It should be noted, however, that even this represents a step forward, as money market shares and RPs were excluded from all of the previously existing definitions of money.

On balance, the Federal Reserve has moved to modernize the transaction-type measure of money but has not gone as far as it might. Nevertheless, it has retained an open mind on the question, recognizing "that no one set of monetary aggregates can satisfy every purpose or every user." As a consequence, it plans to publish regularly all the relevant

---

[16] "The Redefined Monetary Aggregates," *Federal Reserve Bulletin*, February 1980, p. 100. Recall that the changes in the definition of money were introduced prior to the passage of the Deregulation Act.

raw information so that those who would prefer their M-1B with RPs will be able to "roll their own."

**Broader Measures of Money**

We indicated in Chapter 1 that some economists prefer to make use of a broader definition of money that includes assets such as time and savings deposits. So this group would not feel left out, the Federal Reserve has also modernized its broad definitions of money. These are denoted by M-2 and M-3. In addition, the Federal Reserve has begun reporting a very broad measure of liquid assets, which is denoted by the symbol L. All three of these broad measures are defined in Table 17–2.

Generally speaking, M-2 includes savings and small time deposits at all depository institutions as well as money market shares and overnight

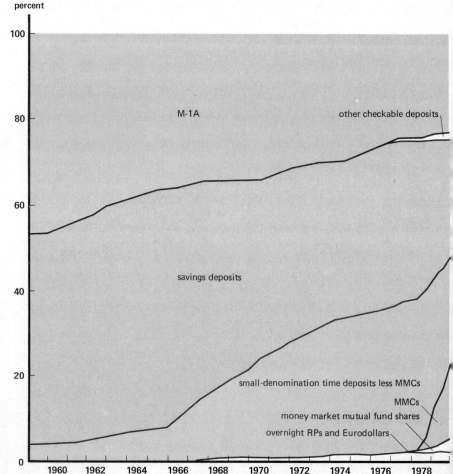

*Principal components of M-2*

Source: *Federal Reserve Bulletin,* February 1980, Washington, D.C., p. 107.

**FIGURE 17–2**

RPs and overnight Eurodollars. Figure 17–2 indicates how the composition of M-2 has varied over time. Quite evidently, money, narrowly defined, has been a decreasing fraction of M-2. The same story is told in another way in Table 17–3, which shows the annual average growth rates for the various measures of money. Since 1960 M-2 has grown substantially faster than M-1A or M1-B, reflecting primarily more rapid growth of time and savings deposits than of demand deposits. The M-3 measure has even grown faster than M-2.

**Why All the Fuss?**

Although we have spared the reader the gory details, before unveiling the revised definitions of money the Federal Reserve expended many resources. First, an Advisory Committee on Monetary Statistics was established. This committee, which issued its report in 1976, entailed considerable effort by economists both inside and outside the Federal Reserve. Before the recommendations of this committee were implemented, however, it became apparent that the rapid evolution of the financial system meant that further study was required. Consequently, substantial additional effort was undertaken, and as we have seen, in early 1980 the new definitions were released.

To the casual observer this scurrying about to produce the "best" definition of money might seem a bit strange. Such a person would undoubtedly agree that it was desirable, at least on aesthetic grounds, to have a sensible and consistent definition of money. Yet all the effort devoted to the question suggests that more than aesthetics is involved, and indeed this is the case. More specifically, how one defines money can have a critical influence on the conduct and success of monetary policy. In this regard several points deserve to be stressed.

1   In carrying out monetary policy the Federal Reserve must be guided by some model of the economy. As we have seen, a critical ingredient of such a model is likely to be the demand function for money. If such a function is to be empirically identified in a reliable way, it is clearly necessary that we define money in the behaviorally most meaningful way. Only in such circumstances is the Federal Reserve likely to be able to carry out a successful policy.

**TABLE 17–3**

*Growth rates of various monetary measures (average annual rates of growth, in percentages)*

| Period | M-1A | M-1B | M-2 | M-3 |
|---|---|---|---|---|
| 1960–1979 | 4.9 | 5.1 | 8.3 | 9.0 |
| 1960–1969 | 3.7 | 3.8 | 6.9 | 7.2 |
| 1970–1979 | 6.0 | 6.4 | 9.6 | 10.8 |

Source: *Federal Reserve Bulletin*, February 1980, p. 103.

2   To put the point another way, even (or perhaps especially) if one were a monetarist who advocated the Friedman rule that the money supply should grow at a constant rate, it is clearly critical how we define the money supply.

3   As hinted at above, economists sometimes use movements in the stock of money as an indicator of the state of the economy. Again, this clearly requires a definition of money that is closely related to underlying economic variables.

4   Not all definitions of money are equally amenable to control by the Federal Reserve. If it turns out that the best definition is only controllable with significant error, then perhaps the Federal Reserve should be provided with additional tools to improve monetary control.

As these points make clear, considerably more than aesthetics is involved in how we define money. What this all suggests is that we need to move from definitional issues to an examination of the role of money in monetary policy. We take up this issue in the next chapter.

**SELECTED READINGS**

Board of Governors of the Federal Reserve System, "A Proposal for Redefining the Monetary Aggregates," *Federal Reserve Bulletin*, January 1979, pp. 13–42.

———, "The Redefined Monetary Aggregates," *Federal Reserve Bulletin*, February 1980, pp. 97–114.

Bowsher, N. N., "Repurchase Agreements," *Review*, Federal Reserve Bank of St. Louis, September 1979, pp. 17–22.

Lovati, J. M., "The Growing Similarity Among Financial Institutions," *Review*, Federal Reserve Bank of St. Louis, October 1977, pp. 2–11.

*Report of the President's Commission on Financial Structure and Regulation*, Washington, D.C., Government Printing Office, 1971.

Roberts, S. M., "Development Money Substitutes," in Federal Reserve System, *Improving the Monetary Aggregates*, Washington, D.C., 1978, pp. 147–165.

Some readers may think the title of this chapter a bit strange, since it probably seems self-evident that money is somehow the essence of monetary policy. Indeed, throughout our discussion of policy from Chapter 14 on, we have fostered this impression by maintaining the assumption that monetary policy involved finding the "right" quantity for the stock of money. To be sure, we have suggested that problems of conflicting goals, lags, uncertainty and financial evolution make this no simple task, but the presumption has been that money and monetary policy are virtually synonomous. While for many purposes this is a useful simplifying assumption, there is, in fact, more to monetary policy than just finding the "right" quantity of money.

For one thing, monetary policy does not necessarily operate by setting the money supply. From 1942 to 1951, for example, the Federal Reserve conducted policy by pegging interest rates and letting the money supply be whatever it turned out to be. In subsequent years, although it abandoned pegging, the Federal Reserve continued to pay more attention to interest rates than to monetary aggregates. It is only in recent years that policy has been seriously concerned with the money supply. Nevertheless, even here there has been more to policy than just picking a monetary target. The reason, of course, is that the Federal Reserve is not endowed with a "money supply dial" that allows it to control the stock of money. Rather, as we shall see, there are serious questions as to the best operating procedures for controlling the money supply.

The purpose, then, of this chapter is to reexamine the nature of monetary policy. The outline of the chapter is as follows: We first address the question of why the Federal Reserve might pay attention to interest rates. Since the wisdom of this depends in part on the stability of the demand for money, we next examine this issue. Following this, we take a detailed look at how the Federal Reserve actually conducts monetary policy, focusing particularly on its choice of operating strategies. Finally, we consider some legislative proposals designed to improve the Federal Reserve's ability to control the money supply.

**MONETARY POLICY TARGETS: MONEY VS. THE INTEREST RATE**

We have just indicated that under some circumstances the Federal Reserve, even if it could directly control the quantity of money, might choose to conduct monetary policy in some other fashion. We shall consider a number of alternative possible strategies below, but here we concentrate on just one strategy that has been frequently advocated, namely, that the Federal Reserve should control the interest rate.[1] This should not be interpreted as meaning that the Federal Reserve necessarily pegs the interest rate for an extended period of time (as it did during World War II). Rather, what the advocates of this strategy have in mind is that the Federal Reserve should select a "reasonable" level for the interest rate and maintain it for some number of months. From a practical point of view, such a strategy is quite easy to carry out via open-market operations. Basically, the Federal Reserve must stand ready to buy or sell securities at the particular price that corresponds to the target interest rate. Of course, under such a strategy the Federal Reserve gives up the ability to control the money supply.

The question naturally arises as to what difference it makes whether the authorities operate by setting the money supply or setting the interest rate. As we shall see, the answer depends on the nature of the uncertainty confronting the policy maker. We have noted that policy makers face various types of uncertainty. Two of the most important of these are uncertainty over the strength of aggregate demand and uncertainty over the strength of the demand for money. In terms of the familiar *IS–LM* framework, uncertainty over the state of aggregate demand means that the monetary authorities are not exactly certain where the *IS* curve is located. They know on average where it will be. But if demand is "surprisingly" strong, then the actual *IS* curve will be farther to the right than the average *IS* curve. And if demand is surprisingly weak, the actual *IS* curve will be to the left of the average *IS* curve. Similarly, because of unexpected variations in the strength of money demand, setting the

---

[1] In couching this strategy in terms of "the" interest rate, we are abstracting from the real-world complexity presented by the existence of many different interest rates. However, our earlier discussion of the structure of interest rates suggests that this is a reasonable simplification.

quantity of money will not precisely pin down the location of the *LM* curve. Again, of course, the authorities will have some notion of where the *LM* curve will be on average.

This then is the setting in which we shall explore the consequences of operating monetary policy by fixing either the money supply or the interest rate. Initially, we shall assume that the price level is fixed, but later we shall consider the case of a variable price level.

**The Case of Certainty**  Figure 18–1 illustrates the two types of monetary policy in the context of the *IS–LM* model. We assume that the authorities desire to bring about a full-employment level of income, $O_e$, and for the moment we ignore the problem of uncertainty. Thus, the position of the *IS* curve is assumed known. To bring about $O_e$ the monetary authorities have two options. First, they could fix the money supply so that the conventional-looking *LM* curve, $L_1M_1$, intersects the *IS* curve at $O_e$. This is possible because we are temporarily ignoring uncertainty about money demand. Alternatively, the authorities could, by appropriate open-market operations, bring the interest rate to $r_e$ and keep it there. This second option amounts to a horizontal *LM* curve, shown as $L_2M_2$. As is clear from Figure 18–1, in the absence of uncertainty it makes little difference which policy is pursued. In either case the equilibrium $(r_e, O_e)$ emerges. When we introduce uncertainty, however, these two policies can diverge.

**The Case of Uncertainty**  We first consider the case in which the uncertainty is solely in the location of the *IS* curve. To keep matters simple, we assume that the *IS* curve is known to lie between the two extremes $I_1S_1$ and $I_2S_2$ in Figure 18–2. If the money supply is set at some fixed level, then the *LM* curve will be $L_1M_1$. Consequently, income will fall somewhere between $O_2$ and $O_3$. Alternatively, suppose the monetary authorities fix the interest

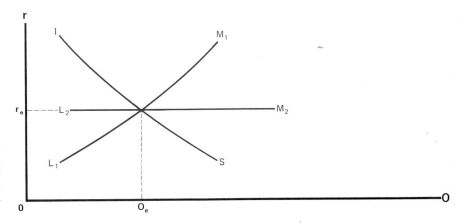

*Money stock and interest rate policies: The certainty case*

**FIGURE 18–1**

rate at $r_e$. The relevant $LM$ curve is $L_2M_2$, and income will vary between $O_1$ and $O_4$, a wider range than $O_2$ to $O_3$. Since on average both policies will produce the desired level $O_e$, the money stock policy is superior to the interest rate policy because it produces a smaller range of variation about that average. The reason for this is that under a money stock policy a random disturbance to the $IS$ curve will affect the interest rate. This in turn will induce a change in investment that partially offsets the initial disturbance.

The opposite polar case is pictured in Figure 18–3. Here we assume that there is no uncertainty about the position of the $IS$ curve. However, unpredictable movements in the demand-for-money function will cause shifts in the $LM$ curve if a money stock policy is followed. As illustrated in Figure 18–3, these shifts are assumed to keep the $LM$ curve between $L_1M_1$ and $L_2M_2$, with the result that income ends up anywhere between $O_1$ and $O_2$. In contrast, however, an interest rate policy keeps the $LM$ curve at $L_3M_3$, so that the desired full-employment level of income, $O_e$,

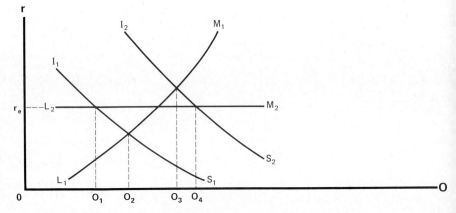

Alternative policies:
IS *uncertainty*

**FIGURE 18–2**

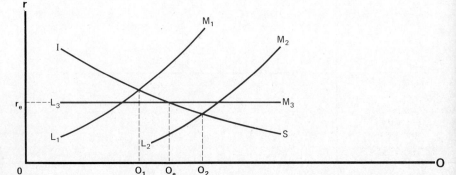

Alternative policies:
LM *uncertainty*

**FIGURE 18–3**

results. This comes about because the stock of money is simply allowed to accommodate any shifts in the demand for money.

We thus see that if uncertainties arise solely from the *IS* or commodity sector, a money stock policy will be superior to an interest rate policy. On the other hand, if the uncertainties arise solely from the *LM* or money sector, an interest rate policy will be superior. In realistic situations, of course, the policy makers are confronted with uncertainty in regard to *both* the *IS* and *LM* curves. Two illustrations of this are depicted in Figures 18–4 and 18–5. In Figure 18–4 the *IS* curve is more unpredictable and, as in the pure case of *IS* uncertainty, the money stock policy is superior—the range is from $O_2$ to $O_3$ instead of $O_1$ to $O_4$. In Figure 18–5

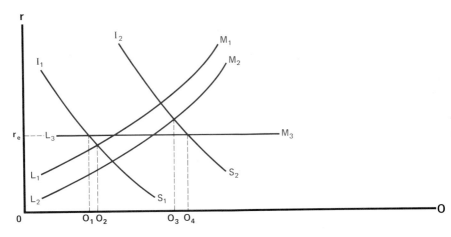

*Alternative policies: IS and LM uncertainty*

**FIGURE 18–4**

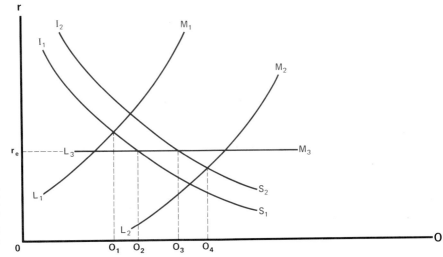

*Alternative policies: IS and LM uncertainty*

**FIGURE 18–5**

the *LM* curve is more variable and, as in Figure 18–3, the interest rate policy is superior.[2]

To a considerable extent these results serve to rationalize the policy recommendations of monetarist economists. In particular, monetarists have frequently stressed their belief that the money-demand function is relatively more stable than the consumption function or the investment function. Thus, they would argue that the situation in Figure 18–4 is more realistic than the one in Figure 18–5. In view of this, it is hardly surprising that the monetarists strongly prefer a money stock policy to an interest rate policy. Furthermore, monetarists emphasize that once the price level is free to vary, there are additional grounds for avoiding an interest rate policy.

**The Interest Rate Policy: A Caveat**

As we saw earlier, in an inflationary environment there is an important distinction between nominal and real rates of interest. Furthermore, it is the real rate of interest that is more relevant for spending behavior.[3] However, since the anticipated rate of inflation is not directly observable, neither is the real rate of interest. Thus, as a practical matter interest rate policies tend to be couched in terms of nominal interest rates. There is a problem here, however, in that the nominal rate of interest incorporates an inflation premium whose size is not precisely known. Hence, it may be difficult to decide whether a given nominal interest rate represents a "tight" or an "easy" monetary policy.

This point has been stressed by monetarists, who have also pointed out the possible undesirable consequences of pursuing an interest rate policy that inadvertently attempts to keep the interest rate below its equilibrium level. They envision a scenario in which the nominal interest rate is reduced by expansionary open-market operations, which leads to an increase in the stock of money outstanding. If this process begins at or near full employment, the initial increase in *M* will lead to a rise in prices, that is, inflation. The actual inflationary experience may generate a rise in the anticipated future rate of inflation. This can lead to a rise in the demand for loanable funds, which will tend to increase interest rates. Thus, still more money would have to be created to prevent interest rates from rising. This could lead to a vicious circle in which further increases in the stock of money produce more inflation, higher antici-

---

[2] For a detailed discussion of these points and a number of extensions see W. Poole, "Optimal Choice of Monetary Policy Instruments in a Simple Stochastic Macro Model," *Quarterly Journal of Economics*, May 1970, pp. 197–216.

[3] Consider, for example, a prospective homeowner faced with a 12 percent mortgage rate. Before deciding this is "high" or "low," our prospective investor obviously examines how fast house prices are likely to appreciate. If, say, they are expected to rise at 12 percent as well, then the mortgage rate is likely to be regarded as a good deal. All we are saying here, of course, is that the investor looks at the real rate of interest (which, in our example, is actually zero).

pated rates of inflation, and greater upward pressure on interest rates. Such a policy may be a perfect recipe for continuing, and probably accelerating, price inflation. In fact, once inflationary expectations become widespread, a level of interest rates that would have maintained price stability under conditions of noninflationary expectations will actually encourage inflation. In this regard it is interesting to note that during World War II, when interest rates were pegged at a low level, at the same time we had price controls to repress the potential inflation. At the end of the war, when controls were lifted but interest rates were kept low, we experienced a serious bout of inflation.

On balance then, it would appear that caution is needed in pursuing an interest rate policy. After much badgering by monetarists, even nonmonetarists have now agreed that there are potential difficulties. Nevertheless, many nonmonetarists still maintain that if uncertainty primarily stems from the LM curve, interest rate policies may be desirable. This is more likely to be the case over short time horizons, when the anticipated rate of inflation does not change very much.

**Overview**    We have considered two alternative operating strategies for monetary policy—money targets and interest rate targets. In neither case, however, should this analysis be interpreted as implying the desirability of a fixed rate. Thus, for example, if the nature of uncertainty is such as to favor a money target, there is no presumption that this target would be chosen by a rule of the Friedman sort. Indeed, this analysis is perfectly consistent with the Federal Reserve's varying the money supply (or interest rate targets) in a discretionary way.

There remains, of course, the issue of which of the two policies we have considered is to be preferred in practice. As we have seen, this depends on whether the uncertainty stems from the IS or the LM side of things. This issue has long been debated, both theoretically and empirically, without a definitive resolution. In a way this should not be surprising, because it is quite likely that the primary source of uncertainty may switch from IS to LM and back again as circumstances change. In recent years it appears that there has been increasing uncertainty in the LM curve. Since the LM curve stems from the equilibrium condition in the money market, this uncertainty could result from the demand or supply of money. In fact, as we shall see, both sides have contributed to increased uncertainty. We first take up the demand for money.

**UNCERTAINTY AND THE DEMAND FOR MONEY**    As just suggested, the recent behavior of the demand for money has been such as to impart increased uncertainty to the LM curve. Since uncertainty might be measured in various ways, we need to be a bit more precise on this point. What we have in mind in referring to uncertainty are the related concepts of *predictability* and *stability*. As we saw in Chapter 12, the major determinants of the demand for money are income (representing transaction needs) and interest rates. If, given these determinants, we could predict the demand for money with a high degree of accuracy, then, in an intuitive sense at least, most observers would agree that money demand is not an important source of uncertainty. A precondition for successful prediction is likely to be a stable demand function for money. That is, the empirical relationship between money and its determinants should remain roughly constant from one period to the next. Until a few years ago most studies had concluded that the demand for money was both stable and quite predictable.[4] In terms of our previous analysis, other things equal, this tended to support the use of monetary targets. In the mid-1970s, however, confidence in the stability of the demand for money was severely shaken.[5]

**The Case of the Missing Money**

As we have identified uncertainty with a lack of predictability, this suggests that we ought to take a look at the forecasting record of the demand-for-money function. This is done in Figure 18–6, where we have plotted the actual quantity of real-money balances along with the quantity predicted by a conventional money demand function for the period from 1974 to 1976.[6]

As may be recalled, the economy experienced a severe recession from the first quarter of 1974 to the first quarter of 1975 and then recovered. Consistent with this, as Figure 18–6 shows, the demand for money was predicted to decline through the first quarter of 1975 and to rise thereafter. Actual money demand did decline, but the drop was much steeper than predicted. Furthermore, as the economy recovered, the actual demand for money rose only very slightly. By mid-1976 the prediction error was a whopping 10 percent—much larger than any previous prediction error. It was thus apparent that the economy was making do with much less money, given the levels of income and interest rates, than had been predicted on the basis of past behavior. In view of this shortfall, this episode is sometimes referred to as "the case of the missing money."

---

[4] See, for example, S. M. Goldfeld, "The Demand for Money Revisited," *Brookings Papers on Ecoomic Activity*, 1973, no. 3, pp. 577–638.

[5] Ironically, as we shall see below, monetary targets were not used during the earlier period of stability but were introduced after signs of instability arose.

[6] The actual money data are based on the M-1 series (what is now called M-1A). In making the predictions the money demand equation was estimated using quarterly data from 1952–1973 and then extrapolated to the period 1974–1976. For details, see S. M. Goldfeld, "The Case of the Missing Money," *Brooking Papers on Economic Activity*, 1976, no. 3, Table 2, p. 687.

The same point can be made in a slightly different way with reference to the concept of the income velocity of money. Velocity, denoted by V, it will be recalled, is defined by the condition

$$MV = Y$$

where Y is nominal GNP. In our earlier discussion we pointed out that there has been a rising trend in velocity in the period since the end of World War II. We also noted that during recessions, when both interest rates and real income generally decline, that velocity also tends to decline. As shown in Figure 18–7, this pattern in velocity is precisely what is predicted by a conventional money demand equation.[7] As that figure also shows, actual velocity continued its upward trend throughout the period, although it did slow slightly during the recessionary quarters. In other words, actual velocity was substantially higher than predicted velocity, so that a given level of income could be supported by a smaller amount of money than would have been predicted.

In summary, as judged by either Figure 18–6 or Figure 18–7, there

---

[7] Predicted velocity in Figure 18–7 ($\hat{V}$) is related to predicted real-money demand in Figure 18–6 ($\hat{M}/P$) by the condition $(\hat{M}/P) \cdot \hat{V} = Y/P$, where P is the price level. In nominal terms this is equivalent to $\hat{M} \cdot \hat{V} = Y$.

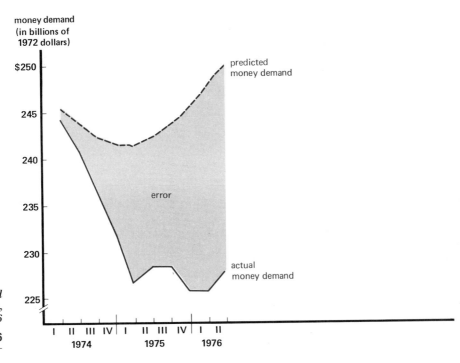

money demand
(in billions of
1972 dollars)

predicted
money demand

error

actual
money demand

*actual and predicted
real-money balances,
1974–1976*

**FIGURE 18–6**

is a clear indication that the demand for money took a sharp and unexpected plunge during the period 1974–1976. Evidence for subsequent years has shown no tendency for money demand to return to its previous track; that is, the shift appears permanent. Furthermore, the most recent data suggest that a further shift appears to be taking place. As already emphasized, these shifts mean that the economy is making do with a smaller volume of currency and demand deposits. More detailed analysis suggests the further finding that virtually all of the shortfall is in demand deposits rather than currency. The question naturally arises as to how and why businesses and households modified their behavior to make do with fewer demand deposit balances.

**Where Did the Missing Money Go?**

One basic way for both firms and individuals to economize on demand deposits is to make use of other financial instruments that serve as a substitute for demand deposits. As our discussion of financial innovation in the last chapter makes clear, there are an expanding number of such substitutes. For households these would include NOW accounts, ATS accounts, money market funds, and telephone transfers. While each of these developments has undoubtedly contributed to a diversion of demand deposits, most of the growth in these categories has been quite recent. As a consequence, these particular substitutes do not explain a very large part of the shortfall pictured in Figure 18–6. In other words, some of the missing money went to these categories, but we have to look elsewhere for the rest.

A second place to look is in the business sector, where in fact much of the shortfall appears to have taken place. One striking development in

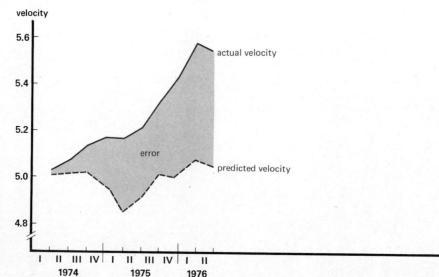

*Actual and predicted velocity, 1974–1976*
Source: S. M. Goldfeld, "The Case of the Missing Money," *Brookings Papers on Economic Activity*, 1976, p. 3.

**FIGURE 18–7**

the business sector has been the use of repurchase agreements (RPs) to manage corporate cash balances. As we have seen, large firms often convert demand deposits to RPs on an overnight basis. Based on this observation, some economists have argued that overnight RPs and demand deposits are the same thing, and have suggested that adding RPs and demand deposits might clear up the puzzling shortfall in Figure 18–6. Unfortunately, there are some data problems that make this hypothesis difficult to test in a precise way. Nevertheless, those tests that have been performed appear to suggest that RPs can explain part but not all of the remaining shortfall.[8] We thus need to look still further.

Thus far we have searched for the missing money among the potentially close substitutes for demand deposits. While some of it appears to be there, there is evidence that individuals and especially firms are getting by with fewer transactions balances in total (i.e., demand deposits plus substitutes). If firms are making do with fewer transactions balances, we ought to be able to find evidence of innovations that have permitted them to economize on such balances. There have, in fact, been numerous such innovations, and the appearance of these has been directly stimulated by the extremely high interest rates of recent years. While it would take us too far afield to discuss these innovations in detail, we can illustrate their nature by just considering two—the lock box and the cash concentration system.

A *lock box* is a device for reducing float. To see how float arises, suppose that a New York customer of a California firm mails a check for payment of services. The check takes a number of days to arrive in California and is then deposited by the firm in its California bank. The bank, however, will make the firm wait until the check clears before letting it use the funds. This whole process might take something like nine days. Enter the lock box. Instead of mailing the check to California, the New York customer mails it to a post office lock box in New York City. Most likely the check will arrive the next day and, when it does, will be collected by a New York City bank. This bank in turn will *wire* the funds to the California firm, and the firm will have immediately usable funds. The net effect is that the California firm has the use of its funds much more quickly. As a result, the company can get by with fewer demand deposit balances; put another way, it has speeded the velocity of its deposits. This is, of course, precisely what figure 18–7 suggests has happened. The funds released by this process can be used by the firm in any way it wishes.

A *cash concentration system* is a second device permitting firms to economize on demand deposits. This typically involves a wire transfer of excess demand balances from local collection banks to a central ac-

---

[8] See R. D. Porter, T. D. Simpson, and E. Mauskopf, "Financial Innovation and the Monetary Aggregates," *Brookings Papers on Economic Activity*, 1979, no. 1, pp. 213–229.

count. Such a system provides the firm with faster and more complete information on its demand balances, while centralization allows the firm to take advantage of offsetting balances at its banks throughout the country. As with the lock box, the end result is to permit a reduction in demand balances and a speedup in velocity.[9]

As should be apparent from this brief introduction to corporate cash management techniques, there are a number of ways in which firms can economize on demand deposits. Many economists feel that the use of such techniques in conjunction with NOWs, RPs, and the like is sufficient to explain the recent behavior of money demand. In principle at least, this "solves" the case of the missing money to the satisfaction of some. As a practical matter, however, things are not so neat and tidy. The reason is that no one has yet managed to produce a widely accepted way of introducing the effects of cash management techniques into an empirical demand-for-money function. As a consequence, there remains a high degree of unpredictability or uncertainty associated with money demand.

**Overview**      The relation between the demand for money balances and its determinants is a fundamental building block in virtually all macroeconomic models. Since it is also a critical component in the formulation of monetary policy, it is not surprising that the money-demand function has been subjected to extensive empirical scrutiny. This scrutiny has revealed that in recent years the demand for money has tended to shift. These shifts, while explainable in principle, have considerably complicated the task of those who conduct monetary policy. Furthermore, in the light of the uncertainty analysis of the previous section, this shifting has cast doubt on the wisdom of couching monetary policy in terms of targets for the monetary aggregates.

Our discussion in this section is obviously closely related to the issue of the definition of money taken up in the previous chapter. Indeed, some of the same factors that made for shifts in money demand (with money defined as currency plus demand deposits) also led to the recently introduced definitional changes. Unfortunately, as our discussion makes clear, these new definitions are not sufficient to explain away completely the shifts that have been observed. Thus, for example, the new M-1B definition would still give a picture qualitatively like that portrayed in Figures 18–6 and 18–7. Some other definitions (e.g., adding RPs to M-1B) would help a bit, but the basic point stands: At the current time there remains considerable uncertainty associated with money

---

[9] For a more complete account of cash concentration systems and cash management techniques more generally, see the appendix to T. D. Simpson, "The Market for Federal Funds and Repurchase Agreements," Board of Governors of the Federal Reserve System Staff Study 106, Washington, D.C., July 1979.

demand, no matter how money is defined. And with the recent authorization of nationwide NOWs—if anything the situation is likely to get worse before it gets better.

At the very least, the Federal Reserve deserves a good deal of sympathy for having to cope with these somewhat hectic developments. Indeed, as we shall see, the life of the Federal Reserve is even more complicated than we have yet let on.

**THE ACTUAL CONDUCT OF MONETARY POLICY**

In discussing procedures for the conduct of monetary policy, we have thus far focused on the choice of money versus the interest rate as an operating target. We have, however, yet to discuss two practical problems: (1) How does the Federal Reserve decide on numerical targets for money and/or the interest rate? (2) How does it actually conduct policy? We have implicitly caricatured these two issues as follows. The Federal Reserve first decides on its goals or objectives regarding the behavior of such measures as real output and employment. In terms of the *IS–LM* framework, for example, these objectives could be summarized by some desired level of output. The Federal Reserve then guesses where the *IS* curve is, and in conjunction with its target level of output, this tells it where the *LM* curve has to go. To accomplish this, it sets the money supply or the interest rate to pin down the *LM* curve. It then sits back and waits until some new data are available, and then it repeats the process.

As in all caricatures, there is an element of truth in this description, but needless to say, it omits many relevant aspects of policy making. For one, the Federal Reserve is faced with incomplete information on the current state of the economy, uncertainty as to its future course, and the fact that monetary policy only works with a lag. Second, the Federal Reserve cannot simply set a dial or thermostat to control the money supply. Rather, it needs to spell out procedures for using its basic tools—open-market operations and reserve requirement changes—to accomplish this. From a practical point of view, all of these issues are supposed to be settled at the meetings of the Federal Open Market Committee (FOMC).

**The FOMC Again**

The FOMC consists of 12 members—the seven members of the Board of Governors of the Federal Reserve System and the presidents of five of the regional Reserve Banks. The committee meets approximately monthly to set monetary policy. The process consists of the following steps.[10]

---

[10] For an insider's description of the FOMC by an ex-governor of the Federal Reserve, see Sherman Maisel, *Managing the Dollar*, New York, W. W. Norton, 1973. The present description of FOMC procedures and the several quotes are from this source.

1   A detailed discussion of the current state of the economy, money and financial markets, and the international situation. For this purpose some several hundred statistical series are studied, their meaning debated, and their accuracy scrutinized.

2   A projection of where the economy seems to be heading. For such projections the FOMC will have to assess factors beyond its control, such as likely future fiscal policies. In actually making the predictions it relies on a mixture of judgmental and econometric forecasting techniques.

3   An analysis of goals and objectives. Here the discussion typically focuses on whether the path of the economy, should current monetary policies be maintained, is likely to lead to a desirable outcome. While in principle, this would be the time for explicit discussion of objectives and proposed trade-offs, this apparently often remains only implicit. As a former governor, Sherman Maisel, has written: "Each member remained free to vote his own value judgments and prejudices without ever having to state or defend his objectives."

4   Choice of an appropriate monetary policy. After the current path of the economy is compared, at least implicitly, with what might be desirable, a course of action is selected. Maisel describes this step as follows: "While disagreements over where the economy is and should be heading are common in FOMC meetings, they pale beside the question of what monetary policy should be adopted to achieve these goals." The basic problem, of course, is that FOMC members, like economists more generally, do not always agree on the likely effect on the economy of a given change in monetary policy. As a consequence, this step of the process is often characterized by heated debate.

5   Issuance of a *directive* to the manager of open-market operations. This function of the directive is to instruct the manager as to how to implement the chosen monetary policy over the next month or so. To do this, it provides various kinds of operating guides, the nature of which has changed considerably over time. Since this is a critical part of the process, we shall examine the directive in more detail.

**THE DIRECTIVE AND OPERATING GUIDES FOR POLICY**

At one end of the monetary policy spectrum we have the tools of policy, such as open-market operations and reserve requirement changes. At the other end are the ultimate policy targets, such as real output, the unemployment rate, and the rate of inflation. In between are a whole spectrum of variables that go by such names as *operating targets* or *intermediate targets*. Examples of these variables are total bank reserves, and, as we have seen, the money supply and interest rates. These variables are "in between" or intermediate in the following sense: An open-market operation first affects bank reserves and extremely short-term interest rates (e.g., the overnight federal funds rate); next it influences various monetary aggregates and longer-term interest rates; and after a still longer lag it affects ultimate policy targets such as GNP.

In its choice of monetary policy, the FOMC naturally thinks in terms of appropriate values for one or more of these operating targets. It is these targets that are communicated, via the directive, to the manager of open-market operations. These targets serve two important purposes: (1) They provide a standard of accountability for the manager; and (2) by observing the actual behavior of the targeted variables, the policy makers get some feedback on the state of the economy and the appropriateness of their policies. This is important, since not all variables are observed with the same frequency. For example, while interest rates may be observed daily, money supply figures are available weekly with considerable inaccuracy or monthly on a more accurate basis, and GNP data are only available quarterly. Thus, if monetary targets are used and it turns out that the actual money supply data are deviating from targeted values, the FOMC gets a chance to consider why this is happening. It may in such circumstances decide that the manager of open-market operations has fallen down on the job, or it may conclude that its targets are inappropriate and adjust them accordingly. In any event, it is clear that these intermediate variables can provide useful information to the FOMC. Below we shall examine some examples of how this is used.

Thus far we have indicated that the FOMC has a number of possible operating guides. In point of fact, it has frequently changed strategies in the last 25 years or so. A brief review of the various operating guides that have been used in the past will provide considerable perspective on the latest strategy change, which was introduced in October 1979.[11]

**Money Market Conditions**    From 1942 to 1951 the Federal Reserve's job was to peg interest rates. Indeed, it was not until 1953 that the Federal Reserve had finally made the transition to a period in which it could freely conduct monetary policy. Its first operating guides in this period were termed *money market conditions*. The particular conditions chosen consisted of changes in certain key short-term interest rates and totals for member bank borrowing and excess reserves at Federal Reserve banks. Gradually the FOMC began to focus on the difference between excess reserves and member borrowing, which is termed *net free reserves* (see Table 18–

---

[11] For an authoritative review of FOMC strategies prior to the most recent change, see H. C. Wallich, "The Role of Operating Guides in U.S. Monetary Policy: A Historical Review," *Federal Reserve Bulletin*, September 1979, pp. 679–691.

1). For about a decade the directive was couched in terms of net free reserves and short-term interest rates.

Around 1960 a number of economists both inside and outside the FOMC began questioning the use of net free reserves as an operating target. They pointed out that the same level of free reserves could have a rather different policy impact, depending on whether credit demands at banks were strong or weak. For instance, maintenance of a given level of free reserves when strong loan demand was tending to use up such reserves would inevitably lead to monetary and credit expansion. In effect, banks would try and lend out their excess reserves and the FOMC would replenish them. If this process were repeated for long, a dangerously expansionary situation could result. On the other hand, holding free reserves constant when loan demand was weak and banks wanted to let their free reserves rise (by accumulating excess reserves and repaying borrowing) would lead to contraction. After several episodes in which a net free reserve strategy led to undesirable effects, the FOMC began to search for other operating guides.

**Money Market Conditions Plus**

A gradual shift in emphasis took place in the mid-1960s as the FOMC started to concern itself more with aggregate quantities such as the volume of bank credit. In the first instance it expressed this by introducing what it termed a *proviso clause* to the directive. An example of this is contained in the directive for November 22, 1966:

> *Open market operations until the next meeting of the Committee shall be conducted with a view to maintaining somewhat easier conditions in the money market, unless bank credit appears to be resuming a rapid rate of expansion.*

This is basically a money market strategy with a proviso (the "unless" part). While not an official part of the directive, supporting documents for the November 1966 meeting indicated that the directive's language was consistent with a roughly zero level of net free reserves, a three-month

---

**TABLE 18–1**

*Various measures of the reserve position of member banks, February 1980 (monthly average of daily figures, in millions of dollars)*

| | |
|---|---:|
| Total reserves | 43,196 |
| **Less:** Borrowed reserves | 1,660 |
| **Equals:** unborrowed reserves | 41,536 |
| Total reserves | 43,196 |
| **Less:** required reserves | |
| **Equals:** excess reserves | 43,026 |
| **Less:** borrowed reserves | 170 |
| **Equals:** free reserves | 1,660 |
| | −1,490 |

*Source: Federal Reserve Bulletin,* March 1980, p. A5.

Treasury bill rate of about 5 percent, and bank credit expansion of from 2 to 4 percent. Interestingly enough, however, the manager was given no explicit guidance as to what to do in the event that not all these (possibly conflicting) general guides could be met.

While the proviso for bank credit represented something of a change in the character of FOMC strategy, until the beginning of 1970 money market conditions remained the critical operating targets. At that time a further modification took place as the role of the proviso and the main part of the directive were interchanged. In particular, directives stressed bank credit and money as primary targets, and relegated money market conditions to the proviso. Furthermore, net free reserves were abandoned as the proviso was typically couched in terms of a range for the federal funds rate.

Although this was a seemingly big change in the direction of a strategy based on monetary aggregates, in practice this was not the case. The reason for this was that the FOMC specified a relatively narrow range for the federal funds rate and the manager was instructed to be bound by the proviso. As a consequence, despite the primary emphasis on money and credit, actual growth in these measures often deviated significantly from the FOMC's specified ranges.

For a brief period the FOMC experimented with various aggregate reserve measures as a substitute for the federal funds rate. These, however, proved difficult to work with. The problem was the complicated structure of reserve requirements that apply to deposits of different types (e.g., demand vs. time) and sizes. As a result, the multiplier between a total reserve measure and the money supply proved unstable.[12] Put another way, this suggests that the simple money-multiplier approach outlined in Chapter 6 must be applied cautiously in practice. If nothing else, this experience indicated that direct control of the money supply is more difficult than might appear at first glance. In any event, after experimenting with reserve measures the FOMC returned to a proviso based on the federal funds rate.

**Monetary Aggregates**  The next stage in the development of an operating guide involved considerably more explicit attention to money supply. The role of bank credit was dramatically reduced and supplanted by targets for the growth of various measures of the money stock—primarily M-1 and M-2 (on the basis of the definitions then prevailing). In this regard, the Federal Reserve was spurred in part by congressional pressure to pay greater attention to monetary aggregates. From 1975 to 1978 the Federal Re-

---

[12] During the period the FOMC made use of both total reserves and "reserves against private deposits." Private deposits exclude Treasury balances at banks, which are quite variable and are not included in the money supply.

serve made quarterly reports to Congress on its twelve-month money growth targets. Since 1978, under the Humphrey-Hawkins bill, these reports have been semiannual, although some technical details in the nature of the reporting were improved with the passage of the Humphrey-Hawkins bill.

Despite the more prominent attention given to the money supply, the FOMC continued to rely on a proviso based on the federal funds rate, and indeed, within a monthly period a fairly narrow range was specified for the funds rate. Furthermore, in those months in which there was an incompatability between the funds rate and the money supply, the funds rate, despite its proviso status, remained the binding constraint. There was a new wrinkle, however, in that if the actual growth of money deviated from the targeted growth rate, the range on the funds rate was adjusted at the next FOMC meeting.

This process is pictured in Figures 18–8 and 18–9, where we have plotted the FOMC ranges for the growth rate of M-1 and the funds rate for the years 1978 and 1979. In April and May of 1978, for example, the actual growth rate of M-1 exceeded the top of its tolerance range (see Figure 18–8). As a consequence, in mid-April, as shown in the figure, the FOMC both shifted up the range on the funds rate and widened the band. In terms of the analysis at the beginning of the chapter, within a month the FOMC was pursuing an interest rate policy (of course, with a range rather than a specific number). Across months, however, it was following what has been termed a *combination policy*. That is, it was adjusting both money and interest targets in the light of new information. While this combination policy in principle gave the FOMC greater control over the monetary aggregates than it would have had under a strict interest rate policy, critics still complained that control was not adequate. In 1979 these complaints grew more vociferous, especially as inflation began accelerating. Feeling the need to "do something," the Federal Reserve announced a major move to tighten monetary policy. Some aspects of this were discussed in Chapter 11. Here we focus on the change in operating strategy.

**Developments of October 6, 1979**

On October 6, 1979, the Federal Reserve announced its intention to achieve tighter control over the money supply. To do this, it proposed to free the manager of open-market operations from the shackles of the federal funds rate and to reduce the importance of the funds rate as a tool of policy. Previously this issue had been something of a vicious circle. The Federal Reserve believed that financial market participants paid close attention to the funds rate, and this inhibited the FOMC's willingness to let the funds rate fluctuate. This inhibition endowed the funds rate with significance and made the whole thing a self-fulfilling prophecy.

By word and deed, the FOMC sought to break this vicious circle.

While it did not totally abandon the proviso clause, it did dramatically widen the permissible range. Thus, for example, in the directive issued on October 6, 1979, the range for the funds rate was set at $11\frac{1}{2}$ to $15\frac{1}{2}$ percent. In contrast, the previous directive had specified a range of $11\frac{1}{4}$ to $11\frac{3}{4}$ percent. The changes in the range and the subsequent marked upward movement in the funds rate are shown in Figure 18–9.

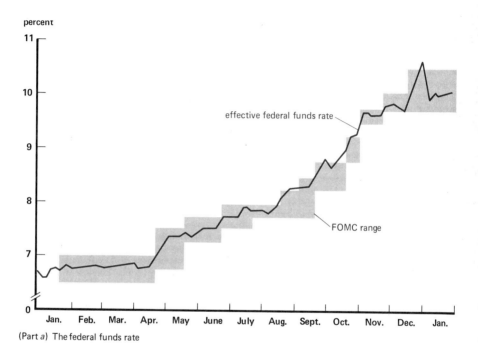

(Part *a*) The federal funds rate

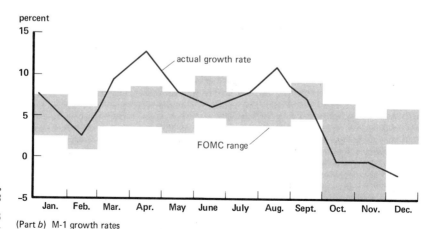

*OMC Policy Ranges, 1978*

**FIGURE 18–8**

(Part *b*) M-1 growth rates

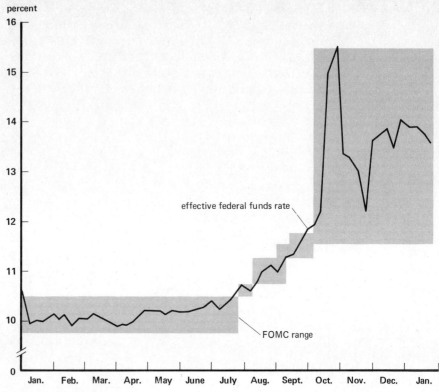

(Part *a*) The federal funds rate

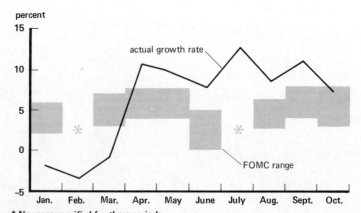

*FOMC Policy Ranges,*
*1979*

**FIGURE 18-9**

* No range specified for these periods

(Part *b*) M-1 growth rates

Overview In choosing to use monetary aggregates as an operating target, the Federal Reserve has, in effect, announced its intention to conduct policy in simple textbook fashion. In many respects the timing of this change is extremely ironic. As we have seen in both this and the previous chapter, at present there is considerable uncertainty as to how to define money. Correspondingly, there appears to be considerable imprecision in the relationship between any particular monetary aggregate and ultimate policy goals such as output, employment, or inflation. Indeed, these very points were acknowledged by the Federal Reserve in its description of the revised money definitions. As a consequence, the wisdom of moving to an operating procedure with increased emphasis on monetary aggregates can certainly be questioned. Of course, some may see virtue in providing greater stability for the monetary aggregates, whatever those aggregates might mean. This certainly explains the monetarists' acceptance, albeit cautiously, of the change in FOMC procedures. Furthermore, in its defense the FOMC might argue that it will focus on several of the money measures and thus avoid being misled by any particular concept. While this makes some sense, the FOMC has yet to evolve workable procedures for coping with multiple monetary targets. What, for example, does it plan to do if one monetary aggregate is growing faster than planned and another is growing more slowly than planned? If the new operating procedures are to lead to an actual improvement in the output of monetary policy, answers to such questions will be needed.[13]

Such issues aside, the usefulness of the new operating procedures will depend critically on the question of *controllability*. That is, it is not sufficient that the FOMC choose a well-defined operating target that is closely related to its ultimate goals. In addition, it must be able to control the chosen operating target with some degree of precision. For example, it would not make sense for the FOMC to use the unemployment rate or retail sales as operating targets, since it cannot readily control these. The various monetary aggregates are, of course, much closer to the daily bread and butter of the FOMC. Indeed, there has always been an implicit presumption that the Federal Reserve could control the money stock if it so chose. While, with some qualification, this was undoubtedly true in the past, it is again a bit of irony that, at the present time and with

---

[13] Another practical issue is raised by the prospect of greater fluctuations in the Federal funds rate. In particular, since individual banks can make reserve adjustments through either the federal funds market or the discount window, the Federal Reserve may need to make the discount rate more flexible so as to keep it in line with the funds rate. Otherwise, if the funds rate were substantially above the discount rate, the Federal Reserve may find overly brisk demand for borrowed reserves.

the new definitions, money may well be less controllable. The Federal Reserve, in fact, is well aware of potential problems on this score and has advocated legislation to improve monetary control.

**IMPROVING MONETARY CONTROL**

"Volcker Warns of Fed Attrition" read a recent headline in the financial press. "Fed attrition," as will be recalled from earlier chapters, refers to the declining membership of commercial banks in the Federal Reserve System. As reported in the article, Volcker, the chairman of the Board of Governors, went on to argue in testimony to Congress that "we cannot responsibly permit attrition from membership to grow to the stage where it seriously disrupts monetary management." In an attempt to prod Congress into action, Volcker added: "I fear we will soon be perilously close to that point." While some may regard this plea as overly melodramatic, there is a real issue here, and it relates directly to the question of the controllability of the monetary aggregates.

As the Federal Reserve perceives it, attrition reduces controllability in two ways. For one, nonmember banks are required to report on their deposits only several times a year. This lack of information complicates the construction of timely and accurate measures of the money supply, and consequently reduces monetary control. This problem could be addressed by a more demanding set of reporting requirements for nonmember banks. This, however, would still leave the fact that nonmember banks are not subject to the reserve requirements of the Federal Reserve.

The Federal Reserve has long regarded reserve requirements as a critical part of the process of monetary control and has argued that control would improve if reserve requirements were applicable to all commercial banks. This, of course, is quite consistent with the Hunt Commission recommendation that similar financial institutions ought to be treated equally in terms of regulations.

**Federal Reserve Membership**

In 1955, deposits at member banks accounted for over 85 percent of total commercial bank deposits. By 1980, this fraction had dropped to about 70 percent and was still heading downward. The primary reason for this decline is that nonmember commercial banks are subject to state reserve requirements, which are more lenient than those imposed by the Federal Reserve. Not only are the percentage requirements lower, but the requirements can be satisfied in several different ways (including, in some cases, holding earning assets). The Federal Reserve does provide its members with a number of services—check clearing, free shipments of currency and coin, use of wire facilities, and access to the discount

## DECIPHERING MONETARY POLICY

The pages of the financial press often feature articles that attempt to figure out what the Federal Reserve is up to. Loosely speaking, what these articles try to sort out is whether the Fed is pursuing a "tighter" or "easier" monetary policy and what the implications of this are for the future course of the economy. As we have seen, since the Fed itself is sometimes unsure as to what its current policy really means, it should not be surprising that outside observers may sometimes be puzzled as to what is going on. This is even more understandable when we recall Maisel's observation that "the Fed has always resisted being too specific about its methods and goals, clothing its operations in a kind of mystique that left it more freedom for maneuver."

To ascertain what the Fed is up to, the interested observer can look at the following sorts of information: (1) quantitative data on the use of the basic policy instruments of the Fed, such as open-market operations, discount rate changes, and reserve requirement changes; (2) various intermediate variables, such as interest rates or money stock measures; (3) speeches and other official policy statements by the Fed members; and (4) the FOMC directive, which is released about 45 days after each FOMC meeting.

While all of this information can contribute to an understanding of the intentions of monetary policy, Fed watchers often go further and try to select some *indicator* of the quantitative thrust of monetary policy. Often this indicator has been chosen from the group of intermediate target variables such as free reserves, interest rates, or the money stock. All of these indicators, however, suffer from a basic flaw: While they are partly influenced by monetary policy, they are affected by many other factors as well. Consequently, they do not provide an unambiguous measure of the thrust of monetary policy. In many respects these measures are analogous to the actual government budget deficit, which we have seen can provide a very misleading indication of fiscal policy. To obtain a true indicator of the quantitative thrust of policy, it is necessary to specify a complete model of the economy and to trace through each policy action in the context of this model.* Unfortunately, this is both a lot of work and subject to debate, since, as already noted, economists do not necessarily agree on an underlying model. It should not be surprising, for example, that fifty years after the fact analysts are still debating whether the Federal Reserve "caused" the Great Depression.

* For one example of this see A. S. Blinder and S. M. Goldfeld, "New Measures of Fiscal and Monetary Policy, 1958–1973," *American Economic Review,* December 1976, pp. 780–796.

window. On balance, however, these services have not been sufficient to stem the tide of attrition.[14]

Two basic approaches have been suggested for coping with the problem of attrition. The first would rely on enticing wayward banks to voluntarily return to the Federal Reserve fold. This might be done by beefing up the list of free services. This, in fact, runs counter to the actual trend, which is to charge for services so that they are utilized rationally. Alternatively, the Federal Reserve could pay interest on reserve balances. While this appeals to many economists, the Treasury has been rather unwilling to forgo any significant amount of revenues (Federal Reserve earnings are in large part turned over to the Treasury). As a consequence, the Federal Reserve has advocated a *mandatory* approach whereby nonmember banks would simply be made subject to the same reserve requirements as member banks. Most recently, the Federal Reserve has gone even further in its advocacy of this principle. In particular, it has asked Congress to extend reserve requirements to thrift institutions. While this is partially viewed as a matter of equity, as the new monetary aggregates include liabilities of the thrift institutions, the Federal Reserve has argued that these reserve requirements are needed to implement its latest operating strategies for controlling the monetary aggregates. In partial compensation, nonmember banks and thrifts could be extended privileges at the discount window and access to other services as well. Needless to say, nonmember banks and thrifts have not been keen on these proposals. Even some member banks, especially those who hold sizable correspondent balances of nonmember banks have been opposed to the idea.[15] Nevertheless, in rough outline this is essentially the proposal that was enacted into law in early 1980.

---

**MONETARY CONTROL ACT OF 1980**

Along with the Depository Institutions Deregulation Act discussed in the previous chapter, the Monetary Control Act was signed into law on March 31, 1980. As its name implies, the intent of the Act is to improve the ability of the Federal Reserve to monitor and control monetary and credit aggregates. Toward that end the Act beefed up reporting requirements for both nonmember banks and thrifts. More importantly, from the Fed's perspective, the Act also considerably expanded the scope of reserve requirements.

---

[14] For a discussion of these issues, see R. A. Gilbert, "Utilization of Federal Reserve Bank Services by Member Banks: Implications for the Costs and Benefits of Membership," *Review*, Federal Reserve Bank of St. Louis, August 1977, pp. 2–15.

[15] Many states permit nonmember banks to use correspondent balances to satisfy state reserve requirements. Under universal reserve requirements the large banks would undoubtedly lose some of these balances.

**Reserve Requirements**     The key feature of the Act in regard to reserve requirements is the establishment of a set of requirements to be uniformly applied to all transactions accounts at *all* depository institutions—that is, commercial banks, mutual savings banks, savings and loans, and credit unions. For this purpose transactions accounts are defined to include demand deposits, NOW accounts, telephone transfers, ATS, and share drafts. The actual requirement was initially set at 3 percent for transaction accounts up to $25 million and 12 percent on the remainder. The Act permits the Federal Reserve to vary the 12 percent requirement within the range 8–14 percent and provides for some indexation of the $25 million breakpoint as transaction balances grow over time. To cushion the impact of these changes on nonmember depository institutions, the Act calls for a gradual phase-in of these requirements over an eight-year period. On the other hand, for commercial banks for whom the new requirements represent a *reduction* in reserves, the phase-down will take place over a four-year period.[16]

In addition to the uniform reserve requirement on transactions accounts, the Control Act also contains a number of other provisions concerning reserve requirements. Among the most noteworthy are the following:

1    All depository institutions will be required to maintain reserves against nonpersonal time deposits. The initial requirement was set at 3 percent but may be varied by the Federal Reserve board in the range 0–9 percent.

2    The Act permits the Board, upon a finding of five of its members that extraordinary circumstances require such action, to impose for a period of up to 180 days reserve requirements on *any* liability of depository institutions and outside the existing limitations on reserve ratios. Prior consultation with the appropriate Congressional committees is required. If the extraordinary circumstances persist, the Board may extend the temporary requirements after explaining its reasons to Congress.

3    The Board is empowered, again upon an affirmative vote of five members, to impose a *supplemental reserve requirement* on every depository institution of not more than 4 percent of its transactions accounts. The Act also provides that depository institutions shall earn interest on their supplemental reserve, with the Federal Reserve given discretion over the relevant rate (up to the Fed's rate of return on its own portfolio).

Taken as a whole, the Control Act provides the Fed with a new arse-

---

[16] The Act is somewhat nasty to those commercial banks that withdrew from membership in the Federal Reserve System after July 1, 1979, and before the passage of the Act. The Act provides that these banks shall be treated as if they were member banks.

nal of reserve requirement tools for the conduct of monetary policy. Given the extensive use made of reserve requirement changes in recent years, we can expect the Fed to put these new tools to active use. It remains to be seen whether these new tools will be sufficient to make the new monetary aggregates controllable in practice. Even the rather monetarist Federal Reserve Bank of St. Louis has expressed doubts on this.[17] Only time will tell.

**Federal Reserve Services**

Along with the imposition of reserve requirements on nonmember banks and the thrift institutions, the Control Act also offered some benefits to these institutions. In particular, the Act provides that any depository institution that holds transactions accounts or nonpersonal time deposits is entitled to the same discount and borrowing privileges as member banks. In addition, nonmember depository institutions will be eligible for other Federal Reserve services as well. These include currency and coin services, check clearing and collection services, wire transfer services, and securities safekeeping services. However, the Act does provide that these services would be priced according to cost, although the same price would be charged all depository institutions.

**Overview**

In conjunction with the Deregulation Act described in the previous chapter, the Monetary Control Act has gone a long way toward implementing the proposals of the Hunt Commission. As implied by its name, the Control Act is designed to improve the conduct of monetary policy by tightening the connection between the tools of the Fed and the monetary aggregates. While this may well improve monetary control, it remains to be seen whether it will lead to an actual improvement in the quality of monetary policy. As this chapter has spelled out, the latter is a considerably more complex issue than controlling a particular monetary aggregate.

**CONCLUSION**

This chapter has tried to give the flavor of some of the key issues faced by the Federal Reserve in the conduct of monetary policy. Running throughout was the theme that uncertainty, in various forms, considerably complicates the Fed's job. In this context, we traced the evolution of the Fed's operating strategy. As indicated, the present policy of exercising greater control over the monetary aggregates is not without problems, both because past and prospective financial innovations have clouded the meaning of the aggregates and because there are questions of controllability. Consequently, we may well expect to see further mod-

---

[17] See J. A. Tatom, "Money Stock Control Under Alternative Definitions of Money," *Review*, Federal Reserve Bank of St. Louis, November 1979, pp. 3–9.

ifications of the Fed's strategy in the future. Indeed, a member of the Board of Governors has recently observed that "no single formula or operating target can be relied on to work effectively in all circumstances." The Fed, at least, is certainly prepared for further change.

**SELECTED READINGS**

Goldfeld, S. M., "The Case of the Missing Money," *Brookings Paper on Economic Activity*, 1976, no, 3, pp. 683–739.

Maisel, S., *Managing the Dollar*, New York, Norton, 1973.

Mayer, T., *Monetary Policy in the United States*, New York, Random House, 1968.

Porter, R. D., T. D. Simpson, and E. Mauskopf, "Financial Innovation and the Monetary Aggregates," *Brookings Papers on Economic Activity*, 1979, no. 1, pp. 213–229.

Wallich, H. C., "The Role of Operating Guides in U.S. Monetary Policy: A Historical Review," *Federal Reserve Bulletin*, September 1979, pp. 679–691.

At selected points throughout this book, we have examined various historical episodes in the conduct of monetary policy. With this chapter we begin a more systematic discussion of American monetary policy.

As noted earlier, the formulation and execution of monetary policy involve at least three elements:

1   Selection of objectives—the choice of goals or purposes to be promoted.
2   Development and use of monetary institutions and instruments to promote the chosen objectives.
3   The use (at least implicitly) of some theory as to the economic effects of the various possible monetary actions.

We shall be interested in the evolution of all these elements in monetary policies. What have been the objectives or goals of our policies? How have these changed through time, and why? How have changing goals affected actions? How has the Federal Reserve developed its control instruments, and how has it used them? In what ways or for what reasons has it changed its use of instruments? What types of monetary theory seem to be the bases for its policies, and how have these changed through time?

Although our primary focus will be on monetary policy, in our discussion we shall also touch on fiscal policy and on policies related to the nature of the international payments mechanism. Like developments in the private sector, each of these influences the environment faced by the

---

[1] Much of the material in this chapter is taken from L. V. Chandler, *Inflation in the United States, 1940–1948*, New York, Harper & Row, 1951.

monetary authorities. As a consequence, we cannot fully understand the actual course followed by monetary policy unless we pay some attention to these factors.

The purpose of this and of the subsequent two chapters is not only to tell the story of past episodes; it is also (1) to give us an opportunity to analyze policy formation and execution in specific situations, (2) to provide a basis for understanding the present status of monetary policy, and (3) to emphasize that monetary policy is continuously — and, at times, discontinuously — in the process of change.

We begin our analysis with the entrance of the United States into World War II in December 1941, when the Federal Reserve again became, as it had been during World War I, a servant of the government's fiscal policy. All conflicting objectives were pushed aside; its overriding objective became that of assuring that the nation's war effort would not suffer from any lack of money. Moreover, it was to assure that the huge war effort would be financed without any rise of interest rates above the low levels prevailing in early 1942.

WARTIME
FISCAL
POLICIES

The federal government's fiscal policy during this period followed the usual pattern for all-out war, but on a huge scale. Its expenditures rose tremendously. Just before the beginning of the defense effort in mid-1940, government expenditures were at an annual rate of about $9 billion. By the fourth quarter of 1941, they had risen to an annual rate of more than $25 billion. By 1944, they were above $95 billion. Thus, at the peak of the war effort federal expenditures were more than 10 times their level before the beginning of the defense program and were themselves greater than total GNP at any time during the 1930s. More than 40 percent of the nation's output was being purchased for government purposes. Between mid-1940, when the accelerated defense program began, and mid-1946, when the wartime deficits ended, federal expenditures totaled more than $383 billion. This was more than twice as much as the federal government had spent during the preceding 150 years, nearly 100 times as much as it spent during the Civil War, and 10 times as much as it spent during World War I (see Table 19–1).

Tax collections were increased greatly, but not nearly as much as expenditures. The result was, of course, huge deficits. These averaged more than $40 billion a year during the period of active participation by the United States in the war; in one year they were nearly $54 billion. For the six years following mid-1940, federal deficits totaled nearly $187 billion. The Treasury therefore faced the necessity of borrowing huge amounts to cover these deficits. In fact, its net borrowings during this six-year period were $199 billion, of which $187 billion was required to cover its deficits and $12 billion was used to increase its money balance (see Table 19–2).

As it had during World War I, the Treasury again tried to borrow as much as it could in ways that would not involve an increase in the money supply. It used all the devices developed during World War I as well as new ones to sell securities to nonbank buyers: great bond-selling campaigns, pleas by movie stars and national heroes; 100 percent clubs;

**TABLE 19–1**

*Cash operating outgo, income, and deficits of the federal government, 1940–1946 (in millions of dollars)*

| Fiscal year ending June 30 | Cash operating outgo | Cash operating income | Cash operating deficit |
|---|---|---|---|
| 1941 | $ 14,060 | $ 9,371 | $ 4,689 |
| 1942 | 34,585 | 15,291 | 19,294 |
| 1943 | 78,979 | 25,245 | 53,734 |
| 1944 | 94,079 | 47,984 | 46,095 |
| 1945 | 95,986 | 51,051 | 44,935 |
| 1946 | 65,683 | 47.784 | 17,899 |
| Total | $383,372 | $196,726 | $186,646 |

*Source:* L. V. Chandler, *Inflation in the United States, 1940–1948.* New York, Harper & Row, 1951, p. 62.

**TABLE 19–2**

*Federal borrowings, their use, and their sources, 1940–1946 (in millions of dollars)*

| Fiscal year ending June 30 | Federal cash operating deficit | Increase or decrease (−) of Treasury's General Fund balance | Net cash borrowing | By nonbank investors | By Federal Reserve and commercial banks | By commercial banks | By Federal Reserve banks |
|---|---|---|---|---|---|---|---|
| 1941 | $ 4,689 | $ 742 | $ 5,431 | $ 2,143 | $ 3,318 | $ 3,600 | −$ 282 |
| 1942 | 19,294 | 358 | 19,652 | 12,869 | 6,761 | 6,300 | 461 |
| 1943 | 53,734 | 6,515 | 60,250 | 28,498 | 30,757 | 26,200 | 4,557 |
| 1944 | 46,095 | -10,662 | 56,757 | 32,913 | 23,899 | 16,200 | 7,699 |
| 1945 | 44,935 | 4,529 | 49,464 | 27,173 | 22,691 | 15,800 | 6,891 |
| 1946 | 17,899 | −10,450 | 7,439 | 5,431 | 2,191 | 200 | 1,991 |
| Total increase for period | $186,646 | $12,356 | $119,003 | $109,027 | $89,617 | $68,300 | $21,317 |

NET INCREASE IN AMOUNT OF FEDERAL INTEREST-BEARING DEBT HELD

*Source:* L. V. Chandler, *Inflation in the United States, 1940–1948,* New York, Harper & Row, 1951, p. 72. This table was computed from various tables in *Treasury Bulletins.* It should be noted that the figures relating to debt reflect only the debt held outside the federal government itself; they do not include an increase of about $22 billion in federal debt held by government agencies and trust funds. These securities involved no borrowing outside the government itself; as the Treasury collected and spent social security taxes, it issued to the trust funds under its control government securities indicating a future obligation to pay social security benefits.

payroll-deduction plans; and so on. It did succeed in getting nonbank investors to increase their holdings of Treasury obligations of $109 billion. But this was not enough; the commercial banks increased their holdings by $68.3 billion, and the Federal Reserve banks by $21.3 billion.

WARTIME
MONETARY
POLICY

Federal Reserve assistance to Treasury financing during World War II differed in at least two important respects from that in World War I. In the earlier war, the Federal Reserve itself bought very few Treasury obligations; it gave its assistance primarily by lending to banks. In World War II, it lent very little to banks; it created additional money primarily by purchasing Treasury obligations, most of them in the open market rather than directly from the Treasury. Interest rate policies also differed markedly in the two wars. Interest rates were allowed to rise during World War I. In general, each new bond issue carried interest rates somewhat above those on earlier issues. During World War II interest rates were not allowed to rise at all.

In March 1942 the Federal Open Market Committee agreed with the Treasury that, in general, the level of interest rates and yields on government securities should not be allowed to rise during the war, and it pledged the full cooperation of the system to this end. This promise was fully kept. Interest rates in general were at that time low by historical standards, and short-term rates were abnormally low relative to longer-term rates. This was partly because of the low demand for investable funds during the depression, partly because of the huge volume of excess reserves in the banking system. At the end of 1941 the latter were still above $3 billion. The pattern of yields stabilized by the Federal Reserve during the war period reflected these conditions. On 90-day maturities, this yield was $\frac{3}{8}$ percent; on 9- to 12-month maturities, it was $\frac{7}{8}$ percent, on 5-year maturities, it was $1\frac{1}{2}$ percent; on 10-year maturities, it was 2 percent; and on the longest marketable Treasury issues, it was $2\frac{1}{2}$ percent. The shape of this yield curve should be noted carefully, because it was to have important consequences.

The Federal Reserve's technique for preventing these various yields from rising—for preventing the prices of the securities from falling—was simple: It merely stood ready to buy without limitation all of these securities offered to it at the selected levels of prices and yields. In short, it stood ready to monetize, with high-powered reserve money, all the government securities offered to it by the banks and all other types of holders. As shown in Table 19–3, the system increased its holdings of Treasury obligations by $21.3 billion between the end of 1941 and June 1946. Its purchases were concentrated in the short maturities; in fact, its holdings of the longer maturities actually declined during the latter part of the war. This was partly because of the very large Treasury issues of short maturities and partly because of the shape of the yield curve. Private investors tended to shun the short maturities with their low yields and to purchase the longer-term, higher-yield obligations. At their Federal Reserve support prices, these longer-term obligations were just as liquid as the shortest maturities. They could be riskier than the short obligations only if purchased above the support price or if the support price were lowered or withdrawn. Most investors were confident that the latter would not happen during the war, and they suspected that support would be continued into the postwar period.

This passive, open-market policy had several important consequences, not only during the war but also in the postwar period.

1  The Federal Reserve thereby abandoned control over its volume of government holdings, the volume of bank reserves, and the money supply. To prevent yields from rising, it had to buy all securities offered to it, regardless of the identity of the seller and regardless of the purpose for which the newly created money would be used. Thus, banks and nonbank investors alike could get new money from the Federal Reserve at will, the only cost being the yield sacrificed on the securities sold. During the six years following 1939, the money supply rose from $36.2 billion to $102.4 billion, for an increase of 183 percent.

2  The cost of getting such funds was the low yield on short-term government securities, because banks and all other types of financial institutions held billions of these.

3  By holding down interest rates on government securities, the Federal Reserve also held down interest rates on loans to private borrowers and assured a highly liberal supply of credit for private uses. The reason was that all holders of government securities retained complete freedom to sell these holdings and to shift to other assets. Thus, not only banks but all other lenders as well could get funds from the Federal Reserve to satisfy private demands, and they would do so in great volume if yields on private obligations tended to rise.

| **TABLE 19–3**<br><br>*Maturities of governments held by the reserve banks, 1941–1946 (last Wednesday of month; in millions of dollars)* | Date | Within 90 days | 90 days to 1 year | 1 year to 2 years | 2 years to 5 years | Over 5 years | Total |
|---|---|---|---|---|---|---|---|
| | December 1941 | 96 | 97 | 247 | 477 | 1,337 | 2,254 |
| | December 1942 | 1,199 | 886 | 242 | 1,408 | 2,254 | 5,989 |
| | December 1943 | 7,256 | 2,457 | 224 | 488 | 1,190 | 11,615 |
| | December 1944 | 12,703 | 4,064 | 760 | 620 | 918 | 19,065 |
| | December 1945 | 15,839 | 7,000 | 0 | 508 | 691 | 24,038 |
| | June 1946 | 17,877 | 4,436 | 46 | 449 | 582 | 23,390 |

While following a passive general monetary policy, the authorities tried to prevent or limit nonessential private borrowing by using selective credit controls. For example, in the autumn of 1941 the Federal Reserve imposed for the first time a selective control over consumer credit, fixing maximum loan values and maximum periods of repayment. Banks were admonished to refuse loans for nonessential purposes. Authorities were established to pass upon the essentiality of new security issues. But these and other selective credit controls were far less effective in containing inflationary pressures, and even in limiting the expansion of credit for private purposes, than were the great variety of direct controls imposed on the economy early in the war.

**THE WARTIME ROLE OF DIRECT CONTROLS**

It soon became evident that the government's fiscal policy would create strong inflationary pressure as output approached capacity levels, if not before. The huge rise of government expenditures directly increased the demand for output; it also contributed greatly increased amounts to private money incomes. Increased tax collections recovered some of this money from the private sector, but not nearly enough to prevent disposable private incomes from increasing greatly. With greater disposable incomes, consumers would, if left free to do so, increase their consumption demands. The multiplier would operate upward, perhaps raising consumer spending at a greater rate than government spending. Something of the same nature would happen to business spending. Prospects for profitable new investment were highly favorable, disposable business income was greatly increased, and credit was cheap. It became clear that something would have to be done to prevent consumers and business from spending as much as they wanted to spend and could afford to spend with their large and rising disposable money incomes. Inflationary pressures would have to be repressed. This was not only to prevent or limit price inflation; it was also to prevent rising private demands from diverting productive resources from the war effort.

A whole series of direct controls was established for these purposes. These controls included price ceilings on virtually every type of output, ceilings on wages, and ceilings on rents. It was illegal for anyone to charge or to pay more than these prices. Also included were many types of controls over the production, distribution, and use of output. In general, producers could buy equipment and supplies only if permitted to do so by the government, and the quantities that they could buy were limited. Thus, total business spending was held down because the quantities of things business could buy were limited and the prices business could pay were limited by ceilings. In short, business was forced to spend less than it wanted to, and this limited its demand for investable funds.

Consumer spending was similarly repressed. Consumers were forbidden to pay prices above the legal ceilings, and the quantities of goods available were limited. Many were rationed. Many others, such as automobiles and most other consumer durables, simply were not produced. Thus, consumer spending was repressed and households were virtually forced to save far more than they would have in the absence of direct controls.

The repression of private spending was not, of course, complete. Consumer spending did rise, as did the wholesale and cost-of-living price indexes. The latter did not reflect actual price increases that occurred through upgrading, quality deterioration, and black markets. Yet the repression was remarkably successful in view of the strength of the inflationary pressures.

In short, the country had not been in the war very long before it was in a state of suppressed inflation, or widespread excess demand. The demand for output at existing prices had become far greater than the available supply. As the war progressed, these inflationary pressures grew—partly as a result of the huge accumulation of private savings. For the years 1940–1945 personal saving amounted to the huge sum of $132.6 billion and corporate net saving aggregated $28.5 billion. Total capital consumption accretions of $72.5 billion also enabled business to increase its liquidity to the extent that these funds could not be spent for replacement of plant and equipment. The private sector used these huge savings in two principal ways: (1) to retire debt—many households and businesses were enabled to retire their debts completely or at least to reduce them markedly; (2) to acquire liquid assets—between the end of 1939 and the end of 1945, individual and business holdings of liquid assets rose from $69 billion to $227.5 billion, an increase of $158.5 billion. Not only the size of this increase but also the liquidity of the assets should be noted. Of the total increase, $59 billion was in holdings of money itself—demand deposits and currency. Another $21.4 billion was in time deposits. Still another $75 billion was in highly liquid Treasury obligations. The nonmarketable issues, such as the E bonds, were redeemable at the Treasury on demand. The marketable issues were, in effect, redeemable on demand at the Federal Reserve at their support prices. The other $3.2 billion increase of liquid assets was in shares of savings and loan associations.

**CONDITIONS AT THE END OF WORLD WAR II**

The country had not escaped overt inflation during the war. By the end of 1945 consumer prices were 31 percent, and wholesale prices 39 percent, above their levels of six years earlier. Repressed inflationary pressures were very strong. The private sectors had accumulated a huge volume of liquid assets. Their money balances were now 183 percent above their level in 1939, and their total holdings of liquid assets were up 230 percent. Moreover, both business firms and households had accumulated unsatisfied wants in large volume. Many business firms that had spent little or nothing for investment purposes during the depression, and had been prevented for spending during the war, now wanted to replace, expand, or modernize their plants and equipment. Large numbers of families, feeling that they had lived like Spartans during the war, now wanted to go on a spending spree and to buy the cars and other things that had not been available during the war. The inflationary potential in increased private spending was large indeed.

But there was another side to the story, a side that led many persons to forecast deep depression and widespread unemployment rather than inflation for the postwar period. Many feared that the decrease of government spending following the cessation of hostilities would bring disaster. The sharp drop of federal expenditures from their level of almost $100 billion a year would directly decrease the demand for output, set off a downward multiplier effect on consumption, and leave industry with so much excess capacity that virtually no investment expenditures would be justified. Such gloomy forecasts were one, but by no means the only, reason for the early dismantling of direct controls. They were also a force for a continued easy-money policy. When the predicted depression did not develop immediately after the war, many people continued to insist that it was "just around the corner."

As the war drew to a close, the government quickly began to relax and to remove the whole complex of direct controls. Prices rose immediately as direct controls were relaxed and removed. During 1946 alone, wholesale prices rose more than they had during the entire 1939 to 1945 period, and the cost of living advanced two-thirds as much as it had during the preceding six years. By August 1948, when prices reached their first postwar peak, wholesale prices had risen 120 percent, and the cost of living 76 percent, since 1939. Two-thirds of the total rise of wholesale prices and three-fifths of the increase in the cost of living had occurred since the end of the war.

**MONETARY POLICY, 1946–1948**

Although direct controls over the economy were removed, Federal Reserve policies remained chained to their wartime objectives and methods of implementation. The system still used its powers to peg the prices and yields on Treasury obligations, and the pegged pattern of yields for some time was the same as it had been through the war. The range was from $\frac{3}{8}$ percent on 90-day maturities to a ceiling of $2\frac{1}{2}$ percent on 25-year Treasury bonds. In short, during a period of full employment and inflation the Federal Reserve was pegging a general level and pattern of interest rates that had evolved during the nation's worst depression. Not until March 1951, more than five years after the end of the war, did the Federal Reserve completely abandon this pegging pattern.

This passive open-market policy of supplying additional Federal Reserve funds to anyone presenting securities at their pegged prices was potentially far more dangerous in the postwar period than it had been during the war. The wartime system of direct controls had effectively limited private demands for credit. As limitations on the quantities that they could purchase and on the prices they could pay limited their total spending, households and business firms limited their demands for credit. But as these limitations were removed, private buyers again became free to bid against each other for larger quantities, to pay higher prices, and to demand larger loans for the purpose. Moreover, all types of financial institutions were in a position to meet almost any foreseeable increase in private demands for credit, and to do so at low interest rates as long as the Federal Reserve pegged yields on government securities, because they held huge amounts of these obligations. For example, at the end of 1945 commercial banks held $90.1 billion; life insurance companies, $20.6 billion; mutual savings banks, $10.7 billion; and savings and loan associations, $2.4 billion. Households and nonfinancial business firms also had large holdings, which they could sell to get money to lend to others or to finance their own spending.

**Reasons for the Pegging Policy**

Why did the Federal Reserve continue, despite inflation, to maintain easy-money conditions through its pegging policy? In part, it was because of the widespread fear of unemployment. The long depression of the 1930s had left an indelible impression, almost a depression psychosis. Almost every year brought new forecasts of a coming decline. Moreover, the nation's new determination to promote the achievement and maintenance of "maximum employment, production, and purchasing power" was embodied in the Employment Act of 1946. Treasury and Federal Reserve officials were reluctant to take any action that might jeopardize the maintenance of prosperity. The policy was also made more acceptable by the lack of faith in the efficacy of monetary policy. There was a widespread feeling that the experience of the 1930s had proved that monetary policy was ineffective in combating depression. Many now asserted that it would be equally useless as an instrument for fighting inflation—that mildly restrictive policies would not be effective and that policies restrictive enough to halt price increases would throw the country into depression.

Concern for Treasury financing and for the prices of outstanding Treasury obligations was a major reason for continuing the policy. The Secretary of the Treasury was a strong and persistent advocate of pegging and a stubborn opponent of increases in interest rates. Several of the relevant arguments are worth noting.

1   Increased rates on the federal debt would add greatly to the already large interest burden.

2   Fluctuating prices and yields on governments would greatly complicate the Treasury's refunding operations, a serious matter with about $50 billion of the debt maturing within a year and nearly $100 billion within five years.

3   An increase of yields on government securities, which without a rise of coupon rates would mean a decline of their prices, would impose capital depreciation on financial institutions and other holders and might lead to panicky selling and loss of confidence in financial institutions. Officials recalled the drastic decline of bond prices in 1920, when the federal debt was only $26 billion, and pointed to the greater possibilities of panic now that the debt was nearly ten times as large and represented about 60 percent of all debt in the country.

4   Disturbances in the prices and yields of government securities would be transmitted to private securities and jeopardize prosperity. It was argued that not only low interest rates but also stability of interest rates and bond prices promoted prosperity.

**Open-Market Policy**   Until July 1947, nearly two years after V-J Day, the Federal Open Market Committee continued to prevent yields on government securities from rising above the pattern selected in early 1942. The first break from the wartime pattern came in July 1947, when the Federal Reserve persuaded the Treasury to allow it to eliminate the $\frac{3}{8}$ percent buying rate on Treasury bills. The next break came the following month, when the Treasury agreed to the elimination of the $\frac{7}{8}$ percent rate on 9- to 12-month certificates of indebtedness. But this did not mean that the Federal Reserve had ceased to limit increases of the yields on these shorter-term obligations. It had merely shifted its policy to one of maintaining the rates fixed by the Treasury on new issues.

Several aspects of open-market policy during the remainder of this period deserve emphasis.

1   Not until March 1951 did the Federal Reserve permit the prices of long-term Treasury securities to fall below par or permit their yields to rise above $2\frac{1}{2}$ percent.

2   In the last analysis, it was the Secretary of the Treasury who set the yields on new issues, and therefore determined the rates to be maintained by the Federal Reserve. And the Secretary consented to rate increases only reluctantly, belatedly, and to a limited extent. By the end of 1948, when the first postwar inflation had reached its peak, the yield on Treasury bills had been allowed to rise only from $\frac{3}{8}$ percent to 1.13 percent, and that on 9- to 12-month certificates from $\frac{7}{8}$ percent to $1\frac{1}{4}$ percent. The results of

these increases could hardly be considered high interest rates for a period of inflation.

3   This willingness of the Federal Reserve to buy government securities in unlimited amounts robbed its other instruments of all, or almost all, of their effectiveness for restrictive purposes. In effect, this policy provided the banking system and others with a means of escape from other Federal Reserve attempts to restrict them.

**Other Monetary Policies**

The Federal Reserve employed two types of selective credit controls during this period. In 1946, as stock market activity began to rise markedly, the Board of Governors raised margin requirements on security loans to 100 percent, thereby putting the stock market on a "cash basis." This action probably inhibited the rise of stock prices and prevented a situation in which a highly speculative stock market might have enhanced inflationary expectations. It did not, of course, restrict the supply of credit for other purposes.

The Federal Reserve also increased discount rates three times. These rate advances probably exerted some influence toward firmness, but their effects were small because the banks were largely out of debt to the Federal Reserve, and were likely to remain so while they held so many short-term Treasury obligations that they could sell to the Federal Reserve at will.

From October 1942 until February 1948, the Board of Governors maintained member bank reserve requirements at the highest levels permitted by law, except that requirements against demand deposits in central reserve city banks were at 20 percent rather than at the maximum level of 26 percent. The Board of Governors then raised these latter requirements to 22 percent in February 1948 and to 24 percent in June. In August, Congress enacted legislation giving the Board temporary permission to raise these requirements above the old maximum levels. The Board thereupon raised requirements against demand deposits at all classes of member banks by 2 percentage points, and against time deposits by $1\frac{1}{2}$ percentage points. In all, these 1948 increases raised required member bank reserves by about $2.5 billion. Such a large increase of requirements would ordinarily have restricted credit markedly. In this case, the major effect was to evoke sales of an additional $2 billion of securities to the Federal Reserve. There was an accompanying slight increase of interest rates, but the effectiveness of the increases in reserve requirements was largely negated by the passive open-market policy.

The main argument of this section is not that these other Federal Reserve actions were wholly ineffective, but that the effectiveness of these restrictive actions was largely offset by the willingness of the Federal Reserve to supply reserve funds by purchasing Treasury obligations at relatively low and relatively stable yields.

MONETARY
POLICY,
1949–MID-1950

After the first postwar peak of prices was reached in August 1948, there followed more than a year of mild deflation. By the end of 1949, the cost of living had fallen 5 percent and wholesale prices were down 11 percent. In fact, 1949 was a year of mild recession, with small declines in both production and employment. The Federal Reserve halted its vain attempts to restrict credit and initiated an easier monetary policy, partly by lowering reserve requirements. In addition, the Treasury lowered somewhat the yields on its new issues, and the Federal Reserve stood ready to prevent market rates from rising above these lowered levels.

Under these conditions of mild deflation, the controversy between the Federal Reserve and the Treasury died down. In such a situation there is no necessary conflict between the objective of promoting general economic stabilization, including stability of price levels, and the objectives of holding down interest costs on the national debt, facilitating Treasury financing operations, and preventing decreases in the prices of outstanding Treasury bonds.

By early 1950 the decline in business activity and prices had stopped and recovery was well under way. As to the future course of business activity and price levels, there was wide disagreement among economic forecasters. The outbreak of fighting in Korea in June 1950 ended this uncertainty and ushered in a new upsurge of inflation.

MONETARY
POLICY DURING
THE KOREAN
WAR

The outbreak of fighting in Korea, and this country's decision to intervene, inspired a surge of buying by consumers and business firms. Remembering the scarcities and price increases of World War II, consumers rushed into the markets to get ahead of the hoarders. Business firms also hastened to replenish their inventories and to make net additions to them. Only later, toward the end of 1950, did the rise of government expenditures for military purposes add its inflationary effects to the rise in private spending. Much of this latter increase was financed by sales of liquid assets, decreases in holdings of idle money balances, and expansions of credit. The velocity of money increased appreciably, redemptions of savings bonds rose, consumer credit expanded, and business loans increased markedly. Between May 1950 and March 1951, the cost of living rose 8 percent and wholesale prices 19 percent. During the rest of 1951, price levels remained relatively constant, the cost of living rising slightly and wholesale prices declining a little.

With the resurgence of inflation, the controversy between the Federal Reserve and the Treasury flared anew. The Federal Reserve wanted to restrict credit to curb the rise of prices, while the Treasury insisted that it continue to hold interest rates at an inflexibly low level. This controversy, which had seethed behind the scenes, came out into the open in August 1950, when the Federal Reserve publicly defied the Treasury. On the same day and at almost the same hour the two issued conflicting public announcements. The Federal Open Market Committee announced the system's determination to fight the current inflation and to use all its powers to this end. At the same time, the Treasury announced a new $13 billion issue of short-term securities with yields no higher than those currently prevailing in the market. Despite this Treasury challenge, the Federal Reserve proceeded to tighten credit. To prevent the Treasury's financing from failing, the system purchased most of the new issue at the yields fixed by the Treasury. Then it sold some of its other holdings in the market on terms that raised the market yields of short-term obligations. It also raised its discount rates from $1\frac{1}{2}$ to $1\frac{3}{4}$ percent. This controversy related only to short-term issues; the Federal Reserve continued to prevent the prices of long-term government bonds from falling below par.

In early 1951 the controversy spread to the prices and yields on long-term Treasury bonds. A major reason for the Federal Reserve's rebellion was its fear that its other attempts to contain inflation would be ineffective as long as it had to peg the prices of these securities. In January it raised member bank reserve requirements against demand deposits by 2 percent. Acting under new congressional authorization, it reimposed selective controls on consumer credit and imposed a similar selective regulation on credit for residential construction. It also encouraged commercial banks, insurance companies, savings banks, and some other financial institutions to enter into a voluntary credit-restraint program to prevent or lessen the extension of credit for "nonessential" purposes. But Federal Reserve officials doubted that these measures alone could stop the inflation. The policy of pegging Treasury bond prices at par would have to end.

In early 1951 the conflict between the Federal Reserve and the Treasury became dramatic. In January, the Secretary of the Treasury publicly announced that during the defense period all the government's issues of marketable securities (for new money as well as for refunding purposes) would bear interest rates no higher than $2\frac{1}{2}$ percent. He also implied, without stating it specifically, that the Federal Reserve had agreed to this policy. Reserve officials denied that this was true. The President and the Council of Economic Advisers then entered the dispute to support the Treasury position. After a White House conference with Federal Reserve officials, the President publicly announced that the Federal Reserve had, in effect, agreed to the Treasury's announced policy. This the Federal Reserve publicly denied. Now that the controversy was common knowledge and involved the President himself, it became a hotly debated issue in Congress, in the newspapers, and in financial circles. The Board of Governors finally informed the Treasury that, as of February 19, it was no longer willing to maintain the existing situation in the government securities market. After further negotiations the Treasury and the Federal Reserve jointly announced, on March 4, 1951, their now-famous accord: "The Treasury and the Federal Reserve System have reached full accord with respect to debt-management and monetary policies to be pursued in furthering their common purpose to assure the successful financing of the Government's requirements and, at the same time, to minimize monetization of the public debt."

The Treasury–Federal Reserve accord of March 4, 1951, stands as a landmark in American monetary history because it marked the end of inflexible pegging of the prices of Treasury obligations. Nine years after it had first adopted the policy (in March 1942), the Federal Reserve had finally regained at least some freedom to refrain from purchasing all securities offered to it, to limit its creation of bank reserves, and to restrict credit when necessary to prevent inflation. To the extent that it was freed from the task of supporting Treasury operations, it could now direct them more toward promoting economic stability.

**SELECTED READINGS**

Brown, A. J., *The Great Inflation, 1939–1951*, London, Oxford University Press, 1955.

Chandler, L. V., *Inflation in the United States, 1940–1948*, New York, Harper & Row, 1951.

Fforde, J. S., *The Federal Reserve System, 1945–1949*, London, Oxford University Press, 1954.

# 20

The Treasury–Federal Reserve accord of March 1951 freed Federal Reserve officials from the shackles of an inflexible pegging policy. It thus gave them the latitude to carry out the mandate set forth five years earlier in the Employment Act of 1946. That act, as we have seen, provided for governmental responsibility in promoting "maximum employment, production, and purchasing power." The Federal Reserve was clearly expected to participate in interpreting and implementing these objectives and readily agreed that its stabilization responsibilities were "to promote continuously high levels of employment, the highest sustainable rate of economic growth, and relative stability of the purchasing power of the dollar." In moving from the era of pegging to one of carrying out this charge, Reserve officials faced the task of developing new patterns of policy implementation. Their problem was not a lack of power; it was rather a problem of deciding how and for what purposes to use their power. We shall highlight three major problems: (1) transition from the period of pegging and determination of the relationship of monetary policy to the management of the national debt; (2) reassessment of the relative roles of policy instruments; and (3) reconciliation of conflicts among objectives, especially in regard to the balance of payments.

**MONETARY
AND DEBT
MANAGEMENT
POLICIES**

During the period of pegging before March 1951, the Federal Reserve entered the government securities market for two principal purposes: (1) to stabilize the prices of securities that were already outstanding and (2) to assist the Treasury in selling new issues, whether these were to secure new money to cover current deficits or to pay off maturing issues.

For the latter purpose the Federal Reserve frequently purchased a part of a new issue that others were not willing to buy at the yield rates fixed by the Treasury, and it sometimes bought outstanding issues of comparable maturities to "make room in the market" for the new Treasury issue.

The immediate purpose of the Federal Reserve at the time of the accord was not to withdraw completely from the government securities market and leave both the prices of outstanding Treasury obligations and current Treasury-financing operations completely on their own. To withdraw support completely and abruptly after such a long period of pegging would have been both impossible and undesirable. Erratic, and perhaps even panicky, declines in the prices of outstanding securities not only would injure holders and jeopardize the future marketability of new long-term issues, but might also disturb the markets for private obligations and upset economic stability. Nor could the Federal Reserve immediately withdraw all support of Treasury financing operations. To permit a new issue to fail and perhaps force the Treasury to default on a part of the national debt was unthinkable. The Federal Reserve's immediate purpose, therefore, was merely to secure somewhat greater flexibility—to permit the prices and yields of oustanding government securities to vary more widely and to induce the Treasury to put more realistic yields on its new issues and to rely less heavily on Federal Reserve support. However, its longer-run purpose was to work toward a situation in which its open-market policies would be shaped almost exclusively by economic-stabilization objectives, and its purchases and sales would again be directed exclusively toward regulating the reserve position of the banking system rather than toward directly influencing the prices of Treasury obligations, new or old.

With respect to outstanding government securities, Federal Reserve policy for some time immediately following the abandonment of pegging was to "maintain an orderly market." Federal Reserve officials insisted that this did not mean that they would limit the extent to which the prices of these securities would be permitted to decline if the price decline was consistent with the attainment of other Federal Reserve objectives. It meant only that they would assist in keeping these adjustments orderly rather than erratic or disorderly. The system then shifted to a policy of preventing a disorderly market. This was not merely an exercise in semantics; it indicated a greater Federal Reserve tolerance of fluctuations in the prices of government securities, reduced readiness to intervene to influence these prices directly, and greater reliance on private purchasers and sellers to maintain orderly conditions.

By the spring of 1953 the Federal Reserve had arrived at a new rule that would normally or ordinarily guide its open-market operations: It would not buy or sell longer-term Treasury obligations (those with maturities of more than one year), but would confine its operations to short maturities, preferably Treasury bills. This has come to be known popularly as the *bills-only doctrine*. The Federal Reserve also decided that thereafter it would not ordinarily engage in *swap operations*, that is, buying some maturities to raise their prices or to limit their price declines, and selling others.

Federal Reserve officials had several closely related reasons for wanting to stay out of the market for long-term obligations and for confining their operations to bills and other short maturities where the direct effects of their purchases and sales on the prices of the securities would be much smaller.

1   They undoubtedly feared that if they continued to operate in the long-term market, they might again be shackled by an inflexible pegging policy. A policy of pegging prices inflexibly at some point below par could be almost as shackling as pegging at par.

2   They wished to avoid possible charges that their sales of long-term securities, or even their refusal to buy them, had unfairly imposed losses on holders.

3   The reason stressed most by Federal Reserve officials was their desire to create conditions in which private buyers and sellers would themselves develop an orderly and self-reliant market. They argued that as long as private operators in this market expected Federal Reserve intervention, they would not perform the ordinary security market functions of taking speculative positions, buying when they thought prices were too low, selling short when they thought prices were too high, and arbitraging among the various issues to establish reasonable yield relationships. It was hoped that after the Federal Reserve's withdrawal from the long-term market, private operators would themselves develop a broad, deep, and resilient market.

The ability of the Federal Reserve to withdraw its support from current Treasury financing operations depended to a great extent on the attitudes and policies of the Treasury. If the latter persisted in fixing low rates on its issues, the Federal Reserve would either have to support them or risk being blamed for the failure of Treasury financing. In fact, however, the Treasury gradually adjusted its financing policies to the current monetary policies of the Federal Reserve and conscientiously tried to make the yields and other terms on its new issues such that they could be sold without Federal Reserve support. The Treasury's cooperation was sufficient to enable the Federal Reserve to adopt two more rules by the spring of 1953: Ordinarily it would not buy any part of a new issue at the time of sale, and it would not at that time buy any outstanding issue of comparable maturity.[1]

---

[1] This was not interpreted as preventing the Federal Reserve from taking part of a new issue in exchange for its holdings of a maturing issue.

Thus, by the spring of 1953 the Federal Reserve had moved far from its policies during the period before March 1951 and had developed four rules that would ordinarily or normally be followed:

1    It would not deal in securities with maturities in excess of a year and would confine its open-market operations to short maturities, preferably bills.
2    It would not engage in swap operations.
3    It would not buy any new Treasury issue at the time of offering.
4    At the time of a new Treasury issue, it would not buy any outstanding securities of comparable maturity.

The Federal Reserve departed from these normal rules only twice during the first five years after their adoption. The first deviation occurred in late 1955, when the system was following a restrictive policy and the Treasury offered a large new issue with a maturity in excess of a year. The Treasury believed the issue had been made sufficiently attractive to enable all of it to be sold to private purchasers, but it soon became apparent that some of the issue would remain unsold. The Federal Reserve thereupon violated three of its rules all at once: It bought some of the new, longer-term issue and then sold some of its holdings of other maturities to mop up the reserves created by its purchases. The second departure occurred in July 1958 after the dispatch of American troops to Lebanon following the revolution in Iraq. The prices of long-term government securities, including prices on a recent issue, declined. Moreover, the Treasury had just announced a new issue, which was not attracting purchasers in sufficient volume. The Federal Reserve intervened to purchase some of the outstanding longer-term issue and some of the new issue. To mop up the reserves created by these purchases, it sold other maturities out of its portfolio.

These exceptions highlight two points. The fact that there were only two exceptions to the normal rules in over five years indicates how far the Federal Reserve had moved away from the policies it had followed before March 1951. It also indicates how far the Treasury, in its debt management policies, was willing to depart from its old objective of borrowing at continuously low interest rates and to move toward adjusting its policies to the economic stabilization policies of the Federal Reserve. But these exceptions also highlight the fact that Federal Reserve policies cannot completely ignore federal debt management.

**RELATIVE ROLES OF FEDERAL RESERVE POLICY INSTRUMENTS**

One reason for the need to reconsider the relative roles of the principal Federal Reserve policy instruments was the virtual disappearance of Federal Reserve lending to member banks during the preceding 17 years. From 1934 to World War II, member banks were so swamped with excess reserves that only a very few banks had any need to borrow. After that time, most members had adjusted their reserve positions through buying and selling government securities. Many bankers, especially younger bankers, had never applied for a loan and knew little or nothing about Federal Reserve lending policies. Moreover, Federal Reserve officials were by now inexperienced in the use of this instrument and needed to reconsider the whole problem of discount policy and discount rates.

Attitudes toward revival of Federal Reserve discounting varied widely. At one extreme, a minority favored not only reviving discounting but also raising its relative importance to the level it had enjoyed in the 1920s. At the other extreme, some people advocated the complete elimination of discounting, considering it to be a "slippage" that decreased the accuracy of Federal Reserve control over the volume of member bank reserves. The outcome was a compromise. Member banks were permitted to borrow, but normally for only limited periods and only to meet such reserve needs as the banks could not reasonably be expected to meet from other sources.

Open-market operations in government securities emerged as the most important policy instrument. The Federal Reserve retained its power to alter member bank reserve requirements, but it used this power only infrequently.

Let us now see how the Federal Reserve used the greater flexibility of action that is regained in March 1951.

---

**FEDERAL RESERVE POLICIES, 1951–1959**

The rise of prices initiated by the Korean conflict ended in March 1951 with the cost of living up 8 percent and wholesale prices up 19 percent from their levels prior to the outbreak. There followed a period of more than four years of relative price stability. In mid-1955 the consumer price index was only 3 percent above its level in March 1951. The wholesale price index actually declined 6 percent. The period up to early 1953 was one of high production and employment. GNP rose substantially, and unemployment was at a minimum. Out of a total labor force of more than 66 million, unemployment averaged only 1.9 million in 1951 and 1.7 million in 1952. In the spring of 1953 it fell to the extraordinarily low level of 1.3 million.

Under these conditions the Federal Reserve allowed interest rates to rise somewhat during the remainder of 1951 and in 1952. It took no action to reduce the volume of bank reserves, but as the demand for bank credit rose it did not supply additional reserves by purchasing government securities. By early 1953 Federal Reserve officials began to fear a resumption of inflation. Prices had not begun to rise, but the economy was already operating at close to capacity levels, unemployment was at a minimum, demand was still rising, and Federal Reserve officials thought they detected a speculative building up of inventories. They therefore intensified their restrictive policy. In January the discount rate was raised from $1\frac{3}{4}$ to 2 percent, its highest level since 1934. Interest rates rose to their highest levels in 20 years. Credit stringency became severe as expectations of still tighter money and even higher interest rates led lenders to withhold funds and borrowers to rush in to anticipate their future needs. In May 1953 the Federal Reserve began to ease the situation. It now became evident that the immediate danger was not inflation but recession.

**Easy Money, 1953–1954**
The recession of 1953–1954 was short and relatively mild. The decline in GNP was accounted for by a shift from inventory accumulation in early 1953 to inventory decumulation, and by an $11 billion decrease in federal expenditures for national security purposes. Other demands for output held up very well, and consumption expenditures actually rose about $4 billion. The latter was due, at least in part, to a $5 billion tax reduction at the beginning of 1954. The number of unemployed rose above its extraordinarily low level of 1.3 million in the spring of 1953, but it did not quite reach 3.5 million, or 5 percent of the labor force.

The Federal Reserve used all its major instruments to ease credit and to combat the recession. Early in May 1953, it began to buy short-term government securities in the open market; by the end of June, it had increased its holdings by nearly $1 billion. Although this action enabled banks to reduce their borrowings and to increase their excess reserves, it did not succeed immediately in lowering interest rates. This failure was, at least in part, because the financial community did not believe that the Federal Reserve had really reversed its tight-money policy and was working toward easier credit conditions. Open-market purchases had not proved to be an effective means of announcing the change of policy. It was partly for this purpose that the Board of Governors reduced member bank reserve requirements against demand deposits at the beginning of July.

The combined effect of these actions was to ease member bank reserve positions markedly. In June and July 1954, the Board again lowered member bank reserve requirements. By mid-1954 credit conditions were very easy. Member bank borrowings were less than $200 million, and excess reserves were above $800 million. The money supply had risen about $3 billion during the preceding year. It rose another $6 billion during the latter half of 1954. Interest rates, which had fallen during 1953, declined still further. The yield on Treasury bills fell below $\frac{3}{4}$ percent. The prices of long-term government securities again rose above par.

This easy-money policy almost certainly helped shorten the recession, reduce its severity, and hasten recovery. It was especially helpful in stimulating residential construction. Some Federal Reserve officials later wondered whether they had not eased credit too much, continued the easy-money policy too long, and provided both the public and the banking system with too much liquidity. This greatly enhanced liquidity of both the public and the banks contributed to the subsequent rise of spending and prices. But it does not necessarily follow that the policies of 1953 and 1954 were too easy and too prolonged. Perhaps the error was in not moving more aggressively as business recovery approached an inflationary stage.

**Tight Money, 1955–1957**      The recession reached its trough in the second quarter of 1954 and was followed first by recovery and then by a boom that culminated in the third quarter of 1957. During this three-year period GNP at current prices rose 24 percent. A major contributor to this was an investment boom that, during this period, produced an increase in gross private domestic investment of more than 40 percent. Unemployment, which was 3.4 million in mid-1954, averaged 2.6 million in 1955 and 1956 and fluctuated around this level during the first ten months of 1957. This represented less than 4 percent of the labor force.

Prices remained stable until mid-1955 and then began to rise, slowly at first and then more rapidly. By October 1957 consumer prices had risen 5.6 percent and wholesale prices 6.6 percent.

The Federal Reserve began to reduce the degree of credit ease as business activity started upward in the latter part of 1954, and then permitted tighter credit conditions to develop during the period from early 1955 to November 1957. The money supply was held approximately constant, despite a substantial increase in the transactions demand for money. Consequently, market rates of interest rose to their highest levels in 25 years, and the 24 percent rise of GNP expenditures was financed almost entirely by an increase in the velocity of money.

We have already seen that these increases in interest rates did not prevent investment expenditures from rising more than 40 percent, that Federal Reserve policies did not prevent total expenditures for output from rising 24 percent, and that they did not prevent the cost of living from rising 5.6 percent and wholesale prices 6.6 percent. This is hardly surprising. One should not necessarily expect a rise of interest rates to prevent a rise of investment expenditures when the rise of rates is itself produced by an upward shift of the investment demand schedule. The investment function undoubtedly shifted sharply upward during this period, so that spenders for investment purposes were willing to spend much more at each level of interest rates or to spend the same amounts at much higher levels of interest rates. An actual rise of investment expenditures could have been prevented only by a sharp decrease in the supply of investable funds at each interest rate, and this did not occur.

The boom reached its peak in the third quarter of 1957 and gave way to recession. By the first quarter of 1958, GNP had fallen nearly 3 percent. Unemployment, which had been 2.5 million in October, averaged above 5.1 million in the first quarter of 1958. Changes in business inventory policies were a major contributor to the recession. But as so often happens, the shift in business inventory policy was induced at least in part by more basic changes in the economy. For one thing, a decline of business expenditures for plant and equipment began. For another, in the autumn federal procurement policies shifted expectations. Perhaps partly to combat inflation, but more for the purpose of holding its expenditures within the total budgeted for the fiscal year and to avoid raising the debt limit, the federal government sharply reduced its new orders for military equipment, reduced its progress payments for military equipment in process of production, and suggested to many firms that they stretch out their production over a longer period. Personal consumption expenditures held up remarkably well, declining less than 1 percent. This was in large part because of the automatic decline of tax liabilities and the automatic rise of unemployment compensation and other transfer payments that bolstered disposable personal incomes.

It was under these conditions that the Federal Reserve relaxed credit restriction and moved toward easy money. In October 1957 its open-market policy was designed to avoid a further tightening of the market and to ease it slightly. The first decisive move came in mid-November, when discount rates were reduced. Market rates of interest, and especially long-term rates, immediately fell sharply. The Federal Open Market Committee cautiously purchased government securities to enable banks to reduce their borrowings and increase their excess reserves.

The Board of Governors also lowered member bank reserve requirements against demand deposits, and the Reserve banks further lowered their discount rates. These liberalizing Federal Reserve actions were accompanied by a sharp decline of short-term interest rates. The yield on Treasury bills, which had averaged about 3.6 percent in October, had fallen well below 1 percent by May. Long-term rates proved less responsive. After dropping sharply immediately after the first reduction of discount rates in mid-November, they began to drift downward much more slowly, and by May had begun to rise. The very easy conditions prevailing in the short-term credit market were not evident in the long-term market, for several reasons. One was the extraordinarily large volume of new long-term bond issues. State and local governments borrowed heavily, both to finance current expenditures and to retire short-term debt issued during the period of high interest rates. So did corporations. The federal government also floated several long-term issues, primarily to retire short-term debt. This became a highly controversial matter, for many believe that in periods of recession the Treasury should borrow only on short-term obligations and should refrain from issuing long-term securities that would compete with private long-term issues and tend to decrease the availability and increase the cost of long-term credit for private investment. These heavy borrowings in the long-term market while short-term loans were being repaid help to explain the disparity in the behavior of short-term and long-term interest rates. Some observers insisted that this was an occasion when the Federal Reserve should have abandoned the bills-only doctrine and bought long-term securities. A majority of Federal Reserve officials rejected this view.

**Tight Money Again, 1958–1959**

The recession that started in the third quarter of 1957 proved to be shorter than many economists had expected, and it reached its low point in April 1958. The economy then began a recovery that continued until the first quarter of 1960. GNP had risen 16 percent by the first quarter of 1960. However, this proved to be the weakest recovery in the postwar period. Demands for output and actual output failed to rise as fast as the productive capacity of the economy. Unemployment, which had claimed 7.4 percent of the labor force in February 1958, did decline to 4.9 percent by mid-1959, but thereafter it climbed to some degree. During the last half of 1959 and the first half of 1960, it averaged 5.5 percent.

Thus, this "prosperity" period was characterized by a level of unemployment comparable to the levels that prevailed during the recessions of 1949 and 1954. There were widespread complaints about the slow rate of economic growth in the United States relative to growth rates abroad. The weakness of the recovery was reflected in the stability of prices. The wholesale price index did not rise, and the consumer price index rose only 1.5 percent from early 1958 to the end of 1959. Nevertheless, fears of inflation were widespread. The almost uninterrupted rise of prices for nearly 20 years and the failure of prices to decline in the 1957–1958 recession convinced many that we were in danger of adopting inflation as a way of life.

It was largely because of fear of inflation that the Federal Reserve abandoned its easy-money policy in May 1958 and initiated a restrictive policy that was to permit interest rates to rise to their highest levels in 30 years. By December 1959, when rates reached their peak, yields on 3-month Treasury bills were around $4\frac{1}{2}$ percent; those on 9- to 12-month Treasury issues, about 5 percent; and those on long-term federal issues, about $4\frac{1}{4}$ percent. In broad outline, Federal Reserve policy during this period was quite similar to that during the 1955–1957 boom. The Federal Reserve did not attempt to reduce the money supply; it only followed a policy of "leaning against the wind," of preventing the money supply from increasing in response to the rising demand for money balances. Total member bank reserves remained almost unchanged during the period. However, banks were able to maintain their reserves at this level only by markedly increasing their borrowings from the Federal Reserve.

After the peak of interest rates was reached around the end of 1959, the Federal Reserve began a cautious relaxation, largely because of the high level of unemployment. In the summer of 1960, as a new recession loomed, the Federal Reserve began to move more positively toward an easy-money policy. Then it was faced by an unhappy fact: Even the United States could have its freedom of action limited by considerations related to balance-of-payments and international reserve positions.

**EVELOPMENTS IN THE NTERNATIONAL MONETARY SITUATION**

While we shall later explore the international aspects of economic policy in considerable detail, it is impossible to understand certain features of monetary policy in the 1960s without some brief attention to the international economic scene.

**Some General Principles**

There are three major types of economic transactions between countries: trade in goods and services, commonly referred to as exports and imports; international gifts and transfer payments; and international capital transactions whereby residents of one country purchase financial claims issued by residents of a second country. The statistical record of all transactions between a nation and the rest of the world is that nation's balance of payments. Speaking very loosely, a country will experience difficulties with its balance of payments whenever its expenditures exceed its receipts. Consider for a moment a situation in which a country's imports exceed its exports and it thus has a trade deficit. As with any deficit, be it of a household, a business, or a governmental unit, a trade deficit can be financed by borrowing. Borrowing, in this context, involves convincing foreigners to acquire additional financial claims (IOUs) issued by the deficit country. Obviously, other things equal, the higher the interest rate on such claims, the more willing foreigners will be to acquire them.

In the event that the deficit cannot be financed by borrowing, the deficit country will be forced to draw on its assets. For this purpose countries keep what are termed *international reserves* (historically in the form of gold or foreign currencies) that can be drawn down as needed. These reserves are generally limited, however, so that continued deficits may require more serious action. Since imports tend to be higher the larger GNP is, one possible way to eliminate a trade deficit is to use restrictive monetary or fiscal policy to damp GNP. Here we have a clear example of a conflict between domestic and international objectives.

**The Experience of the United States**

Beginning in about 1950, the United States began experiencing deficits in its balance of payments. To finance these deficits it resorted to both borrowing and drawing down its gold reserves. Through the 1950s the rest of the world looked somewhat benignly on U.S. deficits, as these deficits provided foreigners with substantial amounts of liquidity in the form of both gold and claims on dollars. By about 1960, however, our short-term dollar liabilities to foreigners exceeded the remaining U.S. gold stock. In effect, the United States was a banker whose ability to deliver on demand was called into question. As a consequence, foreigners began calling for the United States to do something about its payments deficits. As a result, during the period 1960–1965 there was a conflict between the objective of decreasing the deficit in the balance of payments and the desire to increase the rate of real economic growth and lower the unemployment rate. As we proceed to examine monetary policies during this period, we shall see how the monetary authorities attempted to cope with this problem.

**MONETARY POLICIES, 1960–1963**

The economy began to slide into a recession in the first quarter of 1960. The recession was relatively mild, with real GNP decreasing by only slightly more than 1 percent from the first quarter of 1960 to the trough of the recession in the fourth quarter of 1960. However, this small decline of output, together with the continuing growth of the labor force and rising output per unit of labor, produced a sharp rise of unemployment. By the fourth quarter of 1960, unemployment had reached 6.5 percent, and it remained at or above this level for over a year. At the same time, balance-of-payments deficits continued to be a problem. In October 1960, strong speculative pressures drove up the London gold price and the U.S. gold stock declined substantially.

The first response of the Federal Reserve to the onset of the recession was to move toward a more liberal policy, just as it had done in the earlier postwar recessions. It purchased government securities in the open market and lowered member bank reserve requirements, thereby enabling the banks to reduce their borrowings and increase their excess reserves. Moreover, discount rates were lowered. These actions together with decreased demands for funds brought a reduction of market interest rates. For example, the short-term Treasury bill rate declined from 3 percent in the second quarter of 1960 to about 2.4 percent in the third quarter. But there the decline virtually stopped; these rates stayed at about the same level through the third quarter of 1961 and then increased slightly.

Monetary policy during this period of excessive unemployment is best described as only moderately expansionary, and less expansionary than in earlier postwar recessions. For example, Federal Reserve discount rates, which had been reduced to $1\frac{1}{2}$ percent in 1954 and to $1\frac{3}{4}$ percent in 1958, were not reduced below 3 percent in this period. The average annual rate of growth of the money supply was less than 3 percent. The decline of market rates of interest, and especially of short-term rates, was not as great as in earlier recessions. Partly as a consequence of all this, the recovery from the 1960 recession was a relatively weak one. While beginning in 1961 real GNP rose without interruption, its rate of growth was quite sluggish, so that extensive amounts of unemployment and excess capacity persisted. The unemployment rate, for example, averaged 6.7 percent for 1961 and fluctuated between $5\frac{1}{2}$ and 6 percent throughout 1962 and 1963. It appears almost certain that in this period concern about the balance of payments did, to a considerable extent, motivate the Federal Reserve to follow less expansionary policies than it would otherwise have followed.

**Operation Nudge**
In an attempt to reconcile its international and domestic objectives, the Federal Reserve modified its open-market policy, trying to "nudge" short-term rates higher relative to long-term rates. The height of long-term interest rates in the United States relative to those abroad obviously influences the flow of long-term funds to other countries. However, during this period Federal Reserve and Treasury officials believed that short-term rates were more important in determining international flows of funds, whereas long-term rates were more important in determining domestic investment spending. They therefore sought to raise short-term rates relative to long-term rates. Note that they faced two separate policy problems: (1) to regulate the overall reserve positions of the banks, and thus influence the general or average level of interest rates; and (2) to influence the relative heights of short-term and long-term rates. The attempts of the Federal Reserve and the Treasury to raise short-term relative to long-term rates are usually called Operation Nudge, although some people referred to these operations as Operation Twist.

To illustrate the principles involved we assume that the Federal Reserve has already determined the overall reserve position of the banks. The basic technique of the nudge is to increase the supply of Treasury bills and other short issues available to banks and the public relative to the supply of long-term government bonds. This can be done through both Treasury debt management operations and Federal Reserve open-market operations. For its part, the Treasury increases the supply of Treasury bills and other short maturities outstanding. It does this in several ways: through outright "swaps" of Treasury bills for outstanding longer maturities, by concentrating new issues in the short-term area, by purchasing longs rather than shorts for its own investment accounts, and so on.

In comparable ways the Federal Reserve can increase the supply of Treasury bills and other short maturities available to the banks and the public: by selling shorts and buying longs, by purchasing longs rather than shorts to supply bank reserves, and by providing banks with reserves or excess reserves by other means that do not require it to purchase shorts. To do this, however, the Federal Reserve had to abandon its controversial bills-only (or bills-usually) policy. Some steps in this direction were taken in late 1960, when the FOMC began to buy certificates, notes, and bonds with maturities up to 15 months. On February 20, 1961, it abandoned bills-only, announcing, "The System Open-Market Account is purchasing in the open market U.S. government bonds and notes of varying maturities, some of which will exceed five years." Since that time it has dealt in a wide range of maturities. However, its swaps and purchases of long maturities have been in only modest volume.

So much for principles. In actual fact, Operation Nudge was only moderately successful in raising short-term rates relative to long-term ones. The main reason was not that the principles were wrong—after all the Federal Reserve had proved perfectly capable of pegging the interest rate structure during and after World War II—but rather that the operation was conducted on such a limited scale. For its part, the Federal Reserve swaps of short for longs were small, as were its net purchases of longer securities. Moreover, the Treasury actually offset these operations to some extent by issuing longer-term securities. Once again coordination on debt management issues proved to be a tricky business.

There is an interesting postscript to this failure. Recently some economists have concluded that even if Operation Nudge had succeeded in raising short rates relative to long rates, it would probably not have done much to reconcile domestic and international objectives. The reason is that both international capital flows and domestic investment now appear to respond to the entire spectrum of interest rates. As a consequence, these economists argue that the net effect of raising short rates relative to long rates would probably have been negligible.

**OTHER POLICIES**  As we have seen, while the monetary authorities were struggling to reconcile the pursuit of both domestic and international objectives, they followed what at best might be characterized as a moderately expansionary policy. In an attempt both to improve the lackluster performance of the economy and to lessen the problem of conflicting objectives, the government took several steps. In particular, it adopted a more expansionary fiscal policy and introduced the so-called wage–price guideposts.

**Fiscal Policies**

The government hoped that an expansionary fiscal policy, in contrast with an expansionary monetary policy, would lead to less of a conflict between domestic and international objectives. It recognized that a fiscal policy that succeeded in raising domestic income and output would tend to worsen the balance of payments by increasing imports. But, unlike an expansionary monetary policy, it would not tend to lower interest rates or to encourage capital exports. In fact, to the extent that it succeeded in increasing the demand for domestic output and in raising the expected profitability of domestic investment, it would tend to keep funds at home.

In 1962 two steps were taken to encourage private investment. One was a liberalization of depreciation rules, which permitted firms to write off their investments more quickly for tax purposes. The other was enactment of an *investment tax credit* that permitted business firms to deduct from their income tax liabilities an amount equal to 7 percent of their purchases of new plant and equipment. This was, in effect, a subsidy for new investment.

In late 1962 President Kennedy proposed a sizable reduction of personal and corporate income tax rates, but Congress delayed the reduction until 1964. The reduction, which became effective in steps in 1964 and 1965, amounted to $15 billion at the levels of GNP prevailing in 1965. It clearly had the desired effect of increasing the rate of growth of demands for output. It would have been even more useful if it had been instituted at least two years earlier.

**Wage–Price Guideposts**

Although in 1962 the economy was still operating well below its potential, the desire of the government to take significant expansionary action raised the specter of a future conflict between economic growth and low unemployment on the one hand and price stability on the other. To forestall this possibility the Council of Economic Advisers set forth a set of voluntary wage–price guidelines in its *Economic Report* for 1962.

The general principle of the wage guideline was that annual increases in money wage rates should be equal to the average annual increase in output per unit of labor in the economy as a whole. For example, if average output per unit of labor in the entire economy rose by 3 percent a year, it would be appropriate for money wages to rise by the same percentage. This means that labor cost per unit of output would remain unchanged in industries where the increase in labor productivity was equal to the economy-wide average, would fall where the rise of

productivity was above average, and would rise where the rise of productivity was below average. Exceptions to this general wage guideline
were envisaged. For example, larger wage increases would be appropriate where the guideline wage was not high enough to attract sufficient
labor or where this wage was inequitably low.

The general principle of the price guideline is that prices should be
changed only by a percentage equal to the change in labor cost per unit
of output. This means that prices would remain unchanged where the
rise of labor productivity was equal to the national average, would fall
where the rise of productivity was above the national average, and
would rise where the rise of productivity was below the national
average.

In view of their voluntary nature, there has been a fair amount of
controversy over whether the guideposts did actually serve to improve
the trade-off between inflation and unemployment. While the evidence
seems to point to some small salutary effect, it is not fully conclusive,
especially since the guideposts were abandoned when serious inflationary pressures emerged during the Vietnam War.

**DEVELOPMENTS
FROM 1964 TO
LATE 1965**

At the beginning of 1964, when the first round of the substantial tax cuts
just described went into effect, the unemployment rate stood at nearly 6
percent, roughly its average of the previous three years. Then the tempo
of economic activity picked up considerably. Real GNP, which over the
previous three years had advanced at about a 4 percent annual rate, expanded at over a 6 percent rate during the next two years. This gradually
closed the gap between actual and potential GNP, and the Kennedy–
Johnson administrations' interim target of 4 percent unemployment was
reached in late 1965. And all this had occurred without a change in the
rate of inflation. Indeed, the rate of change in the consumer price index
in 1964–1965 was comparable to the performance in 1957–1963, though
some observers thought the upward movement of wholesale prices por-
tended greater inflation in the future. About the only other stabilization
problem was the nagging persistence of the deficits in the balance of
payments. But even these grew somewhat smaller in 1964 and 1965. In
short, who could blame the policy makers for their rosy view of the
world?

But the euphoria did not last long. With the economy close to its potential, defense outlays for the Vietnam War began a significant expansion in late 1965. As these increased outlays were, initially at least, un-
matched by any reduction in fiscal stimulus, monetary policy was
quickly forced to bear the burden of the restraint. Thus began one of the
more dismal periods in the history of economic policy.

CONCLUSION   The period of about nine years extending from the Treasury–Federal Reserve accord in March 1951 until the summer of 1960, when considerations relating to the nation's balance of payments began to influence monetary policy, may be considered to be a reconversion period for the Federal Reserve. At the beginning of the period, the Federal Reserve had not followed a restrictive policy in more than 17 years. For more than nine years its overriding objective, which greatly limited its ability to promote other goals, had been to prevent increases of interest rates on long-term government securities. Now it had regained freedom to elevate other objectives and to develop new ways of using its policy instruments. However, conditions at that time were far different from those of the 1920s and early 1930s. One important change was the great growth of the national debt, which could not be ignored completely. Another change was symbolized by the Employment Act of 1946: The nation was now determined not only to avoid serious depressions but also to maintain continuously "maximum employment, production, and purchasing power."

This chapter has described how the Federal Reserve used its newly regained flexibility of action. It gradually reduced the extent of its direct intervention to stabilize the prices of government securities and to assist in Treasury financing. The two recessions of 1953–1954 and 1957–1958 were countered with expansionary monetary policies. The booms and threatened inflations of 1952–1953, 1955–1957, and 1958–1959 invoked monetary restriction, which consisted mainly of limiting increases in the money supply in the face of rising demands.

At the end of the 1950s the stabilization program had been successful in the sense that there had been no major depression in the fifteen years following World War II. However, there had also been at least partial failures and problems that threatened to persist and perhaps to become more serious. First, there were the three recessions of 1949, 1954, and 1958. Although these were mild and short by historical standards, they were bitter disappointments to those who had hoped for continuously low unemployment and a continuously high rate of economic growth. A second disappointment was the incompatibility of price stability on the one hand and low levels of unemployment and high rates of economic growth on the other. Many people had hoped that stability of price levels could be maintained even with unemployment rates as low as 2 or 3 percent. Now they witnessed price increases while the unemployment rate was 4 percent or even higher.

With the advent of the 1960s, monetary policy found itself increasingly constrained by considerations related to our persistent balance-of-payments deficits. As a consequence, it was extremely cautious in pursuing expansionary policies to bring the economy out of the 1960 recession. The slack was picked up by fiscal policy, and by late 1965, for one brief instant, the economy had seemingly achieved both full employment and relative price stability. Then the bubble burst.

**SELECTED READINGS**

Ahearn, D. S., *Federal Reserve Policy Reappraised, 1951–1959*, New York, Columbia University Press, 1963.

Friedman, M., *Dollars and Deficits*, Englewood Cliffs, N.J., Prentice-Hall, 1968.

The later part of 1965 was, in many ways, a high-water mark for both the economy and economists. For the first time in nearly a decade, the actual performance of the economy was up to its potential. The unemployment rate had declined to its interim target of 4 percent, and the rate of inflation was only slightly over 2 percent per year, almost exactly in line with the behavior of prices during the preceding ten years. Much of the credit for achieving this state of affairs belonged to monetary and, especially, fiscal policy. Indeed, economists who had, seemingly heretically, urged a tax cut in the face of a budget deficit had been vindicated in all respects. The 1964 tax cut not only improved our economic performance but also, precisely because of this improvement, turned around the federal budget so that it showed a surplus in 1965.

Despite this auspicious beginning, the period beginning in late 1965 proved to be an extremely turbulent and problem-filled one. The difficulties began in the last quarter of 1965 with the rapid expansion of defense spending for the Vietnam War. Federal purchases of goods and services, which had shown little increase from 1962 to late 1965 (indeed, they had declined in real terms), spurted ahead. They rose steadily over the next three years, advancing in total by nearly 50 percent. This increase in aggregate demand, superimposed on an economy operating close to capacity, inevitably created inflationary pressures and ushered in a period of marked increases in the aggregate price level. From 1955 to 1965 the GNP implicit price deflator had advanced at about 2 percent per year. In contrast, from 1965 to 1979 this price index rose at about $5\frac{3}{4}$ percent per year. Its performance during the second half of this period, from 1973 to 1979, was an even more dismal $7\frac{3}{4}$ percent annual rate of inflation. Moreover, the rate of inflation was extremely high in 1974 and 1975, precisely the time when the United States was experiencing its severest recession of the post-World War II era. And if these domestic difficulties were not enough, the United States also encountered major problems with the international payments mechanism.

In short, the years 1965–1979 were marked by a substantial variety of serious economic difficulties. These, of course, make the period an extremely instructive one for studying the workings of monetary policy. While this hardly compensates for the fact that our economic performance left much to be desired, a careful examination of the period may at least teach us how to avoid the same mistakes again.

**MONETARY POLICIES, LATE 1965– OCTOBER 1966**

We have already described the upsurge of expenditures by the federal government after mid-1965. These were added to an economy that was already experiencing continuing increases of expenditures by state and local governments and of plant and equipment investment expenditures by private business. Taken together, these induced large increases in consumer spending. Despite these upsurges of spending, no significant federal tax increases were enacted before June 1968.

One effect of these large and rapid increases in expenditures for output was to reduce unemployment. Despite large additions to the labor force, the unemployment rate fell from 4.6 percent in June 1965 to 3.6 percent in November 1966. Another effect was price inflation. Price levels had been relatively stable during the seven years preceding mid-1965. For example, since 1958 the wholesale price index had risen less than 2.5 percent and the consumer price index had risen only about 9 percent. However, between June 1965 and October 1966 wholesale prices rose $3\frac{1}{2}$ percent and consumer prices went up 4 percent.

Thus, in the face of highly expansionary fiscal policies, it became the task of the Federal Reserve to try to contain the inflation by restricting supplies of money and credit while demands for credit were large and rising. The federal government had to borrow large amounts to finance its mounting deficits, and state and local governments were also large net borrowers. Business firms demanded large amounts of funds in both long-term and short-term markets to finance their rising expenditures for fixed equipment and inventory and also, in mid-1966, to meet accelerated tax payments to the government. In the years immediately preceding 1965, nonfinancial corporations received an average of $20 billion a year from outside sources; this rose to $32.7 billion in 1965 and $37.6 billion in 1966. The combination of a restrictive monetary policy and rising total demands for credit in 1966 raised interest rates to their highest levels in more than 40 years.

The first restrictive step was taken by the Federal Reserve in

December 1965, when it increased the discount rate from 4 to $4\frac{1}{2}$ percent. In retrospect, it appears that the increase should have been made earlier. However, President Johnson and many others criticized the increase, asserting that it was premature and would unduly inhibit the growth of employment and output. Perhaps partly because of such criticisms, the Federal Reserve followed a somewhat liberal open-market policy for several weeks. It allowed unborrowed reserves of member banks—that is, their total reserves less amounts borrowed from the Federal Reserve —to rise by $942 million from November 1965 to January 1966. During the same period the money supply expanded by $2.7 billion and total savings and time deposits at commercial banks were increased by $2.5 billion. However, in the spring of 1966 the Federal Reserve began to move toward a highly restrictive policy. By restricting its purchases of government securities, it prevented any significant rise in the supply of unborrowed reserves during the five months following April. The money supply did not increase at all between April and the end of the year, although transactions demands for money balances rose with the continued increase of GNP.

In the meantime banks—and especially large banks—were experiencing unexpected large increases in demands for business loans. Many bankers found to their consternation that while their outstanding loan commitments were far larger than they had thought, some of their most valued depositors unexpectedly demanded accommodation. To meet such demands banks scrambled for funds. They raised their borrowings from the Federal Reserve and attempted to attract more time deposits, but the Federal Reserve refused to raise ceiling rates even though rates on other short-term assets had become higher. As a result, few banks could attract additional time deposits and some suffered net withdrawals, especially of large-denomination CDs. This, for the first time, served notice on the banks that the strategy of liability management was not without its problems. To compensate for the runoff in CDs, the banks sold federal and state and local government securities at large losses; they paid 6 percent or more in the market for federal funds; and some of the most sophisticated banks paid 7 percent or more for Eurodollar loans. By September many banks were forced to use nonprice rationing to limit the increase of business loans, and interest rates were at their highest level in more than four decades. The entire structure of rates shifted upward, but short-term rates rose the most. For example, the rate on 3-month Treasury bills, which had averaged under 4 percent in 1965, rose to $4\frac{1}{2}$ percent in June 1966 and then again to nearly $5\frac{1}{2}$ percent in September 1966.

Disintermediation     As indicated in an earlier chapter, a large part of the public's saving, and especially of household saving, usually flows to financial intermedi-

aries in exchange for such claims as shares in savings and loan associations, deposits at mutual savings banks, and claims against life insurance
companies. This process was shocked severely by the sharp rise of interest rates on competing financial assets between March and September
1966. Hardest hit were the savings and loan associations, which were accustomed to large net inflows of funds. The average monthly increase of
their outstanding shares had been $881 million in 1964 and $698 million
in 1965. Net inflows were far smaller in 1966, and during four months
there were net outflows. At the end of October their total outstanding
shares were slightly below their level at the end of March. Faced with
the virtual cessation of net inflows, and fearing large withdrawals, savings and loan associations found it difficult to meet their outstanding
commitments to lend on mortgages and were unable to make many new
commitments. This was a sharp blow to the residential construction industry, which relies so heavily on these institutions for financing.

Mututal savings banks were also affected, but less severely. Nevertheless, in the first ten months of 1966 their average monthly net inflow
of deposits decreased by over 40 percent from the 1965 level.

Life insurance companies faced a somewhat different problem.
Flows of funds to them did not decrease. However, many of them had
contracted to lend to their policyholders on demand, and at 5 percent,
amounts up to the cash surrender values of their policies. As other interest rates rose, policyholders greatly increased their demand for such
loans. The result was a shrinkage in the net flow of funds available to life
insurance companies for purchasing other types of assets, primarily
mortgages and corporate bonds.

Thus, the three types of financial intermediaries that contribute
most heavily to the financing of the residential construction industry
were forced to restrict their mortgage lending. This restriction, together
with high interest rates, caused a sharp fall in residential construction.
Measured from their levels of a year earlier, new private-housing starts
had fallen 28 percent by July 1966; in October, the decline reached 40
percent. These declines brought loud protests from the building industry, Congress, and some others.

The Federal Reserve was much concerned by these developments.
It feared that nonbank financial intermediaries would be squeezed even
more and would, in at least some isolated cases, suffer large withdrawals.
It was also worried about the heavy impact of these developments on
construction. Thus, it was faced with the problem of determining how to
ameliorate the situation. One approach would have been to shift toward
a less restrictive general monetary policy in order to curb the rise of interest rates, or even to lower them. And this consideration was a factor in
the Board's refusal to approve increases in discount rates during July.
(Seven of the Reserve Banks proposed that their discount rates be raised

from 4½ to 5 or 5½ percent, but the Board disapproved all of these proposals.) But to relax general monetary policy would, of course, increase the danger of inflation. Therefore, the Federal Reserve sought selective measures that would enable it to slow the rate of increase of business loans by banks, reduce the flow of funds into time and savings deposits at commercial banks, and reduce the diversion of funds from nonbank financial intermediaries. It was especially concerned with large banks, whose business loans were expanding most rapidly and who were bidding most actively for funds.

**Selective Measures**     The Federal Reserve adopted several types of selective measures. One was to tighten ceilings on time-deposit rates. Board action in December 1965 had established ceiling rates of 4 percent on savings deposits and 5½ percent on all types of time deposits. As competing market rates rose sharply during the summer, there were widespread requests that the ceilings be raised to enable banks to retain deposits and perhaps attract more. This the Board refused to do. In fact, in July and again in September it actually rolled back ceilings on some types of time deposits. The maximum rate on large-denomination time deposits—those of $100,000 or more—remained at 5½ percent; ceilings on smaller denominations were reduced to 5 percent. These actions had two principal purposes. One was to reduce the diversion of funds from nonbank financial intermediaries. The other was to slow the expansion of business loans by limiting the ability of banks to attract funds. Total savings and time deposits grew very slowly between April and September.

Another action with selective effects was to increase reserve requirements on certain types of time deposits. For nearly four years prior to July 1966, reserve requirements on all classes of savings and time deposits had stood at 4 percent. However, in two actions—one in July and the other in September—the Board changed the regulations. Reserve requirements on savings deposits and on the first $5 million of time deposits at each bank were left unchanged at 4 percent, but those on bank time deposits in excess of $5 million were raised to 6 percent. Thus, the change was directed at the larger banks. Although these actions tended to have some generally tightening effects, their principal purpose was to inhibit the bidding for time deposits by large banks, and thus to lessen their expansion of business loans.

The Federal Reserve also resorted to moral suasion. By early summer, Federal Reserve officials were stating that business loans were expanding too rapidly, that this was inflationary, and that the investment boom might prove unsustainable in the sense that it would lead to a temporary glut of fixed capital and inventory, which would lead to a later decline. Discount officers admonished banks that sought to borrow too frequently or too much while expanding their business loans too rapidly.

The moral-suasion effect culminated in a letter dated September 1 that was sent to all member banks and to the press.[1] The letter made several points:

1 Some expansion of business loans is required, but the national interest would be better served by a lower rate of expansion.

2 Bank liquidation of municipal securities and other investment creates pressures on financial markets; "a greater share of bank adjustments should take the form of moderation in the rate of expansion of loans, and particularly business loans."

3 "Member banks will be expected to cooperate in the System's efforts to hold down the rate of business loan expansion—apart from normal seasonal needs—and to use the discount facilities of the Reserve Banks in a manner consistent with these efforts."

4 Banks cooperating by curtailing business loans rather than by disposing of securities will be eligible for a longer period of discount accommodation if needed.

It is difficult to assess the effects of this letter. The expansion of business loans did begin to slow down at about this time, but not necessarily as a result of the letter. One factor that may have contributed to the slowdown is that many banks had already begun to screen loan applications more closely. Also, demands for business loans were becoming less ebullient. However, it does seem likely that moral suasion by the Federal Reserve, including the September letter, played at least some small role in slowing the expansion of business loans.

The peak of the strains in the financial markets was reached in September. In October, the Federal Reserve decided to move no further toward restriction; in December, it began to move toward a more liberal policy.

---

**MONETARY POLICIES 1966–1971**

**Late 1966–November 1967**

This shift in monetary policy was primarily in response to a weakening of private investment spending, because government expenditures continued to rise without abatement. However, expenditures for residential construction had fallen significantly by the fourth quarter of 1966, business spending for inventory accumulation fell sharply in the first two quarters of 1967, and business expenditures for plant and equipment also declined slightly. To some extent the latter drop reflected the temporary suspension of the investment tax credit in September 1966. There was considerable debate at the time as to whether the so-called credit crunch of late 1966 was about to give rise to a recession. But ultimately all that resulted is what has been termed a mini-pause. In particular,

---

[1] For the text of the letter see *Annual Report of the Board of Governors for 1966*, Washington, D.C., 1967, pp. 103–104.

from the fourth quarter of 1966 to the second quarter of 1967, the annual rate of increase of real GNP slowed to 1.7 percent, a sharp drop from its 6 percent pace of the previous two years.

The Federal Reserve responded to this situation with a number of liberalizing actions. In late December, it quietly withdrew its letter of September 1. In March, it lowered reserve requirements against savings deposits and against the first $5 million of time deposits at each bank from 4 to 3 percent. The effect was, of course, to decrease overall reserve requirements, but also to have most of the initial benefits accrue to the smaller member banks. In April, all the Reserve banks lowered their discount rates from $4\frac{1}{2}$ to 4 percent. The FOMC bought large amounts of government securities. These actions enabled member banks to increase their unborrowed reserves by nearly $2 billion in the year following October 1966; member bank borrowings from the Federal Reserve fell from more than $700 million to less than $100 million, and the money supply rose by about $10 billion, or 6 percent.

Market yields on short-term and long-term debts moved in disparate ways. Short-term yields fell during the first half of 1967 and then rose during the second half—although they did not reach their peaks of 1966. For example, yields on 90-day Treasury bills fell from 5.39 percent in October 1966 to 3.49 percent in July 1967 and then rose to 5.01 percent in December. The decline of market rates on competing short-term assets while ceiling rates remained unchanged permitted a large increase in time deposits at commercial banks, which amounted to more than $13 billion, or 15 percent, during the year following October 1966. These developments also brought large inflows of funds to other financial intermediaries, and especially to savings and loans associations, which helped revive residential construction. On the other hand, yields on long-term debt declined only briefly and then rose to record levels. For example, yields on corporate bonds rated AAA by Moody's declined from 5.44 percent in September 1966 to 5.03 percent in February, and then rose almost continuously to 6.19 percent in December. This disparate behavior of short- and long-term yields resulted from a combination of factors—expectations of continuing inflation and rising rates in the future, fear of unavailability of credit in the future, and the squeeze on liquidity in 1966. Both financial institutions and other business firms had reduced their liquidity markedly by late 1966. Financial institutions preferred short-term liquid assets to rebuild their liquidity, and other business firms issued huge amounts of long-term debt to make sure that they could command funds and to reduce their reliance on bank loans.

In retrospect, it is clear that Federal Reserve policies during this period were excessively expansionary. By October 1967 these policies had become subject to criticism, not only by outsiders but also by a minority within the FOMC. Critics pointed to the continuing rise of government expenditures while Congress still refused to raise taxes, to the renewed increase of private investment spending, to the higher rate of increase of total spending for output, to the continuing domestic price inflation, and to the worsening of the nation's balance of payments. Such considerations alone would probably have led to the adoption of less expansionary monetary policies before the end of 1967 even in the absence of financial disturbances abroad. In fact, however, action was precipitated by events surrounding the devaluation of the British pound on November 18 from a parity of $2.80 to $2.40. This was followed by large capital outflows from the United States.

**November 1967–**
**June 1968**
From November 1967 through June 1968, when Congress finally voted to raise taxes and to decrease federal expenditures, Federal Reserve policies were less expansionary than they had been in the preceding period, but they were still not very restrictive. They probably would have been more restrictive if Federal Reserve officials had not feared that such actions would jeopardize enactment of the tax and expenditure legislation then being considered by Congress. However, a number of restrictive actions were taken. Discount rates were raised from 4 to $4\frac{1}{2}$ percent in November 1967 to 5 percent in March and to $5\frac{1}{2}$ percent in April. Reserve requirements on demand deposits in excess of $5 million at each bank were raised by $\frac{1}{2}$ percent for all classes of member banks. The Federal Reserve did continue to purchase government securities, but at a slower rate.

Both short- and long-term interest rates rose significantly. For example, between October 1967 and June 1968 the yield on 3-month Treasury bills rose from 4.55 to 5.54 percent and that on Aaa corporate bonds rose from 5.82 to 6.28 percent. Judged on the basis of the behavior of monetary aggregates, monetary policies in this period appear less restrictive. The money supply rose at an annual rate of 7.2 percent and time deposits at commercial banks increased at an annual rate of 8.1 percent. In addition to these increases, total expenditure for output rose at an annual rate of 9.7 percent, and the consumer price index increased at an annual rate of 4.5 percent. By this time an increasing number of people were complaining that Federal Reserve policies were being guided too much by the behavior of interest rates and not enough by the behavior of the money supply.

**June–**
**November 1968**
In late June of 1968, a full three years after federal expenditures began their rapid rise, Congress finally passed the Revenue and Expenditure Control Act, which provided for a 10 percent surtax on personal and corporate income taxes and a reduction of $6 billion in federal expenditures. This action was widely expected to be highly effective in restricting the rise of aggregate demands for output, in curbing price

inflation, in lowering interest rates by reducing government borrowing, by lessening inflationary expectations, and by making feasible a less restrictive monetary policy. In fact, some feared an overkill if the restrictive fiscal actions were not accompanied by some relaxation of monetary policies. Federal Reserve officials shared these views. At a meeting on June 18, the FOMC instructed the manager of the open-market account, "that if the proposed fiscal legislation is enacted, operations shall accommodate tendencies for short-term interest rates to decline in connection with such affirmative congressional action on the pending fiscal legislation so long as bank credit expansion does not exceed current projections."[2] Such a policy of accommodation was followed from the end of June through November 1968.

By December, it had become only too clear that the fiscal actions initiated in June were less effective than had been expected. Total expenditures for output were still rising rapidly, and in December 1968 the unemployment rate dipped to 3.3 percent, a fifteen-year low. Furthermore, price inflation continued, and the balance of payments was deteriorating. It was under these conditions that the Federal Reserve shifted to a more restrictive policy in mid-December.

**December 1968–February 1970**

The restrictive policy initiated in mid-December 1968 became more stringent during 1969 and was not terminated until February 1970. Monetary and fiscal policies attempted to slow down the rate of increase of money demands for output, in the hope that the restricted rise of demands, together with the growing productive capacity of the economy, would gradually slow down the rate of price inflation with a minimum of depressing effects on employment and real economic growth. These hopes proved to be overly optimistic.

Monetary policies were highly restrictive. As we shall see later, the money supply was allowed to rise only slightly despite continuing increases in demands for money balances for transactions purposes. And monetary restrictions, together with rising demands for credit, raised market rates of interest, both short-term and long-term, to their highest levels in more than a century. For example, Table 21–1, showing monthly averages of yields, indicates that the peak levels reached during this period were 7.87 percent for 3-month Treasury bills, 8.84 percent for prime commercial paper, 9.19 percent for federal funds, 8.5 percent on bank loans to prime customers, 6.86 percent on long-term government bonds, and 7.91 percent on the highest-grade corporate bonds. In view of both the large rise of interest rates and the high levels reached, it is not surprising that financial markets were at times turbulent, that large

---

[2] *Annual Report of the Board of Governors of the Federal Reserve System*, Washington, D.C., 1968, p. 166.

amounts of funds were diverted away from financial intermediaries and into higher-yielding open-market assets, and that large amounts of funds flowed to the United States from foreign financial centers.

The Federal Reserve used all its major instruments for restrictive purposes. Discount rates were increased from $5\frac{1}{4}$ to $5\frac{3}{4}$ percent in December 1968 and to 6 percent in April. Another action in April raised reserve requirements against demand deposits at all member banks by $\frac{1}{2}$ percent, thus increasing required reserves by about $650 million. Federal Reserve open-market policy was such as to prevent any significant increase in the unborrowed reserves of member banks. During most of 1969, these reserves were at or below the levels prevailing in late 1968, and even in February 1970 they were only 1.5 percent above their level of a year earlier. The banks were faced with a difficult dilemma: While the Federal Reserve refused to provide additional reserves through open-market purchases, consumer demands for bank loans were high and rising rapidly. Banks, therefore, were anxious to obtain funds from whatever source they could find. Their borrowings from the Federal Reserve reached $1.4 billion in May 1969 and averaged more than $1.1 billion through the rest of the year. Banks would have liked to borrow much more from the Reserve banks at the prevailing discount rate of 6 percent, but they knew the Federal Reserve would disapprove, and some considered it prudent to conserve some borrowing power for use in an emergency. Many banks would have liked to have attracted more funds by raising their rates on savings and time deposits, but the Federal

| | | Prime | | Prime | | |
|---|---|---|---|---|---|---|
| | 3-month | 4–6-month | Federal | rate | U.S. | Aaa |
| | Treasury | commercial | funds | charged | Treasury | corporate |
| Period | bills | paper | rate | by banks | bonds | bonds |
| November 1968 | 5.45 | 5.81 | 5.81 | 6.25 | 5.36 | 6.19 |
| December | 5.94 | 6.17 | 6.02 | 6.50–6.75 | 5.65 | 6.45 |
| January 1969 | 6.13 | 6.53 | 6.30 | 7.00 | 5.74 | 6.59 |
| February | 6.12 | 6.62 | 6.64 | 7.00 | 5.86 | 6.66 |
| March | 6.01 | 6.82 | 6.79 | 7.50 | 6.05 | 6.85 |
| April | 6.11 | 7.04 | 7.41 | 7.50 | 5.84 | 6.89 |
| May | 6.03 | 7.35 | 8.67 | 7.50 | 5.85 | 6.79 |
| June | 6.43 | 8.23 | 8.90 | 8.50 | 6.06 | 6.98 |
| July | 6.98 | 8.65 | 8.61 | 8.50 | 6.07 | 7.08 |
| August | 6.97 | 8.33 | 9.19 | 8.50 | 6.02 | 6.97 |
| September | 7.08 | 8.48 | 9.15 | 8.50 | 6.32 | 7.14 |
| October | 6.99 | 8.56 | 9.00 | 8.50 | 6.27 | 7.33 |
| November | 7.24 | 8.46 | 8.85 | 8.50 | 6.51 | 7.35 |
| December | 7.81 | 8.84 | 8.97 | 8.50 | 6.81 | 7.72 |
| January 1970 | 7.87 | 8.78 | 8.98 | 8.50 | 6.86 | 7.91 |
| February | 7.13 | 8.55 | 8.98 | 8.50 | 6.44 | 7.93 |

**TABLE 21–1**

*Market rates of interest, November 1968–February 1970 (yields in percentages per annum)*

Source: *Federal Reserve Bulletin,* various issues.

Reserve refused to raise the ceilings. As yields on competing assets rose, banks in general not only were unable to attract more funds but also suffered net outflows. Withdrawals from large-denomination negotiable CDs were especially large, and the trend of total time and savings deposits at commercial banks was descending through 1969. By December these deposits were 5 percent below their level of a year earlier.

Banks competed with each other in many ways for the existing supply of reserves.

1　They borrowed federal funds. Increased demands for these funds, together with decreases in the supply of excess reserves, pushed the federal funds rate to very high levels. During the last half of 1969 this rate averaged about 9 percent, or 3 percentage points above the Federal Reserve discount rate.

2　They sold some of their holdings of securities, especially obligations of the federal government and of state and local governments, thereby accentuating the rise of yields on these securities.

3　They sold some of their loans and participations in their loans. Some of these sales were outright and some were under repurchase agreement.

4　Their subsidiaries and affiliates issued commercial paper and made the proceeds available to the banks.

5　They borrowed huge amounts of Eurodollars, mostly through their foreign branches. Liabilities of American banks to their foreign branches rose from $8.5 billion in January 1969 to a peak of more than $15 billion in November, and averaged above $14.5 billion during the rest of the year. On many of these borrowings banks paid interest rates in excess of 10 percent.

Despite their competitive scramble for funds, banks were forced to curtail expansion of their loans to customers, including business firms. They did this to some extent by increasing interest rates. For example, the prime rate was increased in three steps to 8.5 percent. However, banks also used various types of nonprice rationing. Firms that could not meet all their needs through bank borrowing turned to other sources – to issues of commercial paper, to expensive long-term financing, to sales of liquid assets, to increases in their accounts payable, and so on. Well before the end of the year, many firms were in a highly illiquid condition.

As in 1966, the sharp rise of market yields was accompanied by financial disintermediation. This was evidenced primarily in a decreased net flow of funds to financial intermediaries, although some institutions suffered net withdrawals. The shrinkage of net inflows was especially severe during the second half of 1969. These developments tended to reduce sharply the supply of mortgage funds, thereby depressing residential construction. The Federal National Mortgage Association and the Federal Home Loan Bank Board supplied some assistance by issuing and selling in the market large amounts of claims against themselves and channeling the proceeds to the principal mortgage lenders. However, these actions were not sufficient to prevent a net reduction in total funds supplied to mortgage markets.

Thus, no matter what criteria one may use, monetary policies in 1969 were highly restrictive. We have already mentioned the rise of interest rates to their highest levels in more than a century, the tight rein kept on the unborrowed reserves of member banks, and the shrinkage of total time and savings deposits at commercial banks. The money supply rose 3.5 percent during 1969, but the annual rate of increase during the second half of the year was only $1\frac{1}{2}$ percent.

In describing this period in his *Newsweek* column in August 1969, Milton Friedman noted:

> *The Federal Reserve System has done it again. Once more it is overreacting as it has so often done in the past . . . Some retardation in growth and some increase in unemployment is an inevitable, if welcome, by-product of stopping inflation. But there is no need for — and every reason to avoid — a retardation of the severity that will be produced by a continuation of the Fed's present monetary overkill.*[3]

We noted earlier that it was hoped that these monetary policies together with fiscal policies would gradually reduce price inflation with a minimum of depressing effects on employment and real economic growth. By the early months of 1970, it was becoming increasingly clear that the plan was not working. On the one hand, price inflation continued unabated. Increases for 1969 as a whole were 6 percent for the consumer price index, 4.8 percent for the wholesale price index, and 5.0 percent for the GNP price deflator. The rate of increase did not fall as the year progressed. On the other hand, real economic growth and employment were affected adversely. Over the first three quarters of the year, real GNP grew at only a 2 percent annual rate; and in the fourth quarter real GNP declined for the first time since the end of 1960. The recession of 1969–1970 had begun. The unemployment rate, which had averaged about 3.3 percent in the first months of 1969, climbed to over 4 percent in early 1970; by year-end it had jumped to over 6 percent.

**February 1970–August 1971**     Federal Reserve officials were in a quandary as they reviewed their policies at the beginning of 1970. They knew that industrial production had been falling for five months, that growth of real GNP had halted, and

---

[3] Cited in R. Dornbusch and S. Fischer, *Macroeconomics*, New York, McGraw-Hill, 1978, p. 522.

that unemployment was rising; they had good reason to believe that the situation would deteriorate further in the absence of positively expansionary actions. But they also knew that there were no signs of a decrease in the rate of price inflation, that inflationary expectations were strong and widespread, that the balance of payments was already in bad condition, and that a more expansionary monetary policy could well lead to large outflows of funds. This mixed situation explains why there were different judgments in the Federal Reserve during the first weeks of 1970, with some officials favoring a continuation of restrictive policies and other advocating relaxation. It also explains why the Federal Reserve moved cautiously for several weeks after it decided, in mid-February, to adopt more expansionary policies.

Not only monetary policies but also federal fiscal policies became more stimulative in 1970. The 10 percent surcharge on income taxes was terminated in two stages; the first of several tax reductions contained in the Tax Reform Act of 1969 became effective; and federal expenditures increased sharply, mainly through larger grants-in-aid to local governments and through transfer payments to individuals. As it moved toward more liberal policies, the Federal Reserve emphasized monetary aggregates—such as the money supply and the volume of bank credit—more than it had in earlier years. However, it continued to devote attention to the behavior of interest rates.

As usual, the Federal Reserve relied primarily on open-market operations to effectuate its policies. It purchased only cautiously at first, but more aggressively after mid-1970. In December, the unborrowed reserves of member banks were 8.5 percent above their level in June and 8 percent above their level in February. Further increases came in early 1971. The downward trend of member bank borrowings from the Federal Reserve was temporarily interrupted during the late spring and early summer of 1970 by disturbances in the commercial paper market associated with the financial distress of the Penn Central Transportation Company. The failure of this firm to meet its maturing commercial paper obligations, and rumors that other important firms might follow suit, led to a sharp reduction of supplies of funds to the commercial paper market and to fears that many businesses would be unable to roll over their commercial paper. The Federal Reserve took two actions to deal with this situation. First, it invited banks to borrow from their Reserve banks the amounts that would be needed to lend to firms that could not roll over their maturing commercial paper. Second, it suspended interest ceilings on large-denomination CDs with maturities of 30 to 89 days, thereby enabling banks to bid freely for these funds. These actions were sufficient to prevent a financial crisis.

Although the Federal Reserve relied primarily on open-market purchases for carrying out its easing of monetary policy, it also reduced both discount rates and reserve requirements against time deposits. In addition, it raised ceiling rates on time and savings deposits by amounts ranging from $\frac{1}{2}$ to $\frac{1}{4}$ percent. Similar actions were taken by the FDIC for nonmember banks and by the Federal Home Loan Bank Board for savings and loan associations. The principal purposes of these actions were to bring ceilings rates more in line with yields on competing assets and to encourage flows of funds to financial intermediaries. The rise of ceilings and the subsequent decline of market yields on competing short-term assets led to a rapid reintermediation. From their February level, total time and savings deposits rose over 30 percent by June 1971. The increase in the money supply over the same period was more than 10 percent. Furthermore, over the 18 months ending in June 1971, outstanding shares at savings and loan associations rose over 20 percent and deposits at mutual savings banks advanced by more than 15 percent. These large inflows played a major role in raising supplies of mortgage funds and in stimulating residential construction.

Both short- and long-term interest rates declined sharply in early 1970 as soon as it became evident that the Federal Reserve planned to relax its restrictive policies. However, after this initial reaction short- and long-term rates behaved in different ways. Short-term rates declined almost continuously until the spring of 1971. In contrast, long-term rates rose sharply for several months and by mid-1970 were even higher than they had been in 1969. There appear to have been two major reasons for this behavior. One was the continuance of strong inflationary expectations, which made some people reluctant to purchase long-term bonds. The other was a huge increase in new bond issues, which rose from $44 billion in 1969 to more than $78 billion in 1970. More than half of the increase was accounted for by government issues, but corporate bond issues rose from $18.3 billion to $30.3 billion. The latter mainly reflected the efforts of business firms to rebuild their liquidity positions, which had deteriorated markedly during the period of monetary restriction.

After reaching their peak in mid-1970, long-term interest rates declined sharply and almost continuously until the spring of 1971.

---

**THE ECONOMY AS OF MID-1971**

**Domestic Aspects**

We have just seen that, following the highly restrictive policies of 1969 and the onset of the 1969–1970 recession, both monetary and fiscal policies became more stimulative in early 1970. The federal government increased its expenditures and lowered taxes, and the Federal Reserve adopted a quite expansionary policy. By July 1971 the money supply had risen 10 percent above its level in February 1970 and time deposits at commercial banks had grown over 30 percent. Both long- and short-term interest rates had fallen sharply.

These policies were accompanied by some increase in real output.

For example, GNP in real terms rose about $2\frac{1}{2}$ percent between the second quarter of 1970 and the second quarter of 1971. However, the growth rate was too small to reduce unemployment. During the summer of 1971, the unemployment rate hovered around 6 percent, about the same level that had prevailed during the preceding eight months and significantly above the levels of early 1970. At the same time, price increases continued at a rate above 5 percent with little sign of abatement and, in fact, with some evidence of acceleration. The question naturally arises as to why the relatively high level of unemployment after mid-1970 failed to slow the rate of inflation. To answer this we must look more closely at the nature of the inflation.

We have emphasized that in the early period of the Vietnam buildup — that is, prior to the third quarter of 1968 — the economy was experiencing a demand pull inflation. The same might be said, although with less certainty, of the first months of 1969. However, by the early months of 1970 the situation had clearly changed. At least partly because of more restrictive federal fiscal policies and very stringent monetary policies in 1969, the rate of increase in aggregate demands for output had slowed down. Moreover, underutilization of labor and plant capacity was becoming more evident. Excess capacity was appearing in industry after industry, and the unemployment rate was rising. The latter rose to 5 percent by mid-1970, rose further to more than 6 percent at the end of the year, and averaged about 6 percent during the first half of 1971. Price inflation continued unabated despite these developments.

By mid-1971 the inflationary process had become in large part a cost push and markup inflation. Hourly wage rates, including fringe benefits, rose much more rapidly than output per unit of labor, thereby increasing labor costs per unit of output. To compensate for these increased costs, most employers tried to increase their prices. Unit labor costs rose more than 4 percent in 1968 and more than 6 percent in both 1969 and 1970. They continued upward in 1971. In view of the strong inflationary expectations that had developed, it is easy to see why demanded increases in money wages were so large. Workers demanded wage increases large enough to offset not only past increases in the cost of living but also expected future increases.

This situation of continued price inflation in the face of excessive unemployment and underutilization of other productive resources presented a dilemma for conventional monetary and fiscal policies. More restrictive policies to combat price inflation would almost certainly lead to increased unemployment, but more expansive policies to promote real economic growth and employment would probably stimulate price inflation and create still stronger inflationary expectations. Because of this dilemma, proposals for some sort of direct wage and price controls or for a wage–price review board received increasing public support. It was thought that direct limitations on wages and prices might combat inflationary expectations, might eliminate or at least lessen cost push pressures, and might allow a larger part of any increase in aggregate demand to be reflected in increases in real output and employment.

**International Aspects**

At the same time that policy makers were faced with a dilemma in the domestic economy with regard to inflation and unemployment, there were also significant difficulties related to international payments. By 1970 these factors had produced a marked deterioration in the nation's balance of payments. In 1970 the deficit in the balance of payments, measured on an official reserve-transactions basis, was $10 billion, far larger than it had been in any preceding year. This deterioration resulted in part from a shrinkage of the balance on the goods and services account, but much more from huge outflows of short-term funds on the private account. The latter was initially in response to widening differentials in interest rates as rates in the United States fell much faster than those in foreign financial centers.

Both the outflow of private funds and the deficit in the balance of payments of the United States were huge during the first half of 1971. For example, as measured on an official reserve-transactions basis, the deficit for the first half of 1971 was $11 billion, and it continued to rise thereafter. In early August, a report by a congressional subcommittee asserted that the dollar had become overvalued and that the situation could be corrected through a general realignment of exchange rates. On the same day, the Treasury reported a $1 billion loss of gold and other international reserves. Outflows of funds accelerated sharply, and over the following week $3.7 billion flowed into foreign central banks. Such were some of the principal developments preceding the President's announcement of August 15.

**Actions of August 15, 1971**

On Sunday evening, August 15, 1971, President Nixon appeared on nationwide television to announce what he described as "the most comprehensive new economic policy to be undertaken by this country in four decades." Although the accuracy of this description is debatable, there can be no doubt that the announced changes were dramatic and sweeping, that at least some of them had not only short-run but also important long-run implications, and that they represented sharp departures from the policies previously followed by Nixon's administration. Up to that time, he had staunchly defended his "game plan" for dealing with domestic inflation and unemployment, and had flatly rejected all proposals for any kind of wage–price guidelines or wage–price review board. Now he imposed a 90-day freeze on wages, prices, and rents; stated that the freeze would be followed for a temporary but indefinite period by a program providing more flexible direct controls; and proposed further tax reductions to combat unemployment. His reversal on international monetary policies was no less dramatic. Prior to this announcement he had affirmed and reaffirmed his determination to maintain the existing exchange rate on the dollar. Now he terminated convertibility of the dollar into gold and other reserve assets, declared his determination that exchange rates on other currencies should rise in terms of the dollar, and imposed a 10 percent surcharge on all dutiable imports. It was hoped that such actions would serve to equilibrate the balance of payments and give monetary and fiscal authorities greater freedom to concentrate on their domestic objectives.

The general public reaction was highly favorable, perhaps not as a result of the specific nature of the actions but as a result of a feeling of relief that "at last something is being done about the economic mess." A complex mess it certainly was: unabating price inflation in the face of excessive unemployment and underutilization of plant capacities, and a deficit in the nation's balance of payments that was not only continuing but growing to mammoth proportions. Some type of comprehensive program was clearly indicated; piecemeal actions would not suffice.

**COMPONENTS OF THE NEW ECONOMIC POLICY**

**Direct Controls of Wages, Prices, and Rents**

As already indicated, the freeze order had several related purposes: to arrest the wage–price spiral, to weaken inflationary expectations, to enable a large part of any rise of demands for output to be reflected in increases of real output and employment, and to make more expansionary monetary and fiscal policies feasible. It was obvious that the freeze itself could be no more than a temporary stopgap, and that over a long period it would become unacceptable and ineffective. One reason was that the freeze included many inequitable and disequilibrium price and wage relationships. For example, some employers had raised wages but had not yet raised their prices; others were in the reverse position. Some recently negotiated wage increases had become effective and were therefore allowable; others had been negotiated but not yet effective and were therefore not allowable; and so on. Such maladjustments might be tolerated for 90 days, but probably not much longer. A second reason that the freeze had to be only temporary was that it relied almost solely on voluntary compliance for enforcement.

When the 90-day freeze terminated in mid-November, it was followed by Phase II—a flexible program to limit, but not prevent, increases of wages and prices. Administration of the program was entrusted to three bodies appointed by the President: (1) the Cost of Living Council, a body within the executive branch; (2) a Pay Board—a tripartite board composed of five public members, five members from labor, and five from business; and (3) a Price Commission composed of seven public members. The Pay Board and Price Commission were given a high degree of autonomy, while the Cost of Living Council intervened only infrequently.

The control authorities faced difficult problems in formulating standards for allowable wage and price increases. The standards announced were that, on the average, wages should rise no more than 5.5 percent and prices no more than 2.5 percent a year. It was believed that these wage and price standards would be mutually consistent if average productivity per unit of labor rose at an annual rate of 3 percent. However, the announcement of such average goals did not really solve the problem of standards, because it left unanswered such questions as: Which wages and prices should be allowed to rise more than the average, and how much more? Which should rise less than the average, and how much less? Under what conditions, and to what extent, should an employer experiencing an increase of wage rates be permitted to raise the prices of products? As might be expected, such questions proved to be highly controversial, and there were many well-publicized disputes in the administration of Phase II.

Despite these difficulties, there is some evidence that the control system was at least partially and temporarily effective in preventing costs and prices from rising as fast as they would have otherwise. Overall, during the period of the initial freeze and Phase II, which lasted until January 1973, the consumer price index rose at an annual rate of 3.3 percent.

At the same time, there were several reasons to believe that this system would become less effective with the passage of time, and especially as employment and output approached their full-employment levels. For example:

1    Excess unemployment and excess plant capacity persisted until the end of 1972. The partial success of the wage–price control system under these conditions provided no basis for expecting similar success as aggregate demands for output rose fast enough to pull employment and output toward their full-employment levels.

2    A large number of products were exempted from price controls, and the system relied heavily on voluntary compliance due to the scarcity of enforcement facilities. These conditions virtually assured that price rises would become increasingly numerous, that those whose prices were more tightly controlled would become increasingly restive, that increases in the cost of living would militate against holding the line on wage increases, and that maladjustments of relative prices and wages would become more widespread.

In response to these kinds of considerations, the administration "decided to modify the price and wage controls program to make it more consistent with the further reduction in excess capacity seen at the time and also move toward the Administration's goal of eventually ending the controls."[4] The new program, known as Phase III, generally reduced controls from those prevailing Phase II and, furthermore, relied on self-administration rather than enforcement. At the time it was widely perceived that the controls were ending. While the move to Phase III undoubtedly reduced the administrative burden of the controls, many economists worried that the controls were being weakened when excess capacity was declining, precisely when they might be needed most. As we shall see shortly, these fears had considerable justification.

International Aspects of the New Economic Plan

Termination of convertibility of the dollar into gold and other reserve assets was a severe shock to the international monetary system. The most immediate impact of the New Economic Plan was on the stability of exchange rates, because the dollar was now free to float. American authorities would no longer sell reserve assets or purchase dollars to limit declines of exchange rates on the dollar, nor would they buy reserve assets or sell dollars to depress the dollar in terms of other currencies. The behavior of exchange rates was to be determined by other participants in the market, including both private transactors and official foreign institutions. However, both the President and the Secretary of the Treasury made clear their determination that exchange rates on other currencies should rise markedly in terms of the dollar. For many weeks they made no specific recommendations, but it was rumored that they would insist on an average appreciation of other currencies in the range of 12 to 15 percent.

The reaction of most foreign officials to changes of such magnitude was shock and disapproval. They contended that such large increases of exchange rates on their currencies would seriously damage both their export industries and their import-competing industries, and might precipitate an economic recession. Nevertheless, most countries allowed their currencies to float, and gradually the exchange rates on their currencies rose.

ECONOMIC DEVELOPMENTS, MID-1971–EARLY 1975

After the introduction of the new "game plan" and more stimulative monetary and fiscal policies, the pace of economic activity quickened. From the third quarter of 1971 to the end of 1972, real GNP grew at an annual rate of $6\frac{1}{2}$ percent. The unemployment rate, which was about 6 percent at mid-1971, stayed at roughly this level for the remainder of

---

[4] *Economic Report of the President*, Washington, D.C., Government Printing Office, February 1974, p. 89.

1971. Then, however, it gradually declined throughout 1972, reaching about 5 percent at year-end. As noted earlier, during this period, which includes the initial freeze and Phase II, the consumer price index rose at an annual rate of 3.3 percent.

The economic record from the beginning of 1973 to mid-1975 is shown in Table 21–2. While starting in 1973 economic policy became more restrictive, economic growth actually accelerated in the first quarter of 1973, with real GNP rising at a 9 percent annual rate. However, policy began to have an effect in the second quarter, and over the last three quarters of the year real GNP grew at less than a 1½ percent annual rate. The unemployment rate, which stood at 5 percent at the beginning of 1973, declined to a low of 4.6 percent in October but by year-end was back to 4.9 percent.

The slowdown in the economy was brought about by fiscal and monetary policy in the hope of moderating inflationary pressures. As such, the actual behavior of prices was an extreme disappointment to policy makers. After rising at 3.3 percent rate during the freeze and Phase II, the consumer price index advanced at an 8.3 percent rate from January to June 1973. The wholesale price index, reflecting a huge 50 percent rate of increase of farm and food prices, advanced at a 24 percent rate over the same period. Spurred by public pressure to "do something," Phase III was abandoned and a second freeze was introduced in June 1973. After 60 days this was replaced by a Phase IV that in several ways was stricter than Phase II. Nevertheless, the rate of inflation did not abate. From June to December 1973 the consumer price index advanced at a 9.6 percent rate. And in the fourth quarter the implicit GNP deflator increased at a 10 percent rate, the largest increase of any quarter during the year. Inflation, if anything, was accelerating, and the economy had yet to feel the full impact of the dramatic fourfold increase in oil prices at the end of 1973.

Quite evidently then, the year 1974 began with the economy in considerable difficulty. And in fact, during 1974 things got distinctly worse. The slowdown in economic growth that had taken place in the last three quarters of 1973 turned into a full-fledged recession in the first quarter of 1974. Real GNP declined for five consecutive quarters and by the first quarter of 1975 stood 6 percent below its peak level in the fourth quarter

| TABLE 21–2 | | 1973 | | | | 1974 | | | | 1975 | |
|---|---|---|---|---|---|---|---|---|---|---|---|
| *Some key economic indicators, quarterly, 1973–1975 (in percentages)* | | I | II | III | IV | I | II | III | IV | I | II |
| | Unemployment rate | 5.0 | 4.9 | 4.8 | 4.8 | 5.0 | 5.1 | 5.6 | 6.7 | 8.2 | 8.9 |
| | Growth rate of real GNP | 9.5 | 0.4 | 1.7 | 2.0 | −3.9 | −1.8 | −2.4 | −5.5 | −9.1 | 6.4 |
| | Inflation rate of GNP deflator | 5.5 | 7.7 | 6.8 | 10.0 | 13.0 | 12.2 | 11.4 | 10.9 | 6.3 | 5.7 |

of 1973. Particularly hard hit was housing, which over the same period declined 40 percent in real terms.

The unemployment rate, which had turned up in late 1973, increased only slowly at first, hitting 5½ percent in July 1974. Thereafter it steadily and dramatically rose, reaching a peak of about 9 percent in May 1975.

Despite the dramatic slowdown in the economy that produced the severest recession of the postwar period, the rate of inflation continued to be high throughout 1974. The consumer price index rose about 12 percent during 1974, the largest increase since 1947. Again, this was a case of cost push inflation. Wage rates accelerated in the face of rising unemployment as workers attempted to catch up with price increases. At the same time, output per unit of labor was falling, so that unit labor costs rose rapidly. In the face of these developments, the controls program embodied in Phase IV was abandoned in April 1974 when its authorization expired. The administration did not try to extend this authorization, nor was there substantial support in Congress for an extension. Despite the good intentions of the controls, it was perceived by many that they had failed to accomplish their objectives. Reasons for this are likely to be debated for many years to come.

**MONETARY AND FISCAL POLICIES, MID-1971– LATE 1973**

As noted earlier, one of the purposes of both the system of wage and price controls and the termination of the convertibility of the dollar was to achieve greater freedom to expand aggregate demand in order to reduce the unemployment and underutilization of capacity that still prevailed in August 1971. Both fiscal and monetary policies were used for this purpose.

**Fiscal Policies**

Expansionary fiscal actions included both tax reductions and expenditure increases by the federal government. Tax reductions were of several types: provision of more liberal depreciation rules for business, a 7 percent tax credit for business purchases of equipment, repeal of the 7 percent excise tax on automobiles, an increase of personal exemptions under the federal income tax from $650 to $675 for 1971 and $750 for 1972, and an increase of the minimum standard deduction on income from $1,000 to $1,300. Federal expenditures began to rise in late 1971 and were accelerated in the first half of 1972 to provide more stimulus to the economy. After a dip in the third quarter, another burst of expenditures took place in the fourth quarter of 1972, primarily reflecting an $8 billion increase in social security benefits and an $11 billion jump in federal grants-in-aid to state and local governments. For 1972 as a whole, federal expenditures rose about $25 billion, or 11 percent.

At the beginning of 1973, fearing a rekindling of inflationary pressures, fiscal policy makers moved toward restraint. Over the next three quarters federal expenditures rose less than 2 percent and tax revenues rose substantially. Part of this was due to the normal growth of revenues as incomes grew, but the increase in tax receipts also reflected a $10 billion boost in social security taxes at the beginning of the year.

In 1974 fiscal policy continued the restrictive stance begun in 1973. Federal expenditures did increase by about 13 percent in nominal terms, but tax revenues were unusually strong for a recession year. There is a tendency, of course, for fiscal policy to cushion a decline in real incomes automatically as tax revenues fall because of lower incomes. In 1974, however, this effect was offset by the rapid inflation that kept nominal incomes growing, so that tax receipts rose substantially. This effect was compounded by the fact that personal exemptions, standard deductions, and tax brackets are fixed in nominal terms. Hence, rapid inflation induced a rise in average tax rates. In effect, fiscal policy tightened because inflation brought about an unlegislated increase in taxation.

At the same time that fiscal policy was tightening because of the automatic responsiveness of the tax system, consideration was being given to discretionary fiscal restrictions. In early October of 1974 President Ford proposed placing a ceiling on federal spending and enacting a 5 percent temporary income tax surcharge on corporations and upper-income families. Thus, the President was advocating a more restrictive stance for fiscal policy just as the recession was assuming epidemic proportions. It was not until early January of 1975 that the President had a change of heart and conceded that it was appropriate to "shift our emphasis from inflation to recession." The result of this was the Tax Reduction Act of 1975, which was signed into law in March. The primary components of the Act were a one-time rebate of 1974 taxes of about $8 billion and a temporary one-year reduction of personal income taxes of about $12 billion. Many economists were disappointed by both the size and the temporary nature of these actions. They regarded them as too little, too late.

Taken as a whole, the fiscal policy record from 1971 to 1975 left much to be desired. As summed up by one perceptive analyst of fiscal matters, Alan Blinder:[5]

> It would be hard to imagine a period of time that provided more ammunition for the opponents of discretionary fiscal policy than did the years 1972 to 1975, when, it seems, fiscal policy did almost everything wrong. With the advantages of hindsight, at least, it is clear that the government pumped up aggregate demand to an unhealthy degree before the 1972 election. Not only did this

[5] A. Blinder, *Economic Policy and the Great Stagflation*, New York, Academic Press, 1979, p. 141.

*undermine the controls program, . . . but also added to the stockpile of suppressed inflation that was awaiting us when controls were lifted. While a shift in policy was clearly imperative in 1973, the turn toward restriction was much too abrupt. . . . Only as the recession hit bottom were antirecessionary tax cuts enacted. And then the authorities weakened the effects by making them temporary.*

This is clearly not a record to be proud of.

**Monetary Policies**

Monetary policy during this period has been indicted along similar lines as fiscal policy. As suggested by Table 21–3, the expansionary monetary policies that had been in effect since early 1970 were maintained after August 1971. During 1972 and early 1973 the growth rate of money was particularly rapid, and by now there is relatively wide agreement that the Fed pumped up the economy to an unhealthy degree during this period. Some have suggested that the Fed was misled by the rising Treasury bill rate during 1972 (see Table 21–3), and therefore interpreted its policy as a restrictive one. If so, we have yet another example of the danger of using interest rates alone as an indicator of the thrust of monetary policy.

Like fiscal policy, monetary policy became somewhat more restrictive as 1973 progressed, and tightened considerably after June. The money supply increased at about an $8\frac{1}{2}$ percent rate in the first quarter of the year but then slowed to about a 5 percent pace. Short-term interest rates soared during the first three quarters of the year and reached record-breaking levels. For example, the Treasury bill rate, which had stood at about 5 percent in December 1972, jumped to over $8\frac{1}{4}$ percent in August 1973. The federal funds rate rose to about 11 percent in September, up from about $5\frac{1}{2}$ percent at the beginning of the year.

As market interest rates rose, as in 1966 and 1969, deposits at commercial banks became less attractive than alternative open-market assets. Contrary to the earlier experience, when there were large outflows of funds from commercial banks, measures were taken to ensure that commercial banks could compete for funds. In particular, interest rate ceilings on large certificates of deposits maturing in 90 days or more

| **TABLE 21-3** | | 1971 | | 1972 | | | | 1973 | | | |
|---|---|---|---|---|---|---|---|---|---|---|---|
| *Key financial variables, 1971–1973 (in percentages)* | | III | IV | I | II | III | IV | I | II | III | IV |
| | Treasury bill rate | 5.0 | 4.2 | 3.4 | 3.8 | 4.2 | 4.9 | 5.7 | 6.6 | 8.3 | 7.5 |
| | Corporate bond rate | 7.6 | 7.3 | 7.2 | 7.3 | 7.2 | 7.1 | 7.2 | 7.3 | 7.6 | 7.7 |
| | Growth rate of M-1B | 4.4 | 4.1 | 10.1 | 5.8 | 10.3 | 10.8 | 8.4 | 4.9 | 4.5 | 4.8 |

were lifted in May 1973. The ceilings on large short-term CDs had been lifted in 1970. As a consequence of these two developments, the volume of large CDs increased from $44 billion in January 1973 to $67 billion in August, a sharp contrast to the sizable decline in 1969. At the same time, however, restraint was maintained by more than doubling the marginal reserve requirement on large CDs.

In late 1973 monetary policy had adopted a slightly easier posture, largely in response to the economic dislocations stemming from the Middle East oil embargo. Short-term interest rates, which had peaked in the third quarter of 1973, gradually declined, and continued to do so until February 1974. The Treasury bill rate, for example, dropped from about $8\frac{1}{2}$ percent to 7 percent, while the federal funds rate fell from 11 percent to $8\frac{1}{2}$ percent. After February 1974, however, the Federal Reserve, once again concerned with inflationary developments, returned to its earlier restrictive stance. In the months that followed, monetary restraint in conjunction with continued rapid inflation and strong business demands for credit combined to produce new historical highs in interest rates. The Treasury bill rate rose to $8\frac{3}{4}$ percent, and the federal funds rate to $13\frac{1}{2}$ percent, shortly after midyear.

The tightening of credit was accompanied by fears of a general liquidity squeeze. These fears were fueled by the well-publicized difficulties (and eventual failure) of the Franklin National Bank in New York. There was also concern that a number of nonfinancial business failures were imminent. To damp these apprehensions, the Federal Reserve announced its willingness to serve as a lender of last resort to nonbanking firms as well as to banks. This helped calm financial markets regarding the possibility of serious financial instability.

Monetary policy during the 1974–1975 recession has been subject to some debate. As the extent of the recession became more apparent, the Fed did take some steps to ease monetary policy. At the time, however, observers with such diverse views as Paul Samuelson and Milton Friedman joined in condemning the Fed for pursuing an overly restrictive policy. Testifying before Congress in February 1975, Friedman cited the small money growth rates between June 1974 and January 1975 and argued that they "surely contributed to the recent deepening of the recession." Soon thereafter Samuelson echoed this view and charged that "if we go into a depression, the Fed will justly bear much of the blame."[6]

In retrospect, while the Fed certainly did not carry out a vigorous antirecessionary program, these assessments probably overstate the restrictive position of monetary policy. The reason for this is, as we have

---

[6] Cited in Blinder, op. cit., p. 189.

seen earlier, that it was during this period that the demand for money was undergoing a substantial shift. As will be recalled, this produced an increase in velocity, which meant that a given volume of money could support a larger volume of transactions. Consequently, the apparently anemic money growth rates during the last two quarters of 1974 and the first quarter of 1975 were not as restrictive as might be thought at first blush. Indeed, by March 1975 the Federal funds rate had dipped to $5\frac{1}{2}$ percent, a far cry from its peak of $13\frac{1}{2}$ percent eight months earlier. In this instance we may have a situation in which money proved to be the deficient indicator and interest rates were perhaps somewhat more reliable. Nevertheless, it should be emphasized that had the shift in money demand not taken place, Samuelson's assessment might have unhappily proved true. Whether one should credit the Fed with blind luck or consummate skill in this matter we leave to the intrepid reader to decide.

## THE RECOVERY PERIOD, 1975–1976

The economy bottomed out in the first quarter of 1975. At that point real GNP stood about 6 percent below its previous peak in the fourth quarter of 1973. Put another way, at the trough of the recession the gap between actual GNP and potential GNP was over $100 billion (in 1972 dollars). Beginning with the spring of 1975, production, employment, and income all started to rise. Over the year from the first quarter of 1975 to the first quarter of 1976, real GNP advanced at a rate of $7\frac{1}{2}$ percent. Even this healthy clip, however, only served to restore real GNP to slightly above its level at the end of 1973.

The unemployment rate, which had reached a peak of about 9 percent in May 1975, declined to just under 8 percent in January 1976. However, after the first quarter of 1976 real GNP advanced at a much-reduced 3 percent rate and progress on the unemployment front slowed. At year-end 1976 the unemployment rate stood at about $7\frac{1}{2}$ percent. The improvement in inflation was somewhat more dramatic as the earlier extended decline in real output finally served to bring down the rate of inflation. From April 1975 to the end of the year, the various price indexes increased in the range of 6–7 percent. And for 1976 as a whole the consumer price index rose at a 5 percent rate. While these rates might have seemed high by historical standards, they marked a substantial slowdown from the double-digit rates of inflation that had prevailed during 1974.

### Policy During the Recovery

In retrospect, the recession appears to have ended at just about the time that Congress was enacting the 1975 tax cuts. While owing to their temporary nature the effectiveness of these tax cuts has been subject to heated debate, they undoubtedly provided support for the recovery. A further stimulus was provided by the extension of these tax cuts into the first half of 1976.

As for monetary policy, there was much debate over the proper course of action during the initial stages of the recovery. In May 1975, for the first time, the Fed publicly announced its target ranges for money growth rates: 5–7½ percent for M-1 and 8½–10½ percent for M-2. Many observers, including some in the Fed, thought these rates would not be adequate to finance the recovery. The chairman of the Board of Governors, Arthur Burns, insisted that they would be adequate because of the rise in velocity that typically accompanied a cyclical upswing. With hindsight he proved correct, although as we have seen, his case was aided by the greater-than-normal increase in velocity stemming from the shift in money demand. Monetary policy in 1976 continued on roughly a 6 percent track for M-1 growth. One observer has described policy during this period as follows:

> *The proceedings of the FOMC in 1976 were characterized by nothing if not blandness. During the entire year, the Committee's basic policy directive never changed, its short-run operating instructions had only minor changes, and there were hardly any dissents from the majority view.*[7]

**ECONOMIC DEVELOPMENTS SINCE 1977**

The recovery of the economy continued in 1977. The growth rate of real GNP picked up from its pace in the last part of 1976 and advanced at a rate of 5.7 percent during 1977 (see Table 21–4). The unemployment rate registered a further improvement and stood at 6.6 percent in the fourth quarter of the year. While the inflation rate did accelerate a bit, it had not yet advanced to a worrisome stage. Indeed, in referring to 1977 in its 1978 *Annual Report*, the Council of Economic Advisers observed

[7] Blinder, op. cit., p. 195.

**TABLE 21–4**

*Some key economic indicators, 1976–1979 (in percentages)*

| | 1976-IV | 1977-IV | 1978-IV | 1979-IV |
|---|---|---|---|---|
| Growth rate of real GNP | 4.9 | 5.7 | 4.8 | 1.0 |
| Inflation rate (CPI) | 5.0 | 6.6 | 9.0 | 12.7 |
| Growth rate of M-1A | 5.5 | 7.7 | 7.4 | 5.5 |
| Growth rate of labor productivity | 3.1 | 1.4 | 0.8 | −2.1 |
| Unemployment rate | 7.7 | 6.6 | 5.8 | 5.9 |
| Treasury bill rate | 4.7 | 6.1 | 8.6 | 11.8 |

*Note:* Growth and inflation rates are for the fourth quarter of each year relative to the fourth quarter of the previous year.

that "the pace of inflation last year was essentially unchanged from 1976, excluding the effects of a few especially volatile factors."[8] Somewhat more worrisome was the slowdown in the rate of growth of *productivity* — the increase in output per hour of labor input. During 1977 the advance in productivity declined to under $1\frac{1}{2}$ percent, a sharp drop from the over 3 percent increase recorded during 1976 (see Table 21–4). Since productivity growth is an important factor in restraining business costs, this did not bode well for the future.

As shown in Table 21–4, the economic expansion continued throughout 1978. The growth of real GNP subsided somewhat, but GNP still grew at a healthy 4.8 percent clip during 1978, and unemployment registered a further improvement. Inflation, however, accelerated to a 9 percent rate. This generated a sufficient concern among policy makers that they began implementing aggregate demand policies to restrict economic growth.

Economic growth did slow to a rate of 1 percent in the first quarter of 1979. In the second quarter, GNP actually declined at a 2 percent annual rate — the first drop in real GNP since 1975. At the time, many economists were forecasting the onset of a full-fledged recession. From the point of view of numerous observers, the recession appeared to be just what the doctor ordered to restrain what by now had turned into a serious inflation. Indeed, at the start of 1979 inflation was racing along at a 13 percent rate. The economy, however, like a recalcitrant patient, refused to take its medicine. Real GNP growth picked up after midyear and advanced at a $2\frac{1}{2}$ percent pace over the last six months of 1979. This did nothing to help the inflation situation, which was further aggravated by a huge runup in energy prices (37 percent for 1979 as a whole).

To many economists, the resiliency of the economy proved surprising. There was some speculation that consumers, rather than being turned off by inflation, actually accelerated their purchases because they expected prices to be still higher in the future. Such considerations are probably particularly important for durable goods, including housing. Thus, for example, high *nominal* mortgage interest rates may have been perceived as quite low (or even negative) *real* rates. Relative to previous periods of high nominal interest rates, in 1979 housing was also spared the effects of financial disintermediation. As we have seen, the major reason for this was the growth of money market certificates, which helped to bolster deposits at thrift institutions.

Although the complete story of the resiliency of the economy is yet to be told, the consequences of that resiliency were all too evident as 1980 began. From November 1979 to March 1980 the CPI advanced at a

---

[8] *Economic Report of the President*, Washington, D.C., Government Printing Office, 1978, p. 46.

16 percent rate, while lurking in the background were further rises in energy costs. Nevertheless, as 1980 unfolded it became increasingly apparent that the long heralded recession had finally arrived.

The somewhat hectic economic developments from 1977 to the present considerably complicated the task of monetary and fiscal policy. It is to a review of these policies that we now turn.

**FISCAL AND MONETARY POLICY SINCE 1977**

We begin our discussion at the start of 1977, when the task of policy makers seemed simple enough—to continue support for the recovery while keeping an eye out for inflationary pressures. As we have seen, of course, our tale does not have a happy ending.

**Fiscal Policy**

Soon after the Carter administration came to office in 1977, it proposed a fiscal stimulus package that would have had a two-year budgetary impact of $31 billion. Its purpose was to raise the growth in real output—which, as we have seen, had slowed to a 3 percent rate over the last three quarters of 1976—and to make further inroads on unemployment. However, during the first quarter of 1977 real-GNP growth accelerated to a nearly 9 percent annual rate. As a consequence, Congress considerably trimmed this proposal. When ultimately enacted, the Tax Reduction and Simplification Act of 1977 provided a relatively minor stimulus package of $14 billion.

Another tax development in 1977, and of considerably more consequence, was the passage of the Social Security Amendments. These provided for major increases in social security taxes, both by raising the maximum amount of wages subject to social security tax and by increasing the tax rate. The first of these changes went into effect on January 1, 1978, when the wage base was raised from $16,500 to $17,700 and the tax rate increased from 11.7 to 12.1 percent. Subsequent increases were scheduled to go into effect on each successive January 1. As of 1980 the wage base stood at $25,900 while the tax rate was 12.26 percent.

One consequence of these amendments was that a considerable degree of fiscal drag was built into the system. A second source of fiscal drag came from the interplay of inflation and the progressive structure of individual income tax rates. In particular, as inflation accelerated, more individuals moved into higher tax brackets and inflation once again was the source of an unlegislated tax increase. It was largely to counter this drag that the President proposed, and Congress enacted, the Revenue Act of 1978. This act, which went into effect in 1979, provided for a $14 billion cut in personal taxes and a $6.5 billion cut in business taxes—less than the tax increase stemming from social security and inflation.

Despite the several tax cuts, over the three years 1977–1979 fiscal policy assumed a progressively tighter stance. Perhaps the simplest measure of this is what we have called the full-employment budget, that is, the surplus or deficit that would prevail if the economy were operating at full employment. In 1977 this budget showed a deficit of $19 billion, in 1978 a smaller deficit of $12 billion, and in 1979 a surplus of about $10 billion.[9] By any standard this represented a steady swing toward fiscal restraint. Nevertheless, while the qualitative direction of fiscal policy was appropriate, in view of the deteriorating inflation performance in 1978, 1979, and early 1980 one can obviously take issue with the quantitative degree of restraint.

**Monetary Policy**

As we have had much to say in previous chapters about monetary developments in the late 1970s, our present discussion can be relatively brief. We need to bear in mind that throughout this period the task of monetary policy was complicated by many new developments in the financial system. These developments served to shift the demand for money about in somewhat unpredictable ways. As a consequence, it was a somewhat tricky business to know the precise degree of restraint represented by any of the monetary aggregates. Furthermore, with high and varying rates of inflation, nominal interest rates were also of questionable use as a precise target of policy. Thus, if it appears that the Fed muddled about in this period, we at least have some feel for why this might be.

Table 21–5 records some of the key financial variables. As with fiscal policy, financial developments in 1977 were relatively calm. The money supply, as measured by M-1B, did grow at a quite rapid rate, but for reasons already indicated, at the time it was difficult to interpret precisely what this meant. Short-term interest rates rose fairly sharply from

---

[9] For the years 1977–1979 the *actual* budget deficits were $46 billion, $28 billion, and $10 billion, respectively. For a comparison of the various budget measures, see the *Economic Report of the President*, Washington, D.C., Government Printing Office, 1980.

**TABLE 21–5**

*Key financial variables, 1977–1979 (in percentages)*

|  | 1977 | | | | 1978 | | | | 1979 | | | | 1980 |
|---|---|---|---|---|---|---|---|---|---|---|---|---|---|
|  | I | II | III | IV | I | II | III | IV | I | II | III | IV | I |
| Treasury bill rate | 4.6 | 4.8 | 5.5 | 6.1 | 6.4 | 6.5 | 7.3 | 8.6 | 9.4 | 9.4 | 9.7 | 11.8 | 13.5 |
| Corporate bond rate | 8.0 | 8.0 | 7.9 | 8.1 | 8.5 | 8.7 | 8.8 | 9.0 | 9.3 | 9.4 | 9.3 | 10.5 | 12.1 |
| Growth rate of M-1B | 9.3 | 6.9 | 6.5 | 8.7 | 7.9 | 9.1 | 7.3 | 7.4 | 4.8 | 10.7 | 10.1 | 5.3 | 7.5 |
| Growth rate of M-2 | 13.7 | 11.2 | 9.6 | 9.7 | 7.5 | 7.5 | 8.2 | 9.5 | 6.3 | 10.2 | 10.3 | 7.2 | 8.7 |

April to October, and the FOMC target for the federal funds rate increased from a range of $4\frac{1}{4}$–5 percent in January 1977 to a range of $6\frac{1}{2}$–7 percent in January 1978.

The growth of M-1B continued at a rapid 8 percent rate over the first half of 1978, but thereafter the pace slowed somewhat. In part this reflected the effects of the introduction of the six-month money market certificates in mid-1978, but it also stemmed from policy moves designed to restrain the growth of the monetary aggregates. Through the year the FOMC gradually raised the tolerance range for the federal funds rate, and in December 1978 it stood at $9\frac{3}{4}$–$10\frac{1}{2}$ percent. Other interest rates generally followed this upward trend, with the Treasury bill rate, for example, moving from 6.1 percent in the fourth quarter of 1977 to 8.6 percent in the fourth quarter of 1978.

These moves to tighten monetary policy were clearly prompted by a deteriorating inflation picture but were also motivated by international considerations. Indeed, on November 1, 1978, the Federal Reserve announced its intention to take action to both fight inflation and restore confidence in the dollar. The steps taken included a 1 percentage point increase in the discount rate, a supplementary reserve requirement of 2 percentage points on large-denomination time deposits, and several actions specifically aimed at the international situation. While these actions brought a temporary improvement in the dollar's exchange rate, a larger-than-expected increase in OPEC oil prices for December 1978 brought about a further deterioration in the dollar. It also set the stage for the poor performance on the inflation front in 1979.

It goes without saying that the principal objective of monetary policy in 1979 was to help check accelerating inflation. However, the extent to which the Fed accomplished this, especially during the first three quarters of the year, is open to question.[10]

As we have noted, the decline in real GNP in the second quarter led to a widespread belief that a recession had begun. In this environment the Fed kept its federal funds operating strategy relatively unchanged. The result was a booming growth in M-1B. Around the middle of the year, the Fed became increasingly uneasy with the rapid growth in the monetary aggregates, and it gradually moved up both the discount rate and the federal funds target. However, with the revival of the economy in the third quarter, the demand for transactions balances mushroomed and the growth of M-1B continued at a 10 percent rate from June to September. At this point the Fed got serious.

---

[10] Similar doubts were expressed, although more circumspectly, in the 1980 *Annual Report* of the Council of Economic Advisers. Some of the following discussion is based on that report. See *Economic Report of the President*, Washington, D.C., Government Printing Office, 1980, pp. 51–58.

As discussed in previous chapters, on October 6, 1979, the Federal Reserve announced a major shift in its technique for implementing monetary policy. In particular, it abandoned adherence to a narrow range for the federal funds rate and proposed to address directly the control of the monetary aggregates via the provision of bank reserves. This, of course, did nothing to clarify the meaning of any particular aggregate. It simply promised better control over the aggregates, whatever they might mean. At the same time, the Federal Reserve raised the discount rate to 12 percent and established an 8 percent marginal reserve requirement on managed liabilities of member banks (see Chapters 7 and 11). Money growth decreased markedly in the wake of the Federal Reserve's action, and during the final quarter of 1979 M-1B rose at an annual rate of only 5 percent. Whether this augurs well for the control of the new complex of monetary aggregates that have recently been introduced, it is too early to tell.

One final development is worthy of note. As we have seen, there was a surge in the inflation rate in early 1980. In response, in February

---

**MONETARY AND CREDIT ACTIONS: MARCH 14, 1980**

In mid-March the Federal Reserve announced a series of monetary and credit actions as part of a general government program to help curb inflationary pressures. A number of the actions were specifically authorized by the President under the provisions of the Credit Control Act of 1969. Overall, the program included the following steps.*

1 A voluntary restraint program on the growth of bank credit aimed at keeping credit growth in the range of 6–9 percent per year.
2 A program of restraint on certain types of consumer credit. The cutting edge of this program was a 15 percent marginal "reserve requirement" on increases in specified kinds of consumer lending.
3 An increase from 8 percent to 10 percent in the marginal reserve requirement on the managed liabilities of large banks and an expansion of the applicability of the requirement. Large nonmember banks were also subject to the 10 percent requirement on managed liabilities.
4 A 15 percent marginal reserve requirement was imposed on increases of total assets of money market mutual funds above the level of March 14.
5 A three percentage point surcharge on discount borrowings by large banks to discourage frequent use of the discount window. Including the surcharge, the discount rate was 16 percent.

* For a detailed description of the program see the *Federal Reserve Bulletin*, April 1980, pp. 314–318.

the Fed jacked up the discount rate from 12 to 13 percent and, through open-market operations, forced the federal funds rate to near 15 percent.[11] Commercial banks quickly raised the prime rate of interest on commercial loans to an all-time record of 16½ percent. Other interest rates similarly established record highs, and the bond markets, to quote the financial press, "were in a state of shock." These records, however, did not last for very long. In the face of continued bad news on the inflation front, the Fed announced yet another tightening of the monetary screws (see "Monetary and Credit Actions: March 14, 1980"). Interest rates soared upward, with the Treasury bill rate reaching 16½ percent and the prime loan rate a whopping 20 percent. It was clearly taking much more than anticipated for the Fed to get things under control.

CONCLUSION

With this chapter we conclude our examination of monetary and fiscal policy. No brief summary of this examination is possible – except perhaps that we have a lot to learn. Nevertheless, it may be helpful to review quickly the progress and problems of policy making.

The Employment Act of 1946 was a major landmark in the history of American economic policy. Even as late as the early 1930s, few people would have believed that in less than two decades the federal government would accept responsibility for promoting "maximum employment, production, and purchasing power." As of 1980, we have achieved one major objective of the Employment Act; we have not had a major depression in the 35 years that have elapsed since World War II. Yet the performance of the economy has failed to meet fully the rising aspirations of the American people. Very large amounts of potential output and employment have been lost during seven economic recessions and some other periods of sluggish economic growth. Also, the economy has proved to be prone to price inflation. Much of the early inflation was associated with the aftermath of World War II, the Korean conflict, and the Vietnam War. While inflation in these periods seems readily explainable as a consequence of excess demand pressures, our recent inflationary experience appears to be a more complex beast. To be sure, excess demand still very much matters, but we have had increasingly to contend with a variety of supply shocks such as OPEC oil price hikes, bad harvests, and our poor productivity performance. As events made clear, we knew a lot more about getting to full employment than we did about staying there in a noninflationary way. Evidently then, the nation still faces the

---

[11] The differential between the discount rate and the funds rate naturally made borrowing from the Fed a rather attractive alternative. Not surprisingly, banks stepped up their borrowing from the Fed, which for the week ending February 20, 1980, averaged a hefty $2.1 billion.

problem of reconciling its objectives of price stability, continuously high levels of employment, and economic growth.

Problems of implementation still remain. It was expected that the objectives of the Employment Act would be promoted primarily through the use of monetary and fiscal policies to regulate the behavior of aggregate demands for output, but the relative roles of monetary and fiscal policies were not specified. The record of fiscal policies for stabilization purposes has been spotty. The automatic fiscal stabilizers have been helpful on many occasions—although they have sometimes inhibited economic recovery, as in the early 1960s—and discretionary tax and expenditure policies have at times contributed to stability. In general, however, fiscal policies have disappointed those who expected them to be adjusted flexibly and quickly. There are many reasons for this: sluggish congressional procedures and an unwillingness to delegate authority to the President; a continued lack of conviction on the part of some congressional leaders that economic stabilization should be a dominant consideration in fiscal policies; partisan politics; and so on. Fiscal policies have not yet made their maximum contribution to economic stabilization. This has shifted a major part of the burden to monetary policy. On some occasions, as in 1966, monetary policy alone bore the burden of combating inflation while fiscal policies were excessively expansionary. The results were the highest interest rates in more than 40 years, heavy impacts on the construction industry and on nonbank financial intermediaries, and unwanted increases of interest rates in foreign financial centers.

Monetary policies since World War II have been superior to those in earlier periods. The Federal Reserve has shown more wisdom in selecting its objectives and more sophistication in the use of the instruments at its command. However, even in the postwar period it was far from able to carry out policy in a precise way. This is partly because of the associated problems of inadequate economic forecasting and of lags in the effect of monetary policy. However, in many instances the Federal Reserve was itself to blame for a poor choice of operating strategies. In more recent years the Federal Reserve has had the added burden of coping with a rapidly changing financial system. It remains to be seen what form the system will ultimately take and whether the Federal Reserve will be able to innovate as quickly as the participants in financial markets seem able to.

There is a growing feeling that even if control of aggregate demand were completely precise, it could not alone reconcile our various economic objectives to an optimum degree. We may well need other measures to achieve more favorable trade-offs between price stability on the one hand and continuously low levels of unemployment and high rates of economic growth on the other. In recent years a number of such measures have been advanced. These include the following: policies designed to increase efficiency in the use of energy and reduce dependence on foreign oil; incentives for increasing investment and encouraging research and development and improvements in productivity; measures to improve labor markets; and reform of the regulatory process to weed out unnecessary and costly regulations. We do not know the precise role such measures will play in our national economic policy. One thing is clear, however: None of them can be a substitute for appropriate control of aggregate demand.

**SELECTED READINGS**

Blinder, A. S., *Economic Policy and the Great Stagflation*, New York, Academic Press, 1979.

*Economic Report of the President*, Wasington, D.C., Government Printing Office, 1980.

Heller, W. W., and M. Friedman, *Monetary vs. Fiscal Policy*, New York, Norton, 1969.

Okun, A. M., *The Political Economy of Prosperity*, Washington, D.C., Brookings Institution, 1970.

# VI INTERNATIONAL MONETARY RELATIONS

# 22

Most of the discussion up to this point has concentrated on domestic aspects of money and finance. However, our financial institutions play an important role in transactions across national boundaries. In addition, our monetary policy has profound effects on other countries, and the financial policies of other countries affect monetary and financial conditions in this country.

The following two chapters explore some of the most important aspects of international financial relationships. In this chapter we examine the functions of money and finance in international transactions, the types of transactions that give rise to international payments flows, and the foreign exchange market. Then, in the following chapter, we explore the principal institutional arrangements that facilitate international payments, international economic interdependence, and the recent history of the international financial system.

**FUNCTIONS OF
MONEY IN
INTERNATIONAL
TRANSACTIONS**

The basic functions of money and finance in international trade are the same as those in domestic exchanges, that is, to facilitate exchange by decreasing the real cost of transacting, and thereby to enable traders to exploit potential gains from trade.

International trade is, in the final analysis, the exchange of goods and services produced in one country for those produced in another. Because of international differences in preferences, endowment of productive factors, and relative efficiencies of producing specific types of commodities and services, the residents of two countries may be able to increase their welfare by trading with each other. Similarly, financial transfers that take advantage of international differences in real rates of return to capital may increase total real income in each of the countries taking part in the transactions.

The extent to which potential gains from trade can be realized depends on the efficiency and smooth functioning of international exchange processes. All of the above types of exchanges might be possible under a barter system, but such a system would be clumsy and inconvenient. It would also be possible to make internatioal payments by shipping precious metals in the form of coin or bullion, or by shipping paper money. However, the shipments of gold or paper money across national boundaries would be expensive and risky. Freight costs would be high, the risk of loss would be omnipresent, and the speed of transferring payments would depend on the speed of the transportation facilities. To avoid these costs and inconveniences, nowadays international payments, like many domestic payments, are generally made by quick electronic transfers of financial claims from payers to payees. The financial claims that serve as *quid pro quo* in international payments are usually deposit liabilities of commercial banks. In the next chapter we shall discuss the role commercial banks play in international financial systems.

**TYPES OF INTERNATIONAL TRANSACTIONS AND THE BALANCE OF PAYMENTS**

There are three broad categories of international transactions that give rise to payments between nations: purchases and sales of goods and services, gifts and grants, and purchases and sales of financial claims. The statistical record of all transactions taking place between one country's residents and the rest of the world is the nation's *balance-of-payments account*.

**Trade in Goods and Services**

American exports of goods and services include not only exports of many types of commodities but also many types of services, such as transportation services, financial services, services to foreign tourists in the United States, and services rendered by American property located abroad. On the other hand, Americans purchase from the rest of the world large amounts of imports of goods and services, including services supplied to American travelers abroad and services rendered by foreign property in the United States.

Our exports of goods and services $(X)$ may be viewed not only as a receipt item in our balance of payments but also as the value of foreign demands for our output and as the value of our output made available for use by the rest of the world. Our imports $(M)$ may be viewed not only as a payment item in our balance of payments but also as the amount of our national income that is used to demand output from the rest of the world. The quantity $(X - M)$ is usually referred to as the *balance on goods and services*. This has been a net-receipt item for the United States during most years since World War II, although it was a net-payment item in 1977, 1978, and 1979.

**International Gifts and Grants**

International gifts and grants are similar to domestic transfer payments in that the donor surrenders goods, services, or purchasing power without directly receiving anything of value in return. In the balance-of-payments accounts, gifts and grants are called *unilateral transfers*. They are a source of receipts when the United States receives gifts and grants from abroad and a payment item when Americans or the U.S. government export goods, services, or purchasing power without receiving compensation. In most years unilateral transfers are a net-payment item for the United States.

**Trade in Financial Claims**

All other transactions in the balance of payments involve purchases and sales of various types of financial claims. There are three broad categories of international transactions between the residents of different countries:

1  *Direct investment* occurs when the residents of one country purchase stocks in order to acquire entrepreneurial control over a business or enterprise in another country. In addition, direct investment occurs when an enterprise of one country starts a new subsidiary in another country.

2  *Long-term portfolio investment* involves international transactions in securities with original terms to maturity of greater than one year.

3  *Short-term capital flows* involve securities with original terms to maturity of less than one year.

Differences in the marginal productivity of capital among countries constitute a basic, long-term force inducing international flows of capital funds. These differences in the marginal productivity of capital from country to country result from differences in stocks of savings and capital goods relative to supplies of natural resources and labor, differences in technology, differences in managerial capacity, and so on. In a world characterized by perfect competition, absence of risk, and unfettered movements of funds, differences in the marginal productivity of capital would be reflected in differences in interest rates; residents in areas with high interest rates would sell financial claims in areas with low interest rates in order to command more capital; and the process would continue until the marginal productivity of capital and interest rates were equalized in all areas. There are, of course, many obstacles to international purchases and sales of financial claims, including government restrictions, incomplete knowledge of opportunities, and fear that property rights will not be protected. However, very large international capital flows do occur. Some of these are in response to basic long-term forces of the type described above, while others are in response to short-run factors such as cyclical fluctuations in national economies. In addition, basic portfolio considerations affect the international flow of financial claims.

For example, when comparing financial investment alternatives at home to those abroad, sophisticated investors seek to achieve the most favorable combination of yield, safety of principal, and liquidity. Other things equal, the proportion of assets held in the form of claims against other countries will vary directly with the level of interest rates abroad relative to those at home. Thus, when interest rates rise in some countries and not in others, funds tend to flow from areas with lower interest rates to areas with higher interest rates. Residents of countries with the higher interest rates tend to lend more at home and less abroad, while residents of countries with the lower interest rates tend to lend less at home and more abroad.

A second factor affecting investors' choices among claims on domestic and foreign entities is relative safety of principal value. Both domestic and foreign claims are subject to default risks and to the market risk that interest rates may increase in the future. Two other related types of risk should be mentioned. The first type, called political risk, results from possibilities of confiscation, refusal to allow payments to foreigners, emergence of a government that will not enforce private property rights, and so on. When such events are expected in a country, large capital outflows are often induced. The other type of risk is exchange risk. Exchange risk arises from the possibility of fluctuations in the exchange rate, that is, in the rate at which one currency trades for another.

Relative liquidity is a third factor affecting investors' choices among domestic and foreign financial claims. The very high liquidity of short-term claims against dollars makes them a popular investment for foreigners. However, expected changes in relative liquidity can induce large-scale movements of funds. For example, threats of war or other developments abroad that reduce expected liquidity of foreign claims can lead to large shifts of funds to the United States.

It it sometimes useful to lump together private sector transactions in short- and long-term financial claims. Americans pay for their purchases of both short- and long-term financial claims by sending liquid purchasing power abroad, Thus, such purchases can be thought of as generating capital outflows or capital exports. On the other hand, the payments generated by sales of both short- and long-term financial claims by Americans to foreigners can be thought of as capital inflows or capital imports to the United States. The quantity (capital exports − capital imports) measures the increase in a country's net financial claims on foreigners and is sometimes called the *balance on capital account*.

The final type of trade in financial claims is trade between central banks. As we shall see in the next chapter, central banks hold stocks of "official reserve assets" in the form of claims against foreign moneys or other things that can be readily exchanged for foreign money, such as gold. When a central bank adds to its stock of official reserve assets by purchasing foreign exchange, it sends its home currency abroad. Sales of official reserve assets, on the other hand, are a source of receipts because buyers must pay for them.

**The Balance-of-Payments Identity**

As already noted, a nation's balance-of-payments account shows for some stated period the flows of that nation's receipts from the rest of the world and its payments to the rest of the world. A schematic version of the balance of payments is given in Table 22–1.

Table 22–1 shows that for any stated period a nation's total receipts from international transactions must equal its total payments on international account. To look at this accounting requirement another way, we can rearrange Table 22–1 as follows:

(Exports of goods and services − imports of goods and services)
  + (unilateral receipts − unilateral payments)
= (capital exports − capital imports) + net change in official reserves

The left-hand side of this equation, which is the sum of the balance on goods and services and net unilateral transfers, is called the *balance on current account*. Also, as defined above, the term (capital exports − capital imports) is known as the *balance on capital account*. Hence, an equivalent way to express Table 22–1 is as follows:

Balance on current account
= balance on capital account + net change in official reserves

This equation, in either of its two equivalent forms, is sometimes called the *balance-of-payments identity*. It indicates that if the United States has a deficit on current account, it must somehow increase its claims against the rest of the world. This may be done by having the private sector import more capital than it exports. For example, capital imports will increase whenever U.S. citizens sell previously held foreign securities

| TABLE 22–1 | Receipts | Payments |
|---|---|---|
| *Components of the U.S. balance of payments* | 1. Exports of goods and services | 1. Imports of goods and services |
| | 2. Unilateral receipts | 2. Unilateral payments |
| | 3. Sales of long-term claims | 3. Purchases of long-term claims |
| | 4. Sales of short-term claims | 4. Purchases of short-term claims |
| | 5. Sales of reserve assets | 5. Purchases of reserve assets |

or foreign citizens decide to increase their holdings of dollar-denominated assets. However, with a current account deficit, if the balance on capital account is not sufficiently negative, then, from the identity above, we see that the government must fill the gap by selling foreign exchange (i.e., decreasing its stock of reserve assets).

**Summarizing the Balance-of-Payments Accounts**

Either from Table 22–1 or, equivalently, from the balance-of-payments identity, we see that total receipts and payments must be equal. Yet a nation is sometimes said to have a surplus or a deficit in its balance of payments, implying inequalities of that country's international receipts and payments. These apparently conflicting views are easily reconciled. It would indeed be rare for a nation to have an exact balance of receipts and payments on every major class of transactions entering into its balance of payments. Instead, it usually experiences net receipts on some types of transactions, which must be balanced by net payments on others. The general notion of a surplus or deficit is fairly straightforward: A nation is considered to have a surplus during a stated period if its net receipts on account of some types of transactions are balanced by net payments on other accounts in such a way as to improve its net international reserve position or its net international liquidity position. This can be reflected in a net increase in its stock of official international reserve assets, a decrease of selected types of debt liabilities to foreigners, or some combination of the two. A nation is said to have a deficit when its net payments on account of some types of transactions are balanced by net receipts on other accounts in such a way as to deteriorate its net international reserve or net international liquidity position. This can be reflected in a net decrease in its stock of official reserve assets, an increase of selected types of debt liabilities to foreigners, or a combination of the two. Unfortunately, however, there is no general agreement on specific definitions of these key terms. Nations use differing definitions, and the United States has employed several.

Since a nation's balance of payments must balance, the key to determining when a country faces an international payments imbalance is the distinction between autonomous and accommodating transactions. *Autonomous transactions* are transactions undertaken for normal commercial motives. Frequently autonomous transactions are influenced by the exchange rate, that is, by the rate at which one currency trades for another. International traders use exchange rates to transfer prices denominated in foreign currencies into their domestic-currency equivalent so that they can "comparison shop" in the international market. We shall discuss exchange rate determination in the following section. *Accommodating transactions* differ from autonomous transactions in that they are not undertaken in pursuit of commercial profit. As we shall see later, one common type of accommodating transaction is undertaken by a government or central bank in order to preserve or enforce a price (the exchange rate) in the foreign exchange market.

Once all international transactions have been classified as autonomous or accommodating, a payments imbalance is defined as a situation in which the sum of all accommodating transactions is nonzero. It should be noted that the balance of payments identity implies that the sum of all accommodating transactions must be equal to but opposite in sign from the sum of all autonomous transactions. Because the distinction between autonomous and accommodating transactions is not definitive, it is possible to construct a wide variety of measures of payments imbalance.

One possible measure of a nation's balance-of-payments position is called the *official reserve transactions* balance. In the United States the official reserve transactions balance is defined as the net change during the period in U.S. official reserve assets plus the net change in U.S. liabilities to foreign official agencies. According to this definition of payments imbalance, all transactions on the current and capital accounts are autonomous. A nonzero reserve transactions balance implies that autonomous receipts from international trade in goods, services, and financial assets did not equal autonomous payments. Table 22–2 illustrates these principles with data for 1977.

Note that in Table 22–2 payments are designated by a minus sign and the absence of a minus sign denotes receipts. The balance on goods and services in 1977 was −$9,423 million. The balance on the official reserve transactions basis was −$36,281. This deficit was financed by net sales of $375 million of U.S. official reserve assets and an increase of $36,656 million in net U.S. government liabilities to foreign official agencies. In other words, the official transactions balance was financed largely through the provision of foreign exchange by foreign govern-

| TABLE 22–2 | | |
|---|---|---|
| *U.S. balance of payments, 1977 (in millions of dollars)* | Balance on goods and services | −$ 9,423 |
| | Net unilateral transfers | − 4,670 |
| | Net long-term capital flows | − 16,073 |
| | Net private short-term capital flows | − 5,178 |
| | Errors and omissions* | − 937 |
| | Balance on official reserve transactions basis | −$36,281 |
| | Settlement of reserve transactions balance | |
| | Net change in U.S. official reserve assets | −$ 375 |
| | Net change in liabilities of foreign official agencies | $36,656 |

*Note:* Minus sign denotes payments; omission of sign denotes receipts.
* This category is in the nature of a statistical discrepancy largely reflecting the failure to identify some organizations properly.
*Source: Survey of Current Business, June 1979.*

ments adding to their holdings of dollar claims, which are, of course, part of their official reserves.

**Economic Interpretation**
Perhaps the simplest way to see what is involved is to refer back to the balance-of-payments identity. As the use of the term *identity* implies, as a matter of accounting this expression must always hold. It is thus analogous to the identity of saving and investment encountered earlier. In that case, we saw that simply satisfying the saving–investment identity did not ensure equilibrium. Equilibrium required that *desired* saving and *desired* investment should be equal. If these two were not equal, then either income or interest rates had to change to bring about equality. Similar considerations apply in the case of the balance of payments.

In particular, equilibrium requires that the quantity of dollars that foreigners desire to hold must be equal to the quantity of dollars Americans are willing to supply. If these two quantities are not equal, then we have a situation of disequilibrium. And it is the extent of this disequilibrium that some particular surplus or deficit measure is trying to capture.

As with saving and investment, if there is a disequilibrium, then certain adjustments must take place. In the short run this may simply take the form of the government stepping in and using its international reserve assets to bring about equality between supply and demand. But this can only temporarily remove a disequilibrium. In the longer run there must be an adjustment in some or all of the following—income, interest rates, prices, or exchange rates—for it is these variables that influence the various entries in the balance-of-payments identity. For example, U.S. income levels and the relative prices of foreign and domestic goods influence the extent to which we will import foreign goods. Similarly, interest rates, both here and abroad, influence the magnitude of capital flows. In the next chapter we shall examine in greater detail the ways in which nations adjust to balance-of-payments disequilibria.

**FOREIGN EXCHANGE MARKETS**
The types of international transactions we described in the preceding sections give rise to a huge volume of exchanges of national moneys. For example, an American who receives a claim against French francs and does not want to spend in France or to hold French francs will offer them in exchange for dollars or for some other nation's money that he or she wants to spend or hold. Other Americans who want to spend or hold moneys of other nations offer dollars in exchange for them. Similar transactions occur all over the world. The term *foreign exchange market* refers to all the facilities and processes involved in the exchange of

claims against the various national moneys. The things bought and sold include small amounts of coin and larger amounts of paper money, but the great bulk of trading is in claims against banks denominated in the various national moneys. Some of these are payable on demand; others, only after a lapse of time. Short-term claims against nonbank debtors are also exchanged in these markets.

Whenever things are exchanged against each other, there must, of course, be some rate or ratio of exchange between them; there must be some type of "price." By the *exchange rate* between two monetary units we mean simply the number of units of one money required to buy one unit of the other. Either monetary unit may be employed as the unit for stating the price of the other. For example, a situation in which 2 German marks exchange for 1 U.S. dollar could be stated either as $1 = 2 marks or as 1 mark = $\frac{1}{2}$ dollar. Also, a change in the exchange rate to $1 = 3 marks can be expressed either as a rise in the exchange rate on the dollar relative to the mark or as a decrease in the exchange rate on the mark relative to the dollar. As we shall see later, an exchange rate may be determined like any other price, that is, by the supply and demand functions for foreign exchange. On the other hand, the exchange rate may also be pegged by an official agency that intervenes in the foreign exchange market by buying or selling official reserve assets to maintain the rate at a certain level.

Virtually all countries have some type of foreign exchange market, but some markets are more highly developed than others. Among the largest and most active are those in New York, London, Paris, Amsterdam, Brussels, Zurich, Frankfurt, and Rome. Exchange rates in different financial centers are kept nearly identical by arbitrage.

**Arbitrage**

*Arbitrage* is a general term in economics for buying something where it is cheap and selling it where it is dear. If the price of Japanese yen in New York falls below that in London by more than a small cost of transacting, profits can be made by buying yen in New York and selling them in London; such a transaction is called *foreign exchange arbitrage.*

Arbitrage also keeps exchange rates consistent across markets. Disregarding transactions costs, suppose you buy $10,000 worth of yen in New York, sell it in London for German deutsche marks (DM), and then sell the DM for dollars in Paris. If you wind up with either more or less than $10,000, the exchange rates were inconsistent across the New York, London, and Paris foreign exchange markets. If you made a profit, you and other arbitragers would continue to transfer funds across the three markets until the exchange rates were driven into consistency. If the proposed transaction involves a loss, then of course it will not be undertaken. However, it would be possible to "reverse" the transaction and make a profit. (Make sure you see why this is so.)

This brings up the question: How are market exchange rates established?

**The Exchange Rate**

As mentioned earlier, exchange rates may be determined by free-market forces, that is, by demand–supply conditions in exchange markets. The free-market or freely floating exchange rate is said to be in equilibrium when it reaches a level at which the nation's autonomous receipts from international trade in goods, services, and financial claims equal its autonomous payments. Equivalently, the equilibrium exchange rate is that rate which clears the market for foreign exchange.

On the other hand, official agencies may intervene in foreign exchange markets to peg exchange rates at particular levels or to influence the behavior of exchange rates. When a government intervenes in the foreign exchange market by buying foreign exchange, the transaction is recorded in the balance-of-payments accounts as an increase in official reserve assets. In addition, the transaction may be interpreted as an accommodating transaction and an indication of balance-of-payments disequilibrium. Similarly, when a government intervenes by selling foreign exchange, the balance-of-payments accounts record a decrease in official reserve assets.

We shall now describe exchange rate determination in detail for each of these two cases. We begin with the case in which there is no official intervention in foreign exchange markets.

**FLEXIBLE EXCHANGE RATES**

When official agencies do not peg exchange rates or otherwise intervene in the foreign exchange market, the exchange rate is determined by free-market forces. To illustrate the principles involved in a system of freely floating exchange rates, we shall analyze the dollar price of the British pound sterling. We shall state our analysis in terms of the supply of and demand for sterling.

By the supply of sterling we mean a function or schedule showing the quantities of sterling that would be supplied in exchange markets per period of time at each of the various possible dollar prices of sterling. Its components are the payment items in the British balance of payments — amounts of sterling supplied to purchase imports of goods and services and to buy various types of financial claims from foreigners. By the demand for sterling we mean a function or schedule showing the quantities of sterling that would be demanded in exchange markets at the various possible dollar prices of sterling. The components of these demands for sterling are the receipt items in the British balance of payments, that is, quantities of sterling demanded to pay for British exports of goods and services and to purchase various types of financial claims from the British. Let us now use simple statics to show how supply and demand functions determine exchange rates.

**The Supply Function for Sterling**

The purpose of a supply schedule stating supply as a function of price is the usual purpose of isolating the effect of price (in this case, the exchange rate) on quantities supplied. Such a curve can be drawn only if we assume that all other conditions affecting supply are given and constant. Listed next are the principal factors that, for the moment, we assume to be given and constant.

1    The level of real income in Britain
2    The level of prices and costs in Britain relative to those of other countries
3    Levels of interest rates in Britain relative to those of other countries
4    Expectations as to future exchange rates on sterling
5    Tastes for British products relative to those of other countries
6    Other factors relevant to the productivity and comparative costs of British and foreign products

Later we shall see how changes in these conditions tend to shift the supply function for sterling.

The supply function of sterling is represented by the SS line in Figure 22–1. It is shown as a positive function of the exchange rate on sterling; that is, the higher the exchange rate on sterling, the greater will be the quantity of sterling offered in the exchange market. The reason for this is that the higher the dollar price of sterling, the cheaper will be the sterling price of imports, the greater will be the quantity of imports demanded by Britain, and the greater will be the sterling value of imports if the price elasticity of British demands for imports, stated in terms of sterling prices, is greater than unity. This becomes clearer as we remember that increases in the dollar price of sterling are accompanied by decreases in the sterling price of the dollar. For example, a rate of £ = $1 is obviously the same as $1 = £1; £1 = $2 is equivalent to $1 = £½; and £1 = $3 is equivalent to $1 = £⅓. Suppose the American price of

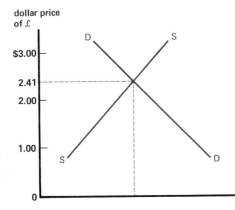

*Demand for and supply of sterling*

**FIGURE 22–1**

some export to Britain is $1 per unit. In terms of sterling, the cost of the import to the British will be £1 if the exchange rate is £1 = $1, only £$\frac{1}{2}$ if the exchange rate is £1 = $2, and only £$\frac{1}{3}$ if the exchange rate is £1 = $3.

It will be helpful to remember that, other things equal, an increase in the exchange rate on a nation's currency tends to encourage its imports, and a decrease in the exchange rate on a nation's currency tends to discourage its imports.

**The Demand Function for Sterling**  The demand function for sterling, represented by the *DD* line in Figure 22–1, assumes that all other conditions except the exchange rate are given and constant. The most important of these conditions are those just listed as influencing the supply function of sterling, with the exception that we would now substitute the level of real income in the rest of the world for the level of real income in Britain. Later we shall see how changes in these conditions can increase or decrease the demand function for sterling. The demand function for sterling is shown as a negative function of the exchange rate on sterling; that is, the higher the exchange rate on sterling, the smaller will be the quantity of sterling demanded in exchange markets. This is because higher exchange rates on sterling make British exports of goods and services more expensive in terms of other currencies. For example, suppose that the sterling price of some British good is £1. The dollar cost of the good will be $1 at an exchange rate of £1 = $1, $2 at an exchange rate of £1 = $2, and $3 at an exchange rate of £1 = $3.

Thus, we find that, other things equal, a nation's exports are discouraged by a rise in the exchange rate on its currency and encouraged by a decrease in the exchange rate on its currency.

It will be remembered that we are dealing with the case in which the authorities do not attempt to peg exchange rates or intervene directly to affect their behavior, but allow exchange rates to be determined by market forces. In this case the exchange rate can be in equilibrium only when the quantity of sterling demanded is exactly equal to the quantity supplied, leaving neither an excess demand nor an excess supply. Figure 22–1 shows that, with the given *DD* and *SS* curves, this can occur only at the exchange rate of £1 = $2.41. At any higher rate there would be an excess supply of sterling. The supply of sterling would be larger because British imports would be cheaper in terms of sterling, and the demand for sterling would be smaller because British exports would be more expensive to foreigners. On the other hand, there would be an excess demand for sterling at any lower exchange rate on sterling. Demands for sterling would be larger because the cost of British exports in terms of foreign currencies would be lower, and supplies of sterling would be smaller because the sterling price of imports would be higher.

**Shifts of Supply and Demand Functions in Exchange Markets**

We shall now use comparative statics to show how changes in selected economic and financial conditions can shift demand and supply functions in exchange markets, thereby tending to change exchange rates. We shall pay special attention to changes in price levels, income levels, and interest rates.

### Changes in Level of British Prices and Costs Relative to Levels Abroad

Suppose, for example, that Britain experiences a domestic inflation of its price and cost levels. As the sterling prices of British products rise, the demand curve for sterling will shift to the left and downward. British goods will now be more expensive at each level of exchange rates, and British exports will be discouraged. This rise of British price levels will also shift the supply curve of sterling downward and to the right. As the prices of competing domestic products rise, the British will demand more imports at each exchange rate on the dollar.

Thus, we find that if British prices rise more than prices elsewhere, the exchange rate on sterling will tend to be lowered, both by a shift in the demand function for sterling downward and to the left and by a shift in the supply function of sterling downward and to the right. When a country inflates its domestic price levels significantly while prices elsewhere remain relatively constant, it usually cannot balance its receipts and payments without reducing its exchange rate to maintain its exports and discourage imports.

### Changes in Level of Real Income in Britain

A rise of real income in Britain would tend to increase British imports at each level of exchange rates and thereby to increase the supply of sterling in exchange markets. It would therefore tend to lower the sterling exchange rate if the demand schedule for sterling remained constant. On the other hand, a fall of real income in Britain would tend to decrease the British demand for imports at each exchange rate, to decrease the supply of sterling at each exchange rate, and to raise the sterling rate in exchange markets.

### Changes in Level of Real Income in the Rest of the World

An increase of real incomes in the rest of the world tends to raise the demand for British exports at each exchange rate, to increase the demand for sterling at each exchange rate, and to raise the rate on sterling. Note that, to the extent that the rise of foreign demands for British exports is allowed to raise the exchange rate on sterling. Britain may be enabled to escape inflationary effects on its domestic price level. On the other hand, a decline of real incomes abroad tends to decrease the demand for British exports at each exchange rate, to lower the demand for sterling at each rate, and to reduce the exchange rate on sterling. By allowing the sterling exchange rate to fall, thereby making British exports cheaper in foreign moneys, Britain may be able to reduce the extent to which the decrease of foreign demand will reduce British exports, and may do this without reducing the sterling prices of its exports.

### Changes in Level of Interest Rates in Britain Relative to Levels Elsewhere

Suppose that British interest rates rise relative to those elsewhere. This will at least reduce capital outflows from Britain, and may induce inflows. Thus, by decreasing the supply of sterling or increasing the demand for sterling, it will tend to raise the sterling exchange rate. A fall of interest rates in Britain relative to levels elsewhere tends to have the opposite effect, that is, to reduce the demand for sterling and increase the supply of sterling for international capital flow purposes.

### Changes in Expectations Concerning Future Sterling Exchange Rates

Changes in expectations may be very important in evoking speculative capital flows. Suppose, for example, that there arise expectations that the rate on sterling will fall sharply in the future. The demand curve for sterling may be shifted to the left and downward immediately as people postpone their purchases of sterling. The supply curve of sterling may be shifted to the right and downward as people sell sterling and buy foreign moneys. Both the decrease in the demand for sterling and the increase in its supply will cause a decrease in the exchange rate on sterling. This decline in the sterling rate will, of course, stimulate British exports and discourage British imports.

Quite evidently, in a system of flexible exchange rates there are many factors that can cause movements in exchange rates. We shall now discuss exchange rate determination in the presence of government intervention in the foreign exchange market.

**PEGGED EXCHANGE RATES** Until quite recently the most common exchange rate policy has been that of pegging exchange rates within narrow limits over considerable periods of time. Almost all of the major national currencies were interlinked through fixed rates under the international gold standard that prevailed during the years preceding World War I. Most nations returned to pegged rates during the 1920s following the breakdown of the old system during World War I. After World War II, an international organization known as the International Monetary Fund (IMF) was established to oversee the functioning of the pegged exchange rate system. Under the initial IMF agreements the exchange rate was permitted to fluctuate within a band from 1 percent above to 1 percent below some fixed rate. Thus, for example, if the dollar price of the British pound was pegged at $2.40, the actual exchange rate could fluctuate between $2.38 and $2.42. We shall discuss the functions of the IMF in greater detail in the next chapter.

The technique of pegging exchange rates, like that of pegging the price of wheat, the price of gold, or the price of a government security, is basically simple. A monetary authority or someone else stands ready to supply at some fixed price all the nation's money that is demanded from it at that price, and to demand at some fixed price all the nation's money that is offered to it at that price. As we saw earlier, actual transactions take place in the foreign exchange market when national moneys are bought and sold. For example, suppose that the British monetary authority undertakes to prevent the exchange rate on sterling from rising above $2.42 and from falling below $2.38. Whenever the exchange rate on the pound rises to $2.42 (that is, when the rate on the dollar falls to £1/$2.42), the monetary authority uses sterling to demand dollars. On the other hand, when the exchange rate on the pound falls to $2.38 (i.e., the exchange rate on the dollar rises to £1/$2.38), the monetary authority sells dollars in exchange for sterling. For this purpose it needs a sufficient supply of dollars, gold, or other official reserve assets that can be sold for dollars, or the ability to borrow dollars.

If nonofficial demands for and supplies of sterling are such as to equalize the demand for and the supply of sterling at some rate between $2.42 and $2.38, the government authority need not intervene at all. But the supply of sterling may exceed other demands for it at the support price. For example, at the rate £1 = $2.38 the supply of sterling may greatly exceed other demands for sterling, so that the authority must sell large amounts of its gold and foreign exchange holdings to buy an amount of sterling equal to the difference between its supply and the demand. Such a situation is depicted in Figure 22–2, where the amount

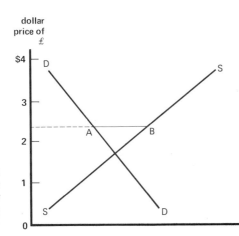

*Disequilibrium with pegged exchange rates*

**FIGURE 22–2**

of disequilibrium is indicated by AB. If this disequilibrium continues for very long, Britain may be drained of all its holdings of gold and foreign exchange.

It should be noted that a government can intervene in the foreign exchange market to influence exchange rate behavior without committing itself to pegging the exchange rate at a particular level for any length of time. When central banks intervene intermittently, we have a system that combines features of freely floating and pegged exchange rate systems. Such a combined system of exchange rate determination is known as a *managed float* or sometimes, more pejoratively, as a *dirty float*. We shall describe the considerations that influence a nation's choice of an exchange rate system in the following chapter.

**FORWARD EXCHANGE MARKETS**

Trading in foreign exchange markets includes not only currencies for immediate delivery, or *spot exchange*, but also *forward exchanges*, or currencies to be delivered on a specified date in the future. Forward contracts generally mature in 30, 60, 90, or more days from the date of execution. Transactions in forward exchange markets are similar to futures transactions in commodity markets.

Participants in forward exchange markets have several different purposes. One is to speculate. For example, suppose today's exchange rate on sterling for delivery in 90 days is £1 = $2.30. A speculator will contract to buy sterling at this rate if she believes that the spot exchange rate in 90 days will be higher than £1 = $2.30. On the other hand, she will sell sterling forward (i.e., promise to deliver sterling in 90 days) if she believes that she will be able to cover the contract by purchasing spot sterling at a rate less than £1 = $2.30 three months hence.

A second major function of forward exchange markets is to reduce exchange risks in international transactions. The following example illustrates the presence of exchange risk in international trade and shows how traders protect themselves from it.

Suppose that an American importer of British goods is obliged to pay the shipper in sterling 90 days hence. The importer can simply wait until the payment is due and then go to the spot market and purchase enough sterling to cover the obligation. However, if he postpones the purchase of sterling for 90 days, he runs the risk that the dollar price of sterling will rise in the interim, thus increasing the dollar equivalent of his original sterling liability. To avoid this risk, the importer can go to the forward exchange market to purchase a contract that promises delivery in 90 days of enough sterling to cover his sterling obligation. This type of transaction in the foreign exchange market is called *hedging*. Hedging reduces or eliminates exchange risk for international traders. International borrowers and lenders also use the forward exchange market to eliminate or reduce their exposure to exchange risk.

Because the currency in which an international loan is denominated may decline in value before the loan is repaid, international lenders face exchange risk. On the other hand, international borrowers face the risk that the currency in which their borrowings are denominated may increase in value before the debts are repaid, thus increasing their liabilities. The forward exchange market allows borrowers and lenders who do not want to risk an exchange rate change to "cover" the exchange risk and insure the domestic currency value of their debts or assets. Such transactions are called *covered interest arbitrage*.

Covered interest arbitrage is not complex in principle, but its mechanics are difficult to remember. An *interest arbitrageur* is an international lender (borrower) who compares interest rates across countries looking for the highest yield (the lowest-cost funds). However, the decisions of interest arbitrageurs are also influenced by spot and forward exchange rates. The following example shows how interest rates and exchange rates interact to determine the most profitable course of action.

We concentrate on two countries, the United States and Britain, and assume that an American lender wishes to invest funds for three months in a government security of one of the two countries. A simplistic approach, which ignores the possibility of changes in the exchange rate, is to compare the U.S. interest rate, $r$, to the British interest rate, $r^*$, and invest in Britain if $r^* > r$. However, to avoid the risk associated with potential changes in the exchange rate, the lender must calculate the rate of return of a series of transactions. More specifically, if our investor starts with $1,000 and wishes to make a covered investment in a British government security, she must take the following steps:

1 Convert her initial pool of dollars into sterling at the spot exchange rate. If the dollar price of sterling in the spot market is denoted by $s$, this conversion will produce $1,000/s$ pounds.

2 Take the proceeds of this conversion and purchase a three-month British government security. Since for every pound invested this will yield $(1 + r^\circ)$ pounds, she will receive sterling proceeds after three months of $1,000 (1 + r^*)/s$.

3 Simultaneous to purchasing the security, she makes a forward sale of the sterling proceeds she will receive when the bill matures. If we denote by $f$ the dollar price of sterling for delivery 90 days hence, the value of her proceeds in dollars can be expressed as

$$1,000 (1 + r^*) \left(\frac{f}{s}\right)$$

Of course, to see whether this is the better of the two investment decisions our lender must compare this amount with the amount forthcoming from investing $1,000 in a three-month U.S. Treasury bill. This amount is clearly 1,000 $(1 + r)$ dollars. Thus, for covered interest arbitrage to be more profitable than an investment in a U.S. Treasury bill, it is necessary that

$$1,000 \ (1 + r) < \ 1,000 \ (1 + r^\circ) \left(\frac{f}{s}\right)$$

Another way to write this condition is

$$\frac{1 + r}{1 + r^\circ} < f/s$$

In this form the condition can be interpreted as follows: Covered interest arbitrage investment in British securities is profitable when the proportion by which the U.S. interest rate exceeds the British interest rate is less than the proportional forward premium on the pound (i.e., $f/s$). This condition indicates that for foreign investment to be profitable it is not necessary that the foreign interest rate exceed the domestic interest rate. If sterling is trading at a forward premium $(f > s)$, interest arbitrageurs might profit by investment in Britain even if Britain has a lower interest rate. Whenever market conditions fail to yield equality between the two sides of the above condition, capital movements are profitable in one direction or the other.

---

CONCLUSION

In this chapter we identified three broad categories of international transactions that give rise to payments between American entities and the rest of the world. We discussed the components of a nation's balance-of-payments accounts and the meaning of payments imbalances. We explained the functioning of foreign exchange markets and the difference between fully floating and pegged exchange rates. Finally, we discussed the purposes of the forward exchange market. In the following chapter we will discuss the institutional features of the international financial system and international financial relationships.

SELECTED READINGS

Chacholiades, M., *International Monetary Theory and Policy*, New York, McGraw-Hill, 1978.

Stern, R., *The Balance of Payments*, Chicago, Aldine, 1973.

Yaeger, L. B., *International Monetary Relationships*, 2nd ed., New York, Harper & Row, 1976.

The preceding chapter discussed international transactions and foreign exchange markets. This chapter will survey the principal institutional arrangements that facilitate international payments.

The international financial system is composed of more than 150 national monetary systems, each of which has its own central bank and determines its own monetary policy. The principal components of each national monetary system are its central bank and financial intermediaries. In addition, there exists one truly international monetary institution, the International Monetary Fund (IMF), which operates through the various national monetary authorities, serving as a source of international liquidity for them and as a channel for consultation and cooperation.

## BANKS AND INTERNATIONAL PAYMENTS

The process of making international payments is greatly facilitated by a network of banking offices within each country and by interrelationships among the banks of the different countries. We have already seen how the thousands of banks in the United States are intertwined in a nationwide system for clearing and collection and in a correspondent banking system. Practically every bank in the country has a correspondent relationship with a bank in New York or with some larger bank that, in turn, has a correspondent in New York. Thus, virtually every bank, large or small, is enabled to provide its customers who wish to make payments abroad with checks drawn on a well-known New York or other metropolitan bank and even with checks drawn on foreign banks with which its city correspondent maintains close relations. In most other countries similar results are achieved through nationwide branch banking systems.

The financial centers and commercial banking networks of various countries are interconnected in two principal ways. First of all, many of the world's largest banks, including such U.S. banks as Chase Manhattan, First National City Bank, Bank of America, Continental Illinois Trust, and Morgan Guaranty Trust operate foreign branches. Foreign branches usually become members of the clearing and collection system of the country in which they are located, establish relations with banks in that country, and engage in banking activity insofar as the laws of the country permit it. For the head office and its correspondents and customers, foreign branches perform many types of services. They supply credit and market information, draw and sell drafts, collect drafts, pay drafts, accept drafts, and so on. In addition to their foreign branches, some American banks have established subsidiaries for the primary purpose of financing international trade. These finance not only trade between the United States and other countries but also trade among foreign countries. Also, some American banks have joined with banks of other countries in establishing and operating banks abroad.

The second type of international connection between commercial banks takes the form of international correspondent relationships. The nature of these relationships can be illustrated by a hypothetical example in which the Chase Manhattan Bank of New York and the Midland Bank, Ltd., of London became correspondents of each other. Under such arrangements each performs many services for the other, compensation being fixed by prior agreement or by later negotiation. Each acts for the other and for the customers and correspondents of the other in paying and collecting checks and other items, presenting bills of exchange for acceptance, and buying and selling securities, and at least one of the banks maintains a deposit account with the other.

It is easy to see how this vast network of correspondent relationships facilitates international payments. Americans are enabled to make payments abroad with written, telegraphic, or cable orders drawn by their banks on American banks or on foreign correspondent banks. And foreigners can make payments in the United States with written, telegraphic, or cable orders drawn by foreign banks on foreign—or U.S.—correspondent banks.

While we have emphasized the importance of commercial banks in international transactions, these transactions have come to play a critical role in the economic well-being of commercial banks. Between 1970 and 1976 the top ten commercial banks in the United States achieved a 30 percent annual rate of growth in overseas earnings. From just $167 million, or $17\frac{1}{2}$ percent of total profits in 1970, their overseas contribution jumped to $825 million, or over half of total profits, in 1976. However, in 1977 and 1978 the overseas earnings of American banks grew by only 10 percent a year, and much of the 1977–1978 increase in overseas earnings came from specialist, fee-based activities such as foreign exchange trading and loan syndications. Figure 23–1 summarizes the sources and uses of funds of overseas branches of American banks as recorded in 1978.

THE
EURODOLLAR
MARKET

Much of the recent rapid growth in the overseas profits of U.S. banks was a result of their participation in the Eurodollar market. *Eurodollars* are dollar-denominated deposits in foreign commercial banks and in the foreign branches of U.S. banks. The phrase "dollar-denominated" signifies that the deposit, which, for example, might be held at a German commercial bank, is stated in terms of dollars rather than in the local currency, which in this case is marks. In this section we shall describe how such deposits might arise.

The Eurodollar market is one of the leading institutions associated with international short-term capital mobility. The Eurodollar market deals in loans and interest-bearing time deposits. It is like any other market for bank loans and bank deposits, except that Eurocurrency transactions are not denominated in the currency of the country in which they take place. Most of the banks issuing Eurodollar deposits are located in Britain and continental Europe. However, banks in the Bahamas, Canada, and Southeast Asia also participate in the Eurodollar market. The term *Eurodollar* is becoming obsolete not only because banks outside continental Europe participate in the "Eurodollar" market but also because banks located in some countries are now issuing deposits denominated in other foreign currencies, such as British sterling, Dutch guilders, German marks, and Swiss francs.

A Sample
Transaction

The following example illustrates a typical Eurodollar transaction. Suppose a large corporation, say IBM, moves $5 million from its account at Chase in New York to a time deposit account at the London branch of

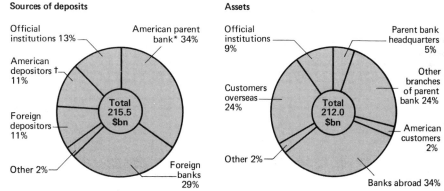

*Sources of deposits*

Official institutions 13% — American parent bank* 34%
American depositors † 11%
Foreign depositors 11%
Other 2%
Foreign banks 29%

**Total 215.5 $bn**

*Assets*

Official institutions 9% — Parent bank headquarters 5%
Customers overseas 24% — Other branches of parent bank 24%
Other 2% — American customers 2%
Banks abroad 34%

**Total 212.0 $bn**

*Where the money comes from . . . and where it goes (overseas branches of American banks, September 1978)*
Source: *The Economist*, March 31, 1979.

**FIGURE 23–1**

*Plus overseas branches of parent bank. † Including other banks.

Citibank.¹ It is simplest to think of IBM as writing a check against Chase and depositing it in Citibank, London, but the actual transaction is effected by wire or telex. Of course, the deposit at Citi London is denominated in dollars.

Table 23–1 spells out what happens to the various balance sheets. It shows that IBM exchanges one asset, $5 million of demand deposits at Chase in New York, for another, $5 million of Euro time deposits at Citi London. As a result of this transaction, Chase loses $5 million in reserves and demand deposits. These reserves and deposits are gained by Citibank, but as Table 23–1 shows, the accounting is a bit complicated. In effect, Citi London has received the deposit but Citi New York has received the reserves. Consequently, Citi New York owes Citi London money, which is reflected in the item "New York office dollar account." This can be thought of as a checking account that Citi London holds with Citi New York. It thus shows up on the asset side of the balance sheet of Citi London and on the liability side of Citi New York (as "London office dollar account").

Two things are noteworthy about Table 23–1. First, while IBM thinks of itself as now holding dollars in London, the dollars never actually left the United States. All that happened was a shift of reserves from Chase to Citi New York. The second point is that Table 23–1 is not the end of the story. Citibank in London, which has a new time deposit on which it has to pay interest, is naturally going to lend those dollars out. As we saw in our discussion of domestic bank expansion, this will set up

¹ With the exception of call money, Eurodeposits have a fixed term. These terms vary from overnight to five years, although the bulk of the transactions are for six months or less.

**TABLE 23–1**

*A sample Eurodollar transaction*

| IBM | | CHASE, NEW YORK | |
|---|---|---|---|
| ASSETS | LIABILITIES | ASSETS | LIABILITIES |
| Demand deposits, Chase, N.Y. −$5 million Euro time deposits Citi London +$5 million | | Reserves −$5 million | Demand deposits −$5 million |

| CITI N.Y. | | CITI LONDON | |
|---|---|---|---|
| ASSETS | LIABILITIES | ASSETS | LIABILITIES |
| Reserves +$5 million | London office dollar account +$5 million | New York office dollar account +$5 million | Euro time deposits + $5 million |

a process of multiple expansion of Eurodollars. The precise size of the multiplier will depend on the size of various leakages (e.g., of deposits out of the Eurobank system and back to the United States) and on reserve requirements. While the details of this process need not concern us, it should be noted that as a result of both initial injections of Eurodollars and the subsequent multiplier process, the Eurodollar market has grown from $65 billion at the end of 1970 to some $450 billion in mid-1979.

**Eurodollars as a Source of Commercial Bank Funds**

As noted previously, commercial banks in the United States have increasingly tended to rely on nondeposit liabilities as a source of funds. They have, for example, made extensive use of the federal funds market to acquire reserves and lendable funds. In this same spirit, they have at various times utilized the Eurodollar market for similar purposes.

The most critical use of Eurodollars as a source of funds for commercial banks in the United States took place in the late 1960s. In particular, in 1968 and 1969 the Regulation Q ceiling kept interest rates on certificates of deposit below those available on other money market instruments. As a consequence, lenders who would normally have purchased CDs turned to other outlets, including Eurodeposits. Commercial banks in the United States, in turn, borrowed these funds back from their overseas branches (the mechanics are, in effect, spelled out in Table 23–1). After 1970, with the lifting of the ceiling on large CDs, commercial banks in the United States reduced their use of Eurodollar borrowings. However, as noted in Chapter 7, beginning in 1979 banks again began making substantial use of Eurodollar borrowings. In addition, as emphasized earlier, Eurodollars more generally have permitted overseas branches of American banks to vastly expand their operations, and have contributed to American bank profits.

**Overview**

The Eurodollar market is extensive and complex. It is not the only means of transferring short- and medium-term funds across national boundaries, but it has greatly increased international capital mobility, and in so doing, it has served several important functions. First, the Eurodollar market intermediates the preferences of the suppliers and users of funds. Second, international flows of Eurodollars have improved economic efficiency: Eurodollar deposits flow from low-interest-rate countries to high-interest-rate countries and thereby reduce interest differentials among nations. However, the Eurodollar market has also compounded the problems of countries whose policy objectives require control of international capital movements.

The Eurodollar market and related international capital markets underwent a severe test after the oil price increase of 1973. In 1974 the oil-exporting countries' export revenues exceeded their import payments by nearly $60 billion. That sum constituted an enormous transfer of purchasing power from oil importers to oil exporters. For the most part, importers sold securities to pay their oil bills. If the exporters had been willing to hold the securities that the importers sold, the purchasing power transfer would not have disturbed international capital markets. However, oil exporters sought highly liquid, low-risk, short-term investments while oil importers were selling longer-term, riskier assets. Eurocurrency banks were hard pressed to find borrowers who would absorb all of the funds that oil exporters had placed in short-term deposits. They found themselves exposed to great risk because their deposits had grown rapidly while their equity capital had remained unchanged. A few banks failed as a result of unsuccessful forward exchange dealings. However, for the most part the system hung together in the face of this massive disturbance.

**CENTRAL BANKS AND INTERNATIONAL LIQUIDITY**

Each nation makes most of its payments to other countries by transferring to them deposit claims against banks. The major source of a nation's capacity to make payments to others is its flow of current receipts from these other countries. However, as noted in the preceding chapter, not infrequently a nation's residents collectively need to be able to spend abroad more than they receive in payments from abroad. In such cases a nation requires a stock of reserve assets that will be acceptable as payment in other countries. This is comparable to an individual's need for a stock of money balances to bridge the gap between excess expenditure and receipts. One of the earliest functions of central banks was to serve as a custodian of the nation's international reserves.

A nation can prepare for a future excess of international payments over international receipts by holding a stock of assets in the form of claims on foreign money or claims on other assets that are readily exchanged for foreign money. For reasons described earlier, gold has long been a popular form of international reserves. However, gold has some disadvantages for its holders. Perhaps most important, it yields no interest or other explicit income. Also, its shipment to make payments is expensive and requires time. It should not be surprising, therefore, that nations have sought some form of asset that would be as good as gold, or almost as good, in terms of acceptability, and would be better than gold in the sense that it would not be inconvenient or costly to ship and would yield an income. Indeed, the importance of gold as a reserve asset has declined markedly over the years.

Most countries now hold the largest part of their international reserves in the form of claims against foreign moneys. The U.S. dollar is by far the most important international reserve currency; however, nations also hold some other currencies for this purpose, including British sterling, German deutsche marks, and Swiss francs. These claims against dollars and other reserve currencies take several forms, such as deposit claims against the central bank, demand deposits against commercial banks, time deposits, Treasury bills, and other short-term government securities. Generally, nations hold working balances of reserves in the form of demand deposits and other nonearning claims and place the remainder of their international reserves in earning assets.

Income-yielding claims against a foreign money may be considered superior to gold as an international reserve as long as that money is freely convertible or exchangeable into the moneys of other nations and there is confidence that it will not depreciate in terms of gold or other moneys. But if fears arise that the money will depreciate, an international reserve system depending heavily on claims against national moneys can create problems not only for the country whose money is used as a reserve but also for the world's monetary system.

The responsibilities of a central bank in the international financial system do not end with serving as a custodian of a nation's international reserves. As we saw in the preceding chapter, a central bank may intervene in the foreign exchange market to influence exchange rate behavior. Where a central bank intervenes to keep the exchange rate from reaching its equilibrium level—that is, to keep the exchange rate from reaching the level at which the nation's international receipts equal its international payments, the central bank must make sure that its international reserve position is adequate to meet the demands for foreign payments that may arise.

The need for international reserves raises some of the most difficult and controversial questions in the field of international financial policy. These include the following:

1    How much international liquidity do nations need, both individually and collectively? This obviously depends in part on the behavior of flows of receipts and payments, because these determine the size of the payments gap that needs to be bridged. In addition, the need for international liquidity depends on the central bank's exchange rate policy. We shall discuss exchange rate policies in subsequent sections of this chapter.

2    On what sources of liquidity should nations rely? To what extent should they rely on holdings of assets in the form of foreign money or things that can be readily exchanged for foreign money, and to what extent on arrangements for borrowing foreign money when needed? What forms of assets should they hold and in what proportions? What types of borrowing arrangements should be made?

3    Who should manage the international liquidity positions of nations, both individually and collectively? To what extent should

this be done by private sectors, by individual central banks and governments, by central banks in cooperation, and by international institutions?

Central banks also serve as agencies for international monetary co-operation. One of the most important forms of central-bank cooperation is the extension of credit among central banks. Some central banks borrow from others to meet unusual short-term needs for international reserves. These loans can take many forms. In some cases, these are bi-lateral transactions; in other cases, large numbers of central banks are involved. For example, ten or more central banks sometimes participate in a loan to a country that is experiencing or is threatened with a crisis in its balance of payments. Central banks also enter into *reciprocal currency* or *swap* agreements in which one agrees to give the other a certain amount of its own money in exchange for an equivalent amount of the money of the other and each allows the other free use of the swapped money as it is needed.

Often central-bank cooperation is orchestrated by the IMF. In the following section we shall explore the role of the IMF in the international financial system.

## THE INTERNATIONAL MONETARY FUND

The International Monetary Fund is an international financial institution established in 1946 as a result of a conference held in Bretton Woods, New Hampshire, in July 1944. The Fund has many purposes, of which the following are the most important:

1   Reestablishment of a system of free multilateral payments, and reduction of other barriers to trade. During the Great Depression and World War II, many countries had adopted various types of exchange restrictions—limitations on freedom to make payments to other countries. One purpose of the Fund was to eliminate these as quickly as possible and to work toward lowering other trade barriers as well.

2   Provision of an orderly system for setting and altering exchange rates. During the period following World War II and into the 1970s, the Fund agreement provided that each member country establish with the Fund an initial exchange rate, and that the exchange rate should thereafter be kept within narrow limits except when the Fund gave permission for a change "to correct a fundamental disequilibrium." In 1978 the IMF officially altered its articles to permit its member countries to choose the option of a floating exchange rate. Floating, however, had been widespread since the early 1970s.

3   Provision of financial aid to member countries needing assistance to meet actual or threatened deficits in their balance of payments.

It is in this function of the Fund as a source of international liquidity that we are especially interested.

**Financial Aid by the Fund**

The transactions through which the Fund makes foreign moneys available to a member are called *sales of currencies* or *drawings on the Fund*. The drawing country obtains foreign money in return for an equal amount of claims on its own money. The amount a country can obtain in this way is related to its quota—the amount of gold and its own currency that it has contributed to the fund—although by presenting justification acceptable to the Fund it can exceed its quota.[2] When a country draws funds that exceed the amount of gold it has subscribed to the Fund, new international reserves are created. In effect, other members, through the intermediary of the Fund, have extended credit to help finance the drawing members's needs. It should be evident, then, that through this mechanism the Fund contributes to the provision of international liquidity. In recent years it has developed another important way to supply international reserve assets: through the use of Special Drawing Rights.

**Special Drawing Rights**

At the beginning of 1970, as mentioned earlier, the IMF initiated a scheme for the creation and issue of special drawing rights (SDRs), sometimes referred to as *paper gold*. These are unconditional rights to draw currencies of other countries and are described by the IMF as "unconditional reserve assets created by the Fund to influence the level of world reserves; they are allocated to participating members in proportion to their Fund quotas."

Since the middle of 1974 SDRs have been valued by using an index constructed from a "market basket" of currencies. In May 1979 there were somewhat over 12 billion SDRs outstanding, and each SDR was valued above $1.30.

SDRs, then, are intended to be used in a fashion similar to foreign exchange reserves in financing balance-of-payments deficits. Within certain limits, members can transfer their SDRs to other members, who are rquired to accept them in international payments. The receiving country thus extends credit to the paying country. With the development of SDRs, the IMF took a step toward becoming an international central bank in that it now issues liabilities that are acceptable as international money. However, the creation of new SDRs requires approval by Fund members, so that considerations of international politics an well influence the outcome.

Nevertheless, it seems likely that SDRs or some similar type of asset

---

[2] By July 1978 the Fund had 137 members, whose quotas totaled $50,714.6 million. The quota of the United States, $10,926.5 million, is by far the largest, accounting for 21.5 percent of the total.

will play an increasing role in the international liquidity system in the future. Such a scheme provides a mechanism through which the world can deliberately regulate the size of total international reserves and their rate of growth, rather than allow them to be determined by the vagaries of gold production, nonmonetary demands for gold, and the balance-of-payments position of a major nation such as the United States.

**Total International Reserves**

We have touched on several types of international reserves but not yet given a complete picture. This is provided in Table 23–2, which shows the international reserve position as of May 1979 for the United States, and the total international reserves of all countries that are members of the IMF. As officially defined by the IMF, the *international reserve position* of a country is the sum of the holdings of gold, SDRs, and foreign exchange by the country's government and central bank plus its reserve position in the IMF. The last-named item is any unused part of its gold quota at the Fund against which it can draw automatically.

As evident from Table 23–2, for IMF members countries as a whole, the bulk of international reserves consists of official holdings of foreign exchange.[3] To a large extent these consist of claims against American dollars. While total reserves appear sizable, what is masked by Table 23–2 is the fact (which is not surprising) that reserves are unevenly distributed across countries. As a consequence, some countries are much better able to withstand balance-of-payments shocks (e.g., oil price increases). We shall examine the effects of this difference as we proceed.

**INTERNATIONAL ADJUSTMENT MECHANISMS**

We noted in the preceding chapter that, in principle, a nation that allows its exchange rate to float freely never experiences a disequilibrium in its balance of payments. Its exchange rate is free to increase or decrease to a

---

[3] The reader should be alerted to one problem with Table 23–2 — the valuation of gold reserves. For purposes of the table, gold is valued at its "official price" per ounce of 35 SDRs, or about $45.50. The market value of this gold is clearly many times this figure. It is with this problem in mind that the IMF has recently taken to reporting gold in ounces rather than in dollars.

---

**TABLE 23–2**

*Official international reserves, United States and world (end of May 1979, in billions of dollars)*

| | United States | All countries |
|---|---|---|
| IMF reserve position | $ 1.2 | $ 17.0 |
| Special drawing rights (SDRs) | 2.6 | 15.9 |
| Foreign exchange | 7.1 | 301.3 |
| Gold | 11.4 | 42.4 |
| Total | $22.2 | $376.6 |

level that equates demand and supply in the foreign exchange market and, equivalently, which equates the nation's international receipts and payments. However, historically many nations have been unwilling to let their exchange rate adjust to clear the foreign exchange market. These nations have pegged their exchange rates through intervention in the foreign exchange market, that is, by adding to or subtracting from their stocks of international reserve assets or by borrowing reserves to meet their needs for international liquidity. Indeed, as we have just seen, the concept of pegged exchange rates was a cornerstone of IMF policy for thirty years.

The existence of international reserve assets and international borrowing facilities do not free a nation from the need to balance its international receipts and payments over a longer period. A country with large and persistent deficits would exhaust its holdings of international reserves and also its borrowing facilities. On the other hand, a country with large and persistent surpluses would be forced to purchase large amounts of foreign exchange and other international reserve assets, thereby creating reserves for its commercial banks and a potential for domestic price inflation. We shall now discuss some of the methods by which a country can equilibrate its balance of international payments in a regime of pegged exchange rates.

What policy should a nation follow when it faces a disequilibrium in its balance of international payments and is balancing its receipts and payments only by drawing down its holdings of international reserve assets or building up large short-term debts to foreigners? Historically, this has been one of the most important policy problems in the entire field of international finance. The nation may, of course, adjust its exchange rate to equalize the demand for and supply of its currency and, equivalently, to equalize its international payments and receipts. Or it may resort to direct controls over its trade and payments in order to eliminate the payments imbalance. However, we shall examine a hypothetical example in which Britain runs a balance-of-payments deficit at its pegged exchange rate of £1 = $2.38 and refuses to resort to exchange rate adjustment or exchange controls to eliminate the payments imbalance.

Figure 23–2 indicates that the drain on Britain's international reserves at the pegged exchange rate of £1 = $2.38 can be ended only by developments that will shift the demand curve for sterling upward and to the right (e.g., from $DD$ to $D^1D^1$) and shift the supply curve for sterling upward and to the left (e.g., from $SS$ to $S^1S^1$), or shift both to a sufficient extent to equalize the demand for sterling and the supply of sterling at a rate equal to or more than £1 = $2.38. Several types of developments in other countries can assist in this process:

1   A rise in price levels abroad would increase the demand for
    sterling at each exchange rate by increasing the demand for
    British exports. It would also tend to reduce the supply of sterling
    by discouraging British imports.
2   A rise in real incomes abroad would shift the demand curve for
    sterling to the right.
3   A decrease in interest rates abroad, to the extent that it lessened
    capital flows out of Britain and induced or increased a flow of
    capital to Britain, would reduce the supply of, and raise the
    demand for, sterling.

All these developments could help to raise the demand for sterling
relative to the supply of it and to ease the drain on Britain's international
reserves. However, if these developments do not occur abroad, or are not
sufficiently strong to close the payments gap, one or more of the following things will have to happen in Britain:

1   A fall of British price levels, which would tend to increase the
    demand for sterling by cheapening British exports and to decrease
    the supply of sterling by reducing British imports.
2   A fall of real income in Britain, which would decrease British
    imports and the supply of sterling.
3   A rise of interest rates, which, to the extent that it reduced the
    outflow of capital from Britain or increased capital inflows, would
    tend to reduce the supply of sterling or to raise the demand for
    sterling.

*Adjustment to
disequilibrium under
pegged exchange rates*

**FIGURE 23–2**

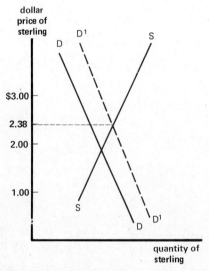

(Part *a*) Demand adjustment

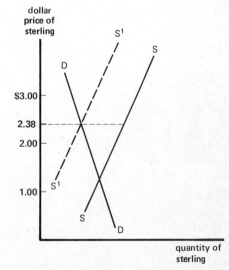

(Part *b*) Supply adjustment

Adjustments of precisely these types will tend to be made "automatically" if the deficit and surplus countries subject their monetary policies to the "discipline of their balance of payments" and "follow the rules of the international gold standard game." These rules originally applied to international gold movements, but they are also applicable to a system of pegged exchange rates in which the central bank buys and sells foreign moneys, thereby tending to create and to decrease bank reserves within the country. The essence of these rules is that the deficit country should allow its loss of gold or other international reserves to restrict its money supply, and that the surplus countries should allow their increases of gold and other international reserves to expand their money supplies.

Suppose that the deficit in the British balance of payments resulted from a decrease of its exports as other countries shifted their demand from British products to their home products. First there are the income effects. Both the decline of demand for its exports and the induced decrease of consumption expenditures at home serve to lower total demands for British output. In the surplus countries the opposite occurs; demands for their output are increased both by the shift from British products to home products and by the induced rise of consumption expenditures.

Then there are the monetary effects. As the Bank of England makes net sales of international reserve assets, it reduces the reserves of British banks, thereby tending to restrict credit and to raise interest rates. It can accentuate monetary restriction by selling securities or calling loans. The monetary restriction and rise of interest rates in Britain serve both to attract funds from abroad (or at least to reduce outflows) and to lower domestic demands for output.

As central banks in the surplus countries make net purchases of international reserve assets, they create reserves for their banks, thereby encouraging expansion of their money supplies and a decrease of interest rates. They can accentuate this if, as their international reserves increase, the central banks buy securities or expand their loans. The fall of interest rates in these surplus countries serve both to encourage outflows of funds to the deficit country and to increase demands for output in the surplus countries.

Such are the automatic processes of equilibrating international receipts and payments if both deficit and surplus countries follow the rules of the game. Capital flows to the deficit country tend to be induced by both the rise of interest rates there and the fall of rates in the surplus countries. More fundamental is the fall of demands for output in the deficit country and the rise of demands for output in the surplus countries. Suppose first that money wage rates and prices are quickly and completely flexible and that changes in demands for output are reflected only in changes in prices. The fall of prices in the deficit country and the rise of prices in the surplus countries will serve to equate international receipts and payments by increasing exports and decreasing imports in the deficit country, and causing the reverse effects in the surplus countries. Thus, if money wage rates and prices are quickly and completely flexible, international payments and receipts may be equated through adjustments of the price levels in the various countries.

What if money wage rates and prices are inflexible, at least in the downward direction? Changes in demands for output can still equate international receipts and payments, but by changing levels of real income. Increases of demands for output in the surplus countries can, by raising their real incomes, increase their demand for the exports of deficit countries. And the fall of demands for output in the deficit country can, by lowering its level of real output and income, decrease its expenditures for imports. The deficit country can become too poor to demand imports in excess of its current international receipts. In other words, it can eliminate the deficit in its balance of payments by creating a deficit in its real income or output.

It is easy to see why countries intent on promoting such domestic objectives as maximum employment and output, rapid economic growth, and price level stability are often highly reluctant to follow rules of the game, which require that their monetary and fiscal policies be dominated by their balance-of-payments and international reserve positions. Countries with surpluses in their balance of payments are sometimes reluctant to expand their money supply for fear of inflationary consequences. Countries with deficits are even more reluctant to follow restrictive monetary and fiscal policies if this threatens their employment and growth objectives. They often take offsetting actions, such as central-bank purchases of securities, to prevent their loss of gold or other international reserves from restricting credit and raising interest rates.

However, if a country insists on pegging its exchange rates at a fixed level and will not adopt restrictive fiscal or monetary policies despite a persistent deficit in its balance of payments, it is likely to be drained of its international reserves, to be forced to impose direct controls over its international trade and payments, or both.

**EXCHANGE RATE SYSTEMS** The preceding discussion indicates that a country's choice of balance-of-payments adjustment policies is closely related to its choices concerning exchange rate systems. For example, to the extent that a nation allows its exchange rate to float freely to eliminate surpluses and deficits, it need not rely on other methods of adjustment. On the other hand, if a country adamantly pegs its exchange rate and if its command over international reserves is limited, it can absorb deficits only for a limited period. In addition, if that country is unwilling to restrict trade and payments, it must fall back on adjustments of levels of income, prices, and interest rates, brought about by monetary and fiscal policies, to equilibrate its payments imbalances.

Evidently then, the choice of an exchange rate system is a major policy decision that critically influences the options available to a nation in dealing with imbalances in international payments. As we have already noted, there are two broad alternatives: fixed (pegged) exchange rates and floating (flexible) exchange rates. We shall now examine some of the features and controversies associated with each system. We shall first consider the general principles involved and then examine the recent history of the world's exchange rate systems.

**Flexible Exchange Rates**

The great advantage claimed for a policy of freely floating exchange rates is that it gives a nation the freedom to pursue domestic economic objectives. If its exchange rate is allowed to adjust in such a way as to equilibrate its balance of payments, a nation need not for this purpose resort to direct controls over international trade and capital movements. And it need not allow concern over the state of its balance of payments and international reserves to influence its monetary and fiscal policies. Such policies can be directed solely to promoting such domestic objectives as full employment, rapid economic growth, and relatively stable price levels.

While the advantages of flexible exchange rates would seem to be considerable, most central bankers and many economists have long resisted the idea. Among the arguments advanced against such exchange rates are the following:

1   Uncertainty as to future exchange rates creates exchange risks and may impede international trade and capital movements. For example, an American who buys exports from Britain and promises to pay in sterling runs the risk that the dollar price of sterling will rise above expected levels. And a British exporter who sells for dollars runs the risk that the sterling price of dollars will fall below expected levels. Exchange risks can be even more serious for capital movements, and especially for long-term capital. As we saw in the preceding chapter, forward exchange markets can lessen the burden of these risks, but these facilities are sometimes expensive and inadequate. They usually are not available to bear exchange risks on long-term lending and borrowing. It is, however, important to note that exchange risk is not necessarily absent under a system of pegged exchange rates, because pegged rates may be changed, sometimes by significant amounts.

2   Changes in a nation's exchange rates that are not necessary for longer-run equilibration of its receipts and payments may cause

unnecessary disturbances in that nation's economy, and especially in its import-competing and export industries. Suppose, for example, that there is an abnormal flow of short-term capital to nation A, which raises the exchange rate on its currency significantly above its longer-term equilibrium level. This increase of its exchange rate will tend to increase the cost of A's exports in terms of foreign currencies, and thus will lower output and employment in its export industries. The rise of the exchange rate will also lower the cost of imports, thus discouraging output and employment in A's import-competing industries. Such domestic disturbances resulting from erratic changes in exchange rates would not be welcome in any nation, least of all in nations heavily dependent on exports and imports.

Attitudes toward a policy of freely floating exchange rates differ widely, largely because of differences of judgment concerning the behavior patterns of rates under such a system. The optimists believe that actual rates would deviate only slightly from their longer-term equilibrium, and that through time adjustments would be relatively smooth and orderly. The pessimists disagree. A basic issue is this: Would private speculation in exchange markets be predominantly and reliably stabilizing, or would it, at least on some occasions, be destabilizing? The optimists argue essentially as follows: Private speculators, or at least those persons who speculate successfully, base their decisions on a careful analysis of the basic factors that determine the longer-run equilibrium level of an exchange rate. When the market rate rises significantly above this level, the speculator will sell the currency, thereby pushing its rate back toward equilibrium. On the other hand, if the speculator buys the currency when its price falls significantly below the long-term equilibrium level, this will tend to raise the currency's price. Thus, the speculators who make money and survive are those who correctly estimate the longer-term equilibrium level of the exchange rate and operate in a stabilizing way. Financial failure will eliminate those speculators who are wrong in their estimate of the level of the longer-term equilibrium rate or who speculate in a destabilizing way.

Pessimists challenge both the conclusion that stabilizing speculation will always predominate and the conclusion that destabilizing speculators will lose money and be eliminated. To make their point, the pessimists sometimes use stock market speculation as an analogy. They admit that much speculation in shares of stock tends to be stabilizing. However, they contend that for considerable periods of time destabilizing types of speculation may predominate and even be highly profitable. For example, suppose that at some time the price of a particular stock is already above what you consider to be its longer-run equilibrium level, but that you expect its price to rise further because of a developing *bullish* sentiment among other participants in the market. Your purchases will be destabilizing in the sense that they will tend to push the price still further above its longer-term equilibrium level, but they will be profitable if you succeed in selling before the price again falls to the level of your purchase price. Similarly, you can reap a profit by selling a stock that is already priced below its longer-run equilibrium level, thereby tending to depress the price, if you are correct in your expectations that other *bearish* sellers will depress the price still further before it rises again. Pessimists may exaggerate the dangers of destabilizing private speculation, but they properly cast doubts on the optimistic contention that such speculation will be predominantly and reliably stabilizing.

Largely because of such doubts, many advocates of flexible exchange rates favor official intervention on at least some occasions. Under such a system the authorities do not peg exchange rates within narrow limits, but they do intervene at times to buy and sell moneys in exchange markets to influence exchange rate behavior. The nature and degree of intervention vary widely. At one extreme, the authorities intervene only infrequently and only for the purpose of preventing "disorderly movements"; they do not attempt to influence the longer-term trends of exchange rates. In other cases, they intervene more frequently and do attempt to affect the level of exchange rates over longer periods. As the authorities try to hold fluctuations within narrower and narrower limits, the system assumes the characteristics of pegged exchange rates.

Official intervention under a policy of flexible exchange rates raises important problems. One problem is the estimation of the longer-term equilibrium level of an exchange rate. There is no assurance that official judgments will be any better than those of private speculators. Moreover, official decisions may be unduly influenced by pressures from economic groups such as exporters and industries competing with imports. When official intervention influences the longer-term level of an exchange rate, there is the problem of determining what that level should be. There is a real danger that some nations will try to manipulate the rate to achieve an undue national advantage. For example, nation A may try to drive down the exchange rate on its money to give greater advantage to its export industries and greater protection to its import-competing industries; nation A may do this despite the fact that it already has a surplus in its balance of payments. Nations B, C, and D may retaliate. The result may be a "war of exchange rates," with disruptive effects on trade and capital movements. Such behavior is most likely to occur in depression periods, when nations try to export their unemployment, but it is by no means unknown in periods of prosperity. These disadvantages of the manipulation of exchange rates highlight the need for an international understanding or agreement concerning the appropriate behavior of exchange rates, as well as the need for some means of promoting cooperation among national exchange authorities.

**Pegged
Exchange Rates**

One of the most controversial issues that arises under a system of pegged exchange rates is the following: What should be the relative responsibilities of surplus and deficit countries for eliminating surpluses and deficits under an international system of fixed exchange rates? Deficit countries usually reply that the surplus countries should solve the problem by increasing their imports, by lending more, or by giving more aid. Surplus countries, on the other hand, often report that the deficit countries should tighten their belts, show some self-discipline, and cease trying to live beyond their means.

Few would contend that surplus countries should make the adjustment when they are already maintaining approximately full employment and stable or rising price levels, and when the deficits of the deficit countries are clearly attributable to their own highly inflationary monetary and fiscal policies. It would be too much to ask surplus countries to eliminate their surpluses by inflating prices at a rapid rate. A more appropriate remedy in this case is for the deficit countries to reform the domestic policies that created their deficits. This may include a realistic adjustment of their exchange rates, accompanied by domestic reforms.

Consider, however, a quite different case, in which the deficit countries have relatively stable price levels and their deficits were created by a sharp fall of real incomes and output in the surplus countries. The surplus of the latter countries was created by the decline of their demands for imports. The deficit countries could, of course, eliminate their deficits by adopting deflationary policies to lower their levels of real incomes and prices. However, a more attractive alternative is for the surplus countries to adopt expansionary monetary and fiscal policies to raise their levels of real income and increase their expenditures for imports.

The following rules of conduct seem appropriate under a system of fixed exchange rates.

1  A deficit country undergoing domestic inflation should solve both problems by adopting restrictive monetary or fiscal policies.
2  A surplus country with domestic output and income well below full-employment levels should solve both problems by adopting expansionary monetary or fiscal policies.

Unhappily, there are many situations that are not covered by these rules. For example, suppose some countries have large surpluses in their balance of payments along with actual or threatened inflation, while others have deficits in their balance of payments despite the presence of unemployment and excess capacity at home. Should the surplus countries inflate still more to equate the balance of payments? Should the deficit countries create still more unemployment to eliminate their deficits? A sensible alternative, if the imbalance of international payments is large and persistent, would be to adjust exchange rates.

**Adjustments
of Pegged Rates**

Although the IMF agreements envisaged virtually a worldwide system of pegged exchange rates, they also provided for adjustments of exchange rate parities "to correct a fundamental disequilibrium." The latter term was not defined, but its general meaning was clear: Exchange rate adjustments were not only permissible but encouraged as a means of dealing with imbalances in international payments that could be remedied otherwise only at excessive cost. Faced with such a basic disequilibrium, a deficit nation should lower its exchange rate to an equilibrium level and peg it there. On the other hand, a nation with a large and persistent surplus should raise the exchange parity on its currency.

The IMF agreements provided no guidelines to regulate the size or the frequency of the adjustments of exchange parities. Such decisions were postponed until they could be based on experience. As the years have gone by, more and more economists and some public officials have come to believe that, in practice, adjustments of parities have been too infrequent and individually too large. Too often adjustments have been made only after a large maldistribution of international reserves has occurred, trade and capital movements have been restricted, and some nations have paid too high a price in terms of output and employment. Such critics believe that if a system of pegged rates is to be retained, parities should be adjusted more promptly and in steps small enough to avoid the large speculative flows of funds that are often induced by prospective large changes in exchange rates.

One proposal for accomplishing this is a scheme of "sliding" or "crawling" parities. These would provide for slow and gradual adjustments of parities in response to the behavior of actual exchange rates during a preceding period. For example, parities might be altered once a month; the parity for a currency during any month would be determined by taking the average of the actual rates for the 12 months immediately preceding the month in question. Thus, as the trend of actual market rates descended from the old parity, both the parity and the band limits would be adjusted downward, but at a pace slow enough to avoid large disturbances to capital flows. The same principles would apply as the trend of actual market rates on a currency increased from its old parity. If such automatic adjustments of parities proved to be inadequate or inappropriate, they could be supplemented or modified through discretionary changes.

**THE
EVOLUTION
OF THE
INTERNATIONAL
MONETARY
SYSTEM**

In the preceding sections we have examined the principal features of fixed and flexible exchange rate systems. We have also indicated that since the early 1970s fixed exchange rates have to a large extent been supplanted by floating rates. The purpose of this section is to explore why this development came about and, in the process, shed a bit more light on exchange rate issues.

**From World War II to 1960**

The restructuring of the international monetary system after World War II had as its foundation a system of pegged exchange rates based on the "golden dollar." Specifically, the price of gold was fixed at $35 an ounce and all other currencies were pegged in relation to this. Gold and the dollar were the two major international reserve assets, and the United States guaranteed the convertibility of dollars in the hands of foreign governments. The U.S. gold stock, which in 1946 accounted for about three quarters of all Western monetary gold, in effect became the central gold reserve for the entire world. These then were the essential elements of the international monetary system as reconstituted at the end of World War II.

In the years immediately following World War II, while war-torn and war-deprived countries were still in the process of restocking and reconstruction, demands for American exports were almost insatiable. Our net exports of goods and services were large enough to enable us to make large loans and grants of foreign aid to the rest of the world and still increase our gold reserves.

By the end of 1949 our gold stock had reached the huge value of $24.6 billion, which was about two-thirds of the world total. However, the situation began to change at about the time of the outbreak of war in Korea, and the large surplus in the U.S. balance of payments was gradually replaced by chronic deficits. Major contributors to this turnabout were the recovery of productive capacity in other major industrial countries, the devaluation of the British pound and several other currencies in 1949, and inflation in the United States during the Korean conflict.

As a result of the large and prolonged deficits in the United States, foreign central bankers added to their foreign exchange reserves by accumulating substantial volumes of dollar claims. Of course, some of these dollars were turned back to the United States for gold, and as shown in Figure 23–3, the net international reserve position of the United States declined markedly. As Figure 23–3 also shows, by 1960 short-term dollar liabilities to foreigners exceeded U.S. international reserves. In essence, the United States was a banker whose ability to deliver on demand was called into question.

**Signs of Strain, 1960–1967**

From their first appearance, in 1950, until about 1960, deficits in the American balance of payments were welcomed as almost wholly beneficial to the rest of the world. Our deficits provided the rest of the world with tremendous amounts of liquidity in the form of both gold and claims on dollars. Attitudes toward deficits in the U.S. balance of payments had begun to change by 1960, and they changed even more during the following years as the deficits continued, as American international reserves shrank and its liquid liabilities to foreigners rose, and as it became increasing clear that the United States would not follow monetary and fiscal policies restrictive enough to terminate the deficits. Deficits that were earlier considered to be beneficial to the world as a whole now came to be regarded as at best dangerous and at worst catastrophic for the international monetary system.

Major criticisms of the balance-of-payments situation were of two related types. The first was that if American deficits were not eradicated, or at least reduced markedly, confidence in the exchange rate on the dollar would deteriorate and the dollar would depreciate in terms of gold. A second criticism was that it was basically unsound to allow the world's supplies of international reserves and liquidity to be so heavily influenced, and even dominated, by the state of the American balance of payments.

As U.S. deficits persisted into the 1960s, the nation's international reserves continued to decline and its liabilities to foreigners grew markedly. This situation gave rise to speculation that the United States might devalue the dollar, thus increasing the value of its gold stock. The price of gold on the London market rose to $40 an ounce. This raised the possibility that foreign central banks would turn in dollars for gold at $35 and resell the gold at a higher price. However, a crisis was avoided when a group of leading central banks banded together to form a *gold pool* aimed at keeping the price of gold at $35. Although the gold market continued to be subjected to speculative waves, the international monetary system managed to limp along. But then, in late 1967, another crisis struck.

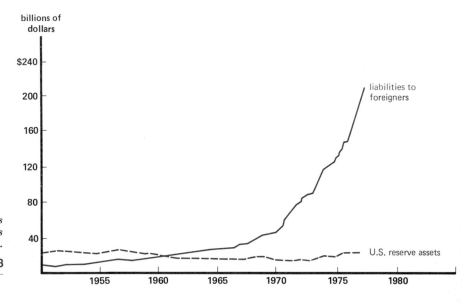

*International reserves and foreign liabilities of the United States.*

**FIGURE 23-3**

**Increasing tension,**
**Late 1967–**
**Late 1971**

In late 1967, with the Vietnam War accelerating the outflow of dollars, it became apparent that attempts to maintain the gold price at $35 would substantially drain the resources of the gold pool. As a consequence, in March 1968 the central banks in the gold pool threw in the towel and a new so-called *two-tier* gold policy was introduced. Under this policy, which sharply distinguished between monetary gold and private gold, the price of gold in the free market was no longer pegged at $35. Existing gold stocks of central banks were still a reserve asset suitable for official international settlements, but only at $35 an ounce. At the same time, the United States stood ready to buy and sell gold for "legitimate monetary purposes" at this price. These actions temporarily served to avert the crisis, but the introduction of the two-tier system did little to solve the longer-run question of international liquidity.

The U.S. gold stock continued to decline, and the U.S. balance of payments continued to deteriorate in a dramatic fashion. In 1970 the deficit on the official reserve-transactions basis was a huge $10 billion, and this soared to over $20 billion for the first three quarters of 1971. Other countries were forced to buy up huge quantities of dollars to maintain fixed exchange rates. As a consequence, in the first four months of 1971 alone, dollar holdings of foreign central banks mushroomed from $20 billion to $32 billion. The new effect was that these countries found themselves losing control over their domestic money supplies. West Germany and the Netherlands were the first to give up the game. Both abandoned fixed exchange rates and let their currencies float. While this eased the situation for a short period of time, in the first half of August 1971 the dollar came under strong attack once again. Faced with $35 billion of outstanding liabilities and with only $10 billion of gold, the United States finally gave up trying to play by the Bretton Woods rules.

**Developments**
**from**
**1971 to 1976**

On August 15, 1971, President Nixon announced that the United States would no longer redeem dollars for gold and that it would not intervene in foreign exchange markets to maintain exchange rates relative to other currencies. The dollar was thus allowed to float, with the expectation that the dollar would be devalued. This indeed happened, although other countries intervened in foreign exchange markets to limit the appreciation in their currencies and thus preserve their relative attractiveness as exporters.

In a last-gasp effort to preserve fixed exchange rates, the major industrial nations met at the Smithsonian Institution in Washington, D.C., in December 1971. The United States agreed to devalue the dollar in terms of gold, raising the price of gold by $8\frac{1}{2}$ percent to $38 an ounce. A number of other countries revalued their currencies in terms of the dollar so that, on average, the dollar was devalued by 12 percent. Pegged exchange rates were reestablished, although fluctuations were allowed within somewhat wider bands. The dollar, however, remained inconvertible into gold.

Viewed with hindsight, the Smithsonian agreement was at best a patchwork effort. It did not deal with the more fundamental problems of international liquidity and adjustment of exchange rates under a system of pegged rates. The system did limp along for about a year, but the international monetary situation again reached critical proportions in early 1973. In February 1973 the United States again devalued the dollar, this time by 11 percent, raising the price of gold from $38 to over $42 an ounce. But even this was not enough to stem the tide, and one month later floating exchange rates were back to stay.

After March 1973 exchange rates floated, albeit in a somewhat "managed" fashion. There were, however, substantial movements in exchange rates, and despite the pessimism of some as to the workability of flexible rates, the international monetary system functioned reasonably well during this period. Indeed, flexible exchange rates were given a rather severe test by quadrupling of the export price of OPEC oil at the end of 1973, which brought about a fundamental change in the international payments structure. In the assessment of the Council of Economic Advisers,

> *The financing of the large external deficits of oil importers over the past 2 years has been accomplished considerably more smoothly than had been anticipated earlier. Financial markets turned out to be very adaptable, and the more flexible exchange rate system helped to avoid the market disruptions so often experienced during past periods of strain.*[4]

**Reform of the IMF**  It should be emphasized that virtually all of the developments since 1971 in regard to exchange rates were, until recently, in technical violation of the rules of the game applicable to members of the IMF. In an effort both to legitimize the status quo and to reform the international monetary system, the Interim Committee of the IMF agreed in January 1976 on a broad package of amendments to the IMF's Articles of Agreement. These were formally approved in 1978, and accomplished the following: "legalize" flexible exchange rates; raise quotas to increase the Fund's resources by over one-third; phase out gold in Fund transactions; and establish a trust fund for the benefit of the poorer members of the IMF. This trust fund will be financed by selling part of the gold holdings of the IMF.

As far as exchange rates are concerned, the new agreement allows for a number of other possibilities in addition to floating rates. A country

---

[4] *Economic Report of the President*, Washington, D.C., Government Printing Office, January 1976, p. 140.

could, for example, choose to peg its currency in terms of SDRs (but not gold). Or a group of countries could cooperate in maintaining their currencies in some fixed relationship to the value of the currency or currencies of other members. The revised Articles even permit, with approval of an 85 percent majority vote, the reestablishment of a set of pegged exchange rates. However, as the United States has approximately 20 percent of the voting strength, this could not be done without U.S. approval.

**Events Since 1976 and Prospects for the Future**

As of this writing, floating rates have been with us for the better part of a decade. Consequently, a brief report card seems in order.

As just indicated, it is generally agreed that floating rates have helped cushion the world economy from a number of major shocks such as the dramatic runup in oil prices. However, while floating rates have clearly performed substantially better than the pessimists had anticipated, the floating system has not lived up to the hopes of its most fervent supporters. As noted above, optimistic supporters of floating thought that the system would allow each country to pursue domestic policies of its choice unimpeded by balance-of-payments constraints. It was also hoped that floating rates would insulate national economies against international disturbances. Actual events, however, turned out somewhat differently, as we see in the following statement by a governor of the Federal Reserve system:

> *The promise of speedy adjustment of payments imbalances through exchange rate movements has remained unfulfilled, perhaps because the very ease with which exchange rates could move has diminished political pressure to adopt appropriate fiscal and monetary policies.*
>
> *The ups and downs of exchange rates have tended to accelerate world inflation because prices rose rapidly where currencies declined but remained sticky where currencies appreciated.*
>
> *Vicious circles seem to have developed in which exchange rate depreciation feeds inflation and accelerating inflation, in turn, feeds back upon the exchange rate. Countries with appreciating currencies have found themselves caught up in virtuous circles, with cheaper imports reducing inflation and reduced inflation further strengthening the currency. These vicious and virtuous circles have threatened to polarize the world into countries with strong and weak currencies, which has come uncomfortably close to splitting the world into strong and weak countries.*[5]

---

[5] Wallich, H. C., "The International Monetary and Cyclical Situation," speech delivered at Lendeszentralbank, Berlin, Germany, June 18, 1979.

In view of this assessment it should not be surprising to learn that the international monetary system has moved into a phase in which there is substantial intervention in exchange markets. As we can illustrate this with reference to two recent examples.

In the face of a continuing depreciation of the dollar (see Figure 23–4), on November 1, 1978, the Federal Reserve announced a major policy move designed to "restore exchange market stability." This new policy included the following measures:

1    A tightening of monetary policy designed both to curb inflation and raise interest rates, thereby increasing the attractiveness of U.S. financial claims.
2    An increase in the magnitude of Treasury gold sales.
3    An $8 billion increase in swap arrangements with Germany, Switzerland, and Japan.
4    The drawing of $3 billion of foreign currencies form the IMF.
5    The sale by the Treasury of up to $10 billion of securities denominated in foreign currencies.

As Figure 23–4 indicates, after November 1 the dollar did improve against other currencies, but then, in late 1979, it again took a turn for the worse. As a consequence, in October 1979, with one eye in international markets, the Federal Reserve was forced to take additional steps.

A different sort of response to dissatisfaction with floating has come from the European Community, which, in March 1979, agreed to attempt to integrate the currencies of its nine member countries. To do this they set up the *European Monetary System* (EMS), whose immediate goal is to reestablish a more fixed set of exchange rates among the nine curren-

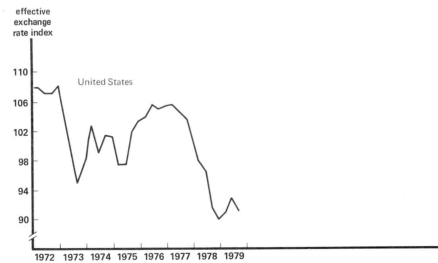

*The value of the U.S. dollar vs other major currencies: the effective exchange rate index (1975 = 100)*

Source: *International Economic Conditions*, Federal Reserve Bank of St. Louis, January 22, 1980, p. 3.

**FIGURE 23–4**

cies. Fixed, of course, does not mean rigidly pegged, and indeed, within the first year of operation of the EMS there were two currency realignments. Over the longer run, the EMS could lead to a single European currency, a European central bank, and a European monetary policy. Given past efforts in this direction, however, skeptics have expressed considerable doubt as to the feasibility of these more grandiose plans, let alone the success of the more limited initial objectives of the EMS.

In summary then, as of early 1980 it was still evident that there remained considerable dissatisfaction with various features of our present international payments system. Indeed, some economists, pointing to the dramatic runup in the prices of both gold and oil, raised doubts about the basic viability of our present system. But while serious problems may confront us in the future, one should not underestimate the resiliency of the international payments system.

**CONCLUSION**   We have now completed our survey of the international monetary system and of international monetary interrelationships and policies. Our survey has devoted special attention to international reserve or liquidity systems, exchange rate systems, and methods of equilibrating international receipts and payments. Each of these fields presents many policy issues with important implications not only for international trade and capital movements but also for the behavior of output, employment, and price levels in the various countries. Moreover, policy choices in any one of these fields have significant consequences for the others.

The following list of some of the basic policy questions in the various fields will suggest both the large number of issues and their interrelatedness.

A. *Issues Relating to the International Liquidity System*
1   How much international liquidity does the world need, and at what rate should it grow to avoid restriction of trade and capital movements and both deflationary and inflationary pressures? The answer depends in part on the nature of the exchange rate system and on the readiness of nations to eliminate deficits and surpluses in their balance of payments. A huge amount of reserves may be required if exchange rates are rigidly pegged over long periods and if nations fail to take quick and effective action to equilibrate their receipts and payments. The reserve requirement will be smaller if exchange rates are flexible or if other actions are taken quickly to equilibrate receipts and payments.
2   What should be the forms and proportions of the various components of international liquidity? What should be the roles of

gold, of SDRs, of holdings of claims against foreign moneys, and of borrowing facilities?

3   Should the existing system be supplemented or replaced by an international central bank with discretionary power to create and regulate international reserves?

### B. Issues Relating to the Exchange Rate System

1   Should exchange rates be rigidly and narrowly pegged over long periods regardless of the cost in terms of other objectives?

2   Should exchange rates be pegged, but adjusted if defense of an existing rate becomes costly? If so, what principles should guide adjustments and what techniques of adjustment should be used?

3   Should rates be allowed to float freely without official intervention?

4   Should rates be flexible, but with official intervention? If so, what should be the criteria for intervention?

### C. Issues Relating to Methods of Eliminating Deficits and Surpluses

1   As a means of equilibrating international receipts and payments, what should be the relative roles of direct controls over trade and payments, adjustments of exchange rates, and adjustments of incomes, price levels, and interest rates? These policy questions are obviously interrelated with those concerning the international liquidity and exchange rate systems.

2   What should be the relative responsibilities of surplus and deficit countries in eliminating imbalances in international payments?

### D. Issues Relating to National Sovereignty and International Economic Interdependence

Among the sovereign rights claimed by each nation is the right to determine its own monetary and fiscal policies. Yet it is an incontrovertible fact that the economic policies of each country affect significantly, and in some cases powerfully, economic developments and welfare in other countries. This situation poses serious economic and political questions.

1   What basic principles should serve as a guideline to resolve these issues?

2   What types of international understandings, agreements, and institutions would best promote workable solutions?

While the recent reform of the IMF discussed in the previous section answers many of these questions, it by no means settles them all. Furthermore, if the history of international monetary relations has taught us anything, it is that answers to policy questions in this area tend to be less than permanent.

**SELECTED READINGS**

International Monetary Fund, *Annual Reports* and *International Financial Statistics* (monthly), Washington, D.C.

Solomon, R., *The International Monetary System, 1945–1976*, New York, Harper & Row, 1977.

Stigum, M. *The Money Market*, Homewood, Ill., Dow-Jones-Irwin, 1978.

Tresize, P. H., ed., *The European Monetary System: Its Promise and Prospects*, Washington, D.C., Brookings Institution, 1979.

Page references in *italics* are to tables and page references in (parentheses) are to illustrations.